ClarisWorks Companion

Jan L. Harrington

CLARIS PRESS

AP PROFESSIONAL

AP PROFESSIONAL
AP Professional is a Division of Academic Press
Boston San Diego New York
London Sydney Tokyo Toronto

This book is printed on acid-free paper. 

AP Professional
1300 Boylston St., Chesnut Hill, MA 02167
An Imprint of Academic Press
A Division of Harcourt Brace & Company
http://www.apnet.com

United Kingdom Edition published by
ACADEMIC PRESS LIMITED
24–28 Oval Road, London NW1 7DX
http://www.hbuk.cc.uk/ap/

Library of Congress Cataloging-in-Publication Data

Library of Congress CIP data pending.

ISBN 0-12-326410-3

CIP

Printed in the United States of America

97 98 99 00 01 CP 9 8 7 6 5 4 3 2 1

Contents

Chapter 9: Data Management: Searching For Data 445

Chapter 10: Data Management Extras 475

These days, the marketplace is flooded with software suites that try to shoe-horn corporate-size applications into your home office, school, or small business computer. The result is a computer that under-performs and is hard to use. Now, ClarisWorks software offers you an inexpensive and slender alternative — without sacrificing the features you really need to be productive.

With the book you have in your hands — the latest offering in the Claris Press series of Claris-authorized guides to our "simply powerful software" — I think you'll find it easy to take advantage of the full range of features and usability enhancements we've built into the latest version of ClarisWorks.

Whether you're publishing information over the Internet, tracking your household budget, or preparing a family or department newsletter, you'll find the guidance you need in Jan Harrington's ClarisWorks Companion, in understandable language and a highly readable format. Memos, letters, presentations, customer lists, mailing labels, and business reports are just some of the documents you can create easily and quickly with ClarisWorks and the helpful tips, insights, and examples in Jan's book.

I'm personally convinced that ClarisWorks is the only productivity software you'll ever need at work, in school, at home, or on the road, and that this informative book will unlock the power of the software for you and make you productive fast. The ClarisWorks Companion and the Claris Press series are proof of our commitment to making complete software solutions for the jobs you have to do. Enjoy!

Valorie Cook Carpenter
Vice President, Worldwide Marketing
Claris Corporation

Preface

ClarisWorks is a computer program that can help you do things such as write letters, analyze your finances, prepare newsletters, create an address book, and prepare documents for World Wide Web pages. If you use your computer at home or in a small business, then ClarisWorks can meet most of your day-to-day computing needs.

The purpose of this book is to help you get the most out of ClarisWorks 5.0. You'll learn to create documents with integrated text and graphics. You'll also learn to create files to store lists of data and to create spreadsheets that can show you how well you are adhering to your budget.

What You Need to Know before You Begin

Before you begin working with this book, there are few skills you should have:

- You should be familiar with the basics of using your computer's user interface. This means you should be able to open, close, move, and resize windows. You should know how to scroll windows, bringing hidden contents into view. You should be able to make choices from menus using either the mouse or the keyboard, whichever is appropriate for your computer.

- You should have some experience with moving, copying, and deleting files.

- You should know how to start (or *launch*) a program.

If you have just taken your first computer out of the box, spend some time with the tutorial that teaches you how to use the computer's user interface before you begin working with this book. The knowledge you gain will make using ClarisWorks much easier.

Conventions Used in This Book

As you read this book, you will find the following typographic conventions used throughout:

- With the exception of menus whose names are icons rather than text, menu selections are indicated by the name of the menu followed by an arrow and the name of the option to be chosen. For example, the

Open option in the File menu is written File -> Open. If a menu option represents a submenu, then the submenu option is again separated by an arrow, as in File -> Macros -> Record Macro.

- The delete (or backspace) key found to the right of the number keys on all keyboards is written as Delete. The forward delete key, which is found above the arrow keys on the extended Macintosh keyboard and most PC keyboards, is written as Del.

- The Macintosh and Windows versions of ClarisWorks are almost identical. However, in the few instances in which there are differences (mostly concerning keyboard equivalents for menu options and dialog boxes that open or save files), you will find platform-specific instructions in tables like the following:

Macintosh	Directions specific to the Macintosh go here.
Windows	Directions specific to Windows go here.

- The Macintosh mouse has only one button, but a Windows mouse typically has two. Whenever a reference is made to the "mouse button," Windows users should use the left mouse button.

ClarisWorks 5.0 and ClarisWorks for Kids

If you have young children in your household or if you are involved in educating young children, you may want to introduce youngsters to ClarisWorks for Kids rather than ClarisWorks 5.0. (Although ClarisWorks for Kids is marketed for ages 5–11 and grades 1–3, most youngsters over the age of 10 can easily handle ClarisWorks 5.0.) Children who have experience with ClarisWorks for Kids will find it very easy to make the transition to ClarisWorks 5.0. Although the look-and-feel of the children's program is different from that of ClarisWorks 5.0, the two programs are nonetheless very similar.

ClarisWorks for Kids includes word processing, painting, spreadsheet, and database modules in an easy-to-use package. The program is full of color and music, and it can read menu options and program messages to users.

ClarisWorks for Kids uses the same basic document creation tools as ClarisWorks 5.0, although their appearance is more colorful. Once you are familiar with using ClarisWorks 5.0, you will recognize the ClarisWorks for Kids tools immediately. Although the tools look a little different, they have similar shapes and positions in the tool panel. You can use the instructions in this book that correspond to the ClarisWorks for Kids tools, because the tools behave the same way in both programs.

Most ClarisWorks for Kids document formatting is handled through templates from which children create their documents. Although ClarisWorks for Kids ships with a good collection of useful templates, you can use ClarisWorks 5.0 to create additional templates or to modify those that come with the program. When you have finished creating or modifying the templates, save them as stationery using the ClarisWorks for Kids file format. (Although ClarisWorks 5.0 can open ClarisWorks for Kids files automatically, ClarisWorks for Kids can't open native ClarisWorks 5.0 files.)

ClarisWorks for Kids organizes document stationery in folders stored in a folder named New Work. Put new word processing templates in the Writing Pad folder and painting templates in the Art Pad folder. Spreadsheet templates go in the Graphing Pad folder, while database templates go in the List Pad folder.

ClarisWorks for Kids doesn't support the full range of document options found in ClarisWorks 5.0. Although you can open and modify any ClarisWorks for Kids document in ClarisWorks 5.0, if you add any elements that aren't supported by ClarisWorks for Kids, those elements won't be translated when you save the document in ClarisWorks for Kids format. The best way to find out what you can import into ClarisWorks for Kids is to explore the sample document templates that accompany the program and to look at the ClarisWorks for Kids menu options.

Acknowledgments

This is the biggest book I've ever written, and it took the cooperation of an entire group of people to get it done. I'd like to thank them all:

- Ken Morton, my editor at AP Professional, who as always, is a joy to work with.

- Linda Hamilton, production editor with Academic Press, who made the whole process go smoothly, even on a very tight timeline.

- Joan Hiraki, at Claris Press, who has been wonderful by providing software and answering questions.

- Robert C. Hunter, the Claris technical reviewer, who really, really knows ClarisWorks inside and out.

- Samantha Libby, AP Professional editorial assistant, who was always there with information when I needed it.
- Carole McClendon, my agent, who always lines up the greatest projects for me.

JLH

http://members.aol.com/blgryph/home.html

1

Introduction

ClarisWorks is an *integrated package,* a piece of software that has programs of more than one type combined into a single unit. Each program within the unit is often called a *module.* As you read this book, you will learn the capabilities of each of ClarisWorks's component modules and how those modules can be used together.

NOTE *One of ClarisWorks's most valuable features is the ease with which you can integrate items prepared with one ClarisWorks module into another ClarisWorks module. You will discover examples of how to make ClarisWorks's parts function together smoothly throughout this book.*

There are several advantages to using an integrated package rather than investing in separate programs:

- An integrated package such as ClarisWorks provides a consistent *user interface* throughout all of its modules. (The user interface is the medium through which a human interacts with a computer.) In terms of an integrated software package, this means that there are many elements of the package that are common to each module. Once you've learned a skill, you can transfer it to other modules. The time it takes to learn the software will be less and you will be less likely to forget skills you've learned, even if you don't use the software every day.

- The consistency among the modules in an integrated package means that the documents you create can work together easily. Although it is true that independent software packages are more compatible with each other today than they were in the past, you will obtain the highest level of integration from ClarisWorks. You can place graphics in a text document that can be edited within the text document; you can place spreadsheets (documents for numerical analysis) within a text document or place a text document within a spreadsheet. In each case, the element that you place within another retains all the capabilities it would have if it were a stand-alone document.

- An integrated package costs less than separate programs. (In fact, if you received ClarisWorks with a new computer, then it didn't cost you much of anything … .)

You may have seen the term "software program" either in printed media or on the Internet. This term, however, is rather silly because both words mean the same thing (a set of instructions that tells a piece of equipment,

or hardware, what to do).Therefore, correct usage is one word or the other, but not both. You can, however, modify either word to indicate the type of hardware to which it applies, as in "computer program" or "computer software."

There are two major types of computer software: system software and application software. System software includes programs that perform management functions for the computer, in particular, the operating system. When you interact with the Macintosh Finder or the Windows desktop, you are working with system software. Application software, on the other hand, is software that performs useful work for you. ClarisWorks is therefore application software.

ClarisWorks Modules

ClarisWorks has six modules:

- Word processing: *Word processing* is designed primarily for the manipulation of text. You can enter, modify, delete, and format text. Along with its basic capabilities, the ClarisWorks word processing module provides headers and footers, footnotes, outlining, and multiple-column layouts. Because word processing forms the basis for so much of what we do with a computer, this book begins with it and devotes three chapters to covering word processing skills.

It's somewhat ironic that word processing has become the preeminent use of today's personal computers. When computers were first developed, in the 1940s and 1950s, they were seen as machines that could process large volumes of numbers ("number crunchers"). In fact, the first commercial computer — ENIAC — was designed to process the U.S. census. The idea that computers could handle text as well as numbers came much later.

- Drawing: ClarisWorks's drawing module provides *object graphics*. It allows you to create illustrations in which each object — for example, a line or an oval — retains its identity as an object, even when it is overlaid by another object. Objects can be moved, resized, and shifted in the layering of objects. Object graphics are well suited for creating charts, technical illustrations, and other structured pictures.

- Painting: ClarisWorks's painting module provides *paint* or *bit-mapped graphics*. This module allows you to create illustrations made up of a pattern of colored dots that is only one layer thick. As you paint shapes on the illustration, lines and colors that overlay existing parts of the illustration replace the previous contents. Bit-mapped graphics are well suited for artistic graphic applications.

- Spreadsheet: A *spreadsheet* is used to analyze numeric data. For example, you might use it to keep a family budget, to figure out whether a small business made a profit, or to project whether an increase in the price of a piece of merchandise will be enough to cover an increase in the costs of raw materials.

- Database: The ClarisWorks database module is a *file manager* that allows you to create and store lists of data that you can view, order, and search in a variety of ways. The data can be text, numbers, or graphics. Things you can do with the database module include keeping a telephone book or a list of clients.

- Communications: The communications module performs *terminal emulation*, permitting your computer to look like a computer terminal when you call a remote computer. Given that most of today's data communications take place over the Internet or with specialized content providers such as America Online, this type of communications software is of far less use than it was even four or five years ago. In addition, the communications module doesn't integrate at all with the rest of the modules. For these reasons, this book doesn't cover the communications module. Should you need to communicate with a host computer using terminal emulation, check with the user support personnel at the site that maintains the host computer to obtain settings that you will need to use with the communications module.

The word processing, spreadsheet, database, painting, and drawing modules share a common user interface. They are also tightly integrated, in that they can be embedded within one another.

The ClarisWorks Working Environment

With the exception of the communications module, ClarisWorks's modules share a common working environment, which you can see in Figure 1.1. At the top of screen, underneath the menu bar, you will find the Button Bar. The Button Bar contains buttons that correspond to commonly used commands, such as those for opening and printing documents. You activate a button with a single click of the mouse button.

The arrow at the far left of the Button Bar drops down a menu with commands for controlling the Button Bar. ClarisWorks lets you configure your own working environment by creating custom Button Bars containing commands that you personally find useful. You can also change the position of the Button Bar on the screen. Details on configuring your working environment in this way can be found in Chapter 11.

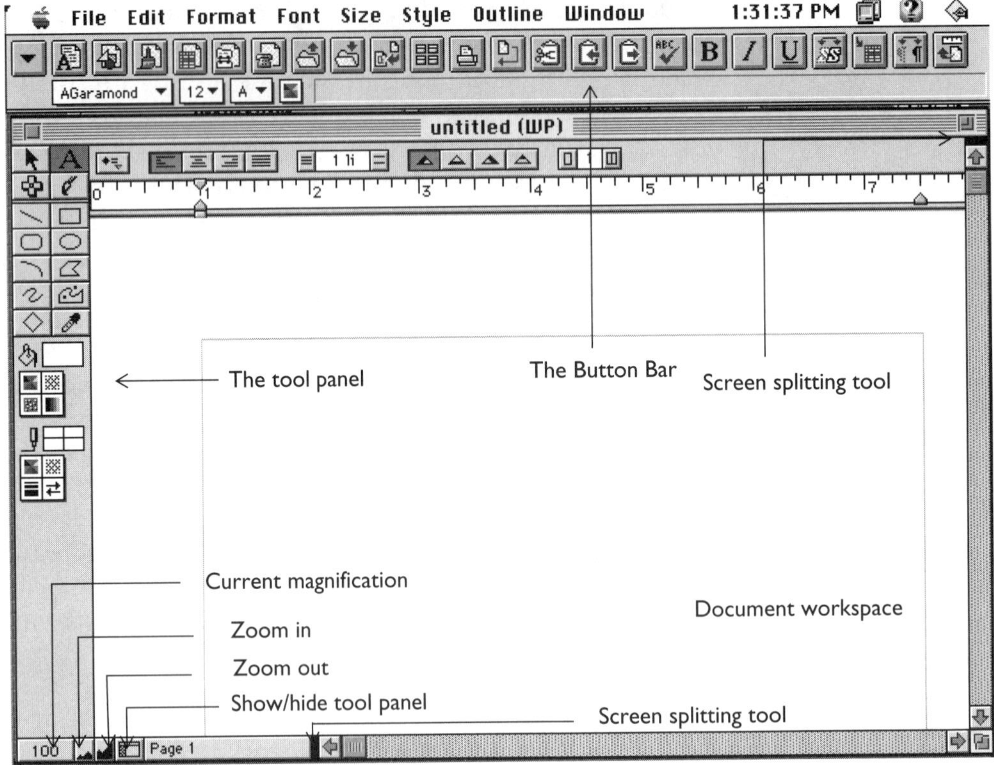

Figure 1.1 The ClarisWorks working environment

The left side of the screen contains the tool panel. The tool panel, which differs slightly depending on the module with which you are working, primarily contains drawing tools. It lets you determine the shape you will draw, as well as setting colors and patterns for text and graphics. You will learn about the specifics of the tool panel as you learn about each ClarisWorks module. Unlike the Button Bar, you won't be able to modify the contents of the tool panel.

The bottom left of the document window contains a switch for hiding and showing the tool panel. Click the icon once to hide the tool panel; click it again to make the tool panel reappear.

The bottom left of the document window also contains buttons for controlling the magnification of the document. Click the Zoom in button (the small mountains) to shrink the document so you can see more of its contents; click the Zoom out button (the large mountains) to enlarge the document. The current magnification appears in the far left bottom corner. This button is also a popup menu that gives you direct access to document magnification settings.

The rest of the screen in Figure 1.1 is occupied by the document workspace. Here you will find the contents of whatever you are working on at any given time. The appearance of the workspace depends, of course, on which module you are using and what text and graphics you have added to your document.

ClarisWorks has only one Button Bar at a time. However, the tool panel is attached to a document window. If you have more than one document open at a time, then each has its own tool panel with its own settings. When you move a document window, the tool panel moves with the window.

Managing Documents

The work that you prepare with ClarisWorks is stored in one or more *documents*, each of which is represented by a single file icon on your computer's desktop. A word processing document, for example, stores text, graphics, and instructions on how the text and graphics should be formatted. A database document stores definitions of what data are stored, layouts for viewing the data in a variety of ways, criteria for finding specific data, and instructions for how data should be sorted, along with the data themselves. Although each ClarisWorks module stores very different things its documents, the way in which you open, close, and save documents is the same.

Creating a New Document

There are two ways to create a new document, using either a menu selection or a button in the Button Bar.

Using a Menu Option

To create a new document using a menu option:

1.

Macintosh	Choose File->New or press ⌘-N.
Windows	Choose File->New, press CTRL-N, or press ALT-F, N.

The New Document dialog box appears (Figure 1.2). Notice that the types of ClarisWorks documents are listed at the left.

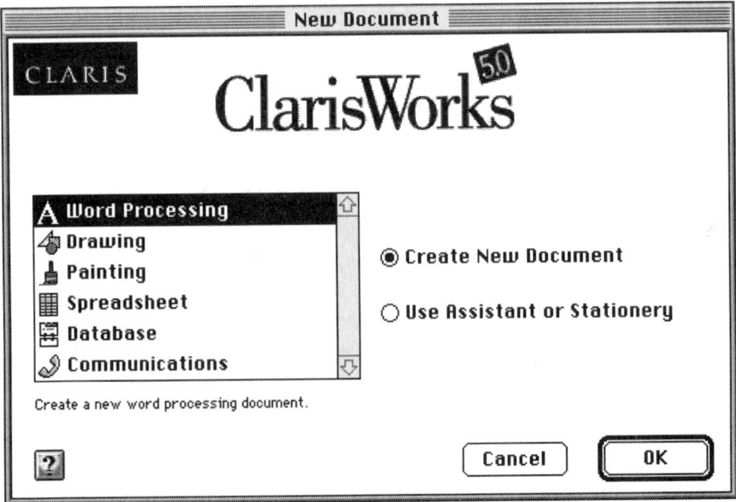

Figure 1.2 The New Document dialog box

2. Click on the type of document you want to create to highlight the type name.

3. Click the OK button or press Enter. ClarisWorks creates a new, untitled document of the type you have selected and opens the document.

Using the Button Bar

The left six options in the default Button Bar (the Button Bar that ClarisWorks displays if you don't make any custom changes) can be used to create new documents without displaying the New Document dialog box. To do so, click on the button that represents the type of document that you want to create (see Figure 1.3). ClarisWorks immediately opens a new, untitled document for you.

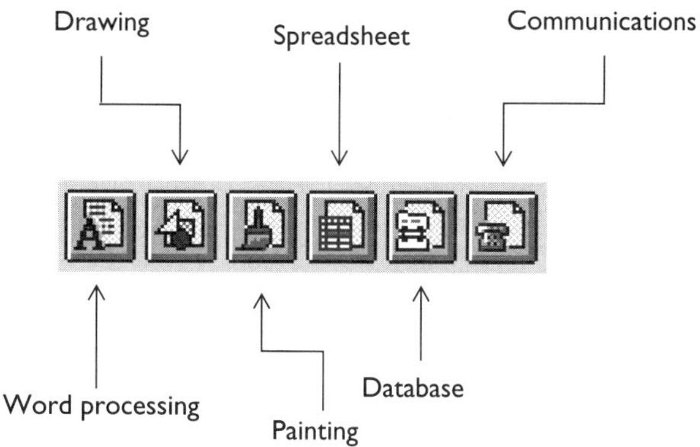

Figure 1.3 Creating new documents using the Button Bar

When you create a new document, ClarisWorks names it "untitled" and places it at the bottom of the Window menu. If other untitled documents are already open, ClarisWorks adds a number to make the window's name unique. Therefore, the second untitled window is named "untitled 2," the third "untitled 3," and so on.

Saving a Document

The way in which you save a document depends on whether you want to save the document under its current name or whether you want to save a copy of the document with a different name.

Save Using the Same Name

To save a document using the same name:

Macintosh	Choose File -> Save or press 1 -S.
Windows	Choose File -> Save, press CTRL-S, or press ALT-F, S.

ClarisWorks *replaces* the existing file on your disk with the contents of the document as they appear on your screen.

Saving under a New Name

To save a copy of a document using a new name:

1.

Macintosh	Choose File -> Save As or press Shift-F7.
Windows	Choose File -> Save As, press SHIFT-CTRL-S, or press ALT-F, A.

The Save File dialog box appears (Figure 1.4 for the Macintosh; Figure 1.5 for Windows).

If you are saving a document that has never been saved, you can perform a Save As by choosing File -> Save or pressing 1 -S, just as you would if the document were already named and saved. ClarisWorks recognizes that the document hasn't been saved and therefore gives you the opportunity to name the document before saving.

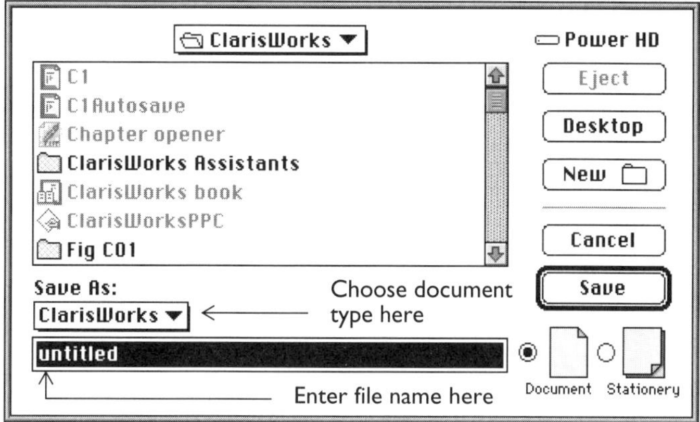

Figure 1.4 The Save File dialog box (Macintosh)

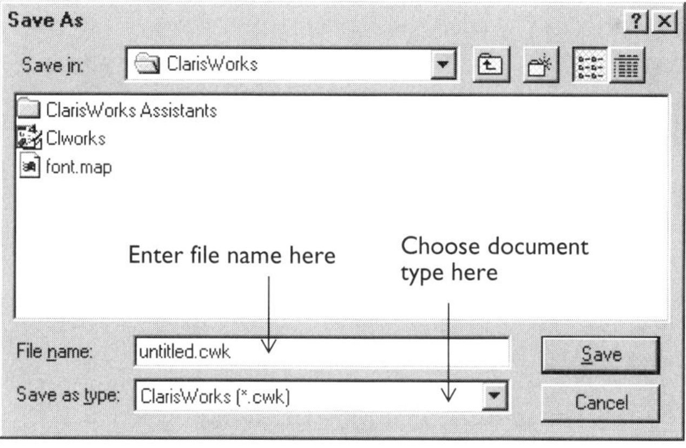

Figure 1.5 The Save File dialog box (Windows)

2. Choose the type of document from the popup menu below the words Save As:. Unless you are exporting the document for use with another program, leave the document type as ClarisWorks.

3. Enter a name for the document's file.

A Macintosh file name can have up to 32 characters. You can use any letter, number, or symbol that you can type on the keyboard, with the exception of the colon (:). A Windows 3.1 file name is limited to eight letters or numbers. The special characters _ and $ are also allowed. (ClarisWorks appends a 3-character extension to the file name so that it can identify the type of document.) Windows 95 allows file names of up to 256 characters.

If you are working under Windows 95 or the Macintosh OS and plan to transfer a file to Windows 3.1, be sure to adhere to the Windows 3.1 file naming rules.

4. Choose a disk location for the document's file.

5. Click the Save button or press Enter.

If a file already exists in the same location with the same name, ClarisWorks asks if you want to replace the file (see Figure 1.6).

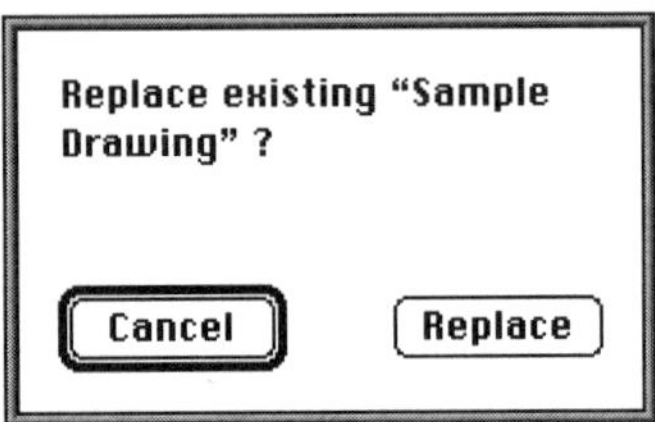

Figure 1.6 Confirming file replacement

Click Replace to replace the existing file with the contents of the document you are saving. Click Cancel to return to the Save File dialog box.

Opening an Existing Document

To open an existing document so that you can modify it:

1.

Macintosh	Choose File -> Open or press 1-O.
Windows	Choose File -> Open, press CTRL-O, or press ALT-F, O.

ClarisWorks displays the Open File dialog box (Figure 1.7 for Macintosh; Figure 1.8 for Windows).

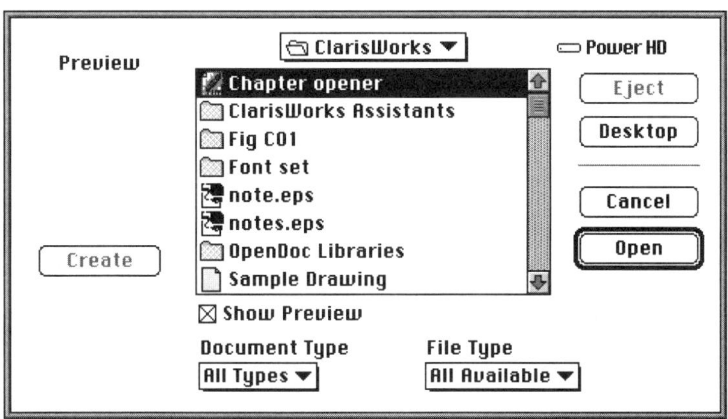

Figure 1.7 The Open File dialog box (Macintosh)

2. Locate the file you want to open and highlight its name.

3. Click the Open button or press Enter. ClarisWorks places the name of the window at the bottom of the Window menu.

tip

You can also select a file by double-clicking on its name.

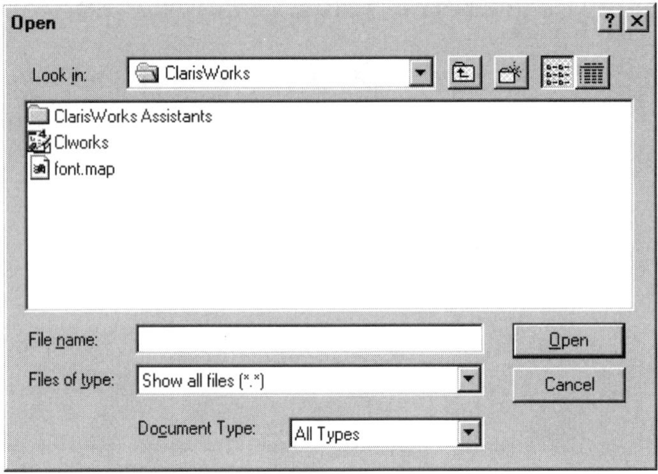

Figure 1.8 The Open File dialog box (Windows)

Switching between Documents

The numbers of windows that you can have open at any one time while working with ClarisWorks is limited only by your computer's main memory. However, you can work in only one window at a time (the *current* window or the *active* window). There are two ways to make a window active:

- Click on any exposed area of the window.
- Choose the window's name from the Window menu. Using the Window menu is particularly helpful if you happen to have many windows open, some of which are completely hidden by others.

Printing Documents

You can print the contents of a ClarisWorks document on any printer to which your computer is connected. Choosing which printer you use and setting printing options depend both on the operating system you are using and the printer you are using.

Printer drivers — the software that acts as an intermediary between application software and the printer — must be installed on your computer before you can print. In most cases, they are installed along with your operating system software. If you need to modify or install additional printer drivers, consult the documentation the accompanies your operating system or printer.

Choosing a Printer (Macintosh Only)

Before you can begin printing on the Macintosh, you must choose which printer you are going to use. Even if only one printer is connected to your Macintosh, you must make sure that it is selected in the Macintosh Chooser before you can print.

To select a printer:

1. If you are going to be using a network printer (for example, a printer connected via LocalTalk or Ethernet), make sure the printer is turned on and warmed up.
2. Select ->Chooser. The Chooser window appears (Figure 1.9).
3. Click on the icon in the list at the left of the window that corresponds to the printer you want to use.
4. If you have selected a network printer, you will see a list of available printers in the right half of the dialog box. Select the printer you want to use.

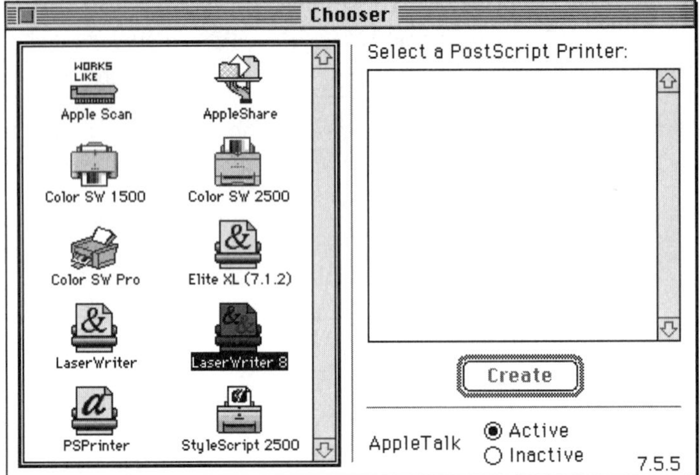

Figure 1.9 The Macintosh Chooser window

5. If you have selected a printer that is connected directly to your Macintosh, you will be asked to choose either the Printer or Modem port. Click the icon that corresponds to the port through which the printer is connected.

6. Click the window's close box or press 1-W to close the window.

7. The Macintosh Operating System warns you with an alert that you have changed your printer settings and that you need to change the page setup for all open documents.

8. Click the OK button to close the alert.

The printer you have just chosen will stay in effect as the computer's default printer until you choose another printer. This means that you don't have to go to the Chooser every time you print, but only when you want to use another printer.

Windows users choose which printer to use when describing paper characteristics for the printer, which is discussed in the next section of this chapter.

Setting Page Options

Before you begin to print, you need to let the printer know some things about the paper (or other medium, such as transparency film) on which you will be printing. In addition, Windows users need to select which printer they are going to use.

Once you set Page/Print options, they stay in effect for each new document you create. You therefore need to access a Page/Print settings dialog box when something changes.

Page Setup (Macintosh)

Basic page setup characteristics for the Macintosh are handled by the Page Setup dialog box. Exactly what the dialog box looks like depends on the printer driver you are using and the version of the Macintosh Operating System running on your computer.

For example, if you are using a printer connected directly to the Macintosh, such as a StyleWriter, your Page Setup dialog box will look something like Figure 1.10. In contrast, if you are using the LaserWriter 8 driver, the Page Setup dialog box appears as in Figure 1.11.

To configure basic page setup options:

1. Choose File->Page Setup. The Page Setup dialog box for the printer driver selected in the Chooser appears.

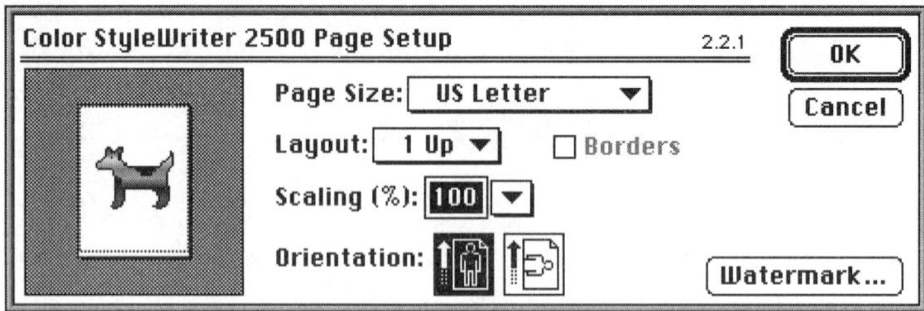

Figure 1.10 The Page Setup dialog box for a StyleWriter

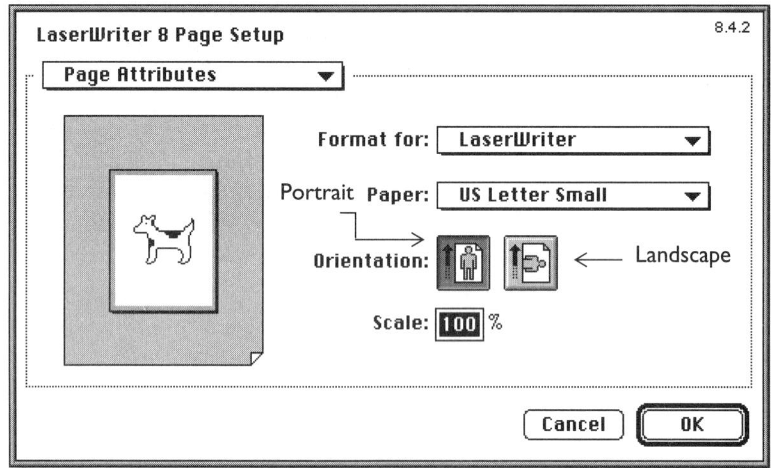

Figure 1.11 The Page Setup dialog box for LaserWriter 8

2. Choose the size of the paper on which you will be printing from the popup menu of paper sizes. In Figure 1.10, the menu is labeled Page Size; in Figure 1.11, it's labeled Paper.

3. By default, the page will print in *portrait* orientation (taller than wide). If you want to print in *landscape* orientation (wider than tall), click the landscape icon (see Figure 1.11).

4. Click the OK button or press Enter to close the dialog box and save your changes.

There are other settings in the Page Setup dialog box that you may want to use at some time. A complete discussion of them, however, is beyond the scope of this book. Consult the manual that came with your Macintosh for details.

The little creature in the sample page in the Page Setup dialog box is known as the dogcow.

Print Setup (Windows)

To set basic print properties and choose a Windows printer:

1. Choose File->Print Setup or press ALT-F, T. The Print Setup dialog box appears (Figure 1.12).

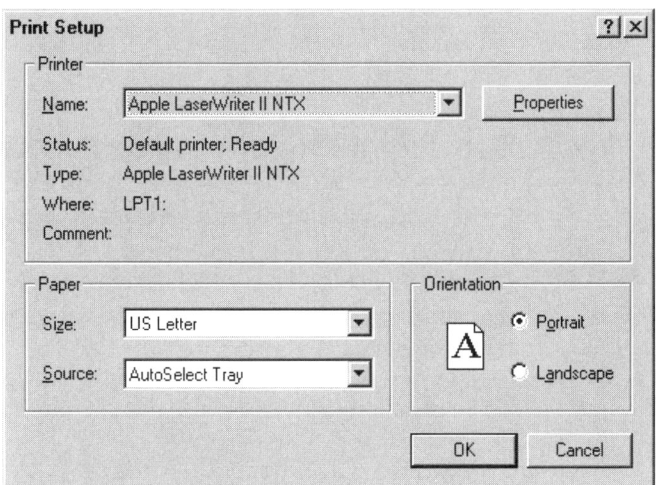

Figure 1.12 The Windows Print Setup dialog box

2. Choose the printer you want to use from the Name dropdown menu.

3. Choose the paper size from the Size dropdown menu.

4. By default, the printer will print your document in *portrait* (taller than wide) orientation. If you want to print using *landscape* (wider than tall) orientation, click the Landscape radio button in the Orientation section of the dialog box.

5. By default, the printer assumes that paper will be fed automatically. If you are going to hand-feed paper, choose that option from the Source dropdown menu.

6. Click the OK button or press Enter to close the dialog box and save your changes.

There are other settings in the Print Setup dialog box that you may want to use at some time. A complete discussion of them, however, is beyond the scope of this book. Consult the manual that came with your Windows software for details.

Sending a Document to Printer

Once you have chosen a printer and configured basic page options, you are ready to print.

Macintosh Printing

To print a document on the Macintosh:

1. Choose File->Print or press 1-P. A Print dialog box appears. If you are using a printer connected directly to the Macintosh, such as a StyleWriter, or the LaserWriter driver, you will see something like Figure 1.13. If you are using LaserWriter 8, you will see the dialog box in Figure 1.14.

Figure 1.13 A Print dialog box for a StyleWriter

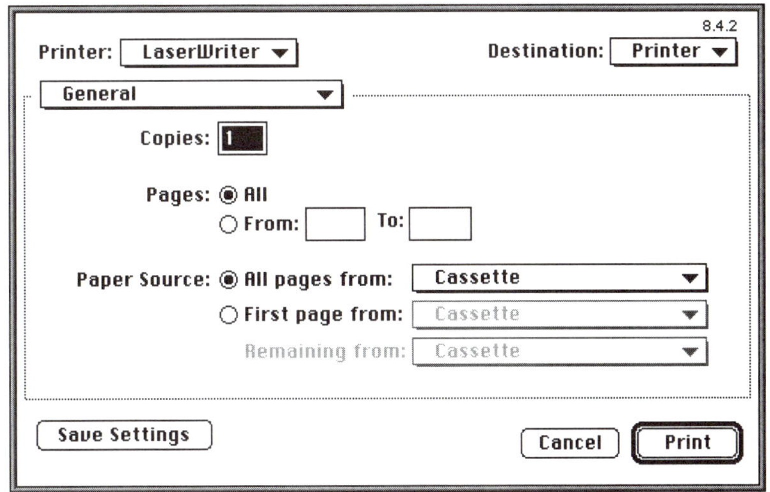

Figure 1.14 The Print dialog box for the LaserWriter 8 driver

You can also initiate printing by clicking the button in the Button Bar. This will send your document to the printer without displaying the Print dialog box. If you want to print using the default print settings, then this is a quick way to start printing.

2. ClarisWorks assumes that you want to print one copy of your document. If you want to print more than one copy, enter the number of copies in the Copies box.

3. ClarisWorks assumes that you want to print all the pages in your document. If you want to print less than the entire document, enter the first page to print in the From box and the last page to print in the To box. To print only one page, enter the same page number in both the From and To boxes.

4. If you are printing on a StyleWriter or ImageWriter, your Print dialog box will have the Print Quality radio buttons that you see in Figure 1.13. Normal quality (the default) provides acceptable output; Best quality takes longer and uses more printer ink or ribbon, but provides the best looking output possible. Click the Best radio button for the highest quality output.

Draft quality output is a holdover from the early days of the Macintosh when printer supplies were very expensive and printers, such as the original ImageWriter, were very slow when printing in Normal or Best mode. Draft quality output typically isn't acceptable by today's standards.

5. If you are working with a laser printer, ClarisWorks assumes that paper will be fed automatically from the paper tray. If you will be hand-feeding paper, choose Hand Feed from the Paper Source popup menu.

6. Click the OK button or press Enter to begin printing.

Print dialog boxes (especially LaserWriter 8) have more options than can be covered in this book. For details, see the documentation that came with both your Macintosh and your printer.

Windows Printing

To print a document from a Windows computer:

1. Choose File->Print, press CTRL-P, or press ALT-F , P. The Print dialog box appears (Figure 1.15).

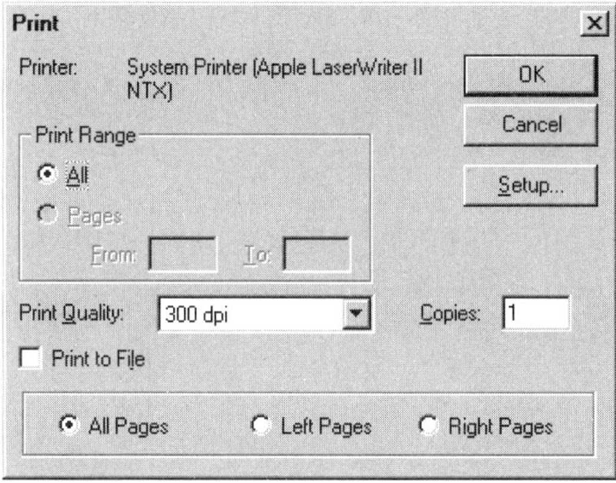

Figure 1.15 The Windows Print dialog box

You can also initiate printing by clicking the [printer button] *button in the Button Bar. This will send your document to the printer without displaying the Print dialog box. If you want to print using the default print settings, then this is a quick way to start printing.*

2. ClarisWorks assumes that you want to print all the pages in the document. If you want to print only a few pages, click the Pages radio button. Then, type the first page to be printed in the From box and the last page to be printed in the To box. If you want to print only one page, put the same page number in both the From and To boxes.

3. ClarisWorks assumes that you want to print one copy of the document. To print more than one copy, enter the number of copies you want to print in the Copies box.

4. Click the OK button or press Enter to begin printing.

The Print dialog box has more options than can be covered in this book. For details, see the documentation that came with both your Windows software and your printer.

Viewing Documents

As you know, a window doesn't necessarily show all of its contents at one time. Often a portion of a window's contents is hidden, in which case you bring hidden portions into view by scrolling the window. Scrolling can become very tedious when a document becomes large, especially if you need to switch back and forth between two widely separated parts of the document. ClarisWorks handles this situation in two ways. First, you can create multiple views of the same document, each of which appears in its own window, that can be manipulated independently of any other views. Second, you can split a single window into regions that scroll independently.

Creating Multiple Views of a Document

When you create multiple views of a document, each view acts like a stand-alone window. This means that you can look at and work on two or more widely separated portions of the document at any time. However, any change you make to one view of a document is reflected immediately in any other open views.

To create a new view:

1. Make the document for which you want to create the new view the active window.

2. Choose Window -> New View.

ClarisWorks adds the names of views to the bottom of the Window menu, just as it does the names of files when they are first created or opened. Each view is numbered. For example, if you open a file named *Drawing*, creating a new view of the document places *Drawing:2* in the Window menu and changes the name of the original document window to *Drawing:1*.

To close a view:

1. Close the view's window.

2. If the view is the last open view for a document, ClarisWorks warns you if there are unsaved changes. You then have the chance to save your work.

Splitting the Screen

At the top of the vertical scroll bar and the left of the horizontal scroll bar in Figure 1.1 you will see two black bands. These let you split the screen into regions, each of which scrolls independently, making it possible to work on more than one part of a document at the same time. For example, in Figure 1.16, a word processing document has been split horizontally into two regions. Each region has its own set of scroll bars and its own black bar for splitting again.

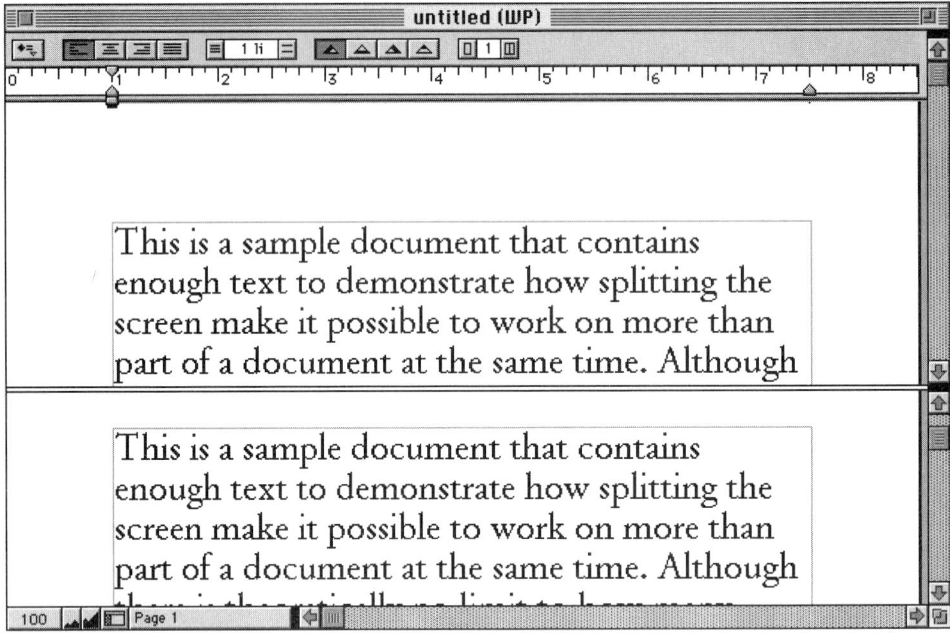

Figure 1.16 A document split into independently scrolling regions

You can split a document into two verticial partitions and two horizontal partitions at the same time. To add a horizontal split, such as that in Figure 1.16, drag the black bar above the vertical scroll bar down. To add a vertical split, drag the black bar at the left of the horizontal scroll bar to the right. To remove a split, drag the black bar back to its original location.

Arranging Windows

Regardless of the size of your monitor, when you have many windows open at the same time, it can be difficult to see more than one or two at once. ClarisWorks therefore provides two methods for quickly arranging windows for easy access.

Tiling Windows

One way to arrange windows is to "tile" them. This means that ClarisWorks will resize all the windows so they fit on your monitor without overlapping. For example, in Figure 1.17 you can see three tiled windows.

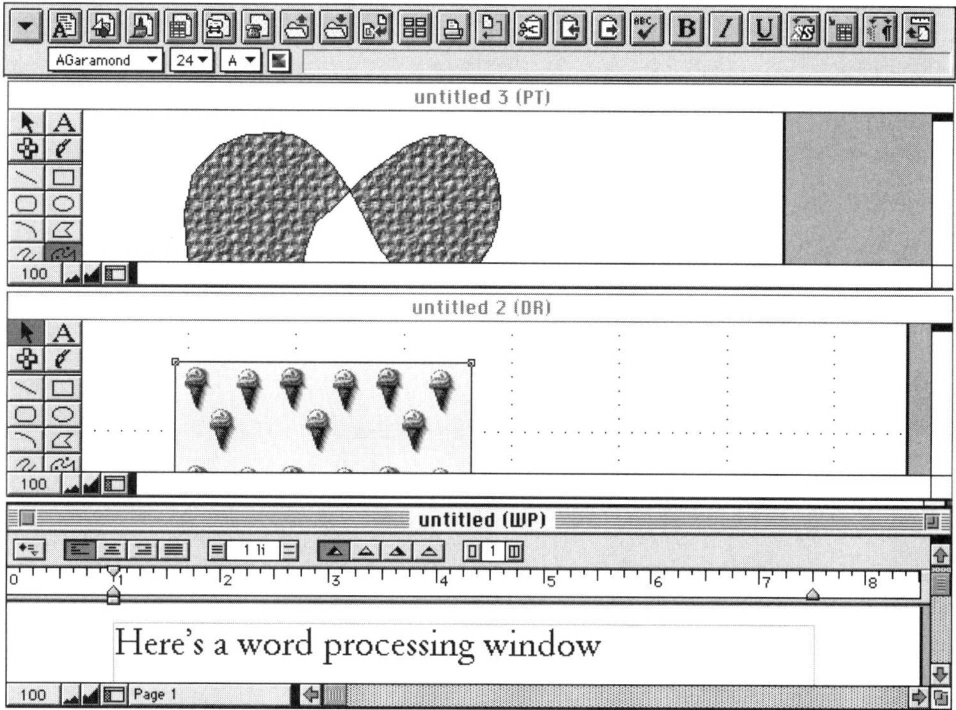

Figure 1.17 Tiled windows

To tile windows:

- Choose Window->Tile Windows or click the button in the Button Bar. (Windows users can also press ALT-W, I.)

Stacking/Cascading Windows

If tiling windows makes the windows too small for you to use, then you may find that asking ClarisWorks to stack (on the Macintosh) or cascade (under Windows) the windows is more convenient. As you can see in Figure 1.18, the windows are staggered on the screen, making them both accessible and as large as possible.

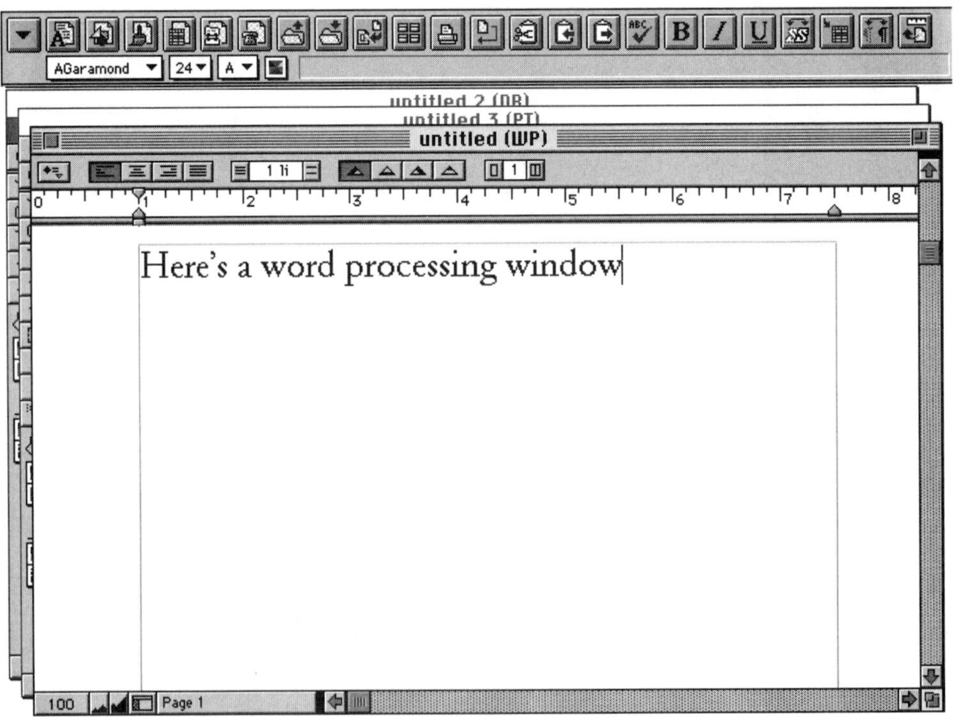

Figure 1.18 Stacked windows

To stack/cascade windows:

Macintosh	Choose Window->Stack Windows
Windows	Choose Window->Cascade or press ALT-W, C

Getting Help

ClarisWorks makes it easy for you to find information about using ClarisWorks while the program is running. If you are working with Windows, then your on-line help comes from the ClarisWorks Help system. If you are working with the Macintosh, then you also have access to Balloon Help.

Using ClarisWorks Help

ClarisWorks Help is a help system that runs as a separate application. Once you begin ClarisWorks Help, you can leave it running while you are working with ClarisWorks or exit Help at any time without affecting any ClarisWorks documents.

Starting ClarisWorks Help

To start ClarisWorks Help:

Macintosh	Choose ClarisWorks Help Contents from the Help menu or press 1-?. If you are using System 7, the Help menu is found at the right side of the menu bar with a question mark icon for its name. (see Figure 1.19). If you are using Mac OS 8, the Help menu is the rightmost menu in the menu bar.
Windows	Choose Help->ClarisWorks Help Contents or press ALT-H, C (see Figure Figure 1.20).

ClarisWorks displays the Help contents (see Figure 1.21). The body of the contents window contains the top-level table of contents of the ClarisWorks Help system.

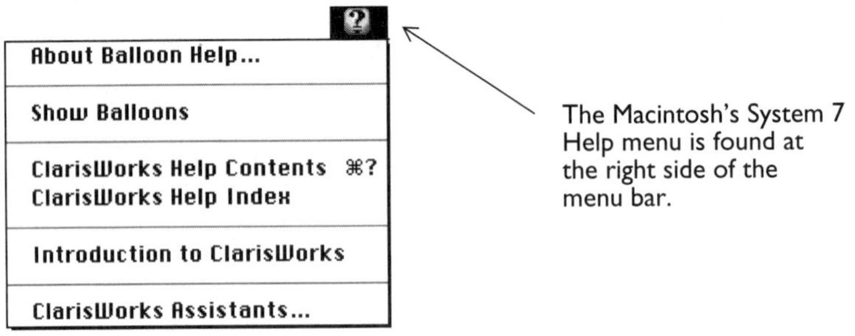

Figure 1.19 The Macintosh System 7 Help menu

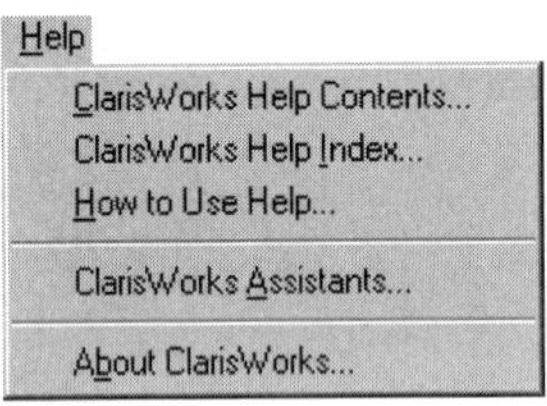

Figure 1.20 The Windows Help menu

The Help Window (Macintosh)

The top of the ClarisWorks Macintosh Help window contains controls for working with the help system (see Figure 1.22). With those controls you can:

- Go directly to the Contents window by clicking on the Contents button.
- Go directly to the Index window by clicking on the Index button. (Using the Help index is discussed later in this section.)
- Go back to the page you viewed just before the current page by clicking the Go Back button.

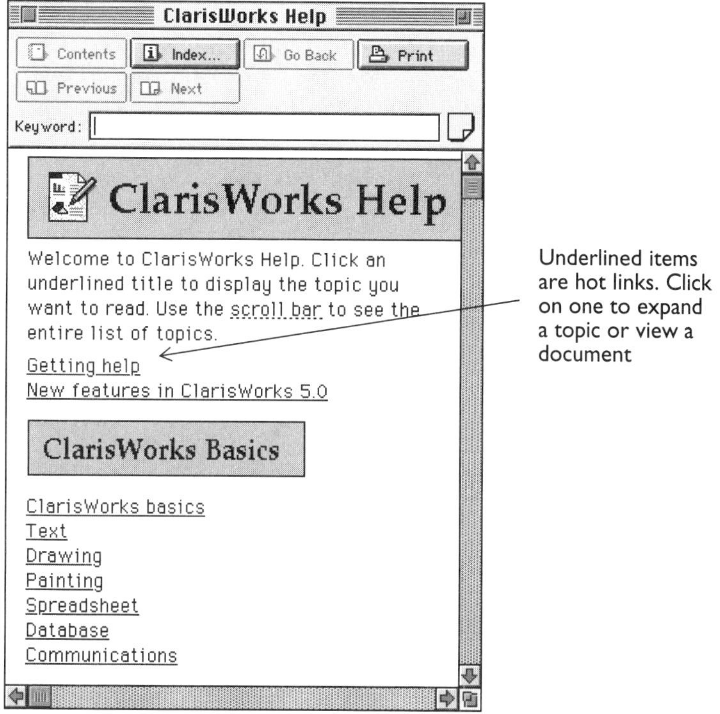

Figure 1.21 Macintosh Help contents

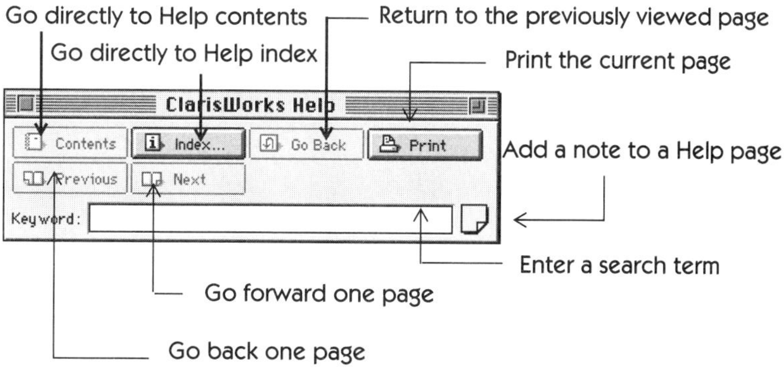

Figure 1.22 ClarisWorks Help controls

- Move back one page in a Help document by clicking the book icon with the left-pointing arrow.
- Move forward one page in a Help document by clicking the book icon with the right-pointing arrow.
- Enter a search term in the Keyword box. (Searching Help is discussed later in this section.)
- Add a note to a Help document. (Adding notes is also discussed shortly.)

The Help Topics and Help Windows (Windows)

The ClarisWorks Windows Help Topics window is a tabbed dialog box. The contents panel that you can see in Figure 1.23 provides a top-level list of help topics. To open one of the books so that you can see its contents, you can either:

- Click on a book and then click the Open button, or
- Double-click on a book.

When opened, a book shows either help documents, represented by icons containing a question mark, or other books (see Figure 1.24).

To open a help document, either:

- Click on the document's icon and click the Open button, or
- Double-click on the icon.

The initial help tabbed dialog box is replaced by a help window displaying the document you selected (Figure 1.25).

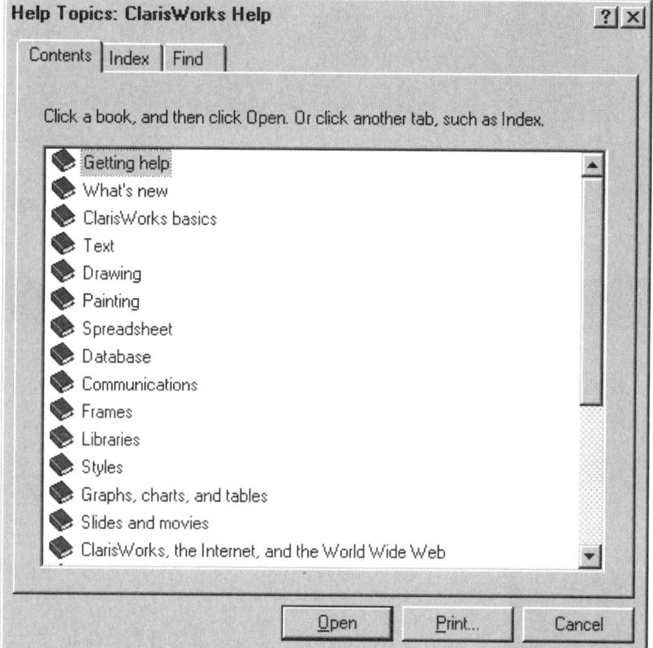

Figure 1.23 The Windows Help window

At the top of this window you will find controls that help you navigate the help system:

- Go directly to the Contents panel of the Help Topics dialog box by clicking on the Contents button.
- Go directly to the Index panel of the Help Topics dialog box by clicking on the Index button. (Using the index is discussed later in this section.)
- Go back to the page you viewed just before the current page by clicking the Back button.
- Print the current document by clicking the Print button.

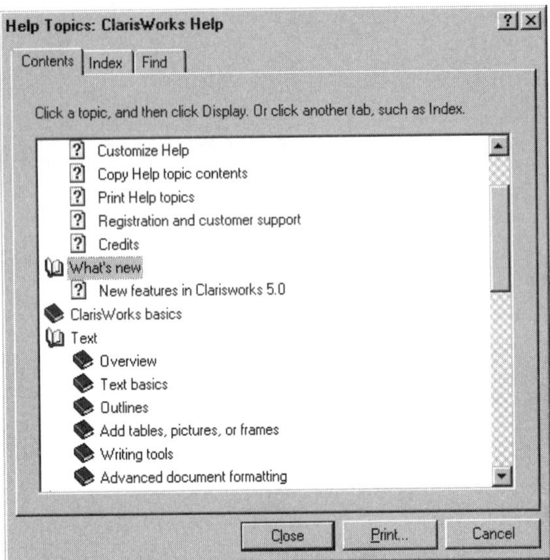

Figure 1.24 Expanding Windows Help topics

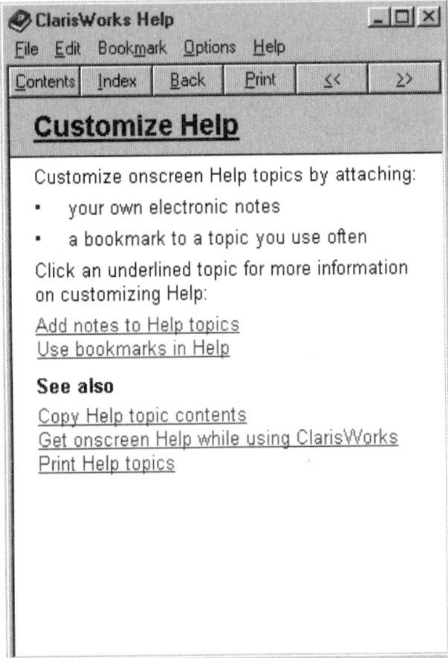

Figure 1.25 A Windows Help document

- Move back one page in a Help document by clicking the left-pointing arrows.
- Move forward one page in a Help document by clicking the right-pointing arrows.

Following Links

The underlined items in Figure 1.21 and Figure 1.25 are *hot links*. When you click on a hot link, ClarisWorks Help either expands a topic (a boldface link) or opens the document associated with the link (a link in regular type).

For example, in Figure 1.26. you can see the expanded contents after clicking on "Getting Help." Clicking on a topic in the expanded list takes you directly to a document that presents information on the topic. In Figure 1.27 you can see the document displayed when you click on the "Learn About ClarisWorks" link from Figure 1.26.

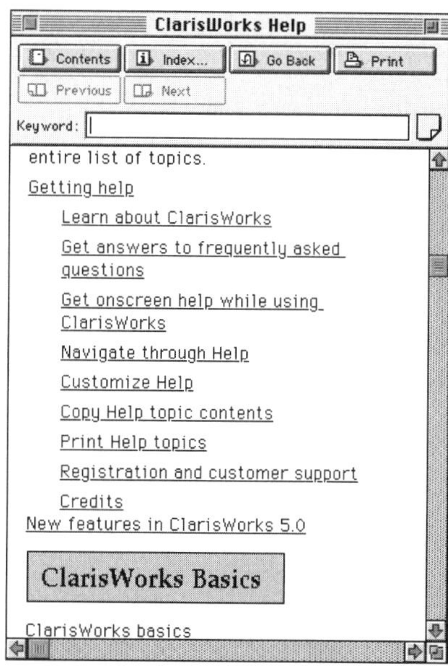

Figure 1.26 Expanded help contents

Using the Help Index

The Help Index (for example, Figure 1.28) contains an alphabetical list of Help topics. There are several ways to reach the index:

Macintosh	Choose Help->ClarisWorks Help Index or click the Index button in the ClarisWorks Help window.
Windows	Choose Help->ClarisWorks Help Index, click the Index tab in the Help Topics dialog box, or click the Index button in the ClarisWorks Help window.

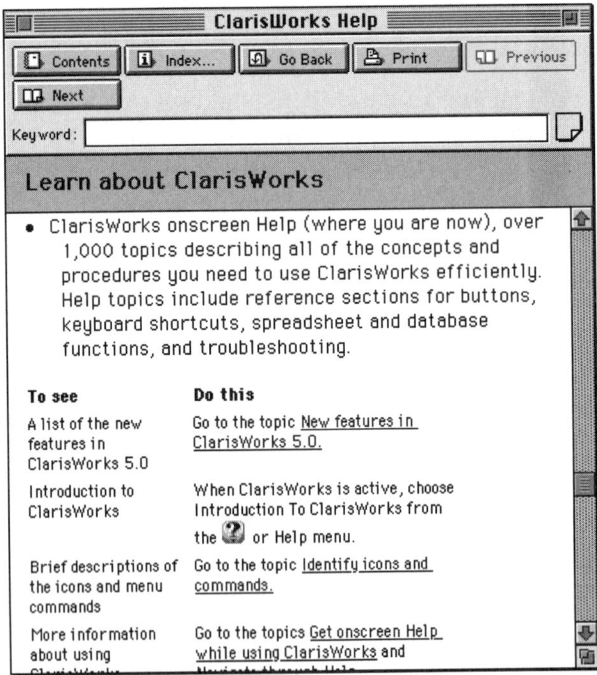

Figure 1.27 A Help document reached by clicking on a link

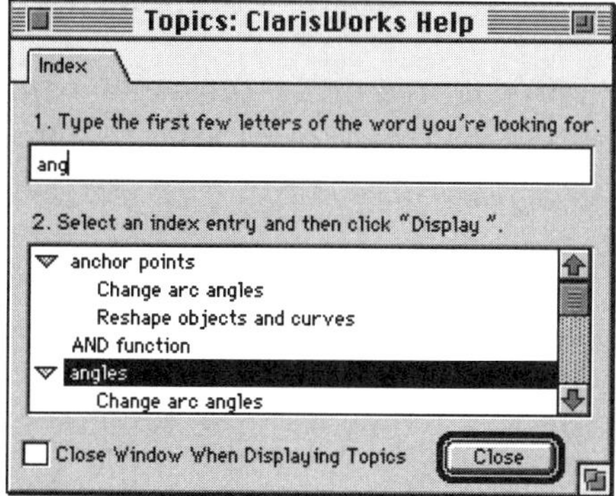

Figure 1.28 ClarisWorks Help Index

To use the Index:

1. Scroll the list to find the topic about which you want more information.

2. Highlight the topic.

3. To display the associated Help document in the Help window:

Macintosh	Click the View Topic button.
Windows	Click the Display button.

On the Macintosh, the Index window remains on the screen. Windows closes the Index window.

4. On the Macintosh, click the Go To Topic button to display the associated Help document and close the Index window.

Performing Keyword Searches (Macintosh)

A Keyword search lets you view topics directly, without needing to scroll through the alphabetical list presented by the index. To perform a Keyword search:

1. Type the first letters of the topic you want to find until ClarisWorks Help displays the closest match to what you have typed in light gray letters. For example, in Figure 1.29, the user has typed "outline f." ClarisWorks Help added "ormat command."

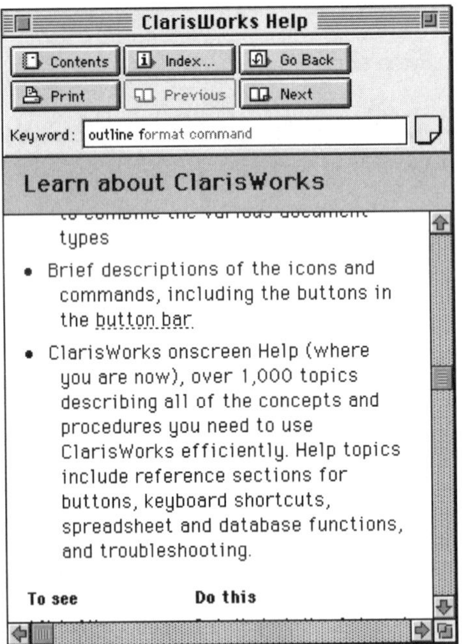

Figure 1.29 Performing a Keyword search

2. If the topic identified by ClarisWorks Help is correct, your search is concluded. Press Enter to display the Help document.

3. However, if the topic is not correct, continue typing the letters of the search term until you find the correct term. Press Enter to display the Help document.

Finding Help Topics (Windows)

You can search for topics in the ClarisWorks Help documents using the Windows Find functions. However, before using Find for the first time, you must let Window build a database to keywords through which it will search.

To build the keyword database:

1. Choose Help->ClarisWorks Help Contents to display the Help Topics dialog box.

2. Click the Find tab. If you haven't attempted a Find before, ClarisWorks displays the Find Setup Wizard (Figure 1.30).

3. ClarisWorks selects the radio button that maximizes the size of the database so that you will have the best chance of finding the topic you want. Unless you are short on hard disk space, leave this option selected.

4. Click the Next button. The wizard displays a second panel indicating that it is ready to create the database.

5. Click the Finish button.

6. Wait while Windows builds the database.

Once the keyword database has been built, you will have access to the Find panel in the Help Topics dialog box (Figure 1.31). Notice that all 851 possible topics are available.

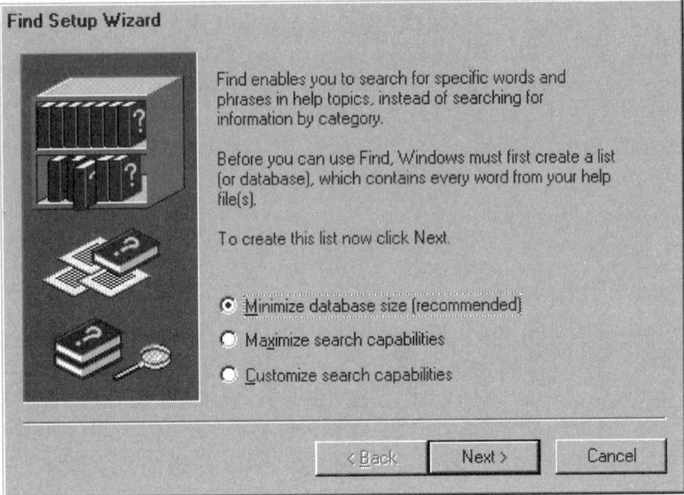

Figure 1.30 The Find Setup Wizard

To perform a search:

1. Type the first letter of the topic you want to find. ClarisWorks narrows the available topics on the basis of that letter.

2. Continue typing the topic. As you type, ClarisWorks adjusts the number of documents that match your search. For example, in Figure 1.32, you can see that the letters *outli* narrow the search to 43 topics.

3. When you have located a topic you want to view, highlight the topic in the scrolling list at the bottom of the Find panel and click the Display button.

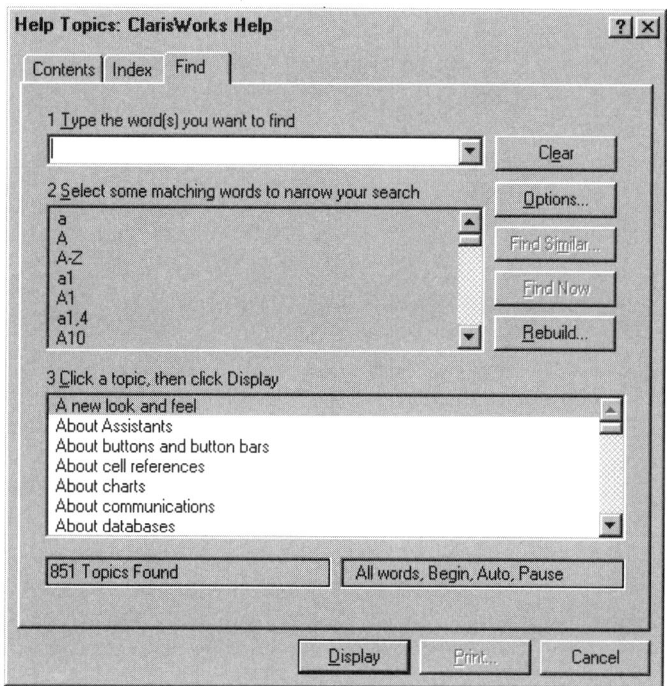

Figure 1.31 The Find panel

Adding Notes to Help (Macintosh)

You can annotate ClarisWorks Help with electronic sticky notes. To place a note in a Help document:

1. Drag a yellow note onto a Help document.
2. Type your note. ClarisWorks Help expands the note as you type (see Figure 1.33).

To remove a note, drag the note to the top of the Help window.

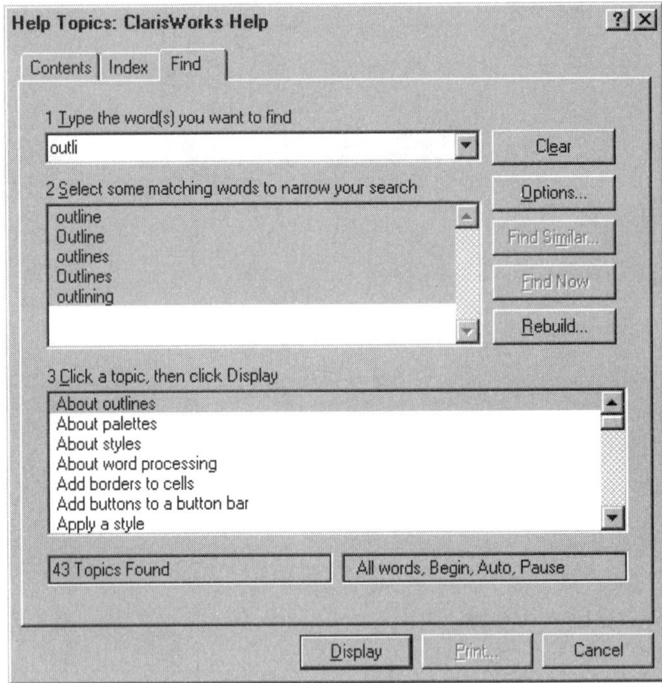

Figure 1.32 Perfoming a Windows Find

Using Balloon Help (Macintosh)

Balloon Help provides cartoon-like balloons that pop up on your screen as you move the mouse pointer onto various elements of the ClarisWorks environment. The contents of the balloon provide information about the element to which the mouse pointer is pointing. For example, in Figure 1.34 you can see a balloon produced by placing the mouse pointer over a button that sets the alignment of text in a word processing document.

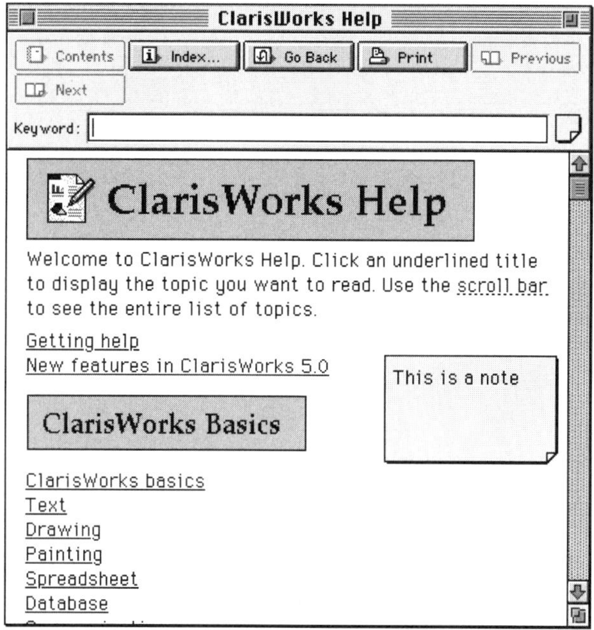

Figure 1.33 Adding a note to a Help document

Turning on Balloon Help

To activate Balloon Help, choose Show Balloons from the Help menu. The Show Balloons option will change to Hide Balloons.

Displaying Balloons

To display balloons, be sure that Balloon Help is turned on. Then move the mouse pointer as needed to perform your work with ClarisWorks. Balloon Help will display all available balloons as the mouse pointer moves on the screen.

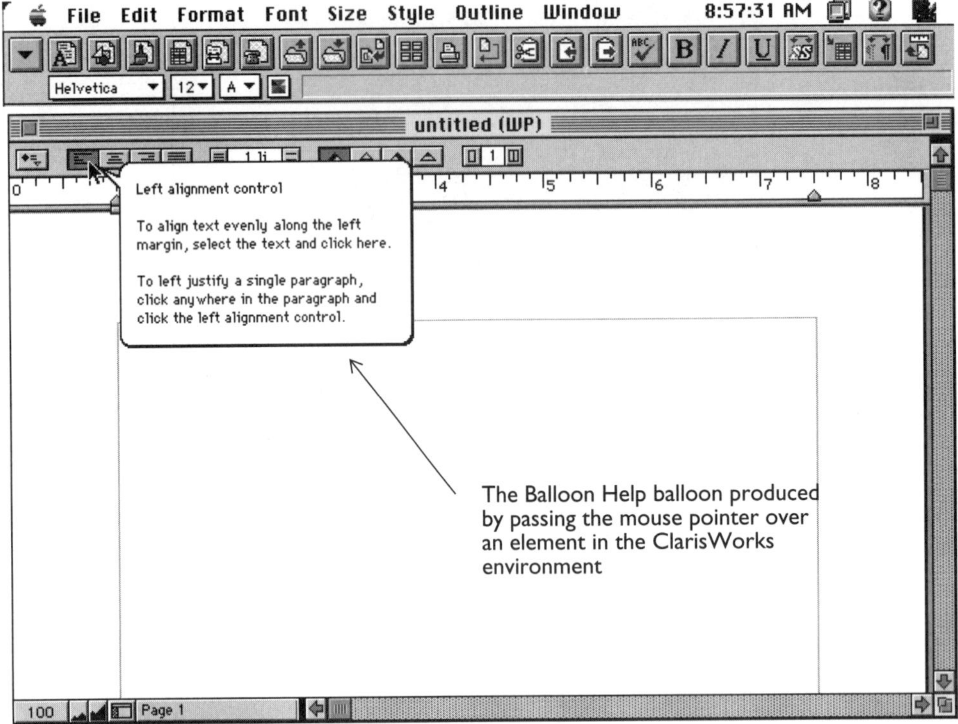

Figure 1.34 A Macintosh Balloon Help balloon

Turning off Balloon Help

To turn off Balloon Help, choose Hide Balloons from the Help menu.

Using Tool Tips (Windows)

Tool tips are labels that show up when you pass the mouse pointer over a button in the Button Bar or the tool panel (for example, see Figure 1.35).

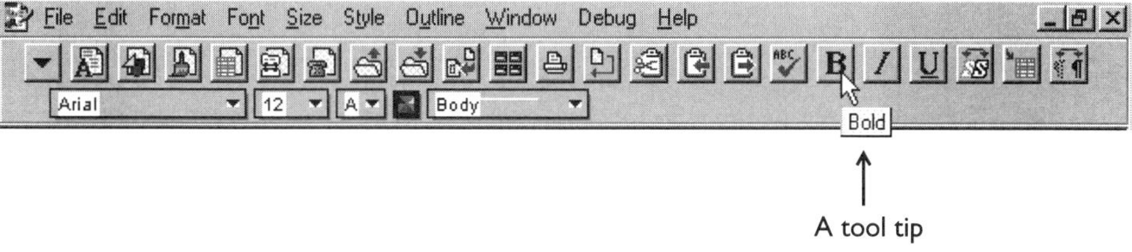

Figure 1.35 A Windows tool tip

If tool tips aren't turned on, do the following to make them visible:

1. Choose Edit->Preferences or press ALT-E, N. The Preferences dialog box appears.

2. Choose General from the Topic popup menu.

3. Click in the Tool Tips check box to place a check mark in the box, as in Figure 1.36.

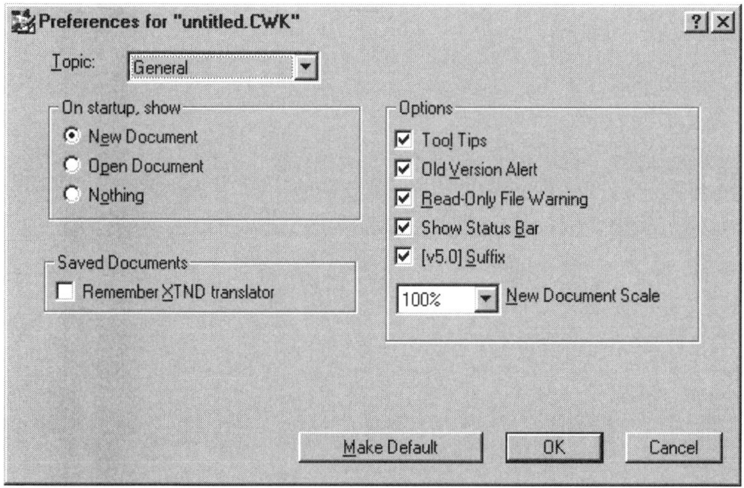

Figure 1.36 Using General preferences to turn on tool tips

4. Click the OK button to save your changes.

To ensure that tool tips are visible whenever you start ClarisWorks, click the Make Default button in the Preference dialog box.

2

Word Processing Basics

Word processing is a computer application that is designed primarily for entering, editing, and formatting text. In this chapter you will be introduced to the basics of the ClarisWorks' word processing module, including fundamental skills such as typing, modifying, and aligning text, setting document and paragraph margins, and setting type characteristics.

ClarisWorks's word processing module is a full-featured word processor. Its capabilities — which are typical of most word processors — include the following:

- Margin settings and tab stops at the paragraph level (different settings for different paragraphs).
- Multicolumn document formatting.
- More than one section in a document, with each section having a different column layout.
- Headers and footers, including automatic page numbering.
- Automatically numbered and placed footnotes.
- Typographic control, including the ability to use multiple typefaces, type styles, and type sizes.
- Styles (collections of formatting) that can be applied as a unit to a paragraph or block of text.
- Outlining.
- Writing tools, such as a spelling checker and thesaurus.
- Embedded graphics. (Although word processors have always been oriented toward handling text, most of today's word processors can also handle graphics.)

The Macintosh version of ClarisWorks also includes an equation editor, a third-party add-on that simplifies the creation of mathematical and scientific formulas. (Using the equation editor is described in Appendix B.) An equation editor is not a typical word processor feature but is often included in a word processor whose developers feel that it might be used for creating technical documents. The inclusion of an equation editor in ClarisWorks means that the word processing module can be used, for example, by students who need to prepare laboratory reports.

The skills that you learn in this chapter for formatting text can be used with other ClarisWorks modules, wherever you happen to be working with text.

Documents versus Frames

ClarisWorks supports two containers for word processing: stand-alone word processing documents and *text frames.* A text frame is a region of a document other than a word processing document that behaves generally like a stand-alone word processing document. Most of what you read about word processing in this chapter and Chapters 3 and 4 applies to text frames as well as stand-alone word processing documents. However, some features — in particular sections and columnar layouts — aren't available in frames.

You will learn about creating text frames in other documents beginning in Chapter 5.

Typing Text

For most people, word processing software replaces the typewriter as a tool for preparing text documents. Although the keyboard we use with a computer looks a great deal like a typewriter keyboard, there are some significant differences between the two that affect your actions with a word processor:

- Using a typewriter, you must press Return at the end of each line. With a word processor, you press Return only at the end of a paragraph. The word processing software takes care of adjusting line endings within a paragraph. By default, ClarisWorks's word processor starts a new line whenever an entire word won't fit on a line (*word wrap*).

In Figure 2.1, for example, you can see a word processing document that contains a single line. There is room for only one character at the end of the line. If you were working with a typewriter, you could type the character and then press Return — if you wanted. However, a word processor won't leave one letter hanging. Instead, it assumes that a word ends with a space. If an entire word won't fit, the word processor automatically moves the whole word to the next line as you are typing. As you can see in Figure 2.2, the word processor has kept words together, even though it means leaving white space at the right edge of the document.

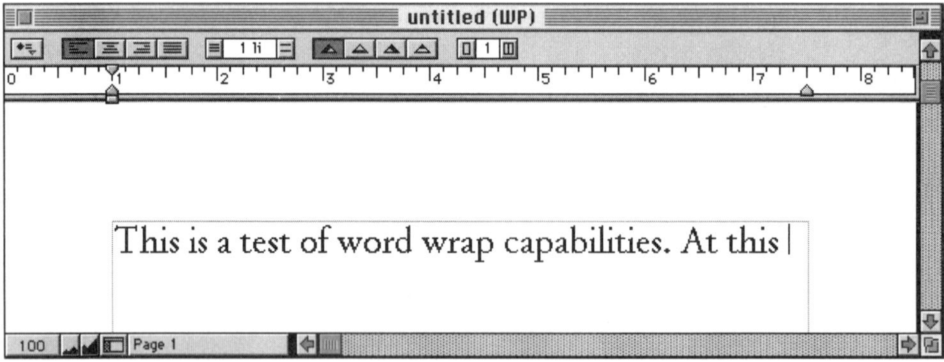

Figure 2.1 Just before word wrap will occur

If you request hyphenation, the word wrap adjusts line endings on the basis of hyphenated parts of words rather than entire words. You will read more about hyphenation in Chapter 4.

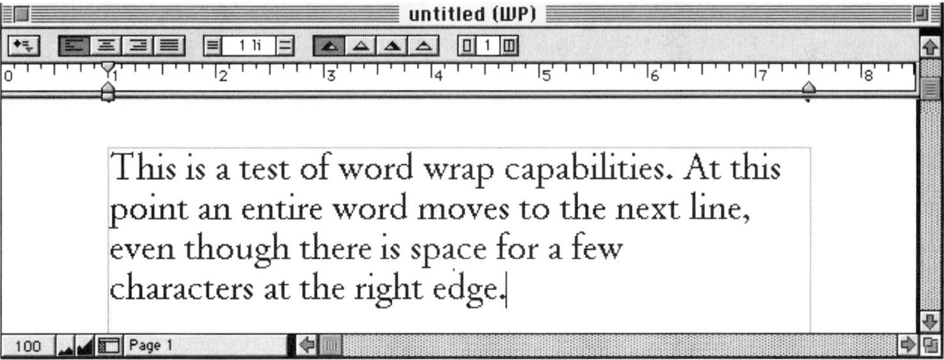

Figure 2.2 After word wrap has occurred

- The letter "O" and the number 0 are interchangeable on a typewriter keyboard. On a computer keyboard they are two different keys. (Whether they actually appear different depends on the typeface you are using.) Although it often makes little difference if you are typing text, you will find that if you want a computer to treat characters as a number — as it may when you are working with the spreadsheet or database module — it is vitally important that you type "O" as a letter and 0 as a number. You should therefore get into the habit of using the correct key even if you are just preparing text that will be read.

- The number 1 is missing from many typewriter keyboards; you use the letter "l" instead. However, when working with a computer, you must be certain to use the letter "l" only within words; use the number 1 in numbers.

- If you hold down a key, rather than just tapping it, the character will repeat until you release the key. (Electric typewriters will do this; manual typewriters won't.)

The bottom line is that when you want to enter text into a word processing document, you just type. When you reach the end of a paragraph, you press Return.

Your word processing document will look more professional if you use only one space between sentences. Although typewritten documents often contain two, typeset documents use only one.

Managing the Insertion Point

The characters you type appear in a word processing document at the *insertion point*, a straight line that flashes. In Figure 2.1, for example, the insertion point is one space beyond the *s* at the right edge of the typed line. In Figure 2.2, the insertion point is after the period at the end of the typing.

To be technically correct, new typing appears to the left of the insertion point, which moves to the right as you type.

You can insert new characters at any place in a word processing document at any time. To do so:

1. Place the mouse pointer at the place where new characters should appear.
2. Click the mouse button. The insertion point appears at the place where you clicked.
3. Start typing. ClarisWorks inserts new characters at the insertion point, pushing existing text to the right and adjusting word wrap as necessary.

Editing Text

One of most delightful things about a word processor is that when you make a change, the change stays put. (This is in direct contrast to the experience many of us have had with a typewriter, where retyping to remove some errors introduces new ones!)

Undoing Actions

If you don't want to keep the last changes you made to a document, you can undo your actions. To perform an Undo:

Macintosh	Choose Edit->Undo or press ⌘-Z.
Windows	Choose Edit->Undo, press CTRL-Z, or press ALT-E, D.
Both	Click the Undo button in the Button Bar.

The Undo mechanism reverses only the last action performed. An "action" is defined as a single editing operation (copying or moving text, for example) or all typing that occurred since the last editing operation.

Making Corrections as You Type

As you are typing, you may realize right away that you have type a few incorrect characters. For example, you notice that you have typed *teh* instead of *the*. The easiest way to correct this type of error is often to delete the incorrect characters and to retype them.

There are two keys that delete characters:

- Delete (on the Macintosh) or Backspace (on Windows): Pressing the Delete or Backspace key, found at the right edge of the number keys, removes one character to the left of the insertion point.
- Del: Pressing the Del key, which is located with other cursor movement keys such as Home and End, removes one character to the right of the insertion point.

The Macintosh standard keyboard and PowerBook keyboards don't have Del keys.

The process for deleting and replacing a few characters as you type is therefore as follows:

1. Move the insertion point to where you want to remove characters.

2. Press Delete/Backspace or Del (whichever is appropriate) to remove the characters you want to replace.

3. Type corrected characters.

Selecting Text

Using the Delete/Backspace or Del key works well when you need to correct only a few characters. However, when you want to delete, replace, or move a large block of text, there is a more efficient way to do so, working with the entire block of text as a unit.

To perform an operation on a block of text, you must first *select* the text. Selected text appears in reverse video (white characters on a black background), as in Figure 2.3.

The actual colors in which selected text appears depend on the colors of your text. If your text, for example, is in colors that are visible on a black background — such as red or blue — then selecting the text simply gives the characters a black background; the text color doesn't change.

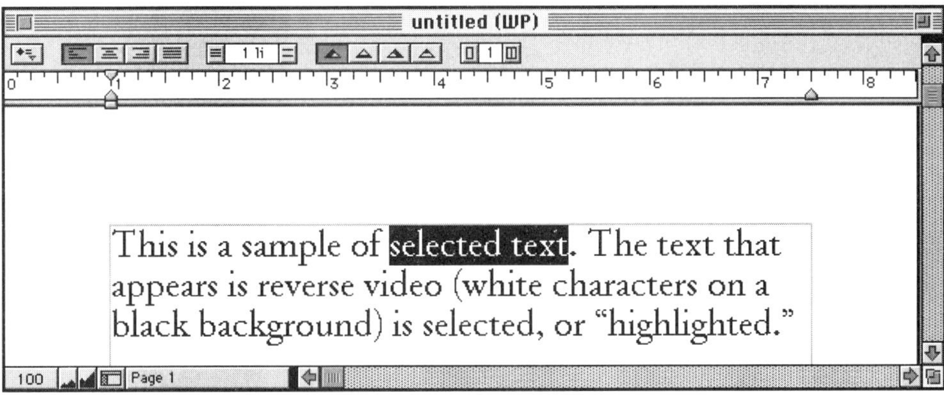

Figure 2.3 Selected text

There are several ways to select text:

- Drag the mouse pointer over the text you want to select. If you move the mouse pointer above or below the workspace, ClarisWorks automatically scrolls the document to extend your selection.
- Double-click on a word to select it.
- Triple-click on a line to select it.
- Quadruple-click on a paragraph to select it.

- Place the insertion point at the beginning of the block of text you want to select. Scroll to the end of the block. Shift-click at the end of the block. ClarisWorks selects everything between the first location of the insertion point and the Shift-click. (This method is much easier to use than dragging if you want to select a large portion of a document.)

- Place the insertion point at the beginning of the block of text you want to select. Hold down the Shift key. While the Shift key is down, press one of the arrow keys to extend the selection. Pressing Shift-right arrow selects one character to the right; pressing Shift-down arrow selects one row down. By the same token, pressing Shift-left arrow selects one character to the left and pressing Shift-up arrow selects one row up.

Once you have selected text, then you can perform operations that affect the entire block of text.

Deleting Text

There are two ways to permanently delete a selected block of text:

- Press the Delete key.

- Choose Edit -> Clear.

Once you have removed text in this way, the only way to recover it is to use the Undo action. However, you must Undo your deletion immediately, before performing another editing action or modifying the contents of the document in any way. Even typing one character will make it impossible to recover your deletion.

Moving a Block of Text

One of the most frequent editing operations we perform when working on a document — whether it be a report, term paper, or letter — is moving text from one location to another. We may also need to move text from one document to another. Word processors support moving text without retyping, so it is easy for us to revise our work.

To move a block of text, a word processor must do the following:

- Delete the text from its original place in the document.
- Adjust word wrap to account for the deleted text.
- Store the deleted text temporarily.
- Let the user indicate where the text is to be placed.
- Copy the text into its new location and adjust word wrap to accommodate it.

The text being moved is stored temporarily on the computer's *Clipboard*, a holding area that can store one item — text, graphics, data, and so on — at a time. When you place an item on the Clipboard, it replaces the Clipboard's previous contents.

The Clipboard is accessible to all applications running on a Macintosh or Windows computer. You can therefore use it for moving items between documents as well as within the same document.

To move a block of text, do the following:

1. Select the text you want to move.

2. *Cut* the text from the document.

Macintosh	Choose Edit->Cut or press ⌘-X.
Windows	Choose Edit->Cut, press CTRL-X, or press ALT-E, T.
Both	Click the Cut button in the Button Bar.

3. If necessary, make the document into which the text will be placed the active document.

4. Move the insertion point to the place in the document where the text should be placed.

5. *Paste* the text into its new location.

Macintosh	Choose Edit->Paste or press ⌘-V.
Windows	Choose Edit->Paste, press CTRL-V, or press ALT-E, P.
Both	Click the Paste button in the Button Bar

Pasting an item *copies* an item from the Clipboard into a document; the contents of the Clipboard remain intact. You can therefore repeatedly copy the contents of the Clipboard into one or more documents. The contents of the Clipboard are modified only when you cut or copy something from a document.

Drag-and-Drop Moving (Macintosh Only)

If you are using ClarisWorks on a Macintosh, then you have one additional method for moving text — *drag and drop*, a technique with which you can use the mouse to drag selected text to a new location in a document.

To move a block of text by dragging:

1. Select the text to be moved. The mouse pointer turns into the *drag cursor* (see Figure 2.4).

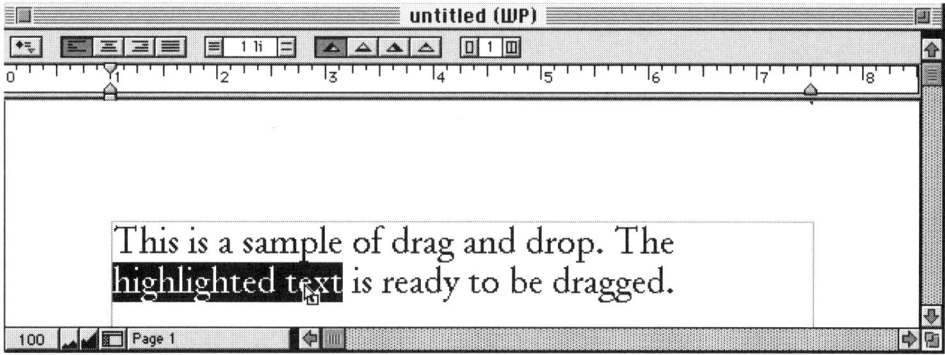

Figure 2.4 The Macintosh drag cursor

2. Hold down the mouse button with the drag cursor over the selected text and drag the text to its new location in the document. An insertion point and a rectangular outline of the highlighted text follow as you drag.

3. When the insertion point is located where you want the highlighted text to appear, release the mouse button. ClarisWorks inserts the text at the insertion point, removing it from its original location.

Copying a Range of Text

We often have text that we use repeatedly, such as a return address or signature line. Rather than typing the same thing over and over again, we can copy the text to the Clipboard — without deleting it from the document — and paste it into another location in the same document or into a different document.

To copy a block of text without deleting it from the document:

1. Select the block of text you want to copy.

2. *Copy* the text to the Clipboard.

Macintosh	Choose Edit->Copy or press ⌘-C.
Windows	Choose Edit->Copy, press CTRL-C, or press ALT-E, C.
Both	Click the Copy button in the Button Bar.

3. If necessary, make the document into which the text will be placed the active document.

4. Move the insertion point to the place in the document where the text should be placed.

5. *Paste* the text into its new location.

Macintosh	Choose Edit->Paste or press ⌘-V.
Windows	Choose Edit->Paste, press CTRL-V, or press ALT-E, P.
Both	Click the Paste button in the Button Bar.

Drag-and-Drop Copying (Macintosh Only)

If you are using ClarisWorks on a Macintosh, you can drag a copy of selected text to a new location in a document:

1. Select the text to be copied. The mouse pointer turns into the drag cursor when it is over the selected text.
2. Hold down the Option key and the mouse button with the drag cursor over the selected text and drag the text to its new location. An insertion point and a rectangular outline of the text follow you as you drag.
3. When the insertion point is located where you want the copy of the selected text to appear, release the Option key and the mouse button. ClarisWorks places a copy of the selected text at the insertion point, without deleting the original selected text.

Basic Formatting

The basic formatting of a word processing document includes setting page size, setting margins for the entire document, changing paragraph margins and indents, setting tab stops, setting paragraph spacing, and setting paragraph alignment. With the exception of page size and document margins, you can apply these settings either from a dialog box or from the ruler that appears at the top of the document window.

The Ruler

Many of ClarisWorks's formatting capabilities are available from the ruler that appears at the top of a document window. There are two types of rulers, text and graphics, and they are controlled by the Rulers Format dialog box.

As you can see in Figure 2.5, the dialog box lets you choose the type of ruler, the display units, and the number of divisions within each major display unit.

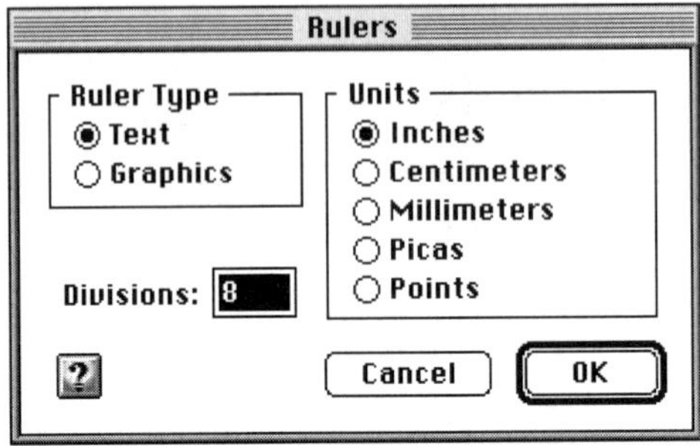

Figure 2.5 The Rulers Format dialog box

Picas and points are units of measurement used by typesetters. There are 6 picas to an inch and 12 points in a pica. Although you may never need to use picas and points when formatting a document, as you will see later in this chapter, type sizes are measured only in points.

Setting Page Size

The size of a word processing document's page is determined by the type of paper on which it will be printed. If you do not set the page size, ClarisWorks automatically uses the size of the page from the last document with which you worked.

To set the page size:

1.

Macintosh	Choose File->Page Setup.
Windows	Choose File->Print Setup.

A dialog box appears (Figure 2.6 for Macintosh; Figure 2.7 for Windows).

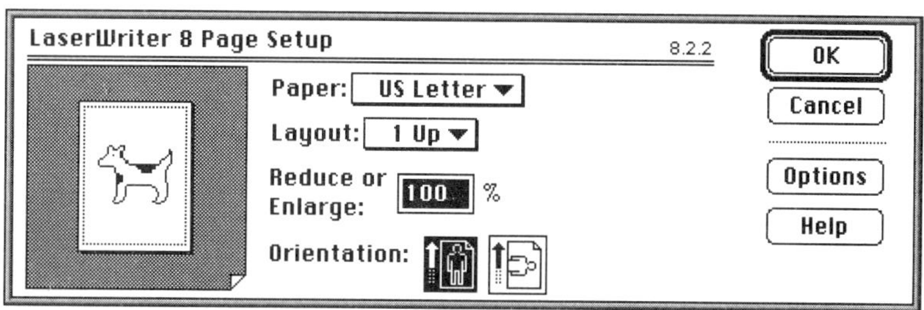

Figure 2.6 The Macintosh Page Setup dialog box

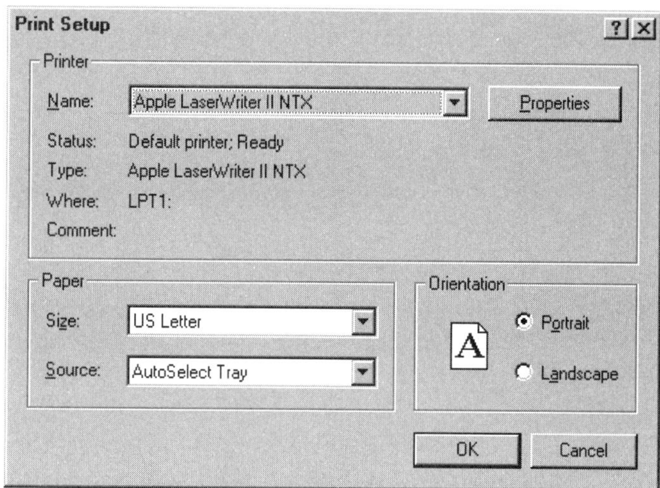

Figure 2.7 The Windows Print Setup dialog box

2. Choose the paper size.

3. Choose the paper orientation. (Portrait is taller than wide; Landscape is wider than tall.)

Working with Document Margins

A word processing document's margins set the outside boundaries within which characters and other document elements (for example, graphics) can appear.

As an example, look at Figure 2.8. The document margins are marked by a light gray box. Inside the margins you can see some text and part of a graphic shape. ClarisWorks simply won't let you type text outside the margins. (If you click the mouse pointer in the margin space, nothing happens!) When the graphic was dragged partially outside the margins, ClarisWorks hid (or *clipped*) the graphic at the margin.

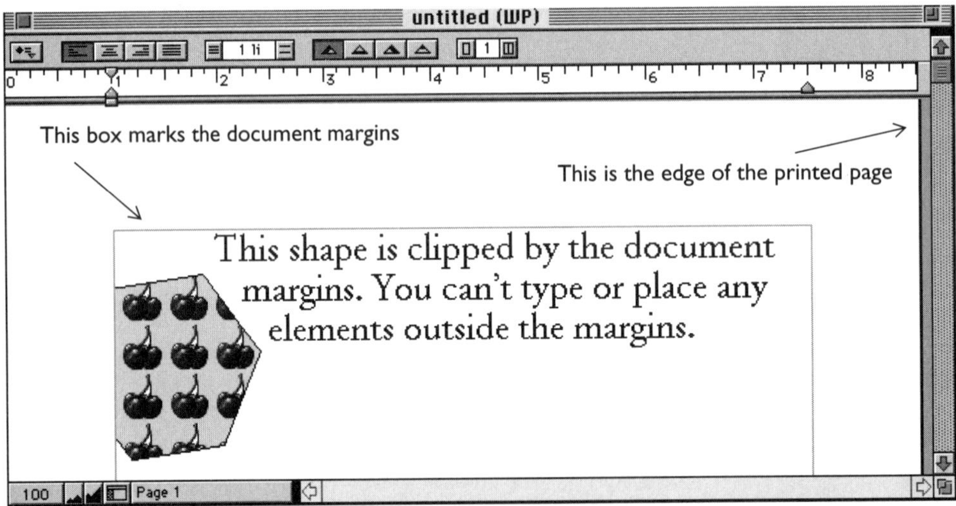

Figure 2.8 How margins restrict the contents of a document

How Document Margins Affect Document Layout

When you set the margins for a document, you specify the amount of empty space that will appear on each of the four sides of a page. Like many word processors, ClarisWorks's word processing module can recognize a variety of types of margin settings, including those where facing pages have mirrored layouts.

In Figure 2.9 you can see the types of available margin layouts. If your document is single sided, then every page will have the same margins. In that case your margins might be regular (left and right the same size) or irregular (left and right different sizes). However, if your document will be printed double sided, then you have three choices. You can use regular margins, where facing pages have the same left and right margins. You can also use irregular margins, where the left and right margins are different on each page, but the same on facing pages.

Alternatively, you can choose a mirrored, irregular layout, where the left and right margins alternate depending on whether the page is a left or right page, as in the bottom illustration in Figure 2.9. A mirrored layout makes it possible to allocate additional space to an inside margin, where the binding of a document takes up part of a page.

Mirrored layouts are also used to leave space at the outside edges of pages for icons (like the tip icon to the left of this note) or other special page design elements. However, because ClarisWorks won't let you work in the margins, if you want to place things in margins you will need to set paragraph margins smaller than the page margins so that the location of the design elements is actually inside the document page margins.

Setting Document Margins

To set the document margins:

1. Choose Format->Document. The Document Format dialog box appears (Figure 2.10).

Identical, regular margins on facing pages

Irregular margins on facing pages (not mirrored)

Irregular margins mirrored on facing pages

Figure 2.9 Possible margin layouts

2. Enter the margins for each side of the page.

3. If you want a mirrored layout, check the *Mirror Facing Pages* check box.

4. If you want to hide the page margins — so they aren't visible on the screen — remove the check from the *Show margins* check box.

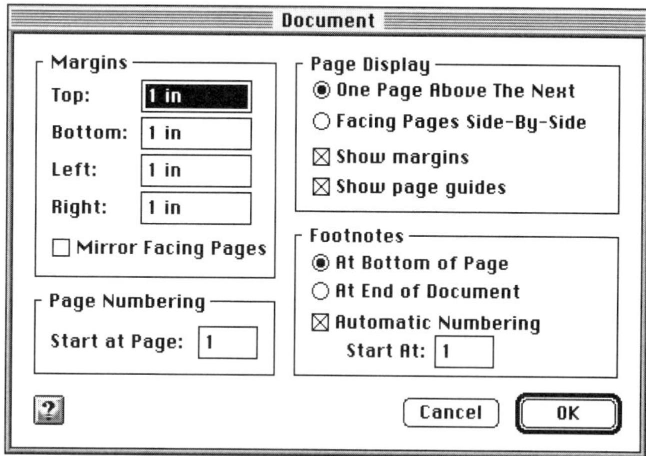

Figure 2.10 Document Format dialog box

5. If you want to hide the box that shows the border between the page margins and the area in which you can enter document elements, remove the check from the *Show page guides* check box.

6. Click the OK button to apply the changes. ClarisWorks reformats the document according to the new page margins.

Setting Paragraph Margins and Indents

Within the page margins, which apply to the entire document, you can change the margins and indentation of any single paragraph or block of paragraphs. These changes can be made using the document's ruler or a dialog box.

A word processing document's ruler has three symbols on it:

- (left indent): The indentation from the left edge of the page.

- (first indent): The indentation of the first line of the paragraph. This is expressed relative to the left indentation.
- (right indent): The indentation from the right edge of the page.

To change an indentation using the ruler, you drag an indentation symbol to a new location.

A change in paragraph margins affects the paragraph containing the insertion point, or — if a block of paragraphs is selected — the entire block. Once you have changed indentation, the change affects all succeeding paragraphs, until the point in the document where different paragraph margins have been applied. To understand how this works, imagine that ClarisWorks places a special, invisible marker in your word processing document each time you change paragraph indentation. ClarisWorks then uses the settings in the marker to format paragraph indentation until it gets new instructions from another marker.

Indenting Entire Paragraphs

When adding long quotations to a document, or other blocks of text that need to be set aside from the body of the document, we usually indent both edges of the paragraph from the page margins, as in Figure 2.11.

To indent from both margins using the ruler:

1. Place the insertion point anywhere in the paragraph to be indented. To indent a range of paragraphs, select all the paragraphs to be indented.
2. Drag both the left indent and the first indent markers together to their new position in the ruler.

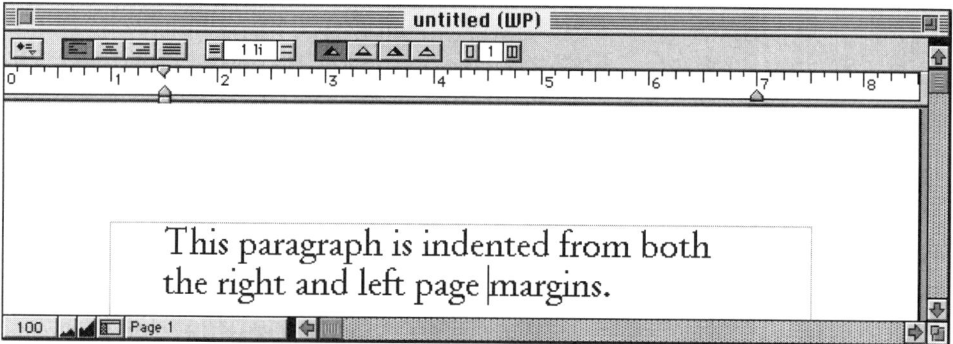

Figure 2.11 Indenting a paragraph from both margins

3. Drag the right indent marker to its new position in the ruler.

To indent from both margins using the Paragraph Format dialog box:

1. Place the insertion point anywhere in the paragraph to be indented. To indent a range of paragraphs, select all the paragraphs to be indented.

2. Choose Format->Paragraph. The Paragraph Format dialog box appears.

3. Enter values for the indentations. Notice in Figure 2.12, for example, that both the left and right indents are expressed in terms of their offset from the page margins. The first line indent is expressed relative to the left indent. In this case, it has a value of 0 because it is the same as the left indent.

4. Click the Apply button or the OK button to apply the changes.

Paragraph

Left Indent: 0.5
First Line: 0 in
Right Indent: 0.5
Label: None
Line Spacing: 1 li
Space Before: 0 li
Space After: 0 li
Alignment: Left
Apply Cancel OK

Figure 2.12 Setting equal left–right indentation using the Paragraph Format dialog box

The Apply, Cancel, and OK buttons you see in Figure 2.12 are present in all the ClarisWorks Format dialog boxes. When you click Apply, ClarisWorks applies your changes but leaves the dialog box on the screen. Because the dialog box is movable, you can move it to another position on the screen to see the effect of the change you've made. However, because the dialog boxes is modal, you must close it before continuing to work on your document. Clicking the OK button applies your changes and closes the dialog box. Clicking the Cancel button undoes all changes made from the time the dialog box was opened and closes the dialog box.

Creating a First Line Indent

Many documents indent the first line of each paragraph to make it easier to see where paragraphs begin (for example, see Figure 2.13)

To create a first line indent using the ruler:

1. Place the insertion point anywhere in the paragraph to be indented. To indent a range of paragraphs, select all the paragraphs to be indented.
2. Drag the first line indent marker to the right until it reaches the location where the first line of the paragraph should begin, as in Figure 2.13.

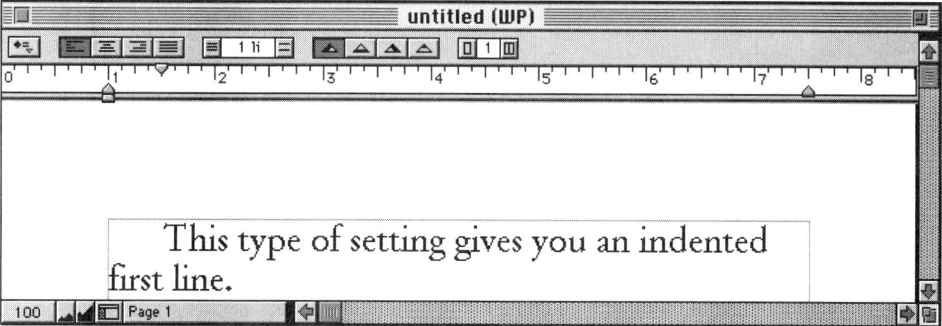

Figure 2.13 Using a first line indent

To create a first line indent using the Paragraph Format dialog box:

1. Place the insertion point anywhere in the paragraph to be indented. To indent a range of paragraphs, select all the paragraphs to be indented.

2. Choose Format->Paragraph. The Paragraph Format dialog box appears.

3. Enter a positive value for First Indent. Keep in mind that this value is added to the value of the Left Indent. In Figure 2.14, for example, the first line indent is 0.5 inch from the left paragraph margin.

4. Click the Apply button or the OK button to apply the changes.

Creating a Hanging Indent

A *hanging indent* occurs when the first line of a paragraph is farther to the left than the rest of the paragraph (see Figure 2.15). Hanging indents are useful, for example, for formatting lists.

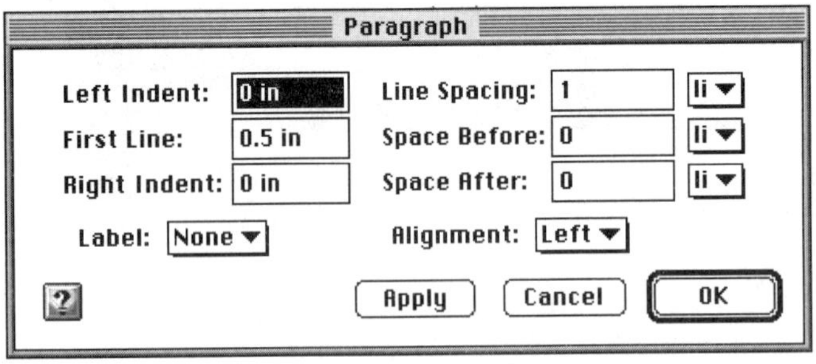

Paragraph

Left Indent: 0 in | Line Spacing: 1 li
First Line: 0.5 in | Space Before: 0 li
Right Indent: 0 in | Space After: 0 li
Label: None | Alignment: Left

Apply | Cancel | OK

Figure 2.14 Setting a first line indent using the Paragraph Format dialog box

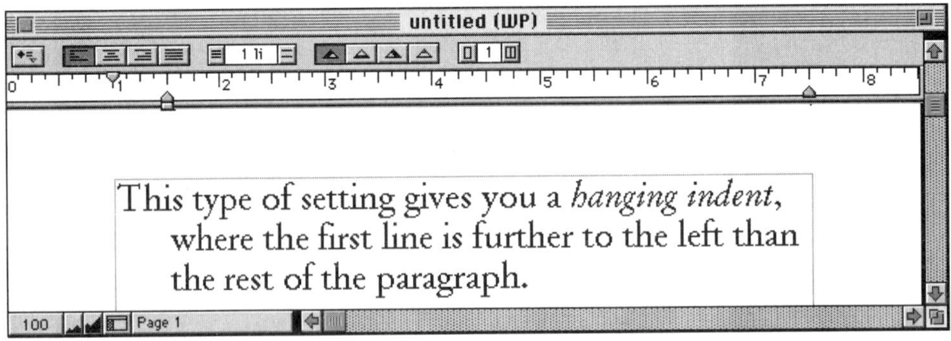

Figure 2.15 Using a handing indent

To format a paragraph with a hanging indent using the ruler:

1. Place the insertion point anywhere in the paragraph to be indented. To indent a range of paragraphs, select all the paragraphs to be indented.

2. Drag the first indent marker to where the left edge of the paragraph (with the exception of the first line) will be.

To format a paragraph with a hanging indent using the Paragraph Format dialog box:

1. Place the insertion point anywhere in the paragraph to be indented. To indent a range of paragraphs, select all the paragraphs to be indented.

2. Choose Format->Paragraph. The Paragraph Format dialog box appears.

3. Enter a left indent for the paragraph.

4. Enter a negative value for the first indent of the paragraph. Keep in mind that this value is relative to the value of the left indent. For example, in Figure 2.16, the left indent is 0.5 inch from the left page margin. The first line indent negative and therefore moves the first line to 0.5 – 0.5 inches, or 0 (aligned with the left page margin).

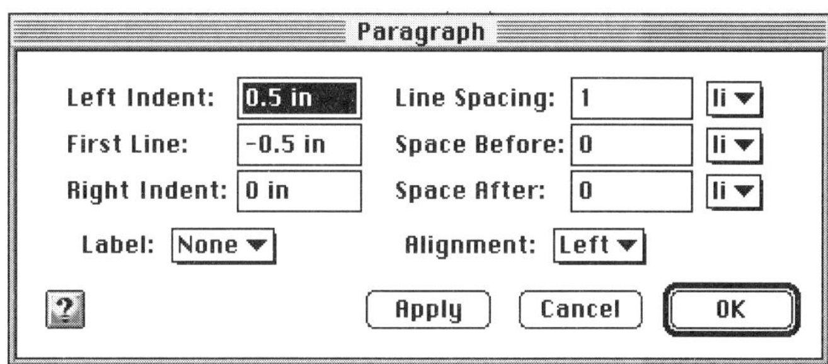

Figure 2.16 Setting a hanging indent using the Paragraph Format dialog box

5. Click the Apply button or the OK button to apply the changes.

Setting Tab Stops

A tab stop marks a spot to which the insertion point will move when you press the Tab key. ClarisWorks supports four kinds of tabs, which are represented by icons:

-  (Left): Text is left aligned with the position of the tab stop.
-  (Center): Text is centered on the position of the tab stop.
-  (Right): Text is right aligned with the position of the tab stop.
-  (Decimal): Text is aligned on a decimal point or any other character you choose.

You may also choose to fill the space between tabs with periods, a straight line, or dashes. A sample of ClarisWorks tab options can be found in Figure 2.17. Notice that the tab stop for all of the samples has been set at the 4" mark in the ruler (3" from the margin).

There are two ways to set tab stops: using the ruler or using a dialog box. The fill character and the alignment character for a decimal tab can be set only from the dialog box. The dialog box also provides more precise control over the placement of a tab.

To set a tab stop using the ruler:

1. Place the insertion point anywhere in a single paragraph or select all paragraphs to which the tab stop will apply.
2. Drag a tab icon from the text ruler into the ruler, *or* click in the ruler where you want the tab stop to

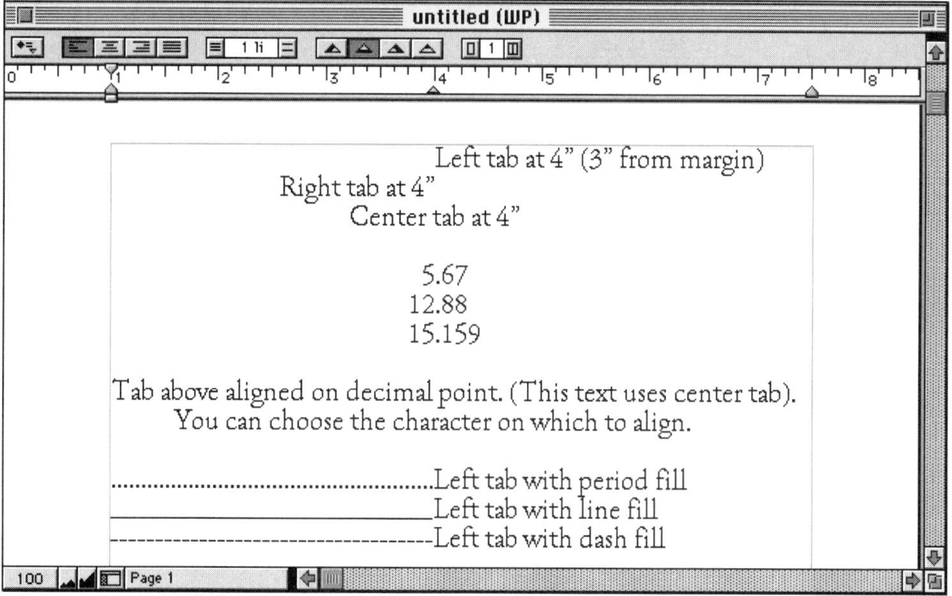

Figure 2.17 ClarisWorks tab options

appear. Drag the tab stop to its position in the ruler. As you drag, ClarisWorks displays a line down your document showing you where the tab stop will align text (see Figure 2.18).

For example, you can see three tab stops (center, left, and decimal) in Figure 2.19.

To set tab stops using the Tab dialog box:

1. Place the insertion point anywhere in a single paragraph the tab stop or select all paragraphs to which the tab stop should apply.

2. Choose Format->Tab. The Tab Format dialog box appears (see Figure 2.20).

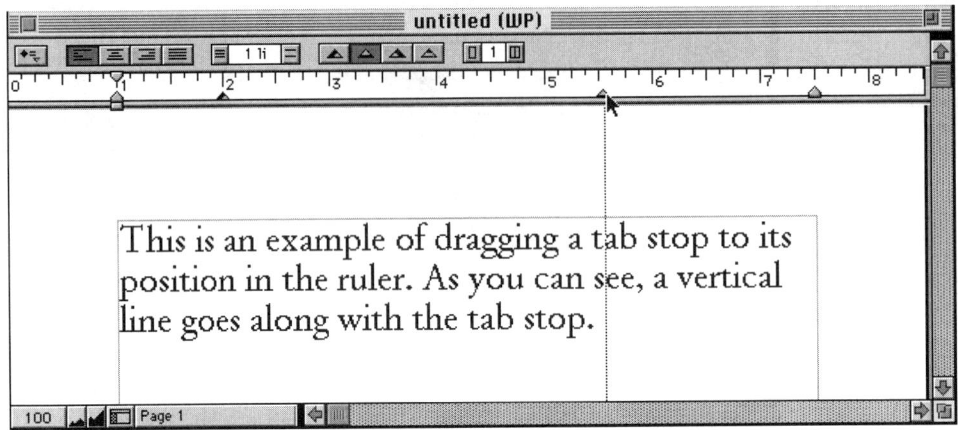

Figure 2.18 Dragging a tab stop into position

untitled (WP)

Drag one of these to here

Item number	Description	Price
1	Red pens	$1.56
2	Blue pens	$0.85
3	Lined paper	$3.25
4	Sticky notes	$0.65

Figure 2.19 Tab stops appearing in the ruler

3. Click the alignment radio button to select the type of tab.

4. If using a decimal tab to be aligned on something other than the decimal point, enter the alignment character.

5. Choose the fill character, if any.

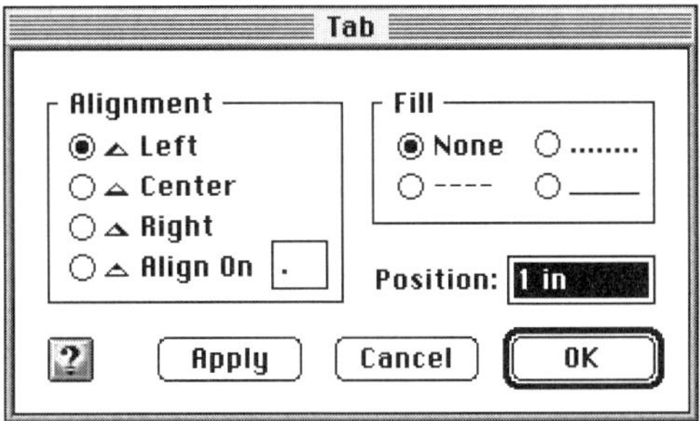

Figure 2.20 The Tab Format dialog box

6. Enter the position of the tab. Note that this measurement is relative to the left margin rather than an absolute measurement. For example, although the tab in Figure 2.17 appears at 4" in the ruler, the Tab Format dialog box setting is 3" because the left margin of the document is set at 1".

7. Click the Apply button or the OK button to apply the changes.

To remove a tab stop:

1. Place the insertion point in the paragraph containing the tab stop you want to remove or select a block of paragraphs.

2. Drag the tab stop marker straight up to the top of the ruler. The tab stop marker will disappear when it reaches the top of the ruler. ClarisWorks then reformats the paragraph containing the insertion point or selected paragraph.

Setting Paragraph Spacing

Professional looking documents have consistent spacing within and between paragraphs. ClarisWorks therefore lets you set three types of paragraph spacing:

- The spacing within a paragraph
- The spacing below a paragraph
- The spacing above a paragraph

For example, in Figure 2.21 you can see paragraphs that have been formatted with one line of extra space below each paragraph. Because the first lines of the paragraphs aren't indented, the extra spacing makes the text easier to read. The user, however, doesn't need to press an extra Return to get the space; ClarisWorks adds it automatically.

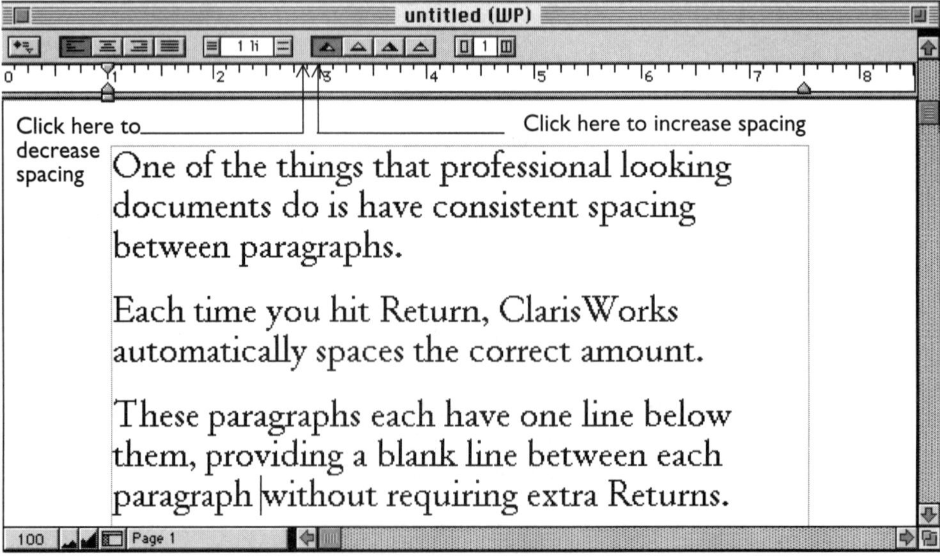

Figure 2.21 Using additional space below a paragraph

If two adjacent paragraphs have extra space below the first paragraph and above the second, ClarisWorks adds the spaces together.

The spacing within a paragraph can be set either from the ruler or the Paragraph Format dialog box. Spacing above and below a paragraph must be set using the dialog box.

To set paragraph spacing within a paragraph using the ruler:

1. Place the insertion point in the paragraph you want the spacing to affect or select a group of paragraphs.
2. Click the widely spaced line icon in the text ruler to increase spacing within the paragraph by 0.5 line. To obtain double spacing you will need to click twice.
3. Click the narrow spaced line icon in the text ruler to decrease spacing within the paragraph by 0.5 line.

ClarisWorks displays the spacing within the current paragraph in the box next to the line spacing icons 1 li.

To set spacing within, above, and below a paragraph using the Paragraph Format dialog box:

1. Place the insertion point in the paragraph you want the spacing to affect or select a group of paragraphs.
2. Choose Format->Paragraph. The Paragraph Format dialog box appears.
3. Enter values for line spacing (spacing within the paragraph), lines below, and lines above. Figure 2.22, for example, was used to create the sample in Figure 2.21, where each paragraph has one line below it.

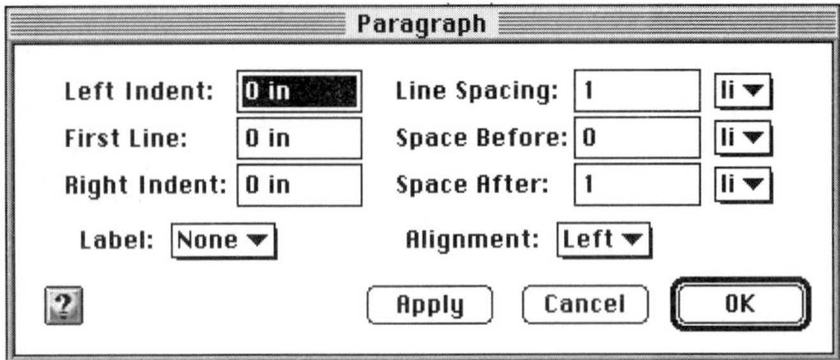

Figure 2.22 Using the Paragraph Format dialog box to set space after a paragraph

4. Choose the unit of measurement in which each spacing setting is expressed (see Figure 2.23).

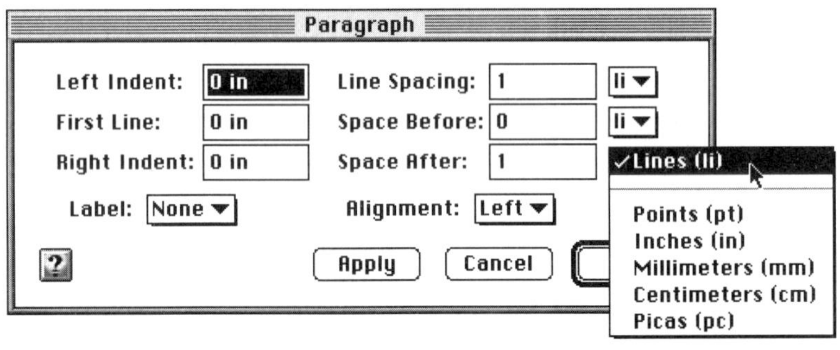

Figure 2.23 Choosing units for paragraph spacing

5. Click the Apply button or the OK button to apply the changes.

Setting Alignment

The term *alignment* refers to how text within a paragraph aligns with the margins. There are four types of alignment, each of which is accessible from an icon in the text ruler:

- (Left): Text aligns with the left margin. The right margin is ragged. This is the setting used in informal documents.
- (Center): Text is centered between the margins. Centered text is used primarily for headings.
- (Right): Text aligns with the right margin. The left margin is ragged. This setting is used for special formatting, such as placing the date or page number at the right edge of a page.
- (Justified): Justified (or full-justified) text aligns with both the left and right margins. ClarisWorks adjusts spacing within a line as necessary. This setting is used in formal documents and most printed materials, such as this book.

You can find a sample of the effect of each of these alignment choices on the appearance of text in Figure 2.24.

Paragraph alignment can be set either from the text ruler or from the Paragraph Format dialog box.

To set alignment using the ruler:

1. Place the insertion point in the paragraph to be affected or select a group of paragraphs.
2. Click the alignment button in the text ruler that represents the new alignment setting. ClarisWorks reformats the selected text.

To set alignment from the Paragraph Format dialog box:

1. Place the insertion point in the paragraph to be affected by the new alignment or select a range of paragraphs.

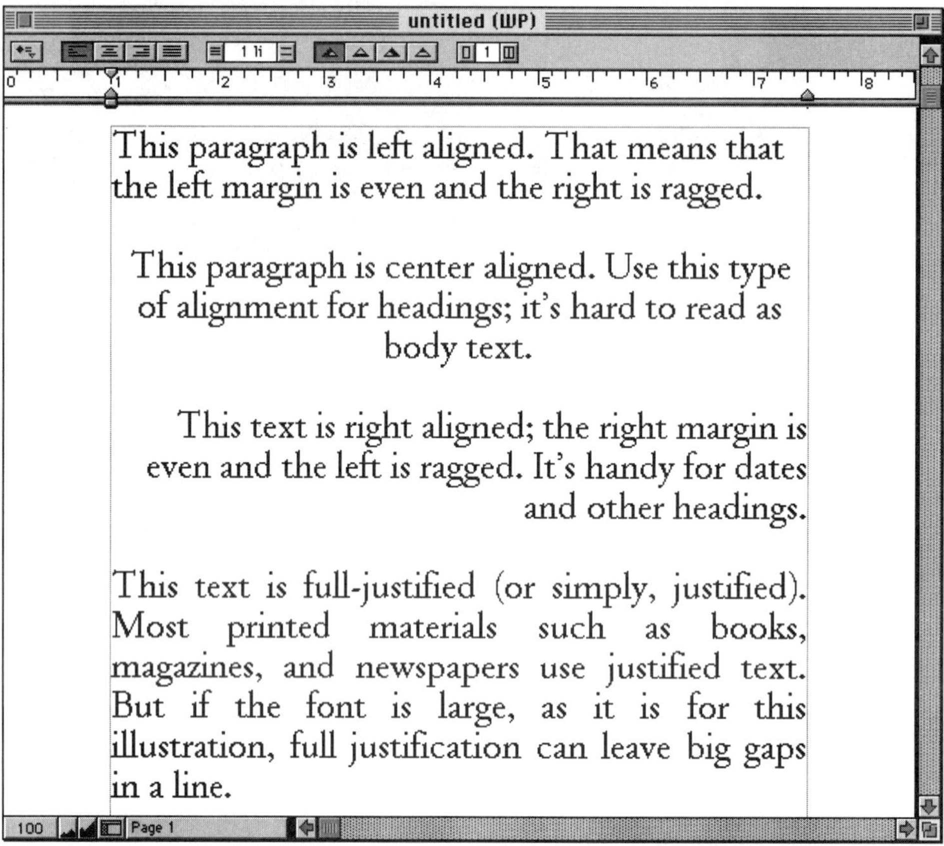

Figure 2.24 Text alignment

2. Choose Format->Paragraph. The Paragraph Format dialog box appears.

3. Choose the new alignment setting from the Alignment menu (see Figure 2.25).

4. Click the Apply button or the OK button to apply the changes.

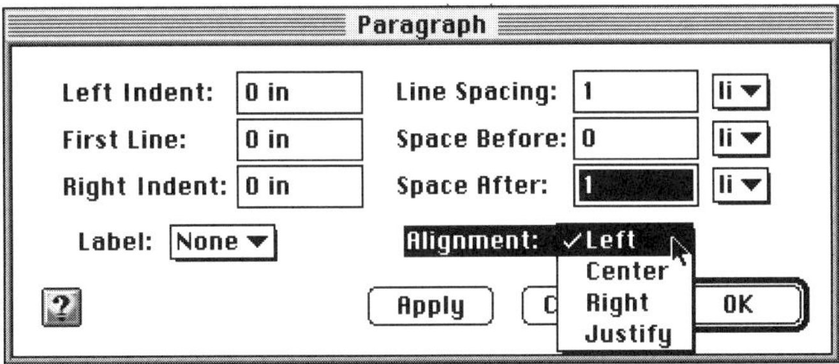

Figure 2.25 Choosing alignment from the Paragraph Format dialog box

Controlling Page Breaks

As you type, ClarisWorks automatically breaks your document into pages on the basis of the paper size and margin settings. However, you can also insert a page break, forcing type to move to the top of the next page, at any time.

To insert a forced page break:

1. Place the insertion point at the place in the document where you want the page break to occur.

2.

Macintosh	Choose Format->Insert Page Break or press SHIFT-NUMENTER.[1]
Windows	Choose Format->Insert Page Break, press CTRL-NUMENTER, or press ALT-M, B.

1. NUMENTER is the Enter key on the numeric keypad. On Macintosh PowerBooks and Duos use the single Enter key.

ClarisWorks moves the text following the insertion point to the top of a new page.

To remove a forced page break:

1. Place the insertion point just after the page break you want to remove.

2. Press Delete.

Formatting Text

The Macintosh 128K of 1984 was the first computer to give users direct control over the appearance of type. Today, however, we take it for granted that we can change just about everything related to the way in which characters appear on the screen.

Like most application programs today, the ClarisWorks word processing module lets you determine how your type will appear. This section therefore begins by talking about the terminology of typography. It then shows you how to set type characteristics in your document.

Understanding Typography

Prior to the use of computers for formatting text, people who performed typesetting had a vocabulary all their own for describing type:

- Typeface: A style of type, such as Times or Palatino.

- Type size: The height of type, measured in points, such as 9 point or 12 point.

- Type style: The style of type, such as plain, boldface, italic, or underlined.

- Font: A single typeface in a single size and style. For example, traditionally 9-point Times boldface is considered a font.

When the Macintosh introduced multiple typefaces, the term *font* was used to refer to all sizes and styles of a single typeface. In many cases, when we talk about working with computer software, this is what we mean; the terms *font* and *typeface* are used interchangeably. (A traditional typographer would call a group of fonts of the same typeface a *type family*.) However, if you purchase software for new typefaces, you will often find that *font* has its original meaning. This confusion means that when you are buying typefaces, you need to pay attention to exactly what is being sold.

When you first starting playing with typography, it's tempting to load your document with a lot of type aces. Resist the temptation at all costs! If you don't, your documents will look very cluttered and unprofessional. Choose at most one typeface for the body of your document and another for headings. You can vary the size and style within each typeface, but stick to just two. This book, for example, uses Palatino for the body text and Gil Sans for most headings. There are also a few specialty fonts used for characters such as ⌘. However, the bulk of this entire book is created from just two typeface families.

Understanding Fonts

Most of today's computers can use three types of fonts:

- Bit-mapped: A font whose characters are created on the screen and on paper using a pattern of dots. Bit-mapped fonts provide the poorest printed output.

- TrueType: A font whose characters are created on paper and the screen by drawing their outlines. TrueType fonts provide excellent printed output with dot-matrix printers, ink-jet printers, and laser printers that don't support PostScript. (They also look good when printed on PostScript printers.)

The fonts that are provided with current versions of the Macintosh OS are all TrueType fonts.

- PostScript: A font whose characters are created on paper by drawing their outlines. The screen image of the font may be drawn by using a pattern of dots or by drawing their outlines (Display PostScript, which currently is not widely used). In most cases, PostScript printer fonts are accompanied by bit-mapped screen fonts used just for screen display, although increasingly some are accompanied by TrueType screen fonts.

  PostScript fonts provide the best printed output with printers and typesetters that use the PostScript Page Description Language. If a printer doesn't use PostScript to describe the page to be printed, a PostScript font performs no better than a bit-mapped font.

If you are working with a simple bit-mapped typeface or a PostScript typeface that is accompanied by bit-mapped screen fonts, a good appearance on the screen requires a bit-mapped font on your computer for the size being displayed. For example, the PostScript printer font Gil Sans is supplied with 12 bit-mapped screen fonts: plain, bold, bold italic, italic, and light italic, each in 10- and 12-point sizes. If you choose to display a character in a size for which a font doesn't exist, then the computer scales the font to the size you request, often producing output that is hard to read (for example, see Figure 2.26). However, when printed, Post-

Script fonts scale correctly, because characters are drawn on the basis of their outlines rather than a scaled pattern of dots. Simple bit-mapped fonts — those without PostScript printer outlines — will print just as you see them on the screen.

You can improve the appearance of the bit-mapped screen fonts that accompany PostScript printer fonts by installing Adobe Type Manager (ATM).This isn't a perfect solution, however. ATM is most effective on large font sizes (greater than 14 points). It also won't help with simple bit-mapped fonts; it works only when a PostScript outline is available for the font.

TrueType fonts scale well on both the screen and printed output. Because TypeType fonts are represented solely as outlines, you don't need separate fonts for each size; only one set of outline descriptions is required. You can also use TrueType fonts with any printer supported by your computer; your printer doesn't need any special page description language. Nonetheless, most publishing professionals believe that the highest quality printed output comes from the outlines provided by PostScript printer fonts.

Setting Type Characteristics

You can set type characteristics as you type or go back later and change the typography of existing text.

To format text as you type:

1. Place the insertion point where the formatted text is to begin.
2. Set the type characteristics.
3. Begin typing.

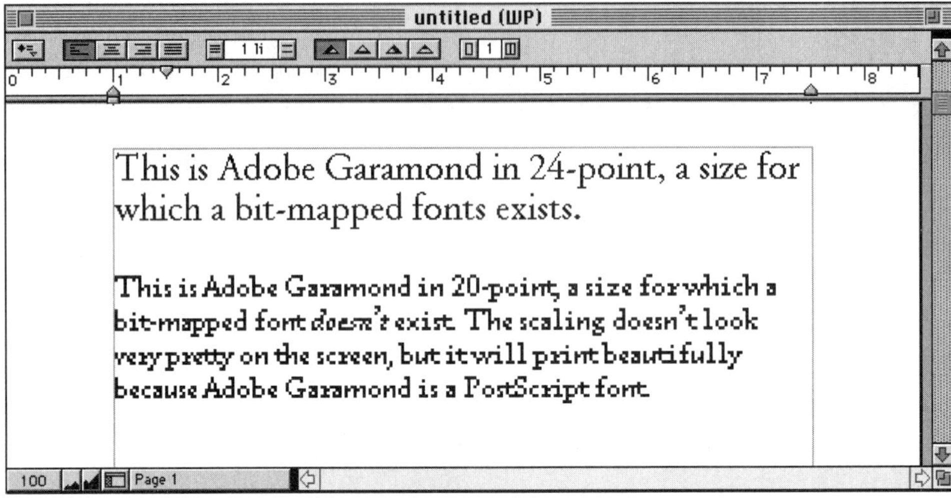

Figure 2.26 Bit-mapped font scaling

To format text after it has been entered:

1. Select the text to be formatted.
2. Set the type characteristics.

Choosing the Typeface

To choose a typeface:

1. Place the insertion point where the typeface is to begin or select the text to be formatted.
2. Choose the name of the typeface or font from the Font menu.

You can find another Font menu at the bottom of the Button Bar (see Figure 2.27).

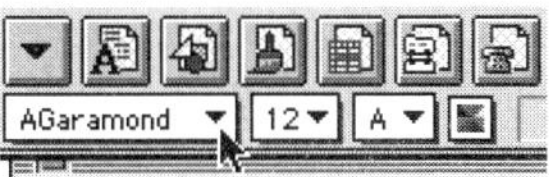

Figure 2.27 The Font menu in the Button Bar

Exactly what you see in your Font menu depends on what fonts are installed on your computer and, in the case of Windows, which fonts you have requested for display.

The Macintosh automatically includes every font in its Font menu. For example, in Figure 2.28 you can see the first portion of the author's Font menu. With the exception of Arial, Ashley, and Avant Garde, all of the fonts are bit-mapped fonts that go along with PostScript printer fonts. Notice that there are multiple entries for each typeface, representing the individual fonts that make up a font family. Arial, however, exists only once because TrueType fonts draw themselves on the basis of instructions that describe their outline, rather than using a preset pattern of dots.

A Windows Font menu looks very similar to a Macintosh Font menu, with one major exception (see Figure 2.29): it doesn't necessarily include every font on the computer. The last option in the menu — Other — provides access to fonts that don't appear.

To gain access to a font that isn't in the Font menu, a Windows user should do the following:

1. Choose Font->Other. The Other Font dialog box appears (see Figure 2.30).
2. Select the font from the scrolling list of fonts at the left of the dialog box.
3. Place a check in the *Appears in Font Menu* check box if you want the font to be added to the Font menu.
4. Click the OK button or press Enter to apply the changes.

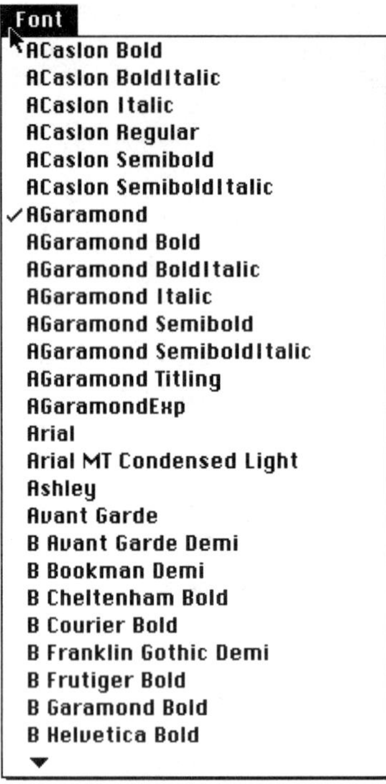

Figure 2.28 A portion of a Macintosh Font menu

Notice in Figure 2.30 that you can tell the type of font by the icon to the left of the font name. A PostScript font has a printer icon; a TrueType font has the TT icon; simple bit-mapped fonts have no icon at all.

Setting a Default Font

After you've been working with a word processor for a while, you will probably discover that there is one particular font that you like to use most of the time for the body of your documents. In that case, you can tell ClarisWorks to select that font whenever you create a new word processing document (a default font).

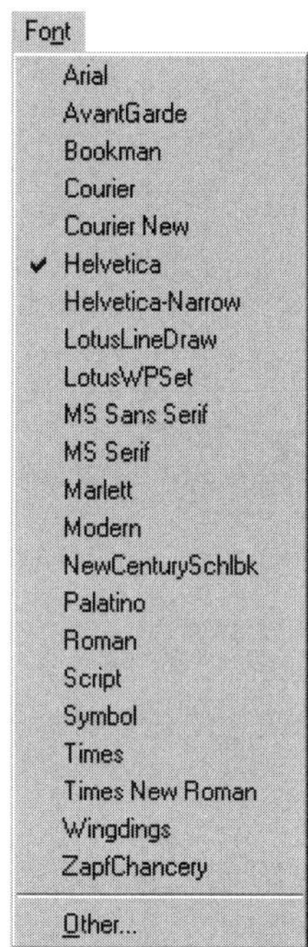

Figure 2.29 A Windows Font menu

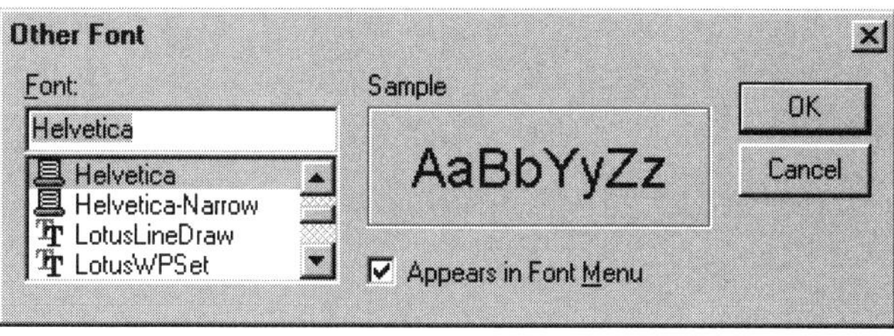

Figure 2.30 Choosing additional Windows fonts

To set a default font:

1. Choose Edit->Preferences. (Windows users can also press ALT-E, N.) The Preferences dialog box appears.
2. Choose Text from the Topics popup menu at the top of the dialog box (see Figure 2.31).

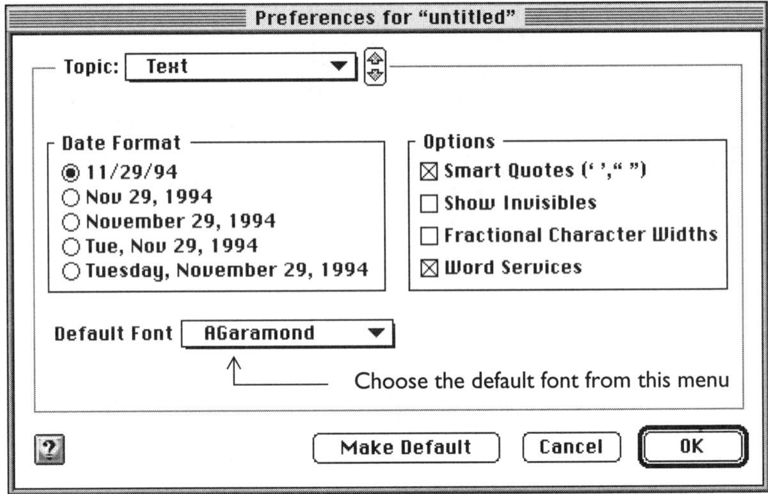

Figure 2.31 Choosing a default font

3. Choose a font from the Default Font menu.

4. Click the Make Default button.

Setting Type Size

As you read earlier, type size is measured in points. To be technically correct, the size is the distance between the lowest *descender* (characters like "y" and "g") and the highest *ascender* (characters like "h" and "b"). Because type measurement doesn't take into account the width of the font or the height of characters such as "x" or "n" (the font's *x-height*), two fonts of the same size can actually appear very different and occupy different amounts of space.

In Figure 2.32, for example, you can see three different typefaces, all in the same size (24 points). The Adobe Garamond at the top appears the smallest because the characters are narrow and the x-height is small relative to the overall height of the font. Times, the middle example, is also relatively narrow, but because it has a greater x-height than Adobe Garamond, it appears a bit larger. The third sample — Chicago — is very wide and has a large x-height. Although it is the same size as the first two examples, it appears much larger.

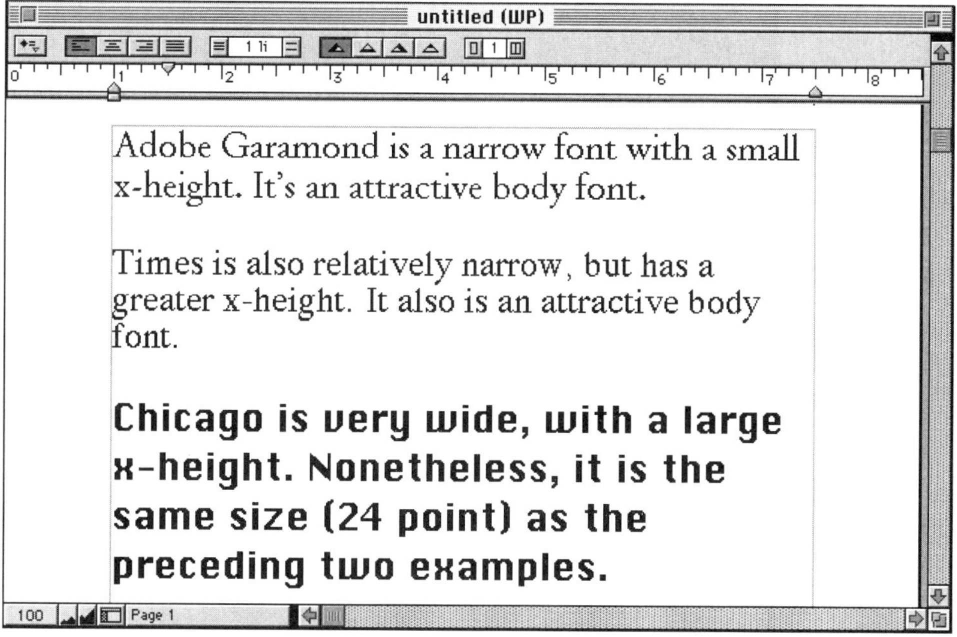

Figure 2.32 Font size differences

There are three methods for changing type size, each of which can be applied to new text as you type or to text already in the document. You can choose a size from the Size menu, enter a size that isn't listed in the menu, or change the size relative to the current type size.

To set text to a specific size in the Size menu:

1. Place the insertion point where the new size is to begin or select existing text.

2. Choose the type size from the Size menu. The Windows Size menu (Figure 2.33) contains a list of the most commonly used screen font sizes. The Macintosh Size menu not only contains the most commonly used sizes but also gives you an indication of which sizes will appear well on the screen. In Figure 2.34, for example, the sizes that will scale nicely are outlined. The TrueType font can scale well to any size; the bit-mapped font (regardless of whether it is a simple bit-map or the bit-map accompanying a PostScript printer font) will appear nicely in only the 10, 12, 14, 18, and 24 point sizes.

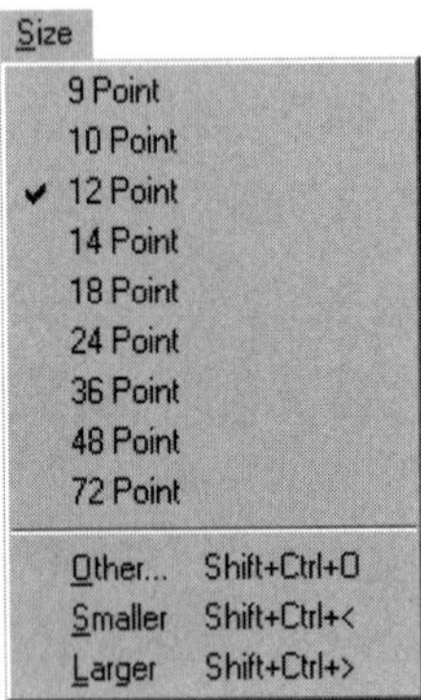

Figure 2.33 A Windows Size menu

To set a type size that isn't listed in the Size menu:

1. Place the insertion point where the new size is to begin or select existing text.

TrueType font

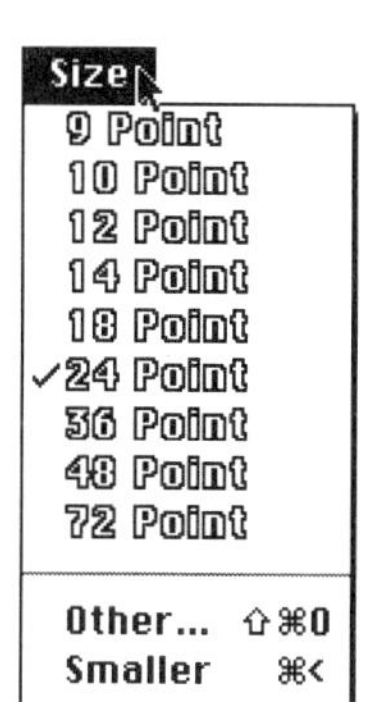

Bit-mapped font (either simple bit-map or PostScript)

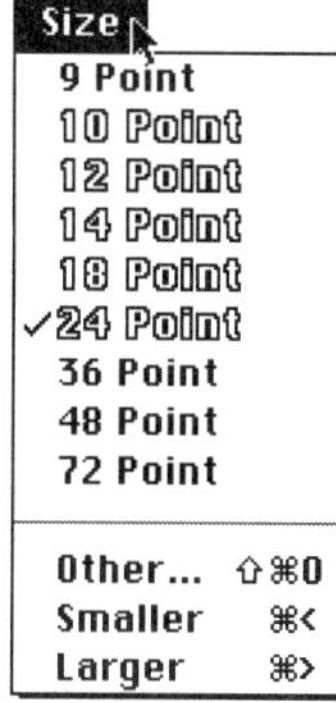

Figure 2.34 Macintosh Size menus

2.

Macintosh	Choose Size->Other or press SHIFT-⌘-O.
Windows	Choose Size->Other, press SHIFT-CTRL-O, or press ALT-S, O.

The Other Font Size dialog box appears.

3. Enter the size of the font in the Other Font Size dialog box (Figure 2.35).

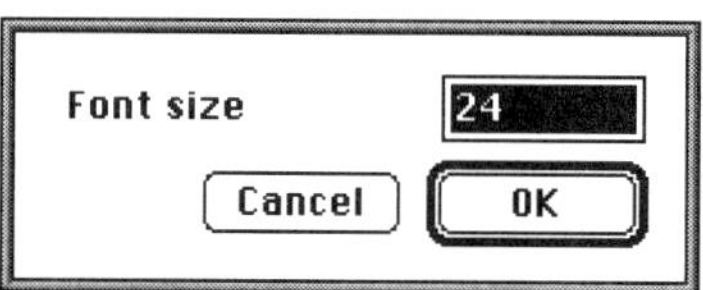

Figure 2.35 Entering an alternative font size

4. Click the OK button or press Return to apply the changes.

Changing size relative to the current type size allows you to increase or decrease type size one point at a time. To make type one point larger:

1. Place the insertion point where the new size is to begin or select existing text.

2.

Macintosh	Choose Size->Larger or press ⌘->. (The keyboard equivalent is the same as ⌘-SHIFT-.)
Windows	Choose Size->Larger, press SHIFT-CTRL->, or press ALT-S, L. (The keyboard shortcut is the same as SHIFT-CTRL-.)

To make type one point smaller:

1. Place the insertion point where the new size is to begin or select existing text.

2.

Macintosh	Choose Size->Smaller or press ⌘-<. (The keyboard equivalent is the same as ⌘-SHIFT-,)
Windows	Choose Size->Smaller, press SHIFT-CTRL-<, or press ALT-S, S. (The keyboard shortcut is the same as SHIFT-CTRL-,)

You can find another Size menu at the bottom of the Button Bar (see Figure 2.36).

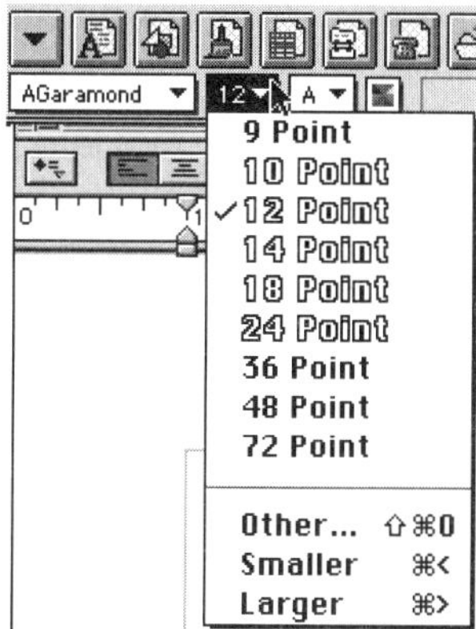

Figure 2.36 The Size menu in the Button Bar

Setting the Type Style

Type styles let you add interest to a document, making it possible to vary the look of the fonts within a single type family. The type styles provided by ClarisWorks can be found in Figure 2.37. Most documents will use plain text, boldface, and italic only. Plain text is used in the body of the document; boldface is used for headings. Italics are used sparingly for emphasis, as they are in this book to highlight new vocabulary words. The remaining styles are for specialty use only and should be used only when absolutely necessary.

Underlining was used as a substitute for italics when people prepared documents with a typewriter. Your documents will look more professional if you use italics in places where you might otherwise use underlining. For example, book titles in a bibliography should be set in italics rather than underlined.

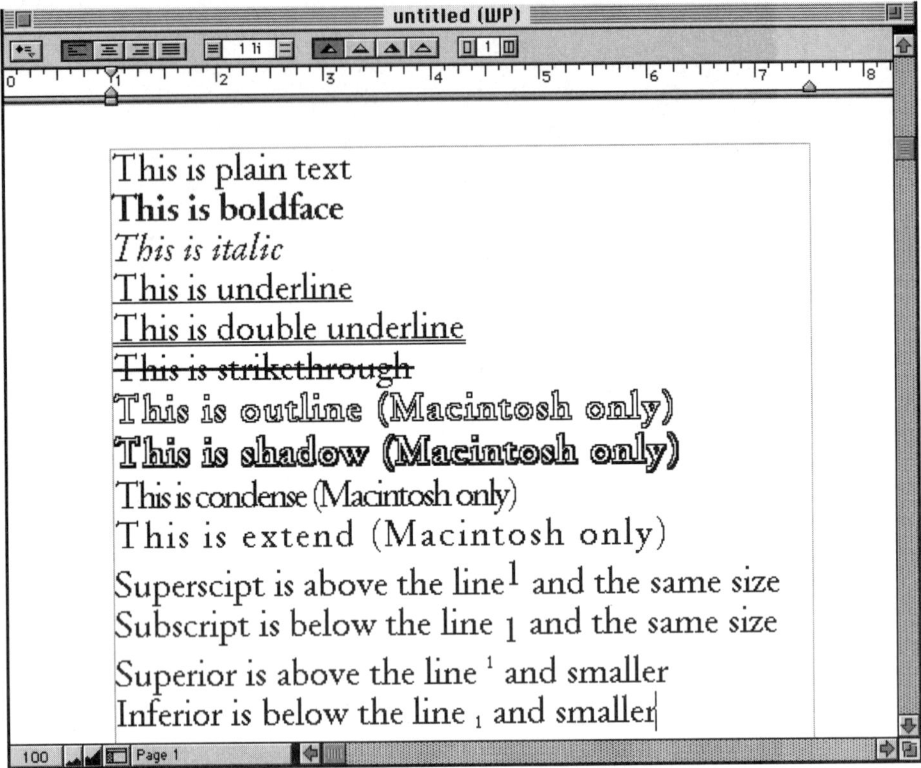

Figure 2.37 ClarisWorks's type styles

In most cases, type styles are additive. This means that it is possible to apply more than one style to the same text. For example, ***this text is bold italic***. Both the boldface and italic styles have been applied. ***You can even underline the bold italic***.

To add a type style:

1. Place the insertion point where the new style is to begin or select existing text.

2. Choose the style you want to apply.

Macintosh	Boldface	Choose Style->Bold, click the  button in the Button bar, or press ⌘-B.
	Italic	Choose Style->Italic, click the  button in the Button Bar, or press ⌘-I.
	Underline	Choose Style->Underline, click the  button in the Button bar, or press ⌘-U.
	Double Underline	Choose Style->Double Underline
	Strike Through	Choose Style->Strike Thru
	Outline	Choose Style->Outline
	Shadow	Choose Style->Shadow
	Condense	Choose Style->Condense
	Extend	Choose Style->Extend
	Superscript	Choose Style->Superscript or press SHIFT-⌘-+
	Subscript	Choose Style->Subscript or press SHIFT-⌘--
	Superior	Choose Style->Superior
	Inferior	Choose Style->Inferior
Windows	Boldface	Choose Style->Bold, click the  button in the Button bar, press CTRL-B, or press ALT-T, -B.
	Italic	Choose Style->Italic, click the  button in the Button bar, press CTRL-I, or press ALT-T, I.

	Underline	Choose Style->Underline, click the U button in the Button bar, press CTRL-U, or press ALT-T, U.
	Double Underline	Choose Style->Double Underline or press ALT-T, D.
	Strike Through	Choose Style->Strike Thru or press ALT-T, S.
	Superscript	Choose Style->Superscript, press SHIFT-CTRL-+, or press ALT-T, E.
	Subscript	Choose Style->Subscript, press SHIFT-CTRL--, or press ALT-T, T.
	Superior	Choose Style->Superior or press ALT-T, -R.
	Inferior	Choose Style->Inferior or press ALT-T, F.

To remove a type style from existing text:

1. Select the text from which the style is to be removed.

2.

Macintosh	Plain text (remove all styles)	Choose Style->Plain Text or press 1-T.
Windows	Plain text (remove all styles)	Choose Style->Plain Text, press CTRL-T, or press ALT-T, P.
Both	Any other style	Repeat the command used to apply the style.

You can find another Style menu at the bottom of the Button Bar (see Figure 2.38).

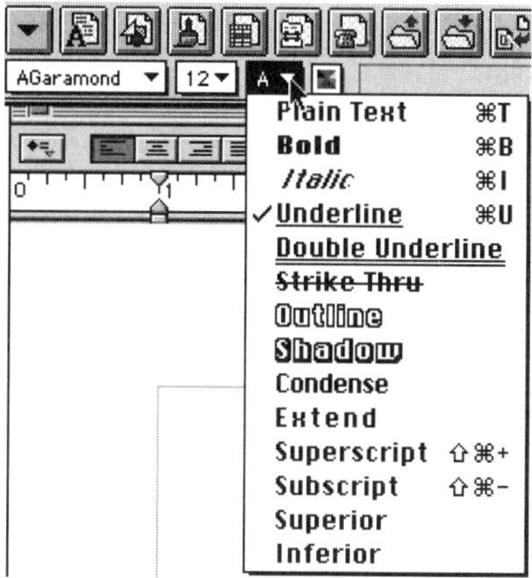

Figure 2.38 The Style menu in the Button Bar

Setting Type Color

ClarisWorks lets you change the color of the text in a word processing document or frame. You might, for example, use red text to emphasize a few words or phrases.

To set text color:

1. Select the text whose color is to be changed or select a block of text.

2. Choose a color from the color palette in the Button Bar or the tool bar (Figure 2.39).

Color is seductive: You may be tempted to use it generously throughout your document. Resist it! There are two good reasons for doing so. First, a document loaded with lots of colors is hard to read and doesn't look very professional. Second, colored text on the screen doesn't do you much good unless you have a color printer. What's a good use of colored text? Try using it for headings or for occasional emphasis.

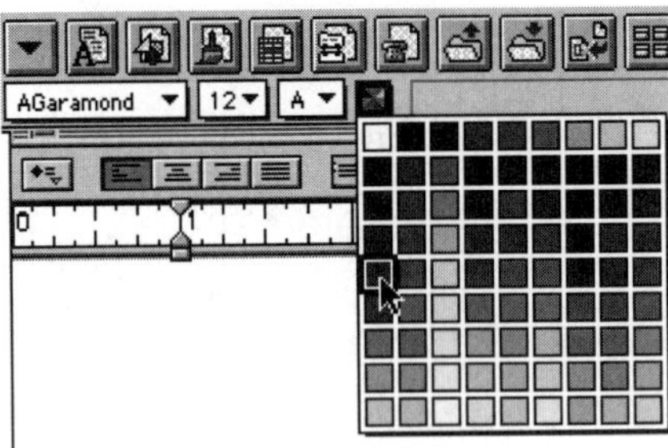

Figure 2.39 The color palette

3

Word Processing Extras

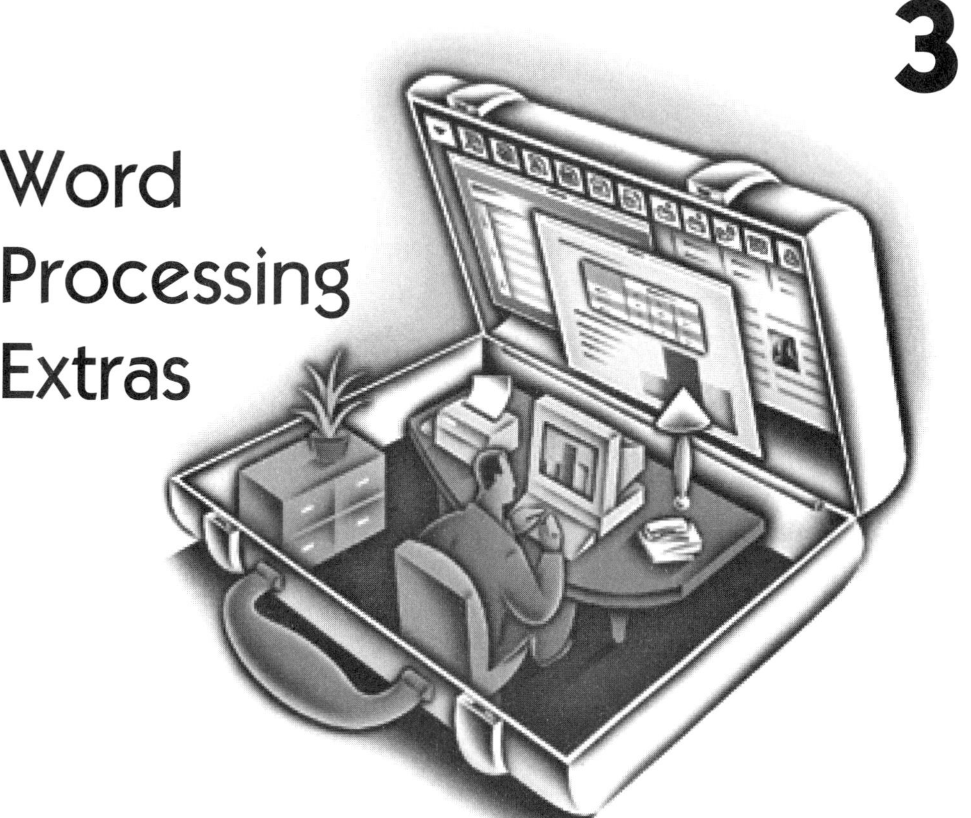

The word processing techniques you read about in Chapter 2 give you basic text document preparation skills. However, today's word processors include many other features — such as outlining, multicolumn layouts, and headers and footers — that make it easy to prepare professional-looking documents.

In this chapter you will read about these more advanced formatting options. They will give you much greater flexibility in the way in which your text documents appear.

Working with Outlines

When most of us were in grade school, we were taught that outlining was the first step to preparing an organized document. Although the process of outlining doesn't work for everyone, there are reasons to use outlines in text documents that have nothing to do with planning before you write:

- An outline can give a technical document structure.
- Outlines can automatically number and format lists of items — including bulleted lists — anywhere within a document.

Regardless of why you choose to use outlining, ClarisWorks provides full support for labeling and formatting items within an outline.

With many word processors, you need to turn outlining on and off. ClarisWorks, however, is always in "outline mode." Every paragraph you type without requesting outlining is the top level of an outline. The top level takes no numbers or letters or special characters; visible outlining — should you request it — begins with the next level down.

As an example, take a look at Figure 3.1. This sample document contains two separate outlines, each of which starts its labeling from the beginning (in this case, with *A*). ClarisWorks assumes that you have finished an outline when you insert a paragraph that has a outline labeling style of *None*. This occurs automatically when a paragraph is aligned with the left margin; you can also add the style explicitly. Once you've used the labeling style of *None*, ClarisWorks begins a new outline the next time you insert a formatted outline topic into the document.

There is one limitation to ClarisWorks outlining of which you should be aware: ClarisWorks assumes that each

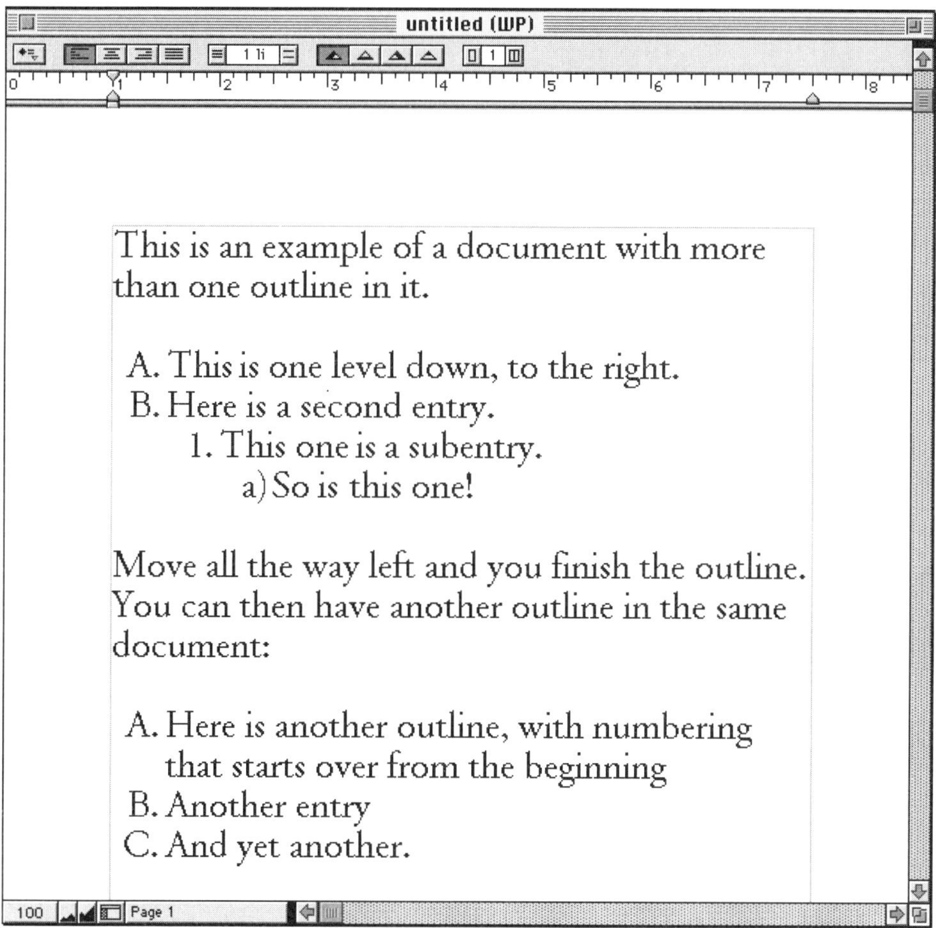

untitled (WP)
This is an example of a document with more than one outline in it.
A. This is one level down, to the right.
B. Here is a second entry.
1. This one is a subentry.
a) So is this one!
Move all the way left and you finish the outline. You can then have another outline in the same document:
A. Here is another outline, with numbering that starts over from the beginning
B. Another entry
C. And yet another.
100
Page 1

Figure 3.1 ClarisWorks outlines

paragraph within an outline should be labeled separately. If you continue an outline topic onto a second paragraph, and remove labeling from that paragraph (giving it a style of *None*), ClarisWorks assumes that you have ended the outline. To ensure that outline labeling works properly, you must confine each element in the outline to one paragraph.

Notice also in Figure 3.1 that ClarisWorks formats outline levels correctly. If the text of an outline entry wraps onto more than one line, ClarisWorks automatically indents the left edge of the text so that it lines up with the beginning of the text on the preceding line. This means that even if you don't want paragraph labeling, you can use outlining for quick formatting of indented items, such as long quotations.

Outline Styles

In school, most of us were taught a single scheme for labeling the paragraphs in an outline. Known as the Harvard style, it begins with capital letters at the topic level and alternates between letters and numbers. ClarisWorks, however, takes a much broader view of how outline paragraphs might be labeled and therefore provides 13 distinct outline styles (including *None*).

ClarisWorks's outline styles are demonstrated in Figure 3.2. Some, like Harvard and Legal, are very traditional. Others, like diamond and check box, are less commonly used.

One of the most interesting aspects of ClarisWorks's outline styles is that the styles are actually applied to individual paragraphs, just like type styles. In other words, when you create a new outline paragraph, ClarisWorks sets the paragraph's margins based on the level within the outline and then applies a style.

This means that you can have more than one style within the same outline. For example, you can have numbered paragraphs with bulleted lists underneath them. In addition, you can format an outline as you type, just as you can format text as you type, or you can apply an outline style to existing text that you have highlighted.

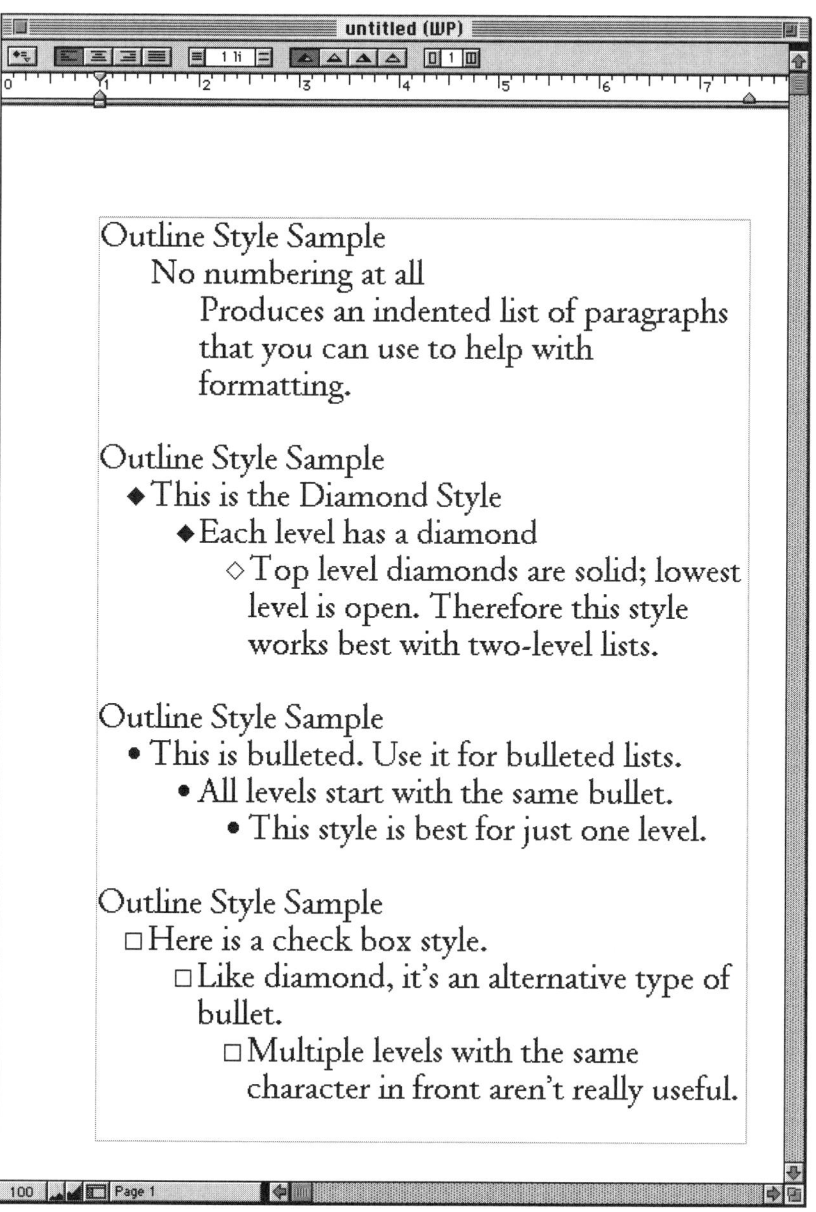

Figure 3.2 ClarisWorks's outline styles

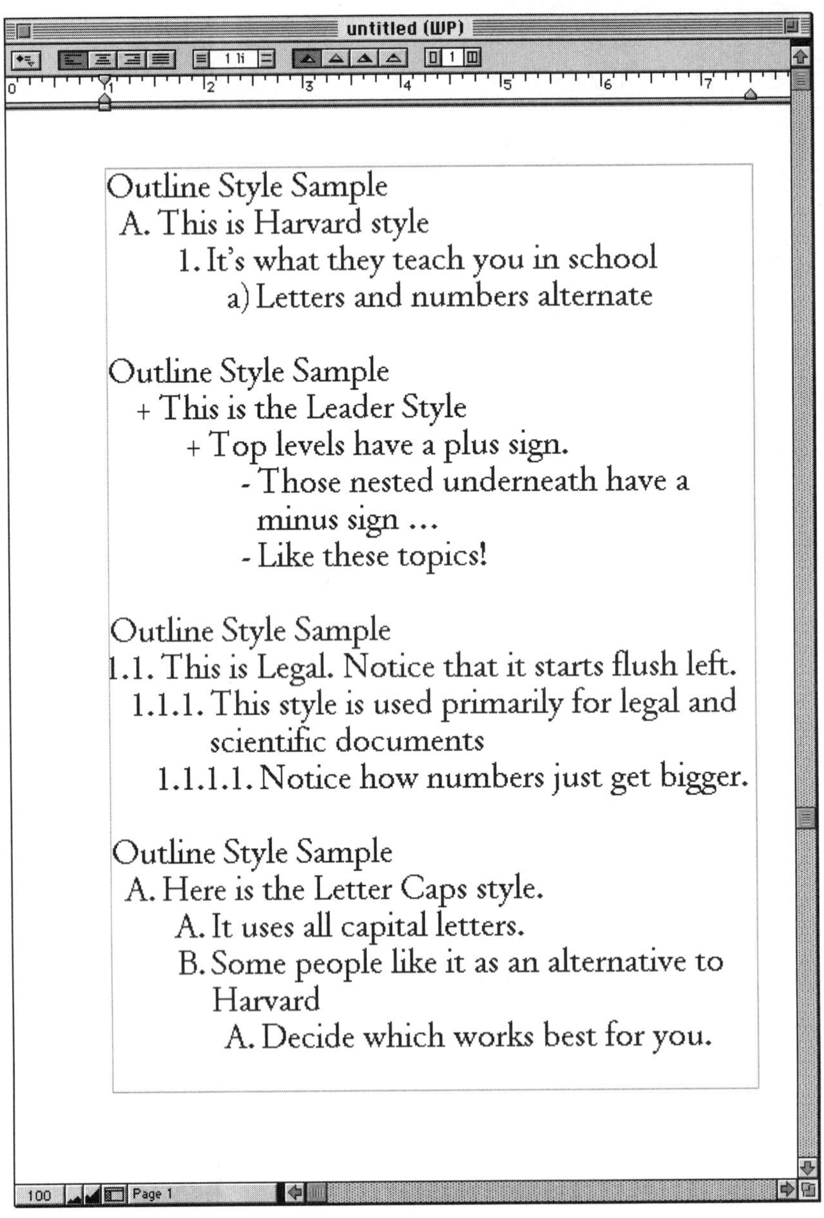

Figure 3.2 (Continued) ClarisWorks's outline styles

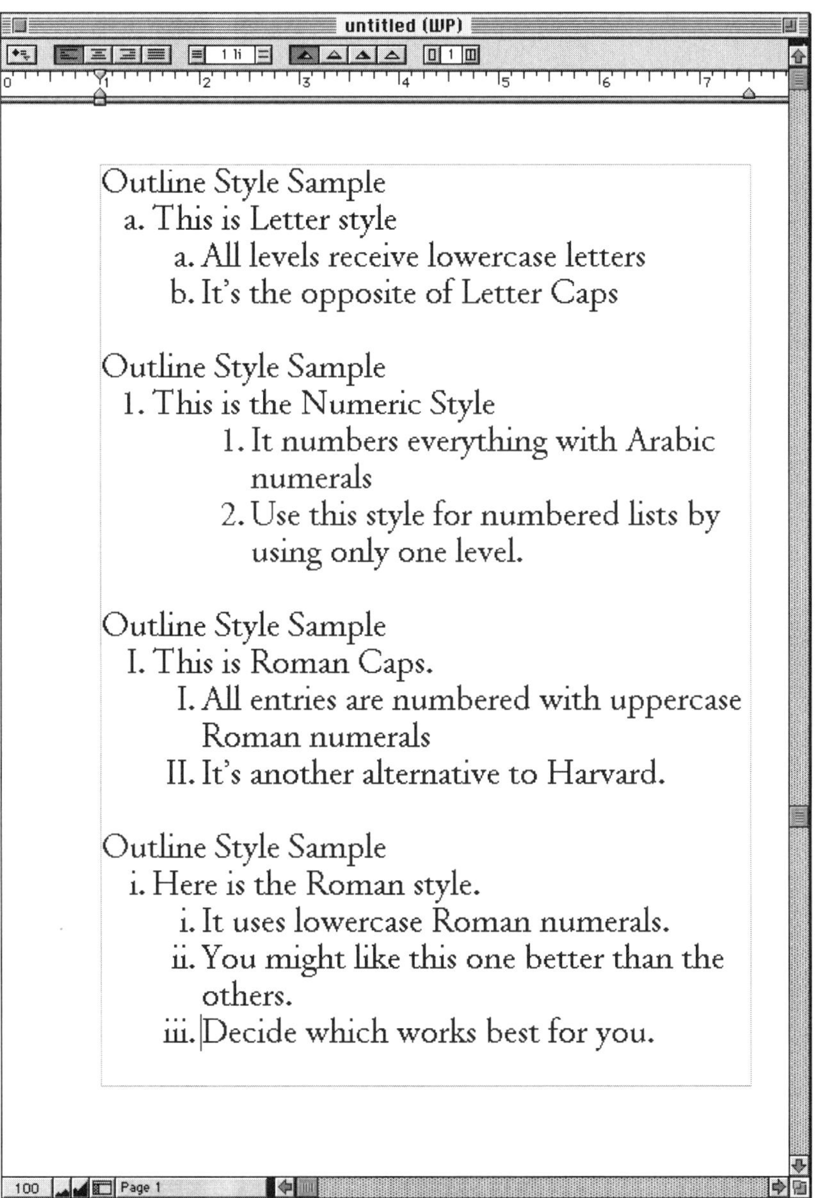

Figure 3.2 (Continued) ClarisWorks's outline styles

To set the outline style:

1. Place the insertion point where the new style is to begin or select a block of text to which the new style is to be applied.

2. Choose the new style from the outline style menu in the text ruler (see Figure 3.3)

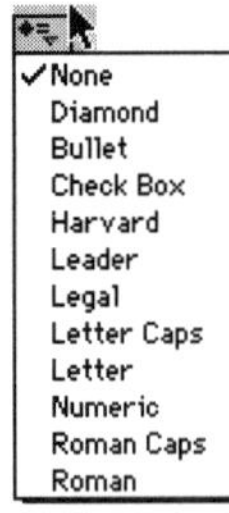

Figure 3.3 The outline styles menu

Adding Topics

There are three locations for the beginning of new paragraphs (known as "topics") in a ClarisWorks outline:

- The same level as the preceding paragraph.
- One level to the left of the preceding paragraph.
- One level to the right of the preceding paragraph.

To add a topic at the same level:

1. Place the insertion point at the end of the preceding paragraph.

2. Press Return, just as if you were completing a paragraph that wasn't part of an outline, *or* choose Outline->New Topic. (Windows users can also press ALT-U, N.)

To add a new topic to the left of the current paragraph:

1. Place the insertion point at the end of the preceding paragraph.

2.

Macintosh	Choose Outline->New Topic Left or press ⌘-L.
Windows	Choose Outline->New Topic Left, press CTRL-L, or press ALT-U, L.

To add a new topic to the right of the current paragraph:

1. Place the insertion point at the end of the preceding paragraph.

2.

Macintosh	Choose Outline->New Topic Right or press ⌘-R.
Windows	Choose Outline->New Topic Right, press CTRL-L, or press ALT-U, R.

When you add a new topic to a ClarisWorks outline, you may not see exactly what you expect in your document. As an example of how the process works, take a look at Figure 3.4. The topic illustration contains a paragraph with an outline style of *Harvard*. (Paragraphs aligned with the left margin don't have labels unless you explicitly add them, regardless of the outline style.) To add a new topic (labeled paragraph) on the line below, you must place the insertion point at the end of the current paragraph. At that point, you can issue the command for a new topic to the right.

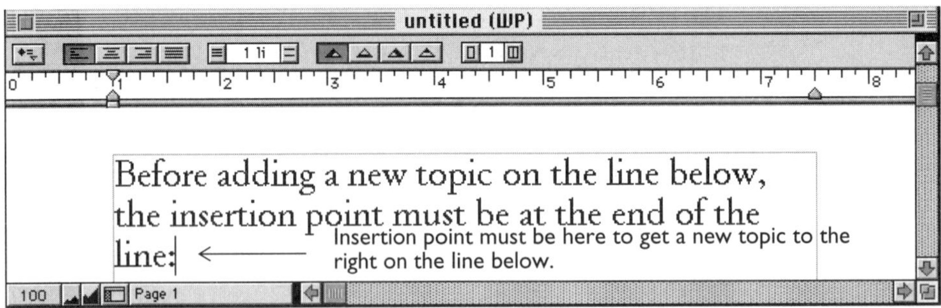

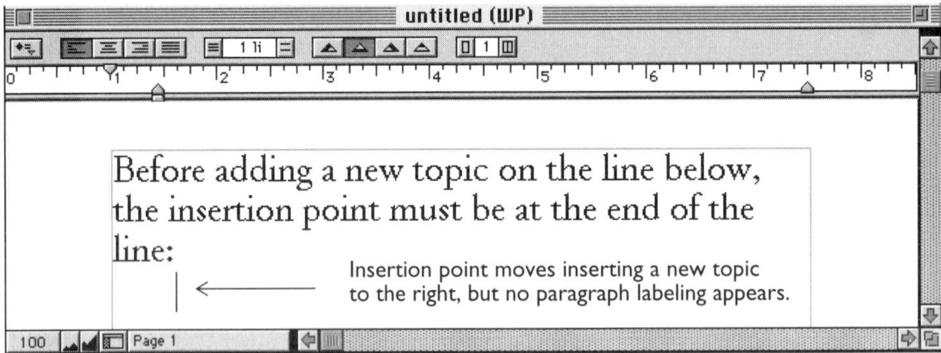

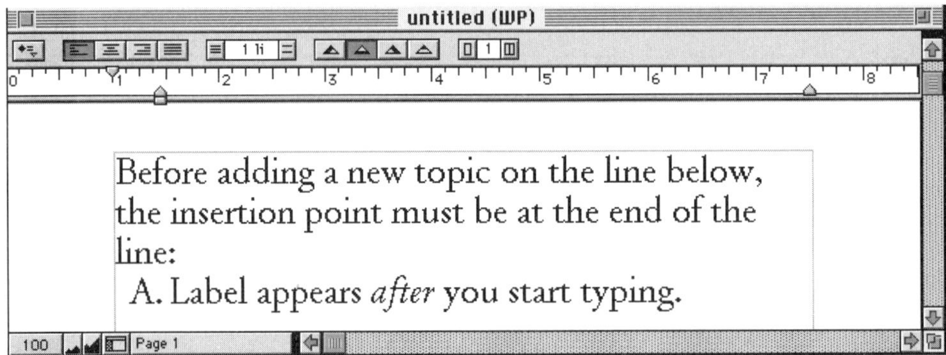

Figure 3.4 Inserting a new topic into an outline

As you can see in the middle illustration in Figure 3.4, the insertion point moves and is indented properly for the new outline paragraph, but the paragraph label doesn't appear.

However, the label will appear as soon as you type the first character of the paragraph.

Changing Topic Levels

Outlines, especially those that are used to organize the logical structure of a document, may need to be changed as you modify your document. In particular, you may decide to change the the level at which a particular paragraph is placed. ClarisWorks lets you move topics left or right, or up or down, and adjusts paragraph labeling appropriately as you do so.

As an example, consider Figure 3.5. The paragraph labeled "1" in the first version of the outline at the top of the illustration has been moved one level to the left in the second version of the outline at the bottom of the illustration. Notice that the paragraph label of the topic that was moved has been changed to match its new level. Also note that all sub-topics of the topic that was moved were moved left as well. Topics labeled with the lower case letters of the third level in the first version are labeled with the Arabic numerals of the second level in the second version.

Moving Topics Right and Left

To move a topic and all its subtopics one level to the left:

1. Place the insertion point anywhere in the paragraph to be moved.

2.

Macintosh	Choose Outline->Move Left or press SHIFT-⌘-L.
Windows	Choose Outline->Move Left, press SHIFT-CTRL-L, or press ALT-U, O.

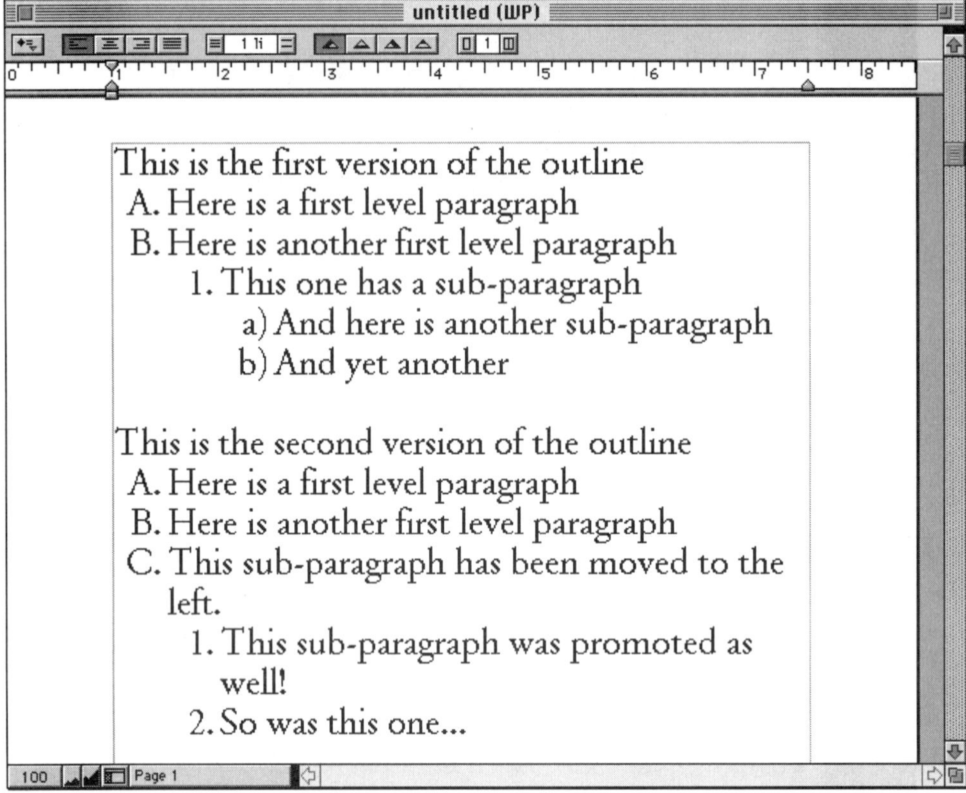

Figure 3.5 Changing outline topic levels

To move a topic and all its sub-topics one level to the right:

1. Place the insertion point anywhere in the paragraph to be moved.

2.

Macintosh	Choose Outline->Move Right or press ⌘-R.
Windows	Choose Outline->Move Right, press SHIFT-CTRL-R, or press ALT-U, V.

Moving Topics Up and Down

As well as changing topic levels by moving topics left and right, ClarisWorks lets you keep topics at the same level but move them up and down. For example, the top sample in Figure 3.6 has two subtopics at level three (labeled with Arabic numerals). Issuing the command to move the sub-topic labeled "1" up takes the paragraph and moves it from a subtopic of "B" to a subtopic of "A." Notice that the remaining subtopic of "B" has been renumbered correctly.

To move a topic up:

1. Place the insertion point in the paragraph to be moved.

2.

Macintosh	Choose Outline->Move Above.
Windows	Choose Outline->Move Above or press ALT-U, A.

To move a topic down:

1. Place the insertion point in the paragraph to be moved.

2.

Macintosh	Choose Outline->Move Below.
Windows	Choose Outline->Move Below or press ALT-U, B.

On the Macintosh, you can also drag topics up and down. To do so, select the topic you want to move. Place the mouse pointer over the selected topic and drag the topic to its new position.

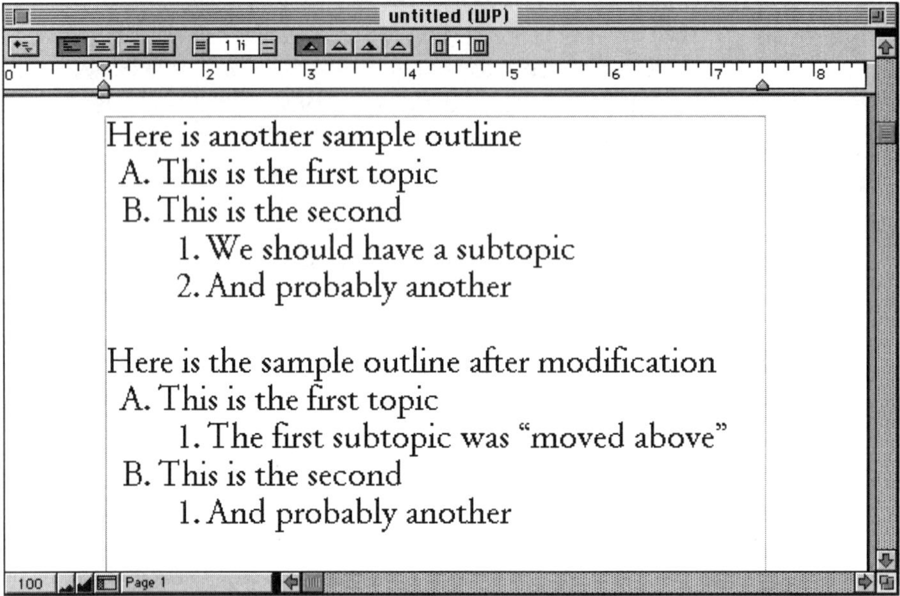

Figure 3.6 Moving outline topics up and down

Raising a Topic

ClarisWorks provides one additional way to change the location of a topic within an outline: raising the topic. If you look at Figure 3.7 you can see that the effect of raising a topic is to promote the topic the next highest level in the outline, regardless of the topic's current position in the outline. (All of the raised topic's subtopics are raised one level as well.) If necessary, ClarisWorks will move the topic to account for its new level, as it did in Figure 3.7.

To raise a topic:

1. Place the insertion point anywhere in the paragraph to be raised.
2. Choose Outline->Raise Topic. (Windows users can also press ALT-U, I.)

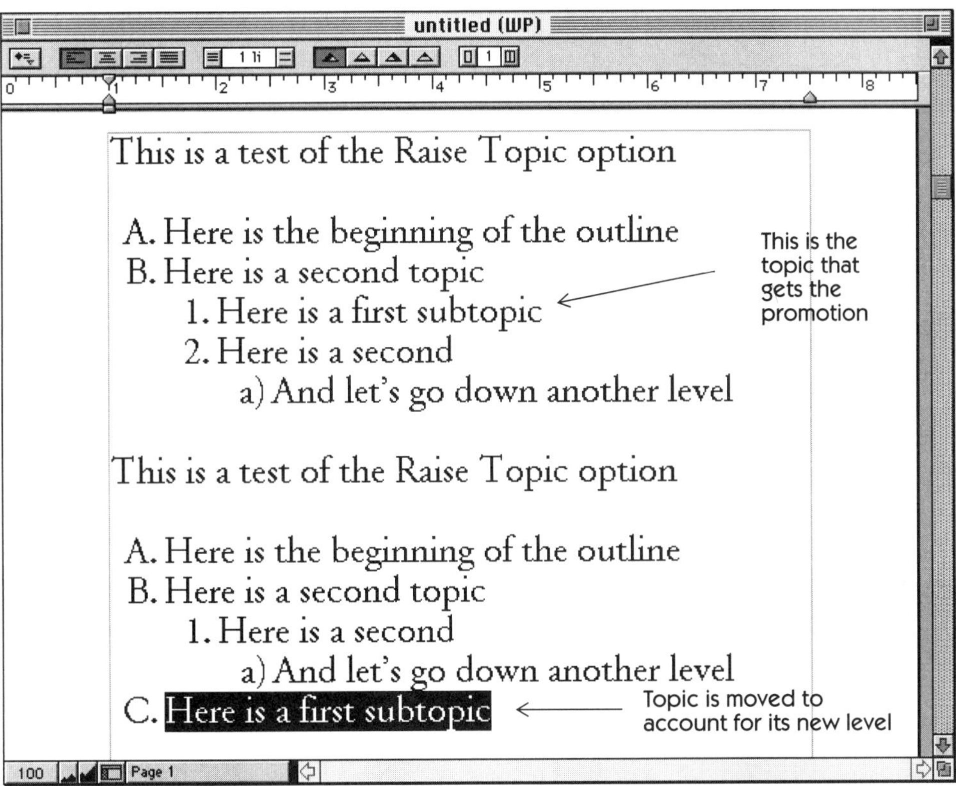

Figure 3.7 Raising a topic

Showing and Hiding Levels

ClarisWorks lets you hide and then redisplay outline paragraphs. For example, you might decide to hide all but the top level in your outline. This makes it easier to see more top-level topics at the same time. Then, you can expand individual topics as you need to see the detail.

For example, in Figure 3.8 you can see a fully expanded outline. When it is fully collapsed (Figure 3.9), all you can see is the top level paragraph. Notice that the paragraph label is underlined, indicating that there are hidden subtopics.

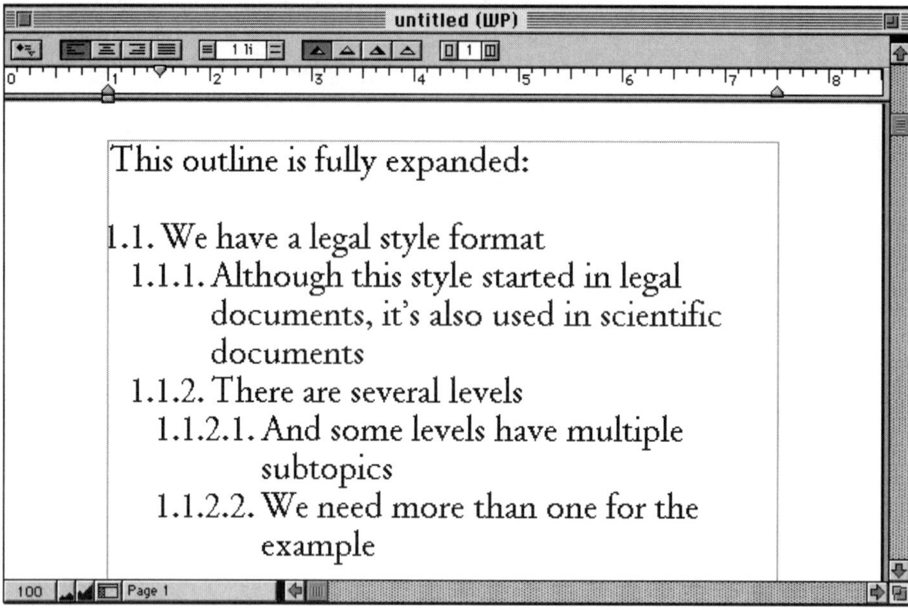

Figure 3.8 A fully expanded outline

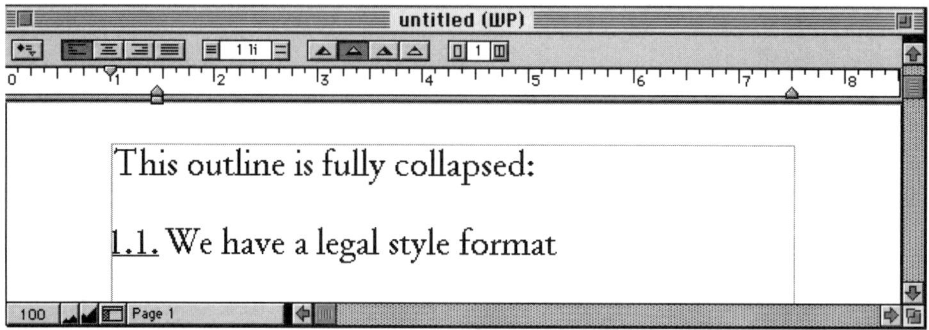

Figure 3.9 A fully collapsed outline

You can collapse or expand topics at any level in an outline. In Figure 3.10, for example, the second- and third-level topics have been expanded, but there are fourth-level topics hidden under "1.1.2," as indicated by the underlining of the label.

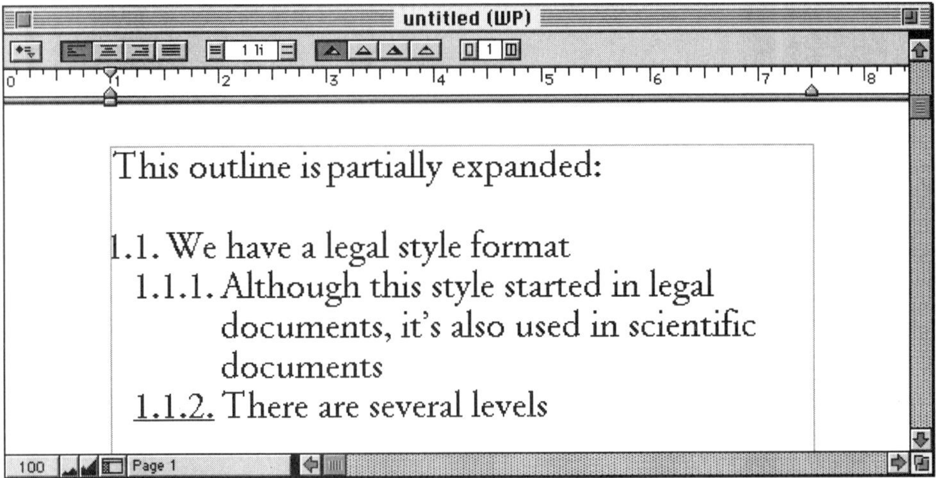

Figure 3.10 A partially expanded outline

To collapse all levels below:

1. Place the insertion point in the paragraph below which topics are to be collapsed.

2. Choose Outline->Collapse. (Windows users can also press ALT-U, C.)

To expand all levels below:

1. Place the insertion point in the paragraph below which all topics are to be expanded.

2. Choose Outline->Expand. (Windows users can also press ALT-U, E.)

To expand topics below to a specific level:

1. Place the insertion point in the paragraph below which some topics are to be expanded.

2. Choose Outline->Expand To. (Windows users can also press ALT-U, X.) The Expand To dialog box appears (Figure 3.11).

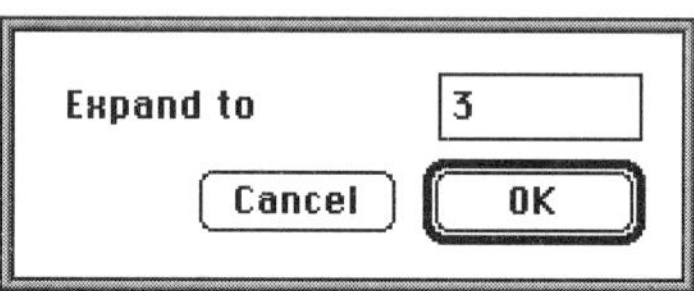

Figure 3.11 The Expand To dialog box

3. Enter the level to which the outline should be expanded. Keep in mind that the unnumbered paragraphs that align with the left margin count as level one.

4. Click the OK button or press Enter to expand the outline.

Adding Document Formatting Extras

Most of what you've read to this point involves the content of a document, rather than its overall structure. However, there are some things you may want to do to the structure of a document to give it a more polished appearance. In this section, you will learn how to break a document into multiple *sections*, each with its own distinct layout, provide multicolumn layouts, and create headers and footers.

Sections

When you create a new word processing document, ClarisWorks assumes that the entire document will have the same overall layout, including the number of columns and headers and footers. However, if you need a document whose layout varies, you can break the document into distinct sections. Layout elements can then be different in each section.

All sections in a document must use the same page margins. However, the rest of page formatting can vary from one section to another.

Creating a New Section

To create a new section in a document:

1. Place the insertion point at the place in the document where the new section should begin. Typically, this will be at the end or beginning of a paragraph.

2.

Macintosh	Choose Format->Insert Section Break or press OPTION-NUMENTER.[1]
Windows	Choose Format->Insert Section Break, press CTRL-NUMENTER, or press ALT-F, I.

1. NUMENTER is the enter key on the numeric keypad.

ClarisWorks inserts a new section beginning at the top of the next page.

Configuring a Section

Once you have the new section in your document, you can set the section's characteristics, including where the new section begins, page numbering, and how headers and footers behave.

To set section characteristics:

1. Place the insertion point in the section whose characteristics you are going to set.

2. Choose Format->Section. (Windows users can also press ALT-F, S.) The Format Section dialog box appears.

3. Choose the location for the start of the section from the Start Section popup menu (Figure 3.12). Notice that as well as beginning a new line or page, a section start can be forced to a new left or right page. If you choose to start the section on a right page (a typical setting when a two-sided document contains multiple chapters), and the previous section ends on a right page, you will get a blank left page in between. The converse, of course, is also true: Starting on a left page after a section that ends with a left page will result in a blank right page in between.

4. If necessary, set page numbering. As you can see in Figure 3.13, numbering can continue from the previous section or can be restarted with any page number you choose. To restart page numbering, click in the Restart Page Number radio button. Enter the beginning page number in the edit box to the right of the radio button.

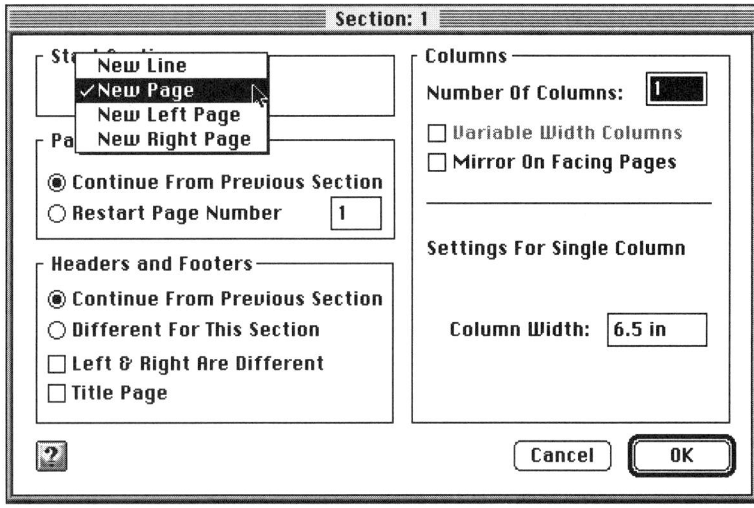

Figure 3.12 Choosing the starting location for a new section

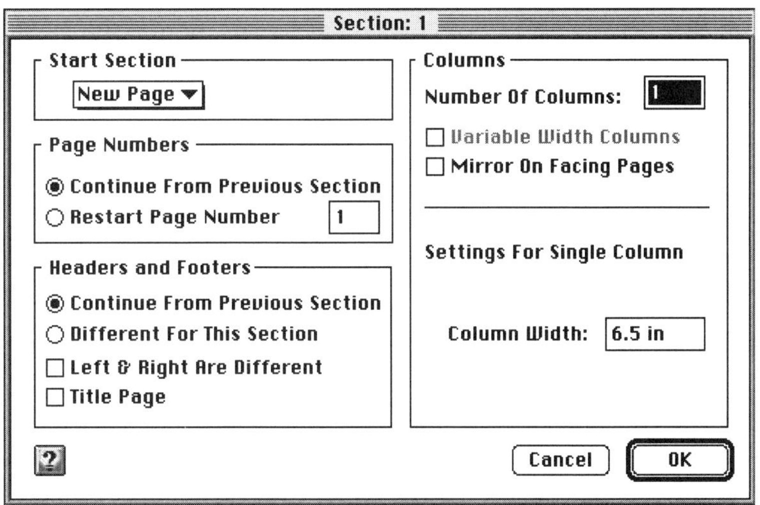

Figure 3.13 Setting other section characteristics

Even if your document has only one section, you can use the Format Document dialog box to change the starting page number. For example, when you are working on a long, multichapter document, you will probably keep each chapter in a separate file. During the final printing of the document, you can set each file to begin printing using a page number one higher than the last page in the previous document.

5. If the new section will have headers and footers that are different from those in the preceding section, click in the Different For This Section radio button. (See the section *Headers and Footers* later in this chapter for details on creating headers and footers.)

6. If the headers and footers will be different on right and left pages, click in the Left & Right Are Different check box.

7. If the section should have a title page — the first page of the section, on which no headers and footers appear — click in the Title Page check box.

Merging Two Sections

When you delete a section break, you merge the section into the preceding section. To delete a section break:

1. Place the insertion point at the beginning of the section to be removed.

2. Press Delete.

When you create a new section, ClarisWorks places an invisible character in your document marking the start of the new section. By pressing Delete, you are actually removing this hidden character. You will learn how to make these hidden characters visible in the last section of this chapter, Viewing Invisible Characters.

Multicolumn Layouts

When you are writing a letter or a report — whether for school or for business — you typically use a document with only one column of text. However, if you happen to be preparing a newsletter or other technical document, you might want a layout with more than one column. The document in Figure 3.14, for example, has two columns separated by approximately 0.17 inch.

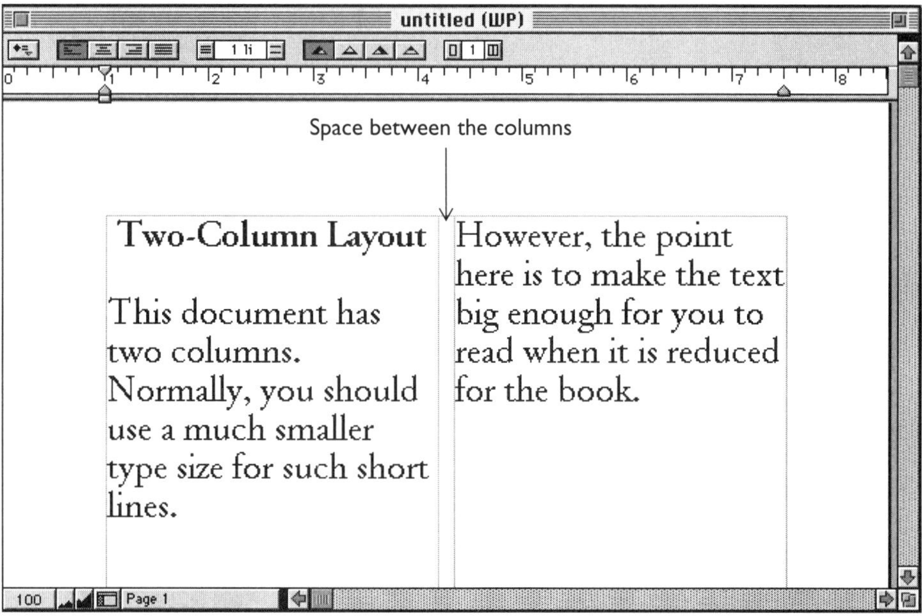

Figure 3.14 A two-column layout

As the number of columns in your document goes up — and the length of the line of type goes down — the size of the type you use should go down. A two-column layout like that in Figure 3.14 looks good with 9, 10, or 11 point type. If the document were only one column, you would probably want to use 11, 12, or 14 point type. This will make your document easier to read.

Column layouts apply to document sections. This means that you use section settings to configure multicolumn layouts, even if your document has only one section (the default). Keep in mind that when you change the number of columns in your document, it affects the entire section. If your document has only one section (in other words, you haven't added any extra sections), then a change in the number of columns affects the entire document.

Changing the Number of Columns

You can change the number of columns in a section either from the text ruler or from the Section Format dialog box. Using the text ruler, all columns will be the same width. If you use the dialog box, you can have columns with different widths.

To use the text ruler:

1. Place the insertion point anywhere in the document section whose number of columns will be modified.

2. Click the double column icon in the text ruler (see Figure 3.15). ClarisWorks adds one column to the section layout and reformats text already in the section.

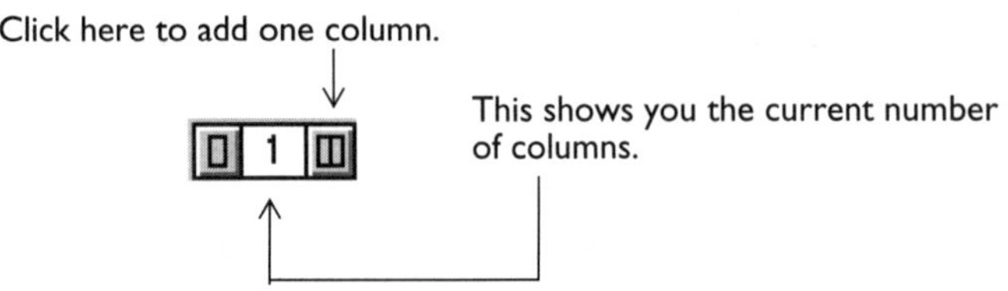
Click here to add one column.
1
This shows you the current number of columns.

Figure 3.15 Adding a column using the text ruler

To use the Section Format dialog box:

1. Choose Format->Section. (Windows users can also press ALT-M, S.) The Section Format dialog box appears (see Figure 3.16).

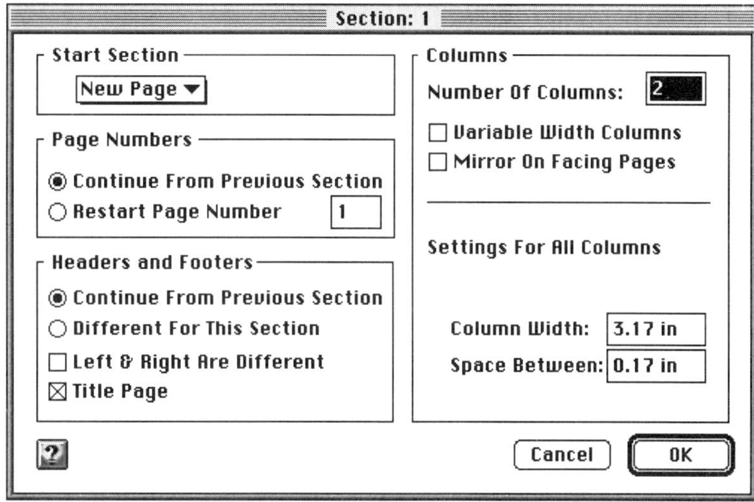

Figure 3.16 The Section Format dialog box

2. Enter the number of columns.

3. Click the OK button or press Enter.

Configuring Column Layout

As you look at Figure 3.16, you notice that there are several settings for column layout:

- Variable column widths
- Mirrored layouts

- Column widths
- Space between columns

If your columns have the same width, the dialog box appears exactly as in Figure 3.16. To set column size for columns with the same width:

1. Display the Section Format dialog box.
2. Enter the width of each column.
3. Enter the space between columns. This space appears only between two columns, not on outside edges next to page margins.

The total width of the columns plus the space in between the columns can be no more than the distance between the page margins.

Variable width columns, such as those in Figure 3.17, are suited for layouts in which you want to put special elements such as headings and graphics in a margin, separate from body text. (Remember that you can't put anything in the page margins!)

To create and configure variable column widths:

1. Display the Section Format dialog box.
2. Click in the Variable Width Columns check box. The Section Format dialog box changes to give you a chance to set a width for each column, as in Figure 3.18.

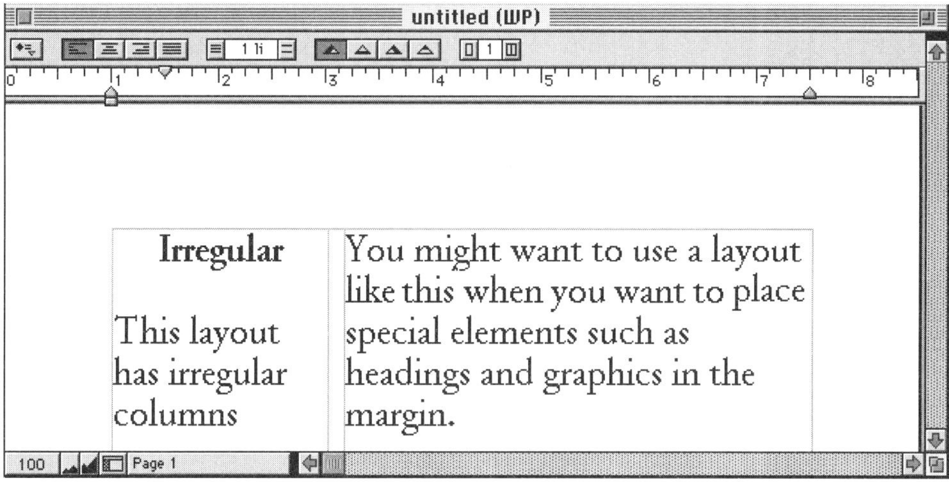

Figure 3.17 Columns with variable widths

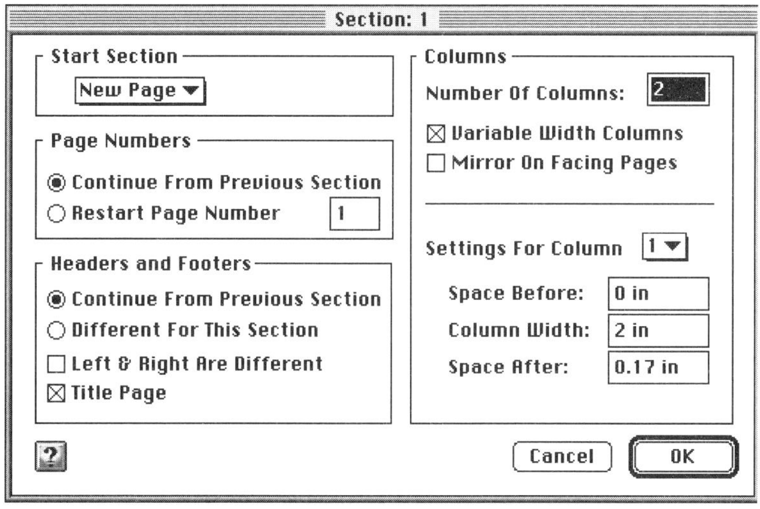

Figure 3.18 Setting the width of a variable width column

3. Enter the settings for the first column. Use the Space Before setting for the amount of space to the left of the column; use the Space After setting for the amount of

space to the right of the column. Use the Column Width setting for the space in which typing can occur. Note that when two columns are next to one another, ClarisWorks adds the Space After of the left column to the Space Before of the right column to produce the total space between the two columns.

4. Choose the next column from the popup menu (see Figure 3.19)

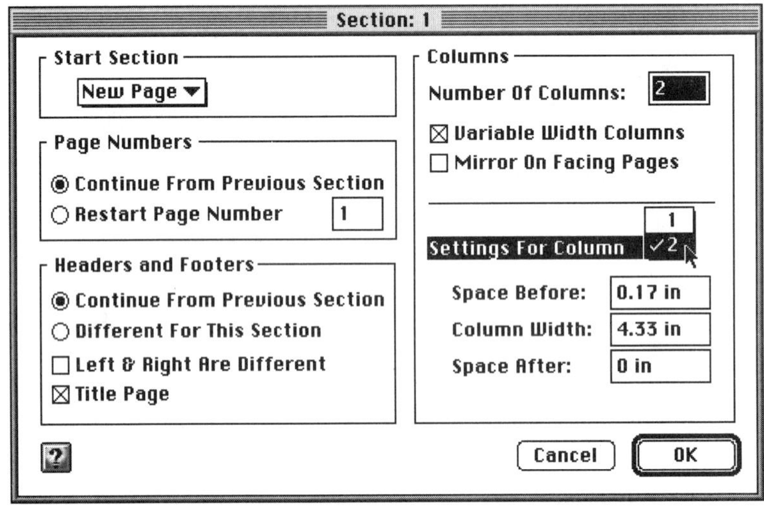

Figure 3.19 Choosing another variable width column to configure

5. Enter the settings for the next column.

6. Repeat steps 4 and 5 until you have configured all columns. Keep in mind that the total width of all columns plus the space between columns can be no more than the distance between the page margins.

7. Click OK or press Enter to apply the settings.

You can adjust column widths manually as well as using the Section Fromat dialog box. To make the adjustments, hold down the Option key (Macintosh) or the Alt key (Windows) and place the mouse pointer over a column divider. Drag the divider right or left to a new location. Hold down the appropriate modifier key, place the mouse pointer in the space between two columns, and drag the space right or left.

Although you can use variable width columns to create small margins for headings and graphics, getting things to line up properly can be awkward. It is usually easier to use linked text frames placed within a drawing document to achieve this type of layout. You will read about how to do this in Chapter 5.

Irregular column layouts, just like irregular page margins, can be the same on facing pages, or can be mirrored. (See Figure 2.9 for examples.) Mirroring is appropriate for double-sided layouts.

To mirror columns on pages with irregular column layouts:

1. Display the Section Format dialog box.

2. Click in the Mirror on Facing Pages check box.

3. Click OK or press Enter to apply the settings.

Inserting a Column Break

As you type into a multicolumn layout, ClarisWorks flows text from the bottom of one column onto the top of another until a page is full, as in Figure 3.20. However, just as you can force a page break, you can also insert a column break before a column is full.

To insert a column break:

1. Place the insertion point at the place where the column break should occur.

2.

Macintosh	Choose Format->Insert Column Break or press NUMENTER.[1]
Windows	Choose Format->Insert Column Break, press NUMENTER, or press ALT-M, U.

1. NUMENTER is the enter key on the numeric keyboard.

Headers and Footers

Headers and footers are document elements that appear at the top or bottom of a page. If you are working with a double-sided document, right and left pages can have different headers and footers. In addition, each section of a document can have its own headers and footers.

Adding a Header

To add a header to a document:

1. Place the insertion point anywhere in the document section that is to receive the header.

2. Choose Format->Insert Header. (Windows users can also press ALT-F, E.) ClarisWorks places a header at the top of the current page, as in Figure 3.21. Notice that the space for the header is allocated at the top of the page but inside the page margins.

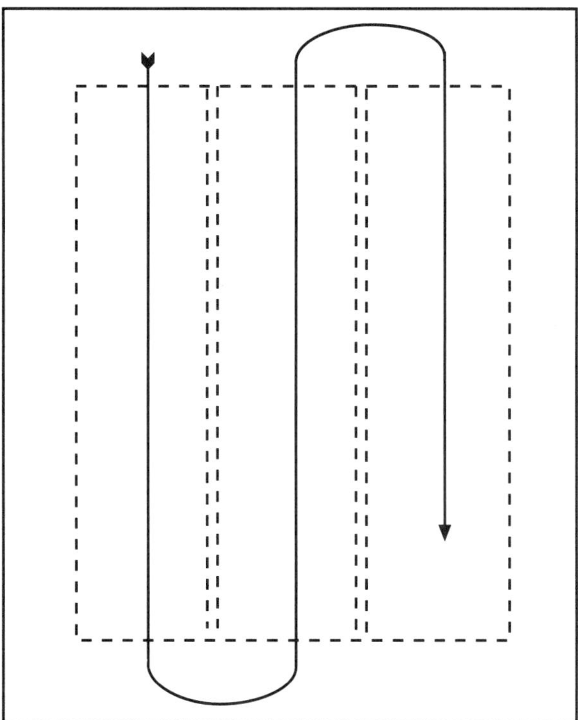

Figure 3.20 Multicolumn text flow

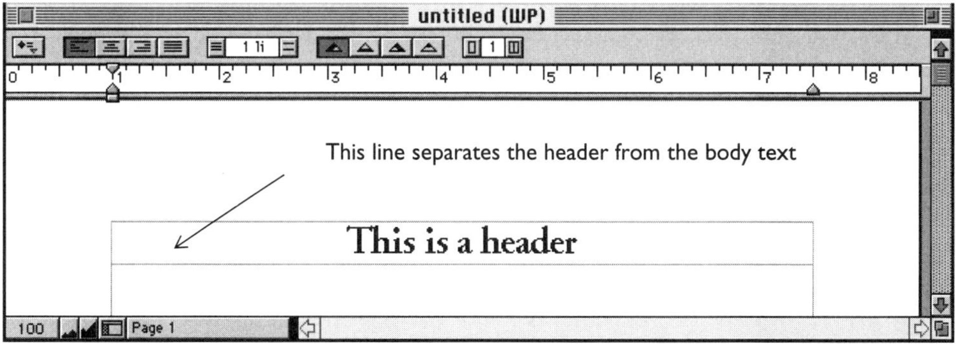

Figure 3.21 A page header

Adding a Footer

To add a footer to a document:

1. Place the insertion point anywhere in the document section that is to receive the footer.

2. Choose Format->Insert Footer. (Windows users can also press ALT-F, O.) ClarisWorks places a footer at the bottom of the current page, inside the page margins.

Editing a Header or Footer

To edit the contents of a header or footer:

1. Place the insertion point in the header or footer whose contents you want to change. Any page on which the header or footer appears will do.
2. Edit the contents of the header or footer, using the same editing techniques you use with the body of the document (for example, alignment and type styles).

A common layout for headers in a single-sided document includes text aligned with both the left and right margins, as in Figure 3.22. To create this type of layout, set the header's paragraph alignment to Left. Then drag a right tab on top of the right page margin.

Removing a Header or Footer

To remove a header or footer:

1. Place the insertion point in the header or footer to be removed.

2. To remove a header, choose Format->Remove Header. (Windows users can also press ALT-F, E.) To remove a footer, choose Format->Remove Footer. (Windows users can also press ALT-F, O.)

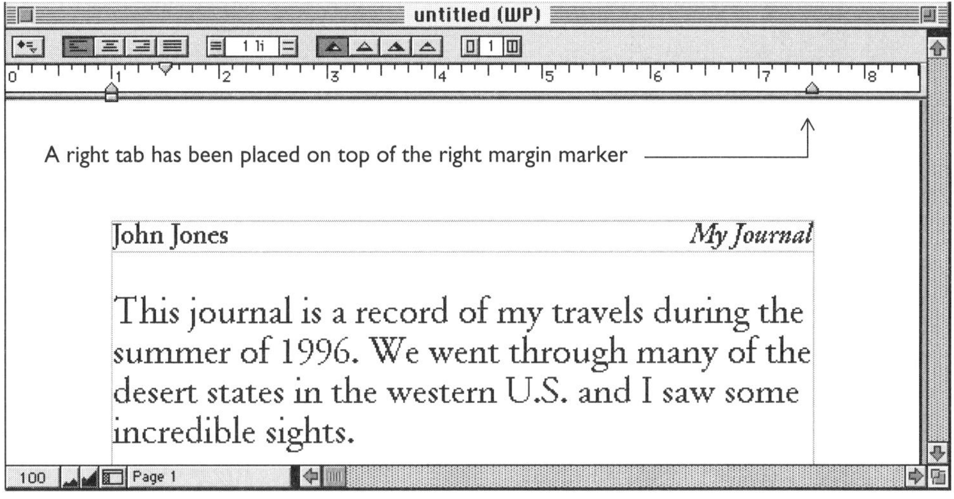

Figure 3.22 A header for a single-sided document

Footnotes and Endnotes

You typically use footnotes, which appear on the bottom of the page, and endnotes, which appear at the end of the document, to indicate the sources of material you are using in a report or paper. You might also use footnotes or endnotes for annotations to text, to contain material that shouldn't be in the main body of the document.

ClarisWorks supports automatic placement and numbering of footnotes and endnotes. By default, footnotes are placed at the bottom of the page on which they are referenced. However, you can also request that all footnotes be turned into endnotes by having them placed on a separate page at the end of the document.

Choosing Footnote or Endnote Placement

To set where footnotes or endnotes will appear:

1. Place the insertion point anywhere in the document.
2. Choose Format->Document. (Windows users can also press ALT-F, D.) The Format Document dialog box appears.

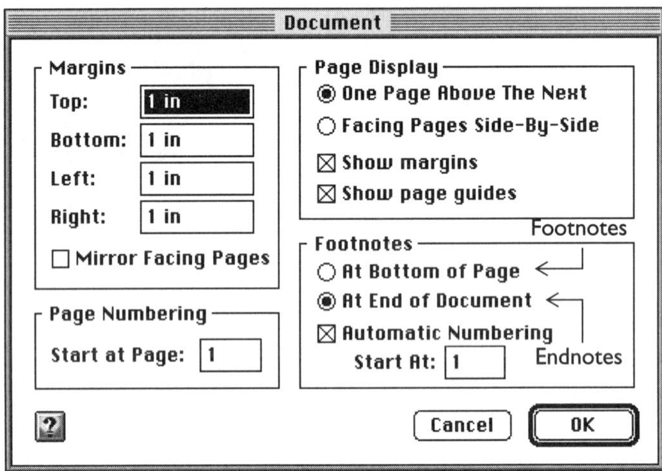

Figure 3.23 Choosing footnotes or endnotes

3. To change from footnotes to endnotes, click in the At End of Document radio button (see Figure 3.23). To return to footnotes, click the At Bottom of Page radio button.

Inserting a Footnote or Endnote

To insert a footnote or endnote:

1. Place the insertion point at the place where the reference to the footnote or endnote should appear.
2. If using footnotes:

Macintosh	Choose Format->Insert Footnote or press SHIFT-⌘-F.
Windows	Choose Format->Insert Footnote, press SHIFT-CTRL-F, or press ALT-F, F.

If using endnotes:

Macintosh	Choose Format->Insert Endnote or press SHIFT-⌘-F.
Windows	Choose Format->Insert Endnote, press SHIFT-CTRL-F, or press ALT-F, F.

ClarisWorks inserts a reference to the footnote or endnote in the document (see Figure 3.24). By default, the reference has the Superior text style. ClarisWorks also places the footnote or endnote in the document. As you can see in Figure 3.25, footnotes are separated from the body of the document by a line. (Endnotes start on a new page at the end of the document.) You can then type anything you want in the space left for the footnote or endnote. You can also apply any type of formatting you want to the text of the note.

Deleting Footnotes and Endnotes

To delete a footnote or endnote:

1. Select the reference to the footnote or endnote in the text.
2. Press Delete. ClarisWorks removes the footnote or endnote and, if automatic numbering is turned on, renumbers all remaining footnotes or endnotes.

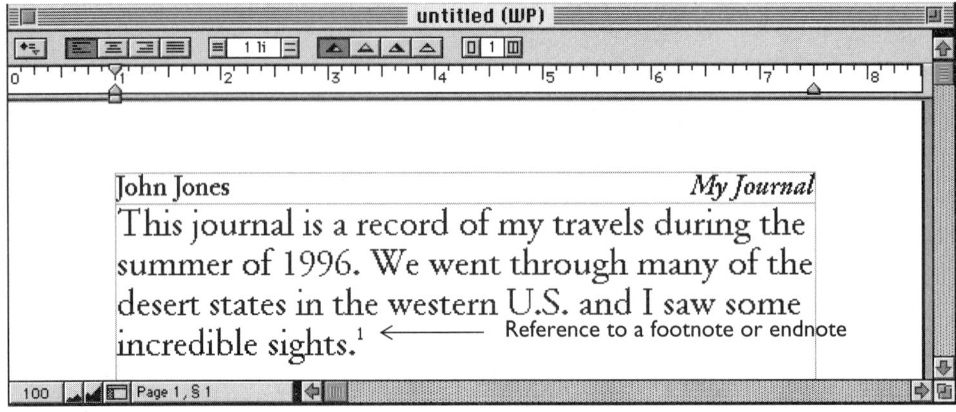

Figure 3.24 A footnote or endnote reference

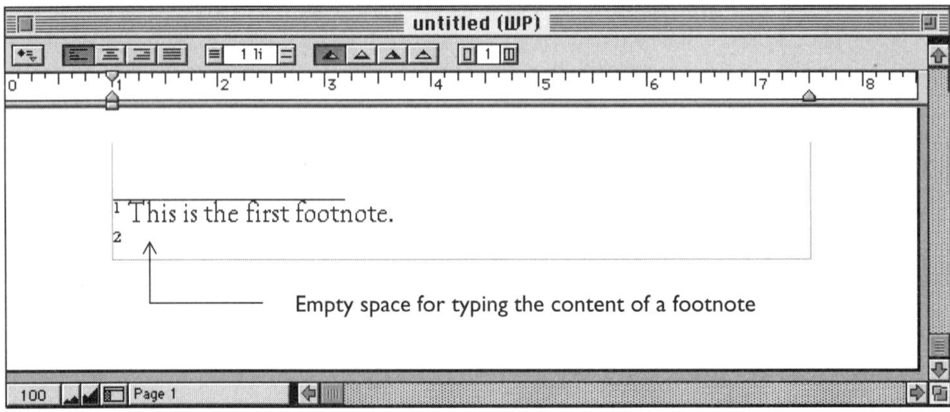

Figure 3.25 Footnotes at the bottom of a page.

Controlling Footnote and Endnote Numbering

By default, ClarisWorks automatically numbers footnotes and endnotes, beginning with 1. However, you can change the starting number or remove automatic numbering altogether and use whatever symbols you choose for your footnotes.

To turn off automatic numbering:

1. Choose Format->Document. (Windows users can also press ALT-F, D.) The Format Document dialog box appears (see Figure 3.23).

2. Click in the Automatic Numbering check box to remove the check.

When automatic numbering has been turned off, ClarisWorks will ask you to indicate the reference character for each footnote you insert. For example, in Figure 3.26, an asterisk has been entered into the Footnote dialog box. When the user clicks OK or presses Enter, the new footnotes will be marked with *.

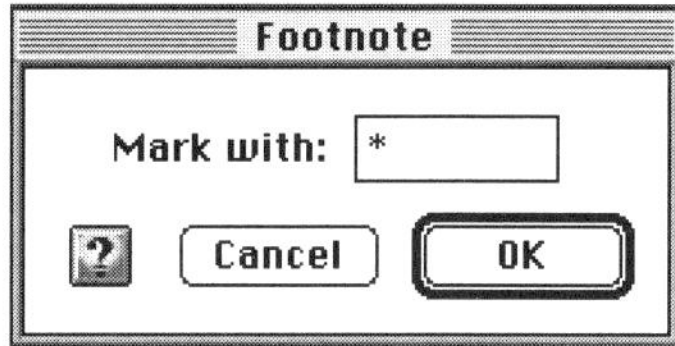

Figure 3.26 Manually entering a character for a footnote or endnote reference

To turn automatic numbering back on:

1. Choose Format->Document. (Windows users can also press ALT-F, D.) The Format Document dialog box appears.

2. Click in the Automatic Numbering check box to place a check in it.

To change the number with which automatic footnote or endnote numbering begins:

1. Choose Format->Document. (Windows users can also press ALT-F, D.) The Format Document dialog box appears.

2. Enter the starting number in the Start At text box in the Footnotes section of the dialog box.

Special Text

Text documents are often marked with the current date and a page number. Some specialized documents (for example, statements of when services were performed) also include the current time. Although you can certainly type dates, times, and page numbers directly into your document, it is easier to let ClarisWorks do it for you. ClarisWorks can also automatically update dates, times, and page numbers.

Adding the Date and Time

There are two types of dates and times you can add to a ClarisWorks document: those that update and those that don't. Dates and times that update will be changed automatically to reflect the current date and time whenever you open, save, or print the document. Dates and times that don't update are like any other kind of text: They retain their values unless you edit them directly.

Adding Dates That Update

To add an automatic date to a document:

1. Place the insertion point at the location where the date should appear.

2. Choose Edit->Insert Date. (Windows users can also press ALT-E, D.)

Adding Dates That Don't Update

To add a date that doesn't update to a document:

1. Place the insertion point at the location where the date should appear.

2.

Macintosh	Hold down the OPTION key and choose Edit->Insert Date.
Windows	Hold down the CTRL key and choose Edit->Insert Date, or press CTRL-ALT-E, D.

Adding Times That Update

To add an automatic time to a document:

1. Place the insertion point at the location where the time should appear.

2. Choose Edit->Insert Time (Windows users can also press ALT-E, T.)

Adding Times That Don't Update

To add a time that doesn't update to a document:

1. Place the insertion point at the location where the time should appear.

2.

Macintosh	Hold down the OPTION key and choose Edit->Insert Time.
Windows	Hold down the CTRL key and choose Edit->Insert Time, or press CTRL-ALT-E, T.

Dates and times are taken directly from your computer's clock. If the computer's clock isn't set accurately, then the values that appear in your ClarisWorks document won't be accurate either.

Choosing a Date Format

ClarisWorks lets you choose the format in which an inserted date will appear. To select the format:

1. Choose Edit->Preferences. (Windows users can also press ALT-E, N.) The Preferences dialog box appears.

2. Choose Text from the Topic popup menu at the top of the dialog box (see Figure 3.27).

3. Click one radio button in the Date Format section of the dialog box to select a date format.

4. Click the OK button or press Enter to save the change for this document only. Click the Make Default button to instruct ClarisWorks to use your choice whenever it creates a new word processing document.

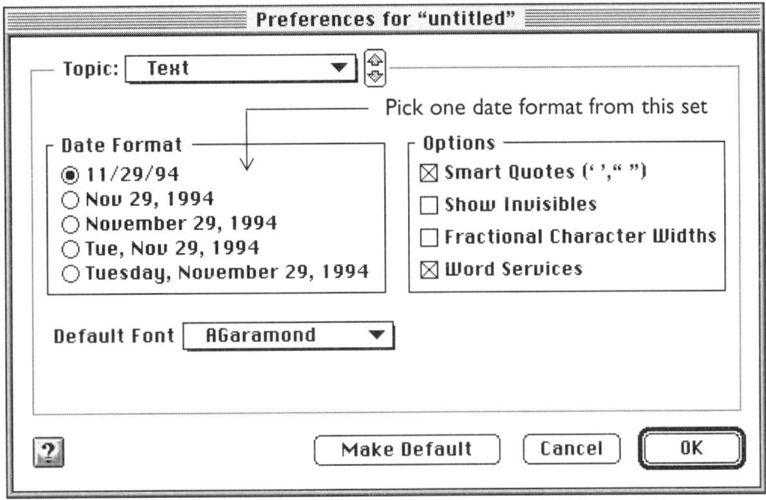

Figure 3.27 Choosing a date format

Page Numbering

ClarisWorks provides several options for numbering pages in a document. In Figure 3.28 you can see the various numbers that ClarisWorks will place in a document and update automatically for you as your document changes. These include the page number, the section number, the section page count (number of pages in the section), and the document page count (number of pages in the document.)

You can combine these numbers in a variety of ways, such as *Page 3 of 15*. To create this, you type the word *Page* followed by a space, insert the page number, type *of* and a space, and then insert the document page count. Keep in mind that ClarisWorks supplies only the numbers; you need to enter any text that surrounds the numbers.

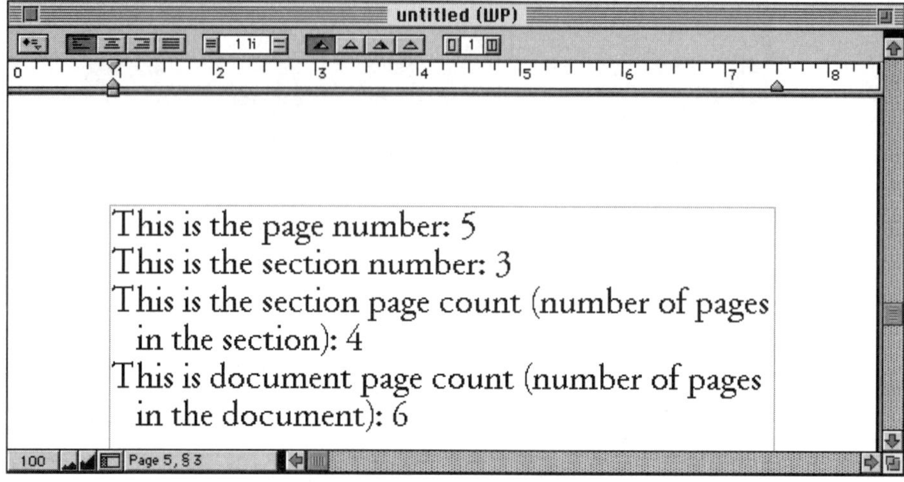
untitled (WP)
This is the page number: 5
This is the section number: 3
This is the section page count (number of pages in the section): 4
This is document page count (number of pages in the document): 6
100
Page 5, § 3

Figure 3.28 Page numbering options

ClarisWorks also gives you five choices of how the numbers appear. As you can see from Figure 3.29, page (or section) numbers can be displayed in Arabic numerals, upper- or lowercase Roman numbers, or upper- or lowercase letters.

To insert a page number:

1. Place the insertion point at the location where the page number should appear. (Often, the location will be in a header or footer.)
2. Choose Edit->Insert Page #. (Windows users can also press ALT-E, G.) The Insert Page Number dialog box appears (Figure 3.30).
3. Choose the type of page number you want from the radio buttons at the top of the dialog box.
4. Choose the style of numbering from the Representation popup menu at the bottom of the dialog box.
5. Click the OK button or press Enter to insert the page number.

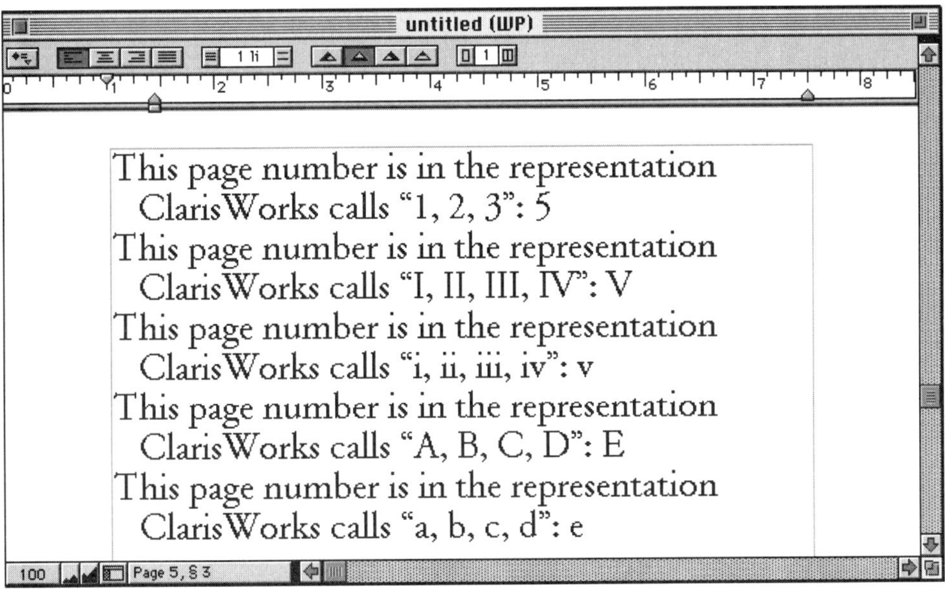

Figure 3.29 Page numbering styles

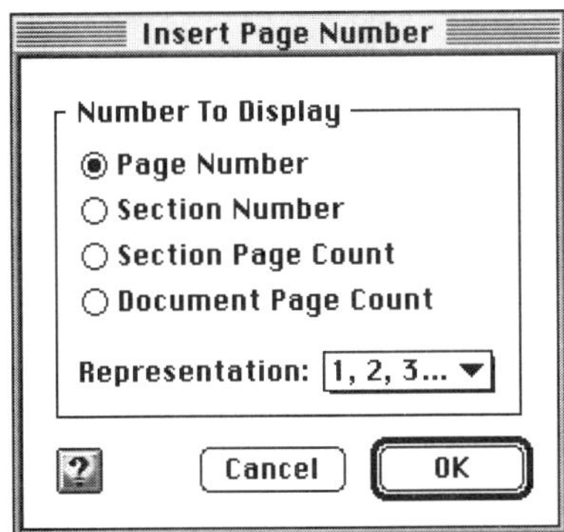

Figure 3.30 Insert Page Number dialog box

Style Sheets

A *style sheet* is a group of formatting characteristics that can be applied together to a portion of a document. The formatting in a style sheet can be applied to a range of text, an entire paragraph, an outline, or a table. (ClarisWorks tables are actually spreadsheets, which are discussed in Chapter 7.) Style sheets make it much easier to keep formatting consistent throughout a long document and between multiple documents.

When you apply a style sheet to a portion of a document, ClarisWorks replaces any existing styles with those specified in the style sheet. This is different from the behavior of some styles when applied directly. For example, if a range of text contains the italic style, applying the bold style directly makes the text both italic and bold. However, the behavior of a style sheet depends on the way in which the style sheet has been defined. If the style sheet has been defined with the Compound Styles option selected, then the style sheet *adds* its styles to any styles that have already been applied to text. However, if the style sheet has been defined without the Compound Styles option, its styles will *replace* those currently applied. For example, if the text's current style sheet includes italic and the style sheet is changed to one that includes bold, the italic will be changed to bold.

Once a portion of a document is tagged with a style sheet, the formatting of that document portion will change whenever the contents of the style sheet change. For example, if the top level headings in your document are formatted with a style sheet that makes them 18-point bold, and you change the style sheet to 24-point plain text, then every portion of the document marked with the modified style sheet will be reformatted with the 24-point plain text.

Style sheets become a part of the document in which they are defined. However, you can export style sheets to a file and then import them into another document. In this way, many documents can share the same set of formatting specifications.

Types of Style Sheets

ClarisWorks has four types of style sheets:

- Basic: Basic styles include text formatting characteristics such as typeface and type size, but no paragraph formatting information. A basic style is therefore usually applied to a selected range of text or individual characters as you type. Basic styles can also be created in other ClarisWorks modules for numbers, graphics, and portions of a spreadsheet.

- Paragraph: Paragraph styles affect an entire paragraph and therefore can include paragraph formatting as well as text styles.

- Outline: Outline styles affect paragraph labeling and formatting within an outline.

- Table: Table formats are applied to portions of a spreadsheet.

ClarisWorks comes with a set of style sheets of each type. You can use these styles as they are or modify them to better suit your needs.

Applying Styles

Styles can be applied from the Button Bar or from the Stylesheet window. To apply a style from the Button Bar:

1. If you are applying a Basic style, place the insertion point where you want the style to begin or select the text to which it should be applied. If you are applying a Paragraph or Outline style, place the insertion point anywhere in the paragraph to be formatted.

2. Select the name of the style from the Styles menu in the Button Bar (see Figure 3.31). ClarisWorks formats the text according to the specifications in the style sheet.

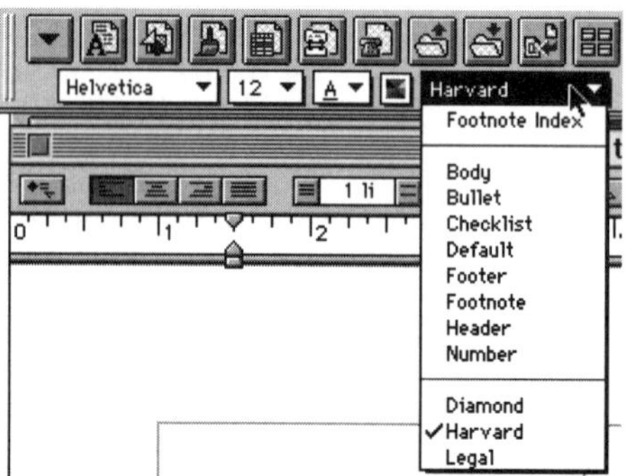

Figure 3.31 Choosing a style sheet from the Styles menu in the Button Bar

To display the Stylesheet window and choose a style from it:

1. If you are applying a Basic style, place the insertion point where you want the style to begin or select the text to which it should be applied. If you are applying a Paragraph or Outline style, place the insertion point anywhere in the paragraph to be formatted.

2.

Macintosh	Choose Window->Show Stylesheet, click the button in the Button Bar, or press SHIFT-1-W.
Windows	Choose Window->Show Stylesheet, click the button in the Button Bar, press SHIFT-CTRL-W, or press ALT-W, Y.

3. The Stylesheet window appears as in Figure 3.32, listing the style sheets that are appropriate for the current document type.

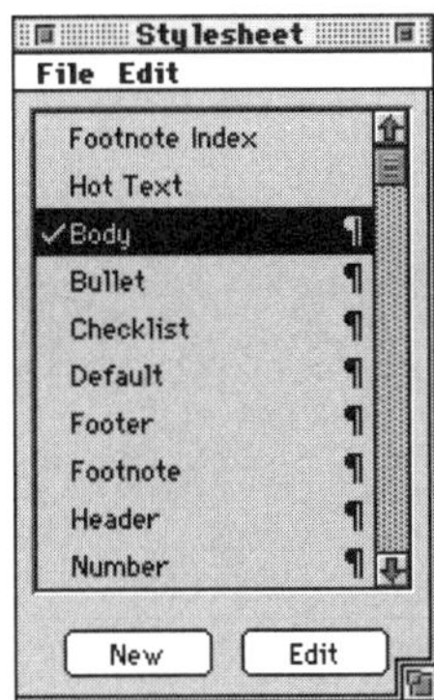

Figure 3.32 The Stylesheet window

4. Click the name of the style sheet you want to use.

The Stylesheet window is a floating window that always stays on top of any document windows. You can get rid of it by clicking in its close box. Alternatively, a Macintosh user can shrink it down to its title bar by clicking on its zoom box.

Creating a New Style Sheet

To create a new style sheet that will be saved with the document in which it was created:

1. If necessary, display the Stylesheet window.
2. Click the Stylesheet window's New button. The New Style dialog box appears.
3. Enter a name for the new style in the Style Name box ("Head 1" in Figure 3.33).

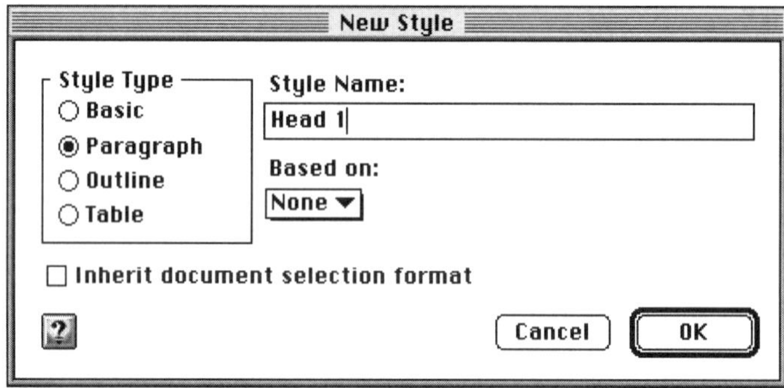

Figure 3.33 The New Style dialog box

4. Click the radio button that corresponds to the Style Type.
5. If you want to begin the new style with the settings from an existing style sheet, choose the style sheet's name from the Based on: popup menu.
6. If you want to use the settings from whatever is currently selected in the document, place a check in the Inherit document selection format check box.

7. If you want the settings in the style sheet to be *added* to whatever settings are currently applied to text, choose Compound Styles from the Stylesheet window's Edit menu. If you want the style sheet settings to *replace* those in existing text, do nothing.

8. Click the OK button or press Enter. The New Style dialog box disappears. The Stylesheet window — now called the Edit Style window — enlarges to show you all style sheets (not just those appropriate for the current document type), with the new style selected. Its current settings appear at the right of the Stylesheet window (see Figure 3.34). The cursor also changes to the Stylesheet cursor ( ). At this point you can set the new style sheet's characteristics as you need.

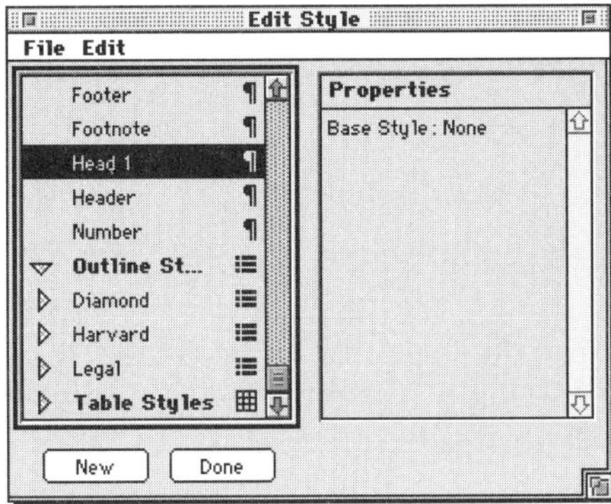

Figure 3.34 The Edit Style window

Setting Style Sheet Properties

To edit a style sheet's properties, you make choices from menus, just as you would if you were formatting a document directly. For Basic styles, choose from the Font, Size, and

Style menus. For Paragraph and Outline styles, you can also use the text ruler, the Paragraph dialog box, and the Tab dialog box. The Head 1 style in Figure 3.35, for example, includes specifications for the typeface, type size, and type style, which were taken from their respective menus. The Head 1 style also specifies one line of extra space below each paragraph, a setting taken from the Paragraph dialog box.

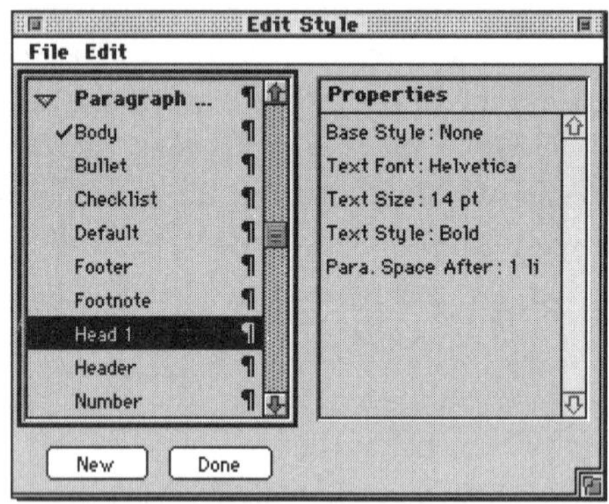

Figure 3.35 Editing a style sheet

To edit a style sheet, setting the style's characteristics:

1. Click the Stylesheet window's Edit button. The Stylesheet window expands and turns into the Edit Style window.

2. Click on the name of the style sheet you want to edit. Its properties appear at the right of the Edit Style window.

3. Make any changes necessary to the characteristics of the style sheet.

4. To finish editing, click the Edit Style window's Done button.

As long as you continue to make menu choices that involve formatting or perform actions in the text ruler, ClarisWorks assumes that you are modifying the style sheet. When you do something that isn't formatting, such as clicking in a document workspace, then ClarisWorks returns the cursor to its original shape and lets you continue working with the document. However, you can return to modifying the style sheet at any time by clicking the Stylesheet window's Edit button.

Moving Style Sheets between Documents

The custom style sheets that you create yourself are stored with the document in which they are defined. To share style sheets between documents, you must export the style sheets to a file and then import them into the document in which you want them to be used.

Exporting Style Sheets

To export style sheets to a disk file:

1. Make sure that the document from which you want to export style sheets is the current document.

2. If necessary, display the Stylesheet window.

3. Choose Export Styles from the Stylesheet or Edit Style window's File menu. The Select Styles to Export dialog box appears.

4. Click in the check box next to each style you want to export, as in Figure 3.36.

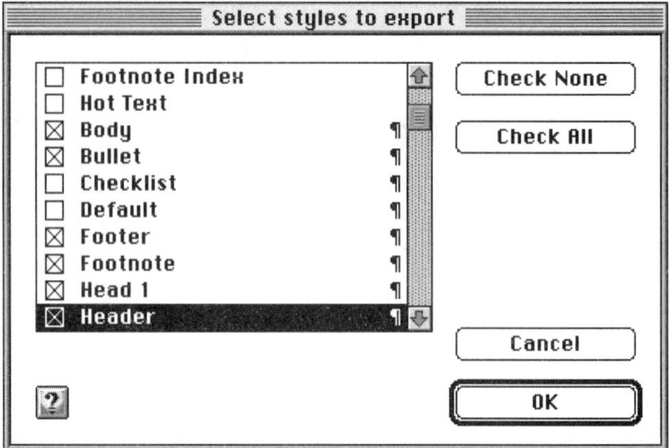

Figure 3.36 Choosing style sheets to export to a file

5. Click the OK button or press Enter. A Save File dialog box appears.

6. Enter a name for the file. Click the OK button or press Enter. ClarisWorks saves the file.

Importing Style Sheets

To import style sheets saved in a disk file:

1. Make sure that the document into which you want to import style sheets is the current document.

2. If necessary, display the Stylesheet window.

3. Choose Import Styles from the Stylesheet or Edit Style window's File menu. An Open File dialog box appears.

4. Choose the name of the file containing the style sheets you want to import. ClarisWorks displays the Select Styles to Import dialog box.

5. Click in the check box next to each style you want to import (see Figure 3.37).

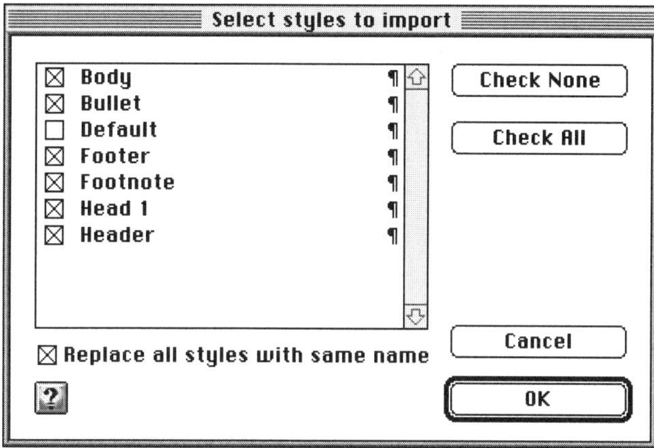

Figure 3.37 Choose style sheets to import

6. ClarisWorks assumes that you want to replace any existing styles with imported styles with the same name. If you do not want to replace styles, click in the "Replace all styles with the same name" check box to remove the check.

7. Click the OK button or press Enter. ClarisWorks reads the selected styles from the file and adds them to the current document. The imported styles will now be available in the Stylesheet window, where they can be used or edited.

Smart Quotes

When you look carefully at typeset material, you'll notice that the quotation marks (both single and double) are curly or slanted (for example, ' 'and " ") rather than straight

(' and "). Unless they are used in measurements (for example, 14"), straight quotes are a holdover from the typewriter. A document looks more professional if it uses matching, curly quotes.

Smart Quotes is a word processing option that automatically provides matching curly quotes as you type. The software makes assumptions, based on spacing, about whether it should insert an opening or a closing quote.

For example, if a double quote follows a space, Smart Quotes assumes that you want an opening quote. If a double quote follows something other than a space, Smart Quotes assumes that you want a closing quote. You can then type:

She said: “My dog has fleas.”

and get correct curly quotes without needing to use any special key combinations. Possessives, such as John’s, will also include a quote curling in the correct direction.

ClarisWorks turns on Smart Quotes for you. If you want to turn them off:

1. Choose Edit->Preferences. (Windows users can also press ALT-E, N.)
2. Choose Text from the Topic popup menu at the top of the dialog box (see Figure 3.27).
3. Click in the Smart Quotes check box to remove the check.
4. Click the OK button or press Enter to apply the change. Click the Make Default button to apply the change and save the setting for all future word processing documents.

When Smart Quotes are turned off, Macintosh users can type curly quotes directly from the keyboard. Press OPTION-[for “, SHIFT-OPTION-[for ”, OPTION-] for ‘, and SHIFT-OPTION-] for ’.

Viewing Invisible Characters

At various places in this chapter and Chapter 2, you have read about the invisible formatting characters that ClarisWorks inserts into a word processing document. Such invisible characters mark things such as page, section, and column breaks. They also mark returns and tabs.

Sometimes it can be hard to remove a page, section, or column break because you don't know exactly where that invisible marker has been placed. The solution to the problem is to ask ClarisWorks to display the markers (see Figure 3.38). These markers, even when visible, will not be printed with your document.

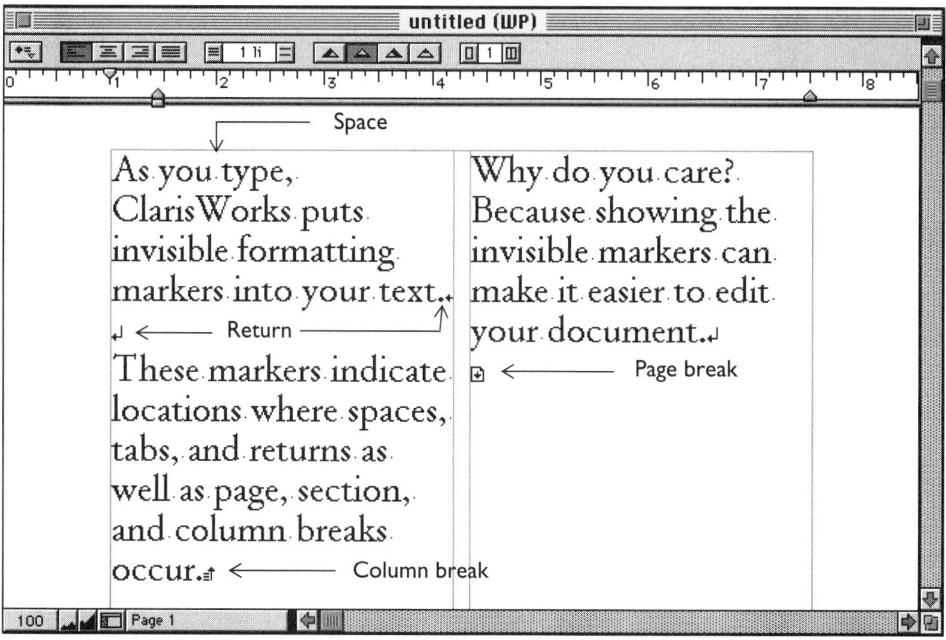

Figure 3.38 Viewing invisible formatting characters

To make the invisible characters visible, click the  button in the Button Bar *or*

1. Choose Edit->Preferences. (Windows users can also press ALT-E, N.) The Preferences dialog box appears.
2. Choose Text from the Topic popup menu at the top of the dialog box (see Figure 3.27).
3. Click in the Show Invisibles check box.

- Click the OK button or press Enter to make the change for the current document. Click Make Default to use the settings for all new word processing documents.

or

Macintosh	Press 1-;
Windows	Press CTRL-;

4

Word Processing Tools

ClarisWorks provides a collection of word processing tools that make working with a text document much easier. Such tools come under the heading "you can live without them but they sure make life easier." This chapter discusses those tools, including finding and changing text, working with hyphenation, using the spelling checker, using the thesaurus, obtaining a word count, and importing documents created with other word processors.

Finding and Changing Text

As a word processing document grows, it becomes harder and harder to find specific text within that document; scanning the document for a particular word or phrase becomes impractical. Word processors therefore provide "find" capabilities, through which you can ask the word processor to find text for you.

Once you have found text, you can automatically replace it with another word or phrase. For example, assume that you have addressed a person as *Mary* throughout a long business letter. Before you mail the letter, someone tells you that Mary will be offended if you use her first name. Therefore, you need a quick way to find every use of *Mary* in the document and to change it to *Ms. Jones*. This is what ClarisWorks's Find/Change capability can do for you.

A ClarisWorks search starts at the current location of the insertion point and works forward in the document. When it reaches the end of the document, it jumps to the beginning of the document and continues the search.

Finding Text

There are two ways to find text, either by selecting the text in the document or by working with the Find/Change dialog box. Although finding selected text is easier, it gives you less control over the way in which ClarisWorks conducts the search than using the Find/Change dialog box.

Finding Selected Text

If there is at least one example of the text you want to find already in the document, then you can select that text and ask ClarisWorks to locate other occurrences.

To find selected text:

1. Select an example of the text you want to find.

2.

Macintosh	Choose Edit->Find/Change->Find Selection or press SHIFT-⌘-E.
Windows	Choose Edit->Find/Change->Find Selection, press SHIFT-CTRL-E, or press ALT-E, F, S.

ClarisWorks searches the document for the selected text. As soon as it finds the first occurrence of the selected text, it stops the search and highlights the found text.

If ClarisWorks can't find any occurrence of the search text in a document, it will tell you with an alert (for example, Figure 4.1).

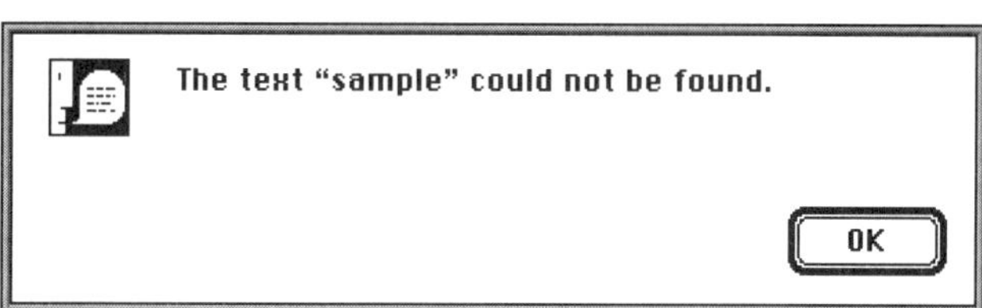
The text "sample" could not be found.
OK

Figure 4.1 A "text not found" alert

Finding Text Using the Find/Change Dialog Box

To find text by entering it into the Find/Change dialog box:

1.

Macintosh	Choose Edit->Find or press ⌘-F.
Windows	Choose Edit->Find, press CTRL-F, or press ALT-E, F, F.

The Find/Change dialog box appears.

2. Type the text you want to find in the Find box (see Figure 4.2).

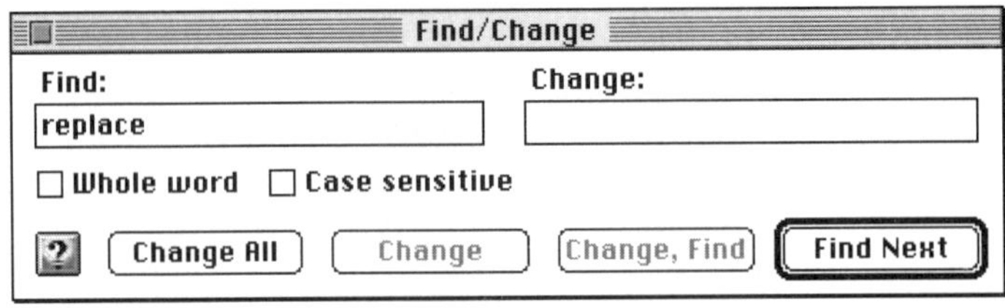

Figure 4.2 The Find/Change dialog box

3. Click the Find Next button or press Enter.

ClarisWorks searches the document for the selected text. When it finds the selected text, it stops the search and highlights the found text. The Find/Change dialog box remains on the screen.

Repeating a Find

When you search for text, ClarisWorks always stops at the first match it finds. If you want to continue the search for the same text, you can tell ClarisWorks to repeat the search without entering the search term again:

- Using the keyboard and mouse:

Macintosh	Choose Edit->Find/Change->Find Again or press 1-E.
Windows	Choose Edit->Find/Change->Find Again, press CTRL-E, or press ALT-E, A.

The preceding keyboard equivalents won't work if the Find/Change dialog box is open.

- Using the Find/Change dialog box: Click the Find Next button or press Enter.

Tailoring Find's Behavior

When you use the Find/Change dialog box, you have some control over the way in which ClarisWorks looks for text. By default, a search is not *case sensitive*. This means that it ignores differences between upper- and lowercase letters. In addition, the search looks for text anywhere within a word. For example, *the* will match *there* and *then* as well as the word *the*.

If you look back at Figure 4.2, you will notice that there are two check boxes in the middle of the dialog box, one for case sensitivity and another for whole-word searching:

- To instruct ClarisWorks to perform a case sensitive search, click in the Case sensitive check box. ClarisWorks will then recognize *Amber* as matching *Amber* but not *amber*.

- To instruct ClarisWorks to search for matches of entire words only, click in the Whole word check box. ClarisWorks will then match *the* with the word *the* but not *then* or *there*.

Changing Text

There are two strategies for changing text:

- You can find each occurrence of the search text and replace it after you verify that it should be changed.

- You can ask ClarisWorks to find and change automatically every occurrence of the search text in the document.

Changing with Verification

To get a chance to decide whether an occurrence of search text should be changed:

1.

Macintosh	Choose Edit->Find or press ⌘-F.
Windows	Choose Edit->Find, press CTRL-F, or press ALT-E, F, F.

The Find/Change dialog box appears.

2. Enter the search text in the Find box.
3. Enter the text that will replace the search text in the Change box. For example, if you were going to replace *Mary* with *Ms. Jones*, you would enter *Mary* in the Find box and *Ms. Jones* in the Change box.
4. Click the Find Next button or press Enter. Claris-Works searches for the text in the Find box, stopping when it locates the first occurrence.
5. To replace the Find text with the Change text and stop the search, click the Change button. To replace the Find text with the Change text and continue the search for the next occurrence of the Find text, click the Change, Find button.

Changing All without Verification

To change all occurrences of text in a document automatically:

1.

Macintosh	Choose Edit->Find or press ⌘-F.
Windows	Choose Edit->Find, press CTRL-F, or press ALT-E, F, F.

The Find/Change dialog box appears.

2. Enter the search text in the Find box.
3. Enter the text that will replace the search text in the Change box. For example, if you were going to replace *Mary* with *Ms. Jones*, you would enter *Mary* in the Find box and *Ms. Jones* in the Change box.
4. Click the Change All button. ClarisWorks warns you that Change All is not undoable (Figure 4.3).

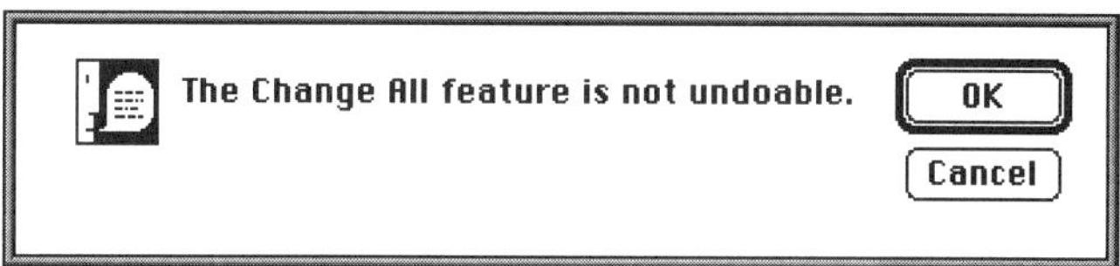

Figure 4.3 The Change All alert

5. If you are sure that you want to perform the Change All operation, click the OK button or press Enter. ClarisWorks automatically searches for every occurrence of the Find text and replaces it with the Change text.

Change All can have unexpected side effects. For example, if you want to change every occurrence of "pen" to "fountain pen," you might end up with "hapfountainpen" because ClarisWorks found "pen" within "happen." Use Change All with great caution.

Working with Hyphenation

Hyphenation can give a document a professional look. It is also very useful when you are working with full justification and you want to avoid large gaps within a line. For example, the text in Figure 4.4 uses full justification without hyphenation. Because the type size is large, there are unsightly gaps in the lines.

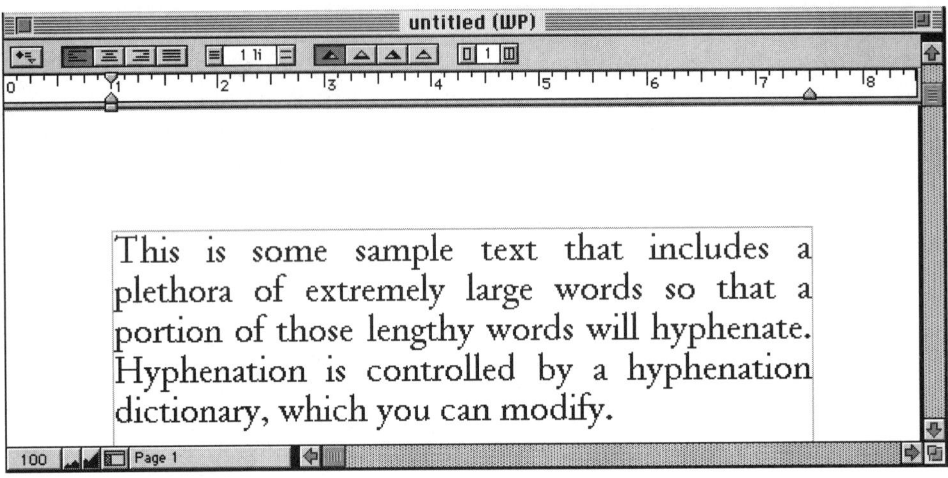

Figure 4.4 Full-justified text without hyphenation

Hyphenation helps the appearance of the text a great deal. However, as you can see in Figure 4.5, the first line still has too much white space between the words. This occurs because hyphenation is controlled by a dictionary that tells ClarisWorks where it can place hyphens. The word *plethora* isn't in the default hyphenation dictionary.

Fortunately, you can add words to the hyphenation dictionary. After adding a hyphenation point for *plethora*, the text takes its final form (see Figure 4.6). Even the first line is now attractively spaced.

Turning Hyphenation On and Off

Hyphenation affects the entire document: Either it's on or it's off. When you turn hyphenation on, ClarisWorks hyphenates the entire document; when you turn hyphenation off, ClarisWorks removes automatic hyphenation from the entire document.

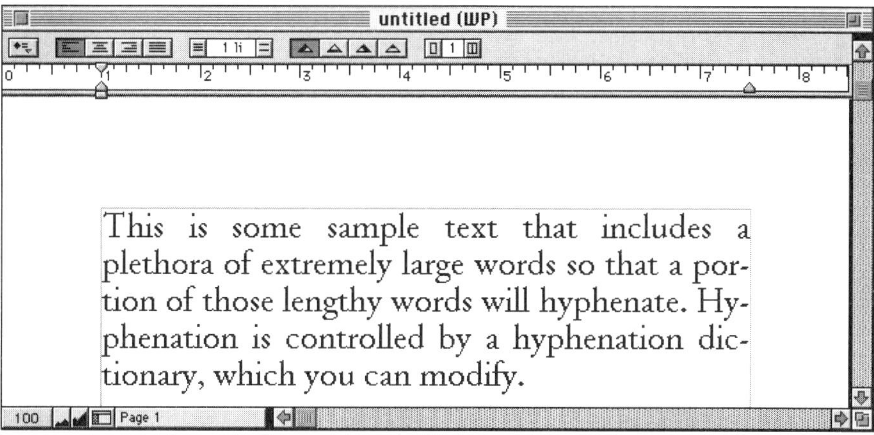

Figure 4.5 Full-justified text using the default hyphenation dictionary

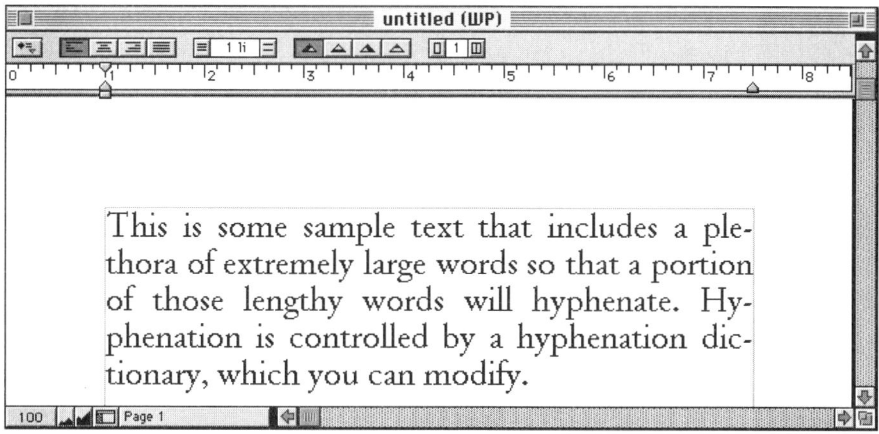

Figure 4.6 Full-justified text using custom and default hyphenation points

To turn automatic hyphenation on:

Choose Edit->Writing Tools->Auto-Hyphenate. (Windows users can also press ALT-E, A.)

ClarisWorks hyphenates the document and places a check mark next to the Auto-Hyphenate menu item.

To turn automatic hyphenation off:

Choose Edit->Writing Tools->Auto-Hyphenate. (Windows users can also press ALT-E, A.)

ClarisWorks removes hyphenation from the entire document and removes the check mark from the Auto-Hyphenate menu item.

Configuring Hyphenation Points

If ClarisWorks does not hyphenate a word that you would like hyphenated, you should enter that word and the places where the word can be hyphenated into the hyphenation dictionary.

To enter a word and its hyphenation points:

1. Display the Edit Hyphenation File window:

Macintosh	Choose Edit->Writing Tools->Edit Hyphenation Dictionary.
Windows	• Choose Edit->WritingTools->Select Dictionaries or press ALT-E, W, I to display the Selection Dictionaries dialog box. • Choose Hyphenation (*.chy) from the "Files of type" popup menu. • Highlight the name of the hyphenation dictionary you want to use. • Click the Edit button.

2. Enter the word to be hyphenated in the Entry box, placing hyphens everywhere the word can be hyphenated. For example, in Figure 4.7, *plethora* is entered as *ple-thora* because it is legal to hyphenate the word at that point.

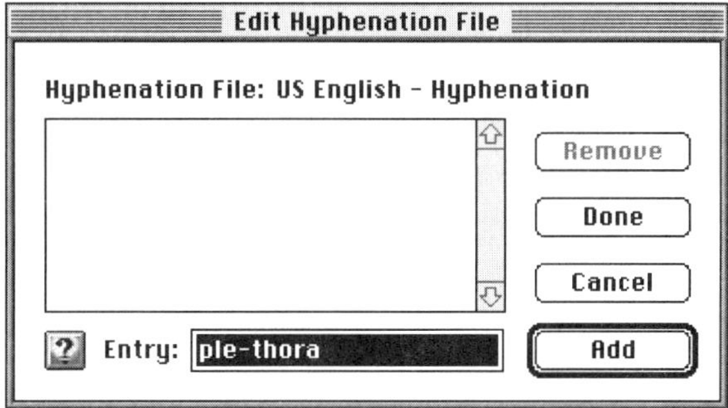

Figure 4.7 Adding a word to the hyphenation dictionary

3. Click the Add button or press Enter. The word and its hyphenation points are added to the hyphenation dictionary.

4. Repeat steps 2 and 3 for each word you want to add.

5. Click the Done button to close the window.

To remove a word from the hyphenation dictionary:

1. Display the Edit Hyphenation File window:

Macintosh	Choose Edit->Writing Tools->Edit Hyphenation Dictionary.
Windows	• Choose Edit->WritingTools->Select Dictionaries or press ALT-E, W, I to display the Selection Dictionaries dialog box. • Choose Hyphenation (*.chy) from the "Files of type" popup menu. • Highlight the name of the hyphenation dictionary you want to use. • Click the Edit button.

2. Highlight the word to be removed in the list of words at the top of the window.

3. Click the Remove button. The word and its hyphenation points are removed from the hyphenation dictionary.
4. Repeat steps 2 and 3 for each word to be removed.
5. Click the Done button to close the window.

Checking Spelling

A *spelling checker* is a word processing tool that identifies incorrectly spelled words in a document and suggests correct spellings. ClarisWorks's spelling checker matches each word in a document against two dictionaries of correct spelling: a main dictionary and a user dictionary. The main dictionary contains words that are most likely to be used in typical documents; the user dictionary contains words that you have added because they are unique to a specific document or set of documents.

ClarisWorks allows you to have many dictionary files. You might, for example, have a user dictionary for technical documents and another user dictionary for letters to family. Details on maintaining dictionary files can be found later in this chapter in the section Working with Dictionaries.

When ClarisWorks identifies a misspelling in a document, you have the following options:

- Skip the word, accepting the word as correctly spelled. The word is not added to a dictionary.
- Replace the word with one of ClarisWorks's suggested correct spellings or with a correct spelling that you type.

- Accept the word as correctly spelled and add it to the current user dictionary. The next time ClarisWorks encounters this word, it will recognize it as a correct spelling.

Starting the Spelling Checker

When you start the spelling checker, ClarisWorks immediately begins scanning the document, looking for words that aren't in the dictionary. It stops either when it finds the first misspelled word or when it has scanned the entire document.

To begin checking spelling:

- Check the entire document:

Macintosh	Choose Edit->Writing Tools->Check Document Spelling, click the button in the Button Bar, or press ⌘-=.
Windows	Choose Edit->Writing Tools-> Check Document Spelling, click the button in the Button Bar, or press CTRL-=, or press ALT-E, W, S.

- Check only the currently selected text:

Macintosh	Choose Edit->Writing Tools->Check Selection Spelling or press SHIFT-⌘-Y.
Windows	Choose Edit->Writing Tools->Check Selection Spelling, press SHIFT-CTRL-Y, or press ALT-E, W, H.

After finding a misspelled word, ClarisWorks displays the Spelling window, showing the misspelled word and any suggested corrections it can identify (for example, Figure 4.8). ClarisWorks also highlights the misspelled word in the document.

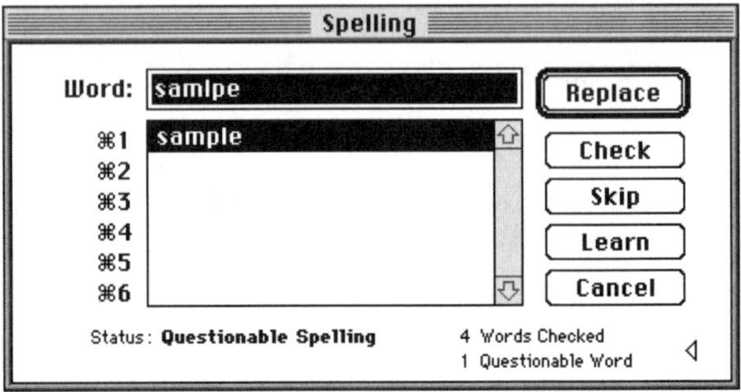

Figure 4.8 The Spelling window with a misspelled word

If you can't see the misspelled word in the document because the Spelling window is in the way and you aren't able to move it easily out of the way, you can expand the Spelling window to show you the immediate context of the misspelled word. To do so, click on the small triangle in the lower right corner of the window. This expands the window to show one line of the document, including the misspelled word, as in Figure 4.9.

Handling Misspelled Words

As you read earlier, there are three things you can do when ClarisWorks finds a misspelled word: You can replace it, skip it, or add it to a dictionary.

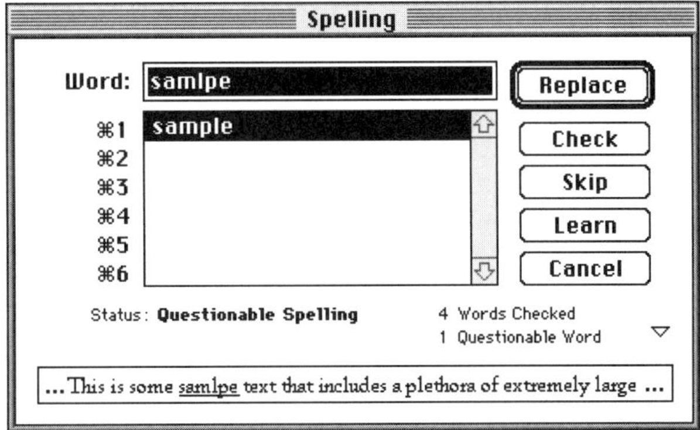

Figure 4.9 The Spelling window, showing the immediate context of a misspelled word

Replacing Misspelled Words

To replace a misspelled word, do any of the following:

- Type a correct spelling in the Word box. Click the Replace button or press Enter.
- Choose one of the first six (Macintosh) or seven (Windows) suggested correct spellings with a key combination:

Macintosh	Press ⌘-Word Number.
Windows	Press CTRL-Word Number.

- Double-click on a suggested correct spelling.

Regardless of which option you use, ClarisWorks replaces the incorrect word with the correction and continues checking for misspelled words.

Skipping Misspelled Words

When your document contains a word that is spelled correctly but that you don't want to add permanently to a dictionary you can instruct ClarisWorks to skip the word.

To skip a word, click the Skip button in the Spelling window. ClarisWorks skips the word throughout the rest of the document. Keep in mind, however, that because the skipped word isn't being added to a dictionary, ClarisWorks will mark it as misspelled the next time you spell check the document.

Adding New Words to a Dictionary

There are some words that you will use frequently—proper names and technical terms, for example—that won't be in ClarisWorks's main dictionary. To prevent ClarisWorks from identifying those words as misspelled, you can add them to a user dictionary. The next time ClarisWorks checks a document, the words you have added to the user dictionary won't be flagged as misspelled.

To add a word to the current user dictionary, click the Learn button in the Spelling window. ClarisWorks adds the word to the current user dictionary and continues spell checking the document.

Be conservative in which words you add to a user dictionary. If you add too many small words, you will find that the effectiveness of the spelling checker goes down. For example, if you were writing a document about publishing, you might talk about "em" dashes (dashes like — that are the width of the character "m"). The spelling checker will identify "em" as a misspelling. Although it is correct in the current document, adding it to a user dictionary would be a mistake because in most documents, "em" is a misspelling. An alternative would be to create a special user dictionary just for the document in which you talked about publishing.

Finishing Checking Spelling

ClarisWorks stops checking spelling when it has checked the entire document (or selected portion of the document). The Spelling window then tells you how many words were checked and how many of those the spelling checker flagged as misspelled ("Questionable words").

If you want to stop checking spelling before ClarisWorks reaches the end of the document, click the Cancel button in the Spelling window.

A spelling checker is no substitute for a good proofreading. Although a spelling checker can catch errors such as "hte" instead of "the," it can't tell you if you've used "it's" instead of "its." Both are correct spellings. The spelling checker is simply matching the words in your document against a dictionary of acceptable spellings. It knows absolutely nothing about the context in which words are used.

Using the Thesaurus

Just like a thesaurus printed on paper, a computer-based thesaurus is a writing tool that helps you find synonyms for words. A computer-based thesaurus is easier to use than a printed one because you can ask the computer to search the thesaurus for you.

There are two ways to search ClarisWorks's thesaurus:

- Select the word for which you want to find a synonym. ClarisWorks's thesaurus will then show you suggestions for synonyms for that word.
- Enter a word directly into the thesaurus window and ask the thesaurus to search for synonyms.

Starting the Thesaurus

To begin using the thesaurus:

1. If the word for which you want to find a synonym is already part of your document, select the word.

2.

Macintosh	Choose Edit->Writing Tools->Thesaurus or press SHIFT-⌘-Z.
Windows	Choose Edit->Writing Tools->Thesaurus, press SHIFT-CTRL-Z, or press ALT-F, W, E.

The Thesaurus window appears. If you have selected a word in the document, the thesaurus shows you suggested synonyms in its word list (see Figure 4.10).

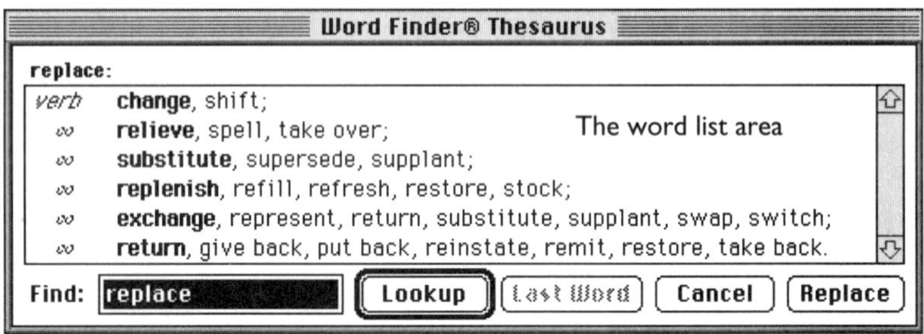

Figure 4.10 Using the thesaurus

Searching for Synonyms

If you did not select a word in your text when you started the thesaurus or if you want to search for another word while the Thesaurus window is open, you can do so.

To perform the search:

1. Click on the word for which you want to find synonyms in the word list *or* type the word in the Find box.

2. Click the Lookup button or press Enter. The thesaurus performs the search and displays synonyms in the word list.

Inserting or Replacing a Synonym

If you have selected text when you start the thesaurus, you can replace that text with a synonym. If no text was selected when you started the thesaurus, you can insert a word from the thesaurus into the document at the current location of the insertion point.

To place a word from the thesaurus into a document:

1. Click on the word you want to place in the document in the word list at the top of the Thesaurus window. The word is transferred to the Find box at the bottom of the window.

2. Click the Replace button.

You can also place a word from the thesaurus into a document by double-clicking on the word in the Thesaurus window's word list.

Working with Dictionaries

As you read earlier in this chapter, ClarisWorks bases its spelling checking on the contents of two dictionaries: a main dictionary and a user dictionary. Hyphenation and the thesaurus also use their own dictionary files. Although ClarisWorks comes with four dictionary files for your use, you can create and use other dictionary files as necessary.

If you work on several types of text documents, it can be extremely useful to keep more than one user dictionary. This is particularly true if some of your documents use a technical or professional vocabulary that isn't used by others. By keeping the user dictionaries specific to the language used in a given document, you can speed up the spell checking process.

In addition, keeping separate user dictionaries can help spell checking be more accurate. For example, in a document discussing computing topics, DOS is a legal spelling. However, in a letter to a retail store describing why the television you purchased isn't working, DOS would probably not be correct. You therefore wouldn't want to use the computing user dictionary to check the spelling of the letter.

Being able to use a variety of dictionary files means that ClarisWorks can also support more than one language. The rules for correct spelling, for example, are different between U.S. and British English. If you are writing for a British audience, you might want to replace the U.S. dictionaries (main, user, hyphenation, and thesaurus) with British dictionaries.

Choosing Dictionaries

Depending on which operating system you are using, you will find the dictionary files buried somewhere among your system files. On the Macintosh, they are stored in a folder named Claris, which is installed in the System folder; under Windows 95, they are stored in Program Files/Claris Corp/ Claris folder.

U.S. ClarisWorks users are supplied with four default dictionary files:

- US English - Hyphenation
- US English - Spelling (the main spelling dictionary)
- US English - Thesaurus
- User Dictionary

You can replace any of these as needed at any time.

To select any alternate dictionary file:

1. Choose Edit->Writing Tools->Select Dictionaries. (Windows users can also press ALT-E, W, I.) The Select Dictionaries dialog box appears (see Figure 4.11 for the Macintosh, Figure 4.12 for Windows).

2. Choose the type of dictionary file you want to select:

Macintosh	Choose the dictionary type from the Select Dictionary Type popup menu at the top of the Select Dictionaries dialog box.
Windows	Choose the dictionary type from the "Files of type" dropdown list in the middle of the Select Dictionaries dialog box.

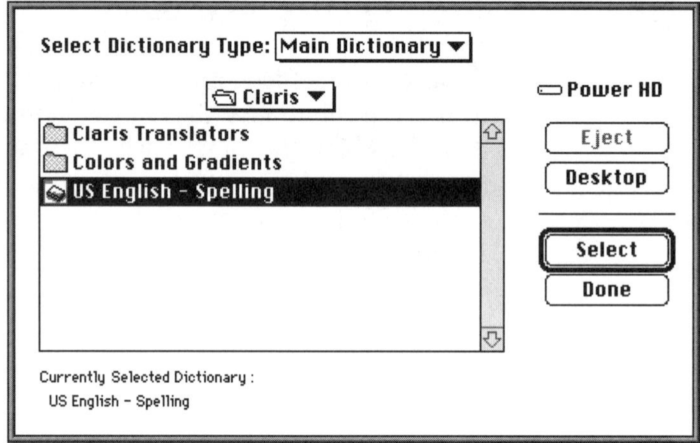

Figure 4.11 The Select Dictionary dialog box (Macintosh)

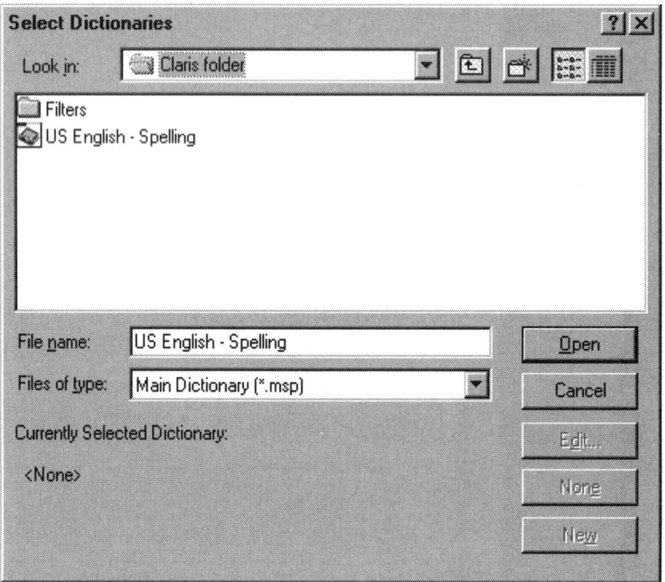

Figure 4.12 The Select Dictionary dialog box (Windows)

3. Locate the dictionary file. In most cases, your default disk directory will be different from that in which the dictionary files are stored. You will therefore probably need to thread your way through the folders on your hard disk to locate the dictionary file.

4. Highlight the dictionary file by clicking on its name.

5. To install the dictionary file:

Macintosh	Click the Select button or press Enter.
Windows	Click the Open button or press Enter.

6. Repeat Steps 2 through 5 for each dictionary file you want to install.

7. To close the Select Dictionaries dialog box:

Macintosh	Click the Done button.
Windows	Click the Cancel button or click the window's close box.

Maintaining a User Dictionary

The contents of a user dictionary are totally under your control. This means that you can add and remove words at any time, even if you aren't checking spelling.

Why might you want to do this? You might want to remove words that you accidentally added to the dictionary, or words that are preventing the spelling checker from catching some errors. By the same token, you can add terms that you know you will be using in a document so that they are present in the user dictionary *before* you begin to check spelling.

Editing the Current User Dictionary

To edit the contents of the current user dictionary:

1. Display the Edit User Dictionary dialog box:

Macintosh	Choose Edit->Writing Tools->Edit User Dictionary.
Windows	• Choose Edit->WritingTools->Select Dictionaries or press ALT-E, W, I to display the Selection Dictionaries dialog box. • Choose User Dicitonary (*.usp) from the "Files of type" popup menu. • Highlight the name of the user dictionary you want to edit. • Click the Edit button.

In Figure 4.13, for example, the current user dictionary is named User Dictionary.

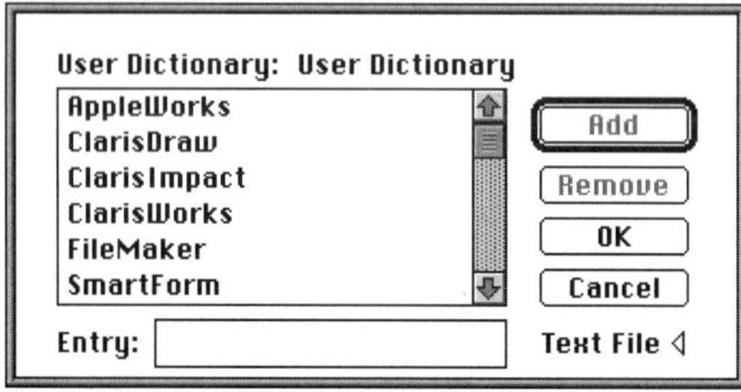

Figure 4.13 Editing the current user dictionary

2. Type a new word to be added to the dictionary in the Entry box.

3. Click the Add button or press Enter to add the word to the dictionary.

4. Repeat steps 2 and 3 for all words to be added.

5. Highlight a word to be removed from the dictionary.

6. Click the Remove button.

7. Repeat steps 5 and 6 for each word to be removed.

8. Click the OK button to close the dialog box and save changes. To close the dialog box without saving changes, click the Cancel button.

Exchanging Word Lists between Dictionaries

You can move word lists between user dictionaries by exporting the contents of one user dictionary to a text file and importing the word list into another user dictionary.

To export a word list:

1. Display the Edit User Dictionary dialog box:

Macintosh	Choose Edit->Writing Tools->Edit User Dictionary.
Windows	• Choose Edit->WritingTools->Select Dictionaries or press ALT-E, W, I to display the Selection Dictionaries dialog box. • Choose User Dicitonary (*.usp) from the "Files of type" popup menu. • Highlight the name of the use dictionary you want to edit. • Click the Edit button.

2. Expand the dialog box to include two more buttons: Import and Export (see Figure 4.14).

Macintosh	Click the diamond in the lower right corner of the dialog box (next to the Text File label).
Windows	Click Text File >> in the lower right corner of the dialog box.

3. Click the Export button. A Save File dialog box appears.

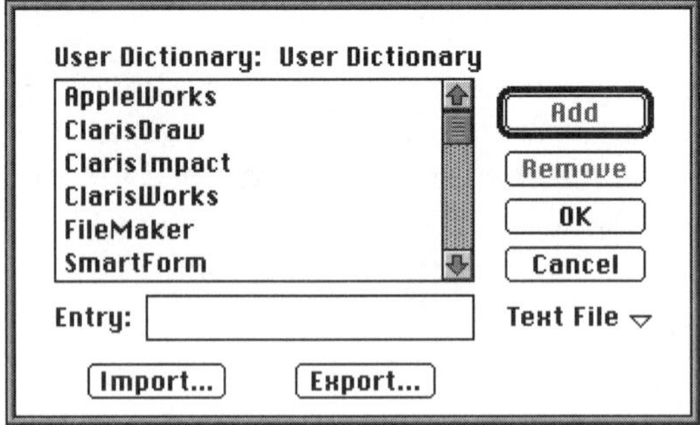

Figure 4.14 The expanded Edit User Dictionary dialog box

4. Choose a location for the file.

5. If you want, change the default name that ClarisWorks gives the file.

6. Click the Save button or press Enter to copy the words in the current user dictionary to the text file. The contents of the user dictionary will not be affected.

To add the words from a file to the current user dictionary:

1. Display the Edit User Dictionary dialog box:

Macintosh	Choose Edit->Writing Tools->Edit User Dictionary.
Windows	• Choose Edit->WritingTools->Select Dictionaries or press ALT-E, W, I to display the Selection Dictionaries dialog box. • Choose User Dicitonary (*.usp) from the "Files of type" popup menu. • Highlight the name of the user dictionary you want to edit. • Click the Edit button.

2. Expand the dialog box to include two more buttons: Import and Export.

Macintosh	Click the diamond in the lower right corner of the dialog box (next to the Text File label).
Windows	Click Text File >> in the lower right corner of the dialog box.

3. Click the Import button. An Open File dialog box appears.

4. Highlight the file containing the words to be imported.

5. Click the Open button or press Enter. ClarisWorks adds the words in the file to the current user dictionary. Duplicate words are ignored.

Creating a New User Dictionary

You will probably choose to create a new user dictionary whenever you have a document or set of documents that uses words that aren't shared by other documents you have created.

To create a new user dictionary file:

1. Choose Edit->Writing Tools->Select Dictionaries. (Windows users can also press ALT-E, W, I.) The Select Dictionaries dialog box appears.

2. Select User Dictionary as the type of dictionary file. The New button in the dialog box becomes active.

3. Click the New button. A Save File dialog box appears.

4. Enter a name for the new user dictionary.

5. Select a location for the new user dictionary. (Although the default User Dictionary file is stored in the same disk directory as the other dictionary files, there is no reason a custom user dictionary must share the same location; you can put it anywhere you want.)

6. Click the Save button or press Enter. ClarisWorks creates a new, empty user dictionary file and makes it the current user dictionary.

Getting a Word Count

One of the handy little things a word processor can do for you is to tell you how many words are in a document. If you've been assigned a 1000-word paper or if you are limited to 500 words in an essay, then it's convenient to have the computer do the counting for you.

To obtain a word count:

1. Choose Edit->Writing Tools->Word Count. (Windows users can also press ALT-E , W, W.) A window containing a count of various elements in the current document appears (see Figure 4.15).

2. Click the OK button or press Enter to close the window.

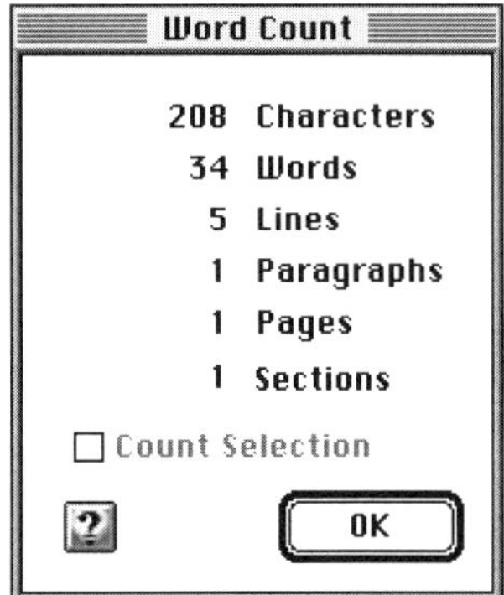

Figure 4.15 A count of a variety of characteristics of a document

By default, the word count function bases its counts on the entire document. However, if you want to count the contents of just a portion of the document:

1. Select the portion of the portion of the document for which you want counts to be computed.

2. Display the Word Count dialog box. ClarisWorks will still count the entire document. However, the Count Selection check box will be active.

3. Click the Count Selection check box. ClarisWorks immediately changes the counts to reflect only the selected portion of the document.

Opening Documents from Other Word Processors

ClarisWorks can read and translate documents created with a wide variety of other word processors and text editors. Exactly which formats it can read well depends on the specific translators that you have installed on your computer.

A set of translators is supplied with ClarisWorks. However, you can also obtain file format translators from other sources. For example, the Macintosh Operating System includes a large set of translators licensed from DataViz (the MacLink Plus translators). ClarisWorks can use these third-party translators along with its own.

To open a document created with another word processor or text editor:

1.

Macintosh	Choose File->Open or press ⌘-O.
Windows	Choose File->Open, press CTRL-O, or press ALT-F, O.

2. Choose Word Processing from the Document Type popup menu (see Figure 4.16).

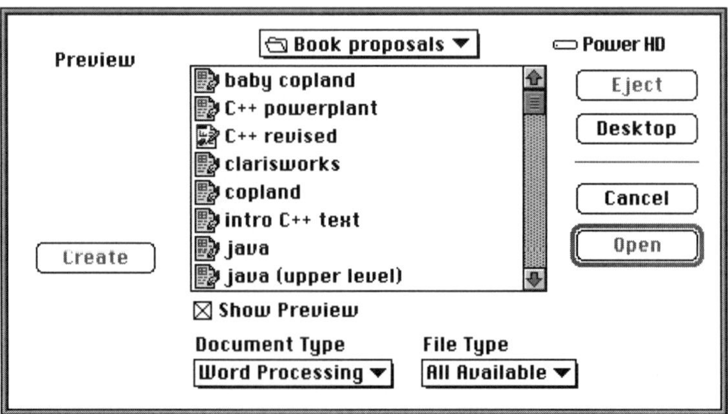

Figure 4.16 Opening a file created with another word processor

3. Choose the type of file you want to open from the File Type popup menu or, to view all files, leave the file type set to All Available.

The File Type popup menu lists all the translators that ClarisWorks has available (for example, see Figure 4.17). Its contents will therefore vary from one computer to another.

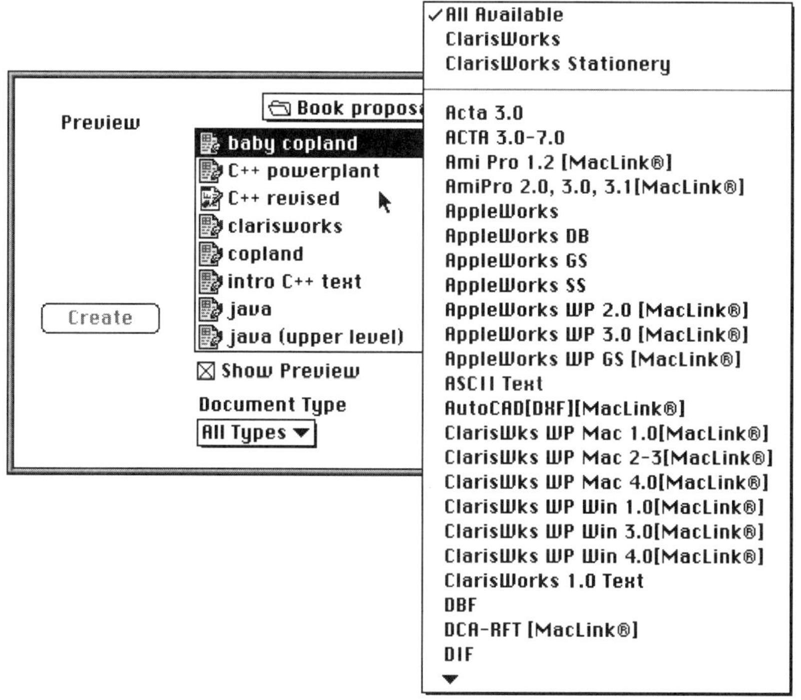

Figure 4.17 A portion of a File Type popup menu

4. Locate the file you want to open.

5. Highlight the file name.

6. Click the Open button or press Enter. ClarisWorks opens and translates the file into ClarisWorks's format. As it opens the file, ClarisWorks tries to preserve as much of the original file's formatting as possible.

You can also choose a file to open by double-clicking on its name.

ClarisWorks opens a file created with another word processor in a new ClarisWorks document. Its title will be the title of the original document with - *Converted* added. Although the new ClarisWorks document has a name, it has not been saved. If you want to keep the ClarisWorks version of the document, you must save it before you exit ClarisWorks.

When you use ClarisWorks to open a file created with a different word processor, the original document is left unchanged.

5

Drawing

ClarisWorks provides two graphics modules: drawing and painting. Although superficially similar, they are very different in the way in which they represent the contents of a document. That difference affects not only how you use the modules, but also the tasks for which each is best suited.

In this chapter, you will first read about the difference between drawing and painting. Then, you will learn to manipulate tools for creating illustrations using the drawing module. In addition, you will see how to integrate word processing frames into a drawing, and how to place drawings into a word processing document.

Drawing Versus Painting

As you read in Chapter 1, the difference between drawing and painting involves the way in which the contents of the document are represented. Drawings are examples of *object graphics*, where each distinct element of the document is represented by a description of its shape, size, color, fill pattern, location in the document, and position in the layering of all document elements.

In contrast, a painting is represented as a pattern of dots, each of which has only a color and position in the document. A painting has no concept of shape per se. Everything in the document is part of the pattern of dots.

To make this distinction a bit clearer, lets look at an example. In Figure 5.1 you can see two overlapped circles in a drawing document. If we create two similar circles in a painting document (Figure 5.2), we can't see much difference. Both illustrations contain two circles, one of which appears to be on the top of the other.

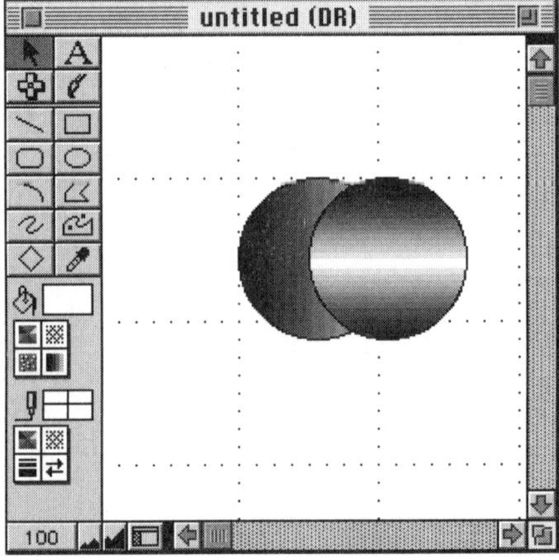

Figure 5.1 Overlapped circles in a drawing document

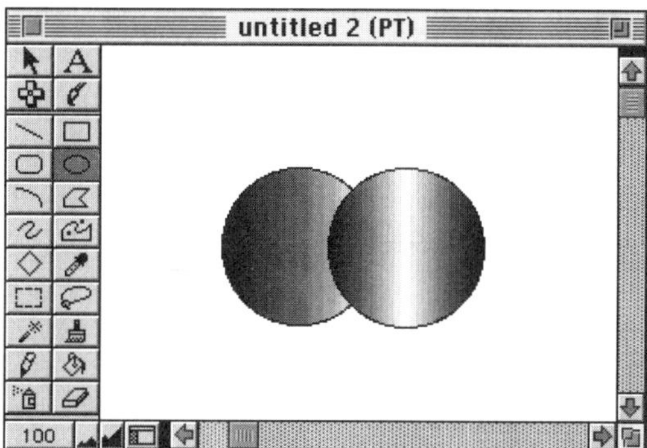

Figure 5.2 Overlapped circles in a painting document

The real difference appears when we try to separate the circles. In the drawing document, we can click on one of the circles to select it and then drag it to one side, producing two complete, independent objects, as in Figure 5.3.

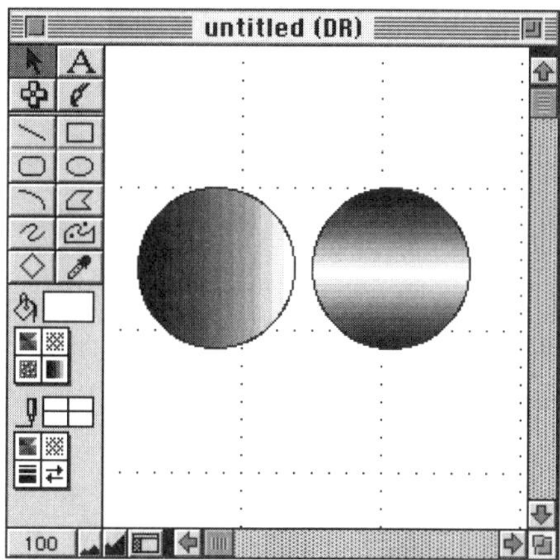

Figure 5.3 Separated circles in a drawing document

However, when we try to separate the circles in the painting document, we discover that we can't. Instead, the best we can do is select a portion of the document, which can then be moved. If you look at Figure 5.4, you can see that a portion of the document has been moved and that anything that was in the selected portion was affected by the move. Once you finish painting a shape, it loses its identity as a shape and simply becomes a portion of the pattern of dots that makes up the illustration's contents.

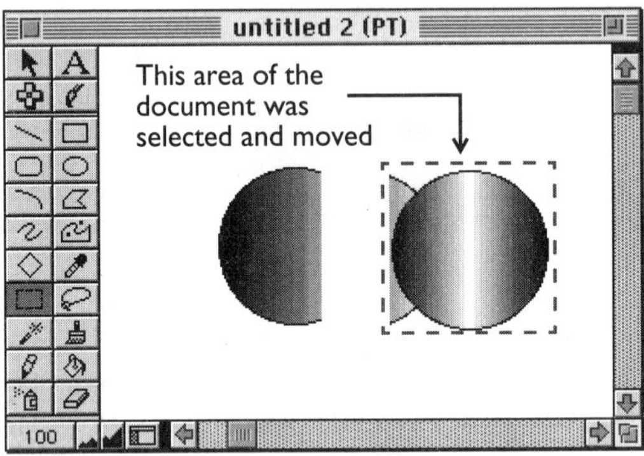

Figure 5.4 The result of attempting to separate the circles in the painting document

What does this mean in terms of when you decide to use which module? In most cases, you will want to use the drawing module for structured illustrations, such as organization charts or technical drawings. In contrast, a painting document is well suited for artistic graphics, such as a picture of a tree or an impressionistic rendering of a landscape.

Using Drawing Tools

When working with text in a word processing document, you have little need to use the ClarisWorks tool panel. However, the tools you use to manipulate a drawing are all part of that tool panel.

The drawing tool panel can be found in Figure 5.5. When you are working with anything other than a painting frame or document, the tool panel will contain the tools you see in the illustration. The selection arrow tool at the top left lets you work with the current document, whatever kind it might be.

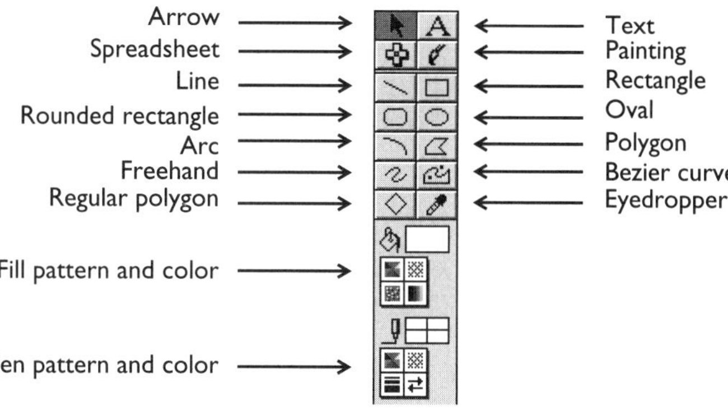

Figure 5.5 The drawing tool panel

The spreadsheet tool right below the selection arrow lets you insert and work with a spreadsheet frame in any type of document. You will read more about spreadsheets in Chapter 7.

The text tool lets you insert and work with a word processing frame in any type of document. When you select the Text tool in anything other than a word processing document, the tool panel won't change. However, whenever the word processing frame is selected so that you can work on it, the menu bar will change so that it includes the word processing menus.

By the same token, the painting tool lets you insert and work with painting frames in another type of document. When you select the painting tool, the tool panel changes to include the painting tools. Menus will also change whenever the painting frame is selected so that you can work on it.

The remainder of the tool panel contains the actual tools that you will use to create the objects in a drawing. The first nine tools create shapes that can be sized, moved, and filled with colors, patterns, textures, and gradients:

- Simple shapes: The line, rectangle, oval, and rounded rectangle tools draw simple shapes that can be sized and filled in a variety of ways.
- Arc: The arc tool draws arcs (portions of an oval) of various sizes. Arcs can be filled with colors and patterns.
- Polygons: The polygon and regular polygon tools draw shapes with multiple sides and vertices. Like other shapes, polygons can be sized and filled with colors and patterns.
- Freehand: The freehand tool draws a shape by following the mouse pointer. The result can therefore be as straight or curving as necessary.
- Bezier curve: A Bezier curve is a shape defined by a set of connected points. To draw the shape, you specify the points; ClarisWorks connects them with a curved line. Although you can also create smooth curves with the freehand tool, unless you have a very steady hand, Bezier curves tend to be smoother than freehand curves.

The other tools give you control over the appearance of the objects you create:

- Eyedropper: The eyedropper tool picks up the color and pattern of any shape on which it is clicked. You can then use that color to fill another shape in the document.

- Fill pattern and color: The set of four buttons under the paint bucket icon expand to show four palettes for specifying fill color, pattern, texture, and gradient.

- Pen pattern and color: The set of four buttons under the pen icon expand to palettes for specifying pen color, pen pattern, pen weight (thickness), and line ends (arrows or no arrows).

Regular Shapes

Many of the drawing tools produce shapes with a predetermined number of sides and angles or, as in the case of the arc, a predetermined shape. For want of a better term, we'll call these objects *regular shapes*. They include rectangles, round-cornered rectangles, ovals, lines, and arcs.

Rectangles and Rounded Rectangles

The rectangle and round-cornered rectangle tool draw similar shapes: four-sided objects. The difference between them is that the corners of a rectangle are square, whereas those of a round-cornered rectangle are rounded.

To draw a rectangle or round-cornered rectangle:

1. Click on the rectangle or rounded rectangle tool.

2. Move the mouse pointer into the drawing document's workspace.

3. Holding down the mouse button, drag the crosshair cursor down and to the right. As you drag, the outline of a rectangle or rounded rectangle appears (see Figure 5.6).

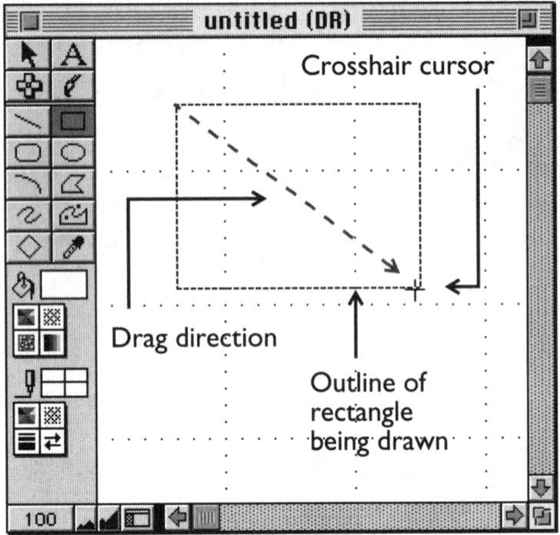

Figure 5.6 Drawing a rectangle

4. When the rectangle or rounded rectangle is the size you want it to be, release the mouse button. ClarisWorks draws the object and automatically switches back to the arrow tool.

If you want to draw more than one shape of the same type, you can prevent ClarisWorks from automatically switching to the arrow tool after you finish drawing a single shape by double-clicking on the tool. The tool will then remain selected until you explicitly select another tool.

When you draw a rounded rectangle, you have control over the curvature of the shape's corners. The curvature is expressed in points, in terms of the radius of a circle that has the same shape as the rounded rectangle's corner. In Figure 5.7, for example, you can see four rounded rectangles, each of which has a corner of a different diameter.

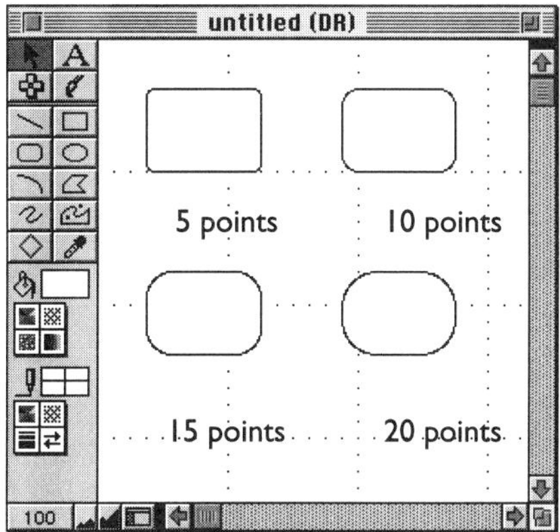

Figure 5.7 Rounded rectangles

To change the diameter of a rounded rectangle's corner:

1. Select the rounded rectangle by clicking anywhere on its outline.
2. Choose Edit->Corner Info. (Windows users can also press ALT-E, I.) The Corner Info dialog box appears.

You can also display the Corner Info dialog box by double-clicking on the outline of a rounded rectangle.

3. Enter a value, in points, for the radius of the corner, as in Figure 5.8.

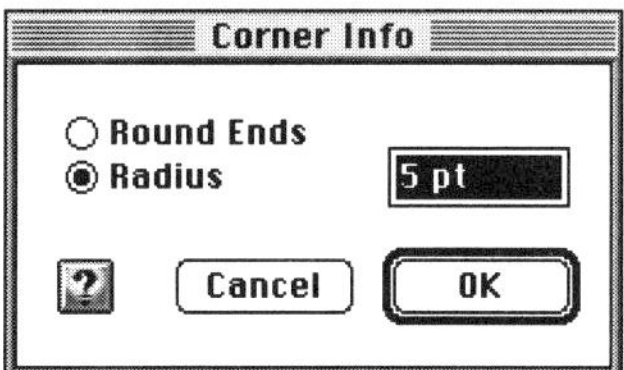

Figure 5.8 Setting the radius of a rounded rectangle's corner

4. Click the OK button or press Enter.

If you want a shape with a 180° arc at each end, choose Round Ends in the Corner Info dialog box. You'll get a shape something like this:

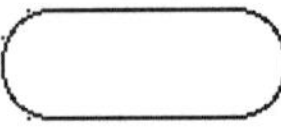

As mentioned earlier, rectangles and rounded rectangles are really the same shape with the exception of their corners. A rectangle is therefore a rounded rectangle with a corner radius of 0. You can turn a rounded rectangle into a rectangle by setting its corner radius to 0. You can also turn a rectangle into a rounded rectangle by opening the Corner Info dialog box for a rectangle and giving the shape a corner radius of something other than 0.

Drawing Squares

A square is nothing more than a rectangle that has all four sides the same length. ClarisWorks makes it easy for you to *constrain* a rectangle or rounded rectangle to a square:

To draw a square:

1. Select the rectangle or rounded rectangle tool.
2. Hold down the SHIFT key.
3. Keeping the SHIFT key down, drag the crosshair cursor to create the square. As long as the SHIFT key is down, ClarisWorks will constrain the shape so that all four sides are of equal length.
4. Release the mouse button.
5. Release the shift key.

Ovals and Circles

The oval tool draws ovals and, when constrained by the SHIFT key, circles. To draw an oval or circle:

1. Click on the oval tool.

2. Move the mouse pointer into the drawing document's workspace.

3. If you want to draw a circle rather than an oval, press down and hold the SHIFT key.

4. Hold down the mouse button and drag down and to the right until the oval or circle is the size and shape you want. An outline of the oval or circle appears as you draw (see Figure 5.9).

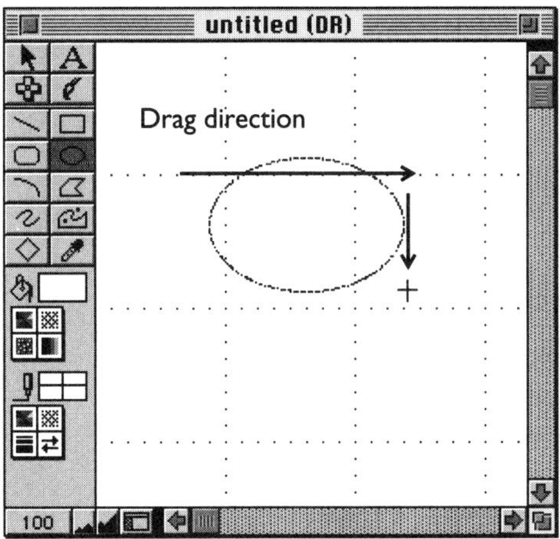

Figure 5.9 Drawing an oval

5. Release the mouse button.

6. If you are drawing a circle, release the SHIFT key.

Lines

To draw a straight line:

1. Click on the line tool.

2. Move the mouse pointer into the drawing document's workspace.

3. Hold down the mouse button and drag down and to the right in the direction you want the line to go.

4. When the line is the length and direction you want, release the mouse button.

If you hold down the SHIFT key while drawing a line, ClarisWorks will constrain the direction of the line to the nearest 45° angle. As you can see in Figure 5.10, constrained lines go straight across, straight along a diagonal, or straight down.

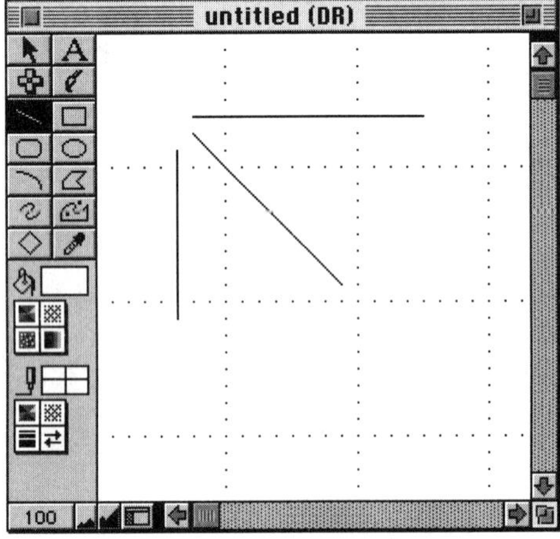

Figure 5.10 Constrained lines

Arcs

An arc is a quarter of an oval, as in Figure 5.11. (When constrained with the SHIFT key, it is a part of a circle.)

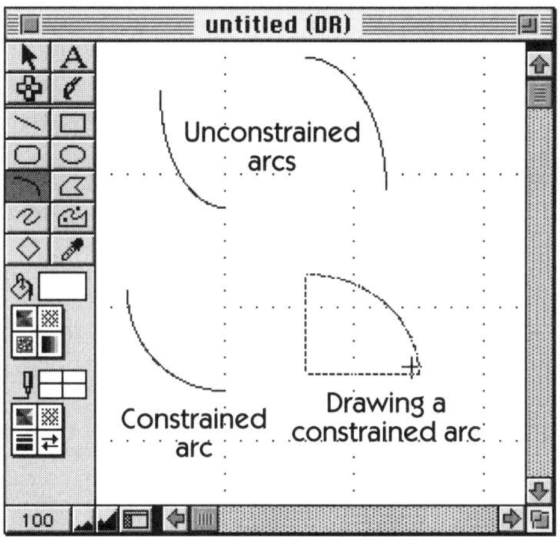

Figure 5.11 Arcs

To draw an arc:

1. Click on the arc tool.
2. Move the mouse pointer into the drawing document's workspace.
3. If you want to constrain the arc to a circle, press and hold down the SHIFT key.
4. Drag down and to the right. The arc and the quarter-oval of which it is a part appear as you drag. (See the illustration in the lower right corner of Figure 5.11.)
5. Release the mouse button.
6. If you are constraining the arc to a circle, release the SHIFT key.

Polygons

A polygon is a shape with straight sides and a variable number of angles. Regular polygons are six-sided by default; irregular polygons can have any number of angles. In Figure 5.12, for example, the irregular polygon has eight angles; the regular polygon has six.

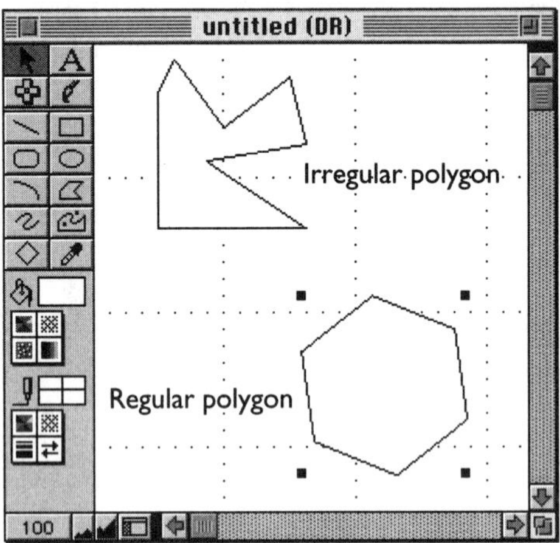

Figure 5.12 Polygons

You can change the number of sides in the default polygon. To do so , select the polygon tool and choose Edit->Polgyon Sides. Enter a number from 3 to 40 in the dialog box and click the OK button or press Enter.

Regular Polygons

To draw a regular polygon:

1. Click on the polygon tool.
2. Move the mouse pointer in the drawing document's workspace.

3. Hold down the mouse button and drag down and to the right to expand the polygon. As you draw, the polygon pivots on its top angle (see Figure 5.13).

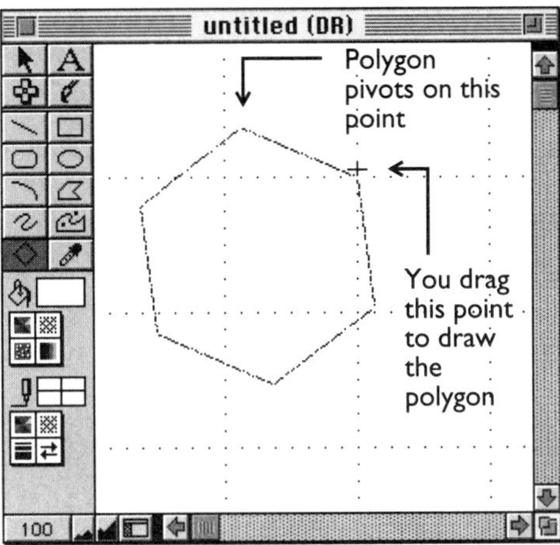

Figure 5.13 Drawing a regular polygon

4. When the size and orientation of the polygon are what you want, release the mouse button.

By default, a regular polygon pivots freely as you draw it. To constrain the angle of the pivot to intervals of 45°, or to the value you have specified in the graphic preferences, hold down the SHIFT *key while you drag.*

Irregular Polygons

An irregular polygon, with its varying number of angles, is defined by a set of points connected by straight lines. You draw the polygon by clicking where you want points to appear; ClarisWorks draws lines between the points for you.

An irregular polygon can be closed or open. In Figure 5.14, the upper irregular polygon is open; there is a gap between its starting and ending points. In contrast, the lower irregular polygon is closed; the starting and ending points are the same.

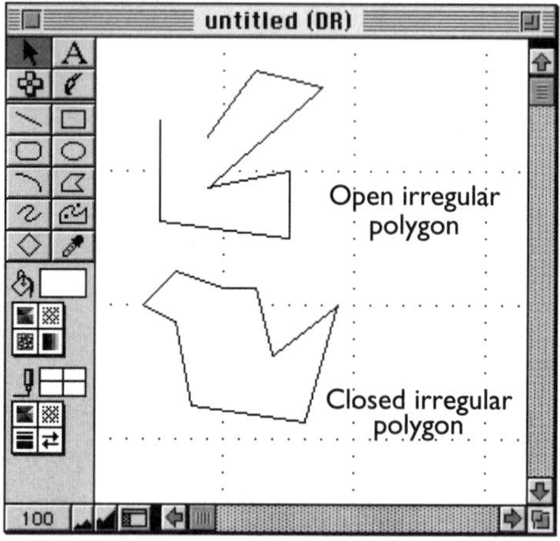

Figure 5.14 Open and close irregular polygons

1. Click on the irregular polygon tool.
2. Move the mouse pointer into the drawing document's workspace.
3. Click the mouse button where you want the first point to appear.
4. Click the mouse button where you want the next point to appear. ClarisWorks draws a line between this point and the previous point.
5. Repeat step 4 until all points except the last point have been placed.
6. Double-click at the location of the last point to finish the polygon. If you are drawing a closed irregular polygon, the last point should be directly on top of the first.

By default, polygons are set to be closed manually. That means that your last point must be on top of your first, as just described. However, if you change the Graphics preferences so that polygons are closed automatically, then all you need to do is double-click the last point and ClarisWorks will automatically draw a line between that point and the first point you placed.

If you want to connect the points in a polygon with curved rather than straight lines, hold down the Option key (Macintosh) or the Alt key (Windows) as you click to place the points. You can mix curved and straight lines in the same polygon by holding down the modifier key when you place some points and releasing it when you place others.

Freehand Objects

A freehand object is an object whose shape you define by the direction in which you drag the mouse pointer. Working with the freehand tool is much like working with a pencil. For example, the shape in Figure 5.15 was drawn by dragging the mouse pointer in a spiral motion.

Freehand shapes can be used to create relatively complex objects. For example, the dog at the top of Figure 5.16 is composed primarily of a single freehand shape. At the bottom of Figure 5.16 you can see the shape with points where the line changes direction highlighted.

In Figure 5.16 the square handles indicate that the shape has been converted into a polygon with straight-line segements. If a shape contains circular handles, then it is either a freehand shape or a polygon with curved (smoothed) segments.

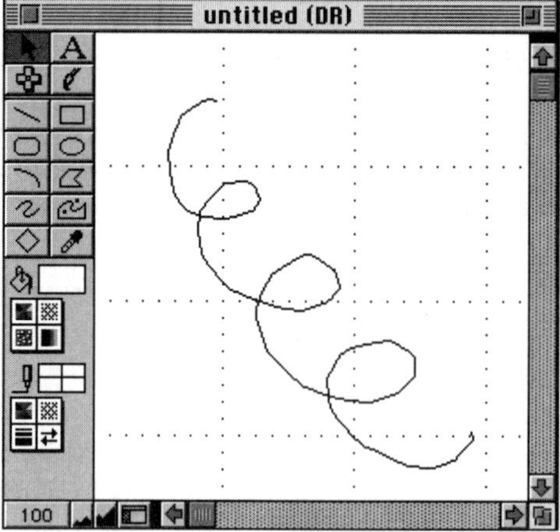

Figure 5.15 A freehand shape

Figure 5.16 Creating a complex object out of a freehand shape

To draw a shape using the freehand tool:

1. Click on the freehand tool.
2. Move the mouse pointer into the drawing document's workspace and place it at the location where the freehand shape will begin.
3. Drag the mouse pointer to draw the shape.
4. When the shape is complete, release the mouse pointer.

Bezier Curves

A Bezier curve is a freehand shape that is defined by a set of points joined by curved lines. It is drawn in the same way as an irregular polygon but often looks more like a freehand shape.

To draw a Bezier curve:

1. Click on the Bezier curve tool.
2. Move the mouse pointer into the drawing document's workspace.
3. Click the mouse button where the first point of the curve should appear.
4. Move the mouse pointer to where the next point of the curve should be placed. ClarisWorks draws a curved line from the previous point to the location of the mouse pointer, as in Figure 5.17.
5. Click the mouse button to place the next point.

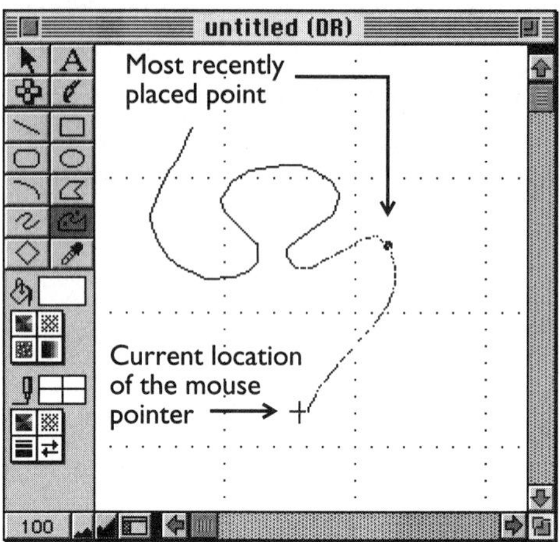

Figure 5.17 Drawing a Bezier curve

6. Repeat steps 4 and 5 until all points except the last have been placed.

7. Double-click to place the last point and finish the shape.

If you hold down the Option key (Macintosh) or the Alt key (Windows) when you place a point on a Bezier curve, the new point will be connected to the previous point with a straight rather than a curved line.

ClarisWorks calls a shape created with the Bezier curve tool a "Bezigon."

Editing Objects

Part of the joy of creating graphics on a computer is the ease with which you can modify objects once they have been drawn. ClarisWorks lets you move, resize, reshape, duplicate, and rotate objects.

Selecting and Moving Objects

The easiest way to move an object is to select it and then drag it from one place to another on the screen. To place an object more precisely, you position it visually relative to the rulers or specify its position relative to the edges of the document.

Selecting Objects

When an object is selected, it has visible *handles*, small squares that mark the edges of the object (see Figure 5.18).

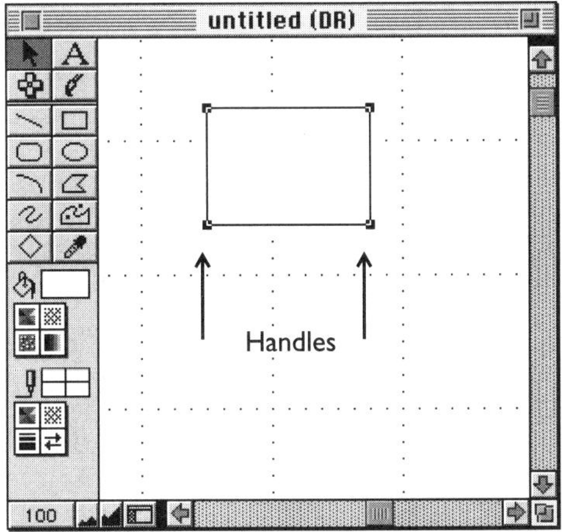

Figure 5.18 Handles on a selected object

There are three ways to select a single object:

- Click on any visible portion of the object. For example, as you can see in Figure 5.19, clicking on the visible border of a rectangle will select the rectangle. Because the rectangle is filled with white, you can also click anywhere inside the rectangle to select it.
- Drag the mouse pointer around the outside edges of the object, as in Figure 5.20

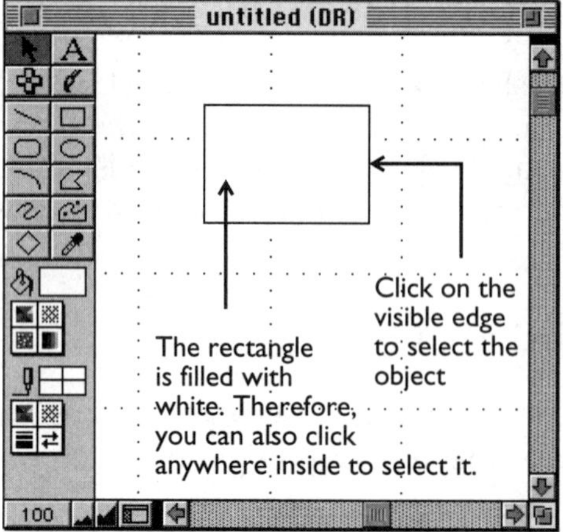

Figure 5.19 Clicking to select an object

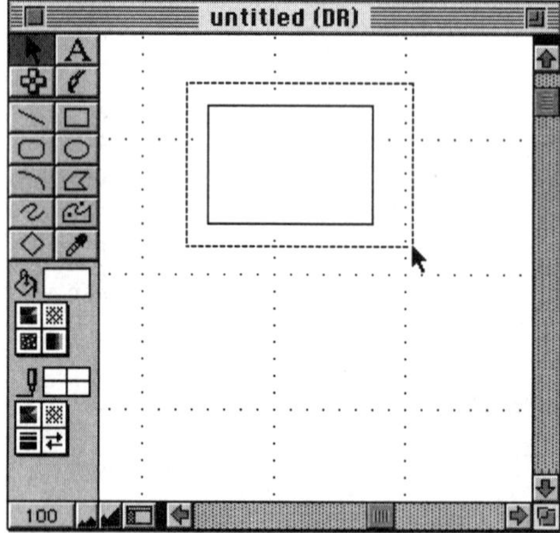

Figure 5.20 Dragging to select a single object

- Hold down the 1 key (Macintosh) or the CTRL key (Windows) and drag across any portion of the imaginary rectangle that completely encloses the object. For example, 1 /CTRL dragging across the round-cornered rectangle in Figure 5.21 selects the entire round-cornered rectangle.

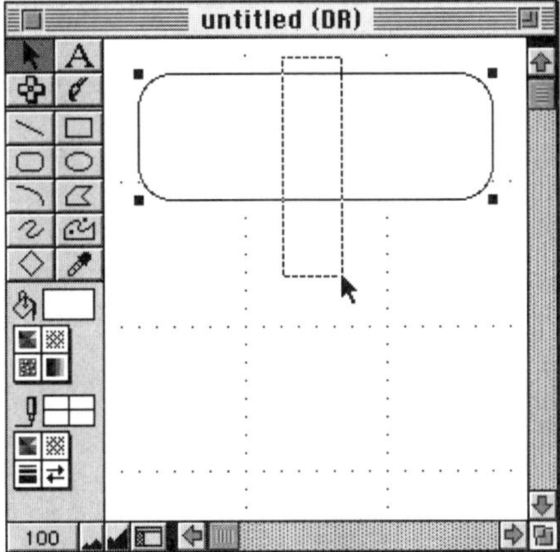

Figure 5.21 1/CTRL dragging to select

If you select more than one object, you can move all the objects together. To select multiple objects:

- Drag the mouse pointer around the outside edges of all the objects you want to select.
- Click on the first object to select it. Hold down the SHIFT key and click on the second object to select it. Repeat the SHIFT-Click for each additional object you want to select.
- To select all objects in the document:

Macintosh	Choose Edit->Select All or press 1-A.
Windows	Choose Edit->Select All, press CTRL-A, or press ALT-E, A.

Using the Rulers

You can visually place an object using ClarisWorks rulers. As you can see in Figure 5.22, the rulers display the current location of the cursor. As you move the cursor, the lines in the ruler indicating the cursor's position move as well.

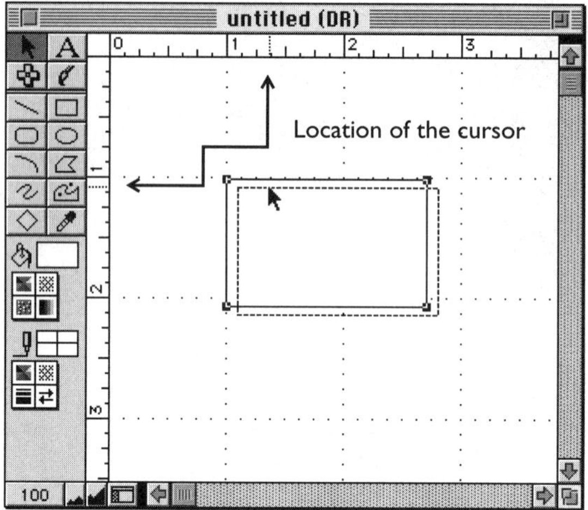

Figure 5.22 Using the rulers to position an object

There is one drawback to using the rulers to position an object: The lines in the rulers show the *cursor's* position, not the position of the corner of the object. If you happen to drag one of the handles at the corner of an object, you'll resize the object rather than move it.

Positioning Objects Precisely

To position an object precisely, you specify its distance from the edges of the document:

1. Select the object you want to position.

2. Choose Options->Object Size. (Windows users can also press ALT-O, O.) The Size window appears.

   As you can see in Figure 5.23, the top four entries in the window indicate where the object is located. If the object isn't a rectangle, the position in the Size window refers to a rectangle that completely encloses the

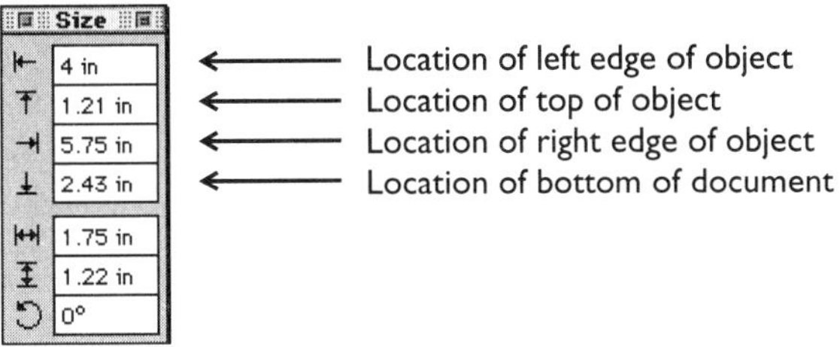

Figure 5.23 Specifying an object's location

object. The left and right edge measurements are expressed relative to the left edge of the document; the top and bottom measurements are expressed relative to the top of the document.

3. Enter a new value for one of the object's edges.
4. Press Enter. ClarisWorks moves the object and adjusts the values for the object's other edges.
5. Repeat steps 3 and 4 as necessary to place the object where you want it.

The Size window is a floating palette that rests on top of all open documents. You can leave it open and continue to work on your drawing. To close the Size window, click on its close box. To roll it up into a title bar to get it out of the way, Macintosh users can click on its zoom box; Windows users can click on its Minimize box. Click the Zoom/Minimize button again to return it to its original size.

Deleting Objects

To delete one or more objects from a drawing:

1. Select the object or objects to be deleted.
2. Press the Delete key.

You can also delete selected objects with the Edit->Clear menu option or the Edit->Cut menu option. Clear removes the objects from the document completely; Cut removes the objects from the document, placing them on the Clipboard.

Resizing Objects

Because objects in a drawing retain their identify as objects once they are placed in a document, objects can be resized as needed. There are three basic ways to resize an object: by dragging, by scaling, and by specifying precise object dimensions.

Resizing by Dragging

To resize an object by dragging:

1. Select the object to be resized.
2. Place the mouse pointer over one of the object's handles.
3. Drag the handle in the direction in which you want to expand or contract the object. All the handles except the one you are dragging remain in their original position. As you can see in Figure 5.24, an outline of the object's new size appears as you drag
4. When the object is the size you want, release the mouse button.

You can constrain an object to retain its current proportions if you hold down the SHIFT key while you drag.

You can resize more than one object at the same time by selecting more than one object. Then, drag any handle. Each selected object will be resized in the amount and direction of whichever handle you drag.

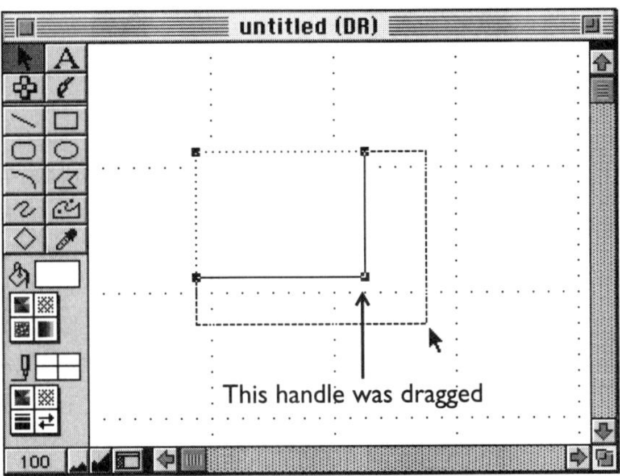

Figure 5.24 Resizing an object by dragging one of its handles

Resizing by Scaling

Scaling gives you precise control over the amount by which an object is resized. You express an object's new size as a percentage of its current size (less than 100% for a smaller object, greater than 100% for a larger object).

To resize an object by scaling:

1. Select the object you want to resize.

2. Choose Arrange->Scale By Percent. (Windows users can also press ALT-A, P.) The Scale By Percent dialog box appears (Figure 5.25).

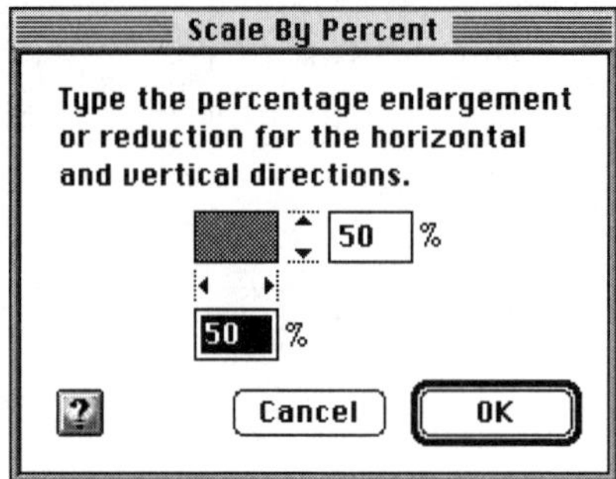

Figure 5.25 Resizing an object by providing a scaling percentage

3. Enter the percentage by which the object should be scaled. If you enter the same percentage for horizontal and vertical directions, the object will retain its current proportions. Different values for horizontal and vertical will distort the object's shape.

4. Click the OK button or press Enter. ClarisWorks resizes the object according to the percentages you entered.

You can resize more than one object at a time using percentages if multiple objects are selected when you display the Scale By Percent dialog box.

Resizing by Specifying Object Dimensions

If you want to be very precise about the size of an object, you can specify its measurements. To set an object's size by giving the object's dimensions:

1. Select the object you want to resize.

2. Choose Options->Object Size. (Windows users can also press ALT-O, O.) The Size window appears

(Figure 5.26). The height and width of the object appear at the bottom of the window. It the object isn't rectangular, the dimensions apply to a rectangle that encloses the entire object.

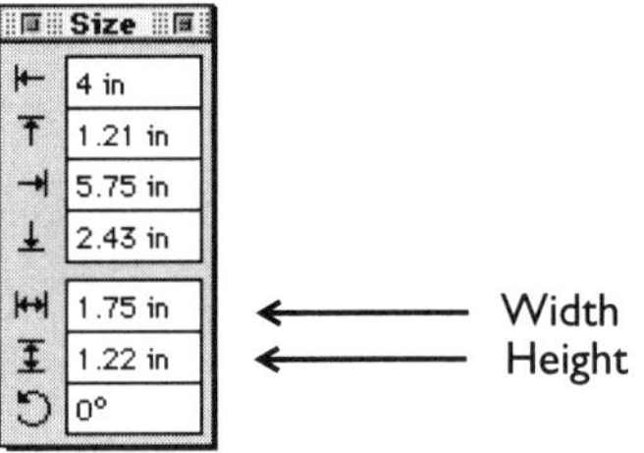

Figure 5.26 Specifying the dimensions of an object

3. Enter a new height and/or width for the object.

4. Press Enter. ClarisWorks applies the new dimensions to the object.

Reshaping Polygons, Freehand Objects, and Bezier Curves

Resizing an object can change an object's proportions but doesn't change the object's basic shape: A rectangle is still a rectangle; an oval is still an oval. However, polygons, freehand objects, and Bezier curves don't have predetermined forms. Therefore, ClarisWorks lets you change whatever shape you have given these irregular objects at any time.

There are two parts to reshaping an irregular polygon. First, you can add additional points to the object's outline. Second, you can move a point to change the object's shape.

Working with Polygons and Freehand Objects

To reshape a polygon or freehand object:

1.

Macintosh	Choose Arrange->Reshape or press 1-R.
Windows	Choose Arrange->Reshape, press CTRL-R, or press ALT-A, S.

ClarisWorks places a check mark next to the Reshape menu option. The cursor changes to the reshape cursor (the square with a plus sign through it that you can see in Figure 5.27).

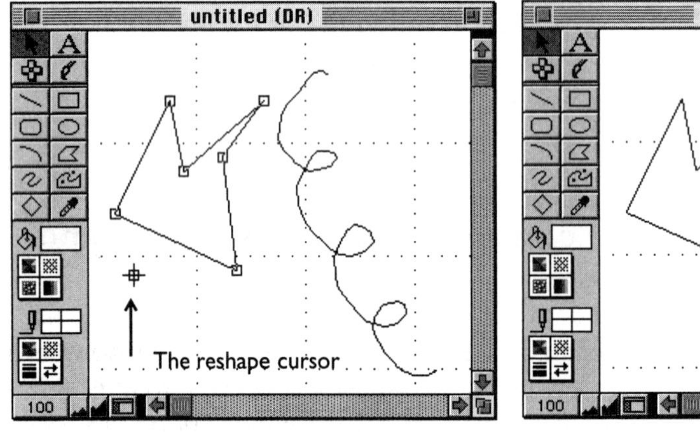

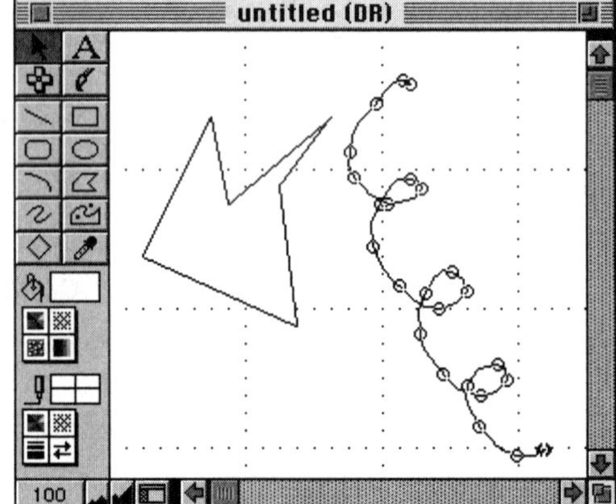

Figure 5.27 Reshape points on a polygon and a freehand object

2. Select the object you want to reshape. The object's handles appear. Notice in Figure 5.27 that the handles are square for a polygon and circular for a freehand shape.

When you are using the reshape cursor, you can select only one object at a time.

3. Drag any handle with the reshape cursor to a new location. The new outline of the shape follows the reshape cursor, as in Figure 5.28.

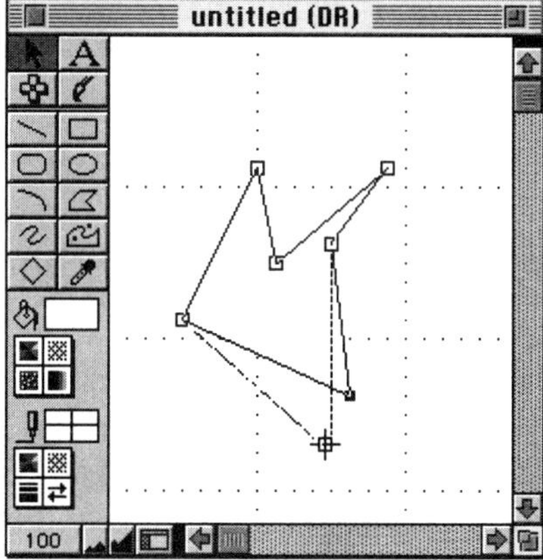

Figure 5.28 Dragging a handle to reshape a polygon

You can SHIFT*-click to select more then one handle. When multiple handles are selected, dragging one selected handle moves all selected handles at the same time.*

4. If the current handles on the object won't let you form the object into the shape you want, add additional handles. To add a new handle, click anywhere on the object's outline with the reshape cursor. You can then drag the new handle to any position you like.

To remove a handle, click on the handle with the reshape cursor to select it and press the Delete/Backspace key.

5. Repeat steps 3 and 4 as necessary until the object is the shape you want.

6. To return to the arrow cursor:

Macintosh	Choose Arrange->Reshape or press ⌘-R.
Windows	Choose Arrange->Reshape, press CTRL-R, or press ALT-A ALT-S.

Working with Bezier Curves

The principles of reshaping a Bezier curve are similar to those of reshaping a polygon or freehand object, but Bezier curve points can move differently.

To reshape a Bezier curve:

1.

Macintosh	Choose Arrange->Reshape or press ⌘-R.
Windows	Choose Arrange->Reshape, press CTRL-R, or press ALT-A, S.

ClarisWorks displays the reshape cursor.

2. Select the Bezier curve you want to reshape. ClarisWorks displays the object's handles. At this point, the object looks very similar to a freehand object selected with the reshape cursor.

3. Click on the handle whose position you want to change. As you can see in Figure 5.29, the selected point has a straight line through it with a handle at each end of the line.

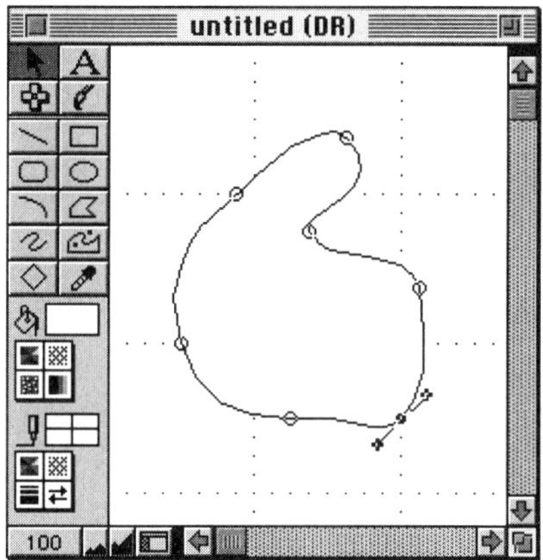

Figure 5.29 A selected point on a Bezier curve

4. Drag a selected handle to a new location. ClarisWorks reshapes the curve as you drag. (This is exactly the same as the way you reshape polygons and freehand objects.)

5. Drag either of the handles at the end of the line through the selected point to pivot the shape about the point, as in Figure 5.30. The point itself stays fixed in place, but the shape of the curve changes as you rotate the line.

6. To add another point to the curve, click anywhere on the object's outline with the reshape cursor.

7. Repeat steps 4 through 6 as necessary to create the shape you want.

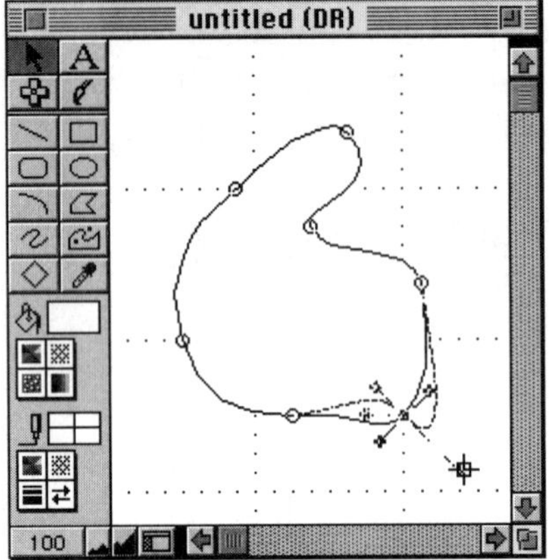

Figure 5.30 Rotating a point on a Bezier curve

8. To return to the arrow cursor:

Macintosh	Choose Arrange->Reshape or press ⌘-R.
Windows	Choose Arrange->Reshape, press CTRL-R, or press ALT-A, S.

Duplicating Objects

When you are working on a document that contains multiple objects of the same shape and size, it is easier to duplicate an existing object than it is to try to draw many objects exactly the same way.

To duplicate one or more objects:

1. Select the object or objects to be duplicated.

2.

Macintosh	Choose Edit->Duplicate or press ⌘-D.
Windows	Choose Edit->Duplicate, press CTRL-D, or press ALT-E, U.

ClarisWorks creates a duplicate of the selected object or objects, placing the new shapes a bit down and to the right of the original (see Figure 5.31).

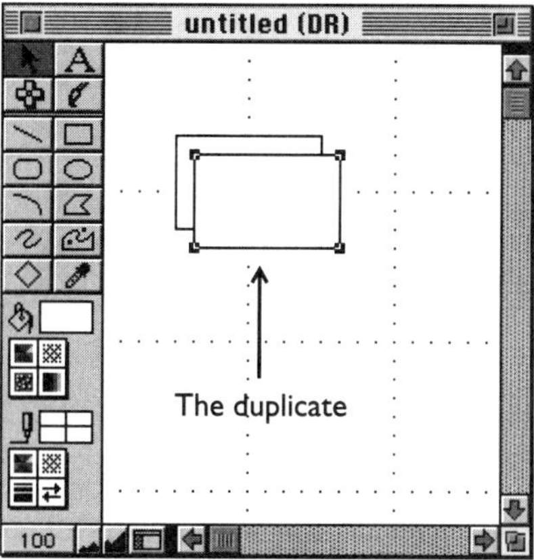

Figure 5.31 A duplicated shape

You can also duplicate objects by using Edit->Copy to copy selected objects to the Clipboard, followed by Edit->Paste to place a copy of what's on the Clipboard into the document.

If you move a duplicated object and then duplicate it again, the newest object will be the same distance from the first duplicate as the first duplicate is from the original. For example, if the the first duplicate is two inches down and one inch right of the original, the second will be two inches down and one inch right of the first. ClarisWorks maintains this relative positioning until you either move one of the duplicates to establish a new relative position or perform some other action with the document.

Rotating Objects

When you add an object to a drawing, it is oriented with its top to the top of the document. If you want to change that orientation, you can rotate an object by pivoting it around any of its handles or by specifying the number of degrees the object should be rotated.

Rotating by Dragging

When you drag to rotate, the rotation occurs relative to the object's current position in the document. To rotate an object by dragging:

1.

Macintosh	Choose Arrange->Free Rotate or press SHIFT-⌘-R.
Windows	Choose Arrange->Free Rotate, press SHIFT-CTRL-R, or press ALT-A, R.

The cursor changes to the rotate cursor (see Figure 5.32).

2. Select the object or objects you want to rotate.

3. Drag a handle of any selected object in the direction in which you want to rotate the object. ClarisWorks displays an outline of the object's new position as you rotate, as in Figure 5.32.

4. When the object has reached its new position, release the mouse button.

5. To return to the arrow cursor, repeat step 1.

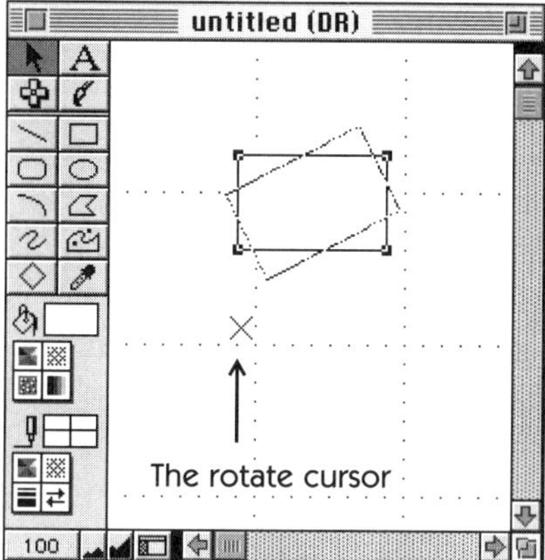

Figure 5.32 Rotating an object

You can constrain rotation to a default 45° angle by holding down the SHIFT key while you rotate. You can change the constraint angle in the Graphics panel of the Preferences dialog box.

Specifying Absolute Rotation

Absolute rotation is the number of degrees an object is to be rotated from its original position in the document. To specify an absolute rotation:

1. Select the object to be rotated.

2. Choose Options->Object Size. (Windows users can also press ALT-O, O.) The Size window appears (Figure 5.33).

3. Enter the number of degrees the object should be rotated.

4. Press Enter. ClarisWorks rotates the object.

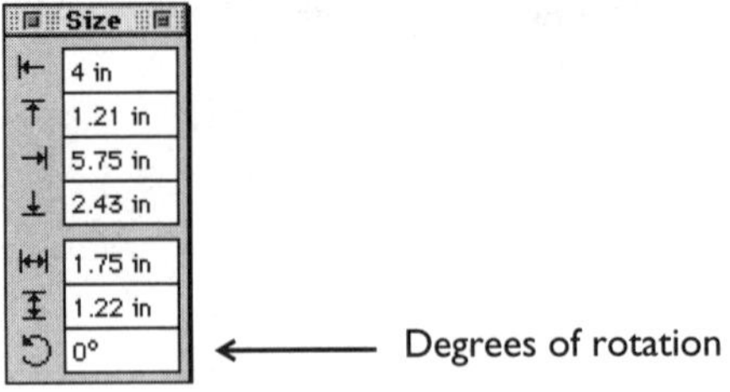

Figure 5.33 Specifying degrees of rotation

Flipping Objects

If you simply want to flip objects—either horizontally or vertically—you can do so with a single command. For example, in Figure 5.34 you can see that flipping horizontally turns an object into its mirror image; flipping an object vertically turns an object upside down.

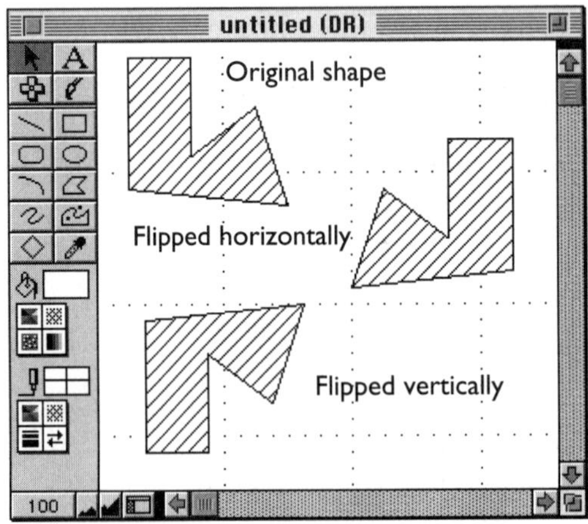

Figure 5.34 Flipped objects

To flip one or more objects:

1. Select the object or objects to be flipped.
2. To flip horizontally, choose Arrange->Flip Horizontally. (Windows users can also press ALT-A, H.)
3. To flip vertically, choose Arrange->Flip Vertically. (Windows users can also press ALT-A, V.)
4. Repeat steps 3 and 4 as needed until the shape is oriented the way you want.

Organizing Objects

Although you can place any object in a drawing document by dragging the object wherever you want, it can often be difficult to place objects exactly. ClarisWorks therefore provides several ways to place and organize objects precisely. You can align objects to a grid, align objects to each other, change the layering of objects, group objects into a larger object, and lock objects so they can't be moved.

Using the Grid

The illustrations that you have seen so far in this chapter have all had a faint grid pattern in the background. This grid, which doesn't print when you print a drawing, can be used to line up objects automatically.

The divisions in the grid correspond to the divisions in the graphics ruler. For example, in Figure 5.35 you can see a graphics ruler that has 1/8" divisions. The visible grid lines line up with the inch markings. However, there are also invisible grid lines at 1/8" intervals.

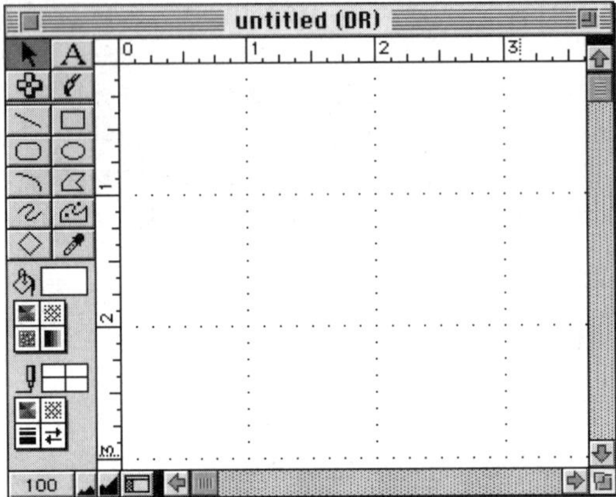

Figure 5.35 The graphics grid and graphics rulers

Turning Grid Alignment Off and On

By default, grid alignment is turned on. However, you may find that you need to position objects between grid markings and that automatic grid alignment makes positioning impossible.

To turn grid alignment off:

Macintosh	Choose Options->Turn Autogrid Off or press ⌘-Y.
Windows	Choose Options->Turn Autogrid Off, press CTRL-Y, or press ALT-O, A.

Once you've turned grid alignment off, the Options menu option changes to Turn Autogrid On. To turn grid alignment back on, select the Turn Autogrid On option, which returns the menu option to its original Turn Autogrid Off.

Aligning Objects to the Grid

An easy way to align objects with one another is to align them on the same grid position. There are two ways to align objects to the nearest grid line:

- If the grid is turned on, all objects that you draw or move are automatically aligned with the nearest grid line.
- If the grid is turned off, you can use a menu option to align selected objects to the grid.

To align objects to the grid when automatic grid alignment is turned off:

1. Select the object or objects to be aligned with the nearest grid line.
2.

Macintosh	Choose Arrange->Align to Grid or press ⌘-K.
Windows	Choose Arrange->Align to Grid, press CTRL-K, or press ALT-A, A.

Changing the Rulers and Grid

To change the spacing of the grid, you change the spacing of the graphics rulers:

1. Choose Format->Rulers. (Windows users can also press ALT-F, R.) The Rulers dialog box appears (Figure 5.36).
2. To change the units in which the rulers and grid are measured, click the radio button that corresponds to the type of units you want. For example, if you want to work with the metric system, you could choose Centimeters.

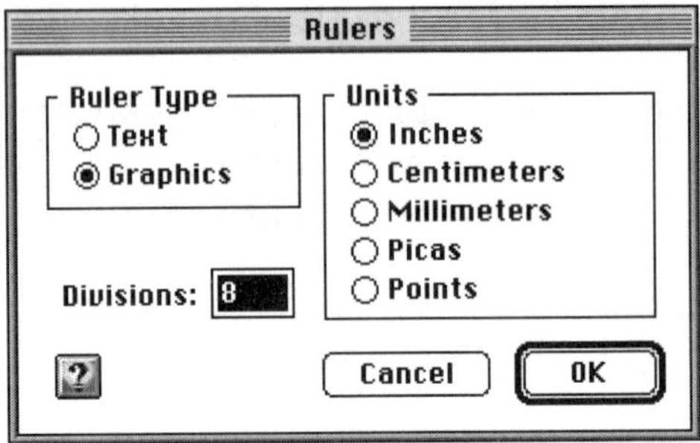

Figure 5.36 The Rulers dialog box

3. To change the number of divisions per major unit, enter a value in the Divisions box. For example, if the rulers were using centimeters, then you would probably want 10 divisions. (Millimeters would be a bit small to be practical.)

4. Click the OK button or press Enter to apply the changes and close the dialog box.

Hiding and Showing the Grid

Regardless of whether automatic grid alignment is on or off, the grid lines can be visible or invisible.

To turn grid lines off, choose Options->Hide Graphics Grid. (Windows users can also press ALT-O, G.) The grid lines disappear and the menu option changes to Show Graphics Grid.

To turn grid lines back on, choose Options->Show Graphics Grid. (Windows users can also press ALT-O, G.) The grid lines reappear and the menu option changes to Hide Graphics Grid.

Aligning and Distributing Objects

Drawings often require elements to be aligned or distributed relative to one another. For example, in Figure 5.37, each text frame is centered relative to both the top and bottom edges and the left and right edges of its enclosing rectangle. The three rectangles on the lower level are aligned by their tops; the single rectangle on the upper level is left and right centered with the middle rectangle in the lower level. In addition, the three rectangles on the lower level are evenly spaced (evenly distributed).

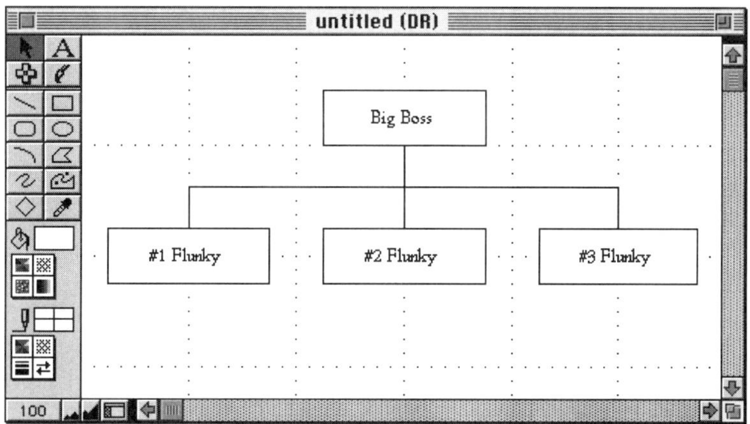

Figure 5.37 An organization chart with elements that have been aligned

Aligning Objects

To align objects to one another:

1. Select the objects to be aligned.
2.

Macintosh	Choose Arrange->Align Objects or press SHIFT-⌘-K.
Windows	Choose Arrange->Align Objects, press SHIFT-CTRL-K, or press ALT-A, O.

The Align Objects dialog box appears (Figure 5.38).

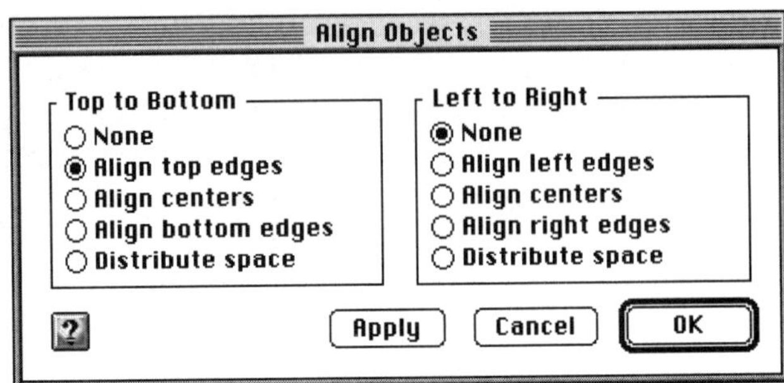

Figure 5.38 The Align Objects dialog box

3. Click the radio buttons that correspond to the type of alignment you want.

4. Click the Apply button to apply the alignment and leave the Align Objects dialog box open. Click the OK button or press Enter to apply the alignment and close the dialog box.

You can align selected objects quickly by using buttons in the Button Bar. The button aligns the tops of all selected objects to the topmost object. The button aligns the left edge of all selected objects to the leftmost object. The button aligns the bottom edges of all selected objects to the lowest object. Note that the default Button Bar doesn't include a right alignment button, but you can add that button if you need to. See Chapter 11 for details.

Distributing Objects

The bottom radio buttons in the Top to Bottom and Left to Right sets in the Align Objects dialog box don't perform alignment. Instead, they distribute objects to provide even spacing between them.

Distributing is effective only when three or more objects are involved. If you distribute from Top to Bottom, ClarisWorks leaves the top and bottom objects in place but spaces all other objects evenly between them. If you distribute from Left to Right, ClarisWorks leaves the most left and right objects in place, but spaces all other objects evenly between them.

To distribute objects:

1. Select at least three objects to be spaced.

2.

Macintosh	Choose Arrange->Align Objects or press SHIFT-⌘-K.
Windows	Choose Arrange->Align Objects, press SHIFT-CTRL-K, or press ALT-A, O.

3. Choose the Distribute space radio button for Top to Bottom and/or Left to Right spacing.

4. Click the Apply button to distribute the objects and leave the Align Objects dialog box open. Click the OK button or press Enter to distribute the objects and close the dialog box.

Changing Object Layering

As you add objects to a drawing, new objects are placed on top of existing objects. ClarisWorks keeps track of where each object is in the stack of objects. As long as objects don't overlap, you probably won't care about object layering. However, you may need to change the layering of objects that partially obscure other objects.

As an example, consider the slightly modified organization chart in Figure 5.39. Each of the rectangles now has a drop shadow, created by placing a rectangle filled with a gray pattern behind and just to one side.

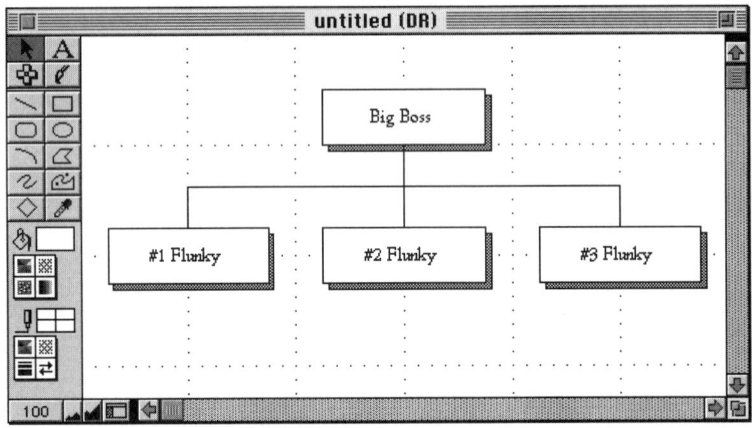

Figure 5.39 The organization chart with drop shadows

If we assume that the rectangles that form the drop shadows are added *after* the rectangles containing text, then when first placed on the document, the drop shadow rectangles lie on top of the rectangles containing text, as in Figure 5.40. To make the drawing look like Figure 5.39, we need to move the drop shadow rectangle behind the rectangle containing text.

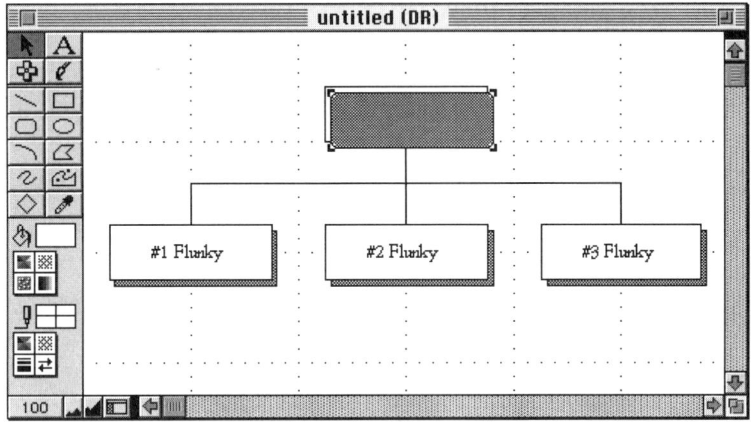

Figure 5.40 An object lying on top of another object

To change object layering:

1. Select the object or objects whose position in the stack of objects you want to change.
2.

Macintosh	To move one position up	Choose Arrange->Move Forward or press SHIFT-⌘-+.
	To move to the top of the stack	Choose Arrange->Move To Front.
	To move one position down	Choose Arrange->Move Backward or press SHIFT-⌘--.
	To move to the bottom of the stack	Choose Arrange->Move To Back
Windows	To move one position up	Choose Arrange->Move Forward, press SHIFT-CTRL-+, or press ALT-A, F.
	To move to the top of the stack	Choose Arrange->Move To Front or press ALT-A, -E.
	To move one position down	Choose Arrange->Move Backward, press SHIFT-CTRL--, or press ALT-A, B.
	To move to the bottom of the stack	Choose Arrange->Move To Back or press ALT-A, M.

Grouping and Ungrouping Objects

When you have complex objects whose parts consist of many other objects, it can be easier to work with all of the parts of an object as a group. You can then move, resize, reshape, and add color and fill patterns to the entire group.

For example, consider the bar chart in Figure 5.41. Each bar in this illustration is a separate object; so are each line and the white circles that overlie the x and y axes. If you want to move or resize this chart, the easiest way to do so is to group all of the individual pieces into a single object.

To group objects:

1. Select all of the objects that are to be part of the group.
2.

Macintosh	Choose Arrange->Group of press ⌘-G.
Windows	Choose Arrange->Group, press CTRL-G, or press ALT-A, G.

To ungroup a grouped object:

1. Select the object you want to ungroup.
2.

Macintosh	Choose Arrange->Ungroup of press SHIFT-⌘-G.
Windows	Choose Arrange->Ungroup, press SHIFT-CTRL-G, or press ALT-A, U.

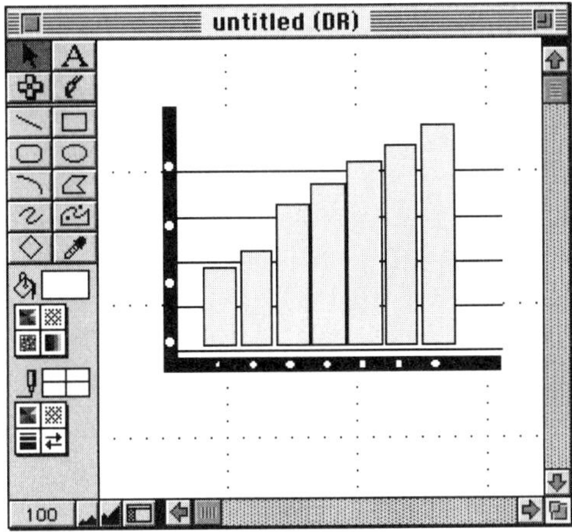

Figure 5.41 A bar chart made up of many individual objects

Locking and Unlocking Objects

By default, every object in a drawing is movable and modifiable. If you drag it, it will move; if you drag its handles, it will change size. However, there are circumstances in which you want to make sure that you don't accidentally move one or more objects while you are working on other parts of the document.

For example, assume you are working on the drawing in Figure 5.42. You want to move the three inner circles. However, every time you try to move just those three, you end up accidentally selecting the outer circle and moving it as well. What can you do? You can lock the outer circle in place so that even if it is accidentally selected, it won't move with the inner three. Locked objects can be selected and copied, but they can't be colored, filled, moved, resized, or reshaped.

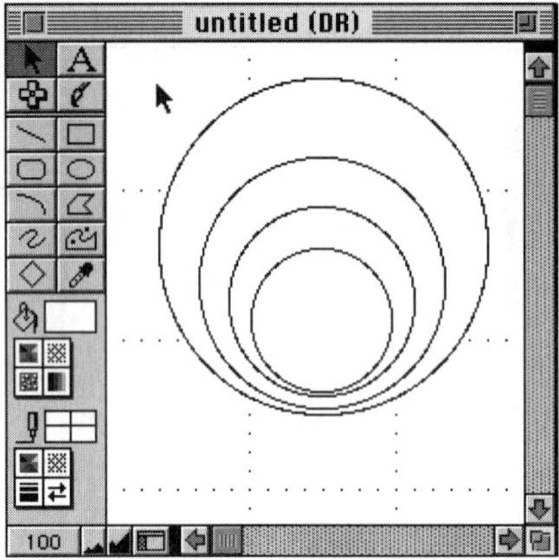

Figure 5.42 A drawing in which locking will make modifying objects easier

To lock one or more objects:

1. Select the object or objects to be locked.

2.

Macintosh	Choose Arrange->Lock or press 1-H.
Windows	Choose Arrange->Lock, press CTRL-H, or press ALT-A, L.

To unlock one or more objects so they can be moved or modified:

1. Select the object or objects to be unlocked.

2.

Macintosh	Choose Arrange->Unlock or press SHIFT-1-H.
Windows	Choose Arrange->Unlock, press SHIFT-CTRL-H, or press ALT-A, N.

Adding Color, Patterns, and Gradients to Objects

To this point, most of the shapes you have seen have been empty: they have borders, but no interior colors or patterns. (The major exceptions were the drop shadow rectangles in the organization chart, which were filled with a solid shade of gray.) Many drawings, however, have at least some objects filled with colors, patterns, and gradients. Drawings also contain various types of lines for object borders. For example, the butterfly in Figure 5.43 has fill colors of black and a shade of gray for the insect's body and portions of the wings.

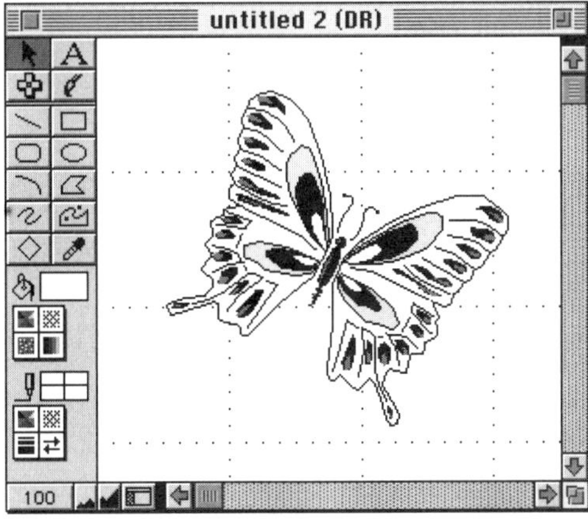

Figure 5.43 A drawing that contains filled objects

Filling Objects

The color and/or pattern with which the interior of an object is filled is controlled by the fill controls. As you can see in Figure 5.44, there are four fill controls (color, black and white pattern, fill texture, gradient), each of which expands into a tear-off palette that you can leave on the screen, floating above all open documents. Next to the paint bucket icon is a small rectangle that contains a sample of the fill settings for the currently selected object.

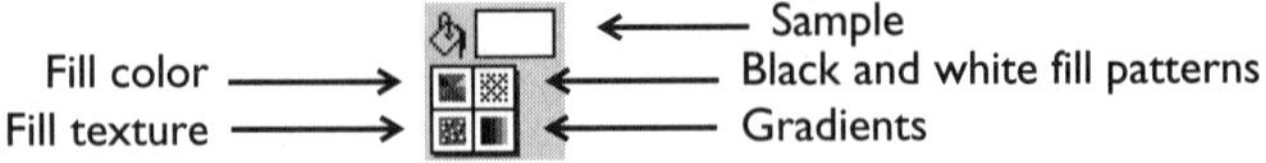

Figure 5.44 The fill controls

The fill color palette (top left in Figure 5.45) contains solid colors with which you can fill any shape. The fill pattern palette (top right in Figure 5.45) contains patterns that can fill any shape. The basic patterns are black and white. However, you can apply a color from the fill color palette to any of the patterns.

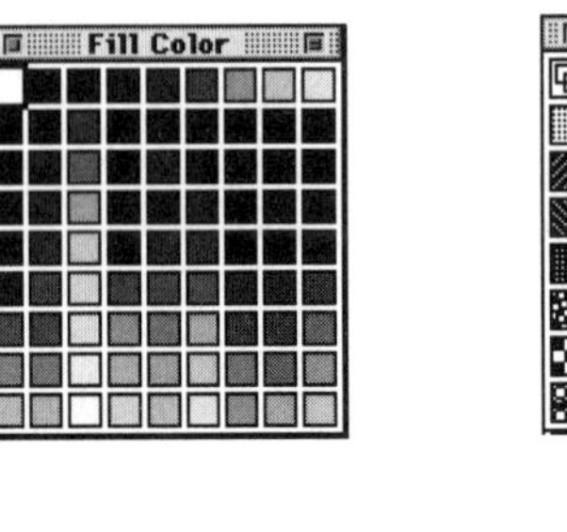

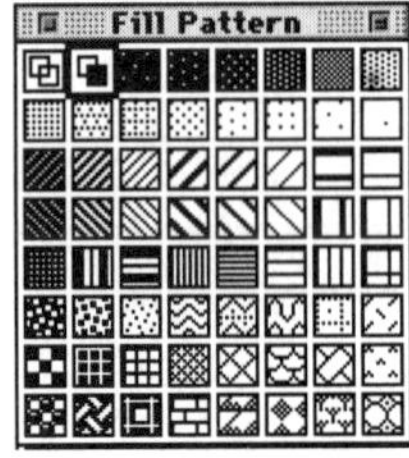

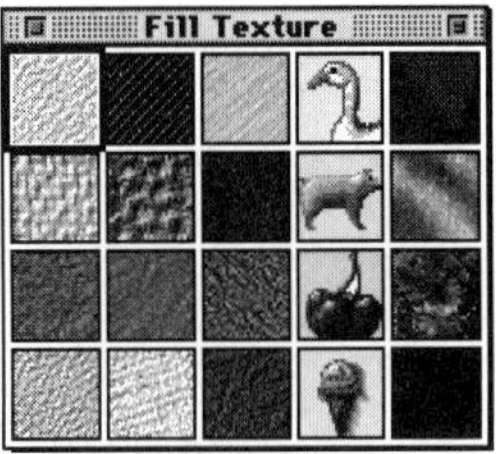

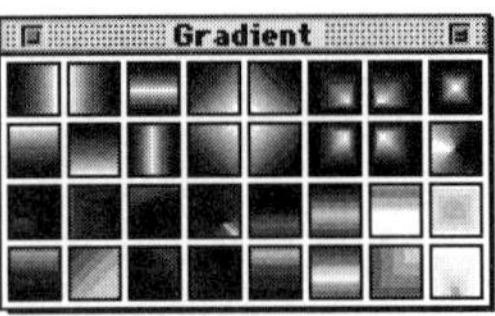

Figure 5.45 The fill palettes

The fill texture palette (bottom left in Figure 5.45) applies specialty textures to objects. When you apply a texture, it replaces any existing fill pattern, color, or gradient.

The gradient palette (bottom right in Figure 5.45) applies fills that shade objects with a sequence of grays or colors. The effect of a gradient is to give an object a three-dimensional appearance. As you can see in Figure 5.46, the gradients shade from light to dark, giving the appearance that a light source is coming from one specific direction.

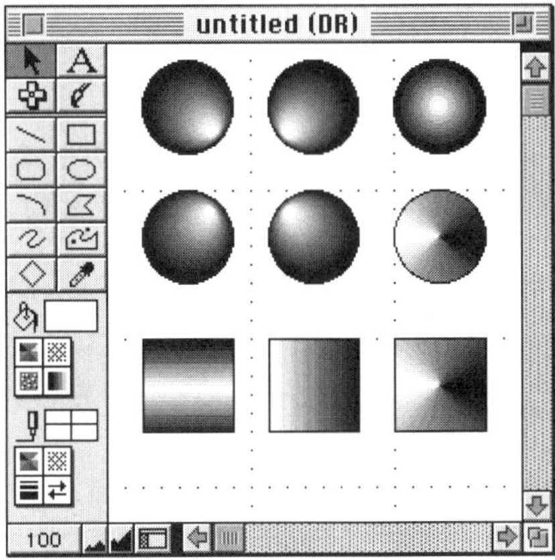

Figure 5.46 Gradients

Applying Fills

To apply a selection from any of the fill palettes to one or more objects:

1. Select the object or objects to be filled.
2. Click and hold down the mouse button on the control that represents the palette you want to use.

3. Drag the mouse pointer to the palette square you want to select (see Figure 5.47).

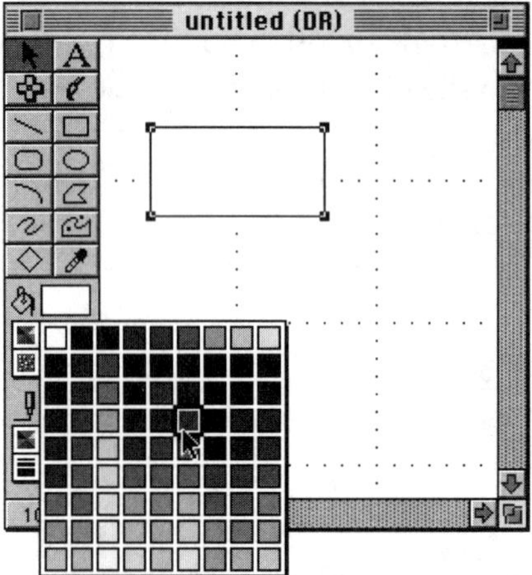

Figure 5.47 Choosing from a palette

4. Release the mouse button. ClarisWorks applies the fill.

You can select from a palette by clicking on its control to expose the palette and then dragging to the selection, as described earlier. However, if you plan to make many selections from the same palette, it's easier to tear off the palette and let it float on top of your documents.

If you make selections from the fill palettes when no object is selected, the next object you draw will use your selections.

Transparent versus Opaque Objects

The two selections at the left edge of the top row of the fill pattern palette are different from the selections in any other palette. Rather than affecting the fill of an object, they control whether an object is transparent or opaque. The far left selection produces a transparent object; the selection to the right of it (the default) produces an opaque object.

Transparent objects allow objects behind them to show through. For example, in Figure 5.48, the empty rectangle is actually on top of the filled rectangle. However, because the empty rectangle is transparent, the filled rectangle behind is completely visible.

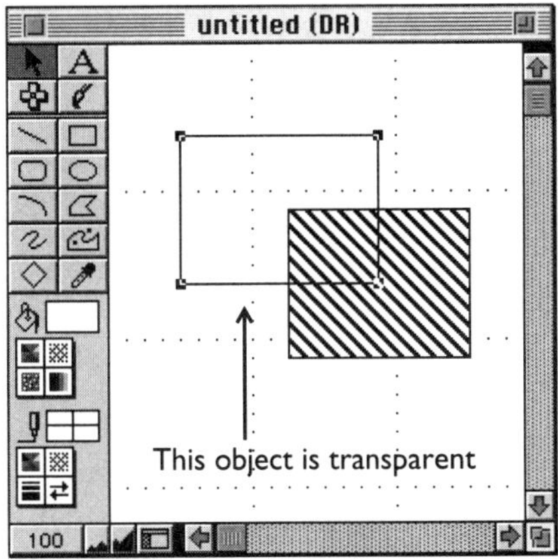

Figure 5.48 A transparent object

To make an object transparent, select the top left square of the fill pattern palette. Because transparent objects have no fill pattern or color, any pattern or color the object has will disappear.

To make a transparent object opaque, select the second square from the left in the top row of the fill pattern palette *or* give the object a fill pattern or color.

Customizing Lines

Changing the fill color or pattern affects only the inside of an object; it doesn't affect the line that forms an object's outside border. To customize the border of an object, you need to work with the pen controls.

As you can see in Figure 5.49, there are four pen controls, each of which expands to a tear-off palette. The controls also provide a sample of the current pen pattern.

The pen color palette (top left in Figure 5.50) controls the color applied to the outside of an object. The pen pattern palette (top right in Figure 5.50) contains black and white patterns that can give a line a dashed or other nonsolid appearance. Pen colors and patterns can be applied together, just like fill colors and patterns.

Figure 5.49 The line controls

The width palette (bottom left in Figure 5.50) sets the width of a line. If you choose None, the line will be transparent. Use this setting if you want to draw a shape without a visible border. The remainder of the settings set the width of a line, measured in points. (A hairline is 0.02 point.)

You can also obtain an invisible line by making the line transparent. To do so, select the transparent pen pattern (the top left square in the pen pattern palette).

The arrow palette (bottom right in Figure 5.50) applies only to straight lines. Use selections from this palette to place arrowheads at one or more ends of a line. The reference to

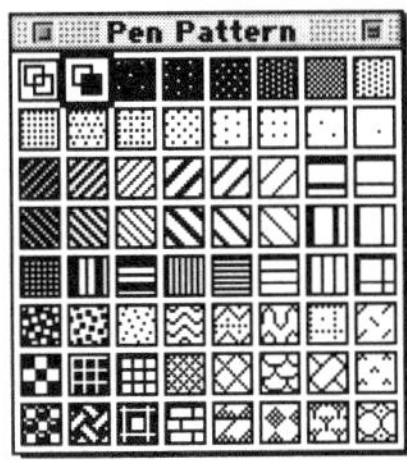

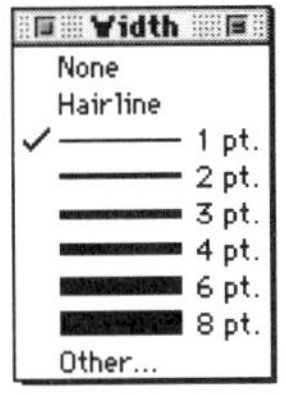

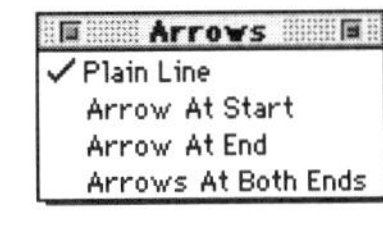

Figure 5.50 The pen palettes

"start" in the palette is the end of the line where you started drawing; the "end" is the end of the line where drawing finished.

Applying Pen Settings

To change the appearance of a line:

1. Select the object or objects whose line you want to change.
2. Click and hold the mouse pointer over the control whose palette you want to use.
3. Drag the mouse pointer to the palette square or option you want to select.
4. Release the mouse button.

If you make selections from the pen palettes when no objects are selected, the next line you draw will use your selections.

Picking up Settings with the Eyedropper

The eyedropper tools can make it easy to use the same fill and pen settings on multiple objects. When you click on an existing object with the eyedropper, the fill and pen settings are set to match those of the clicked object. Each object you draw from that point takes on those settings, until such time as you change them.

To use the eyedropper tool:

1. Click on any object that currently has the fill and pen settings you want to duplicate. ClarisWorks picks up those settings and makes then the current settings.

2. Draw another object. The new object will use the settings you picked up in Step 1.

You can also use the eyedropper to pick up settings and apply them to existing objects. First, double-click on the eyedropper. Then click on the object whose settings you want to pick up. The settings will be transferred to the fill, pen, pattern, and gradient palettes. To apply those settings 1-*click (Macintosh) or* CTRL-*click (Windows) on the objects whose settings you want to change.*

Importing Clip Art

You don't need to be an artist to create great drawings: You can import and modify clip art drawings. *Clip art* is electronic images that are sold for use in printed form. Typically, you can include clip art images in your own printed documents, either modified or unmodified, in any way you choose. However, the electronic clip art files can't be distributed in electronic form.

The use of clip art images on the Web World Web presents an interesting copyright dilemma. If you can prevent the images from being downloaded by a user, then it's OK to include them on a web page. In that case, the image isn't any different from a clip art image used in a printed document. However, there's no simple way to make an image on a web page read-only.

Where do you get clip art? There are several sources. You can purchase it; you will also find that many programs, like ClarisWorks, come with a collection of clip art for your use. Some images are available freely from on-line services and the World Wide Web. You can also create your own clip art by saving images that you create and use often in a ClarisWorks library.

Clip art collections are available in many graphics formats. With a full set of Claris file format translators installed, you can open and work with drawings in EPS, PICT, JPEG, and GIF formats. EPS (Encapsulated PostScript) is a cross-platform format that describes the contents of a drawing using the PostScript page description language. PICT is a Macintosh format that uses QuickDraw commands from the Macintosh ToolBox to describe the contents of a document. JPEG and GIF are compressed bit-mapped formats used primarily on the World Wide Web.

Using ClarisWorks Libraries

A ClarisWorks library is a collection of images that can be dragged into a document. You might, for example, put a company logo in a library, or you might have a decorative bar that you use in all your slides, such as the bar in Figure 5.51.

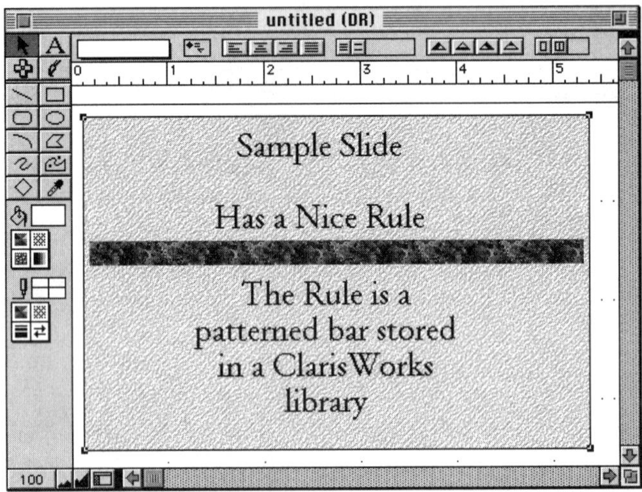

Figure 5.51 A drawing containing an image (the bar) copied from a library

Creating a New Library

A library is a special file that stores images for you. To create a new, empty library:

1. Open or create the document that contains one or more images that you want to store in a library.

2. Choose File->Library->New. (Windows users can also press ALT-F, L, N.) An empty library window appears (Figure 5.52). This window floats on top of all open documents.

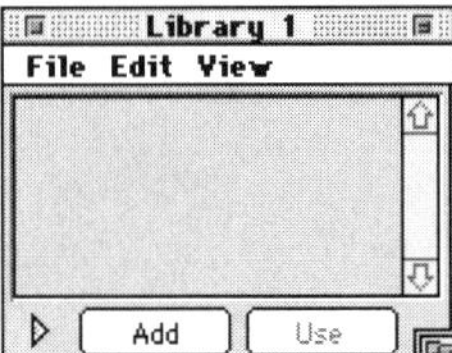

Figure 5.52 An empty library window

Opening an Existing Library

To open a library file that you have already created:

1. Choose File->Library->Open. (Windows users can also press ALT-F, L, O.)

Adding Images to a Library

To add images to a library:

1. Highlight the object that you want to add to the library.
2. Click the library window's Add button. ClarisWorks copies the image to the library (for example, see Figure 5.53).

Macintosh users can also drag images into a library window.

Renaming Library Objects

When you add an image to a library, ClarisWorks gives it a default name of *Object n*, where *n* is the next number in the sequence of objects. However, if you want to be able to search the library using object names, you will need to give each image a meaningful name.

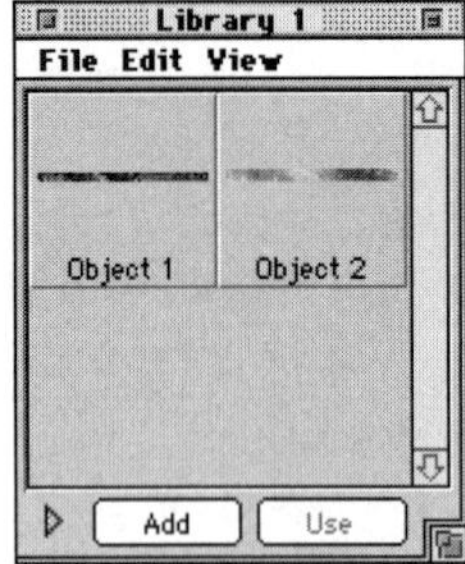

Figure 5.53 Objects in a library

To change a library object's name:

1. Click the right-facing triangle to the left of the Add button in the library window. The window expands to expose two additional buttons (Rename and Find).

2. Select the object in the library you want to rename.

3. Type its name in the Name box, as in Figure 5.54.

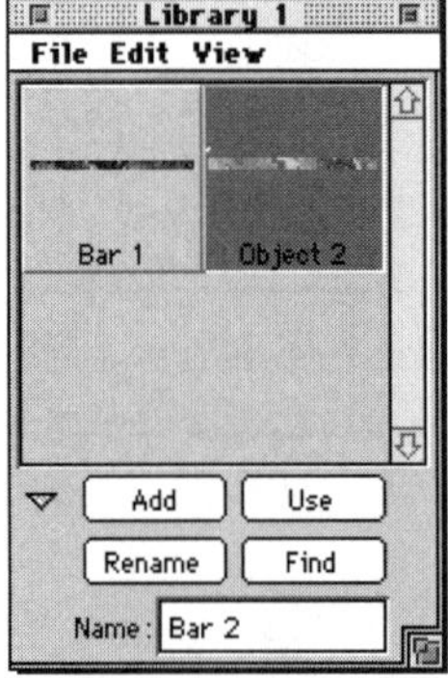

Figure 5.54 Renaming an image in a library

4. Press Enter to apply the new name.

Searching a Library

As the number of objects in a library grows, it can become difficult to locate the specific image you want. Assuming you have given the images meaningful names, you can use those names to search the library.

To search a library:

1. Click the right-facing triangle to the left of the Add button in the library window. The window expands to expose two additional buttons (Rename and Find).

2. Enter the name of the image you want to locate in the Name box.

3. Click the Find button. ClarisWorks locates the image with the matching name and selects it in the library window. If no match is found, ClarisWorks beeps the computer's speaker.

Using Images Stored in a Library

To copy an image from a library to a document:

1. Open the document into which the image will be copied and make it the current document.

2. Open the library containing the image.

3. Select the image, either by clicking on it or by searching for it.

4. Click the Use button. ClarisWorks copies the image into the current document.

Macintosh users can also drag an image from a library into a document.

Removing Objects from a Library

To remove an image from a library:

1. Open the library from which an object is to be removed.
2. Select the object to be removed.
3. Choose Delete from the library window's Edit menu.

Using Artwork from External Sources

As mentioned earlier, ClarisWorks can open documents in a variety of graphics formats, providing you with access to a huge body of clip art. However, there is something you need to be aware of when you import clip art prepared in EPS or PICT format. Depending on the type and/or complexity of the image, you may or may not be able to ungroup and modify it in the ClarisWorks drawing module.

Because you can't count on being able to modify the content of EPS or PICT clip art, in most cases you will need to use the images as they are shipped, making them part of your own drawings without modification.

Many of the images that can't be modified in the drawing modules can be modified in the painting module.

Integrating Drawing and Word Processing

Some of the illustrations you've seen in this chapter have included text, but you haven't read anything yet about how to add text to a drawing. This is because any text you place in a drawing is really a text frame, a miniature word processing document. In this section we'll look at text frames and compare their behavior with that of stand-alone word processing documents. In addition, you'll see how to create linked text frames so that text flows automatically from one frame to the next. Finally, we'll turn the tables around and discuss how you can place drawing frames in a word processing document.

Placing Text Frames in Drawing Documents

As you just read, any text that you place in a drawing document is a text frame, a miniature word processing document that has all the formatting capabilities of a stand-alone word processing document. However, a text frame is an object that can be moved, rotated, flipped, and filled, just like any other object in a drawing.

Drawing a Text Frame

To draw a text frame:

1. Click the text tool **A** in the tool panel. The drawing menus in the menu bar are replaced with the word processing menus.

2. Move the mouse pointer into the document's workspace. The mouse pointer turns into the I-beam cursor.

3. Drag the cursor down and to the right to give the text frame its initial size and shape, as in Figure 5.55.

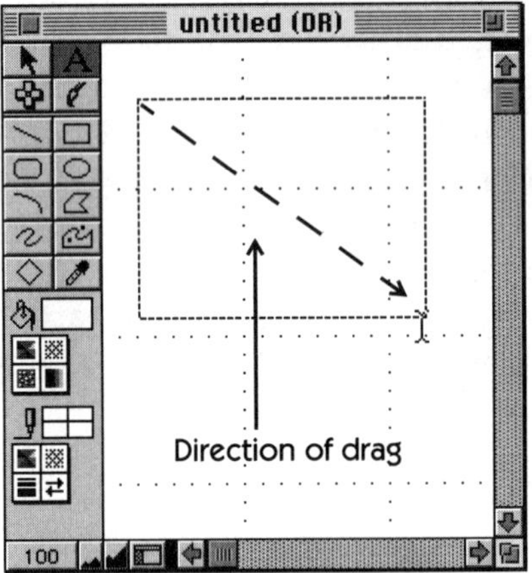

Figure 5.55 Drawing a text frame

4. Release the mouse button when the frame is the shape and size you want.

An insertion point will appear at the top left corner of the frame. At this point, you can type text, using any of the word processing tools available to a stand-alone word processing document.

Switching to the Text Ruler

By default, a drawing document displays the graphics ruler. However, it is easier to work with a text frame if you have access to the text ruler.

To switch to the text ruler:

1. Choose Format->Rulers. (Windows users can also press ALT-M, R.) The Rulers Format dialog box appears.

2. Click the Text radio button in the Ruler Type box.

3. Click the OK button or press Enter to change the ruler.

To return to the graphics ruler, repeat the preceding process but select the Graphics radio button.

Selecting and Modifying Text Frames

When you finish working with a text frame, you can click on any other drawing tool (including the text tool) to continue working on your document. You can then return to a text frame at a later time to modify it.

Use the following techniques to work with a text frame:

- To select a text frame, make sure the arrow tool is selected in the tool panel. Then click anywhere on the visible text in the frame. When selected, handles appear at the four corners of the frame, as in Figure 5.56.

- To resize a text frame, select the frame and drag one of its handles, just as you would when resizing any other object.

- To move a text frame, select the frame and drag it to its new location.

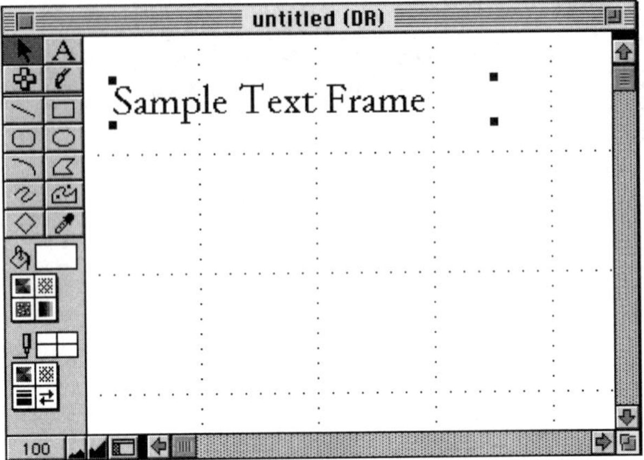

Figure 5.56 A selected text frame

- To rotate, flip, or change the layering of a text frame, select the frame and follow the procedures described earlier in this chapter for manipulating objects.
- To change the text inside a text frame, double-click on the text in the frame. ClarisWorks selects the text tool in the tool panel and places an insertion point in the text.
- To stop working with the text frame, click the mouse pointer anywhere outside the text frame's borders.

Linking Text Frames

By default, the text frames that you place in a drawing document are independent objects. However, you can link frames together so that text flows automatically from one to the other.

For example, the text frames in Figure 5.57 are linked. The top of the first frame in the chain of linked frames is marked with an empty rectangle; the bottom of the last frame in the chain is marked with a rectangle filled with a down arrow (the *continue indicator*). The tops and bottoms of all other parts of the chain are marked with the *link indicator* (⊡).

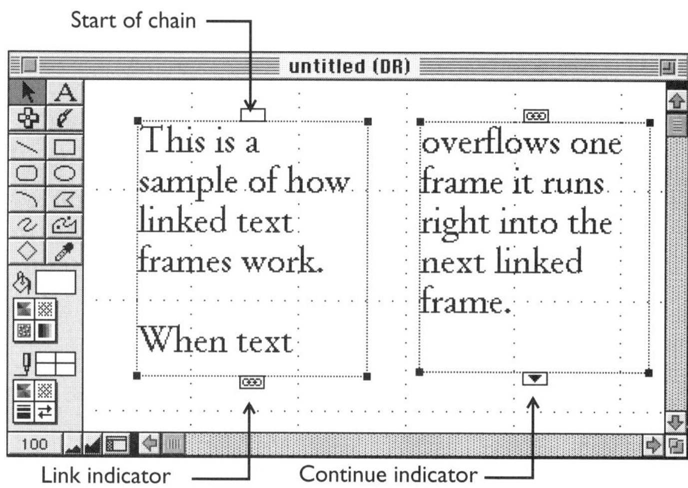

Figure 5.57 Linked text frames

One common use of linked text frames is to create a newsletter in which text is automatically continued from one column to another. Unlike a word processing document, in which a multicolumn layout flows text into contiguous columns, linked text frames can be placed anywhere on a drawing, making it easy to place graphics or other elements between the individual frames in the linked chain. This gives you more flexibility in your layout than working with a word processing document.

To create linked text frames:

1. Draw the first frame and add some text to it. (If you don't add any text, the frame will disappear when you click outside the frame's borders.)
2. Select the frame.

3.

Macintosh	Choose Options->Frame Links or press ⌘-L.
Windows	Choose Options->Frame Links, press CTRL-L, or press ALT-O, L..

The selected text frame gets a continue indicator at the bottom.

4. Click on the selected frame's continue indicator. The mouse pointer changes to an I-beam with a crosshair ⌶.

5. Drag to create the next frame in the chain. The continue indicator on the first frame changes to a link indicator. The new text frame has a link indicator at the top and a continue indicator at the bottom.

6. Repeat step 5 until you have drawn all the text frames in the chain.

To add more links to the chain at a later time:

1. Select the last frame in the chain.
2. Click on the frame's continue indicator.
3. Drawing another frame.
4. Repeat step 3 until all frames have been drawn.

If you enter more text than will fit in a set of linked text frames, ClarisWorks stores the text, displays as much text as it can, and then places an overflow indicator in the lower right corner of the last frame in the chain (see Figure 5.58).

When an overflow occurs, you can make the size of the type smaller to display more text, delete some of the text, or add a frame to the chain to provide more space.

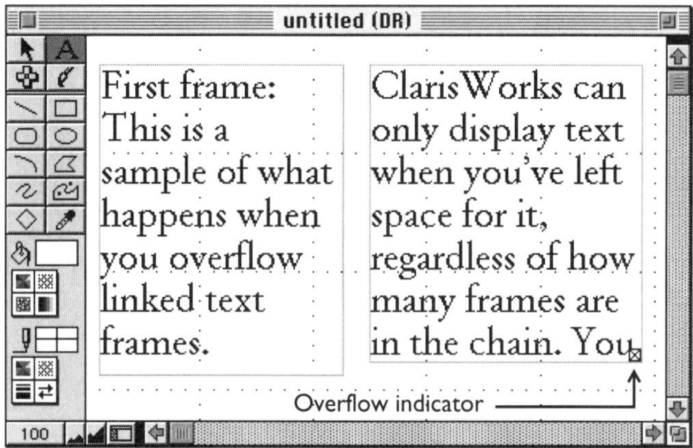

Figure 5.58 Overflowing linked text frames

Placing Drawings in Word Processing Documents

Because the elements of a drawing are individual objects, they can be placed in a word processing document without creating a frame to hold them. When you add an object to a word processing document, it has the following properties:

- The object is fixed to its location on the page. It doesn't move as text is added to or removed from the document.
- When first drawn, the object lies on top of the text. However, you can use the graphics commands that change the layer of objects to move it behind the text (for example, Arrange->Move To Back). For example, Figure 5.59 contains white text centered on a black

rectangle to provide a banner for the first page of a newsletter.

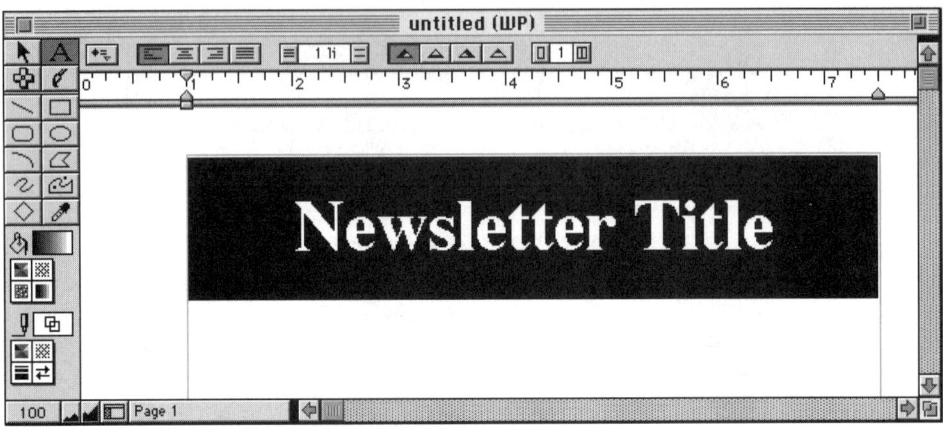

Figure 5.59 White text centered on a black rectangle

- By default, text flows over graphics objects as if the graphics objects weren't there. This is what is occurring in Figure 5.59, for example. However, you can ask ClarisWorks to wrap the text around the objects. (See *Adjusting Text Wrap* later in this section.)

Adding Graphics Objects

To add a graphics object to a word processing document:

1. If it is not already visible, display the tool panel.
2. Click on the arrow tool. The menus in the menu bar change to the drawing menus.
3. Click on the graphics tool you want to use.
4. Draw the object in the word processing document. You can modify the document using any of the drawing techniques discussed in this chapter.

Switching between Drawing and Word Processing

To return to working with text after you have modified a graphic object, you can:

- Click on existing text in the document, or
- Click anywhere in the text area of the document not occupied by a graphic object, or
- Click the A button in the tool panel.

To return to working with graphics, click the button in the tool panel.

Adjusting Text Wrap

The term *text wrap* refers to the way in which text behaves when it encounters a graphic. As you read earlier, the default is to have text flow across (or under, depending on layering) the graphic as if the graphic wasn't present. However, you can also ask ClarisWorks to flow text around the graphic.

Aside from having no text wrap at all, there are two text wrap settings:

- Text can flow around the object as if it were a rectangle. In Figure 5.60, for example, text flows around an invisible rectangle that encloses the polygon.
- Text can flow around the precise shape of the document. In Figure 5.61, for example, the text wrap follows the outline of the polygon.

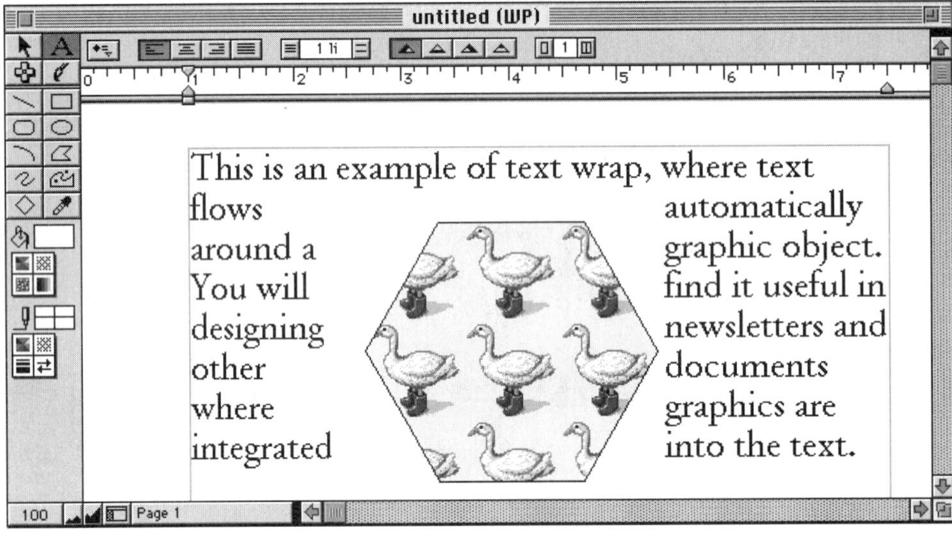

Figure 5.60 Regular text wrap

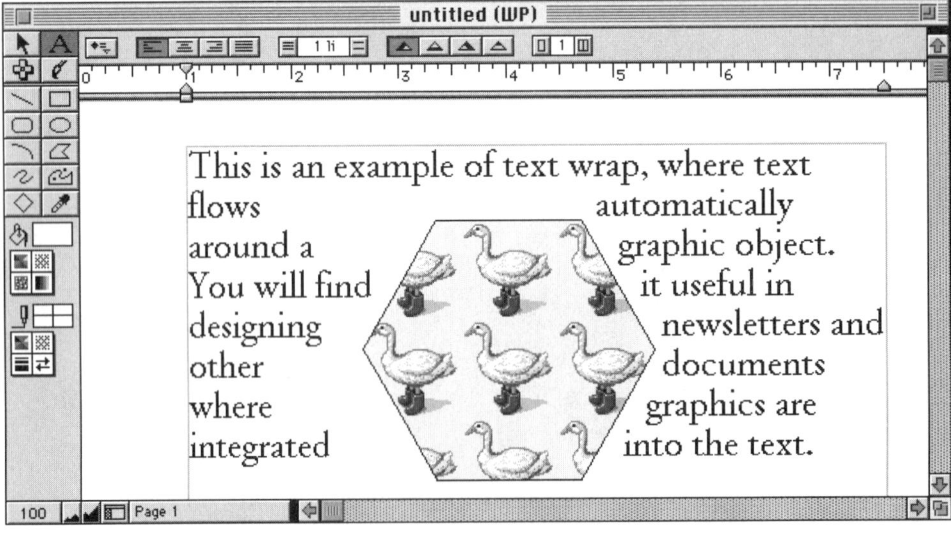

Figure 5.61 Irregular text wrap

In addition, you have control over the distance between the edge of the graphic (or the invisible rectangle enclosing it) and the text.

To set text wrap:

1. Select the object or objects whose text wrap you want to set.

2. Choose Options->Text Wrap. (Windows users can also press ALT-O, T.) The Text Wrap dialog box appears (Figure 5.62).

3. Click on the icon that represents the type of text wrap you want.

4. Enter the amount of space, in points, to be left between the object and text in the Gutter box.

5. Click the OK button or press Enter to apply the text wrap settings and close the dialog box.

To get text wrap to work in a drawing document, you must be working with linked ext frames.

Figure 5.62 The Text Wrap dialog box

6

Painting

ClarisWorks's painting module lets you create images made up of a single layer of dots. Commonly also called *bit-mapped graphics*, paintings are useful for graphics that are to be displayed on a computer screen. For example, the graphics that are displayed in World Wide Web pages are bit-mapped graphics.

The process of working with a painting is more like working with charcoal, or pastels, or even oils than drawing. In the past, people viewed painting as artistic, whereas they viewed drawing as more akin to drafting. Today, however, drawing software is flexible enough that you can use it to create artistic images, and because the contents of a drawing are represented by the outlines of their shapes, they provide better printed images than painting. Therefore, we typically use drawings when we are going to be producing printed images and painting when designing images for viewing on the screen (particularly the World Wide Web).

If you're going to be doing a lot of artistic graphics, consider getting a graphics tablet. A graphics tablet lets you use a pen-like stylus in place of a mouse, trackball, or trackpad, something many artists feel is more like working on paper or canvas. Using the stylus is also easier on the wrist than constant use of other pointing devices.

Unlike a drawing, in which each object retains its identity as an object, a painting is an undifferentiated pattern of colored dots. Whereas objects in a drawing lie on top of one another, anything added to a painting replaces whatever it overlies. Painting uses many of the same tools as drawing, and the way in which you use those tools is the same, but the effect on the document is significantly different.

The dots that make up a painting image are known as *bits* or *pixels*. The term *pixel* is short for "picture element" and refers to one dot on a computer's screen. In the context of a painting, a *bit* is one dot in the image, regardless of whether it is on paper or on the screen.

"Bit" is actually short for "binary digit," a 0 or 1 that is used in the binary number system. Each dot in a painting is represented internally by a binary code (a pattern of 0s and 1s) that identifies the dot's color. Paintings are therefore "bit-mapped" because they are stored as nothing more than a sequence of binary codes.

One unfortunate effect of paintings being made up of a pattern of dots is that elements in a painting don't resize as nicely as elements in a drawing. As you can see in Figure 6.1, as the image is made smaller, it loses detail. There simply aren't enough pixels available in the smaller versions of the image to represent the entire image. Objects in a drawing, however, retain all their detail as they are made smaller because they are described by their outlines rather than by a pattern of dots.

Figure 6.1 Resizing portions of a painting

By the same token, if you enlarge a small area of a painting, it will lose its smooth edges as it becomes larger. Notice in Figure 6.2, for example, that the two larger images have jagged edges. They were created by duplicating the portion of the painting containing the smallest image and then enlarging the selected portion.

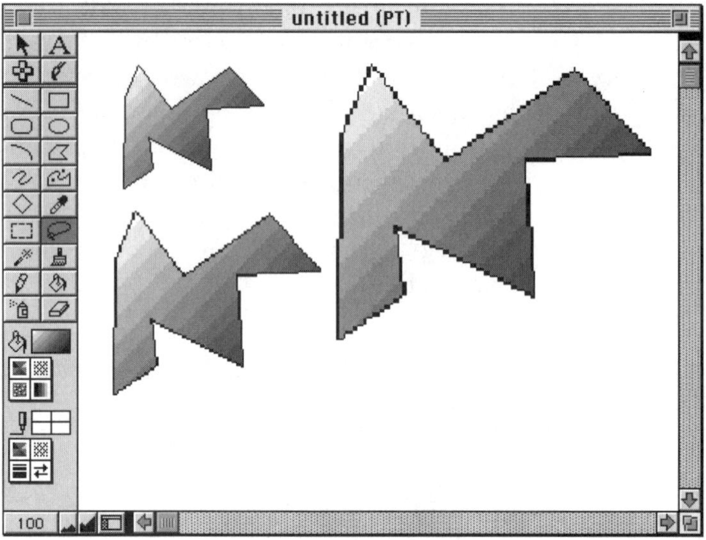

Figure 6.2 The effect of enlarging parts of a painting

It is important to remember that drawings also show problems with resizing when they are displayed on the screen because screen displays are bit-mapped. However, the difference between drawing and painting appears when you print them. A painting prints exactly as it appears on the screen; the objects in a drawing will print with smooth edges and all detail intact.

The Painting Tool Panel

The painting tool panel can be found in Figure 6.3. Notice that the top seven rows in the tool panel are identical to those in the drawing tool panel; the tools used for setting patterns and colors are identical as well. However, the painting module has some tools for selecting parts of a painting and tools for painting using special effects that are all its own.

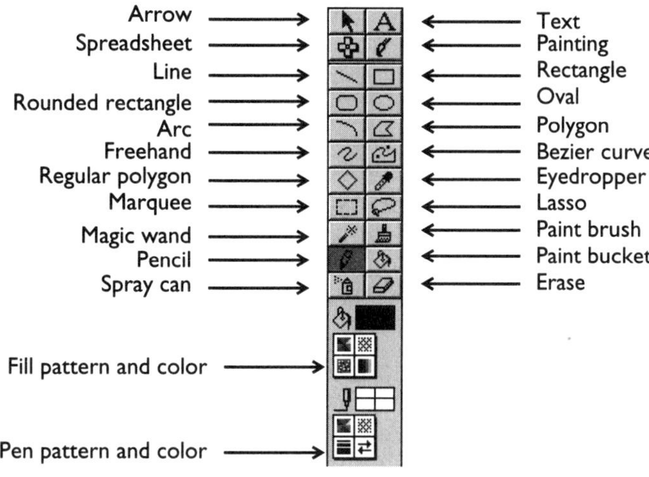

Figure 6.3 The Painting tool panel

The top four tools (arrow, text, spreadsheet, painting) control which type of frame you are creating at any given time. Keep in mind, however, that although you can place text and spreadsheet frames in a painting, once you have finished creating them, they become a part of the painting and lose their identity as individual frames. (You can find more details about incorporating text into paintings later in this chapter. Spreadsheets are discussed in Chapter 7.)

The regular shape tools (line, rectangle, rounded rectangle, oval, arc, regular polygon) paint areas with predetermined shapes. The irregular shape tools (freehand, polygon, Bezier curve) paint areas without predetermined shapes. The eyedropper tool picks up colors, just as it does in a drawing.

There are three tools for selecting parts of a painting:

- Marquee: The marquee selects a rectangular area.
- Lasso: The lasso selects all painted areas (in other words, nonwhite) encircled by the tool.

- Magic wand: The magic wand selects all adjacent areas of the same color.

In addition, four tools have been included specifically for painting:

- Pencil: The pencil modifies one bit in the image at a time. Typically, you magnify an image so that you can see the individual bits. Then you can change them with the pencil.

- Paintbrush: The brush works much like a paintbrush that you hold in your hand. It paints whatever is under its path as you drag. ClarisWorks gives you control over the size of the brush.

- Paint bucket: The paint bucket fills irregularly shaped areas with color or patterns.

- Spray can: The spray can applies color and patterns as if you were using spray paint.

Finally, the eraser tool erases portions of a painting.

Painting Basic Shapes

You use shape tools in a painting document in exactly the same way that you use them in a drawing document. Therefore, rather than repeat the same material that is found in Chapter 5, here's where you can find the details for using those tools:

- Rectangles and rounded rectangles: page 197

- Squares: page 200

- Ovals and circles: page 201
- Lines: page 202
- Arcs: page 203
- Regular polygons: page 204
- Irregular polygons: page 205
- Freehand objects: page 207
- Bezier curves: page 209

Keep in mind that although irregular polygons and Bezier curves are painted by placing points on the painting with the mouse pointer—just as they are in a drawing—once you have finished painting the shape, the shape is merged into the single layer of bits in the painting. You will not be able to access those points again to select, move, resize, or reshape what you have painted. This doesn't mean that you can't modify what you've painted, but with a painting you perform the modifications in another way.

Using Specialty Painting Tools

Because painting software is the electronic version of working with artists' tools, simply having tools that draw shapes isn't enough. You need tools that simulate the pens, pencils, and brushes that artists actually use. ClarisWorks therefore provides you with three specialty painting tools: the pencil, the paintbrush, and the spray can.

Using the Pencil

The pencil tool changes the color of any pixel it touches. You can draw with it much as you would draw with the freehand tool. However, the pencil's most effective use is to tweak individual pixels in a magnified image.

Assume, for example, that you are working with the painting in Figure 6.4. You want to add a few streaks of white to the painter's brush. Because this is a small detail, the easiest way to make the change is to display the painting at 800% so that you can see the individual pixels, as in Figure 6.5. At that point, you can click the pencil anywhere you want to make a change.

Figure 6.4 A full-sized painting

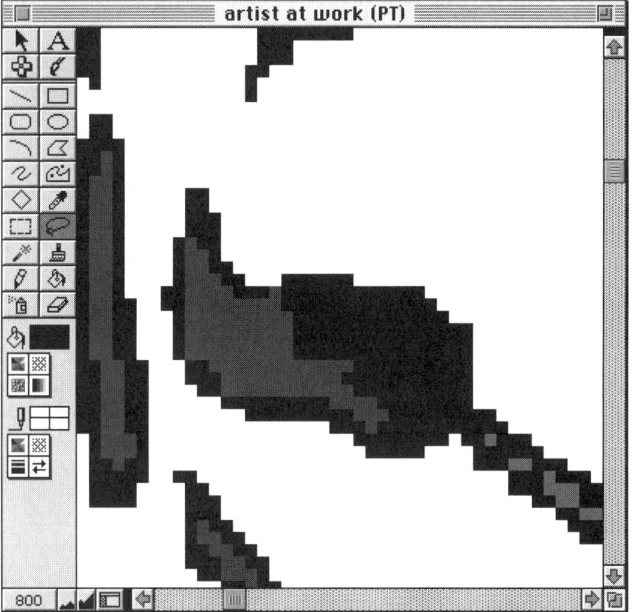

Figure 6.5 The enlarged painting, showing individual pixels

The pencil works in the following way:

- If you click (or drag) on a pixel that is currently painted with white, the pixel takes on the current fill color and/or pattern.
- If you click (or drag) on a pixel that is currently painted a color or pattern other than white, the pixel becomes white.

To use the pencil:

1. Click on the pencil tool in the tool panel.
2. If necessary, enlarge the painting so that you can see individual pixels.

3. If necessary, change the fill color and/or pattern.

4. Click the pencil on a pixel whose color you want to change or drag the pencil across a group of pixels whose color you want to change.

5. Repeat step 4 until all pixels have been changed.

Using the Paintbrush

The paintbrush tool provides you with a set of artist's brushes. When you drag the paintbrush, it paints using the current fill color and/or pattern.

To use the paintbrush:

1. Click on the paintbrush tool in the tool panel.

2. If necessary, set the fill color and/or pattern.

3. Drag the paintbrush in the painting document to create the image you want.

Setting the Brush Size and Shape

Although the paintbrush does only one thing at a time, ClarisWorks gives you control over the size and shape of the brush, as well as providing several special painting effects. For example, the lines in Figure 6.6 were all drawn using black as the fill color but with different brush shapes.

The square in Figure 6.7 was drawn with a gray fill color. Then the fill color was set to black. The paintbrush was set to the largest square shape. Each of the lines drawn across the gray square, however, represents a different paintbrush effect. The blur and tint lines were drawn by dragging once

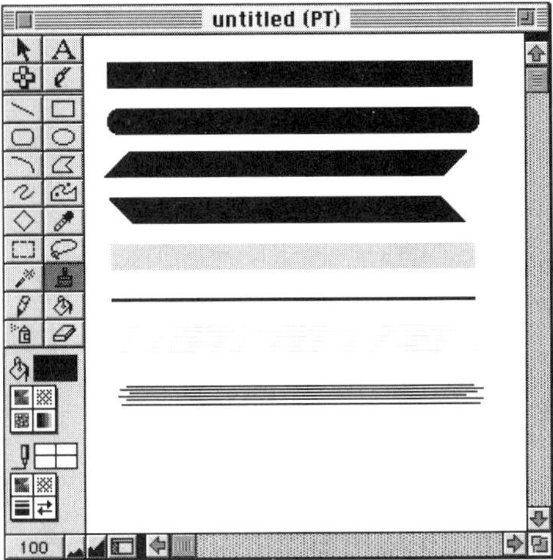

Figure 6.6 Lines drawn with different brush shapes

across the gray square; the lighten and darken lines were drawn by dragging back and forth across the gray square, with each drag shorter than the other.

To set the paintbrush shape and effect:

1. Choose Options->Brush Shape. (Windows users can also press ALT-O, B.) The Brush Shape dialog box appears (Figure 6.8).

You can also display the Brush Shape dialog box by double-clicking on the paintbrush tool in the tool panel.

2. Click on the brush shape you want.
3. If desired, choose an effect from the Effects popup menu.
4. Click the OK button or press Enter to set the new shape and close the dialog box.

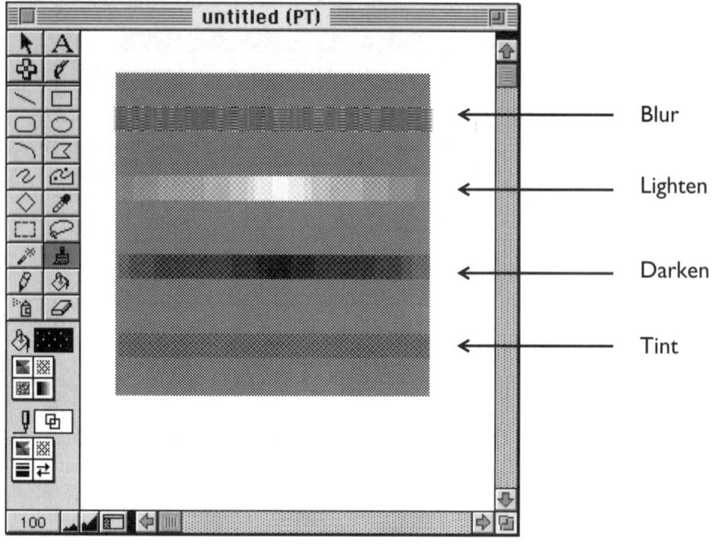

Figure 6.7 Special paintbrush effects

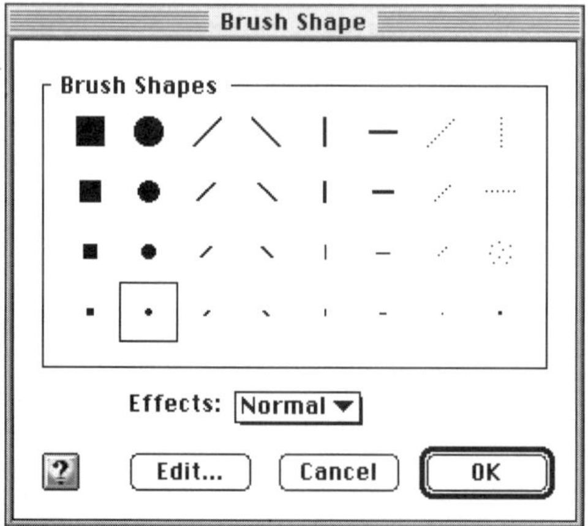

Figure 6.8 The Brush Shape dialog box

If none of the existing brush shapes meet your needs, you can design your own brush. To do so,

1. Display the Brush Shape dialog box.
2. Click on the brush shape you want to replace with a different brush shape.
3. Click the Edit button. The Brush Editor dialog box appears, showing the current shape of the paintbrush (Figure 6.9) in a 16-by-16-pixel square.

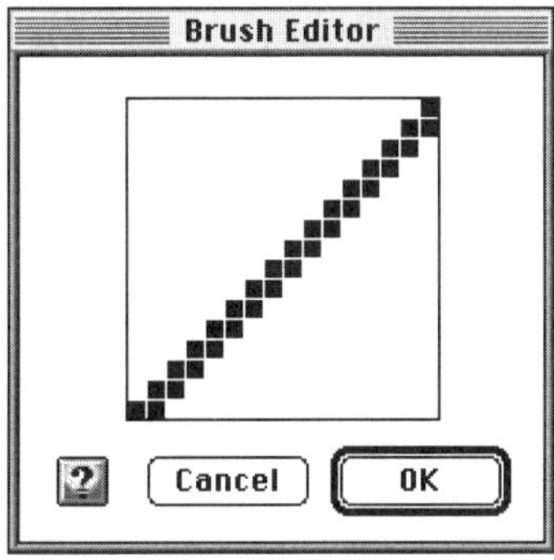

Figure 6.9 The Brush Editor dialog box

4. Click or drag the mouse pointer on any pixel you want to change. Clicking or dragging on a black pixel turns it white; clicking or dragging on a white pixel turns it black.
5. Repeat step 3 until the brush is the shape you want.
6. Click the OK button or press Enter. The new brush shape replaces the shape selected when you displayed the Brush Editor dialog box.
7. Click the OK button or press Enter to close the Brush Shape dialog box. You will now be ready to use the new brush shape.

You can also lighten, darken, tint, and blur areas of a painting by first selecting the area of the painting you want to affect and then choosing the effect from the Transform menu.

Using the Spray Can

The spray can creates a pattern of dots, much as you might expect to get if you were actually working with a spray can. For example, the leaves of the tree in Figure 6.10 were created by setting the fill pattern to a gradient and then dragging the spray can in a swirling motion.

Figure 6.10 A tree with "spray can" leaves

When you drag using the spray can tool, ClarisWorks applies color in the current fill color and/or pattern in a circular area. The longer you hold the spray can in the same spot on the painting, the more "paint" you apply. In other words, the longer the spray can stays in the same place, the darker the paint becomes.

To use the spray can:

1. Click on the spray can tool in the tool panel.
2. Drag the spray can to paint.

Setting Spray Can Action

Because the spray can tool works much like an actual can of spray paint, you can adjust the size of the area it affects and how fast it paints.

To change the size and rate of the spray can:

1. Choose Options->Spray Can. (Windows users can also press ALT-O, C.) The Edit Spray Can dialog box appears (Figure 6.11).

You can also display the Edit Spray Can dialog box by double-clicking on the spray can tool in the tool panel.

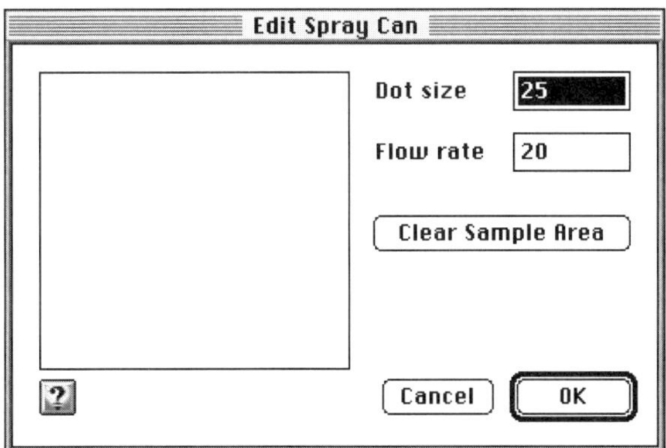

Figure 6.11 The Edit Spray Can dialog box

2. Enter the size of the area the spray can affects in the Dot size box. The value should be between 1 and 72.
3. Enter how fast color should be applied in the Flow rate box. The value should be between 1 and 100.
4. Test your new spray can by dragging in the box at the left of the dialog box.
5. To clear the box, click the Clear Sample Area button.
6. Repeat steps 2 through 5 until the spray can acts the way you want.
7. Click the OK button or press Enter to close the dialog box. You are now ready to spray with the new settings.

Painting Modes (Macintosh Only)

As you have read, when you add something to a painting, the new image replaces whatever it is drawn on top of. However, the Macintosh version of ClarisWorks gives you some control over how that replacement works with its painting modes.

There are three painting modes (see Figure 6.12):

- Opaque: Whatever you draw completely replaces anything it overlaps.
- Transparent: When drawing with white, whatever is in the background shows through.
- Tint: Drawing occurs in a tint of the current fill color and/pattern. Overlapped areas are darker than areas that haven't been overlapped, as if the tints have been added together in the overlapped portions.

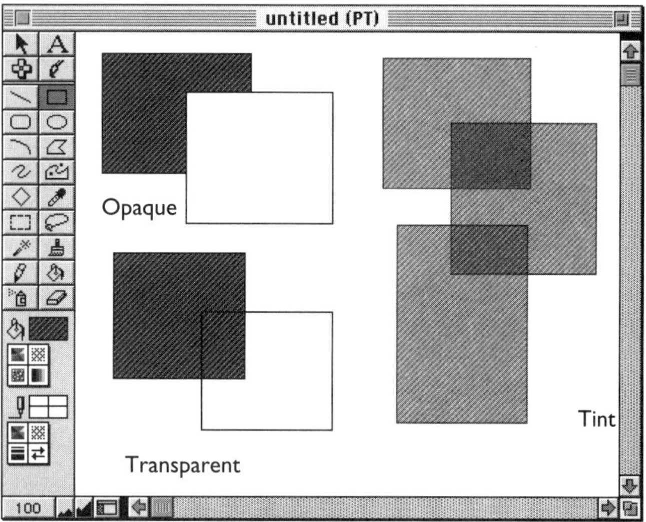

Figure 6.12 Painting modes

To set the painting mode:

1. Choose Options->Paint Mode. The Painting Mode dialog box appears (Figure 6.13).

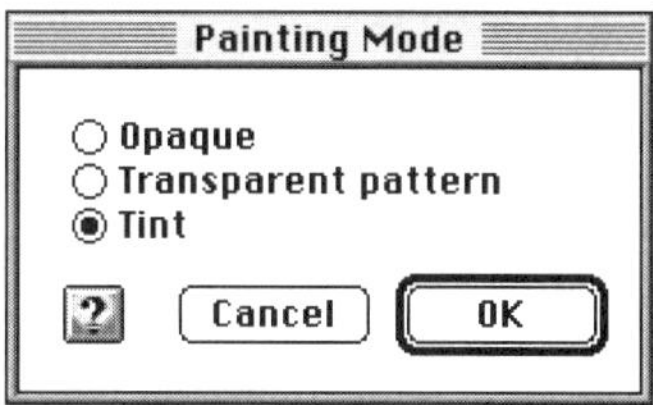

Figure 6.13 The Painting Mode dialog box

2. Click the radio button for the painting mode you want to use.

3. Click the OK button or press Enter to close the dialog box. You are now ready to work with the selected painting mode.

Adding Text

When you add text to a painting, you have access to all of ClarisWorks's word processing formatting options—but only until you stop working with the text frame the very first time. Once you move on to another text frame or another painting tool, the text becomes part of the painting's bit-map and therefore loses its identity as individual formatted characters. The text can be modified later, but only as individual bits, not as characters.

For example, in Figure 6.14 you can see a text frame in a painting. At this point, the text has been typed but the user hasn't selected any other painting tool. The text can therefore be edited and formatted just like a word processing document.

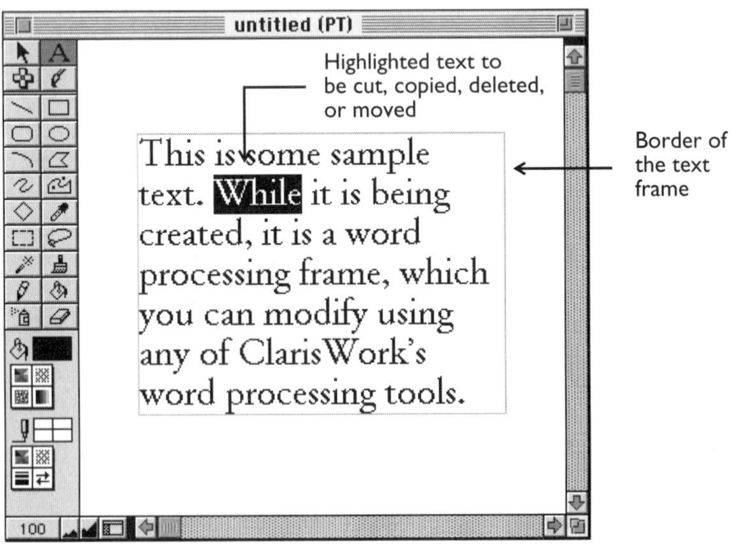

Figure 6.14 A text frame to a painting

However, if you choose another tool and then return to working with text, you'll find that an attempt to place the insertion point in the text only creates another text frame. If you look closely at Figure 6.15, you'll see the text frame that ClarisWorks placed on the painting when the user attempted to locate an insertion point in existing text. This means that when you add text to a painting, you must either get it right the first time or erase the existing text and start over!

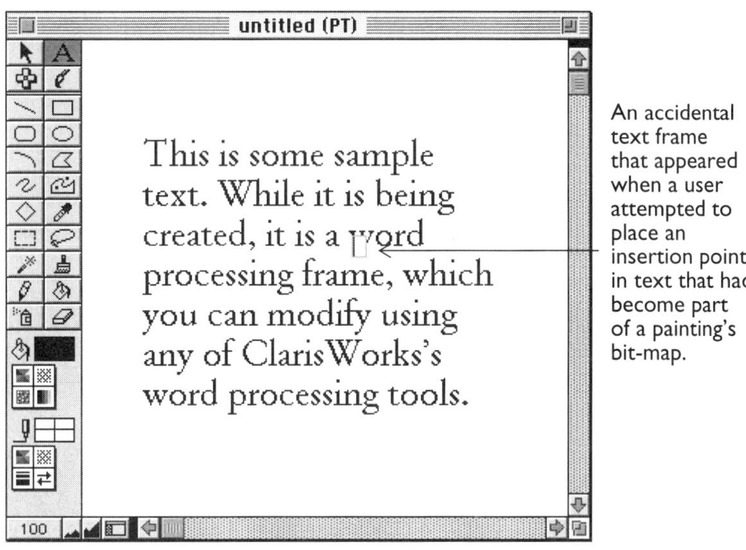

Figure 6.15 Attempting to edit text in a painting

To add text to a painting:

1. Select the text tool [A] in the tool panel.
2. Drag the cursor down and to the right to create a rectangular area for the text frame, as in Figure 6.16.
3. Type and format text as desired. As you enter text, ClarisWorks performs word wrap at the right edge of the text frame; the width of the frame won't change.

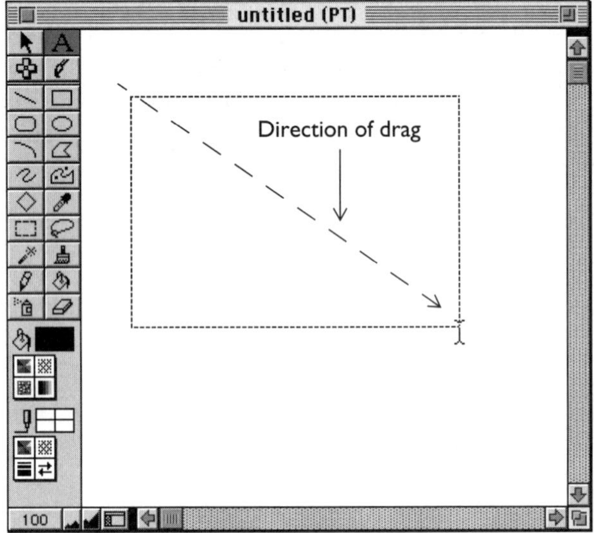

Figure 6.16 Drawing a text frame

However, the text frame expands automatically at the bottom as text overflows the currently available space.

4. To finish editing text, select another tool or click anywhere in the painting outside the text frame.

Editing a Painting

There are two basic strategies for editing a painting:

- You can paint new images on top of existing images, replacing whatever the new images overlie.
- You can move, duplicate, or erase parts of a painting.

Selecting an Area of a Painting

Before you can move or duplicate part of a painting, you need to select it using either the marquee or lasso tool. The marquee selects a rectangular area; the lasso selects all non-white pixels that it surrounds.

To use the marquee tool:

1. Select the marquee tool in the tool panel.
2. Drag a rectangle around the area you want to select. As you can see in Figure 6.17, the selected area is surrounded by a rectangle with a dashed border.

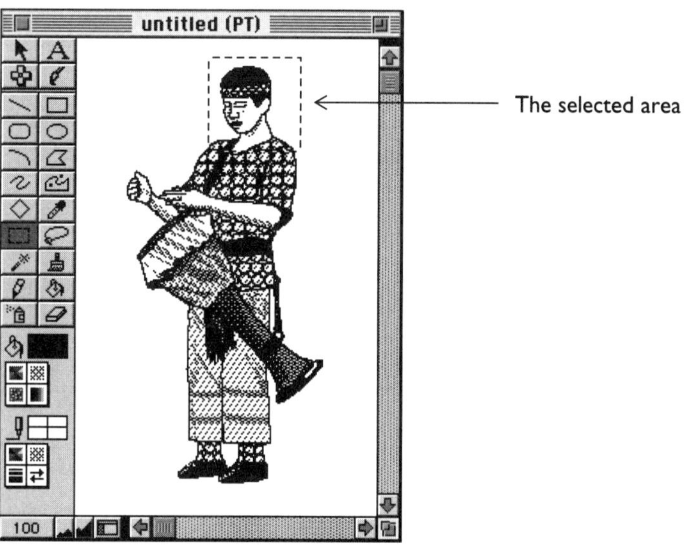

Figure 6.17 A portion of a painting selected with the marquee

To select the entire document, double-click on the marquee tool.

To use the lasso tool:

1. Select the lasso tool [lasso icon] in the tool panel.

2. Drag around the area you want to select. As you can

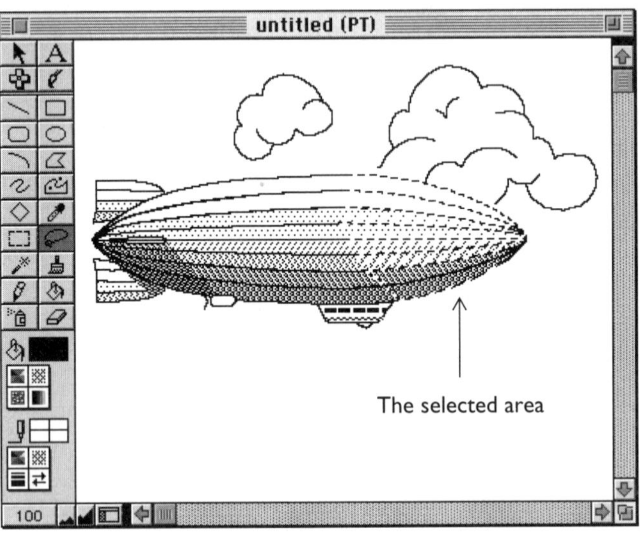

Figure 6.18 A portion of a painting selected with the lasso

see in Figure 6.18, the selected portion of the document appears a bit lighter than the rest. (In fact, it shimmers.) Notice also that the white pixels surrounding the image are *not* selected.

tip

To select all nonwhite pixels in a document, double-click on the lasso tool.

Moving Parts of a Painting

To move a selected part of a painting:

1. Select the area to be moved.
2. Drag the selected area to its new location. As you can see in Figure 6.19, the pixels in the dragged image's original location are filled with white.

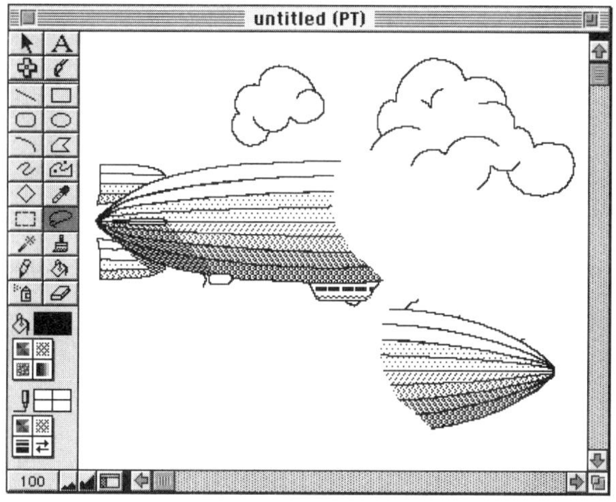

Figure 6.19 Moving a part of a painting

Duplicating Parts of a Painting

To duplicate parts of a painting:

1. Select the area to be duplicated.
2.

Macintosh	Hold down the OPTION key and drag the selected area to a new location.
Windows	Hold down the ALT key and drag the selected area to a new location.

As you can see in Figure 6.20, ClarisWorks leaves the original selected area untouched and places a copy in the new location.

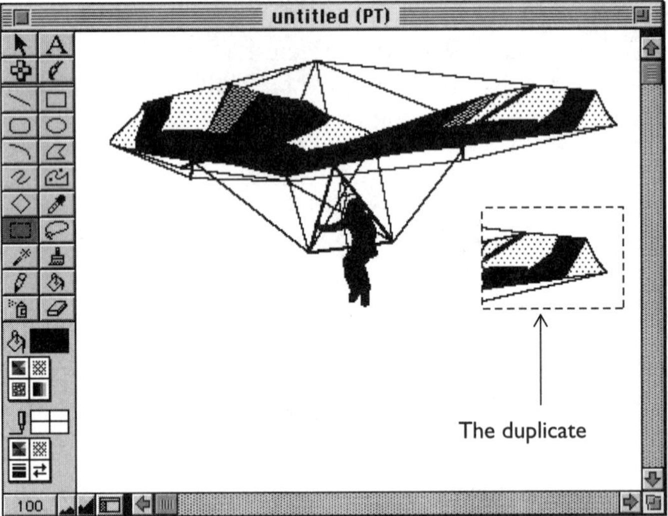

Figure 6.20 Duplicating a part of a painting by dragging

You can also copy a selected portion of a painting to the Clipboard and then paste a copy back into the document.

Erasing Parts of a Painting

There are three ways to erase part of a painting:

- Select a portion of the painting and then press Delete.
- Select a portion of the painting and then use either the Edit->Cut or Edit-Clear menu command.
- Erase a portion of the painting with the eraser tool.

To use the eraser tool:

1. Select the eraser tool in the tool panel.
2. Click or drag the eraser in the painting. Everything under the eraser when you click or drag is replaced with white pixels, as in Figure 6.21

Figure 6.21 Using the eraser

You can constrain the direction of the eraser to a straight line by holding down the SHIFT *key while you drag.*

To erase the entire contents of the document, double-click on the eraser tool.

At 100% magnification, the eraser is too large for fine work. However, if you magnify the painting to 400% or 800%, you can erase much smaller areas of the painting.

Adding Colors, Patterns, and Gradients

When you are working with a painting, there are three general schemes for adding colors, patterns, gradients, and textures:

- You can select fill and pen colors, patterns, textures, and/or gradients for use as you paint.
- You can apply colors, patterns, textures, or gradients to enclosed areas of a painting.
- You can apply colors, patterns, textures, or gradients to selected areas of a document.

To do the first, you use the same techniques as you would if you were working with a drawing. To do the second, you use the paint bucket tool.

Setting Fill and Pen Colors, Patterns, or Gradients

If you want to set fill and pen colors, patterns, and/or gradients as you paint, you make choices from the fill and pen controls *before* you paint a shape. The process is exactly the same as setting the fill and pen colors for a drawing document, which is discussed in depth in Chapter 5. You can find those instructions at the following locations:

- To set the fill color, see pages 241 through 243.
- To set pen color and line endings, see pages 246 through 247.

Once you have selected fill and pen settings, the settings stay in effect until you explicitly change them. Everything new you add to the painting uses the current fill and pen settings.

Using the Paint Bucket

The paint bucket tool lets you apply color, patterns, and/or gradients to existing areas of a painting. If you click the paint bucket tool on a painting, ClarisWorks fills the area in which you click with the current fill settings.

The behavior of the paint bucket can sometimes be a bit unexpected. As a first example, consider Figure 6.22. The painting contains two overlapping, unfilled rectangles. When you use the paint bucket in an attempt to fill one of them, ClarisWorks fills only the enclosed area in which the paint bucket was clicked. The area where the two rectangles overlap is a separate enclosed area. If you want that area filled, you must click the paint bucket tool in that area.

Because the paint bucket fills an enclosed area, you must be very careful to close shapes that you intend to fill in this way. In Figure 6.23 you can see an irregular polygon that isn't completely closed. When you try to fill this shape using the paint bucket, paint "leaks" out the opening and fills the entire painting (see Figure 6.24).

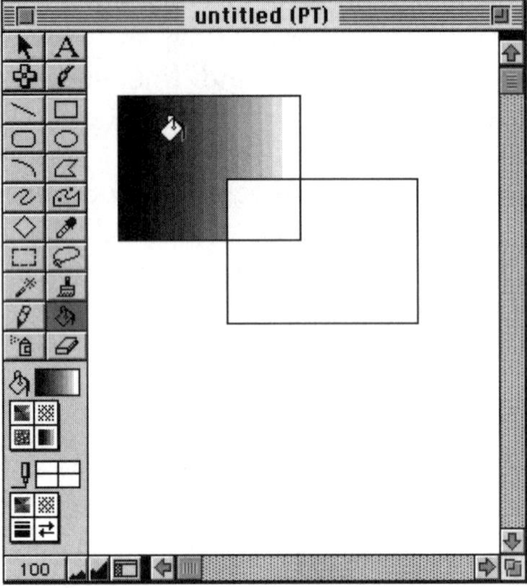

Figure 6.22 Filling an area with the paint bucket

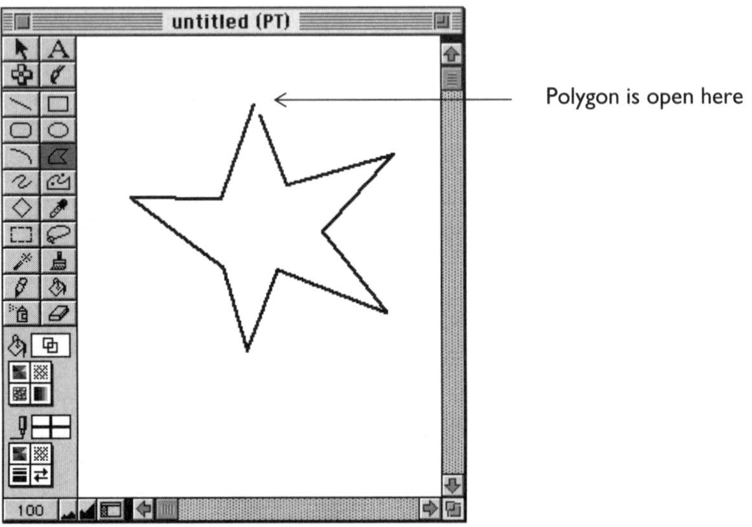

Figure 6.23 An irregular polygon that hasn't been closed

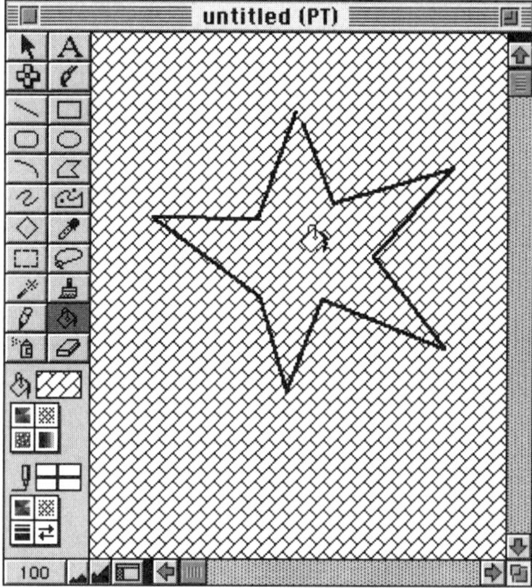

Figure 6.24 An unexpected paint bucket effect

To use the paint bucket tool:

1. Click on the paint bucket tool in the tool panel.
2. Use the fill controls to set the color, pattern, or gradient with which you want to paint.
3. Click the paint bucket in the area of the painting you want to fill.

Filling Selected Areas

To fill a selected area of a painting:

1. Select the area of the painting you want to fill, using either the marquee or the lasso tool.
2. Set the fill color, pattern, or gradient using the fill controls.

3. Choose Transform->Fill. (Windows users can also press ALT-T, F.) ClarisWorks fills the selected area with the current fill settings.

As discussed earlier, you can use the pencil tool to apply color one pixel at a time.

Special Painting Effects

In addition to the standard tools about which you have been reading, ClarisWorks's painting module provides specialty painting effects for modifying the contents of a painting in unusual ways. Known as *transformations*, these effects let you reshape selected areas of a painting.

Shear

As you can see in Figure 6.25, shear lets you distort a selected area of a painting by dragging the corner of a rectangle surrounding the selected area. You can drag only one corner at a time. As you do, ClarisWorks keeps the other three corners in a rectangular position.

To shear a selected area of a painting:

1. Select the area of the painting you want to shear.

2. Choose Transform->Shear. (Windows users can also press ALT-T, S.)

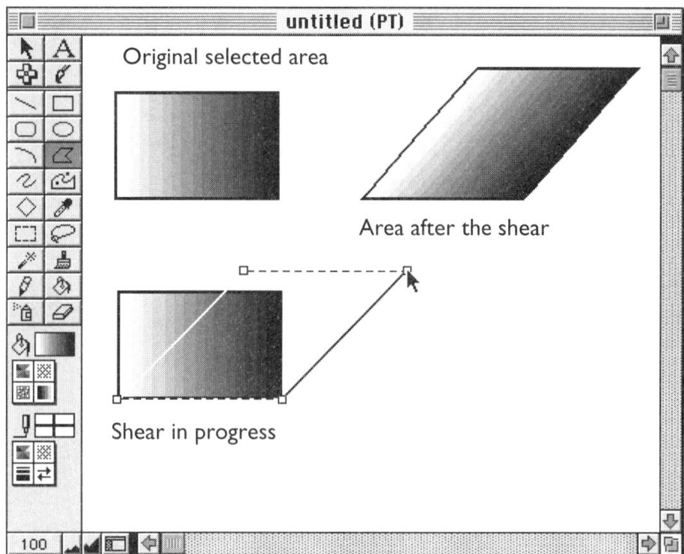

Figure 6.25 Shear

3. Drag any corner of the selected area to a new location.

4. Repeat step 3 until the selected area is the shape you want.

Distort

Distort lets you change the shape of a selected area of a painting by dragging one of the corners of a rectangle surrounding the selected area. Unlike shear, distort does not maintain a rectangle shape as you drag (see Figure 6.26).

To distort an area of a painting:

1. Select the area of the painting you want to distort.

2. Choose Transform->Distort. (Windows users can also press ALT-T, D.)

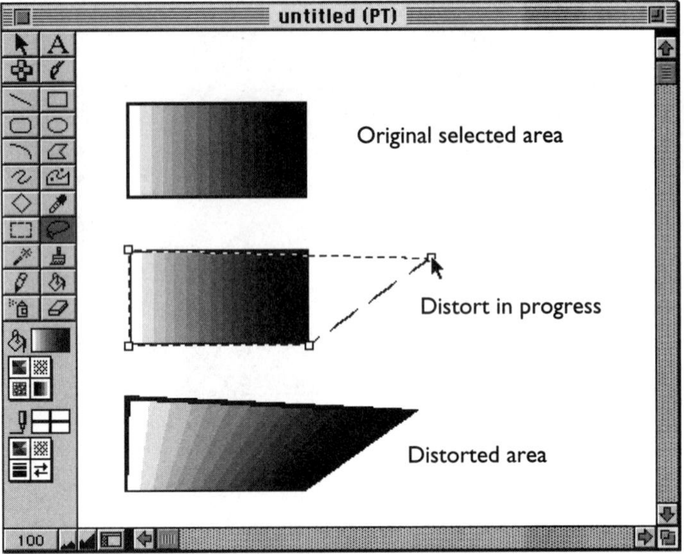

Figure 6.26 Distort

3. Drag any of the selected area's corners in the direction in which you want to distort the area.

4. Repeat step 3 until the selected area is the shape you want.

Perspective

Perspective gives you the height or width of one side of a rectangle that encloses a selected area of a painting. As you can see in Figure 6.27, the corners opposite the drag stay fixed in place. The corner on the same side as the corner being dragged moves with the drag.

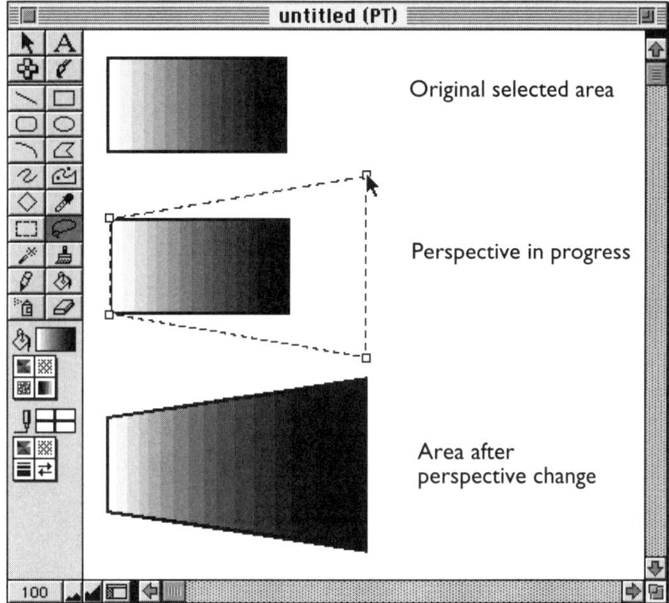

Figure 6.27 Perspective

To change the perspective of an area of a painting:

1. Select the area of the painting whose perspective you want to change.

2. Choose Transform->Perspective. (Windows users can also press ALT-T, P.)

3. Drag a corner of the selected area. If you drag up or down, the height of the area will change. If you drag left or right, the width of the area will change.

4. Repeat step 3 until the selected area is the shape you want.

Invert

When you invert a selected area of a painting, you replace existing colors with their complementary colors. Black becomes white, red becomes blue, and so on. In Figure 6.28, for example, the selected area (a rectangle) was drawn with a thick black border and filled with a gradient that is light on the left and dark on the right. After being inverted, the border is white—and therefore invisible on the painting's white background—and the gradient is dark on the left and white on the right.

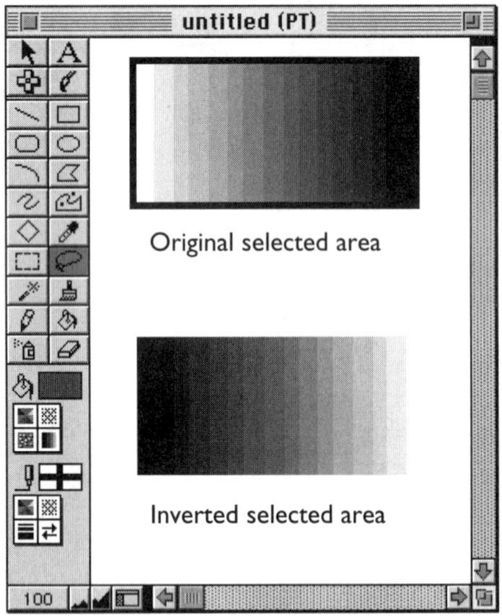

Figure 6.28 Invert

To invert the color of a selected area of a painting:

1. Select the area whose color you want to invert.

2. Choose Transform->Invert. (Windows users can also press ALT-T , I.)

Blend

Blend mixes the colors in a selected area of a painting so that the differences between the colors aren't as pronounced. In Figure 6.29, for example, the original selected area of the painting has a thick black edge and a gray fill pattern. After blending once, the fill is a bit darker and the border between the edge and the fill is a bit less distinct. The effect is even more pronounced after the blend command has been used three times.

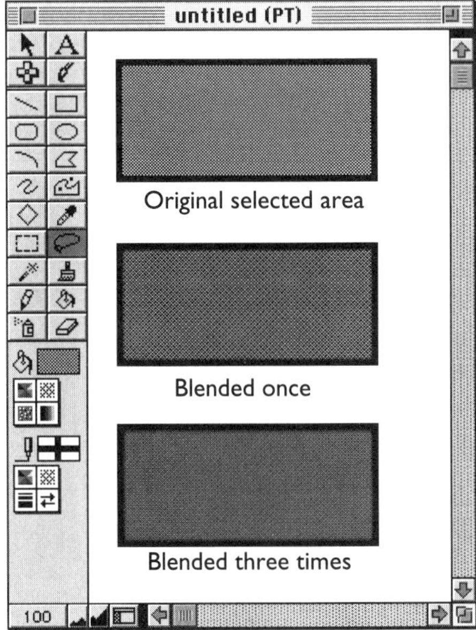

Figure 6.29 Blend

To blend the colors of a selected area of a painting:

1. Select the area to be blended.
2. Choose Transform->Blend. (Windows users can also press ALT-T, B.)

Resizing, Rotating, and Flipping Parts of a Painting

Selected areas of a painting can be resized, flipped, and rotated, just like parts of a drawing. Performing most of these actions is discussed at length in Chapter 5. Rather than repeat the same material here, you can use the instructions in Chapter 5. Just remember that when Chapter 5 refers to an "object," you should think "selected area of a painting."

- To resize a selected area of a painting, see pages 216 through 218. (Note that although you can resize by dragging and by scaling, you can't resize by specifying dimensions.)
- To rotate selected portions of a painting by dragging, see page 226.
- To rotate by specifying degrees of rotation, select the area to be rotated and choose Transform->Rotate. (Windows users can press ALT-T, R.) Enter the degrees of rotation and press Enter (see Figure 6.30).

Figure 6.30 Specifying degrees of rotation for a selected area of a painting

- To flip selected portions of a painting, see page 228.

Adjusting Resolution and Depth

The amount of memory a painting uses, the overall size of the painting, and how many colors are available are all a function of the painting's resolution and depth. The term *resolution* applies to the density of the pixels, measured in "dots per inch" or DPI. The *depth* of a painting refers to the total number of colors available for use in the painting.

By default, ClarisWorks sets the resolution and depth of a painting equal to the resolution and depth of your startup monitor. However, you can change those settings if you choose.

To change the resolution and depth:

1. Choose Format->Resolution and Depth. (Windows users can also press ALT-F, L.) The Resolution and Depth dialog box appears (Figure 6.31).

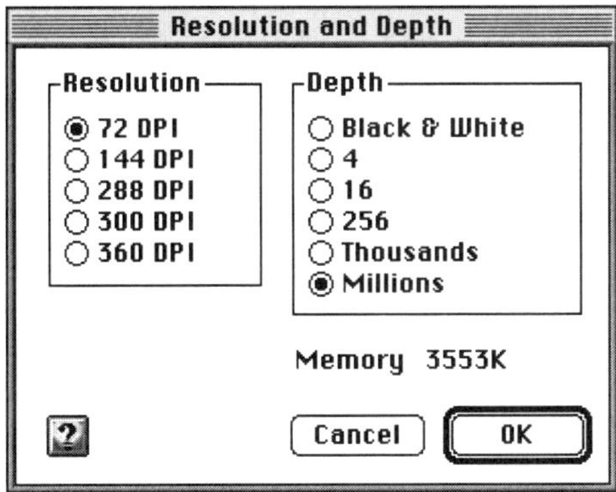

Figure 6.31 Setting a painting's resolution and depth

2. Click the radio button that corresponds to the resolution you want.

Notice in Figure 6.32 that the overall size of the painting decreases as the resolution increases. This is because the number of pixels in the painting doesn't change as you increase the resolution. Instead, the same number of pixels are packed more closely, thus shrinking the area that they cover.

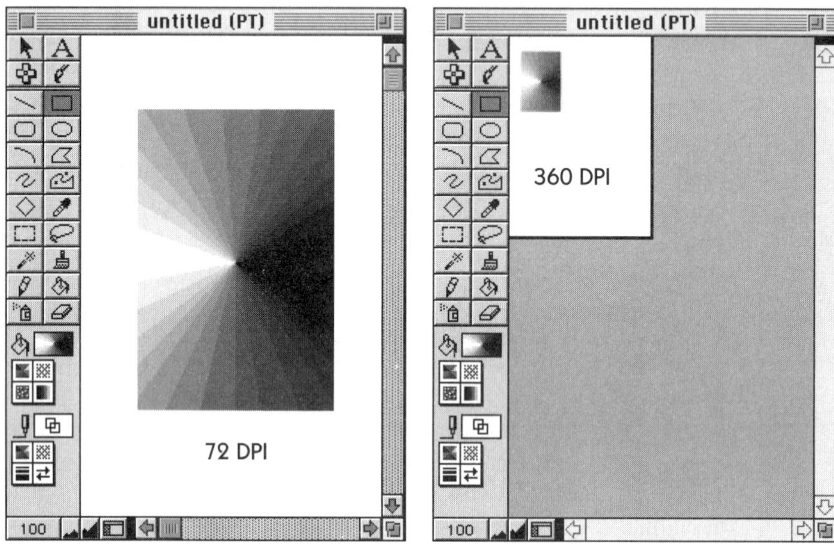

Figure 6.32 The effect of resolution changes

3. Click the color depth you want. ClarisWorks adjusts the painting to the new color settings.

When you set a depth lower than the depth with which the painting was original created, ClarisWorks substitutes colors available at the lower depth for those used at the higher depth. You will be unable to regain those transformed colors should you later return the document to a higher depth.

You can set a color depth for a document higher than the number of colors your monitor can display. This means that you can work with a larger palette of colors than you can see. The drawback to setting the depth higher than the depth of your monitor is that you won't be able to see the extra colors. (Keep in mind that ClarisWorks's color palette holds only 256 colors at a time. You can switch those colors at any time, however. See Chapter 11 for details.)

4. Click the OK button or press Enter to apply the resolution and depth settings and close the dialog box.

Placing Painting Frames in Other Documents

A painting frame that you place in another type of ClarisWorks document is a miniature painting. You can work with it just as you would a stand-alone painting. In addition, the frame itself is an object that can be moved around the document in which it has been placed.

Adding a Painting Frame

To add a painting frame to a word processing, drawing, or spreadsheet document or to a database layout:

1. Click on the painting tool in the tool panel. The mouse pointer turns into a paintbrush.

2. Drag a rectangle in the document to define the borders of the painting frame, as in Figure 6.33.

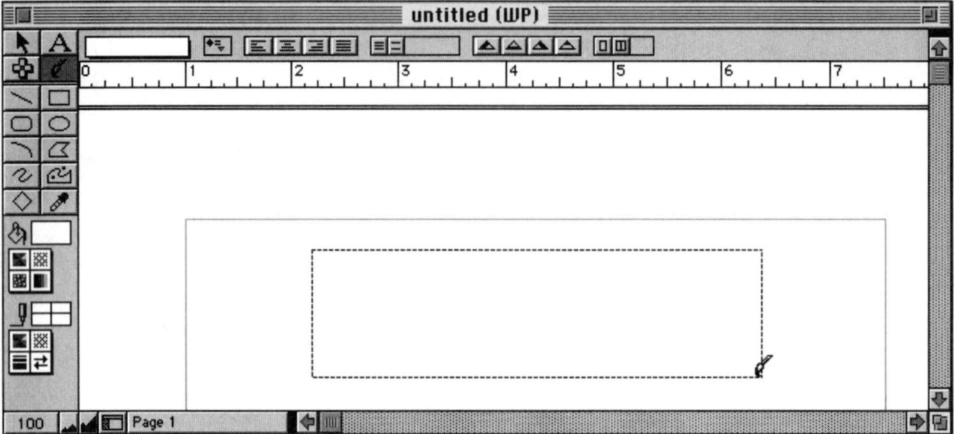

Figure 6.33 Drawing a painting frame

Adding Contents to a Painting Frame

Because a painting frame is just a painting document in miniature, you can use any of the painting tools and effects in the frame. As you can see in Figure 6.34, when you are working with the painting frame, the tool panel changes to provide you with the painting tools. The painting menus are also available.

To work within a painting frame:

1. Click on the painting tool in the tool panel.
2. Click the mouse pointer—which looks like a paintbrush—anywhere in the painting frame.

The painting frame itself behaves like an object in a drawing. In particular, this means that if you want to make its border invisible, you should select the frame by clicking on it with the arrow tool and then choosing the transparent option from the pen pattern palette.

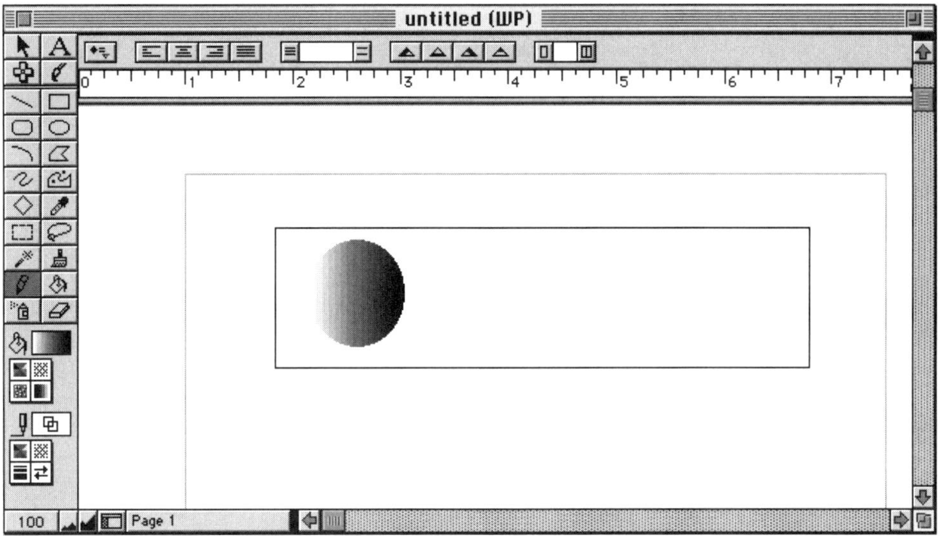

Figure 6.34 Working with a painting frame

Moving and Resizing a Painting Frame

When you place a painting frame in another document, the frame's position is fixed on the page where you draw it. However, you can move and/or resize the frame as needed.

To move or resize a painting frame:

1. Click the arrow tool in the tool panel.
2. Click anywhere on the border of the painting frame. Handles appear at the corners.
3. To move the frame, drag it by any border edge to its new location, as in Figure 6.35.
4. To change the size of a painting frame, drag any of its handles.

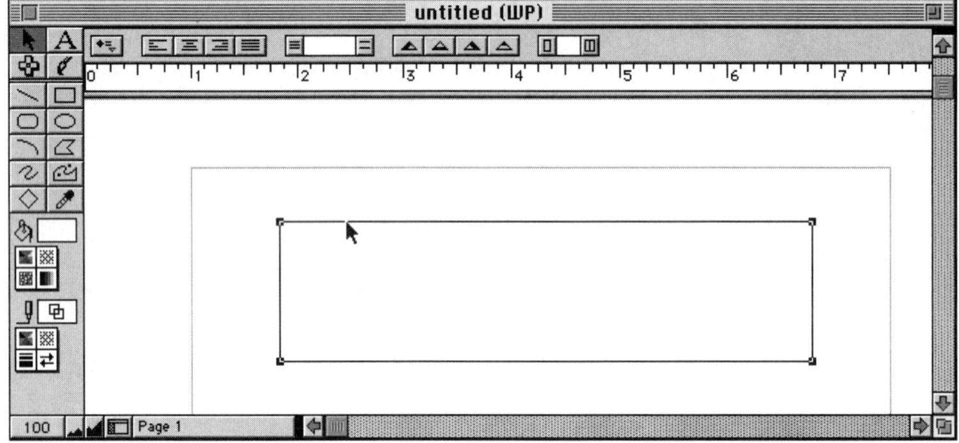

Figure 6.35 Moving a painting frame

When you place a painting frame in a word processing document, you can adjust the way text flows around the frame. For more details, see page 263.

Working with Clip Art

ClarisWorks can open documents in several bit-mapped formats, including the following:

- MacPaint: The original paint document format, pioneered by the MacPaint application that shipped with the original Macintosh in 1984.

- TIFF: A cross-platform file format used to prepare bit-mapped images for printing. For example, the screen shots used as illustrations in this book are TIFFs.

- GIF: A cross-platform file format created by CompuServe and now used extensively for graphics that are displayed over the World Wide Web.

- JPEG: A compressed cross-platfrom format used extensively for images on the World Wide Web.

- BMP: A Windows bit-mapped format.

Bit-mapped clip art that you open with ClarisWorks is more flexible than object graphics. Once you have opened a bit-mapped graphics file, you can modify its contents using any of ClarisWorks's painting tools.

For details on open files not created with ClarisWorks, see page 254. For details on keeping clip art and other images in ClarisWorks libraries, see page 250.

7

Spreadsheets

A *spreadsheet* is the electronic equivalent of the paper-based ledger sheets used by bookkeepers and accountants. It is a grid of columns and rows into which you can enter numbers that the spreadsheet can manipulate for you, including almost any arithmetic transformation you can imagine. Electronic spreadsheets can also graph data and perform *"what if" analyses*, through which you can vary one or more values in an arithmetic formula to see what effect the changing values have on the end result.

A Bit of History

If it weren't for an electronic spreadsheet, microcomputers might still be viewed as toys for hobbyists rather than as serious business equipment. In the late 1970s, the Apple II computer line was selling to electronics hobbyists but had little impact on business. Then, a software developer named Dan Bricklin created the first electronic spreadsheet program: VisiCalc.

VisiCalc was the first program truly designed for business. Users loved it. The size of the spreadsheet itself was no longer limited by the physical size of the paper. Because the computer could scroll the visible area, the spreadsheet could be much larger than what you could see at any one time. Perhaps even more important, when the computer did calculations, they were correct. Much of the risk of inaccurate computation was removed.

Business users realized that the microcomputer wasn't a toy, that it had serious business applications. They bought Apple II computers so that they could run VisiCalc. Other software developers saw that many computers were appearing in business, so they began to write more software for that market. More business software meant more microcomputer sales, and more computer sales meant more software and more entrants into the hardware market, including IBM. Although certainly no one can be sure that the micrcomputer market wouldn't have arisen anyway, it is true that VisiCalc was the spark that started the entire business microcomputing revolution.

Uses of a Spreadsheet

Spreadsheets were originally used primarily as business tools. Therefore, most of their uses center around processing numbers and performing analyses of those numbers. Uses of a spreadsheet include:

- Budgeting: A budget spreadsheet contains income and expenses. It will probably compute totals of each and determine whether there is a surplus or a deficit at the end of each budget period. Budget spreadsheets are therefore useful for both home and business users.

- Profit and loss analysis: A profit and loss spreadsheet contains the cost of producing a product or server and the income gained from sales. The spreadsheet then usually computes profit. This type of spreadsheet is often used for "what if" analyses. The user can vary costs and sales to see how profits might be affected.

- Gradebook maintenance: A gradebook spreadsheet holds the names of students and the grades they are assigned. The spreadsheet is usually set up to calculate final grades on the basis of whatever weighting the teacher chooses.

- Sports analysis: A sports analysis spreadsheet contains the names and statistics of sports participants. The spreadsheet can then calcuate averages for individual athletes or for a team as a whole.

As you can see, although electronic spreadsheets were originally designed only for business accounting uses, they have applications in a wide variety of settings in which it makes sense to store and analyze numbers in a grid of columns and rows.

The beauty of a spreadsheet becomes apparent when you realize that many of the values you see on a spreadsheet are interrelated by mathematical formulas. When you change one value, any calculated values based on that value are recomputed.

As an example, take a look at the profit and loss statement in Figure 7.1. The price of the items sold, the expenses per unit, the number sold, and the tax rate were typed directly onto the spreadsheet. However, the remainder of the values are calculated.

profit/loss statement (SS)

F20

	A	B	C	D	E
1	Sales analysis	Fall quarter 1998			
2					
3	**Income**				
4		**Price**	**Number sold**	**Revenue**	
5		$3.45	10,088	$34,803.60	
6		$4.99	102,000	$508,980.00	
7		$5.25	35,625	$187,031.25	
8	**Total**		147,713	$730,814.85	
9					
10	**Expenses**	**Each**		**Cost**	
11	Materials	0.89		$131,464.57	
12	Overhead	0.25		$36,928.25	
13	Labor	1.16		$171,347.08	
14	**Total**			$339,739.90	
15					
16	**Net before taxes**			$391,074.95	
17					
18	**Tax**	33.00%		$129,054.73	
19					
20	**Net after taxes**			$262,020.22	
21					

100

Figure 7.1 A profit and loss spreadsheet

If the user changes the number sold at $5.25, then ClarisWorks recalculates all the values that depend on that quantity, as in Figure 7.2. (This is one way for the user to get an answer to the question, "*What if* we sold more items at the higher price?")

profit/loss statement (SS)

F20

	A	B	C	D	E
1	Sales analysis	Fall quarter 1998			
2					
3	**Income**				
4		**Price**	**Number sold**	**Revenue**	
5		$3.45	10,088	$34,803.60	
6		$4.99	102,000	$508,980.00	
7		$5.25	100,012	$525,063.00	
8	**Total**		212,100	$1,068,846.60	
9					
10	**Expenses**	**Each**		**Cost**	
11	Materials	0.89		$188,769.00	
12	Overhead	0.25		$53,025.00	
13	Labor	1.16		$246,036.00	
14	**Total**			$487,830.00	
15					
16	**Net before taxes**			$581,016.60	
17					
18	**Tax**	33.00%		$191,735.48	
19					
20	**Net after taxes**			$389,281.12	
21					

Figure 7.2 The profit and loss spreadsheet with recalculated values

As you can see, not only has the revenue value for that price changed, but so have the total number sold and the expenses. (Expenses depend on the total number sold.) In addition, total revenue, net income before taxes, the tax to be paid, and the net after taxes have been recalulated. Keep in mind that all the user had to do was modify one value. Because of the way the spreadsheet was constructed, changing that value allowed the entire spreadsheet to update itself without the user needing to perform any calculations.

Anatomy of a Spreadsheet

In Figure 7.3 you can see an empty spreadsheet document. Unlike word processing, drawing, and painting documents, which present you with a blank canvas that you can format, a spreadsheet document has a layout already set for you in a pattern of columns and rows.

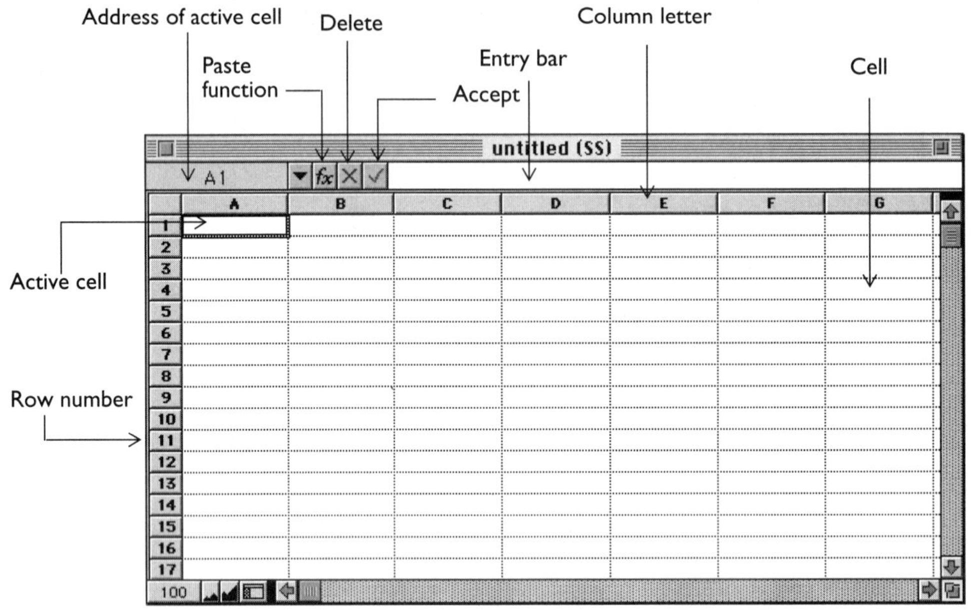

Figure 7.3 A spreadsheet document

You can configure ClarisWorks so that you don't see the boundaries of the columns and rows or their labels, and you can change the size of the columns and rows. Nonetheless, the basic layout of a spreadsheet always remains in columns and rows.

As you can see in Figure 7.3, columns are identified by letters and rows by numbers. The 26th column is Z; the 27th column is AA, the 28th AB, and so on. By default, ClarisWorks provides 500 rows and 40 columns. However, you can add more of both if you need them.

The intersection of a column and a row is called a *cell*. 4A cell's *address* (its location in the spreadsheet) is its column letter followed by its row number. Actions that you take with a spreadsheet affect the currently selected cell (the *active cell*). As you can see in Figure 7.3, the active cell has a highlighted border. The address of the active cell apears at the top left corner of the spreadsheet document.

Spreadsheets work not only with individual selected cells but also with blocks of contiguous cells, known as *ranges*. A range, like that in Figure 7.4, is defined by the cell in its top left corner (B5 in this example) and the cell in its bottom right corner (D10 in this example). However, the spreadsheet shows only the top left cell as the active cell.

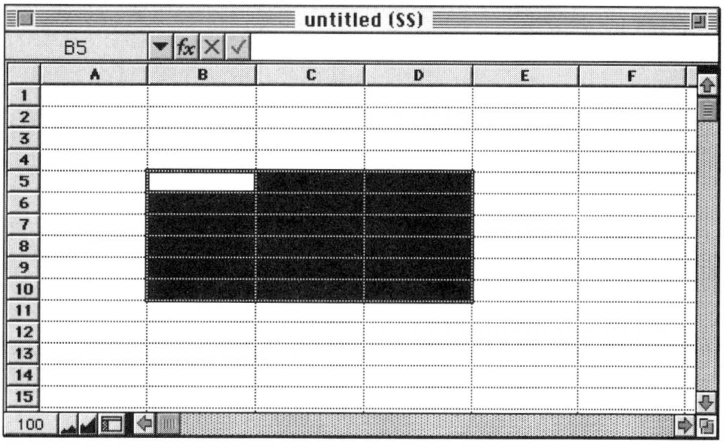

Figure 7.4 A range of selected cells

The notation used for a range when a range is part of a formula places two dots between the corners of the range, as in B5..D10. This notation has no special meaning; it's just been a part of spreadsheets since the VisiCalc days.

Unlike word processing, drawing, and painting, you don't enter anything directly into a spreadsheet document.

You can format cells directly, but all data entry takes place in the Entry bar. When an entry is complete, you press the Enter key (or click the Accept button in the Entry bar) to transfer the entry into the spreadsheet. This makes it possible to create a cell entry — in particular, a mathematical formula — that is different from what a user sees in the body of the spreadsheet. When you enter a formula, the spreadsheet calculates the result of the formula and displays the result; the underlying formula itself is visible only in the Entry bar.

Moving around a Spreadsheet

A spreadsheet's active cell (or range of selected cells) determines the portion of the spreadsheet that will be affected by a change you make. Therefore, you need methods for navigating around a spreadsheet, changing the active cell as you go.

You can change the active cell in any of the following ways:

- Scroll to bring the cell you want into view and then click in the cell.

Scrolling by itself does not change the active cell. It merely brings a different portion of the spreadsheet into view.

- Click on the address of the active cell in the upper left corner of the spreadsheet. The Go To Cell dialog box appears (Figure 7.5). Type the address of the cell that you want to make the active cell. Click the OK button or press Enter.

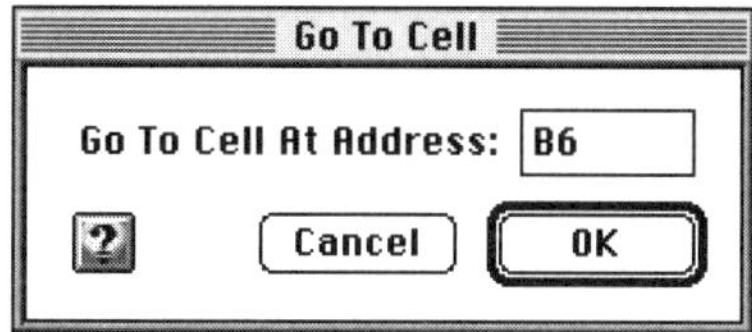

Figure 7.5 The Go To Cell dialog box

- Display the Go To Cell dialog box using a menu option:

Macintosh	Choose Options->Go To Cell or press ⌘-G.
Windows	Choose Options->Go To Cell, press CTRL-G, or press ALT-O, G.

- Move one cell in any direction by pressing the associated arrow key. For example, use the up arrow key to move up one row and the right arrow key to move right one column.

- Move one cell to the right by pressing the Tab key; move one cell to the left by pressing SHIFT-Tab.

- Move one cell down by pressing the Enter key; move one cell up by pressing SHIFT-Enter.

The way in which the arrow keys, Tab, and Enter work actually depends on settings in the Spreadsheet preferences panel (Figure 7.6). By default, the arrow keys move the insertion point in the Entry bar whenever there is something in the Entry bar that hasn't been transfered to the body of the spreadsheet. However, when there is no pending entry, the arrows keys move from one cell to another. If you want the arrow keys always to move the active cell, choose the Always Selects Another Cell radio button.

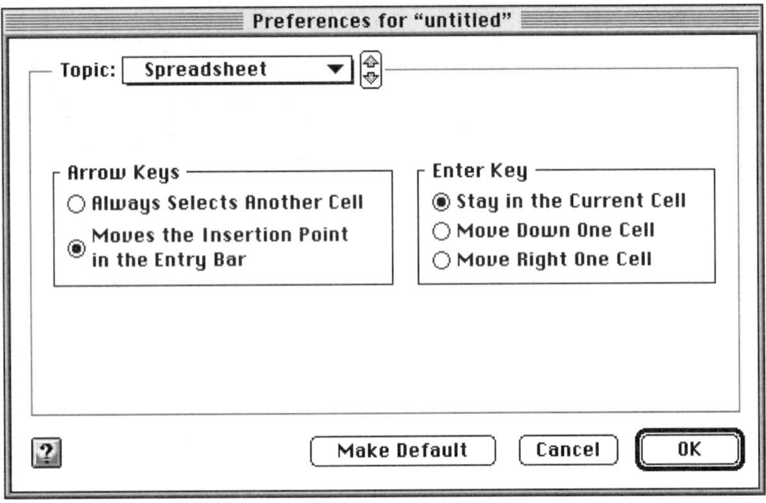

Figure 7.6 Spreadsheet preferences

By default, whenever there is a pending entry in the Entry bar, the Enter key transfers an entry to the spreadsheet and leaves the active cell untouched. It moves one cell down when there is no pending entry. However, if you are doing a great deal of data entry into adjacent cells, it can be easier to have the Enter key move the active cell as well as transfer an entry. In that case, you may want to select either the Move Down One Cell or Move Right One Cell radio button so that you are automatically positioned in the next cell where you want to place a value.

To display the Preferences dialog box, choose Edit->Preferences. (Windows users can also press ALT-E *, N.) Then choose Spreadsheet from the Topic popup menu.*

Entering Data

The values that appear in a spreadsheet can come from two primary sources: They can be constants, in which case they are simply typed on the keyboard, or they can be the result of calculations, in which case the spreadsheet performs a calculation and displays its result. For example, in Figure 7.7, all of the text you see is labels. The numbers on the Income and Expenses lines are numeric constants. However, the number on the Surplus/Deficit line is obtained by computing the value of a formula.

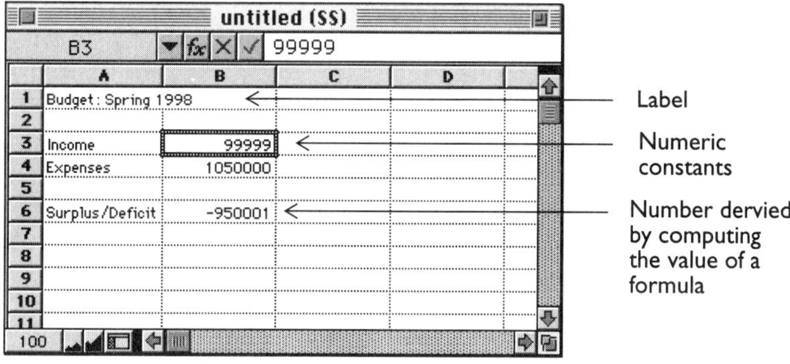

Figure 7.7 Spreadsheet constants

In this section we will look at entering the two types of constants, numbers and labels. (You will read about formulas in the following section.)

Numeric Constants

A numeric constant is a single value that you type in the Entry bar and transfer to the spreadsheet. Once you enter a numeric constant, its value will not change unless you make its cell the active cell and modify the value in the Entry bar.

To enter a numeric constant:

1. Make the cell in which you want the numeric constant to appear the active cell.

2. Type the value in the Entry bar.

3. Press Enter or click the Accept button in the Entry bar. ClarisWorks transfers the value to the body of the spreadsheet.

Labels

Labels are text constants that you can place anywhere on a spreadsheet to make the contents of the spreadsheet easier to understand. In fact, your goal with labels should be to make the spreadsheet self-documenting. Anyone looking at the spreadsheet, assuming they have knowledge of the spreadsheet's topic, should be able to understand what it is presented without resorting to additional documentation.

To enter a label:

1. Make the cell in which you want the label to begin the active cell.

2. Type the label in the Entry bar.

3. Press Enter or click the Accept button in the Enter bar. ClarisWorks transfers the value to the body of the spreadsheet.

If a label is too wide to fit across the width of the column in which it is located, ClarisWorks automatically spans adjacent, empty cells to the right. This means that all of a long label appears, unless its path is blocked by a cell that already has something in it. For example, in Figure 7.8, all of the label in A2 can be seen because nothing is blocking it. However, the label in A4 is truncated because there is a value in B4 in the way. Notice that even though the label in A4 is truncated on the worksheet, the entire label can be seen in the Entry bar when A4 is the active cell.

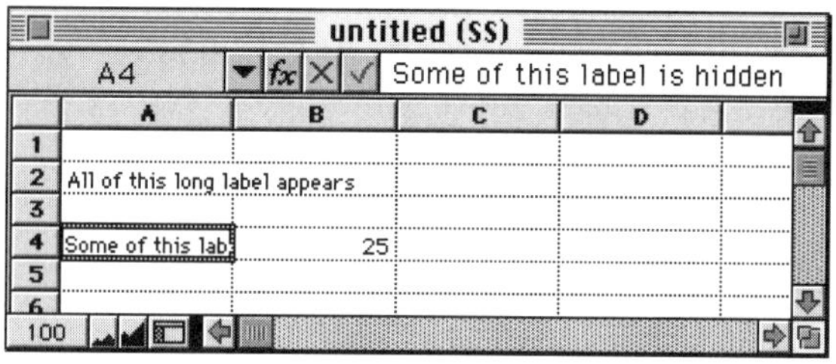

Figure 7.8 Labels

Editing Cell Contents

You can change the contents of a cell, even after it has been transferred from the Entry bar to the body of the spreadsheet. To modify a cell's contents:

1. Select the cell whose contents will be modified. The contents of the cell appear in the Entry bar.

2. Modify the contents of the Entry bar.

3. Press Enter or click the Accept button to transfer the modified contents back to the body of the spreadsheet.

The editing techniques you can use in the entry bar include the following:

- Select characters with the mouse and delete them by pressing Delete or by choosing Edit->Clear.
- Move the insertion point with the mouse and enter new characters.
- Delete characters with the Delete and Del keys.

Defining Formulas

A formula is an expression of the way in which you would like ClarisWorks to manipulate data. The simple budget in Figure 7.9, for example, uses formulas to obtain the contents of cells B6, B16, and B18.

There are several basic elements in a formula:

- Numeric constants: ClarisWorks uses the value of the constants exactly as you typed them when it calculates the value of the formula.
- Cell addresses: ClarisWorks uses the value stored in the cell address when it computes the value of a formula.
- Functions: A function is a small program that performs one specific action, such as finding the average of the values in a range of cells. ClarisWorks executes each function it finds in a formula and uses the result when it computes the final value of the formula. ClarisWorks has just over 100 functions that you can use in spreadsheet formulas.

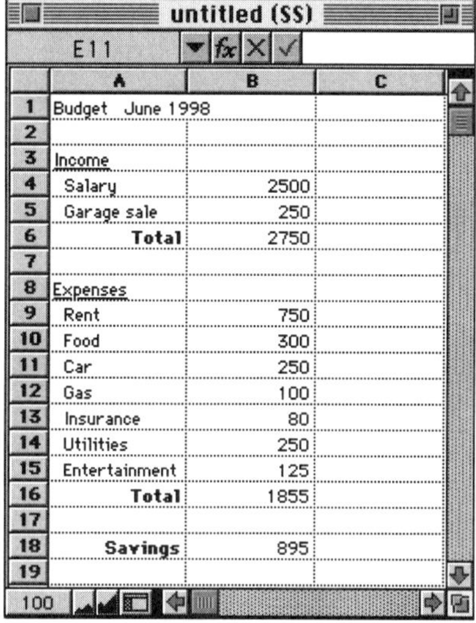

Figure 7.9 A simple budget spreadsheet using formulas to add and subtract

- Operators: Operators tell ClarisWorks what to do with the values in a formula. The ClarisWorks operators include the basic mathematical operators with which you are probably familiar, including addition, subtraction, multiplication, and division.

Entering Formulas

To enter a formula:

1. Make the cell that will display the value of the formula the active cell.

2. Type an equals sign (=) in the Entry bar.

ClarisWorks assumes that anything that begins with an equals sign is a formula. Everything else is a constant.

3. Type the formula in the Entry bar.

4. Press Enter or click the Accept button in the Entry bar. ClarisWorks calculates the value of the formula and displays it on the spreadsheet.

Constructing Formulas

As discussed earlier, ClarisWorks formulas are a combination of constants, operators, cell addresses, and functions. In this section we will look these elements and at how they perform within a formula.

Arithmetic Operators

The arithmetic operators that you can use in a formula can be found in Table 7.1. Although these are the same operators that you use in everyday math, notice that some of the symbols are a bit different. In particular, computers use * for multiplication, / for division, and ^ for raising a number to a power (exponentiation).

Because a spreadsheet computes the value of a formula for you, you can use a spreadsheet as a simple calculator. For example, if you type =125 ^ 5 (125 raised to the fifth power) in the Entry bar and then press Enter, ClarisWorks will perform the math for you. This is particularly useful if you need to work with numbers that are too large for your pocket calculator. A spreadsheet can handle them!

Table 7.1 ClarisWorks arithmetic operators

Operator	Action
+	When used by itself in front of a value, preserves the sign of the value. When used between two values, adds them together.
-	When used by itself in front of a value, changes the sign of the value. When used between two values, subtracts the value on the right from the value on the left.
*	Multiplies two values.
/	Divides two values.
^	Raises the value on the left to the power on the right.

Precedence

There is theorectically no limit to the number of arithmetic operators you can place in a single formula. However, when you have operators of more than one type in the same formula, sometimes the results can be somewhat unexpected. This is the result of *precedence*, the rules by which a computer determines the order in which it will evaluate parts of an arithmetic expression.

As an example, consider the arithmetic expression 10/2+3. Depending on whether the division or addition is performed first, the answer could be 8 or 2.

Most computer software uses the following general rules of arithmetic precedence when there is more than one arithmetic operator in an expression:

- The unary + and - operators (those that preserve and change the sign of a number) are applied first.
- Exponentiation is performed second.
- Multiplication and division are performed next.

- Addition and subtraction are performed last.
- When there is more than one operator with the same precedence, they are evaluated from left to right.

In our example, this default precedence would produce the result 8 rather than 2.

However, if you really want the computer to perform the addition first, you can surround the parts of the expression that should have highest precedence with parentheses. A computer evaluates whatever is within parentheses first. Therefore, 10/(2+3) produces a result of 2.

Parentheses can be nested. For example, the expression 12/(2*(1+2)) first performs the addition in the innermost parentheses, followed by the multiplication, and finally the division, producing a result of 2. If there were no parentheses, the expression 12/2*1+2 would first perform the division, then the multiplication, followed by the addition, producing a result of 8.

The most important thing to keep in mind is to be sure that you have an opening parenthesis for each closing parenthesis!

Using Cell Addresses

Most of the formulas that we use in a spreadsheet include cell addresses. For example, the formula for computing the monthly savings in Figure 7.9 is =B6-B16. This tells ClarisWorks to take the value it finds in cell B16 and subtract it from the value it finds in cell B6. If the contents of a cell are defined by a formula, then ClarisWorks uses the value of the formula rather than the formula's definition.

There are two ways to enter a cell address into a formula:

- Type the cell address. The column letter does not need to be capitalized. ClarisWorks recognizes both upper- and lowercase letters.
- Click on the cell. From the time you enter an equals sign to start a formula until you press the Enter key to store the formula, ClarisWorks assumes that the address of every cell on which you click should be placed in the Entry bar as part of the formula.

Although you see a cell's address in the Entry bar, by default ClarisWorks actually doesn't store the address. Instead, it stores the position of the address relative to the cell in which the formula is stored. For example, when we place the formula =B6-B16 into cell B18 of the simple budget spreadsheet in Figure 7.9, ClarisWorks actually stores B16 as something like "the cell two rows up in the same column." This is known as a *relative address*.

If you want ClarisWorks to store an actual cell address, then you want an *absolute address*. To get an absolute address, you place a dollar sign ($) in front of the row or column that you want stored absolute rather than relative. For example, B6 stores a B and a 6; $B6 stores a B and a relative reference for row 6.

At this point, differentiating between absolute and relative addresses probably doesn't make much sense. However, you will see both in action shortly and understand the importance of the difference when we talk about copying formulas from one cell to another.

Using Functions

As mentioned earlier, a function is a small program that performs a single operation for you. For example, the SUM function adds a group of values. Those values might be in a range, or they might be scattered throughout a spreadsheet.

Each function has a name and a list of *arguments,* which provide the input data that the function needs to complete its work. The SUM function, for example, needs the values it is to add. The format of the function begins with the name, followed by the arguments in parentheses: SUM(B6,B12,B18). When there are multiple arguments, they are separated by commas.

Many functions, like SUM, can take a range of cells as arguments. For example, to add up the expenses in the simple budget spreadsheet from Figure 7.9, the cell B16 contains the formula =SUM (B9..B15). To enter a range in a formula, you can type the corners of the range, separated by two commas, or you can drag the mouse pointer across the range.

Some commonly used functions include:

- AVERAGE (number1, number2, ...): AVERAGE computes the average value in a group of cells. The arguments can be any number of numeric constants or the addresses of cells containing numbers, separated by commas. Any of the arguments can also be a range of cells containing numbers.
- SQRT (number): SQRT computes the square root of a number. The argument can be specified as a numeric constant or as the address of a cell containing a number.
- MAX (number1, number2, ...): MAX finds the maximum value in a group of cells. The arguments can be any number of numeric constants or the addresses of cells containing numbers, separated by commas. Any of the arguments can also be a range of cells containing numbers.
- TRUNC (number): TRUNC removes the fractional portion of a number, truncating it to an integer. The single argument can be specified as a numeric constant or as the address of a cell containing a number.

ClarisWorks's functions can be used in computed fields in the database module as well as in spreadsheet formulas. Therefore, the full range of functions are document in Appendix D.

To enter a function, you can type the entire function, including name and arguments, in the Entry bar. Alternatively, you can paste the function into the Entry bar. To do so:

1. Choose Edit->Paste function or click on the Paste Function button in the Entry bar. (Windows users can also press ALT-E, U.) The Paste Function dialog box appears (Figure 7.10).

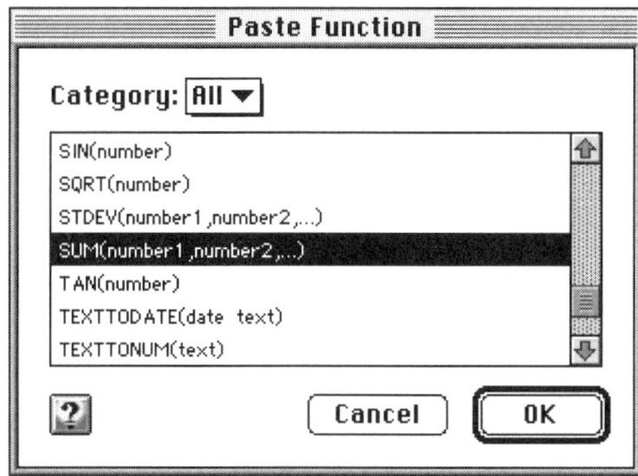

Figure 7.10 The Paste Function dialog box

2. Highlight the function you want to insert.

3. Click the OK button or press Enter. ClarisWorks pastes the function into the entry bar with specifications for the types of data needed for its arguments as placeholders.

4. Replace the argument placeholders with constants or cell addresses.

5. Repeat steps 1 through 4 for each function you want to paste into the formula.

Viewing Formulas

By default, ClarisWorks shows you formulas only in the Entry bar. The body of the spreadsheet contains the results of evaluating the formulas. However, if you want to see the formulas in the spreadsheet:

1. Choose Options->Display. (Windows users can also press ALT-O, D.) The Display dialog box appears (Figure 7.11).

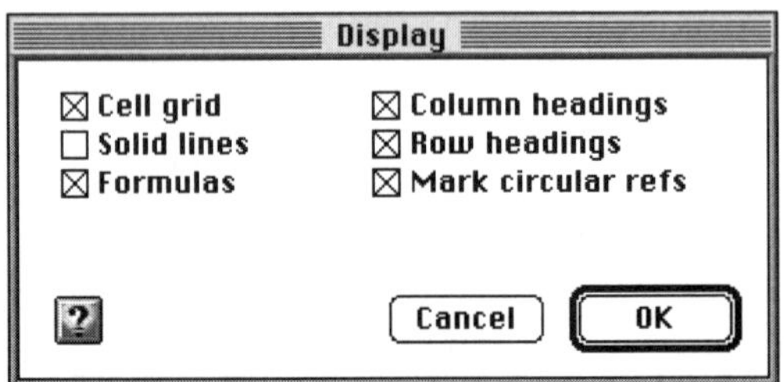

Figure 7.11 The Display dialog box

2. Click the Formulas check box to place an X in it.

3. Click the OK button or press Enter.

ClarisWorks replaces the calculations on the spreadsheet with the formulas. Figure 7.12, for example, shows you the formulas underlying the profit and loss spreadsheet from Figure 7.1.

profit/loss statement (SS)

D20 =D16-D18

	A	B	C	D
1	Sales analysis	Fall quarter 1998		
2				
3	**Income**			
4		**Price**	**Number sold**	**Revenue**
5		$3.45	10,088	=C5*B5
6		$4.99	102,000	=C6*B6
7		$5.25	35,625	=C7*B7
8	**Total**		=SUM(C5..C7)	=SUM(D5..D7)
9				
10	**Expenses**	**Each**		**Cost**
11	Materials	0.89		=B11*C8
12	Overhead	0.25		=B12*C8
13	Labor	1.16		=B13*C8
14	**Total**			=SUM(D11..D1
15				
16	**Net before taxes**			=D8-D14
17				
18	**Tax**	33.00%		=D16*B18
19				
20	**Net after taxes**			=D16-D18
21				

Figure 7.12 Viewing formulas

Copying Formulas

It is not unusual for many cells in a spreadsheet to contain similar formulas. In fact, the formulas may be identical except for cell addresses. As an example, look again at Figure 7.12. The formulas in D5, D6, and D7 fit this pattern; so do the formulas in D11, D12, and D13. Each of the first group takes the value in the cell two columns to the left and multiplies it by the value in the cell one column to the left. In the second group, the values are in cells two columns to the left, and two columns to the left and six rows above. (Here's where those relative addresses make sense.)

You could certainly enter these similar formulas by typing the same formula multiple times. However, there is an easier way: You can type a formula once and then *copy* it into other cells.

When you copy a formula, the internal representation of addresses stay the same. The result is that when a formula contains a relative address, copying maintains the relative position of the addresses in the formula to the cell where the formula is copied. For example, if cell D5 contains =C5*B5, then copying the formula into D6 produces =D6*B6 because the original formula was stored as "two cells to the left in the same row * one cell to the left in the same row."

Absolute addresses, which are stored with specific row numbers and/or column letters, are copied exactly. Therefore B6 will always copy as B6, regardless of the cell into which you copy it.

There are two basic ways to copy a formula, using copy and paste or filling right or down. You use the copy and paste technique to place formulas anywhere on a spreadsheet. The fill technique can only be used with adjacent cells.

To copy a formula using copy and paste:

1. Select the cell containing the formula to be copied.

2. Copy to the Clipboard. (For instructions on how to copy parts of a document, see page 60.)

3. Select the cell or range of cells into which the formula will be copied.

If you copy a single cell and paste into a range of selected cells, ClarisWorks pastes only the single copied cell, placing it in the top left corner of the selected range.

4. Paste the copied formula into the selected cells. (For instructions pasting objects into a document, see page 60.)

To copy a fomula into adjacent cells below:

1. Select the cell containing the formula and cells below. For example, in Figure 7.13, the formula for computing a student's final grade has been entered into cell H4. The user has then selected H4 and cells directly below it, into which the formula will be copied.

gradesheet (SS)

H4 =(C4+D4+E4)/3*0.3+F4*0.5+G4*0.2

	A	B	C	D	E	F	G	H	I
1	Student grades	English 101							
2									
3			A1	A2	A3	Exam	Paper	Total	
4	Anderson	Jane	85	100	85	100	94	95.8	
5	Baker	Billy	100	95	100	95	75		
6	Collins	Mary	75	80	75	80	75		
7	Davis	Tom	90	75	90	75	100		
8	Eng	Will	75	100	75	100	100		
9	Franklin	David	100	60	100	60	80		
10	Gamble	Jane	85	85	85	85	85		
11	Harris	Ellen	80	80	80	80	83		
12	Jackson	Amy	80	100	80	100	100		
13	Kahn	Craig	60	80	60	80	90		
14	Lewis	David	75	80	75	80	95		

100

Figure 7.13 Selecting a range of cells to fill with a copied formula

2.

Macintosh	Choose Calculate->Fill Down or press ⌘-D.
Windows	Choose Calculate->Fill Down, press CTRL-D, or press ALT-C, D.

To copy into adjacent cells to the right:

1. Select the cell containing the formula and cells to the right.

2.

Macintosh	Choose Calculate->Fill Right or press ⌘-R.
Windows	Choose Calculate->Fill Right, press CTRL-R, or press ALT-C, R.

Paste Special

When you copy and paste a formula, ClarisWorks pastes the formula and displays the result of the formula based on its new location. However, if you want to copy the *result* of a fomula rather than the formula itself, you can use the Paste Special command.

To paste the result of a formula:

1. Copy the cell or cells whose values you want to place in other cells.

2. Select the target cell or cells.

3. Choose Edit->Paste Special. The Paste Special dialog box appears (Figure 7.14).

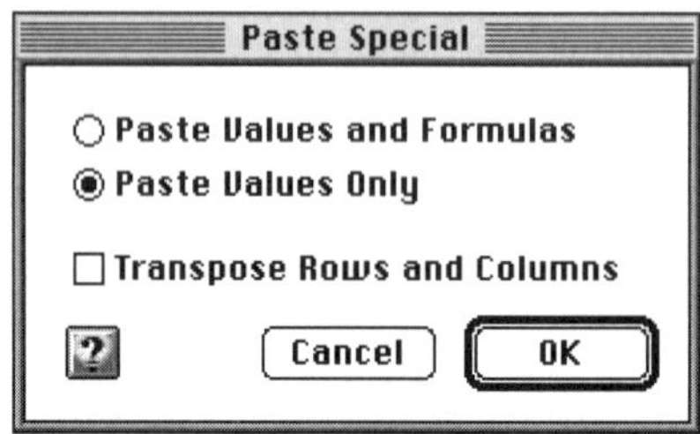

Figure 7.14 The Paste Special dialog box

4. Leave the Paste Values Only radio button selected.

5. Click the OK button or press Enter.

Controlling Formula Recalculation

Unless you specify otherwise, ClarisWorks recalculates the values of all formulas every time you make any change on the spreadsheet that affects a formula. However, if a spreadsheet contains a number of very complex formulas, then recalculating every time there's a change in the spreadsheet can greatly slow down data entry. In such a case, you might want to prevent ClarisWorks from recalculating until you have finished entering all your data.

To prevent automatic recalculation:

1. Choose Calculate->Auto Calc to remove the check from the Auto Calc menu item. (Windows users can also press ALT-C, A.)

To recalculate the entire spreadsheet when auto recalculation is turned off:

1.

Macintosh	Choose Calculate->Calculate Now or press SHIFT-1-=.
Windows	Choose Calculate->Calculate Now, press SHIFT-CTRL-=, or press ALT-C, N.

To turn automatic recalculation back on:

1. Choose Calculate->Auto Calc to place a check on the Auto Calc menu item. (Windows users can also press ALT-C, A.)

Working with Named Ranges

The traditional way to specify a spreadsheet range is to give the addresses of the range's top left and bottom right cells. However, ClarisWorks makes it much easier by allowing you to assign a name to a range of cells. You can then use that name in any formulas that would otherwise require the range's coordinates.

Using ranges with meaningful names makes it easier to understand what spreadsheet formulas are doing. For example, the formula SUM(Revenue) is clearer than SUM(A6..A8).

Naming a Range

To give a range of cells a name:

1. Select the range you want to name.
2. Choose Define Name from the Range menu (the down arrow to the right of the address of the current cell, as in Figure 7.15). The Define Named Range dialog box appears.

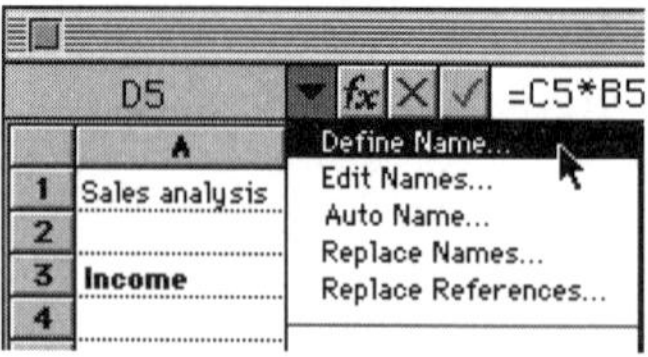

Figure 7.15 The Range menu

If a vertical range has a label in the cell directly above, ClarisWorks assumes that label will be the name (see Figure 7.16). ClarisWorks will also pick up a label that is in the cell directly to the right of a horizontal range.

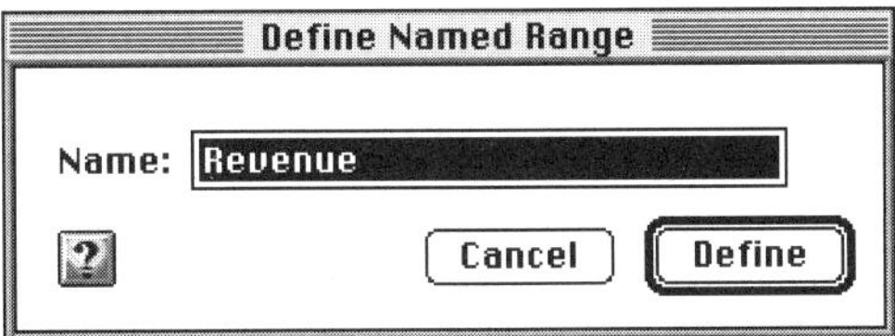

Figure 7.16 Entering a name for a range

3. If necessary, enter a name for the range.

4. Click the Define button or press Enter. ClarisWorks stores the name for the range and adds it to the bottom of the Range menu.

Using a Named Range

You can use the name of a range anywhere you would use the range's coordinates. To use a name you can either select the name from the bottom of the Range menu or type the name directly into a formula.

Switching Names and Coordinates

ClarisWorks keeps track of the range coordinates that correspond to each named range. That means that you can switch between coordinates and names at any time.

To replace names with coordinates:

1. Select the cell or cells containing the names you want to replace with coordinates.

2. Choose Replace Names from the Range menu. The Replace Names dialog box appears, showing you the names and coordinates for all named ranges in the current selection (Figure 7.17).

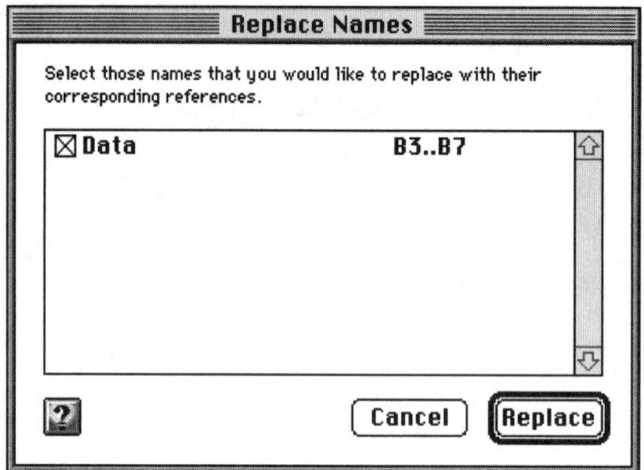

Figure 7.17 Replacing names with coordinates

3. Click in the check box next to any names you *don't* want to replace to remove the X.

4. Click the Replace button or press Enter.

To replace coordinates with names:

1. Select the cell or cells containing the coordinates you want to replace with names.

2. Choose Replace References from the Range menu. The Replace References dialog box appears, showing you the names and coordinates for all named ranges in the current selection (Figure 7.18).

3. Click in the check box next to any coordinates you *don't* want to replace to remove the X.

4. Click the Replace button or press Enter.

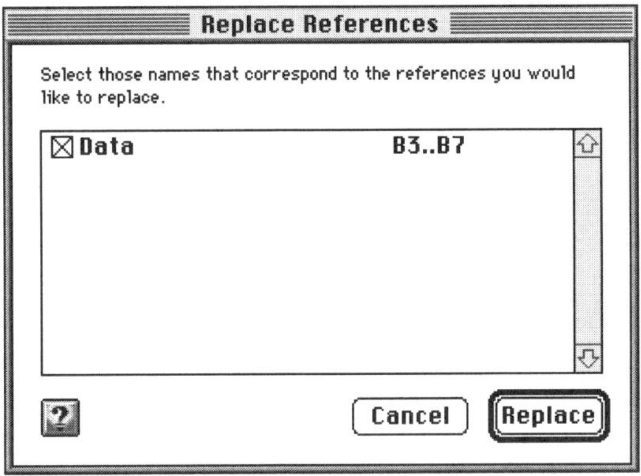

Figure 7.18 Replacing coordinates with names

Formatting a Spreadsheet

You apply formatting to a spreadsheet to make it easier to read and understand. (Remember that the goal of spreadsheet design is to make the spreadsheet understandable by anyone with the appropriate knowledge of the subject area of the spreadsheet, without needing to give that person extra documentation.) To this end, you can format text, the appearance of numbers, and the cells of the spreadsheet itself.

Text Formats

Text formatting in a spreadsheet can be applied to labels and to values. This means you can set the font, style, size, color, and alignment of any characters you see on a spreadsheet, regardless of whether they are used in calculations.

When you are working with a spreadsheet, the menu bar does not contain individual formatting menus. Instead, the text formatting options are gathered together as submenus of the Format menu, as in Figure 7.19. (For details on text formatting, including shortcut keys that you can use, see page 88 through page 101.)

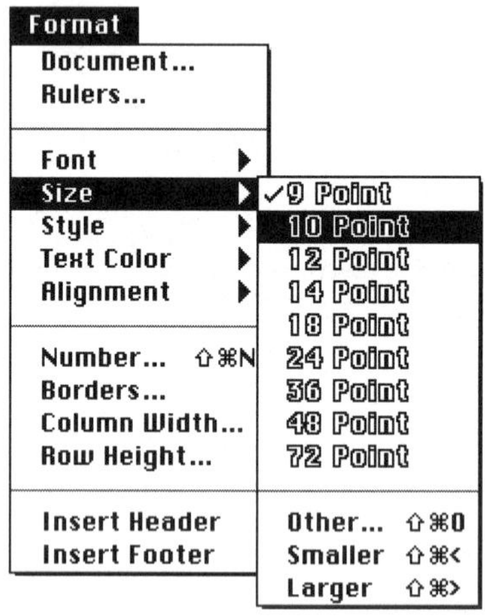

Figure 7.19 Accessing formatting options from a spreadsheet menu

To set text formatting:

1. Select the cell or cells to which you want the formatting to apply.
2. Make a choice from one of the Format menu's submenus.
3. Repeat step 2 until all formatting has been applied.

To set cell alignment quickly, use one of the alignment buttons in the Button Bar .

Number Formats

Number formatting refers to the way in which numbers appear on a spreadsheet. You can set the precision of a number (the number of digits that appear to the right of the decimal point), whether it includes commas or a dollar sign, whether it appears as a percentage, and so on.

There are five number formats, all of which are demonstrated in Figure 7.20:

untitled (SS)

A11

	A	B
1	Number Formatting Example	
2		
3	Original value (default General format):	12345.678
4	Currency format	$12345.68
5	Percent format	1234567.80%
6	Scientific format	1.23e+4
7	Fixed format (precision = 2)	12345.68
8		

100

Figure 7.20 Number formats

- General: General format (the default) displays all digits that you have entered. There are no trailing zeros. Decimal fractions have a leading zero, such as 0.68. Negative numbers have a - as the first character.

- Currency: Currency format displays a dollar sign in front of the number and by default includes two digits to the right of the decimal, filling in trailing zeros if necessary. If the original number has a higher precision, ClarisWorks rounds the number.

- Percent: Percent format multiplies the value by 100 and displays it with a trailing percent sign. By default, percent format includes two digits to the right of the decimal point, filling in trailing zeros if necessary. If the original number has a higher precision, ClarisWorks rounds the number.

- Scientific: Scientific format presents the value in the format X.XXXeEE, where EE is the exponent to which 10 is raised. By default, ClarisWorks includes two digits to the right of the decimal point, rounding the number when the original has higher precision.

- Fixed: Fixed format allows you to specify precision (default is two digits).

To set the number format:

1. Select the cell or cells to which formatting will be applied.

2.

Macintosh	Choose Format->Number or press SHIFT-1-N.
Windows	Choose Format->Number, press SHIFT-CTRL-N, or press ALT-M, N.

The Format Number, Date, and Time dialog box appears (Figure 7.21).

3. Click the radio button that corresponds to the number formatting you want.

4. Click in the Commas check box to place commas between groups of three numbers in the whole number portion of a number.

5. Click in the Negatives in () check box to place parentheses around negative values instead of the default leading -.

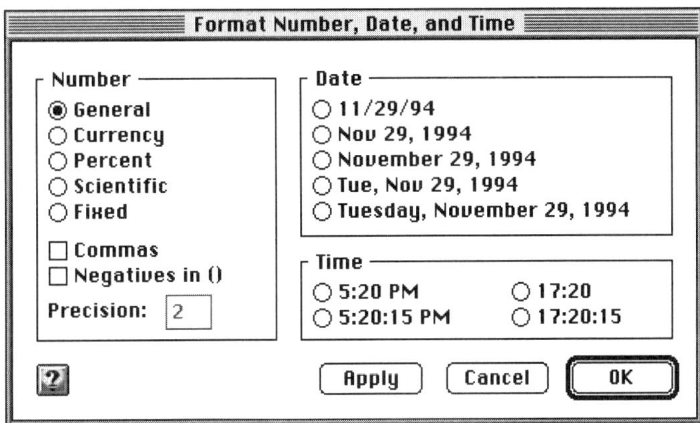

Figure 7.21 The Format Number, Date, and Time dialog box

6. For formats that allow you to set precision (all except General), enter the number of digits that should appear to the right of the decimal point in the Precision box.

7. Click the Apply button to apply the formatting and leave the dialog box on the screen. Click the OK button to apply formatting and remove the dialog box from the screen.

Cell Formats

In additon to formatting the text and numbers that appear on a spreadsheet, you can add formatting to the cells themselves, including cell borders and fill colors and patterns.

Setting Cell Borders

By default, a cell has no visible borders. What you have been seeing in the illustrations in this chapter is the spreadsheet's grid, which can be turned off. (For details, see Adjusting the

Spreadsheet Display, later in this chapter.) When the grid is off, the body of the spreadsheet is empty, just like the body of a word processing, drawing, or painting document (for example, see Figure 7.22).

profit/loss statement (SS)

G19

	A	B	C	D
1	Sales analysis	Fall quarter 1998		
2				
3	**Income**			
4		**Price**	**Number sold**	**Revenue**
5		$3.45	10,088	$34,803.60
6		$4.99	102,000	$508,980.00
7		$5.25	35,625	$187,031.25
8	**Total**		147,713	$730,814.85
9				
10	**Expenses**	**Each**		**Cost**
11	Materials	0.89		$131,464.57
12	Overhead	0.25		$36,928.25
13	Labor	1.16		$171,347.08
14	**Total**			$339,739.90
15				
16	**Net before taxes**			$391,074.95
17				
18	**Tax**	33.00%		$129,054.73
19				
20	**Net after taxes**			$262,020.22

100

Figure 7.22 The profit and loss spreadsheet displayed without the cell grid

To display solid borders around cells when the grid is off:

1. Select the cell or cells to which you want to give a border.
2. Choose Format->Border. (Windows users can also press ALT-M, B.) The Borders dialog box appears (Figure 7.23).
3. To place a border around all four sides of the cell, click in the Outline check box. (The next time you return to the dialog box, the other check boxes will be checked as well.) To place a border around selected sides, click in the check boxes that correspond to the sides where you want the border to appear.

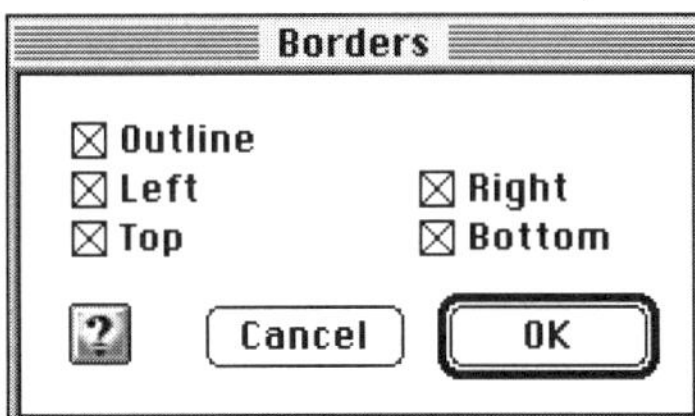

Figure 7.23 The Borders dialog box

4. Click the OK button or press Enter to apply the border and close the dialog box.

Adding Color to Borders

Once a cell has a border, you can give that border color. To add color to a border:

1. Select the cell or cells whose borders are to be colored.
2. If necessary, display the tool panel.
3. Choose the color from the pen color palette, as in Figure 7.24.

Adding Fill Colors and Patterns

Spreadsheet cells can accept fills colors and patterns but not textures or gradients. To add a fill color or pattern:

1. Select the cell or cells to be filled.
2. If necessary, display the tool panel.
3. Choose a color or pattern from the fill color or fill pattern palette, as in Figure 7.25.

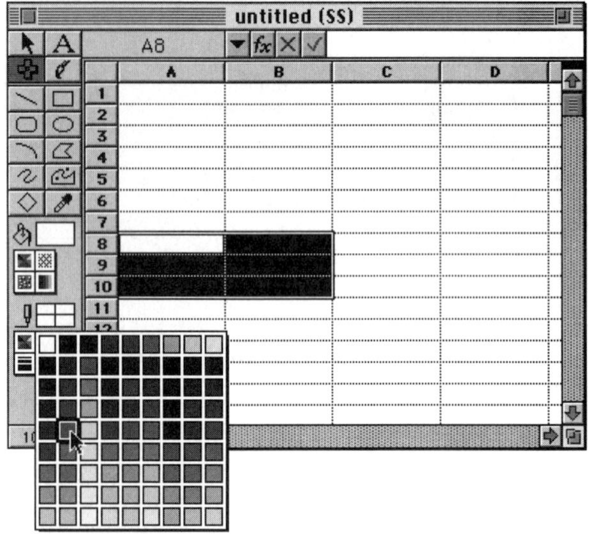

Figure 7.24 Adding color to cell borders

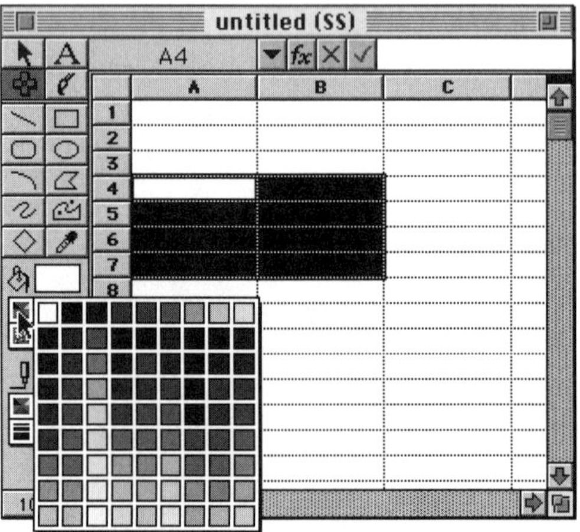

Figure 7.25 Adding fill color to a cell

For additional information on using the fill and pen palettes, see page 241 through page 248.

Be conservative in your use of color on a spreadsheet. Keep in mind that in most cases, text on top of color is hard to read. In addition, unless you use a color printer, color on a spreadsheet will be visible only on the screen and may make a printed black-and-white copy hard to read.

Sorting Rows

ClarisWorks can sort data in a range of cells. This is particularly handy if you want to maintain data in a specific order but it's not convenient to enter the data in that way. For example, a teacher might enter students into a spreadsheet as he or she grades papers. Once the grades have been entered, the teacher can sort the spreadsheet by the students' last names.

To sort spreadsheet cells:

1. Select the entire range of cells that should be sorted. As you can see in Figure 7.26, the selected range includes not only the column by which the data should be sorted (column A, the sort key) but all columns that should be included in the sort (columns B through H).

2.

Macintosh	Choose Calculate->Sort or press ⌘-J.
Windows	Choose Calculate->Sort, press CTRL-J, or press ALT-C, S.

The Sort dialog box appears (Figure 7.27).

gradesheet (SS)

A4 | Anderson

	A	B	C	D	E	F	G	H
1	Student grades	English 101						
2								
3			A1	A2	A3	Exam	Paper	Total
4	Anderson	Jane	85	100	85	100	94	95.8
5	Collins	Mary	75	80	75	80	75	78
6	Kahn	Craig	60	80	60	80	90	78
7	Davis	Tom	90	75	90	75	100	83
8	Eng	Will	75	100	75	100	100	95
9	Baker	Billy	100	95	100	95	75	92
10	Franklin	David	100	60	100	60	80	72
11	Harris	Ellen	80	80	80	80	83	80.6
12	Jackson	Amy	80	100	80	100	100	96
13	Lewis	David	75	80	75	80	95	82
14	Gamble	Jane	85	85	85	85	85	85
15								

Figure 7.26 Cells selected for sorting

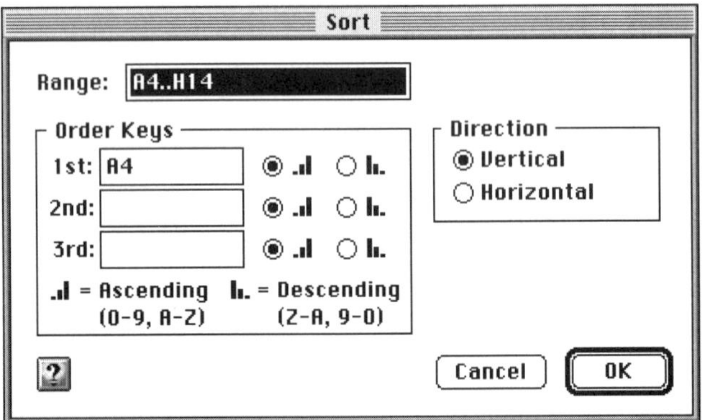

Figure 7.27 The Sort dialog box

3. ClarisWorks assumes that the top left corner of the selected range contains the first cell to be sorted (the outermost sort key). If this is not the case, change the cell address in the 1st box under the Order Keys section of the dialog box.

4. By default, ClarisWorks sorts in ascending order (.ıl = Ascending). If you want to sort in descending order, click the radio button next to the descending icon (lı. = Descending).

5. To sort by more than one key, enter the address of second sort key in the 2nd box and, if necessary, the address of a third sort key in the 3rd box. For example, if the gradesheet were to be sorted by last name and then first name, the 2nd box would contain B4, the first cell in the column containing the second sort key.

6. If necessary, choose ascending or descending sorting for the second and third sort keys.

7. By default, ClarisWorks assumes that the cells containing values on which the sort is to be based are in the column below the cell in the top left corner of the selected range. It therefore selects the Vertical radio button in the Directions section of the box. However, if the sort values are in the row of the cell in the top left corner of the selected range, click the Horizontal radio button.

8. Click the OK button or press Enter to close the dialog box and sort the spreadsheet.

Manipulating Cells

As you develop a spreadsheet, you may need to add or delete rows and columns. You might also need to move the contents of cells around the spreadsheet. In addition, the size of the values in a column may mean you need to change its width.

Larger font sizes often require taller rows. In this section you will therefore read about a variety of techniques for manipulating a spreadsheet's columns and rows.

Adding Rows

To add a new row:

1. Select the row above which you want to insert a new row by clicking on the row's number, as in Figure 7.28.

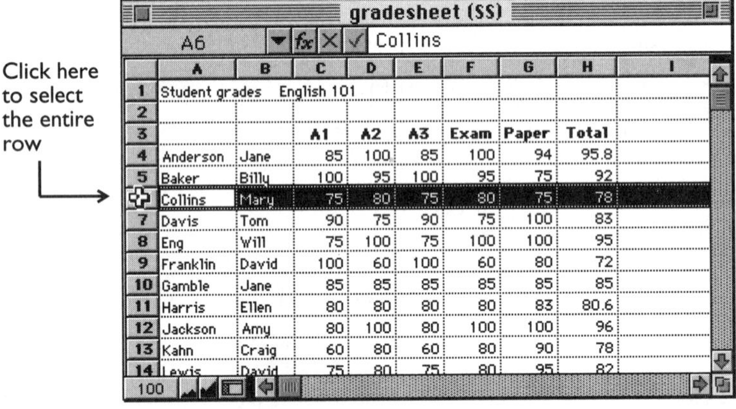

Figure 7.28 Selecting an entire row

2.

Macintosh	Choose Calculate->Insert Cells or press SHIFT-1 -I.
Windows	Choose Calculate->Insert Cells, press SHIFT-CTRL-I, or press ALT-C, I.

ClarisWorks inserts a new row above the selected row.

To insert more than one row or column at the same time, select the number of rows or columns you want to insert before issuing the Insert Cells command.

Adding Columns

To add a new column:

1. Select the column that will be to the left of the new column by clicking on its column letter, as in Figure 7.29.

Click here to select an entire colum

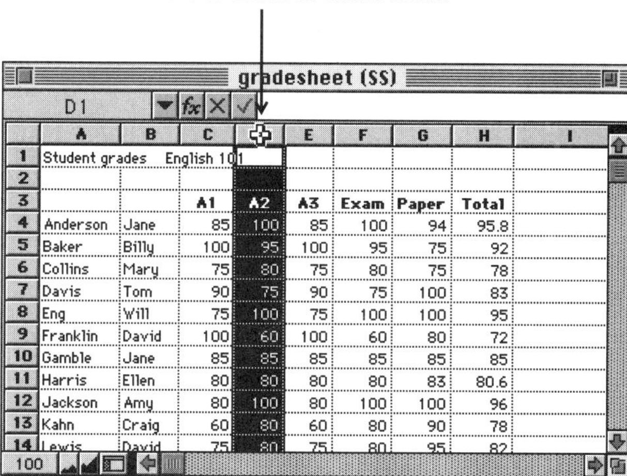

Figure 7.29 Selecting an entire column

2.

Macintosh	Choose Calculate->Insert Cells or press SHIFT-⌘-I.
Windows	Choose Calculate->Insert Cells, press SHIFT-CTRL-I, or press ALT-C, I.

ClarisWorks inserts a new column to the left of the selected column.

Deleting Rows and Columns

To delete rows or columns:

1. Select the rows or columns to be deleted.

2.

Macintosh	Choose Calculate->Delete Cells or press SHIFT-⌘-K.
Windows	Choose Calculate->Delete Cells, press SHIFT-CTRL-K, or press ALT-C, E

Moving Cells

You can move the contents of entire columns and rows or ranges of cells using Cut and Paste. If you are working on the Macintosh, you can also drag selected portions of a spreadsheet to a new location.

Moving with Cut and Paste

To move cells using Cut and Paste:

1. Select the rows, columns, or range whose contents you want to move.

2. If necessary, add new rows or columns to contain the cells being moved.

3. Cut the contents of the selected cells from the spreadsheet and onto the Clipboard. The selected cells themselves will be emptied and remain part of the spreadsheet.

4. Select the rows, columns, or range into which the cells will be placed.

If you are pasting a range of cells, rather than entire rows or columns, all you need to select is the top left cell of the area into which cell contents will be pasted.

5. Paste the contents of the Clipboard into the selected area of the spreadsheet.

Moving by Dragging (Macintosh Only)

To move rows, columns, or a selected range by dragging:

1. Select the rows, columns, or range of cells whose contents are to be moved.
2. If necessary, add rows or columns to contain the moved contents.
3. Drag the selected portion of the spreadsheet to its new location, as in Figure 7.30. The cells from which you drag will be left empty on the spreadsheet.

Resizing Columns

When a value is too wide to be displayed in a spreadsheet cell, ClarisWorks displays asterisks instead of the value (for example, see Figure 7.31). When that happens, you will need to make the column wide so the value can be seen.

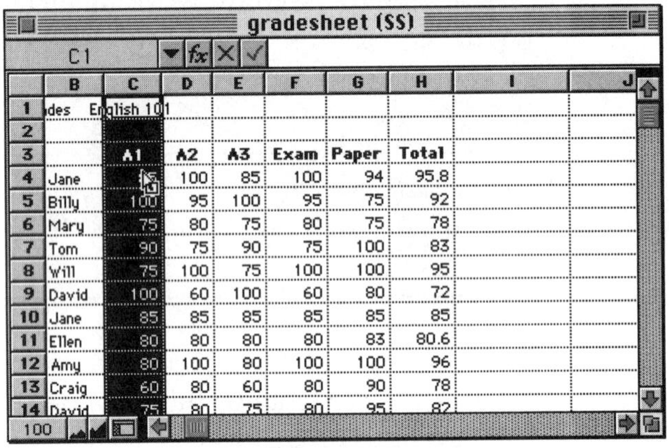

Figure 7.30 Dragging to move cell contents

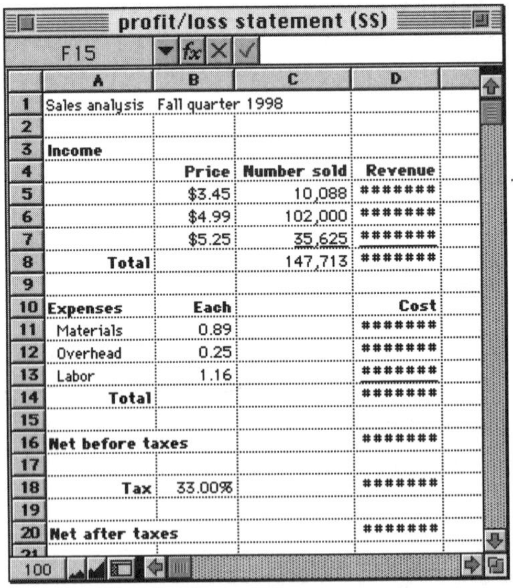

Figure 7.31 The default display of values that are too wide for a column

There are two ways to make columns wider. You can drag the cell border or you can specify a numeric width for the column.

To resize a column by dragging:

1. Move the mouse pointer over the border between two column letters. The mouse pointer changes shape, as in Figure 7.32.

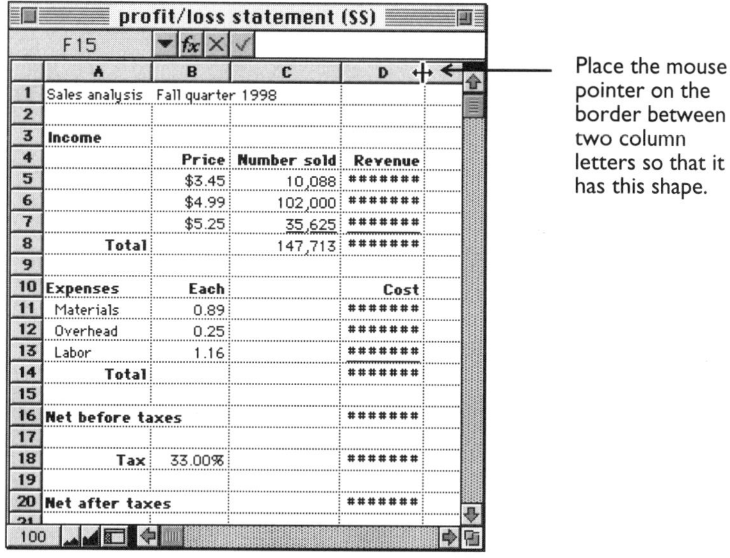

Figure 7.32 Dragging to enlarge a column

2. Drag the column border to the right to make the column wider. Drag the column border to the left to make the column smaller.

To resize a column by specifying a measurement:

1. Select the column or columns whose width you want to change.

2. Choose Format->Column Width. (Windows users can also press ALT-M, W.) The Column Width dialog box appears (Figure 7.33).

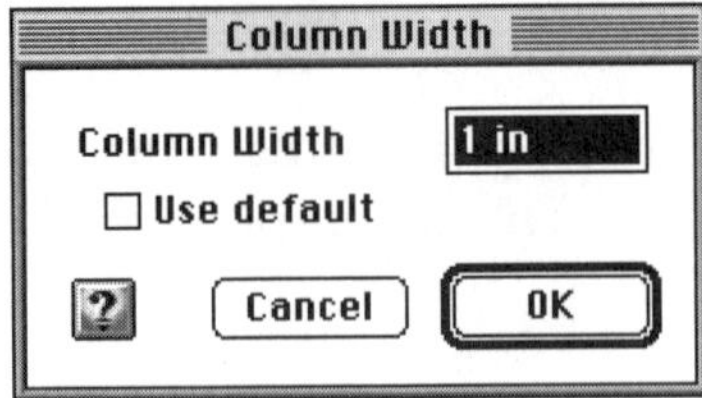

Figure 7.33 The Column Width dialog box

3. Enter the new width for the selected columns.

4. Click the OK button or press Enter. ClarisWorks closes the dialog box and resizes the selected columns.

Resizing Rows

When you increase the size of the font in a spreadsheet cell, the row doesn't automatically become taller to accommodate the bigger letters. You will therefore need to change the height of the row. As with changing column sizes, you can change a row's size by dragging or by specifying a measurement.

To change a row's height by dragging:

1. Move the mouse pointer over the border between two row numbers. The mouse pointer changes shape, as in Figure 7.34.

2. Drag the row border down to make the row taller. Drag the row border up to make the row smaller.

profit/loss statement (SS)

F19

	A	B	C	D
1	Sales analysis	Fall quarter 1998		
2				
3	**Income**			
4		**Price**	**Number sold**	**Revenue**
5		$3.45	10,088	$34,803.60
6		$4.99	102,000	$508,980.00
7		$5.25	35,625	$187,031.25
8	**Total**		147,713	$730,814.85
9				
10	**Expenses**	**Each**		**Cost**
11	Materials	0.89		$131,464.57
12	Overhead	0.25		$36,928.25
13	Labor	1.16		$171,347.08
14	**Total**			$339,739.90
15				
16	**Net before taxes**			$391,074.95
17				
18	**Tax**	33.00%		$129,054.73
19				
20	**Net after taxes**			$262,020.22
21				

Figure 7.34 Dragging to enlarge a row

To resize a row by specifying a measurement:

1. Select the row or rows whose height you want to change.

2. Choose Format->Row Height. (Windows users can also press ALT-M, H.) The Row Height dialog box appears (Figure 7.35).

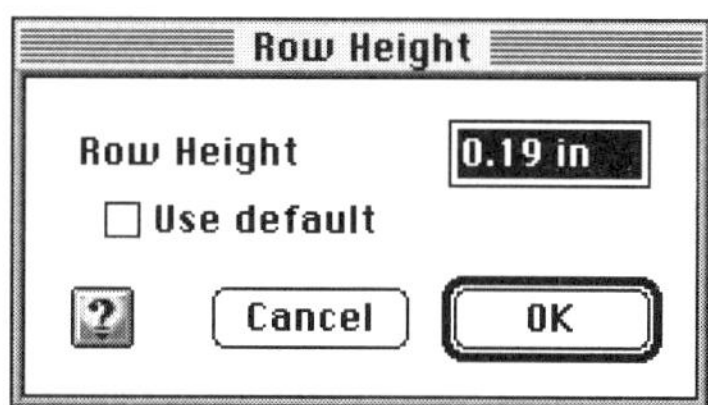

Figure 7.35 The Row Height dialog box

3. Enter the new height for the selected rows.

4. Click the OK button or press Enter. ClarisWorks closes the dialog box and resizes the selected rows.

Locking Parts of a Spreadsheet

The idea of "locking" parts of a spreadsheet means that you prevent parts of it from changing. You can lock individual cells or lock title rows and columns so they don't scroll with the rest of the spreadsheet.

Locking Cells

The contents of a locked cell can't be changed. You might, for example, choose to lock constants on which parts of a formula are based so that users don't change them accidentally.

To lock cells:

1. Select the cell or cells to be locked.

2.

Macintosh	Choose Options->Lock Cells or press ⌘-H.
Windows	Choose Options->Lock Cells, press CTRL-H, or press ALT-O, L.

To unlock cells so their contents can be modified again:

1. Select the cell or cells to be unlocked.

2.

Macintosh	Choose Options->Unlock Cells or press SHIFT-⌘-H.
Windows	Choose Options->Unlock Cells, press SHIFT-CTRL-H, or press ALT-O, U.

Locking Titles

A typical way to set up a spreadsheet is to place title information that labels the data at the top and left of the spreadsheet. Then you enter data to the right. The problem with this layout is that as you enter a great deal of data, you need to scroll the spreadsheet and the labels scroll out of sight. For example, in Figure 7.36, the names of students in a gradesheet have disappeared as the teacher scrolled the document to enter more grades.

gradesheet (SS)

A15

	D	E	F	G	H	I	J
1	1						
2							
3	A2	A3	A4	A5	Exam	Paper	Total
4	100	85	100	85	100	94	95.8
5	95	100	95	100	95	75	92
6	80	75	80	75	80	75	78
7	75	90	75	90	75	100	83
8	100	75	100	75	100	100	95
9	60	100	60	100	60	80	72
10	85	85	85	85	85	85	85
11	80	80	80	80	80	83	80.6
12	100	80	100	80	100	100	96
13	80	60	80	60	80	90	78
14	80	75	80	75	80	95	82
15							

100

Figure 7.36 Disappearing titles

The solution is to lock the title rows and columns in place so that when the rest of the spreadsheet scrolls, the teacher can still see the students' names. As you can see in Figure 7.37, columns A and B are still visible, even though the spreadsheet has been scrolled horizontally.

gradesheet (SS)

E12 | 80

	A	B	G	H	I	J
1	Student grades	Er				
2						
3			A5	Exam	Paper	Total
4	Anderson	Jane	85	100	94	95.8
5	Baker	Billy	100	95	75	92
6	Collins	Mary	75	80	75	78
7	Davis	Tom	90	75	100	83
8	Eng	Will	75	100	100	95
9	Franklin	David	100	60	80	72
10	Gamble	Jane	85	85	85	85
11	Harris	Ellen	80	80	83	80.6
12	Jackson	Amy	80	100	100	96
13	Kahn	Craig	60	80	90	78
14	Lewis	David	75	80	95	82
15						

100

Figure 7.37 The effect of locking titles

To lock either row or column titles:

1. Select adjacent rows or columns in which the titles appear, as in Figure 7.38.

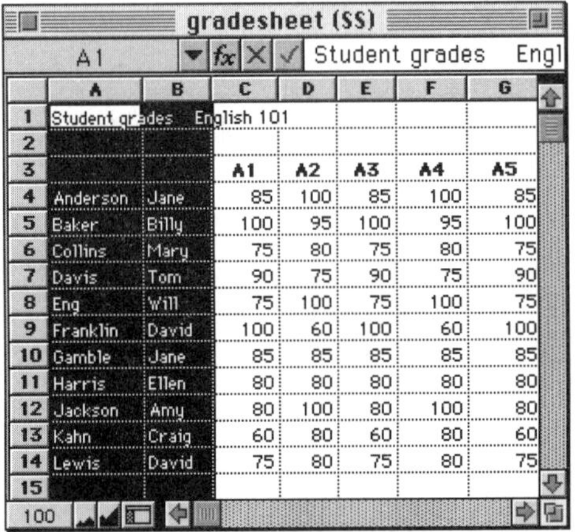

gradesheet (SS)

A1 | Student grades English 101

	A	B	C	D	E	F	G
1	Student grades	English 101					
2							
3			A1	A2	A3	A4	A5
4	Anderson	Jane	85	100	85	100	85
5	Baker	Billy	100	95	100	95	100
6	Collins	Mary	75	80	75	80	75
7	Davis	Tom	90	75	90	75	90
8	Eng	Will	75	100	75	100	75
9	Franklin	David	100	60	100	60	100
10	Gamble	Jane	85	85	85	85	85
11	Harris	Ellen	80	80	80	80	80
12	Jackson	Amy	80	100	80	100	80
13	Kahn	Craig	60	80	60	80	60
14	Lewis	David	75	80	75	80	75
15							

100

Figure 7.38 Selecting columns for title locking

2. Choose Options->Lock Title Position. (Windows users can also press ALT-O, T.) ClarisWorks places a check in front of the menu option.

You can lock either row titles or column titles but not both at the same time.

To unlock title rows or columns, choose Options->Lock Title Position once more.

Printing a Spreadsheet

For the most part, printing a spreadsheet is like printing any other document. However, unlike other documents, you can't specify a portion of a spreadsheet for printing with a page number. A spreadsheet has a rectangular organization rather than a linear page organization.

By default, ClarisWorks prints the rectangular area defined by all cells that contain data. However, if you want to print a different range, you need to set that print range *before* you issue the print command.

To set the print range:

1. Choose Options->Set Print Range. (Windows users can also press ALT-O, I.) The Print Range dialog box appears (Figure 7.39).

2. Click in the Print Cell Range radio button.

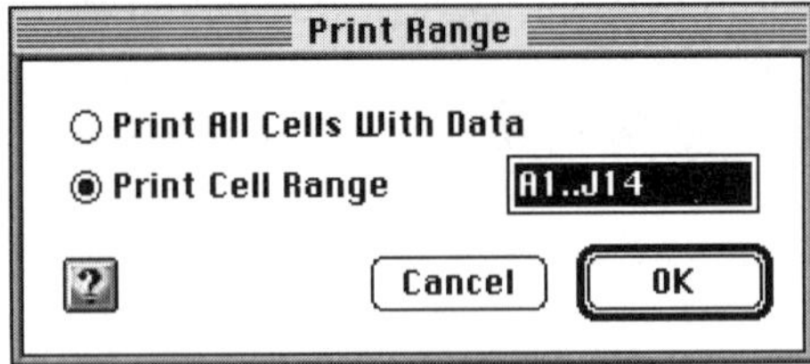

Figure 7.39 The Print Range db

3. Enter the range to be printed in the Cell Range box.

4. Click the OK button or press Enter to close the dialog box and set the print range.

If you select the range of cells to be printed before displaying the Print Range dialog box, ClarisWorks will select the Print Cell Range radio button for you and enter the selected range. Then, all you have to do is press Enter.

Previewing the Printed Page

The typical spreadsheet display shows you only the borders and body of the spreadsheet. You don't see the margins of the page on which the spreadsheet will be printed. However, if you want to see the entire page, do the following:

Macintosh	Choose Window->Page View or press SHIFT-⌘-P.
Windows	Choose Window->Page View, press AHIFT-CTRL-P, or press ALT-W, -P.

To exit page view mode and return to seeing just the spreadsheet borders and body, repeat the preceding command.

Adding Headers and Footers

Much like a word processing document, a spreadsheet document can have page headers and footers. Headers and footers are visible only in page view mode. However, once you have added them to a spreadsheet document, they remain in place even after exiting page view mode.

For information on adding, modifying, and removing headers and footers, see page 132 through page 135.

Adjusting the Spreadsheet Display

Although the grid lines that separate cells in a spreadsheet are very useful when you are preparing the spreadsheet for use, you may not want those lines to appear when you print the spreadsheet. ClarisWorks therefore lets you hide a variety of elements of the spreadsheet displays, including the grid lines, the column letters, and the row numbers.

To adjust the spreadsheet display:

1. Choose Options->Display. (Windows users can also press ALT-O, D.) The Display dialog box appears (Figure 7.40).

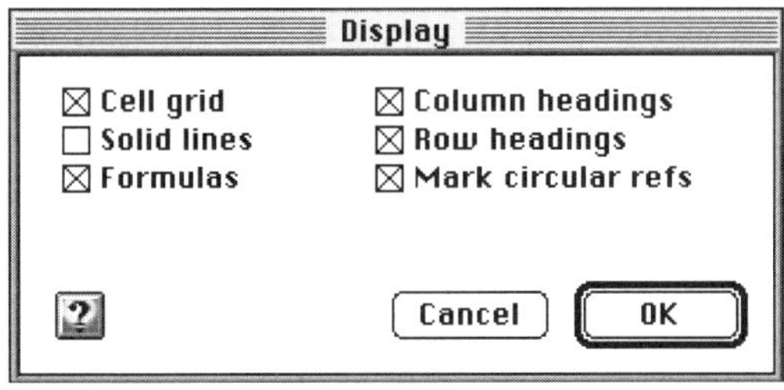

Figure 7.40 The Display dialog box

2. Place a check mark in each check box that represents something you would like to see on the spreadsheet.

3. Click the OK button or press Enter to make the changes to the spreadsheet display and close the dialog box.

The options available in the Display dialog box are:

- Cell grid: When this box is checked, you will see dotted lines around each cell.

- Solid lines: When this box is checked, the dotted lines surrounding the cells are replaced with solid lines. This check box is available only when the Cell grid check box is checked.

- Fomulas: As you saw earlier in this chapter, when the Formulas box is checked, the spreadsheet body displays formulas rather than the results of formulas.

- Column headings: When this box is checked, you will see the column letters.

- Row headings: When this box is checked, you will see the row numbers.

- Circular references: A *circular reference* is a formula that in some way uses itself in its formula. A spreadsheet cannot evaluate this type of formula. When this box is checked, cells containing circular references will be surrounded by ovals so that you can find them easily and make changes to remove the problem.

Spreadsheet Charts

As well as performing calculations with data, spreadsheets can draw graphs — known as *charts* — using stored data. Because charts make it easy to visualize data quickly, they are used frequently to summarize spreadsheet contents.

Assume, for example, that we are working with the simple sales summary spreadsheet in Figure 7.41. The spreadsheet contains the number of units of something sold by each salesperson in each quarter of the preceding year. Notice that the labels (the names of the salespeople and the quarters) are in rows and cells adjacent to the data. This type of layout is important for simplifying generating charts.

sales summary (SS)

D15

	A	B	C	D	E	F
1	**Sales Summary**					
2						
3	**Salesperson**	**Units Sold Per Quarter**				
4		**Q1**	**Q2**	**Q3**	**Q4**	
5	Martin, Mary	10,000	9,500	10,000	10,500	
6	Jones, Sam	9,000	9,500	10,000	9,500	
7	Hilton, Jonathan	10,100	11,000	9,500	8,500	
8	Willis, Ellen	10,000	9,000	9,500	11,000	
9	**Totals:**	39,100	39,000	39,000	39,500	156,600
10						

100

Figure 7.41 A sales summary spreadsheet.

One easy way to view the company's performance is to create a chart summarizing sales. In Figure 7.42, for example, you can see the total units sold per quarter. From that chart you can tell that although the number of units sold by each salesperson varied slightly from one quarter to the next, their performance was, on average, about the same. The bad news for this company is that the total height of the bars indicates that sales didn't really grow in the preceding year.

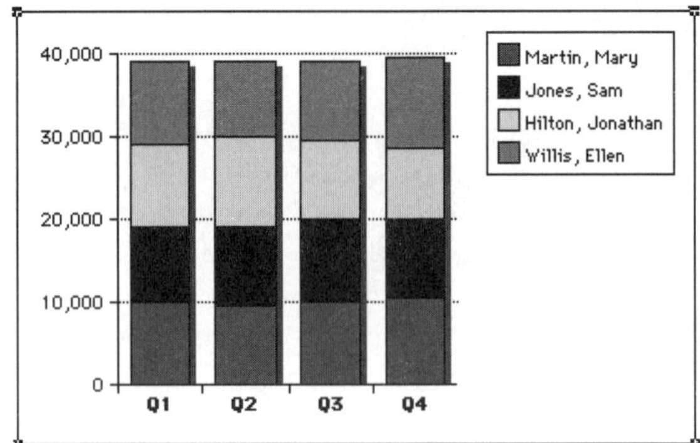

Figure 7.42 A stacked bar chart

If we want to compare the performance of the individual salespeople, then we probably want a chart like Figure 7.43. Now we can see that Sam Jones didn't do quite as well as his co-workers.

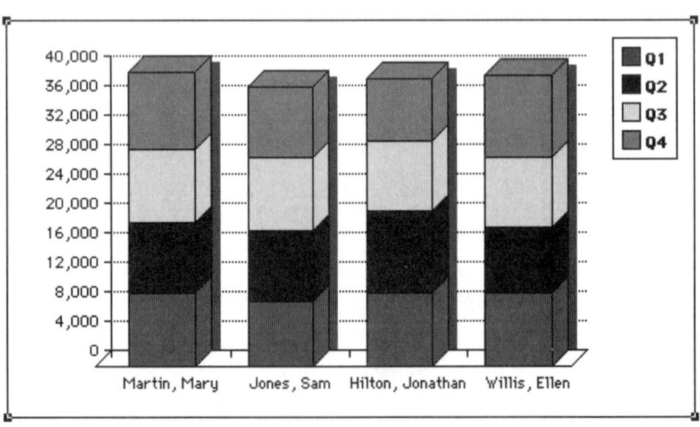

Figure 7.43 A second stacked bar chart

A spreadsheet chart is linked to the cells on the spreadsheet from which its data series are taken. This means that if you change the data on the spreadsheet, ClarisWorks will automatically update the chart.

A spreadsheet chart is a graphic object that floats above the body of the spreadsheet. When a chart is selected, ClarisWorks provides you with the drawing menus. The chart therefore can be modified using many of the drawing techniques discussed in Chapter 5. As you will see shortly, there are also some special techniques used to specify the look of elements of a chart.

Anatomy of a Spreadsheet Chart

A spreadsheet chart has some special vocabulary that describes the various elements in the chart (see Figure 7.44). First, most charts are plotted using two axes, called X (horizontal) and Y (vertical). In Figure 7.44, the tick marks on the Y axis represent the number of units sold. The X axis represents the individual salespeople.

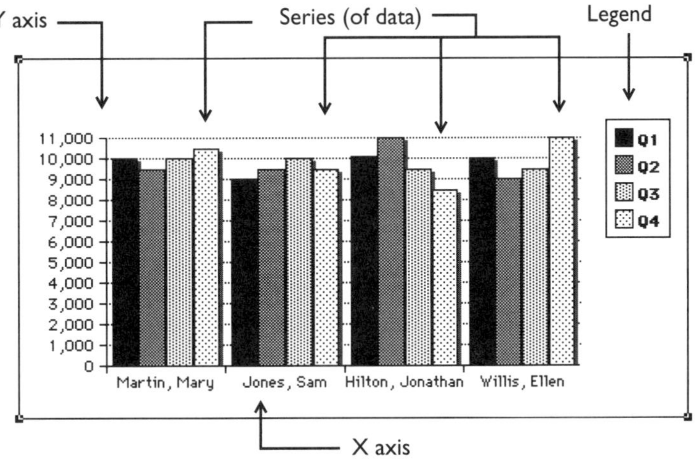

Figure 7.44 The parts of a spreadsheet chart

The divisions on an axis can represent either continuous data, such as the number of units sold, or discrete data, such as people. It is up to you to choose the correct type of chart for continuous or discrete data.

Each group of data in the chart — for example, all the sales for one quarter or all the sales made by one salesperson — is known as a *series*. A series of data is taken from one spreadsheet row or one spreadsheet column. (You choose the direction when you create the chart.)

The chart's *legend* provides a directory for the meaning of the contents of the chart. In Figure 7.44, for example, the legend tells you the pattern assigned to bars representing sales from a given quarter. The legend therefore identifies each data series in the chart.

The tick marks in the Y axis are labeled automatically based on the range of data values in all series plotted on the chart. The X axis and legend labels are taken from the spreadsheet itself in a manner you will see shortly.

Preparing to Create a Chart

The first step in creating a chart is to make sure that the underlying spreadsheet is set up properly. As mentioned earlier, the spreadsheet in Figure 7.41 has been laid out with no intervening columns between the salespeople's names and the data. By the same token, the column labels are in the row directly above the data. This type of layout greatly simplifies chart creation because ClarisWorks can automatically label the X axis and put the series names in the legend.

Assuming your spreadsheet is designed properly, you can then begin to create the chart:

1. Select the cells in the spreadsheet that contain the X axis labels, the data series, and the series names that should appear in the legend, as in Figure 7.45.

sales summary (SS)

A4

	A	B	C	D	E	F
1	Sales Summary					
2						
3	Salesperson	Units Sold Per Quarter				
4		Q1	Q2	Q3	Q4	
5	Martin, Mary	10,000	9,500	10,000	10,500	
6	Jones, Sam	9,000	9,500	10,000	9,500	
7	Hilton, Jonathan	10,100	11,000	9,500	8,500	
8	Willis, Ellen	10,000	9,000	9,500	11,000	
9	Totals:	39,100	39,000	39,000	39,500	156,600
10						

100

Figure 7.45 Selecting a spreadsheet range for charting

2.

Macintosh	Choose Options->Make Chart of press 1-M.
Windows	Choose Options->Make Chart, press CTRL-M, or press ALT-O, C.

The Chart Options dialog box appears, presenting you with a wide variety of options for designing and labeling the chart. Each of the buttons in the dialog box selects a different panel of options.

3. Select the button that brings up the panel containing options you want to set. (Each panel will be discussed in the following sections of this chapter.)

4. Make any needed changes.

5. Click the OK button or press Enter to apply the changes and close the dialog box.

Once you've created a chart, you can display the Chart Options dialog box by double-clicking on the chart. You can then make any changes you want to the chart. The specific panel that you see when double-clicking depends on where you click on the chart. For example, if you click on the Y axis, you will see the Axes panel. If you click on a bar, line, or other piece of plotted data, you will see the General panel.

You can create any number of charts for a spreadsheet document. Each chart is a distinct graphics object that floats above the spreadsheet. When you add a new chart, it is placed on top of all other charts, just as a new object added to a drawing is "on top of" all other objects in the drawing. You can change the layering of overlapping chart objects in the same way as you change layering of objects in a drawing (see page 236).

Choosing the Chart Type (the Gallery Panel)

The first thing you should do when creating a chart is decide which type of chart to use. As you can see in Figure 7.46, ClarisWorks can create 12 different types of charts, not all of which are appropriate for all types of data.

Some of the more commonly used chart types, and the kinds of data for which they are appropriate, include the following

- For discrete data, where the series include data related to distinct units such as people or products, use a bar, stacked bar, pictogram, or stacked pictogram chart (for example, Figure 7.47).

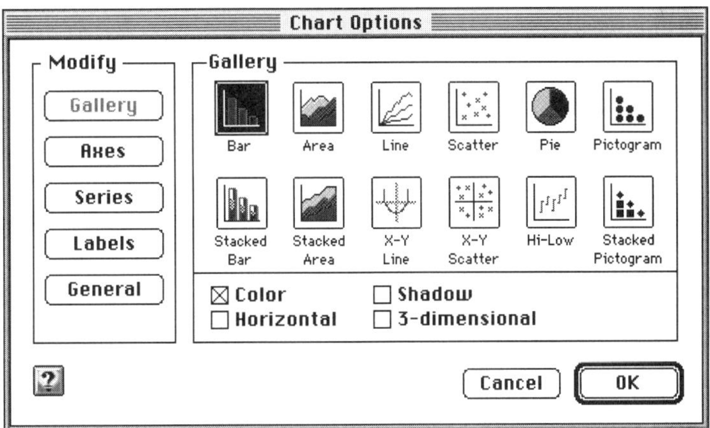

Figure 7.46 ClarisWorks chart types

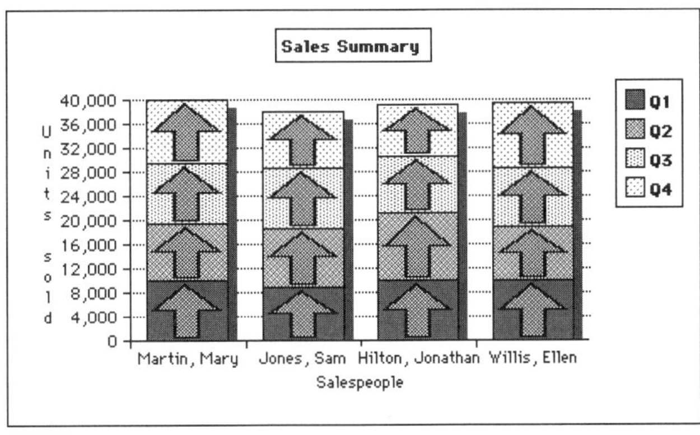

Figure 7.47 A stacked pictogram chart

- For continuous data, such as stock prices throughout a week or temperatures measured over several days, you can use line or area graphs. Bar, stacked bar, pictogram, and stacked pictogram charts may also be appropriate.

- Each pie chart graphs only one series of data. Pie charts are therefore useful for viewing proportions of a whole. For example, pie charts created from the sales summary spreadsheet we have been using as an example would show the percentage of a salesperson's total sales that were made in each quarter (Figure 7.48).

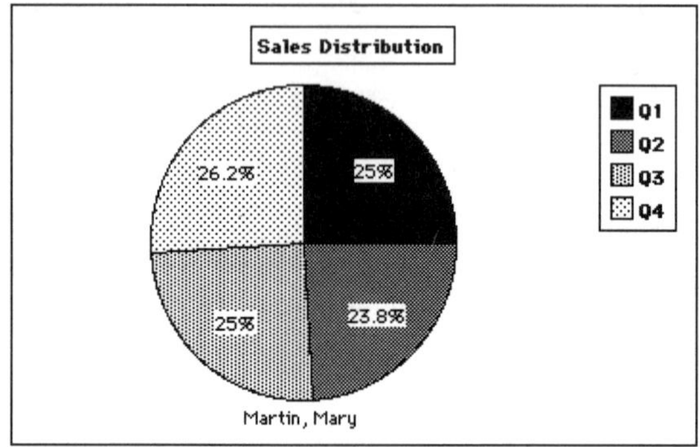

Figure 7.48 A pie chart

There are check boxes at the bottom of the Gallery panel that apply to the currently selected type of chart. (These vary somewhat from one type of chart to another.)

- The Color check box, which appears for all types of charts, determines whether the graph will use colors (box checked) or patterns (box not checked) to distinguish between the series in a graph.

- Checking the Horizontal check box turns most graphs 45°, transposing the X and Y axes.

- Checking the Shadow check box adds a shadow to whatever lines, bars, or other shapes appear in the chart.

- Checking the 3-dimensional check box gives a three-dimensional appearance to whatever shapes appear in the chart.

- The Tilt check box, which appears for pie charts only, determines whether the pie is visible from the top (box not checked) or from the side (box checked.)

Setting General Chart Characteristics

As you can see in Figure 7.49, a chart's General options let you change the range of cells used in the chart and determine whether the series are defined by the columns or rows in the selected range. By default, ClarisWorks defines series in columns; click the Rows radio button to change the definition to rows of data.

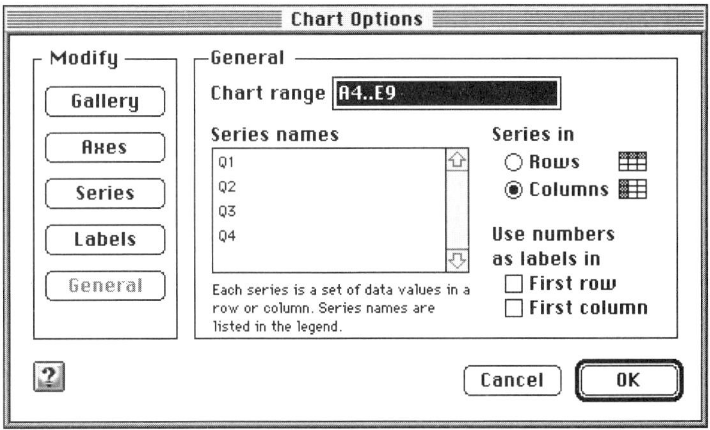

Figure 7.49 General chart options

You have already seen one example of the difference between defining the data series as columns or rows earlier in this chapter. In Figure 7.42, the series were defined by rows; in Figure 7.43, the series were defined by columns. The chart in Figure 7.42 therefore provides an analysis by quarter (one series for each salesperson containing data for all quarters), whereas the chart in Figure 7.43 provides an analysis by salesperson (one series for each quarter containing data for all salespeole).

To help make this a bit clearer, take a look at the line chart in Figure 7.50, which compares daily high temperatures for 3 weeks. Although we are viewing the temperatures by day along the X axis, each series contains a single week's temperature readings and is therefore represented by one line. Assuming that the spreadsheet is set up as in Figure 7.51, then the series for the chart have been defined by the columns.

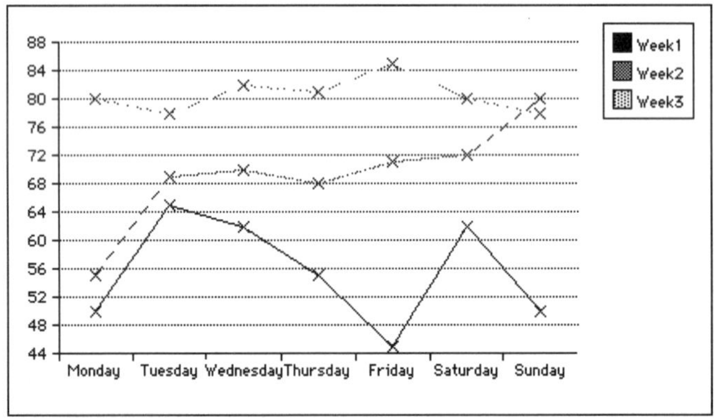

Figure 7.50 A line chart

The General options panel also includes two check boxes labeled "First row" and "Second row." These appear because if the labels you want for the series happen to be numbers, rather than words, ClarisWorks will assume the numbers are part of your data. Therefore if you are defining series by rows and your series labels are numeric, the labels will be in the First column. If you are defining series by columns and your series labels are numeric, the labels will be in the First row.

temperatures (SS)

	A	B	C	D
2				
3		Week1	Week2	Week3
4	Monday	50	55	80
5	Tuesday	65	69	78
6	Wednesday	62	70	82
7	Thursday	55	68	81
8	Friday	45	71	85
9	Saturday	62	72	80
10	Sunday	50	80	78

Figure 7.51 The temperatures spreadsheet

As an example, look at Figure 7.52. The series labels are the various prices charged for a product. However, when the column containing those prices is selected for inclusion in a chart, ClarisWorks can't tell the difference between the prices and the number of units sold during the four quarters on the spreadsheet. (As far as ClarisWorks is concerned, a number is a number is a number … .)

In this case, the series are defined by the rows. (Each row contains the data for 1 year.) Therefore, the series labels are defined as the values in the first column of the range.

Configuring the Axes

The Axis panel in the Chart Options dialog box (Figure 7.53) lets you place a label on each axis and configure the calibration of each axis. You work with each axis separately. Click on the X axis or Y axis radio button at the top of the panel to determine which axis you want to affect.

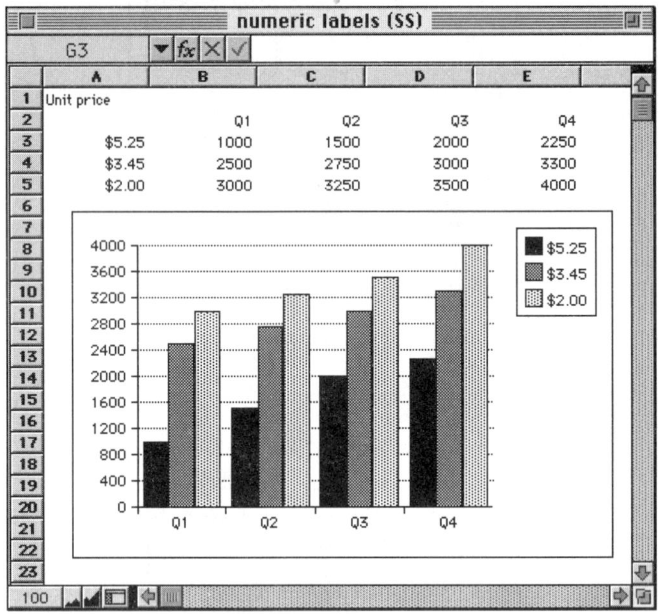

Figure 7.52 Numeric series labels

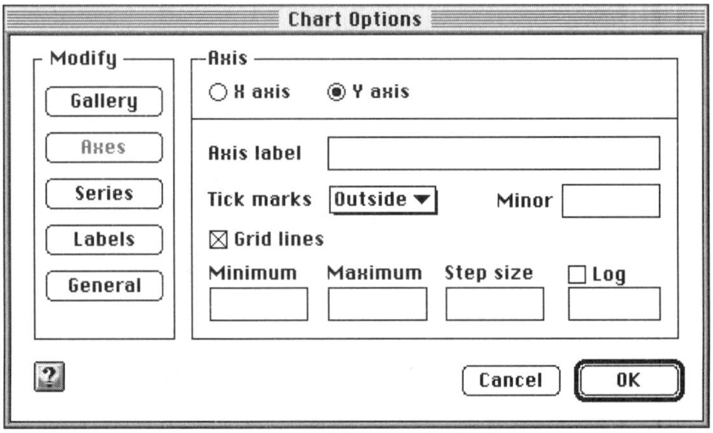

Chart Options

Modify
Gallery
Axes
Series
Labels
General

Axis
X axis
Y axis
Axis label
Tick marks Outside
Minor
Grid lines
Minimum Maximum Step size Log
Cancel
OK

Figure 7.53 Chart axis options

Once you have chosen the axis with which you want to work, you can do the following:

- Set an axis label: Type the label in the Axis label edit box. By default, a Y axis label appears vertically to the left of the Y axis. An X axis label appears horizontally underneath the X axis, as in Figure 7.54.

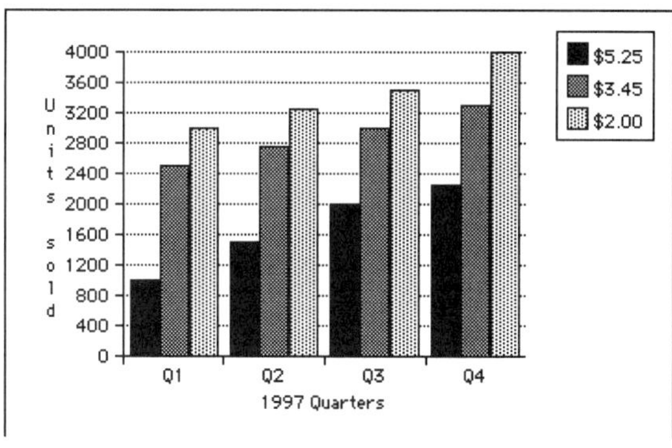

Figure 7.54 A chart with labeled axes

- Modify the scaling and/or calibration of an axis. For example, by default ClarisWorks calibrates the Y axis by taking the highest and lowest values in the range of data being graphed and then dividing that range into equal intervals. To change that calibration:
  - Enter a new minimum value for the axis in the Minimum edit box.
  - Enter a new maximum value for the axis in the Maximum edit box.
  - Edit the distance between grid marks on the axis in the Step size edit box.

- If you want a logarithmic scale for the axis, check the Log check box and enter the base of the logarithm (by default, 10) in the Log edit box.

- To change the tick marks on an axis, make a choice from the Tick marks menu. You can remove tick marks altogether or display them on the outside of the axis, the inside of the axis, or across the axis.
- If you want to remove the grid lines from the chart (for example, the horizontal grid lines that appear in Figure 7.54), remove the check from the Grid lines check box.

Configuring Data Series

The Series panel (Figure 7.55) allows you to configure how you want the data series on your chart to appear. By carefully making choices from this panel, you can actually combine more than one chart type (for example, a bar chart and a line chart). You can also display data values on the chart itself.

To configure the series on a chart:

1. Determine which series on the chart will be affected by changes that you make by choosing the series from the Edit series menu. To affect all series, choose the All option; otherwise, choose just one series.
2. Choose the type of display to be used for the selected series from the Display as menu. Even if you have selected a bar chart for the entire graph, you can use this menu to set the display type for a single series to something else, such as line or pictogram.

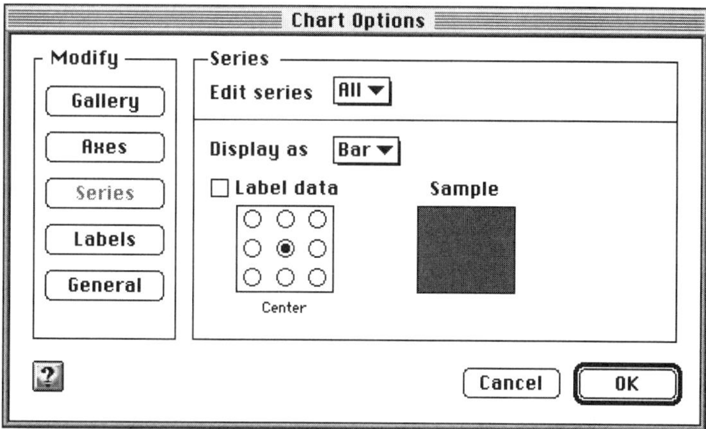

Figure 7.55 Setting series options

3. If you want to see the data values of each symbol on a chart, click the Label data check box. Then, click one of the radio buttons in the grid of nine below the check to determine where the data will appear within the symbol.

Adding Labels

As a finishing touch to your chart, you may want to add a title, letting the spreadsheet user know exactly what the chart represents. The Labels panel (Figure 7.56) lets you add a chart label and also determine whether and where the legend appears.

To add a title to a chart:

1. Enter the title in the Title edit box.

2. Choose the position of the title by clicking a radio button to the right of the Title edit box.

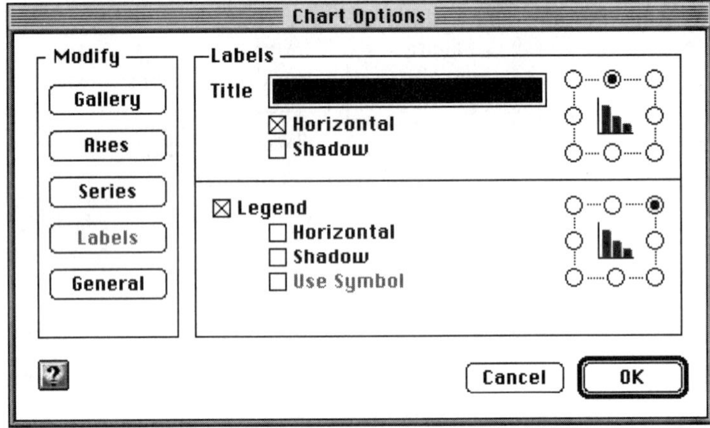

Figure 7.56 Adding chart labels

3. If the title will appear on the top or bottom of the chart, leave the Horizontal check box checked. However, if the title will appear on either side of the chart, remove the check from the Horizontal check box so that the title will appear vertically.

4. Check the Shadow box to give the title a drop shadow, as in Figure 7.57.

By default, ClarisWorks includes a legend on a chart and places it in the upper right corner of the chart. You can change those options in the following ways:

- Remove the legend entirely by removing the check from the Legend check box.

- Change the position of the legend by clicking one of the radio buttons in the square in the lower right corner of the Titles panel.

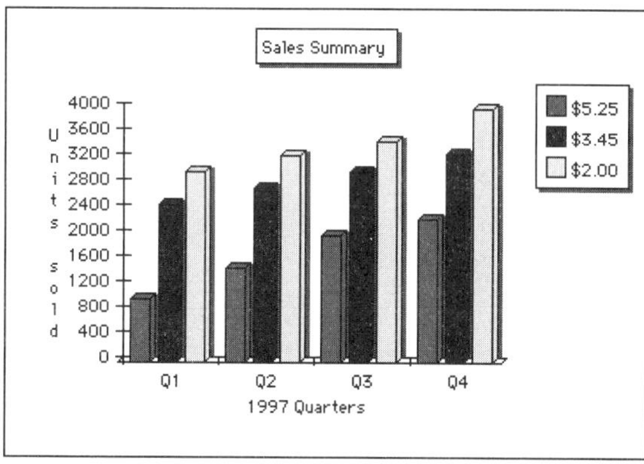

Figure 7.57 A chart containing a title

- Change the position of the elements in the legend from vertical (the default) to horizontal by clicking the Horizontal check box. This option is appropriate when the legend is displayed along the top or bottom of the chart, rather than in one of the corners.

- Give the legend a drop shadow, as it has in Figure 7.57, by clicking the Shadow check box.

Adding Frames to Spreadsheets

A spreadsheet document can include word processing and painting frames. It can also include drawing objects. Any frame or object that you add to a spreadsheet floats on top of the spreadsheet, just like a spreadsheet chart. Once a frame or object is placed on the spreadsheet, you can modify it using the tools appropriate for the type of frame or object (for example, word processing tools for a word processing frame and painting tools for a painting frame).

To add a frame or graphic object to a spreadsheet:

1. If necessary, display the tool panel.
2. For a word processing frame, click on the text tool [A]. For a painting frame, click on the paint tool [paint tool]. For a graphic object, click on the graphic tool that represents the shape you want to draw (for example, the rectangle or polygon tool).
3. Move the mouse pointer over the body of the spreadsheet and drag to draw the frame or graphic object.
4. Modify the contents of the frame or graphic object as desired.

Keep in mind that word processing and painting frames are handled as individual objects when placed in a spreadsheet document. This means that when you move them or change their position in the object layering stack, you affect the entire frame as a unit.

Spreadsheets in Other Documents

Spreadsheet frames can be placed in word processing, drawing, and painting documents. When inside a word processing or drawing document, spreadsheet frames retain their identity as spreadsheets and can be modified at any time. However, a spreadsheet in a painting document becomes a part of the painting's bit map as soon as you click the mouse pointer outside the spreadsheet frame. It therefore loses its identity as a spreadsheet, becoming incapable of performing calculations, creating charts, and so on. In other words, it becomes a painting of a spreadsheet rather than a live, functional spreadsheet. Modifications to it are no different from modifications to any other portion of a painting's bit map.

Once you have placed a spreadsheet frame in a word processing or drawing document, you can work with that frame as if it were a stand-alone spreadsheet document. In particular, this means that you can create charts from that spreadsheet frame. The charts become objects that you can place anywhere in the parent document you like. As long as the spreadsheet frame and the charts are in the same document, the charts remain linked to the spreadsheet. Any changes you make to graphed values in the spreadsheet frame will be automatically reflected in the chart.

Because spreadsheet frames act like graphic objects in word processing and drawing documents, you can adjust their layering and text wrap characteristics. For example, in Figure 7.58, the text wrap has been turned on so that text flows around — rather than on top of — the spreadsheet frame and chart.

Working with Spreadsheet Frames

To place a spreadsheet frame in a word processing, drawing, or painting document:

1. If necessary, display the tool panel.
2. Click on the spreadsheet tool.
3. Move the mouse pointer into the document body.
4. Drag to set the size of the spreadsheet frame.

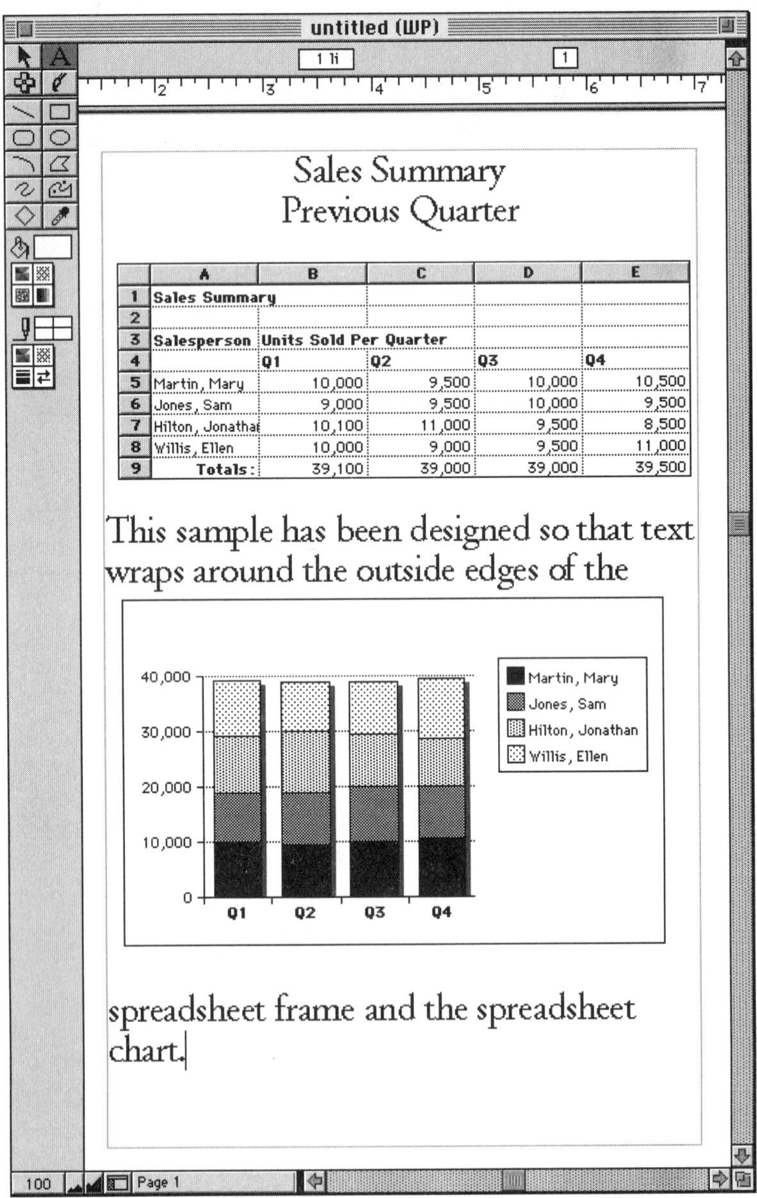

untitled (WP)

Sales Summary
Previous Quarter

	A	B	C	D	E
1	**Sales Summary**				
2					
3	**Salesperson**	**Units Sold Per Quarter**			
4		**Q1**	**Q2**	**Q3**	**Q4**
5	Martin, Mary	10,000	9,500	10,000	10,500
6	Jones, Sam	9,000	9,500	10,000	9,500
7	Hilton, Jonatha	10,100	11,000	9,500	8,500
8	Willis, Ellen	10,000	9,000	9,500	11,000
9	**Totals:**	39,100	39,000	39,000	39,500

This sample has been designed so that text wraps around the outside edges of the spreadsheet frame and the spreadsheet chart.

Figure 7.58 A spreadsheet frame and chart in a word processing document

If you are working in a painting document, the size of a spreadsheet frame can't be changed once you have finished your initial drag. However, the size of spreadsheet frames placed in word processing or drawing documents can be changed at any time by selecting the frame and dragging one of its corners.

5. Use any of the techniques discussed in this chapter to modify the contents of the spreadsheet frame and to create charts from it.

Using Spreadsheet Frames as Tables

In addition to acting like stand-alone spreadsheet documents, spreadsheets can be used in word processing documents to format tables. Because a spreadsheet cell can contain text as well as numbers, you can take advantage of the spreadsheet's grid organization to make it easy to line up elements in a table. For example, the table in Figure 7.59 is actually a spreadsheet frame for which the grid lines, column letters, and row numbers have been hidden.

There are two general strategies for creating tables:

- Open a spreadsheet document and create the table, formatting it as needed. When the table is formatted as you would like, create a spreadsheet frame in the word processing document. Then copy the contents of the table from the spreadsheet document into the spreadsheet frame.

- Create a spreadsheet frame in the word processing document. Format the table while the frame is sitting in the word processing document.

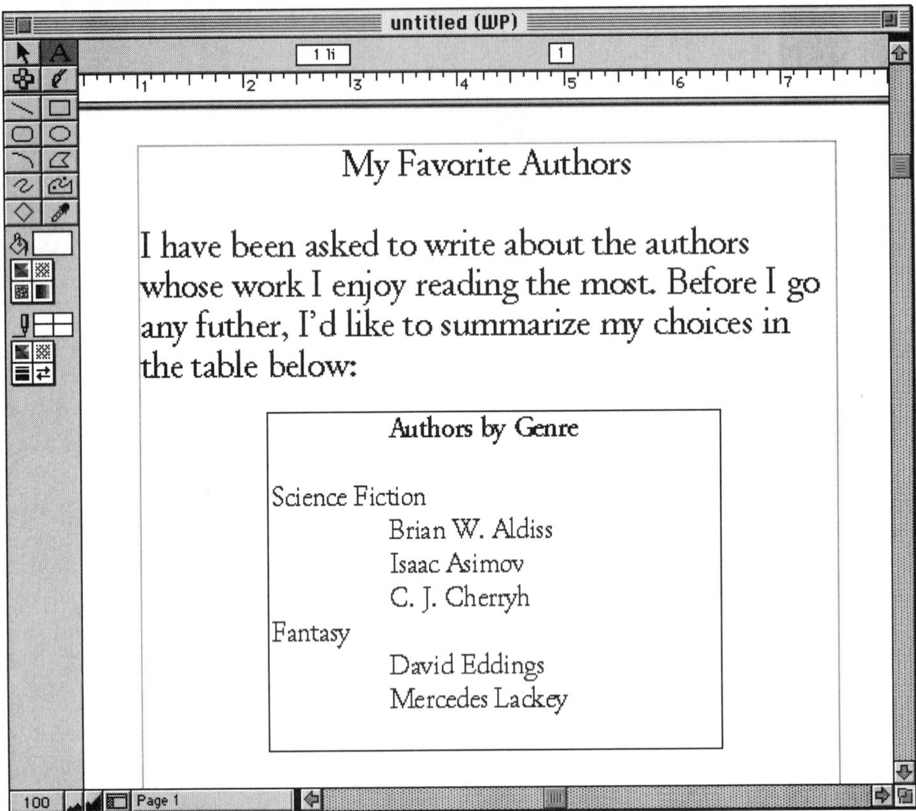

Figure 7.59 A spreadsheet frame used as a table

You can create style sheets for tables to make common table formatting easier. When you give a new style sheet a type of Table, you will have access to the spreadsheet menus so that you can set characteristics such as table and cell borders, number formatting, and cell alignment. For details on creating and using style sheets, see page 146 through page 155.

8

Data Management Basics

The ClarisWorks database module lets you store, modify, search, and format lists of data. You might, for example, use the database module to manage an address book, the roster of players on a ball team, or the customers that a salesperson gets in touch with regularly.

In this chapter you will learn how the ClarisWorks database module organizes data and how you can prepare screen layouts for entering, modifying, and finding data.

But first, it is vital that you understand exactly what the ClarisWorks database module can do and what it can't do. The trick to getting the most out of this module is using it for the right purposes and not trying to force it to do something it can't.

Understanding Data Management

The term *database* is one of the most misunderstood in all of personal computing. The results have been the misuse of a great deal of data management software and users who are frustrated because either their software won't do what they want or they have a great deal of inaccurate, inconsistent data in their files.

To understand exactly what a database is, let's first look at the kinds of things about which we might want to store data. If we were running a mail-order company, for example, we would need to store data about our products, our customers, and the orders the customers place. In database terms, each of these things is an *entity*.

Entities have properties (or *attributes*) that describe them. For example, a customer entity might have a customer number, name, address, and telephone number. We represent an entity in a database by storing values for the entity's attributes.

However, it isn't enough just to represent the entities. If our mail-order database is to be useful, we need to know which customers placed which orders and which products appear on which orders. In other words, we need to store information about how the entities relate to one another.

A database must therefore store two things: data describing the entities stored in the database *and* information about the relationships between the entities. Any file or group of files that is to be considered a database must include both of these elements.

The software that manipulates the data stored in a database is known as a *database management system*, or DBMS. To be considered a DBMS, software must be able not only to store and retrieve data but also to retrieve data on the basis of stored relationships between entities. For example, it must be able to answer data retrieval requests such as "Show me all the orders placed by Customer #6."

The ClarisWorks database module creates a data file that stores data along with tools for viewing the data in many ways. However, it does not store data relationships. This means that each new ClarisWorks database file you create is really designed to manipulate data about one entity at a time. It is therefore not really a database but a data file. The ClarisWorks database module isn't a substitute for a DBMS; it is a what is more correctly called a *file manager*.

The ClarisWorks database module is most effective when you use it to handle data about one entity at a time. Mailing lists, rosters, customer lists, simple inventories — all of these are good uses for this module. However, if you attempt to place more than one entity in a single file, you will eventually run into problems with unnecessary duplicated data and other data inconsistencies.

If you find that your data management needs require data relationships, then consider migrating to a DBMS. The easiest transition from ClarisWorks is probably to FileMaker Pro, a Claris DBMS with an interface much like the ClarisWorks database module. If you decide that FileMaker Pro isn't flexible enough, consider either Helix Express or 4th Dimension, both of which are high-end, programmable DBMSs.

The ClarisWorks Data Management Environment

When you work with a word processing, painting, drawing, or spreadsheet document, each file contains a single document. Where a ClarisWorks database file is concerned, however, the term *document* really doesn't apply. Each database file contains a group of elements for working with a collection of data.

ClarisWorks can store all of the following inside a single database file:

- Definitions of the types of data stored in the file. These are called *fields*. ("Field" is a file manager's term for an attribute.)
- Characteristics of the fields (field options), such as whether values are required or whether values must be within a given range.
- Data values for the fields. The data that describe each individual entity stored in the database are grouped into *records*.
- One or more *layouts* that format the data for viewing. For example, in Figure 8.1 you can see a portion of a mailing list being viewed through a layout that is prepared for printing mailing labels.
- One or more ways to sort the data.
- One or more ways to search the data.
- One or more report specifications that combine a layout, a sort, and a search.

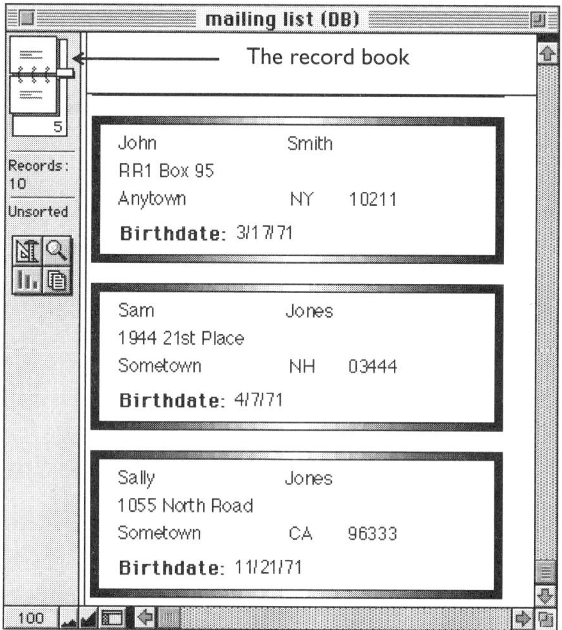

Figure 8.1 Mailing list data viewing through a layout in browse mode

A database document can be viewed in one of four ways:

- Browse mode: Browse mode, which appears in Figure 8.1, lets you view and modify data. The tool panel contains a book for moving through records one at a time, in order. The tool panel also tells you how many records are in the file and, if some of those records have been selected in a search, how many are currently visible. The palette of four tools in the middle of the tool panel provides access to layouts, searches, sorts, and reports.

- Layout mode: You use layout mode to design layout formats. As you can see in Figure 8.2, layout mode provides you with a drawing tool panel so that you can manipulate the objects on a layout just as you would manipulate objects in a drawing.

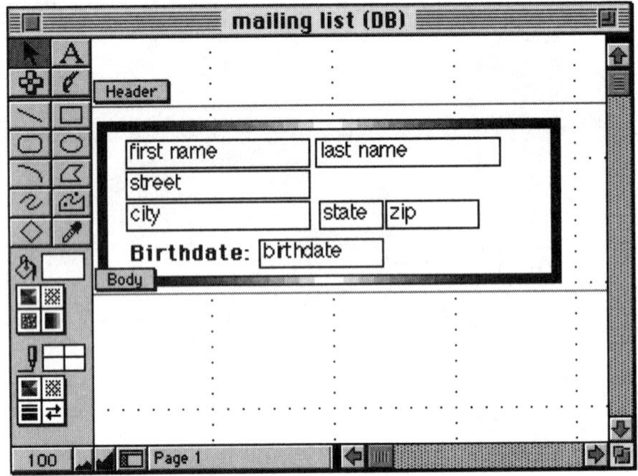

Figure 8.2 Layout mode

- Find mode: Find mode (Figure 8.3) provides a way to enter criteria for searching for specific records. (In addition to using Find mode, you can match records. Finding and matching are discussed later in this chapter.)

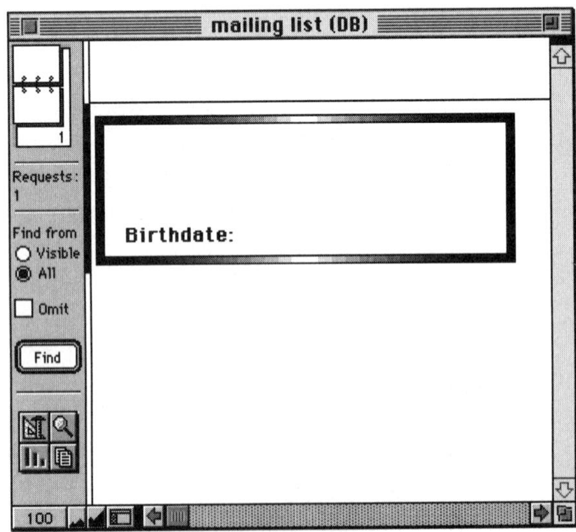

Figure 8.3 Find mode

- List mode: List mode is similar to layout mode in that you can use it to view and modify data. However, list mode provides a grid-like layout (Figure 8.4) that can't be modified other than changing the width of the columns and the order in which they appear. List mode is therefore very useful for quickly entering and viewing large amounts of data because it presents data as compactly as possible.

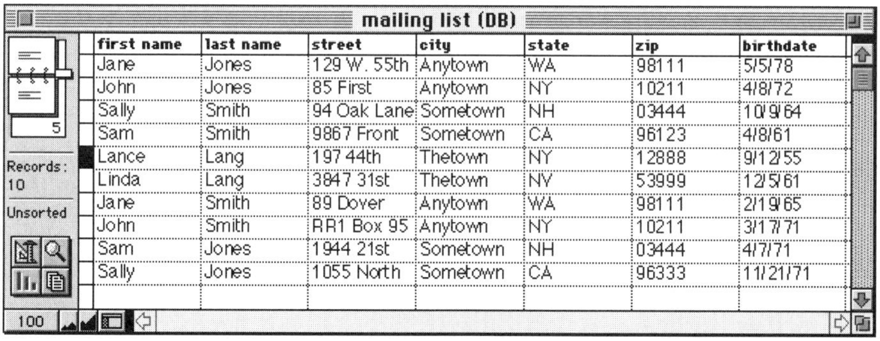

mailing list (DB)

Records: 10

Unsorted

first name	last name	street	city	state	zip	birthdate
Jane	Jones	129 W. 55th	Anytown	WA	98111	5/5/78
John	Jones	85 First	Anytown	NY	10211	4/8/72
Sally	Smith	94 Oak Lane	Sometown	NH	03444	10/9/64
Sam	Smith	9867 Front	Sometown	CA	96123	4/8/61
Lance	Lang	197 44th	Thetown	NY	12888	9/12/55
Linda	Lang	3847 31st	Thetown	NY	53999	12/5/61
Jane	Smith	89 Dover	Anytown	WA	98111	2/19/65
John	Smith	RR1 Box 95	Anytown	NY	10211	3/17/71
Sam	Jones	1944 21st	Sometown	NH	03444	4/7/71
Sally	Jones	1055 North	Sometown	CA	96333	11/21/71

Figure 8.4 List mode

Field Data Types

When you create a new database file, ClarisWorks doesn't simply place an empty document on your screen for you to fill up with something. Instead, you must define the fields that will be stored in your database file. Because field definition comes first, you should spend a bit of time planning your database file before you begin working on the computer. There are two sets of decisions you need to make: the fields that will be part of your file (that's up to you) and the data type of each field.

A field's data type specifies the type of data you can store in a field. Choosing the right data type for a field can make it easier to ensure that data are entered accurately and can simplify sorting and searching the field.

The data types provided by ClarisWorks include:

- Text: A Text field can store anything you can type from the keyboard. If none of the other field types makes sense for a field, use Text. The contents of a Text field are limited to 1020 characters. However, each time you change the style of the text in a field, you take up space for 20 characters.

- Number: A Number field stores a computational quantity. If you are going to be doing arithmetic with a value, then it must be stored in a Number field. (You can't do arithmetic with numbers stored in Text fields.) Number fields can hold up to 255 characters, including the sign (if present) and decimal point (if present).

- Date: A Date field stores a date. Use this type of field for all dates so that dates will be sorted and searched in correct chronological order.

- Time: A Time field stores a time. Use this type of field for all times so that times will be sorted and searched in correct chronological order.

- Name: A Name field holds a person's name. When you sort a Name field, ClarisWorks sorts first by the last word in the field. Therefore, if you store *John Smith* and *Adam Wilson* in a Name field, ClarisWorks will sort *Smith* before *Wilson*.

If you intermix company names with human names in a Name field, you will probably want records containing company names to be sorted by the first word in the field. In that case, place an @ in front of the data when you enter the data. You won't see the @ when you view the data, but it will affect sorting.

- Popup Menu: A Popup Menu field provides the user with a list of options from which he or she can pick. Popup menus are convenient when a field can accept one of only a few values. This not only makes it easier for the user but also ensures that the values are entered correctly.

- Radio Buttons: A Radio Buttons field provides a set of radio buttons from which a user can choose one. If a field can take less than seven values, then a set of radio buttons usually works well.

- Check Box: A Check Box field accepts only a "yes" or "no" (true/false) value.

- Serial Number: A Serial Number field automatically numbers each record.

- Value List: A Value List field provides the user with a scrolling list of values. The user can either make a choice from the list or enter a different value.

- Multimedia Frame: A Multimedia Frame field provides an area in which you can place multimedia documents, such as QuickTime movies.

- Record Info: A Record Info field contains information about the record that ClarisWorks will insert automatically. You can choose from among values such as the date or time the record was created and the date or time the record was last modified.

- Calculation: The contents of a Calculation field are generated by combining the contents of one or more other fields using a formula that you define.

- Summary: Summary fields contain data computed about groups of records, such as totals and subtotals. You place Summary fields on layouts that group data. (Summary fields are discussed in Chapter 10.)

The sample database file that we'll be using for many of the examples in this chapter is a mailing list that contains some fields just for demonstration purposes. Its design is as follows:

- ID number: A Serial Number field that automatically numbers each record.

- Name: A Name field containing the name of the person.

- Street: A Text field containing the street portion of the person's address.

- City: A Value List field whose scrolling list contains the cities most commonly used in the data file.

- State: A Popup Menu listing the states used in the data file.

- Zip: A Text field containing the person's zip code.

Always store zip codes as Text. There are three reasons for this. First, even if you are using only the five-digit U.S. zip codes, some zip codes begin with 0 and if they were stored as numbers, that leading zero would disappear. Second, the U.S. nine-digit zip codes aren't legal numbers because they have a dash in them. Third, you may need to store Canadian postal codes, which include letters.

- Photo: A Multimedia Frame field for the person's photo.
- Birthdate: A Date field for the person's birthdate.
- Send Gift: A Check Box field indicating whether a birthday gift should be sent to this person.
- Maximum Gift$: A Number field specifying the maximum amount available to spend on a birthday gift for the person.
- Gender: A Radio Buttons field indicating whether the person is male or female.
- Date modified: A Record Info field storing the date when the record was last modified.

Creating Fields

When you create a new database file, ClarisWorks automatically displays the Define Database Fields dialog box (Figure 8.5). After you have finished creating your initial fields, you can return to this dialog box to add other fields by doing the following:

Macintosh	Choose Layout->Define Fields or press SHIFT-1 -D.
Windows	Choose Layout->Define Fields, press SHIFT-CTRL-D, or press ALT-L, D.

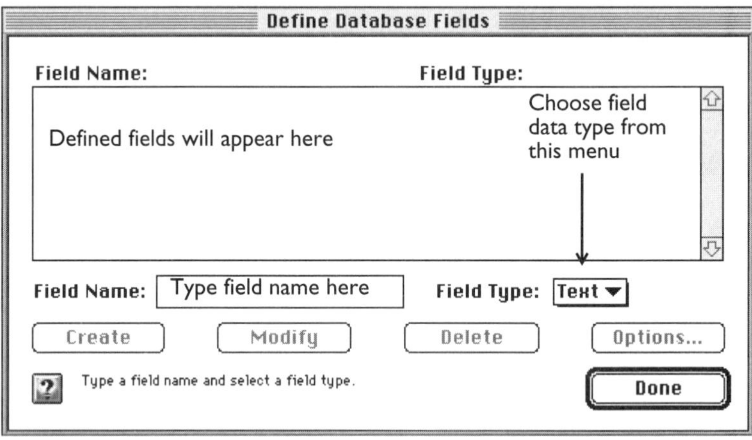

Figure 8.5 The Define Database Fields dialog box

To create a new field:

1. Type a name for the field in the Field Name edit box.

2. Choose a data type for the field from the Field Type menu.

3. Click the Create button or press Enter to create the field. ClarisWorks transfers the field name to the top of the dialog box.

4. Click the Options button or press Enter to configure the field. An Options dialog box appears. Options differ for each type of field and therefore will be discussed individually later in this section.

In some cases — in particular Value List, Popup Menu, Radio Button, and Record Info fields — options are required. Therefore, the Options dialog box appears automatically when you create a field of that type. In contrast, a Multimedia Frame field has no options and therefore the Options button won't become active when you create a field.

5. Repeat steps 1 through 4 for each field you want to add to the file.

6. Click the Done button to close the dialog box. ClarisWorks creates a default layout for you, including all the fields you have defined (for example, see Figure 8.6).

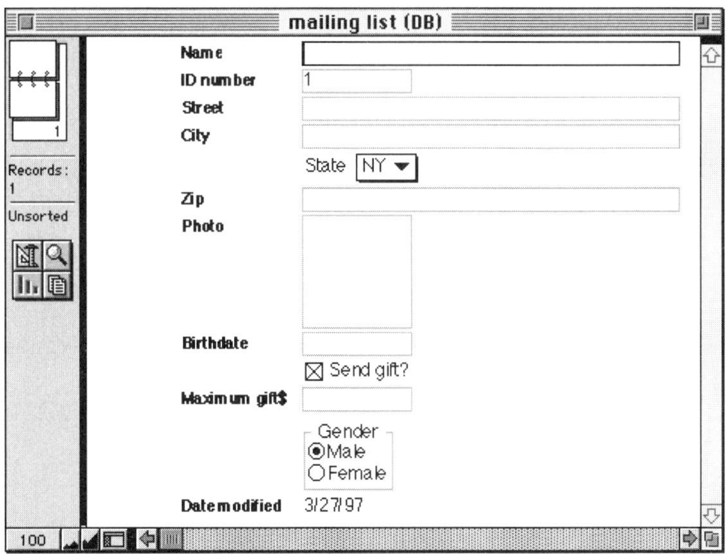

Figure 8.6 A default layout

Text Fields

When you create a text field, you can ask ClarisWorks to perform some simple data validation on that field and also insert a default value (Figure 8.7):

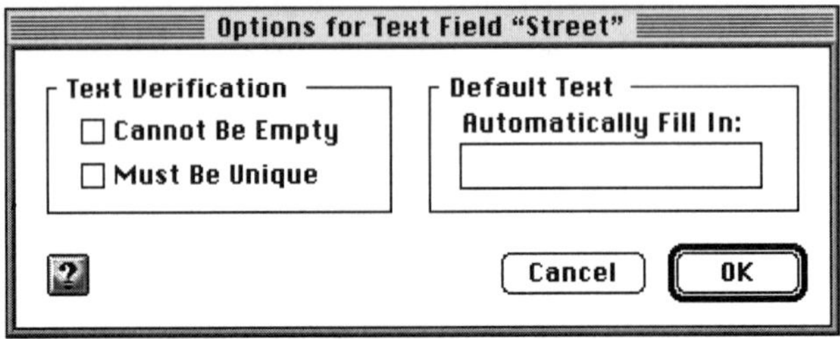

Figure 8.7 Text field options

- To require the user to enter a value in the field, place a check in the Cannot Be Empty check box.
- To require the value to be unique throughout the file, place a check in the Must Be Unique check box. Keep in mind that uniqueness verification applies only to this particular field. If a duplicate of a value in this field appears in a different field, ClarisWorks won't detect it.
- To provide a default value that ClarisWorks fills in automatically every time you create a new record, enter the default value in the Automatically Fill In edit box.

Default values can greatly simplify data entry. Therefore, if you have a field that takes one value most of the time, then it makes sense to provide a default value so the user doesn't have to type it.

Number Fields

Like text fields, number fields (Figure 8.8) can be validated in several ways and can also accept default values:

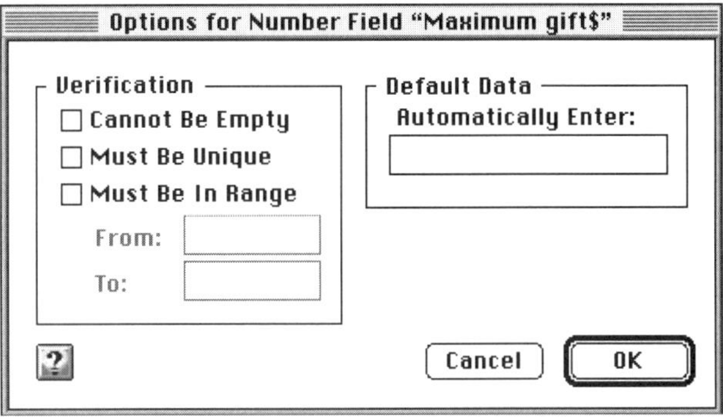

Figure 8.8 Number field options

- To require the user to enter a value in the field, place a check in the Cannot Be Empty check box.

- To require the value in the field to be unique within the file, place a check in the Must Be Unique check box.

- To enter a validation range — a range within which the values in the field must fall — place a check in the Must Be In Range check box. Then enter the lowest permitted value in the From edit box and the highest permitted value in the To edit box.

- To provide a default value that ClarisWorks will automatically enter whenever you create a new record, enter a value in the Automatically Enter edit box.

Date Fields

Date fields (Figure 8.9) can be validated and also given a default value:

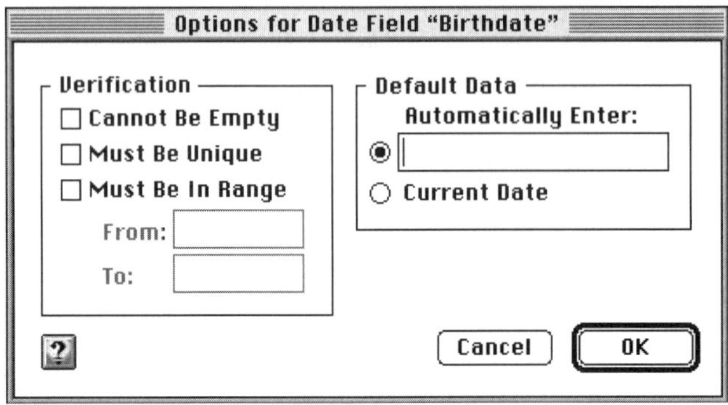

Figure 8.9 Date field options

- To require the user to enter a value in the field, place a check in the Cannot Be Empty check box.
- To require the value in the field to be unique throughout the file, place a check in the Must Be Unique check box.
- To validate that the date falls within a specified range, place a check in the Must Be In Range check box. Then place the earliest permitted date in the From edit box and the latest permitted date in the To edit box.
- To enter the current system date in the field automatically, click the Current Date radio button.
- To give the field a default value other than the current system date, enter the value in the Automatically Enter edit box.

Time Fields

Time field options (Figure 8.10) are very similar to date field options:

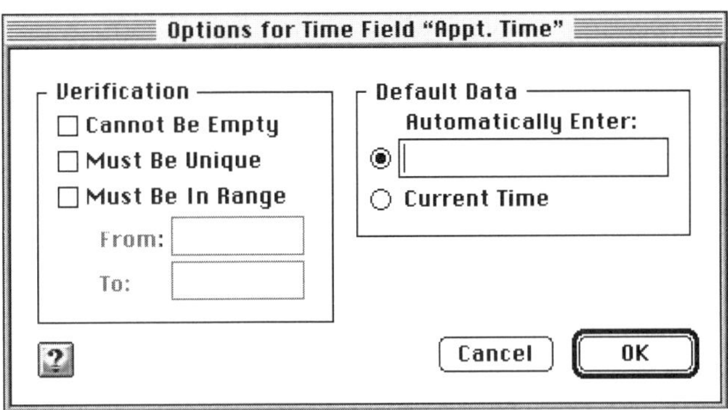

Figure 8.10 Time field options

- To require the user to enter a value in the field, place a check in the Cannot Be Empty check box.
- To require the value in the field to be unique throughout the file, place a check in the Must Be Unique check box.
- To validate that the date falls within a specified range, place a check in the Must Be In Range check box. Then place the earliest permitted time in the From edit box and the latest permitted time in the To edit box.
- To enter the current system time in the field automatically, click the Current Time radio button.
- To give the field a default value other than the current system time, enter the value in the Automatically Enter edit box.

Name Fields

Name fields (Figure 8.11), which are text fields that sort by the last word in the field rather than the first, have the following options:

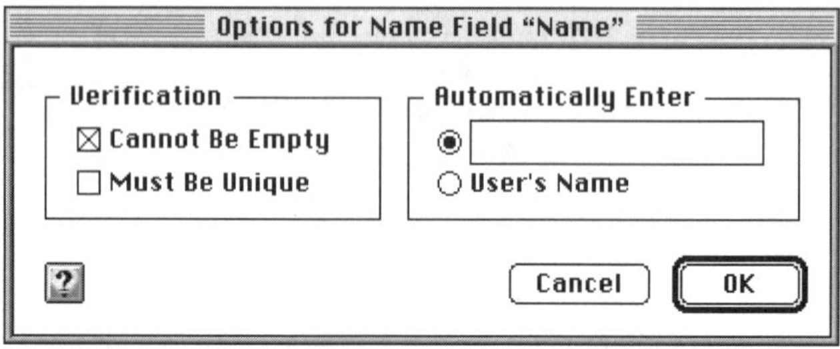

Figure 8.11 Name field options

- To require the user to enter to enter a value in the field, place a check in the Cannot be Empty check box.
- To require the value to be unique throughout the file, place a check in the Must Be Unique check box.
- To enter the current user's name in the field automatically, click the User's Name radio button. On the Macintosh, this value is taken from the Network Identity section of the Sharing Setup dialog box. Under Windows, the source of the name depends on whether your computer is set for one or more user desktop configurations. If every user works with the same desktop configuration, then ClarisWorks uses the name entered when Windows 95 was last configured. However, if your machine is set up to allow multiple user configurations, ClarisWorks takes the name from the name and password dialog box the user completes when he or she logs in. Using the User's Name option is therefore a convenient way to keep track of who modified a record.

- To provide a default value other than the current user, enter that value in the Automatically Enter edit box.

Popup Menu Fields

When you create a popup menu field, ClarisWorks automatically displays the options dialog box (Figure 8.12) so that you can specify the contents of the menu. Initially the "Items for control" list will contain one item named *Item 1*. That value will also be highlighted in the Item Label edit box.

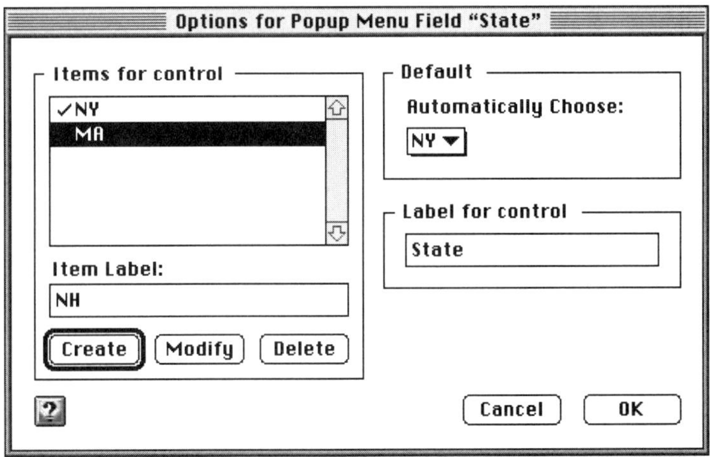

Figure 8.12 Popup menu field options

To configure your own list of popup menu items:

1. Type the first value that should appear in the popup menu in the Item Label edit box. The Modify button will be the default button.

2. Click the Modify button or press Enter to replace *Item 1* with your value.

3. Enter another value for the popup menu in the Item Label edit box. The Create button will be the default button.

4. Click the Create button or press Enter to add the new item to the list of items.

5. Repeat steps 3 and 4 for all items you want to add to the menu.

6. Set the default value (the menu item that will be selected when a new record is created) for the menu by choosing one value from the Automatically Choose popup menu.

7. ClarisWorks fills in the name of the field as the label that will be given to the popup menu when it is placed on a layout. To provide another label, enter the label value in the Label for control edit field.

Radio Buttons

A Radio Buttons field consists of two or more radio buttons from among which the user can pick one. When you create a Radio Buttons field, ClarisWorks automatically displays the options dialog box (Figure 8.13) so that you can set up the radio buttons that define the field's possible values.

When it first appears, the Radio Buttons options dialog box contains two items in its Items for control list: *Item 1* and *Item 2*. You will need to replace these two default items and then add any other items you want.

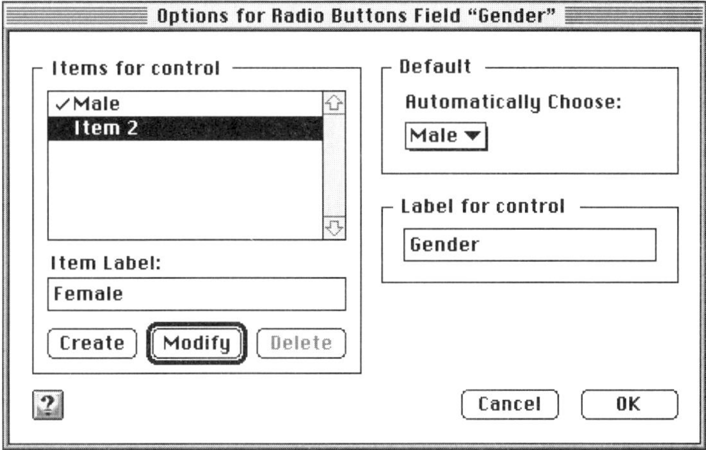

Figure 8.13 Radio Buttons field options

To configure a set of radio buttons:

1. Highlight the *Item 1* that appears in the Item Label edit box.

2. Type a new item label.

3. Click the Modify button or press Enter. ClarisWorks replaces *Item 1* with your label.

4. Click on *Item 2* in the list of items.

5. Repeat steps 2 and 3 for *Item 2*.

6. Enter a new label in the Item Label text box. The Create button becomes the default button.

7. Click the Create button or press Enter to add another item to the list.

8. Repeat steps 6 and 7 for any remaining radio buttons that should be part of this field.

9. To set the radio button that should be highlighted whenever you create a new record, choose one item's name from the Automatically Choose menu.

10. ClarisWorks fills in the name of the field as the label that will be given to the group of radio buttons when it is placed on a layout. To provide another label, enter the label value in the Label for Control edit field.

Check Box Fields

A check box field takes one of only two values, which can be viewed as yes/no or true/false. Its options (Figure 8.14) are therefore somewhat limited:

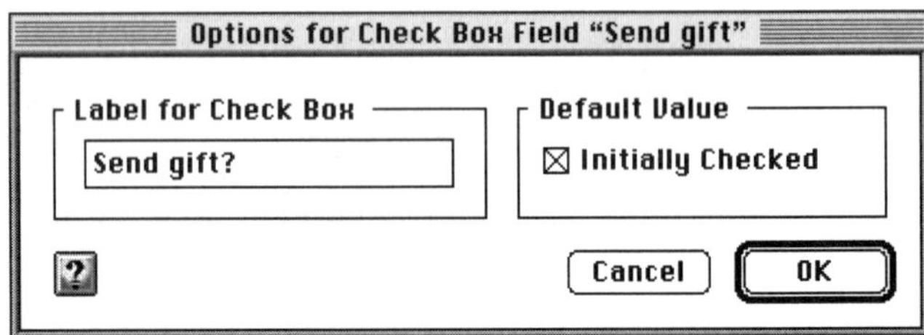

Figure 8.14 Check box field options

- ClarisWorks fills in the name of the field as the label that should be placed next to the check box on a layout. To provide another label, enter the label value in the Label for Check Box edit field.

- When you create a new record, the check box field can be checked or not checked. To have the field checked whenever you create a new record, check the Initially Checked check box.

Serial Number Fields

A serial number field lets you automatically number your records. The contents of the field appear whenever a new record is created. However, the user can change the automatically generated value (Figure 8.15).

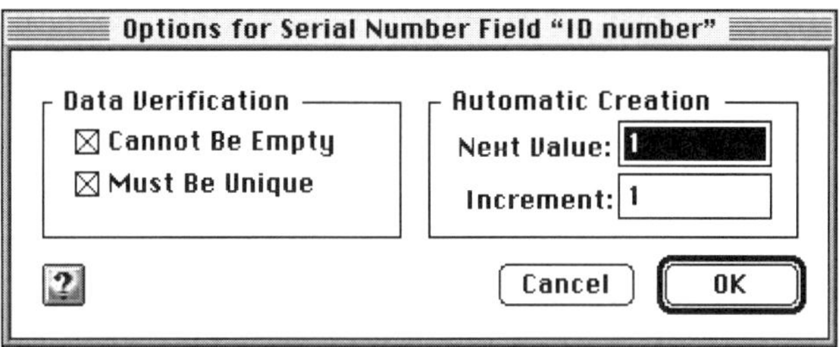

Figure 8.15 Serial number field options

Do the following to configure a serial number field:

- To require a value in the field, place a check in the Cannot Be Empty check box.
- To require that the serial number be unique, place a check in the Must Be Unique check box.
- To set the value for the next automatic serial number, enter a number in the Next Value edit box.
- To set the amount ClarisWorks will add to the Next Value to generate a new serial number, enter a number in the Increment edit box. For example, if the Next Value is 210 and the Increment is 5, ClarisWorks will give the next new record a serial number of 215.

Value List Fields

A value list field is similar to a popup menu field in that it gives the user a list from which to pick. However, whereas the options in a popup menu are fixed, a value list field gives the user the option to enter a different value if he or she can't find an appropriate value in the list. Value lists also contain scroll bars, which means they are better suited to long lists than popup menus.

When you create a value list field, ClarisWorks automatically displays the options dialog box (Figure 8.16) and places one item in the list of items (*Item 1*).

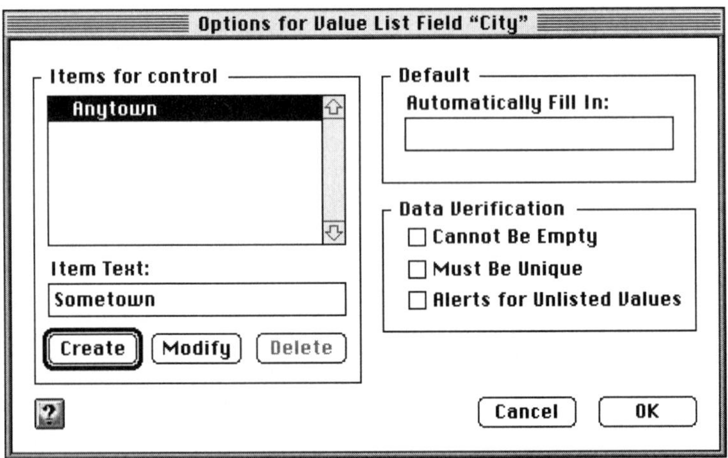

Figure 8.16 Value list field options

To configure your own value list field:

1. If it isn't already selected, highlight *Item 1* in the Item Text edit box.

2. Type the first item that is to appear in the list.

3. Click the Modify button or press Enter. ClarisWorks replaces *Item 1* with your text.

4. Enter a new item in the Item Text box.

5. Click the Create button or press Enter.

6. Repeat steps 4 and 5 for all items that are to appear in the value list.

7. If you want ClarisWorks to enter a default value in the field whenever you create a new record, type that value in the Automatically Fill In edit box.

8. To require that the field have a value, place a check in the Cannot Be Empty check box.

9. To require that the value in the field be unique, place a check in the Must Be Unique check box.

10. To warn the user whenever he or she enters a value in the field that isn't in the list, place a check in the Alerts for Unlisted Values check box.

Record Info Fields

When you create a record info field, ClarisWorks automatically displays the options dialog box (Figure 8.17) so that you can choose the value that ClarisWorks should place in the field whenever a new record is created. To make the choice, click the radio button that corresponds to the value you want.

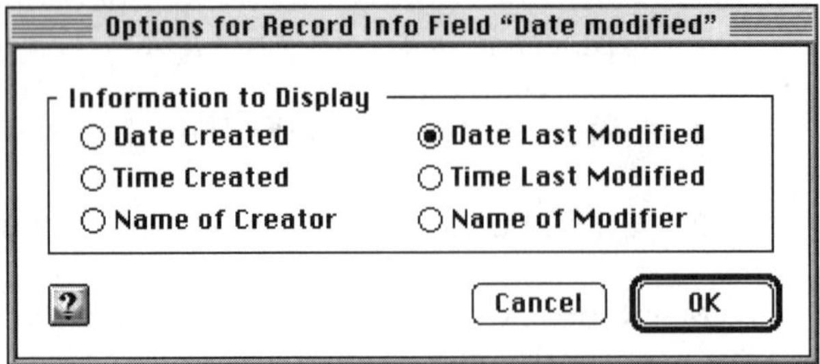

Figure 8.17 Record info field options

Although a record info field can hold only one value at a time, there is no reason that you can't include more than one record info field — each with a different content — in a file if you need to capture more than just one type of system information.

Entering Data

As soon as you have finished defining the fields for your database file, ClarisWorks creates a default layout for you and enters one blank record. If you look back at Figure 8.6, you will notice that all of the default values have already been placed in the record. This includes the ID number generated by the serial number field.

The first task when you are dealing with a new file is to enter data into that first blank record. Then you can add more records, which in turn can be filled with data.

The way in which you enter data depends on the type of field with which you are working. For some field types, you simply type. Other types require pointing, clicking, and even making menu choices.

To enter or modify data, you must be in Layout or List mode.

Text, Name, Number, Date, and Time Fields

To enter data into text, name, number, date, and time fields:

1. Click in the field to make it active.
2. Type the value you want to appear in the field.

Once you have made one field active, you can use the Tab key to move to the next field on the layout.

Value List Fields

Because a value list field lets the user either pick from a list or type a value, there are several ways to place data in the field. Begin by clicking in the field or tabbing to the field to make it active. The value list will appear. At that point, you can do any of the following:

- To enter a value that is not in the list, click in the field once more to get an insertion point. Type the value.
- Double-click on a value in the list to place it in the field.
- Use the down arrow key to select the first item in the list, as in Figure 8.18. Then continue to press the down

arrow key until you reach the value you want. Press Enter to transfer the value to the field.

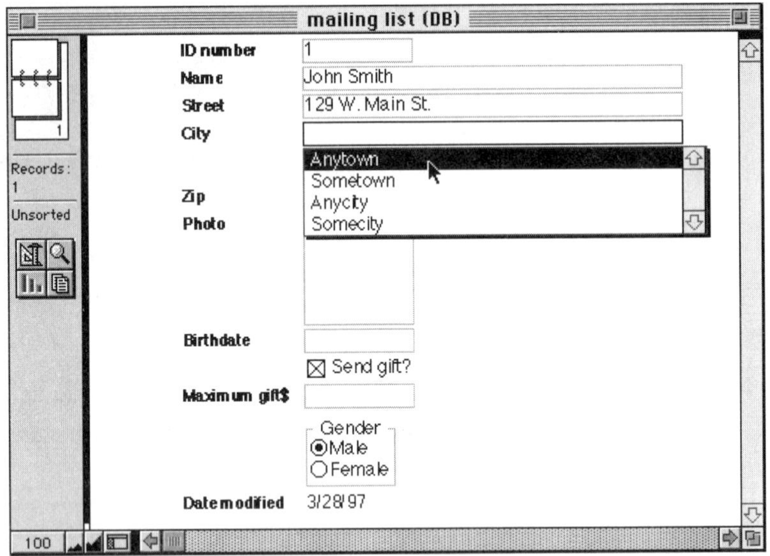

Figure 8.18 Choosing from a value list

- Press the first letter of the value you want. ClarisWorks takes you to the first value that begins with that letter. If this isn't the value you want, you can use the up or down arrow key to select a different value. When the correct value is highlighted, press Enter to transfer the value to the field.

Popup Menu Fields

To enter data into a popup menu field:

1. Click on the popup menu to expose its options (see Figure 8.19).

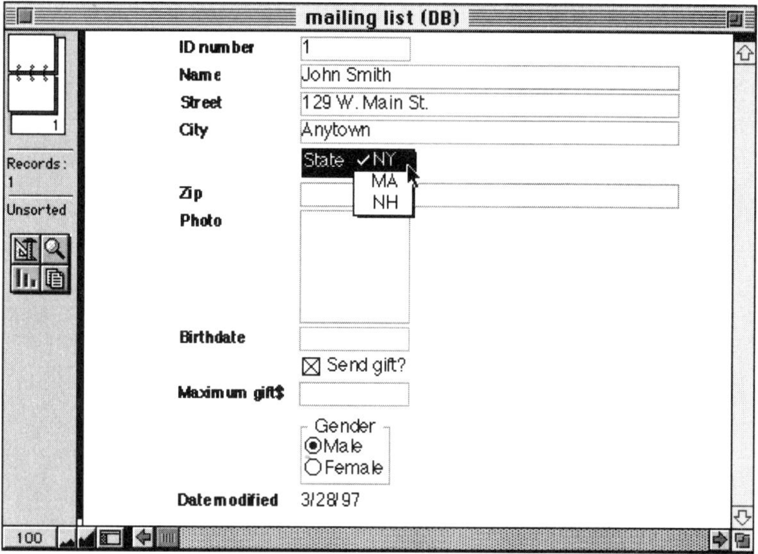

Figure 8.19 Choosing from a popup menu

2. Drag to highlight the value you want.

3. Release the mouse button to enter the value in the field.

Check Box Fields

To change the value in a check box field, click in the box. Clicking a checked box removes the X; clicking in an empty box inserts an X.

Radio Button Fields

A radio button field, which is made up of a group of radio buttons, allows only one button in the group to be selected at a time. To make a selection from the group, click on one button. The button that was selected prior to your click will be deselected.

Multimedia Frame Fields

A multimedia frame field can store many types of graphics, sounds, and QuickTime movies. When you do so, ClarisWorks copies graphics and sounds into your database file. QuickTime movies are "linked" to the file. This means that ClarisWorks stores the name and location of the file, rather than copying in the entire file.

Although it is often exciting to include multimedia in a file, you should be aware that multimedia content can make the file size grow significantly. (This is because graphic and sound files are actually copied into the ClarisWorks document, rather than simply being linked by their names.)

To enter a multimedia element into a multimedia frame field:

1. Click in the field or tab to the field to make it active.
2. Choose File->Insert. (Windows users can also press ALT-F, I.) An Open File dialog box appears.
3. Choose the file containing the multimedia item you want to store. ClarisWorks copies the item into the field.

If the value in a multimedia frame field is a QuickTime movie, you can play the movie by double-clicking on the field (see Figure 8.20).

You can also place data into fields discussed in this section by pasting values from the Clipboard.

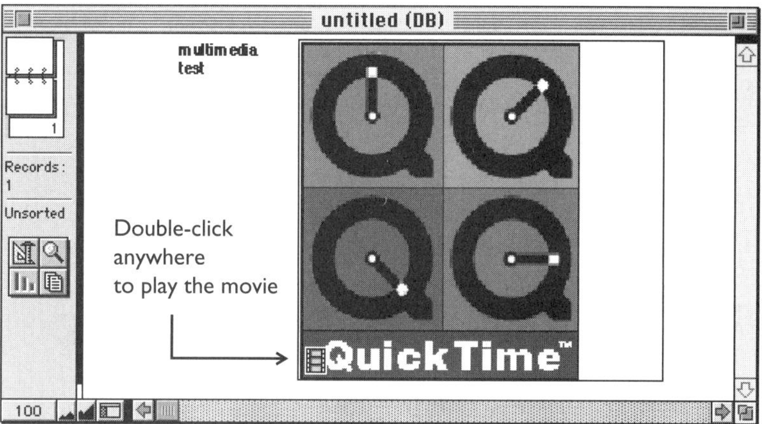

Figure 8.20 Playing a QuickTime movie in a multimedia frame field

Adding New Records

There are two ways to add new records to a file. You can add a blank record, or you can duplicate the currently active record:

- To add a blank record at the end of the file:

Macintosh	Choose Edit->New Record or press ⌘-R.
Windows	Choose Edit->New Record, press CTRL-R, or press ALT-E, R.

- To add a record that is a duplicate of the current record:

Macintosh	Choose Edit->Duplicate Record or press ⌘-D.
Windows	Choose Edit->Duplicate Record, press CTRL-D, or press ALT-E, U.

You can also add a new record by clicking the  *button in the Button Bar.*

Modifying Data

Modifying data is a three-step process:

1. Find the record containing the record you want to modify. (You'll be introduced to several ways to locate records in Chapter 9.)

2. Click in a field to make it the active field.

3. Change the data as needed.

The technique you can use for making changes depends on the type of field:

- For fields that contain characters that you can type (for example, text, name, or value list fields in which you have entered a value not in the list), click in the field to make it active. Then you can do any of the following:

  - Type new characters into the field.

  - Use the Delete key to delete characters to the left of the insertion point.

  - Use the Del key to delete characters to the right of the insertion point.

  - Drag across a group of characters to select them. At that point, you can delete the selection by pressing Delete, or you can cut or copy it to the Clipboard.

  - Paste characters into the field from the Clipboard.

- For fields that provide a list from which you can pick (for example, popup menus, value lists, and radio buttons), choose a different value, using the same process you used to place the initial value in the field.

- When a multimedia frame field is the active field, you can delete the current contents by pressing the Delete key. Then, you can insert a new graphic, sound, or movie.

Working in List Mode

List mode provides a quick way to view your data in a grid layout that contains all the fields in the file. When in List mode, you can also add new records and modify data in existing records.

As you can see in Figure 8.21, List mode preserves some of the characteristics of field data types. For example, the popup menu for the State field is still available. The value list for the City field is also there. However, radio button fields are turned into popup menus.

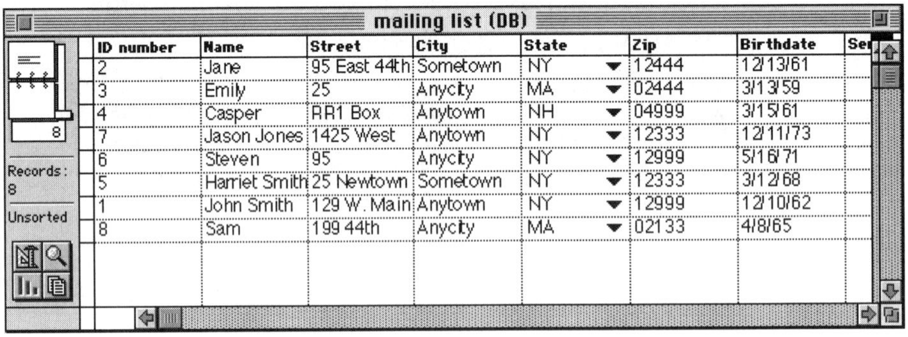

mailing list (DB)

8

Records: 8

Unsorted

ID number	Name	Street	City	State	Zip	Birthdate	Se
2	Jane	95 East 44th	Sometown	NY	12444	12/13/61	
3	Emily	25	Anycity	MA	02444	3/13/59	
4	Casper	RR1 Box	Anytown	NH	04999	3/15/61	
7	Jason Jones	1425 West	Anytown	NY	12333	12/11/73	
6	Steven	95	Anycity	NY	12999	5/16/71	
5	Harriet Smith	25 Newtown	Sometown	NY	12333	3/12/68	
1	John Smith	129 W. Main	Anytown	NY	12999	12/10/62	
8	Sam	199 44th	Anycity	MA	02133	4/8/65	

Figure 8.21 List mode with a variety of field types

You can control the look of the List view in three ways:

- You can change the width of a column. To do so, move the mouse pointer to the column label row at the top of the window and over the divider between two columns. The mouse pointer turns into the double-arrow pointer (see Figure 8.22). Drag the divider to the left to make the column to the left narrower. Drag the divider to the right to make the column to the left wider.

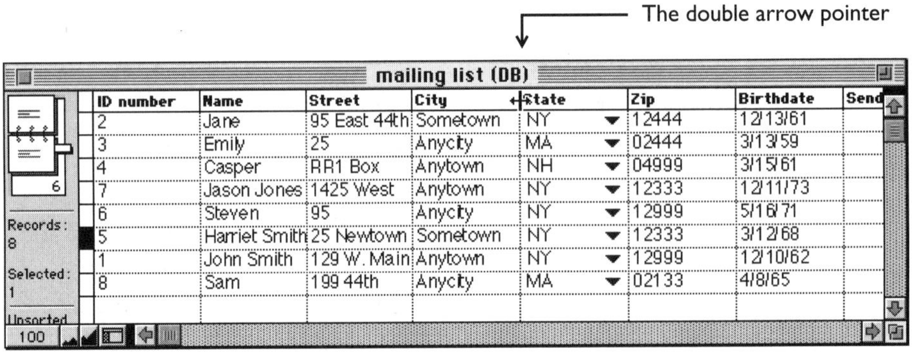

The double arrow pointer

mailing list (DB)

6

Records: 8

Selected: 1

Unsorted

100

ID number	Name	Street	City	State	Zip	Birthdate	Send
2	Jane	95 East 44th	Sometown	NY	12444	12/13/61	
3	Emily	25	Anycity	MA	02444	3/13/59	
4	Casper	RR1 Box	Anytown	NH	04999	3/15/61	
7	Jason Jones	1425 West	Anytown	NY	12333	12/11/73	
6	Steven	95	Anycity	NY	12999	5/16/71	
5	Harriet Smith	25 Newtown	Sometown	NY	12333	3/12/68	
1	John Smith	129 W. Main	Anytown	NY	12999	12/10/62	
8	Sam	199 44th	Anycity	MA	02133	4/8/65	

Figure 8.22 Changing the width of a List mode column

- You can make rows taller or shorter. To do so, move the mouse pointer to the left edge of the rows and over a divider between two rows. The mouse pointer turns into the double-arrow pointer (see Figure 8.23). Drag the divider down to make the row taller. Drag the divider up to make the row shorter.

The double-arrow pointer

mailing list (DB)

Records: 8
Selected: 1
Unsorted
100

ID number	Name	Street	City	State	Zip	Birthdate	Send
2	Jane	95 East 44th	Sometown	NY	12444	12/13/61	
3	Emily	25	Anycity	MA	02444	3/13/59	
4	Casper	RR1 Box	Anytown	NH	04999	3/15/61	
7	Jason Jones	1425 West	Anytown	NY	12333	12/11/73	
6	Steven	95	Anycity	NY	12999	5/16/71	
5	Harriet Smith	25 Newtown	Sometown	NY	12333	3/12/68	
1	John Smith	129 W. Main	Anytown	NY	12999	12/10/62	
8	Sam	199 44th	Anycity	MA	02133	4/8/65	

Figure 8.23 Changing the height of a row in List mode

- You can change the position of a column in the display. To do so, move the mouse pointer to the column label row at the top of the window. Place the mouse pointer within a column rather than over a divider so that the pointer turns into the hollow double arrow (see Figure 8.24). Then drag the column either right or left to its new location.

Hollow double-arrow pointer

mailing list (DB)

Records: 8
Selected: 1
Unsorted
100

ID number	Name	Street	City	State	Zip	Birthdate	Send
2	Jane	95 East 44th	Sometown	NY	12444	12/13/61	
3	Emily	25	Anycity	MA	02444	3/13/59	
4	Casper	RR1 Box	Anytown	NH	04999	3/15/61	
7	Jason Jones	1425 West	Anytown	NY	12333	12/11/73	
6	Steven	95	Anycity	NY	12999	5/16/71	
5	Harriet Smith	25 Newtown	Sometown	NY	12333	3/12/68	
1	John Smith	129 W. Main	Anytown	NY	12999	12/10/62	
8	Sam	199 44th	Anycity	MA	02133	4/8/65	

Figure 8.24 Moving columns in List mode

ClarisWorks saves the changes you make to the look of List mode. Therefore, each time you return to List mode, it will be exactly as you left. (This assumes, of course, that you save your file.)

The one thing you can't do in List mode is control which fields appear in the grid. You get them all, whether you want them or not! List mode therefore isn't a substitute for layouts, which provide complete control over what appears on the screen.

Creating and Modifying Basic Layouts

A layout provides a completely configurable way to view the data you have stored in a ClarisWorks database file. The fields that you choose to include on a layout in no way affect data stored in the file. This means that you can use all, or just some, of the fields in a file. You can also rearrange them on the layout to view them in any order you choose. A layout is therefore a window to your data, making it possible for you to look at the data in whatever way makes most sense to you.

In this section you will be introduced to the types of layouts ClarisWorks provides and how you can begin to tailor those layouts to your particular needs.

Creating a New Layout

To create a new layout:

1. Do either of the following:

- Choose New Layout from the Layout tool in the tool panel (see Figure 8.25).

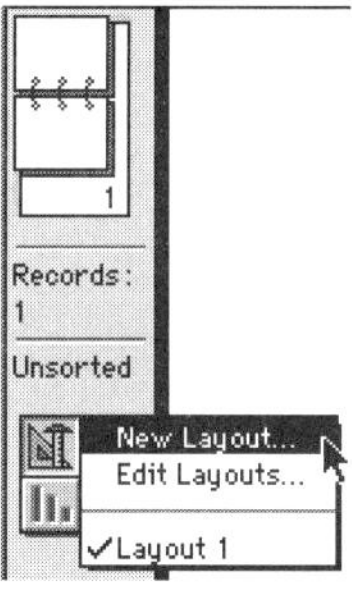

Figure 8.25 Creating a new layout using the tool panel

- Choose Layout->New Layout. (Windows users can also press ALT-L, N.)

  In either case, the New Layout dialog box appears (Figure 8.26).

2. Type a name for the layout in the Name box.

3. Click a radio button to indicate the type of layout you want ClarisWorks to create. (Layout types are discussed in the next section of this chapter.)

4. Click the OK button or press Enter. ClarisWorks creates the layout, which you can then modify by working in Layout mode. The name of the layout is also added to the bottom of the Layout menu and to the Layout tool's popup menu in the Tool panel.

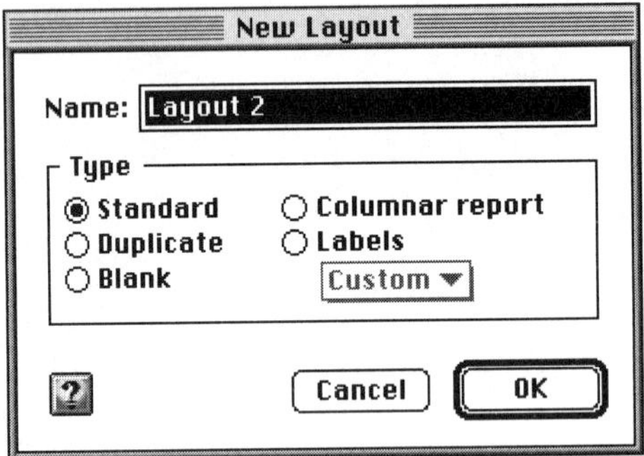

Figure 8.26 The New Layout dialog box

Types of Layouts

As you can see in Figure 8.26, ClarisWorks provides five types of layouts:

- Standard: A Standard layout, such as that in Figure 8.6, includes all of the fields in the file. Each field is displayed on a separate line.
- Duplicate: A Duplicate layout is an exact duplicate of whichever layout is currently being used. This option is handy when you need very similar layouts and don't want to create a new one from scratch.
- Blank: A Blank layout is an empty layout. You will need to add and place all layout elements yourself.
- Columnar report: A Columnar report places fields horizontally across the layout, as in Figure 8.27. When you create a Columnar report, you choose which fields should appear (see Figure 8.28).

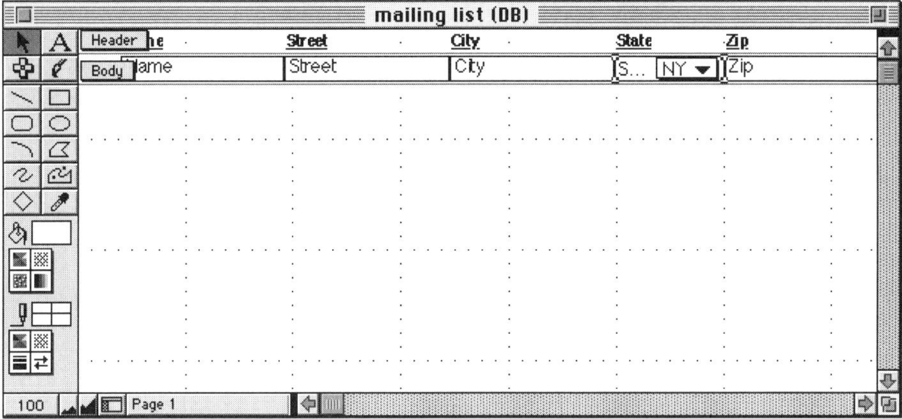

Figure 8.27 A columnar report layout

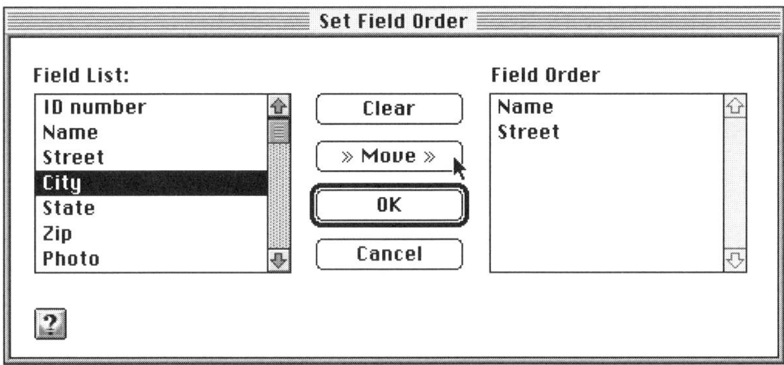

Figure 8.28 Choosing fields for a columnar report layout

- Labels: A Labels layout formats data for printing mailing labels. When you click the Labels radio button in the New Layout dialog box, the Custom popup menu becomes active. If you are going to be working with a specific type of Avery mailing label stock (or another type of label for which you have the equivalent Avery product numbers), you can choose the label type from the Custom menu and be assured that your layout matches the label stock you will be using.

Layout Parts

When you look Figure 8.27, you notice that there are horizontal lines dividing the layout into two sections, one of which is labeled Header and the other Body. These represent layout *parts*. The elements that you place on a layout behave differently in Browse mode and when the layout is printed depending on the part in which they appear.

There are three basic layout parts:

- Header: Anything you place in a Header part appears at the top of the Browse screen and at the top of every printed page. Typically, a Header part includes elements such as column labels.
- Body: The Body part is used for elements that should be repeated for every record being viewed. This includes most fields and, depending on the type of field, some labels. The Body part is the only part of a layout that is required.
- Footer: Anything you place in a Footer part appears at the bottom of the Browse screen and at the bottom of every printed page.

The Header and Footer parts are not the same as a printed page header and footer. You can add page headers and footers to a database document, just as you would to a word processing document. For details, see page 132 through page 135.

There are three other types of parts that will be discussed in Chapter 10

Adding a Part

Columnar report layouts provide you with a Header and a Body part, but no footer part. If you want a footer, for example, you will need to add the part yourself.

To add a part to a layout:

1. Display the layout you want to modify in Layout mode.

2. Choose Layout->Insert Part. (Windows users can also press ALT-L, P.) The Insert Part dialog box appears.

3. Click the radio button for the type of part you want to insert. For example, in Figure 8.29, someone is getting ready to insert a Footer part.

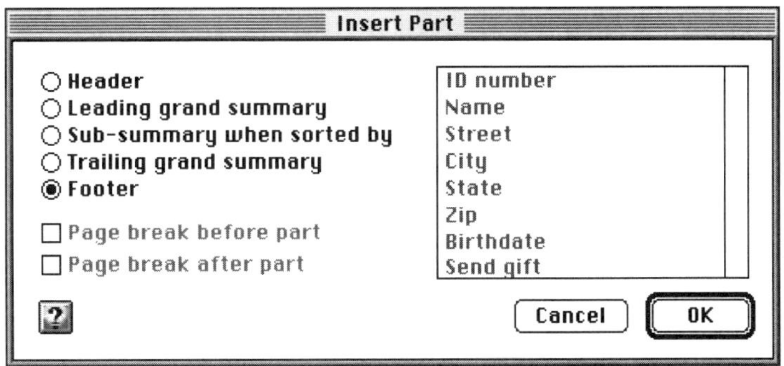

Figure 8.29 The Insert Part dialog box

4. Click the OK button or press Enter. ClarisWorks places the part on the layout. In the case of the Footer part, it will appear below the Body part.

Resizing a Part

The height of a part is up to you. To make a part taller of shorter, do the following:

1. Move the mouse pointer over the horizontal line at the bottom of the part whose size you want to change or move the mouse pointer over the part's name. The cursor changes to the drag cursor.

2. Drag the part's lower border up or down as needed. As you can see in Figure 8.30, an outline of the part's border and name follows as you drag.

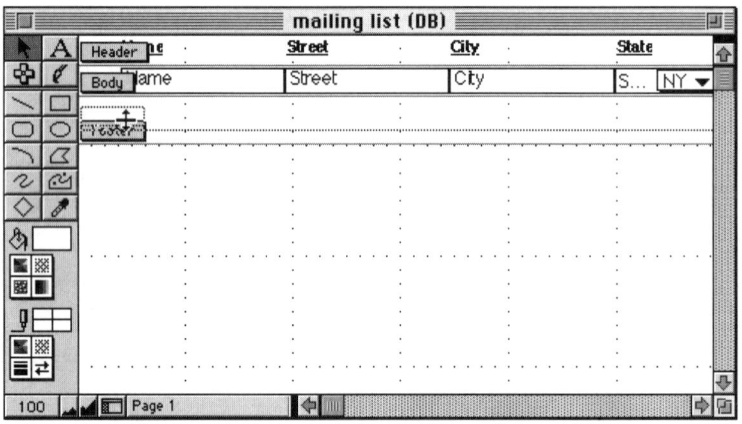

Figure 8.30 Resizing a part

3. Release the mouse button when the part is the size you want.

Deleting a Part

To delete a part, drag the part's name to the top of the part. In other words, drag the part's name over the name of the part above it. In the case of the Footer part we just added, it can be removed by dragging it on top of the Body part.

Editing the Layout

When you create a layout on which ClarisWorks places fields and field labels, you will probably want to change the way in which those elements appear. You may also want to add some graphics to the layout to make it more attractive.

You don't need to be artistic to create appealing layouts. The layout in Figure 8.31, for example, was created by modifying a Standard layout. The background is a gray-filled rectangle that was drawn over the entire layout and then moved behind all other elements. The fields were filled with white. Some labels were removed. Those that remain have been given a text color of white; the text was also made larger. In addition, elements were moved to more logical positions.

The Columnar report layout in Figure 8.32 has been modified by adding elements to the Header part. A gray-filled rectangle has been placed in back of all other elements. A text frame was added to contain the layout's title. The envelope graphic was created by combining a white-filled rectangle with two lines.

Accessing Layouts for Modification

To access a layout in Layout mode so that you can edit it, choose the layout's name from the bottom of the Layout menu. If you aren't in Layout mode, enter Layout mode.

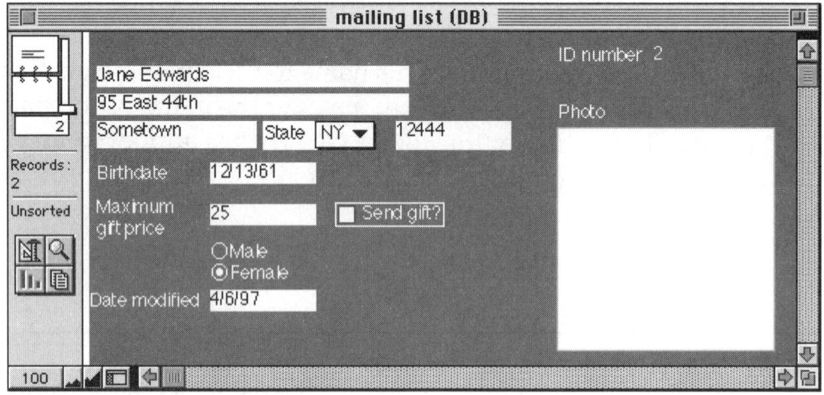

Figure 8.31 A modified Standard layout

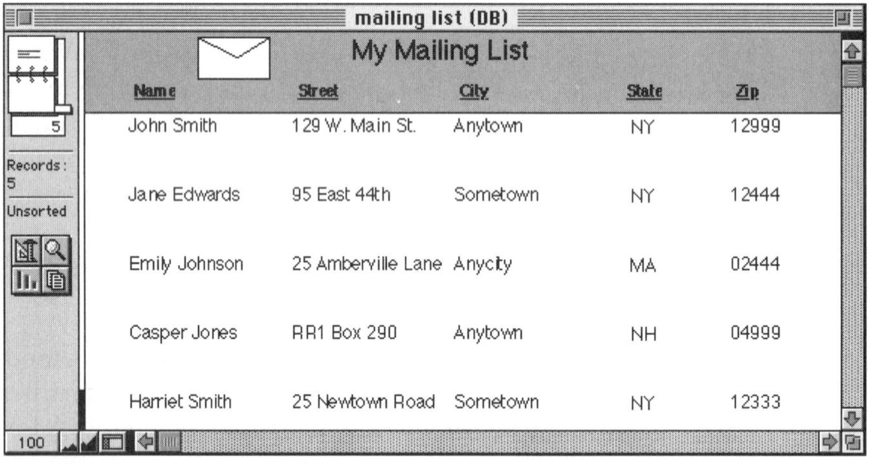

Figure 8.32 A modified Columnar report layout

Moving Elements

The elements on a layout are actually drawing objects. This means that they can be selected and moved by dragging, or by nudging with the arrow keys. For details on moving objects, see page 211.

Adding and Manipulating Layout Elements

If you look back at Figure 8.30, you'll notice that the Tool panel in Layout mode is identical to the drawing Tool panel. You can therefore place any drawing objects you want on a layout, in any part of a layout you want.

Objects on a layout are layered, just like those on a drawing. They can be aligned, grouped and ungrouped, locked and unlocked, resized, rotated, filled, and modified just as if they were part of a drawing document. For details on manipulating drawing objects, see page 194 through page 248.

Deleting Elements

Because the elements you place on a layout are the same as drawing objects, you can delete them in the same way. For details see page 215.

Placing Fields

If you create a blank layout, ClarisWorks won't place any fields on the layout for you. You must therefore add the fields you want manually. (You can also add fields to any other layout at any time using the technique that follows.)

To add a field to a layout:

1. Display the layout to which you want to add fields in Layout mode.
2. Choose Layout->Insert Field. (Windows users can also press ALT-L, S.) The Insert Fields dialog box appears

3. Highlight the field you want to place on the layout, as in Figure 8.33.

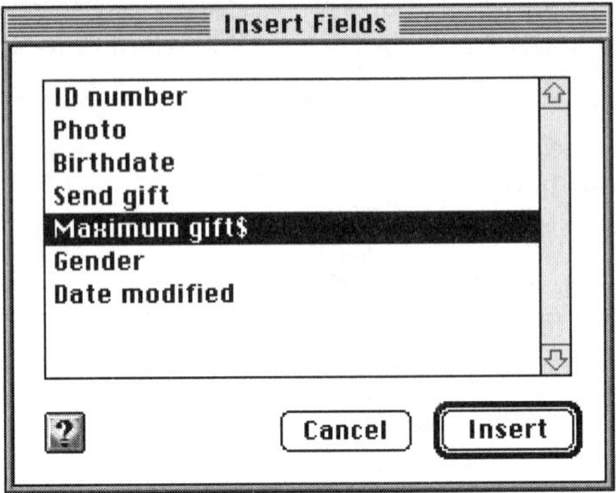

Figure 8.33 The Insert Fields dialog box

4. Click the OK button or press Enter. ClarisWorks places a rectangle for the field and a field label on the layout.

You can select more than one field at a time in the Insert Field dialog box. To select a group of adjacent fields in the list, highlight the first field and then SHIFT*-click on the last field. To select fields that aren't adjacent to each other, hold down the* 1 *key (Macintosh users) or the* CTRL *key (Windows users) while clicking on field names.*

Using Layouts

As your database file matures, you will probably accumulate a collection of layouts, some of which you use for data entry (those that contain every field in the file) and some of which you use for viewing data.

To change the layout with which you are currently working (regardless of the mode), either:

- Choose the layout's name from the bottom of the Layout window, or
- Choose the layout's name from the Layout tool's popup menu in the tool panel (Figure 8.34).

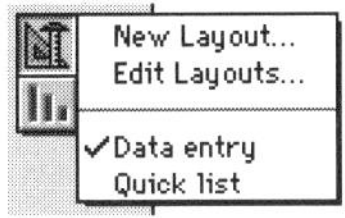

Figure 8.34 Layout names in the Layout tool's popup menu

Deleting Layouts

To delete a layout:

1. Choose Edit Layouts from the Layout tool's popup menu in the Tool panel. The Edit Layouts dialog box appears (Figure 8.35).
2. Highlight the name of the layout you want to delete.
3. Click the Delete button. ClarisWorks asks you to confirm the deletion (Figure 8.36).
4. Click the OK button or press Enter. ClarisWorks removes the confirmation alert from the screen and returns you to the Edit Layouts dialog box.
5. Repeat steps 2 through 4 for each layout you want to delete.

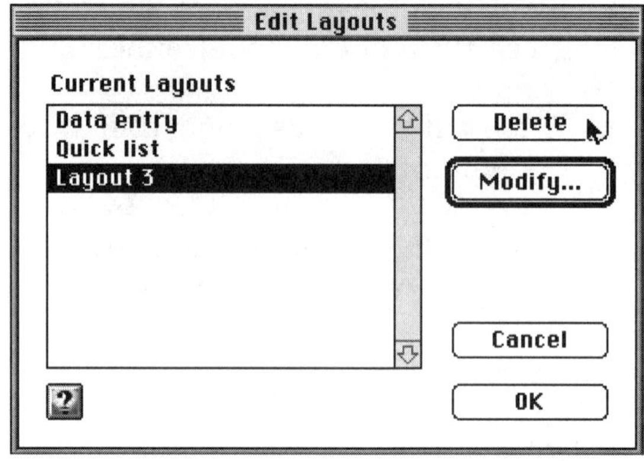

Figure 8.35 The Edit Layouts dialog box

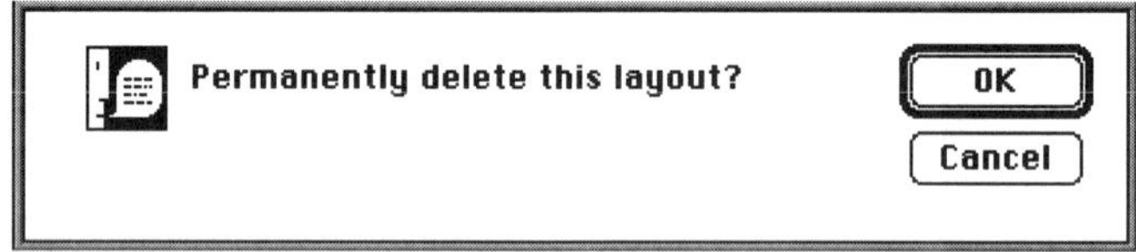

Figure 8.36 Confirming the deletion of a layout

6. Click the OK button to close the Edit Layouts dialog box.

Sorting Data

When you add a new record to a file, ClarisWorks puts that new record at the end of the file. This means that unless you do something to change the order of the records, they remain in the order in which you entered them.

Sorting records lets you change record order. You can base the ordering on a field or combination of fields that you choose.

ClarisWorks lets you name and save your sort specifications. For example, if you want to keep a mailing list in name order, you can define the sort criteria and then call the search Name Order. As you add more records to the file, the file will no longer be in order. Then, you can simply run the named, stored sort without needing to define it again. You might also define a Zip Code order sort that you would use when preparing labels for a bulk mailing.

Don't forget that one of the reasons you choose specific data types for fields is to ensure that sorting will order them properly. For example, using a Date field ensures that dates will sort in correct chronological order; using a Name field makes it easy to keep names in a single field yet still have them sorted by last name.

Quick Sorts on a Single Field

If you want to sort records by a single field, you can do so quickly by using the Button Bar:

1. Click in the field on which you want to sort to make it active.
2. To sort in ascending order (for example, A to Z) by the active field, click the button in the Button Bar. To sort in descending order (for example, Z through A) by the active field, click the button in the Button Bar.

Sorts Using One or More Fields

To sort the data in a file:

1. For a one-time sort (one that will not be saved):

Macintosh	Choose Organize->Sort Records or press ⌘-J.
Windows	Choose Organize->Sort Records, press CTRL-J, or press ALT-R, R.

For a new named sort, choose New Sort from the Sort tool in the Tool panel (see Figure 8.37).

Figure 8.37 Creating a new sort

In both cases, the Sort Records dialog box appears (Figure 8.38). If you are creating a named sort, the dialog box will also have an edit box for entering the sort's name.

2. Highlight the first field on which you want to sort in the Field List list box. The arrows in the Move button point toward the Sort Order list box.

3. Click the Move button. ClarisWorks copies the field name into the Sort Order list box (Figure 8.39).

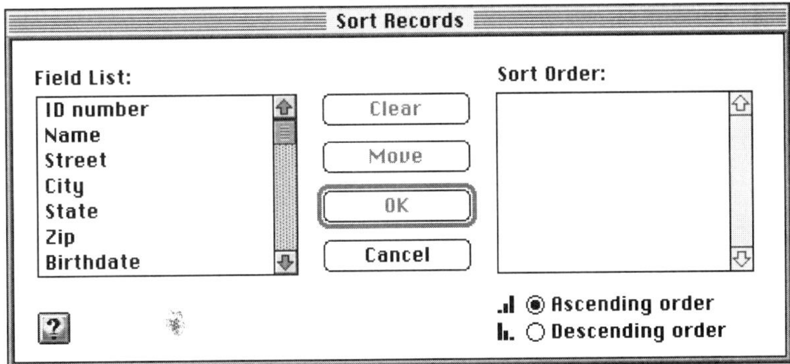

Figure 8.38 An empty Sort Records dialog box

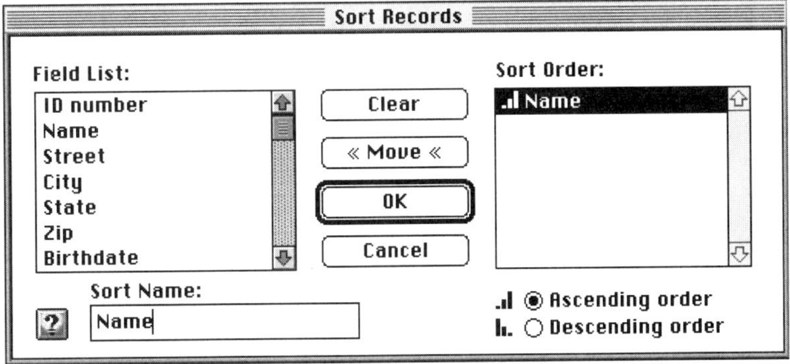

Figure 8.39 The Sort Records dialog box containing a field on which records are to be sorted

4. ClarisWorks makes the assumption that sorting will be in ascending order (from low to high). To change the order of a field in the Sort Order list box, click the Descending order radio button in the bottom right corner of the dialog box.

You can quickly copy fields from the Field List list box to the Sort Order list box by double-clicking on field names in the Field List list box.

5. Repeat steps 2 through 4 for any additional sort fields.

6. Click the OK button or press Enter. If you are performing a one-time sort, ClarisWorks immediately sorts the data. If you are creating a named sort, ClarisWorks stores the sort criteria but does not sort the records.

Using Named Sorts

When you create a named sort, ClarisWorks places the name of that sort at the bottom of the Sort tool's popup menu (Figure 8.40). To sort the records in the file using a named sort, choose the sort's name from the Sort tool's popup menu.

Figure 8.40 A named sort in the Sort tool's popup menu

You can resort the file by the most recently used sort criteria by clicking the 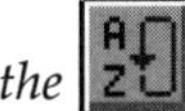 *button in the Button Bar.*

Changing One-Time Sort Criteria

ClarisWorks remembers the last sort criteria used during each ClarisWorks session. Therefore, if you return to the Sort Records dialog box to perform a one-time sort after you have already sorted the file, the dialog box won't be empty.

There are three techniques you can use to change the sort criteria:

- Highlight a field in the Sort Order list box. The arrows in the Move button will point toward the Field List list box. Click the Move button to remove the field from the Sort Order list box. Repeat the process for any fields you want to remove.

- Click the Clear button to remove all fields from the Sort Order list box.

- Highlight a field in the Sort Order list box. Then, click the Ascending order or Descending order radio button to change the direction in which the highlighted field is sorted.

Editing or Deleting a Named Sort

To change the criteria stored in a named sort:

1. Select Edit Sorts from the Sort tool's popup menu in the Tool panel. The Edit Sorts dialog box appears, listing all named sorts (Figure 8.41).

2. Highlight the name of the sort you want to modify or delete.

3. Click the Delete button to delete the named sort.

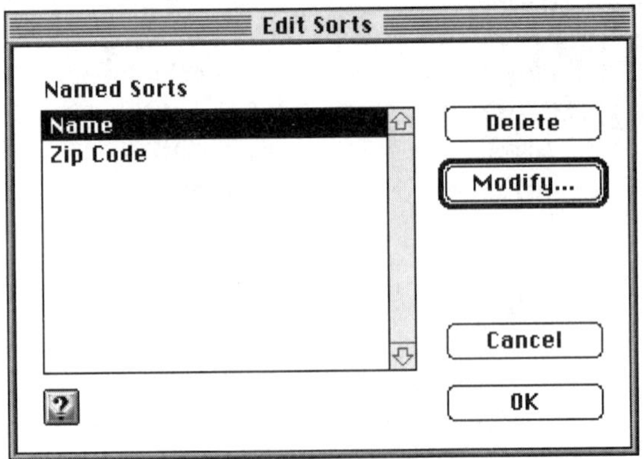

Figure 8.41 The Edit Sorts dialog box

ClarisWorks will not ask you to confirm the deletion of a sort. Be very sure that you want to remove the named sort before you click that Delete button!

4. Click the Modify button to change the sort criteria stored in a named sort. ClarisWorks displays the Sort Records dialog box. You can use the techniques described in the section "Changing One-Time Sort Criteria" to modify the sort.

Sorting and Data Modification

After you sort the records in a file, ClarisWorks changes the word "Unsorted" in the Tool panel to "Sorted." This lets you know that the records are now in order.

However, there are two things you can do that can make the sort order invalid, only one of which ClarisWorks can detect:

- When you add a new record to a file, ClarisWorks automatically assumes that the file will be out of order. Therefore, "Sorted" changes back to "Unsorted."
- If you modify the data in a record so that the record is out of order (for example, changing a last name in a Name field from "Johnson" to "Anderson"), ClarisWorks will not detect that the change affects the sort order. You will therefore need to be aware when this occurs and resort the file even though ClarisWorks thinks it is still sorted.

Viewing Records in Order

One of the ways you can view the data in a ClarisWorks database file is to look at the records in order. There are two ways to do so:

- Use the document window's scroll bars. When you scroll through the records in a file, you view them without selecting them.
- Use the record book in the tool panel. When you use the record book, you select and view records at the same time.

Using the Record Book

As you can see in Figure 8.42, the record book has several tools designed for selecting and viewing records:

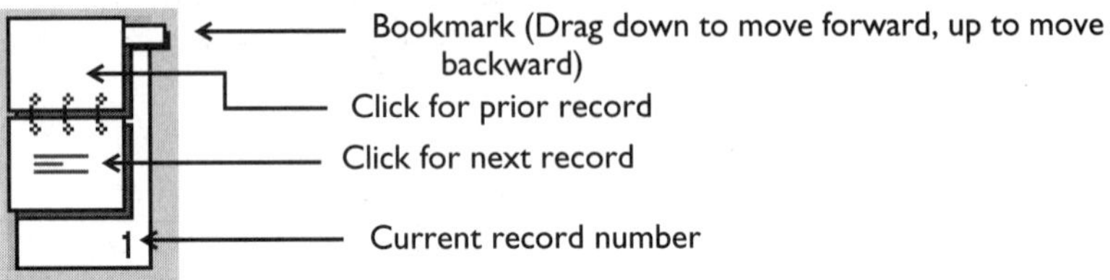

Figure 8.42 Using the record book

- Click the bottom page in the record book to select the next record.
- Click the top page in the record book to select the prior record.
- Drag the bookmark down to move forward in the file. (The number of records you move is proportional to the distance dragged.)
- Drag the bookmark up to move backward in the file.

The record number of the currently selected record appears in the lower right corner of the record book.

The record number assigned to a record is its current position in the file. This value may change each time you sort the file. Therefore, if you want to assign serial numbers to the records in your file, you should do so using a Serial number field. You can't rely on the record number remaining constant.

9

Data Management: Searching For Data

One of the major benefits of storing your data in a ClarisWorks database file is that it makes it easy to search for data that meet some type of logical criteria. (There's no point in storing data in a file if you can't retrieve the data when you need them!) For example, in the sample mailing list you have seen throughout Chapter 8, you might want to find all people whose birthdays fall in a given month or all the people who live in the same town. In this chapter you will therefore be introduced to how to perform ClarisWorks searches.

Understanding Logical Queries

A search that is applied to data stored in a ClarisWorks database file is made up of logical criteria the data must meet. If the data in a record meet the criteria, then the record satisfies the search and is included in the search result. If the data don't meet the search criteria, then the record is excluded from the search result. The key to a search is therefore the logical criteria against which data are evaluated.

Simple Logical Operators

The simplest type of search you can create is to ask ClarisWorks to evaluate the data in one field against a value. There are six relationships you can test:

- Equal to: When you ask for data equal to a value, ClarisWorks looks for all records that match the value exactly. The equal to relationship uses the symbol =. For example, the criterion "=15" matches all records that have the exact value of 15 in the field to which the criterion has been attached.

- Greater than: When you ask for data greater than a value, ClarisWorks looks for all records that have a value greater than what you have entered. The greater than relationship uses the symbol > (SHIFT-period on your keyboard). For example, the criterion ">15" matches all records that have a value greater than 15 in the field to which the criterion has been attached. All records with values of 15 or less won't satisfy the criterion.

- Greater than or equal to: When you ask for data that are greater than or equal to a value, ClarisWorks looks for all records with values that match or exceed the value you have entered. The greater than or equal to relationship uses the symbol >= or ≥ (OPTION-period on the Macintosh keyboard). For example, the criterion ">=15" matches all records that have a value of 15 or higher in the field to which the criterion has been attached.

- Less than: When you ask for data that are less than a value, ClarisWorks looks for all records with values that are less than the value you have entered. The less than relationship uses the symbol < (SHIFT-comma on your keyboard). For example, the criterion "<15" matches all records that have a value of less than 15 in the field to which the criterion has been attached.

- Less than or equal to: When you ask for data that are less than or equal to a value, ClarisWorks looks for all records with values that match or are less than the value you have entered. The less than or equal to relationship uses the symbol <= or ≤ (OPTION-comma on the Macintosh keyboard). For example, the criterion "<=15" matches all records that have a value of 15 or less in the field to which the criterion has been attached.

- Not equal to: When you ask for data that are not equal to a value, ClarisWorks looks for all records that don't match the value you have entered. The not equal to relationship uses either the symbol <> (the less than symbol followed by the greater than symbol) or the symbol ≠ (OPTION-= on the Macintosh keyboard). The behavior of the not equal to relationship is a bit more complex than that of the other relationships. For more details, see the section titled "Search Criteria and Nulls" that follows shortly.

Searches and Data Types

In Chapter 8 you read that one of the reasons it was important to choose the right data types for fields is so that fields will be ordered correctly. For example, if you want to search for all dates prior to some given date, then you want ClarisWorks to evaluate the dates in chronological order. This will occur only if the dates are stored in a date field.

The ordering that ClarisWorks uses when searching (and sorting) various types of fields is as follows:

- Text: Text fields are evaluated in alphabetical order, starting at the leftmost character in the field.
- Name: Name fields are evaluated like text fields, in alphabetical order starting at the leftmost character in the field. (However, sorting begins at the last word in the field.)
- Number: Number fields are evaluated in numeric order.
- Date: Date fields are evaluated in chronological order.
- Time: Time fields are evaluated in chronological order.
- Radio buttons: Radio button fields support only the equal to operator. When creating a search in Find mode, you select one of the radio buttons in the set for ClarisWorks to match.
- Value list: Value list fields are evaluated like text fields, in alphabetical order starting at the leftmost character in the field.

- Popup menu: Popup menu fields support only the equal to operator. When creating a search, you can select one value in the menu for ClarisWorks to match. In Find mode, the popup menu will also contain an option named "don't care." If you select this option, ClarisWorks will ignore the value in the popup menu field during the search.

- Check box: Check box fields support only the equal to operator. Either the value in the field is true, the value is false, or you don't care what the value is. When you view a layout in Find mode that contains a check box, a dash in the box (-) means that the value in that field will be ignored in the search.

- Multimedia frame: Multimedia frame fields cannot be the basis of a search.

Search Criteria and Nulls

One of the things that complicates the interpretation of a search is the presence of fields that don't contain any data. (For example, in the mailing list, people to whom birthday presents aren't set won't have a value in the field for the maximum gift price.) In database terms, an empty field really isn't' empty; it contains a value known as *null*, which means "unknown." Null isn't the same as zero or a blank; it is a special value that tells that database that the value in the field isn't known.

What should ClarisWorks do when it encounters fields with nulls? When it comes to the equal to relationship, ClarisWorks omits records with nulls. A record containing a null won't match any criteria you might enter. The same is true for greater than, greater than or equal to, less than, and less than or equal to. ClarisWorks excludes records with nulls.

However, what should happen with the not equal to relationship? To see why this is a bit of a problem, assume you wanted to see all records in the mailing list for which the maximum gift price was not equal to 15. There are three records with maximum gift values of 25, 35, and 50. Certainly those records meet the search criterion.

But what about the records with null for the maximum gift value? Null is definitely not equal to 15. However, ClarisWorks will not retrieve those records. As with the other relationships, a not equal to search ignores records containing nulls in the field being searched. Depending on what you really want from the search, this behavior can be a bit misleading and hard to interpret.

If you want a not equal to search to include records with null values, you must approach the task in a different way. You perform an equal to search and then tell ClarisWorks to omit all records that meet the criteria. In the mailing list example, you specify =15 as the search criterion and then ask for all records that *don't* meet it.

Complex Search Criteria

The search criteria you have read about to this point have involved only a single relationship and value in a single field. However, sometimes you want to request records that meet multiple criteria. For example, you might want to view records in the mailing list for all women to whom you send birthday gifts. Alternatively, you might want to view records in the mailing list for all people who live in either New York or New Hampshire.

A search criterion that requires a record to meet multiple criteria conceptually uses the logical operator AND. The mailing list query about women and birthday gifts is therefore:

Gender = female AND Send gift = true

When you create criteria of this type, a record must meet *every* condition before it is retrieved.

ClarisWorks uses the symbol & to represent the logical operator AND. Because field names can be more than one word long, they must be enclosed in a pair of single quotes; text values must be surrounded by double quotes. The preceding expression would therefore be written:

'Gender' = "female" & 'Send gift' = true

A search criterion that requires a record to meet only one of a group of criteria conceptually uses the logical operator OR. The mailing list query about the states in which people live is therefore:

State = NY OR State = NH

When you create criteria of this type, a record needs to meet only one of the criteria.

ClarisWorks uses the symbol ^ to represent the logical operator OR. Therefore, when including the preceding expression in a ClarisWorks search, you would use:

'State' = "NY" ^ 'State' = "NH"

As you will see shortly, ClarisWorks has techniques for performing searches involving AND and OR that don't require you to type the words for relatively simple queries.

Because of the way in which ClarisWorks stores data in some types of fields, you will not always be able to construct logical search expressions without first converting the data into a different type. You will read more details about this later in this chapter in the section on matching records.

Find versus Match

ClarisWorks provides two techniques for searching for records: finding and matching. Each has its own capabilities and situations in which it is most appropriate.

Searches with Find

When you use Find, you work with a layout into which you enter search criteria. With Find, you don't need to type a logical expression. Find is therefore easy to use.

However, without resorting to a special trick, you can't use Find to construct a logical expression that involves two fields in the same record. (You'll see how to implement this little trick in Chapter 10, with the discussion of calculated fields.)

For example, assume that you are using a database file to store your office supplies inventory. You have a field that holds the quantity in stock and another field that holds the reorder point. To determine which items need to be reordered, you want to locate records that meet the following criteria:

'Quantity in stock' <= 'Reorder point'

Because these two fields are part of the same record, Find won't be able to create this expression.

When you execute a Find, ClarisWorks locates the records that meet the search criteria. Then, by default it hides the records that *don't* meet the criteria. You can then work with the chosen records (the *found set*) as if the records that aren't part of the found set weren't part of the file. The found set will be the only records to appear in a layout or in List mode. They can also be sorted independently of the records that weren't found.

The search criteria that make up a Find can be named and saved. They can therefore be combined with a named sort and a layout to produce a report.

Searches with Match

A search using Match requires you to build a logical expression, using the syntax you saw earlier in this chapter. Although you don't necessarily need to type all the elements of the expression — you can select many of the elements from scrolling lists of possibilities — you nonetheless must know how the expression should appear.

Because Match allows you to enter a logical expression, you can use it to perform searches that compare two fields in the same record. In addition, the logical expressions you create can use functions. In terms of the types of searches it can perform, Match is therefore more flexible, but more difficult to use, than Find.

When you execute a Match, ClarisWorks *selects* the records that meet the search criteria; they aren't hidden. However, once the Match has been completed, you can hide the selected records. This means that if you want to view records that Match a specific criterion, you will need to write the Match expression so that records that *don't* meet the criterion are selected. Then you can hide them.

Match criteria cannot be named and saved. Therefore, they cannot become part of a ClarisWorks report.

Performing Quick Matches

You can quickly match records that meet a single criterion by using buttons in the Button Bar. Suppose, for example, that you want to locate all people in the mailing list to whom you don't send gifts. You can do this without resorting to Find mode or creating a matching expression.

To perform a quick match:

1. Make sure that you are in either Browse or List mode.
2. Display any record that contains the value you want to use in a Match expression.
3. Click in the field containing the value.
4. Click an operator button in the Button Bar. The possible operators are:

Operator button	Expression ClarisWorks creates
=	'Field' = value
≠	'Field' ≠ value
<	'Field' < value
>	'Field' > value

ClarisWorks performs the search and selects all records that meet the search criterion.

Finding Records

Find mode makes it easy to construct a search because you can "fill in the blanks" on a layout. Each layout that you fill in is known as a *Find request*. To perform a Find, you will need a layout that contains all the fields on which you want to search. (It doesn't matter if the layout contains fields that aren't going to be part of the search.)

Creating a Simple Find Expression

The simplest Find expression you can create involves one field value and one relationship operator. For example, you might want to find all the people in the mailing list database to whom you send gifts more than $15 in value.

To create a simple Find:

1. Select the layout you want to use to perform the Find. The only criterion for the layout is that it contain the field on which the Find will be based.
2. Enter Find mode:

Macintosh	Choose Layout->Find or press SHIFT-⌘-F.
Windows	Choose Layout->Find, press SHIFT-CTRL-F, or press ALT-L, F.

   The tool panel changes to provide the Find tools, as in Figure 9.1.

3. Enter the relationship operator and the value to evaluate in the field to which it applies. In this example, you would enter >15 in the Maximum gift price field (see Figure 9.2).

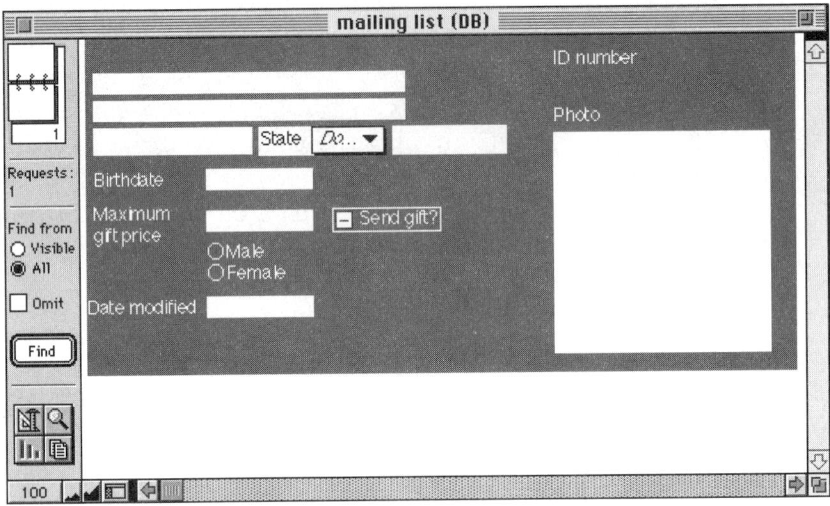

Figure 9.1 Find mode

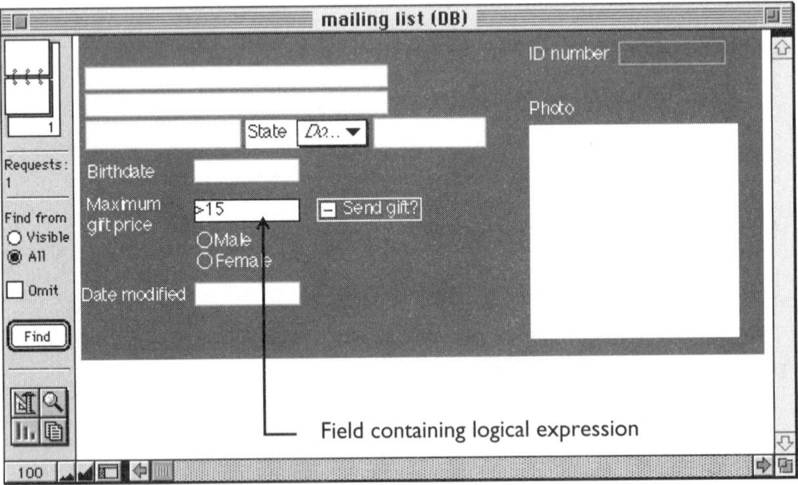

Figure 9.2 A Find expression in a layout

4. Click the Find button or press Enter. ClarisWorks locates the records that match the Find criterion and hides those that don't match from view. You will be returned to Browse mode. As you can see in Figure 9.3, the tool panel shows you how many records of the total were found, in the format *found (total)*.

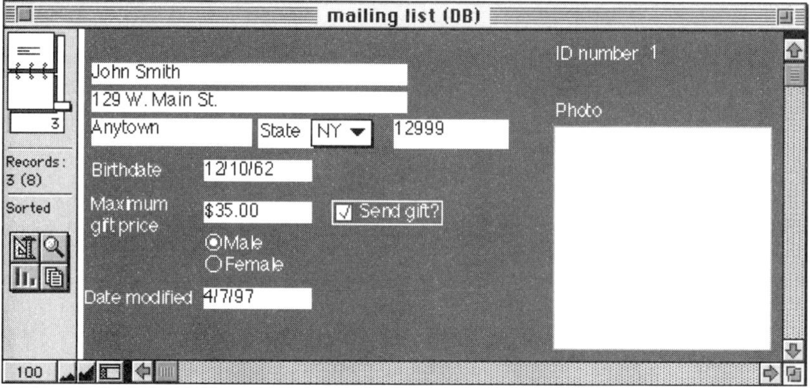

Figure 9.3 The result of a Find

Restoring All Records

When you have finished using the records found by a Find, you can recall all the records in the file with:

Macintosh	Choose Organize->Show All Records or press SHIFT-1-A.
Windows	Choose Organize->Show All Records, press SHIFT-CTRL-A, or press ALT-R, A.

tip

You can also restore all records by clicking the [button] *button in the Button Bar.*

Creating Searches That Use AND

If you place criteria in more than one field in a layout, then ClarisWorks performs an AND. For example, the Find request in Figure 9.4 is the same as the expression

Maximum gift price > 15 AND Gender = female

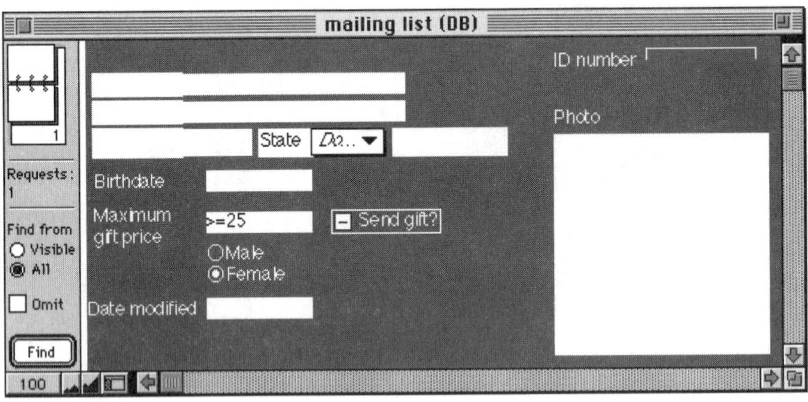

Figure 9.4 A Find request that specifies two simple expressions linked by AND

A record will therefore need to match both criteria if it is to be included in the found set.

Creating Searches That Use OR

Searches that link simple expressions with OR present a bit of a challenge because you can't put more than one expression in a field on a Find mode layout. The trick is therefore to have more than one copy of the layout. In other words, you add additional Find requests to the search.

Assume, for example, that you want to use Find to locate records for all people living in either NY or NH. To perform that search you would do the following:

1. Enter Find mode and choose the layout you want to use.

2. Enter the first search criterion. As you can see in Figure 9.5, the request contains the value NY in the State field.

3. Add another Find request:

Macintosh	Choose Edit->New Request or press ⌘-R.
Windows	Choose Edit->New Request, press CTRL-R, or press ALT-E, R.

4. Enter search criteria in the new request. As you can see in Figure 9.6, the second request appears as another copy of the layout.

5. Repeat steps 3 and 4 for all expressions that should be connected with OR.

Within any individual Find request, you can have multiple conditions that will be connected with AND.

6. Click the Find button or press Enter to process the search.

Find Requests and the Record Book

When you are in Find mode, the record book counts the number of Find requests, rather than the number of records as it does in Browse mode. You can therefore use the record

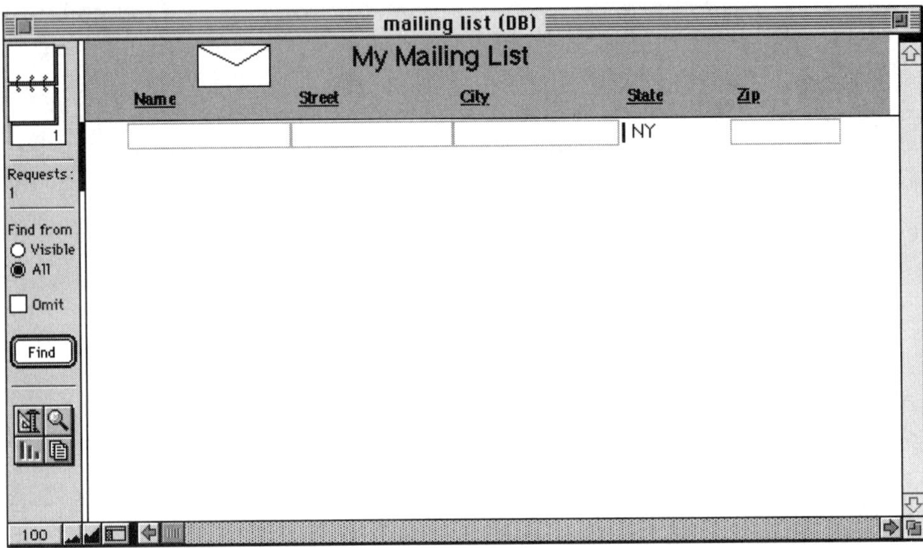

Figure 9.5 The first Find request in a multiple-request search

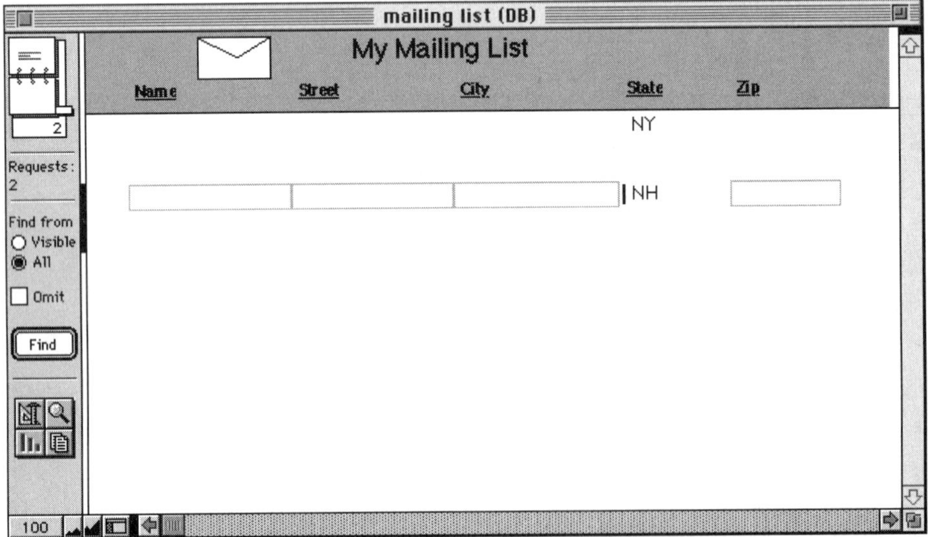

Figure 9.6 A second Find request

book to move through the requests. This is particularly useful if the layout you are using is so large that you can see only one Find request at a time.

Duplicating Requests

If you want to add a Find request that is a duplicate of the preceding request:

Macintosh	Choose Edit->Duplicate Request or press ⌘-D.
Windows	Choose Edit->Duplicate Request, press CTRL-D, or press ALT-E, D.

Deleting Requests

To remove a Find request from the Find mode window:

1. Select the request to be removed by clicking anywhere in the request.
2. Choose Edit->Delete Request.

Negative Searches: Omitting Records

One of the ways to perform a search that contains negative criteria (for example, all values not equal to another value) is to define a Find request that is the opposite of what you want and then ask ClarisWorks to omit records that meet the criteria from the found set. (You read about searches of this type earlier in this chapter in the context of handling records with null values.)

Assume, for example, that you want to locate all the records in the mailing list for people who don't live in NY. Because the State field is a popup menu, there is no way to enter an operator in the field. The only thing you can do is choose a value to match using the equal to operator or indicate that you don't care about the value in the field. However, what you can do is configure the Find request so that it omits all records with the value of NY for the State, leaving you with records for those who don't live in NY.

To perform a Find search that omits records:

1. Enter Find mode and select the layout without which you want to work.

2. Create a Find request that will identify records that you want left out of the found set.

3. Click the Omit check box in the tool panel. For example, the Find request in Figure 9.7 will match records with a value of NY for State. However, those records will be omitted from the found set because the Omit check box is checked.

4. Click the OK button or press Enter to perform the search.

Controlling the Search Set

A Find can be performed either on all records in a file or on the records in the found set ("Visible" records).

To restrict a search to visible records, click the Visible radio button in the tool panel. To return to searching the entire file, click the All radio button in the tool panel.

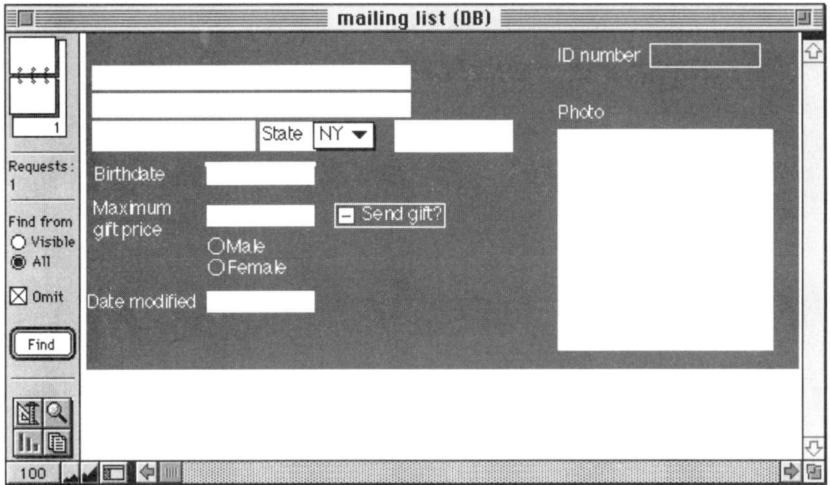

Figure 9.7 A Find request that omits matching records

Creating Named Searches

One of the benefits of using Find rather than Match is that you can name and save searches for later use. A named search can then become part of a report, which groups together a layout, named sort, and named find.

To create a named search:

1. Choose New Search from the search tool's popup menu in the Tool panel (see Figure 9.8). A dialog box appears into which you can enter a name for the search.

2. Enter the search's name, as in Figure 9.9.

Figure 9.8 Creating a new named search

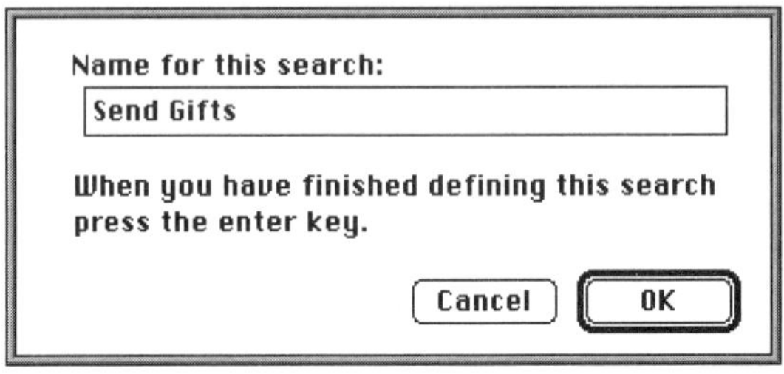

Figure 9.9 Naming a search

3. Click the OK button or press Enter. ClarisWorks takes you to Find mode. Notice in Figure 9.10 that the Find button has been replaced with a Store button.

4. Enter search criteria into the Find mode layout, creating additional Find requests as needed.

5. Click the Store button or press Enter. ClarisWorks stores the named search and adds its name to the bottom of the Search tool's popup menu.

Editing Named Searches

You can change the criteria in a named search at any time. To do so:

1. Choose Edit Searches from the Search tool's popup menu. A dialog box containing all named searches appears (see Figure 9.11).

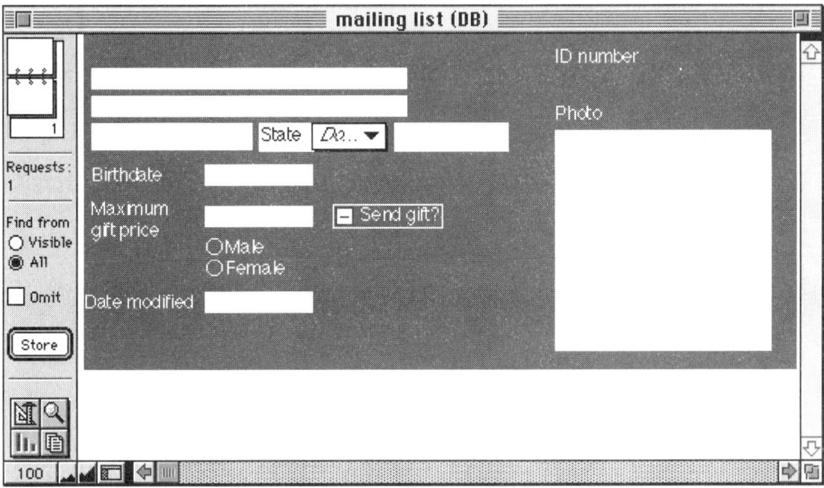

Figure 9.10 Find mode for creating a named search

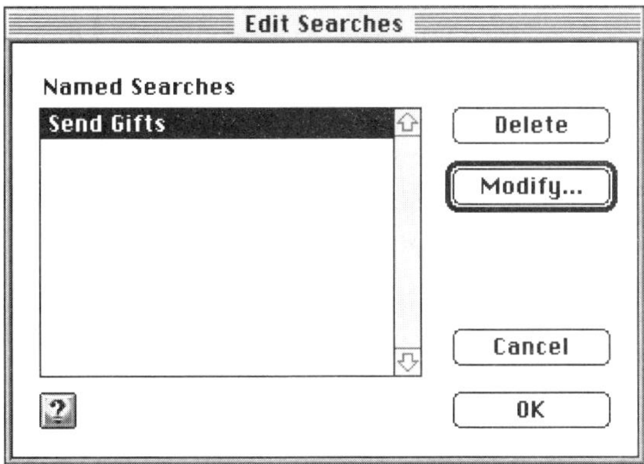

Figure 9.11 Choosing a named search to edit

2. Highlight the name of the search you want to modify.

3. Click the Modify button or press Enter.

4. ClarisWorks displays a dialog box giving you a chance to change the search's name (see Figure 9.9).

5. Click the OK button or press Enter. ClarisWorks returns you to Find mode so that you can modify the search.

To delete a named search, highlight the search name in the Edit Searches dialog box and click the Delete button.

Using a Named Search

To use a named search, select the search's name from the Search tool's popup menu in the tool panel.

Matching Records

As you read earlier in this chapter, matching records allows you to construct logical expressions against which records are then evaluated. Matching selects the records that meet the criteria in the match expression. You can then hide either the selected or unselected records.

Entering the Match Expressions

To perform a match:

1. Make sure that you are in Browse mode.

2.

Macintosh	Choose Organize->Match Records or press ⌘-M.
Windows	Choose Organize->Match Records, press CTRL-M, or press ALT-R, M.

The Enter Match Records Condition dialog box appears (Figure 9.12).

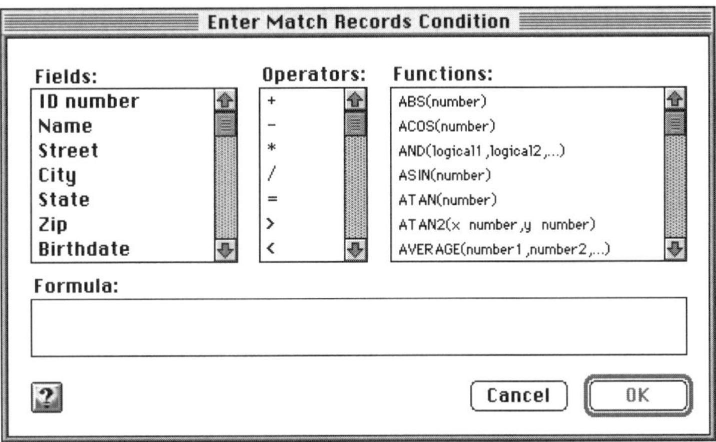

Figure 9.12 The Enter Match Records Condition dialog box

The logical expression against which data will be matched appears in the Formula edit box. You can edit the contents of this box directly or you can double-click on entries in the scrolling lists at the top of the dialog box to transfer elements to the Formula box.

The Fields list contains a list of all fields in the file. The Operators list contains all the relationship and logical operators, including & for AND, ^ for OR. The rightmost list provides ClarisWorks functions (the same functions that can be used in a spreadsheet). To transfer an element from a list to the expression in the Formula box, double click on whatever you want to transfer.

3. Construct the match expression by double-clicking on list elements, typing into the Formula box, or whatever combination of both is needed to create your expression.

4. Click the OK button or press Enter. ClarisWorks closes the Enter Match Records Condition dialog box and performs the search. You are returned to Browse mode, where records that meet the search condition will be selected.

Creating Match Expressions

Match expressions that include text or numeric fields are usually straightforward. However, when you work with date, radio button, popup menu, or check box fields, the match expressions usually require the use of special functions that convert between the way in which ClarisWorks stores data internally and values on which you would like to search. This section therefore includes some examples of matching on these types of fields.

Working with Dates

ClarisWorks stores a date as a single number that represents the number of days elapsed since January 1, 1904. This means that an expression such as

'Birthdate' = 12/12/65

simply won't work. To match against a specific date, you need to convert the date to text and then compare it to a text value.

For example, the preceding expression needs to be written as:

TEXTTODATE ('Birthdate', 0) = "12/12/65"

The first argument in the TEXTTODATE function is the name of a date field. The second represents the format in which the date should be placed. The format numbers you can use are as follows:

Format number	Format
0	12/12/65
1	Dec 12, 1965
2	December 12, 1965
3	Wed, December 12, 1965
4	Wednesday, December 12, 1965

With the help of functions, you can also extract the month or year from a date. For example, if you want to find all the people in the mailing list who have birthdays in April, you could use the expression

MONTH ('Birthdate') = 4

Notice that the MONTH function has only one argument, a date field, and that it returns the number of the month.

By the same token, if you want to find all the people who were born after 1970, you could use

YEAR ('Birthdate') > 1970

Like MONTH, the YEAR function requires just a date field as an argument.

You might, for example, want to match records for all people who have birthdays in the current month. The match expression would be written

MONTH ('Birthdate') = MONTH (NOW())

The NOW function, which takes no arguments, gives you the current system date. Placing it in the MONTH function extracts the current month, which can then be compared to the month portion of the contents of the Birthdate field. If you want all the records for people who have birthdays in the *next* month, simply add one:

MONTH ('Birthdate') = MONTH (NOW()) + 1

Times are stored as the elapsed time since midnight. You must therefore also convert times to text with the TIMETOTEXT function before using them in a match expression. You can extract portions of a time field with the HOUR, MINUTE, and SECOND functions.

Working with Radio Button and Popup Menu Fields

ClarisWorks assigns numbers to each radio button in a radio button field. ClarisWorks also numbers the options in a popup menu. This means that you need to convert that number to its text equivalent for matching. For example, if you wanted to find all the women in the mailing list, you would use an expression like

NUMTOTEXT ('Gender') = "Female"

If you wanted to find all the people who live in New York State, your expression would be

NUMTOTEXT ('State') = "NY"

The NUMTOTEXT function accepts any numeric value as an argument, including any field that stores a number.

Working with Check Box Fields

If a check box field contains an X, ClarisWorks stores the value *true*. When a check box is empty, ClarisWorks stores *false*. A match expression including a check box field must therefore use only those values. For example, to find all the people in the mailing list to whom you send gifts, the expression would be

'Send gift' = true

Hiding Unselected Records

The result of a match is selected records. For example, the records selected in Figure 9.13 are the result of a match using the expression in the preceding section ('Send gift' = true). In this case, you are looking at List mode.

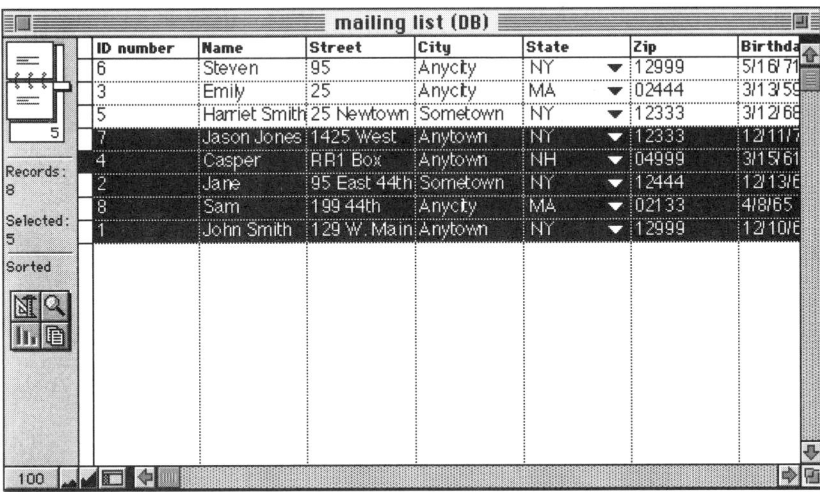

Figure 9.13 Matched records

Notice that the record book tells you how many records out of the total are selected. In addition, the current record (in this example, the record with ID number 4) is indicated by a black box to its very left. The current record (the one you would see if you were looking at a layout that showed only one record at a time) may or may not be one of the records identified by a match.

To hide unselected records (those that didn't meet the criteria in the match expression):

Macintosh	Choose Organize->Hide Unselected or press 1-).
Windows	Choose Organize->Hide Unselected, press CTRL-), or press ALT-R, U.

As you can see in Figure 9.14, the record book now indicates that only five of eight records are visible — 5(8) — and that all five are selected.

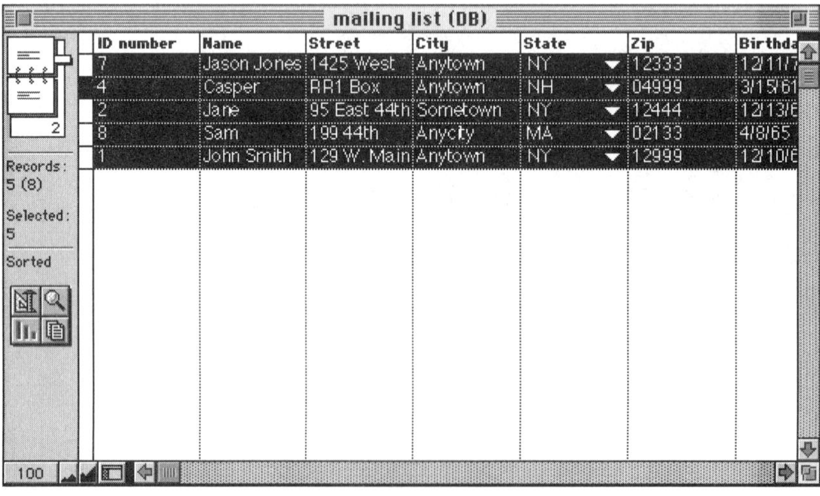

Figure 9.14 List mode where unselected records have been hidden

At this point, the records have been divided into two sets: visible and not visible. You can now perform any actions you need on the visible set, including sorting and finding.

Rather than hiding unselected records, you may choose to hide selected records, leaving you with records that *don't* meet the search criteria. (This is very much like using Find mode's Omit option.)

To hide selected records:

Macintosh	Choose Organize->Hide Selected or press 1-(.
Windows	Choose Organize->Hide Selected, press CTRL-(, or press ALT-R, S.

To restore all records, use Organize->Show All Records just as you would to restore all records after a Find.

10

Data Management Extras

If you have been reading the data management chapters in order, then at this point you know all the basics of ClarisWorks data management. However, there are some additional things you can do to give your data management extra sophistication.

In this chapter, you will read about using calculation fields. You will also learn to create reports that use summary fields to display totals and subtotals. In addition, this chapter enhances your knowledge of layout customization techniques and introduces you to mail merge, with which you can combine word processing and data management to produce customized mailings.

Adding Calculation Fields

A calculation field is a field whose contents are determined by some type of formula. The formulas can include any of the ClarisWorks arithmetic operators and/or functions that make sense for the type of data being manipulated.

For example, if you wanted to know how much a gift would cost after adding 7.5% sales tax, you could create a calculation field with the formula:

'Maximum gift$' * 1.075

Although you can place calculation fields on a layout along with fields of any other type, a user cannot modify the contents of the field in Browse or List mode. In fact, the user won't even be able to click in the field to make it active. However, you will be able to access the field in Find mode so that you can enter search criteria using that field.

To create a calculation field:

1. Display the Define Database Fields dialog box.

2. Enter a name for the field.

3. Choose Calculation as the field's type (see Figure 10.1).

4. Click the Create button or press Enter. ClarisWorks displays the Enter Formula dialog box in which you can enter the formula that will generate the field's contents.

5. Enter the formula for the field, as in Figure 10.2.

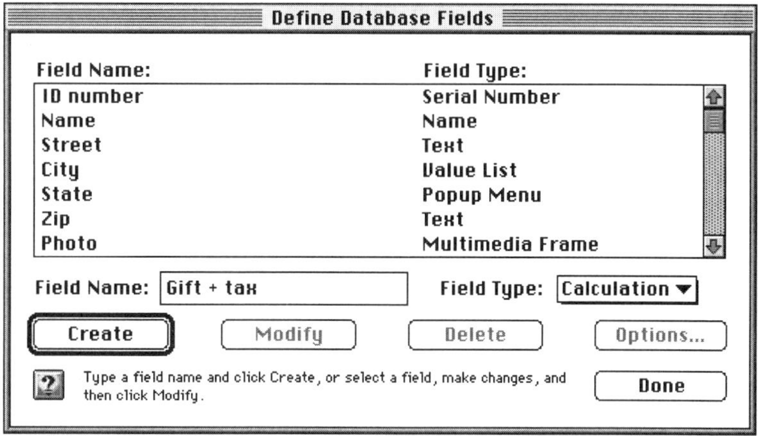

Figure 10.1 Adding a calculation field

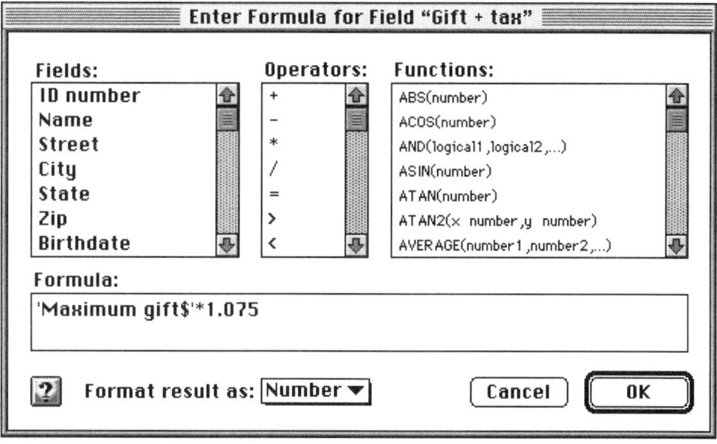

Figure 10.2 Entering the formula for a calculation field

6. Choose a data type for the field from the "Format result as" popup menu. In the mailing list example, the result should be left as a Number.

7. Click the OK button or press Enter. ClarisWorks adds the field to the field list and shows its formula in the Define Database Fields dialog box (see Figure 10.3).

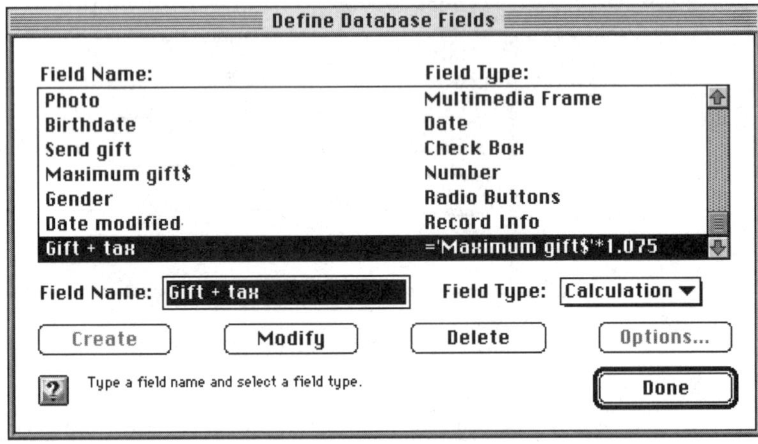

Figure 10.3 A calculation field in the Define Database Fields dialog box

8. Click the OK button or press Enter to close the Define Database Fields dialog box. ClarisWorks places the new field on the current layout and calculates its contents for all records currently in the file.

The Effect of New Fields on Existing Layouts

When you add a new field to a file, ClarisWorks automatically adds that field and a field label to the current layout (see Figure 10.4). If you have customized your layout, then you may not want the field in the place where ClarisWorks puts it, or you may not want the field to appear at all.

If you aren't happy with where ClarisWorks places the new field and its label, you will need to edit the layout to change or remove the new elements.

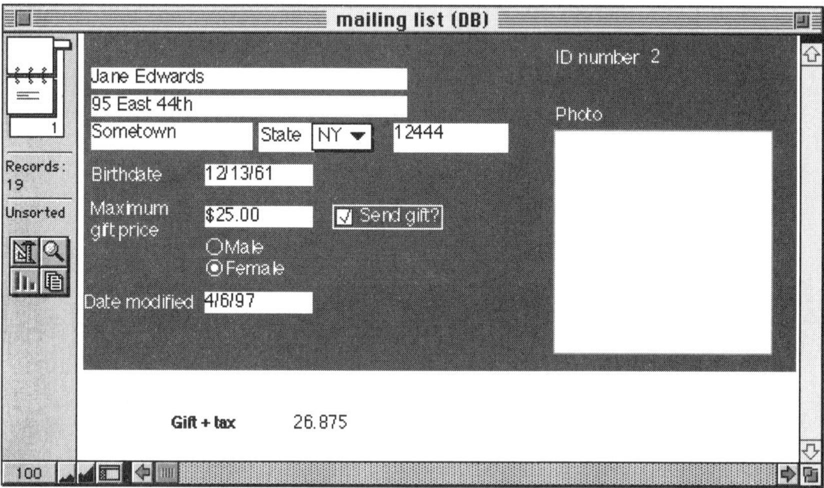

Figure 10.4 A new field added to the current layout

Recalculation

Once a calculation field is part of a database file, ClarisWorks retains the contents of that calculation field. However, the calculation field is linked to the fields used in its formula. This means that if you change the value in a field on which a calculation depends, ClarisWorks will automatically recalculate the value in the calculation field.

Using Calculation Fields to Support Find

One of the biggest limitations to Find mode is that there are some searches that you simply can't perform. As you may remember from Chapter 9, Find can't compare data from two fields in the same record. For example, Find can't compare the current inventory level of a supply item with the reorder point to determine whether the item should be reordered. However, with a little help from a calculated field, you can actually include this type of a search in a Find.

The trick is to create a calculation field that contains the difference between the current inventory level and the reorder point. The formula for the field is

'Inventory level' - 'Reorder point'

As long as there are more items in inventory than the reorder point, the value in the calculation field will be greater than 0. However, when the two are equal, or the inventory level drops below the reorder point, the value in the field will be equal to or less than 0. Therefore, to find items that need to be reordered, you place the following expression in the calculation field:

<= 0

Keep in mind that this works because every time you change the value in the Inventory level field, ClarisWorks automatically updates the value in the calculation field.

It would also be nice to be able to create a named Find for the mailing list that identified all people with birthdays in the current month. However, as you will see, although you can create an expression that works, updating the expression is a major problem.

To store the relationship between the current month and the month in a birthdate, you could create a calculation field that contains the expression

MONTH('Birthday') = MONTH(NOW())

If the expression is true, ClarisWorks puts a 1 in the calculation field; if the expression is false, ClarisWorks stores a 0.

Unfortunately, because ClarisWorks updates calculation fields only when the field(s) on which the calculation is based is modified, the contents of the calculation field in this case will be correct only at the time the field is created. You won't be updating birthdates regularly, so there is nothing to trigger the recalculation of the contents of the calculation field.

Creating and Using Layouts with Totals and Subtotals

One of the common things people do with data is to prepare summary reports. For example, in Figure 10.5 you can see a summary of the maximum amount of money that the owner of the mailing list will spend on birthday gifts during a year. The report is organized by month. It shows the name of each month, the maximum amount to be spent during that month, and details about the people whose birthdays fall in that month. The bottom of the report contains the total amount to be spent.

Reports of this type are known as *control break reports* because they use the value in a field to identify the breaks between groups of data. In this particular example, the groups break on the value of a calculation field that contains the month of each birthdate.

Preparing a control break report using ClarisWorks isn't difficult, although it does require a bit of careful preparation. To make the process clearer, we'll go through it step by step. But first, let's take a look at the finished layout.

mailing list (DB)

Records: 20

Sorted

Yearly Gift Spending Summary

March		**Amount to be Spent**	$0.00
	Emily Johnson	3/13/59	
	Peter Smith	3/6/72	
	Casper Jones	3/15/61	
	Harriet Smith	3/12/68	
April		**Amount to be Spent**	$25.00
	Sam Johnson	4/8/65	
	Terry Jones	4/18/73	
	Jason Edwards	4/21/71	
	Lori Smith	4/19/61	
	Pamela Smith	4/18/71	
May		**Amount to be Spent**	$0.00
	Steven Jones	5/16/70	
	James Johnson	5/15/78	
June		**Amount to be Spent**	$40.00
	Terry Jones	6/15/68	
	Jane Edwards	6/12/63	
	Leslie Jones	6/21/73	
July		**Amount to be Spent**	$50.00
	Lori Edwards	7/12/72	
August		**Amount to be Spent**	$15.00
	Peter Edwards	8/15/62	
October		**Amount to be Spent**	$25.00
	Melanie Johnson	10/10/68	
December		**Amount to be Spent**	$15.00
	Jason Jones	12/11/73	
	John Smith	12/10/62	
	Michael Johnson	12/15/73	
		Total to be Spent	$398.00

100 Page 1

Figure 10.5 A summary report with subtotals and a grand total

A Layout for a Control Break Report

The completed layout for the gift summary report can be found in Figure 10.6. Like other layouts you have seen, it has a Body part and a Header part. The Body part contains the data that should be repeated within each group (in this case, a person's name and birthdate). The Header part contains text for the report's title.

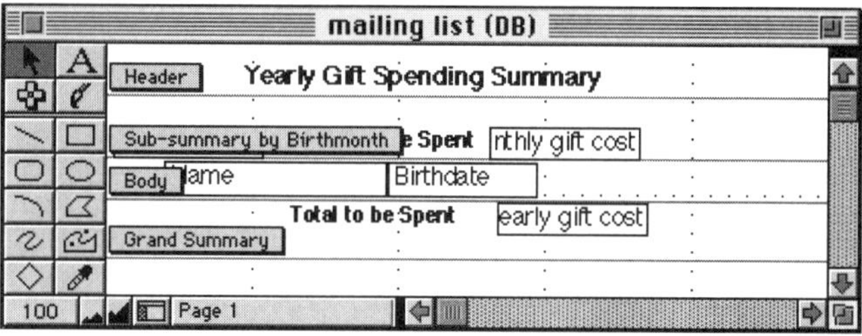

Figure 10.6 A layout for a control break report

The layout contains two new parts:

- Sub-summary: A Sub-summary part groups records on the basis of the values in one or more fields. It can appear above or below the records it is grouping. In our example, the grouping is made on the value of a calculation field called Birthmonth, whose contents are defined by the expression

  MONTHNAME(MONTH('Birthdate')

  The MONTH function extracts the month from the Birthdate field as a number, but we want the month to appear as a word on the report. We therefore use the MONTHNAME function, which takes a month number and translates it into the name of the month. In this particular example, the Birthmonth field appears in the Sub-summary part — you can't see it because it is hidden by the part label — but there is no requirement that it be there.

- Grand summary: A Grand summary part contains data that apply to the file as a whole. It can be placed at the beginning of the report or at the end.

Preparing the Report: Summary Fields

Summary fields are fields whose values are computed from groups of records. They can appear only in Sub-summary or Grand summary parts. The first step in preparing a control break report is therefore to create any needed Summary fields.

The report we are preparing requires a subtotal in a Sub-summary part and a grand total in a Grand summary part. Because each Summary field can appear only once on a layout, we will need two Summary fields, even though both will be defined by exactly the same formula.

To create a Summary field:

1. Display the Define Database Fields dialog box.
2. Enter a name for the field. (In this example, the fields are named Monthly gift cost and Yearly gift cost.)
3. Choose a field type of Summary.
4. Click the Create button or press Enter. ClarisWorks displays the Enter Formula dialog box for you to enter the formula that will define the value in the field.

5. Enter the formula. As you can see in Figure 10.7, the formula in the mailing list example uses the SUM function to total the values in the Maximum gift$ field.

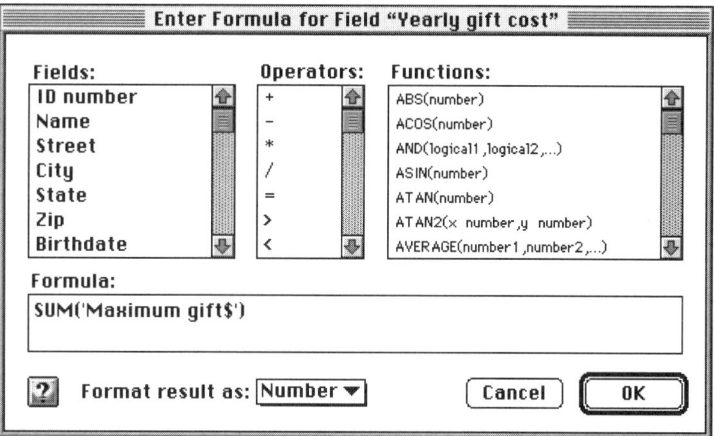

Figure 10.7 Entering a formula for a Summary field

6. Click OK or press Enter. ClarisWorks stores the newly created field in the field (see Figure 10.8).

When you add a Calculation field to a file, ClarisWorks automatically places that field on the current layout. However, unless the current layout has a Sub-summary or Grand summary part, a newly created Summary field will not appear automatically on the layout.

Preparing the Report: Creating the Initial Layout

Control break reports are typically based on columnar layouts (although there is nothing that would prevent you from

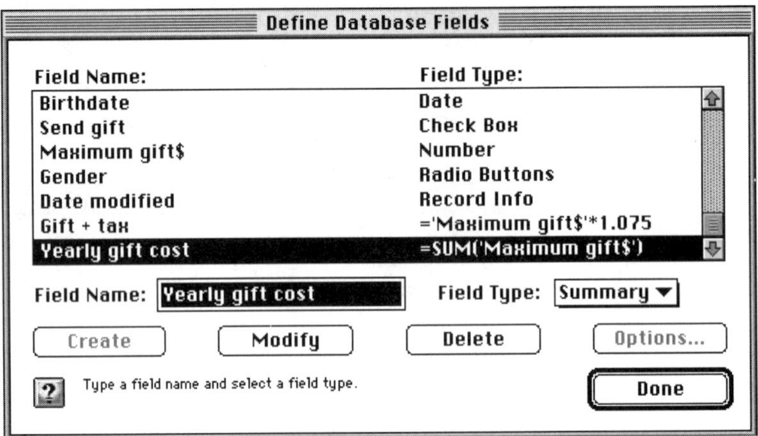

Figure 10.8 A Summary field in the Define Database Fields dialog box

using any other type). To create the basic layout, to which you will later add Sub-summary and Grand summary parts, do the following:

1. Create a new columnar layout (Figure 10.9).

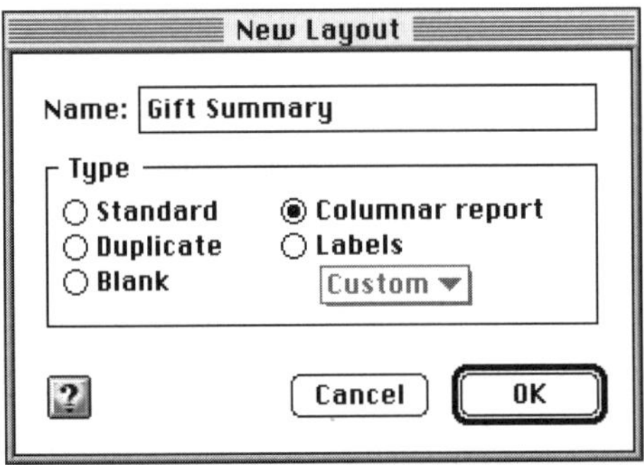

Figure 10.9 Creating a columnar layout for a control break report

2. Add the fields that will appear in the Body part. These should be fields for which you want to see values from every row. For example, the gift summary

report displays the name and birthdate of every person (see Figure 10.10).

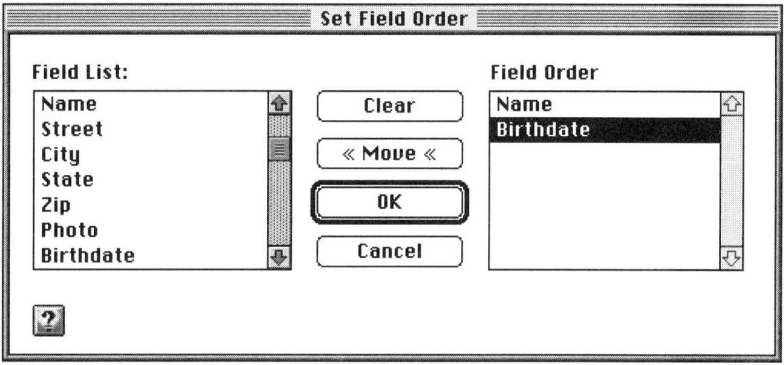

Figure 10.10 Choosing fields for the Body part of a control break report

3. Move the fields within the Body part so that they are located where you want them to appear.

4. If desired, remove the field labels from the Header part, as was done for the gift summary report.

Preparing the Report: Adding the Sub-Summary Part

Once you have the Summary field(s) you need, you can proceed to add Sub-summary and Grand summary parts to the file. (It really doesn't matter which you add first.)

To add a Sub-summary part to a layout:

1. Display the Insert Part dialog box.

2. Click the Sub-summary when sorted by radio button.

3. Highlight the field that will form the groups. In this example, the field is Birthmonth (see Figure 10.11).

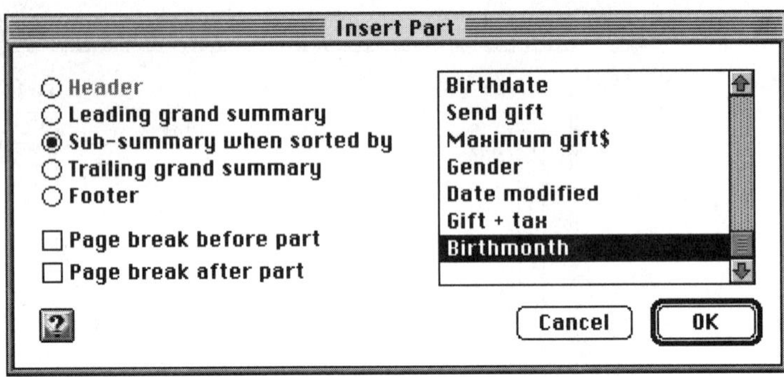

Figure 10.11 Inserting a Sub-summary part

4. Click the OK button or press Enter. ClarisWorks asks you whether the part should go above or below the records being grouped (Figure 10.12).

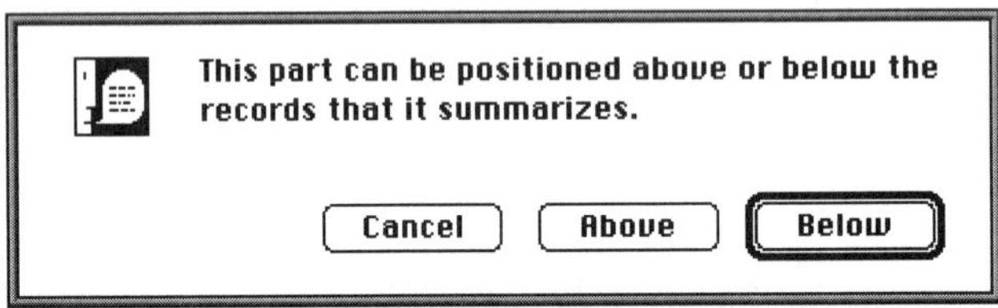

Figure 10.12 Choosing the placement of a Sub-summary part

5. To place the part below the Body part, click the OK button or press Enter. To place the part above the Body part — as was done in our example — click the Above button. ClarisWorks places an empty part on the layout.

ClarisWorks will let you place more than one Sub-summary part on a layout. A additional Sub-summary part represents an "outer" grouping, with the other Sub-summary parts within it. For example, if you were to add a Sub-summary part grouping by State to the gift summary report we have been using as an example, the records would first be grouped by state and then, within each state, by birth month.

Preparing the Report: Adding Fields to a Sub-Summary Part

You place fields that contain values that describe all the records in a group in a Sub-summary part. For example, in the gift summary report, the name of the month and the total amount to be spent on gifts during that month apply to the entire group, rather than to individual records.

To place fields in the Sub-summary part:

1. Display the Insert Fields dialog box.
2. Highlight the name of the field you want to add to the layout (Figure 10.13).
3. Click the Insert button or press Enter. ClarisWorks places the field and a label for the field in the Body part.
4. Move the field into the Sub-summary part.
5. Move the label for the field into the Sub-summary part or delete the label, whichever is appropriate for your layout.
6. If ClarisWorks made the Body part bigger to accommodate the added field, resize the Body part back to its original height.

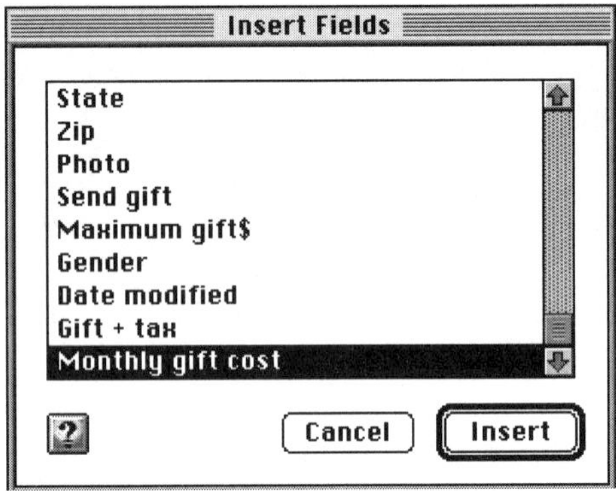

Figure 10.13 Inserting a Summary field

Preparing the Report: Adding the Grand Summary Part

A layout can have two Grand summary parts, one at the top of the layout and one at the bottom. Each can contain different Summary fields that provide information about all the records in the layout.

To add a Grand summary part:

1. Display the Insert Part dialog box.
2. To place a Grand summary part at the top of the layout, click the Leading grand summary radio button. To place a Grand summary part at the bottom of the layout, click the Trailing grand summary radio button, as in Figure 10.14.
3. Click the OK button or press Enter. ClarisWorks places an empty part on the layout.

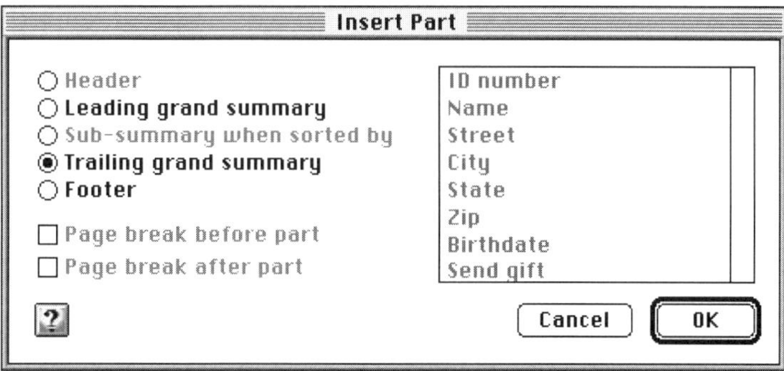

Figure 10.14 Inserting a Grand summary part

Preparing the Report: Adding Fields to a Grand Summary Part

The final step in preparing the control break report is to add fields to the Grand summary part, which will contain Summary fields whose contents pertain to all the records displayed on the layout.

The procedure is exactly the same as adding fields to a Sub-summary part:

1. Display the Insert Fields dialog box.
2. Highlight the field you want to place on the layout. In this example, it will be the Yearly gift cost summary field.
3. Click the OK button or press Enter. ClarisWorks places the field and a label for the field in the Body part.
4. Move the field to the Grand summary part.

5. Move the field label or delete the field label, whichever is appropriate for the layout.

6. If ClarisWorks made the Body part larger to accommodate the new field, resize the Body part back to its original height.

Viewing a Control Break Report

After you have created a layout, there are two things you must do to view a control break report correctly:

- Sort the file by the field or fields that define report groupings.
- Be sure that you are in Page View. Otherwise, the grouping and summarizing will not appear.

To understand why the sorting is necessary, you need to know something about how ClarisWorks assembles a control break report. The process is as follows:

1. ClarisWorks checks the first record for the value of the field whose value determines the groups. This will be the value of the first group.

2. ClarisWorks checks the next record. If the value in the group-determining field is the same as the preceding record, then the current record belongs in the same group. If the value in the group-determining field is not the same as the preceding record, then the current record represents the beginning of a new group.

3. When a new group is detected, ClarisWorks performs any necessary calculations for the just completed group.

4. ClarisWorks repeats steps 2 and 3 until all records have been processed.

The important thing to notice about this procedure is that ClarisWorks is scanning the records in order, from first, to next, to next, and so on. Therefore, all the records that make up one group must be next to each other in the file. If they are not, there will be no way for ClarisWorks to find all the records for each group. We get the records together by sorting them on the grouping field.

Creating and Using Named Reports

A *named report* is a collection of a layout, a named search, and a named sort that can be executed as a unit. Using named reports can simplify creating commonly used displays of data.

Creating a Named Report

To create a named report:

1. Choose New Report from the Report tool's popup menu in the Tool panel (see Figure 10.15). The New Report dialog box appears.

Figure 10.15 The Report tool's popup menu

2. Enter a name for the report.

3. Choose the layout, named search, and named sort you want to use from the popup menus, as in Figure 10.16.

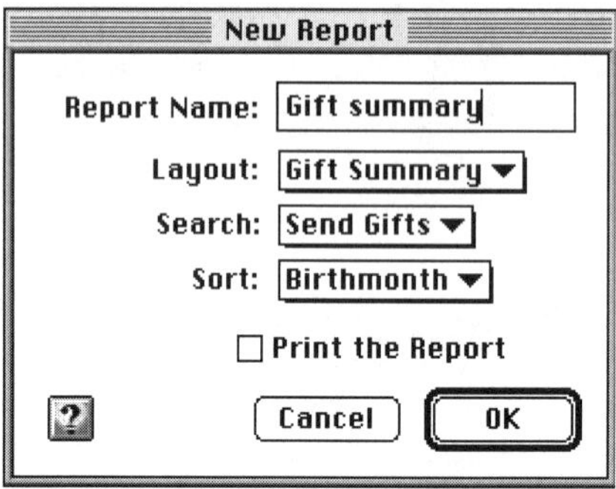

Figure 10.16 Creating a new report

4. Click the OK button or press Enter. ClarisWorks saves the report specifications and adds the name of the report to the Report tool's popup menu.

Using a Named Report

To use a named report, choose the report's name from the Report tool's popup menu. ClarisWorks sorts the data, performs the search, and displays the results in Browse mode using the chosen layout.

You cannot instruct a named report to switch ClarisWorks automatically to Page View for correct viewing of control page reports. You will need to do that manually.

Modifying and Deleting Named Reports

To change or delete a named report:

1. Choose Edit Reports from the Report tool's popup menu in the Tool panel. The Edit Reports dialog box appears, listing all named reports (Figure 10.17).

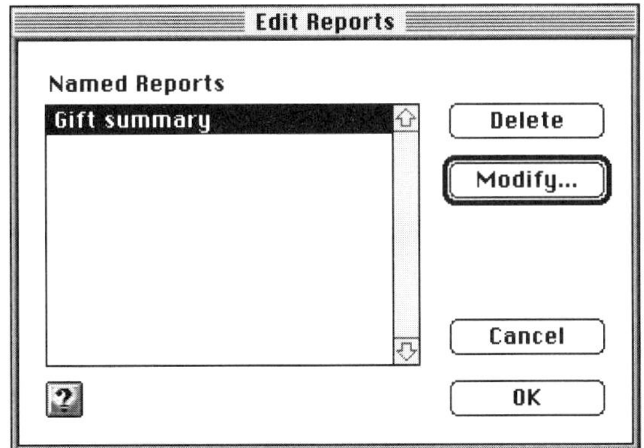

Figure 10.17 Selecting a named report to edit

2. Highlight the name of the report you want to delete or modify.

3. Click the Modify button or press Enter to edit the report. Click the Delete button to delete the report.

ClarisWorks does not ask you to confirm the deletion of a report. Although you can still abort the delete by using the Cancel button to close the Edit Reports dialog box, you should still be very sure you mean it when you delete a report.

4. If you are modifying the report, ClarisWorks displays the dialog box in Figure 10.16. Make any changes needed.

5. Click the OK button or press Enter to save your changes.

Additional Layout Configuration Techniques

To this point, you have read about methods for creating layouts that include placing and moving fields, adding graphics, and changing the type styles of labels. This section presents some additional techniques that can help you make layouts look exactly as you want them to.

Changing Field Display Formats

If you look back at Figure 10.5, you'll notice that the sums of the amounts to be spent on gifts have been formatted as currency, with dollar signs and two places to the right of the decimal point. You add formatting of this type to fields after they have been placed on a layout.

The basic technique is to double-click on a field to display a dialog box in which you can make formatting choices. The specific choices available depend on the type of field.

Formatting for Text Fields

You can choose the font, size, style, and color of text in a Text or Name field on a layout (see Figure 10.18). The same characteristics can also be set by making choices from the Format menu. Two other characteristics — text alignment and line spacing — can be set only from the Format menu.

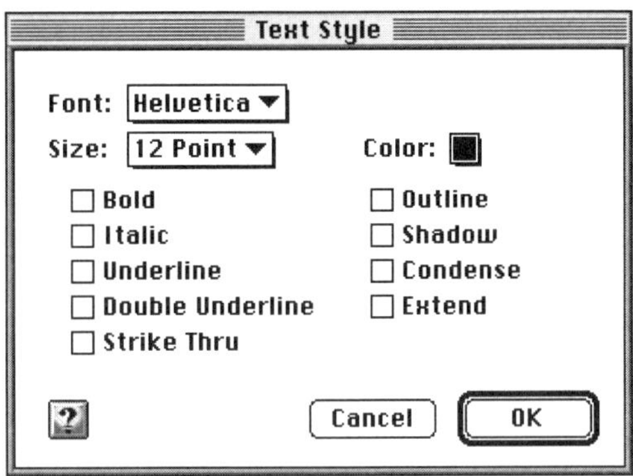

Figure 10.18 Text field formatting options

Formatting for Number Fields

The format dialog box for number fields (Figure 10.19) lets you determine the way in which the value of the number will appear. Text characteristics (font, size, style, color) and alignment can be set from the Format menu.

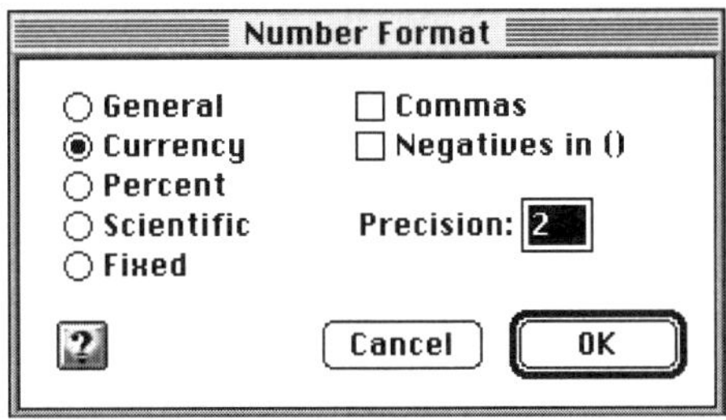

Figure 10.19 Number field formatting options

Formatting for Date Fields

The Date Format dialog box (Figure 10.20) lets you choose among several date display formats. Text characteristics (font, size, style, color) and alignment can be set from the Format menu.

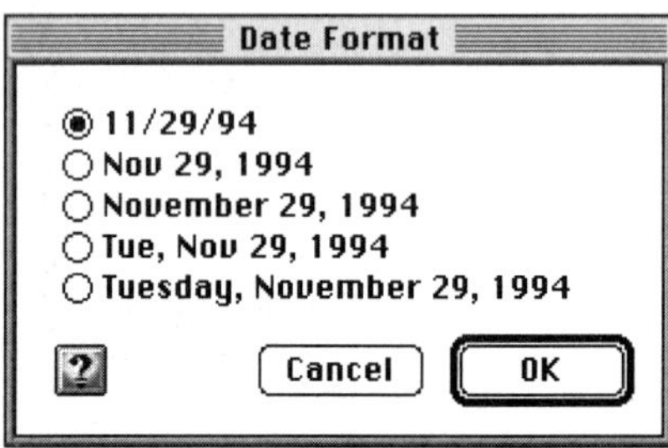

Figure 10.20 Date field formatting options

Formatting for Time Fields

The Time Format dialog box (Figure 10.21) lets you choose between 12- and 24-hour time display formats. Text characteristics (font, size, style, color) and alignment can be set from the Format menu.

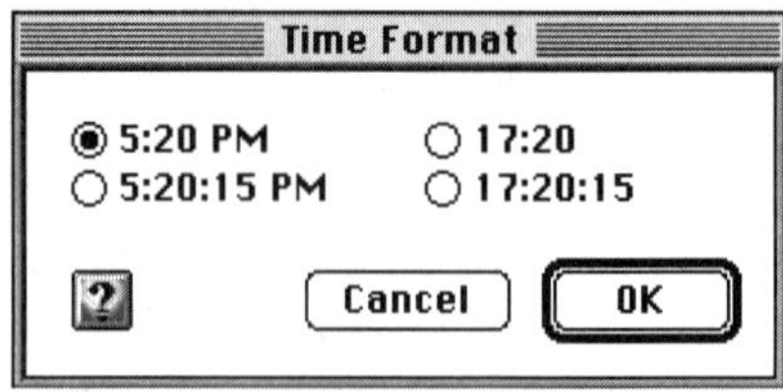

Figure 10.21 Time field formatting options

Formatting for Check Box Fields

The Check Box Style dialog box (Figure 10.22) lets you set the font, size, style, and color of a check box field's label. It also lets you determine whether the label is visible (the Show Label check box) and whether the field displays an X or a ✓ when the box is checked (the Use ✓ mark check box). No other formatting options are applicable to a check box field.

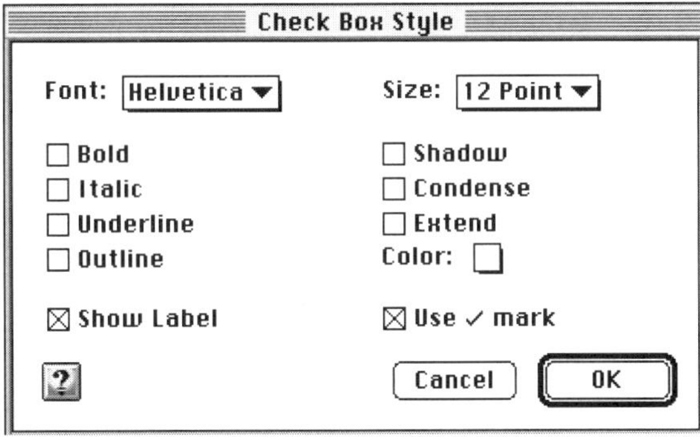

Figure 10.22 Check box field formatting options

Formatting for Radio Button Fields

The Radio Button Style dialog box (Figure 10.23) lets you set the font, size, style, and color of a radio button field's label. It also lets you determine whether the label appears on the layout (the Show label check box). No other formatting options are applicable to a radio button field.

Formatting Popup Menu Fields

The Popup Menu Style dialog box (Figure 10.24) lets you set the font, size, style, and color of the menu's label. Note that you have no control over the appearance of text in the popup menu itself.

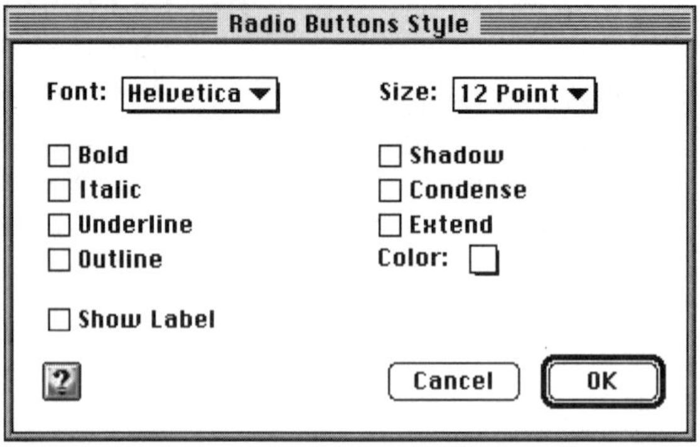

Figure 10.23 Radio button field formatting options

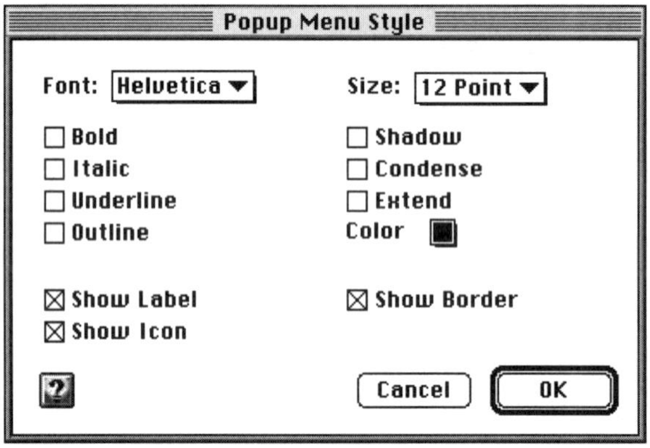

Figure 10.24 Popup menu field formatting options

The three check boxes at the bottom of the dialog box determine the following:

- Show Label: Whether the label appears to the left of the popup menu.
- Show Icon: Whether the menu contains a downward pointing arrow.
- Show Border: Whether the popup menu has a border around it.

If you are displaying a popup menu field in a columnar list, especially if you plan to print the listing, you may want to hide the fact that the field has a menu attached to it. In other words, you may want it to look like a standard text field. In that case, you would remove the checks from all three of the check boxes. The field will still function like a popup menu if a user clicks in it, but in printed output the field's contents will appear without the visual elements of a popup menu.

Formatting Multimedia Frame Fields

The Multimedia Field dialog box (Figure 10.25) provides the only place where you can set characteristics for a Multimedia frame field. The radio buttons at the top of the dialog box determine what happens if an image isn't exactly the same size as its rectangle on the layout.

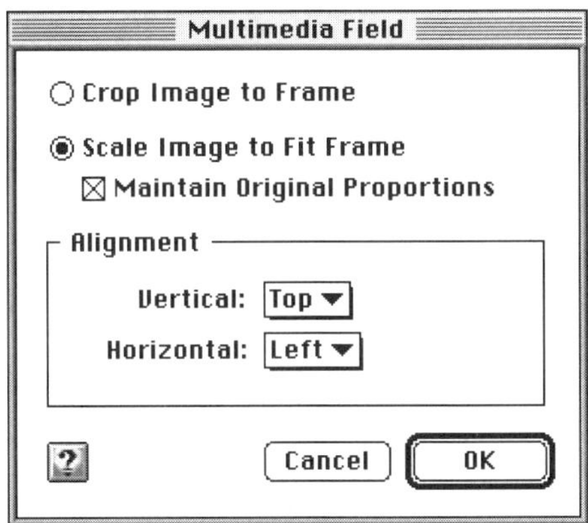

Figure 10.25 Multimedia field formatting options

If the Crop Image radio button is selected, ClarisWorks will display as much of the image as will fit in the rectangle, hiding whatever can't been seen. If the Scale Image radio button is checked, ClarisWorks will change the size of the image so that it fills the rectangle. You will get the best result from this option if you also check the Maintain Original Proportions check box. This ensures that both horizontal and vertical scaling are the same, even if the resulting image doesn't completely fill the rectangle. (Without maintaining proportions, the image may be distorted.)

Given that most images — even those that are scaled proportionately — won't be exactly the same size as the rectangle in which they are displayed, ClarisWorks lets you set the alignment of the image within the rectangle. Use the Vertical and Horizontal alignment popup menus to choose how the image should be aligned to its rectangle.

The formatting options for Record info, Value list, Calculation, and Summary fields depend on the type of data in the field.

Changing the Tab Order

As you know, you can move the cursor from one field to another on a layout by pressing the Tab key. By default, ClarisWorks sets the order in which the Tab key selects fields to match the order in which the fields were defined. You can, however, change the tab order on each layout so that it provides a more logical way to move through the fields.

To change the tab order:

1. Display the layout whose tab order you want to change. Make sure that you are in either Browse or Layout mode.

2. Choose Layout->Tab Order. (Windows users can also press ALT-L, T.) The Tab Order dialog box appears, showing the current tab order (Figure 10.26).

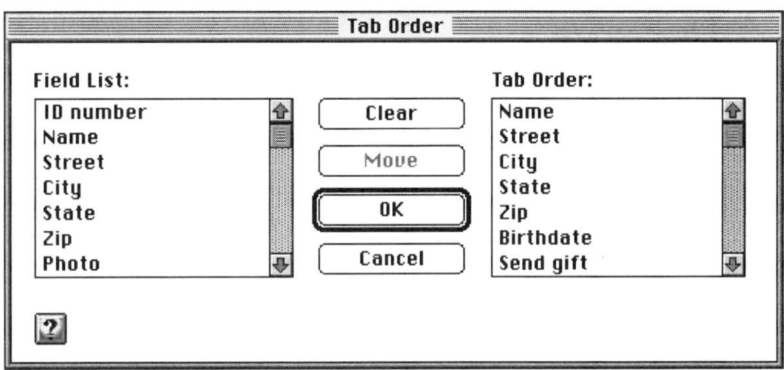

Figure 10.26 The Tab Order dialog box

3. Modify the tab order in any of the following ways:

Move a field out of the tab order	Highlight the field in the Tab Order list and click the Move button. Macintosh users can also press ⌘-M; Windows users can press CTRL-M.
Move a single field to the end of the tab order	Highlight the field in the Field List and click the Move button. Macintosh users can also press ⌘-M; Windows users can press CTRL-M.
Move several contiguous fields.	Highlight the first field. SHIFT-click to select the last field. Click the Move button. Macintosh users can also press ⌘-M; Windows users can press CTRL-M.
Move several non-contiguous fields.	Highlight the first field. Macintosh users should ⌘-click to select additional fields; Windows users should CTRL-click. Click the Move button. Macintosh users can also press ⌘-M; Windows users can press CTRL-M.
Remove all fields from the Tab Order list	Click the Clear button. Macintosh users can also press ⌘-R; Windows users can press CTRL-R.

4. Click the OK button to press Enter to close the dialog box and save the new tab order.

There are two things to keep in mind when working with the tab order:

- The process is somewhat clumsy because the only place you can add a field is at the very end. It may be easier to clear all fields from the tab order and start from scratch than it is to try to maneuver to get one or two fields in specific locations.
- If you leave a field out of the tab order, the user won't be able to tab to the field, but the field can still be selected by clicking in it. In other words, removing a field from the tab order doesn't make it read-only.

Viewing One or More Records at a Time

When you view data through a columnar list type of layout, your intent is to see more than one record at a time. In contrast, when you are performing data entry, you may want to work with only one record.

ClarisWorks doesn't distinguish between layouts that are meant to show one record and those that are meant to show multiple records. However, you can instruct ClarisWorks to show only one record at a time.

By default, ClarisWorks displays as many records as will fit on the screen. To show only one record at a time, choose Layout->Show Multiple. Doing so removes the ✓ from the Show Multiple menu option and restricts the display to a single record. To return to viewing multiple records, choose Layout->Show Multiple again, reinstalling the ✓ on the menu option.

Integrating Data and Word Processing: Mail Merge

Mail merge is the process of creating customized documents by inserting data from a database file into a word processing document or frame. This is the way in which all those "John Doe, you may have won $10,000,000" letters are prepared.

To perform mail merge, you insert placeholders for database data into a word processing document. When the document is printed, ClarisWorks prints one document for each record in the database. As an example, we will be using the mailing list database to help prepare that well-loved American tradition: the holiday letter extolling all the wonderful things that happened during the past year.

ClarisWorks also supports mail merge into a spreadsheet document or frame. However, mail merge using a word processing document is by far the more common usage.

Database Setup

The database used in a mail merge can be any ClarisWorks database file. There are, however, a couple of things to keep in mind when preparing the file.

Preparing the Necessary Fields

When you insert a field placeholder into a word processing document, ClarisWorks will take the entire contents of the field. By the same token, you can't insert anything that isn't stored in the database file. You should therefore give some thought to exactly what you want to appear in the document. For example, you may want to include an appellation (Ms., Mrs., Mr., Dr., and so on) and will therefore need a field to store that value. In contrast, the mailing list stores a person's entire name in a single field, but the greeting of the holiday letter should use just the person's first name.

The solution to the mailing list's problem is to create a Calculation field that extracts the first name from the Name field. The trick is recognizing that a blank follows the first name. Therefore, if we can find the blank, we can figure out which characters to extract. The formula for the Calculation field is:

LEFT ('Name', FIND (" ", 'Name',0)-1)

The LEFT function extracts characters from a string of text beginning at the left edge. It requires two arguments: the field from which the text should be taken (in this example, Name) and the number of characters to copy.

The FIND function locates one or more characters in a string of text and returns a number indicating where the characters begin. Its three arguments are the characters to find (in this example, a blank between two double quotes), the field to search (Name), and the offset from the start of the text (in this case, 0 because we want to start with the first character). The formula subtracts 1 from the value to exclude the blank.

Assume, for example, that you have the name John Smith. The FIND function returns a 5, because the blank is the fifth character. Since we want to copy only four characters, the formula subtracts 1 from the 5, producing the correct number of characters.

Sorting and Searching

When you print a mail merge document, ClarisWorks prints one copy of the document for each visible record in the database file. The documents are also printed in the same order as the database records. There are two implications of this behavior:

- If you want to restrict the records for which mail merge documents are printed, perform a search on the database file that hides the records for which mail merge should *not* be performed.
- Sort the database file in the order in which you want the mail merge documents to be printed.

Word Processing Setup

Once you have the database prepared, you should create the word processing document. Type and format the document as you would any other word processing document. However, leave space for the data that will come from the database file. For example, in Figure 10.27, you can see a portion of the holiday letter. It is missing the inside address and a first name following the salutation.

Selecting the Database File

The first step in the actual mail merge process is to identify the database file from which the merge data will be taken:

1. Make sure the word processing document you will be using is open.

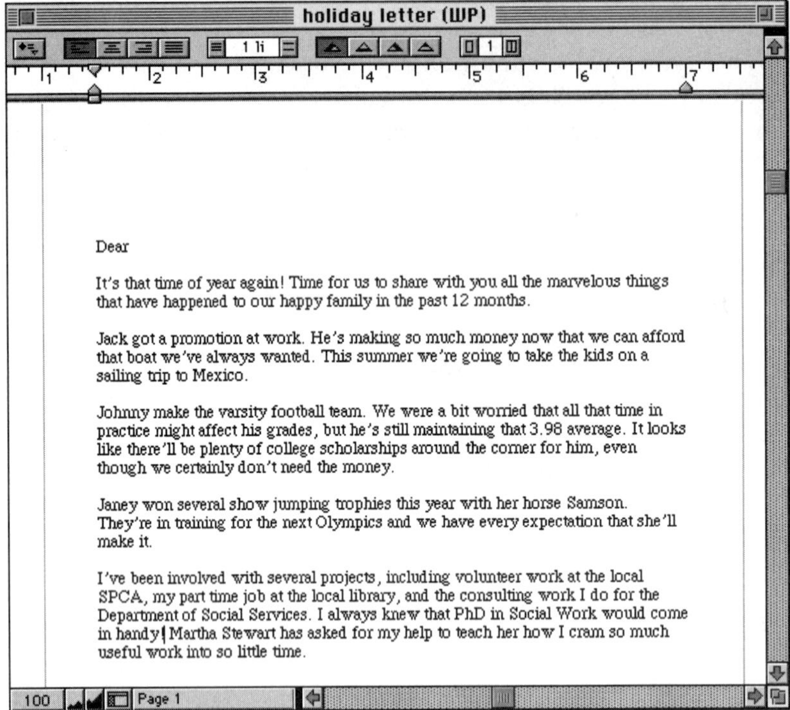

Dear

It's that time of year again! Time for us to share with you all the marvelous things that have happened to our happy family in the past 12 months.

Jack got a promotion at work. He's making so much money now that we can afford that boat we've always wanted. This summer we're going to take the kids on a sailing trip to Mexico.

Johnny make the varsity football team. We were a bit worried that all that time in practice might affect his grades, but he's still maintaining that 3.98 average. It looks like there'll be plenty of college scholarships around the corner for him, even though we certainly don't need the money.

Janey won several show jumping trophies this year with her horse Samson. They're in training for the next Olympics and we have every expectation that she'll make it.

I've been involved with several projects, including volunteer work at the local SPCA, my part time job at the local library, and the consulting work I do for the Department of Social Services. I always knew that PhD in Social Work would come in handy! Martha Stewart has asked for my help to teach her how I cram so much useful work into so little time.

Figure 10.27 A word processing document ready for mail merge elements

2. Choose File->Mail Merge. (Windows users can also press ALT-F, M.) An Open File dialog box appears (Figure 10.28).

3. Double-click on the name of the database file you want to use. ClarisWorks opens the database file if it isn't already open and displays the Mail Merge window (Figure 10.29). This palette will float on top of all other windows. Even if you are clicking and scrolling in another document, the Mail Merge window will still be visible.

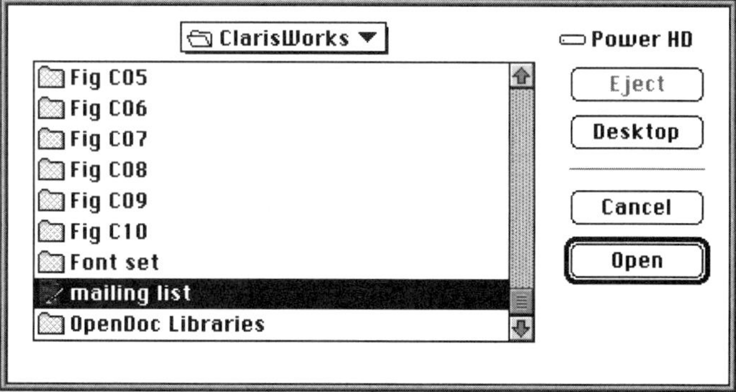

Figure 10.28 Choosing a database file for mail merge

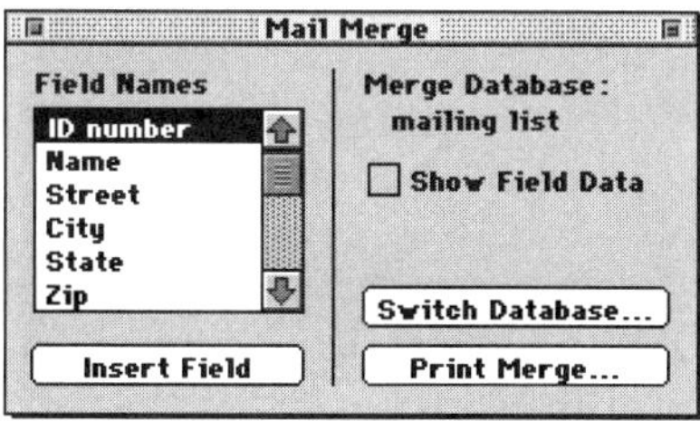

Figure 10.29 The Mail Merge window

Adding Field Placeholders

The next step is to insert placeholders for database fields into the word processing document. To do so:

1. Place the insertion point at a place in the word processing document where you want data from the database to appear.

2. Highlight the field name in the Field Names list in the Mail Merge window.

3. Click the Insert Field button in the Mail Merge window. ClarisWorks inserts a field placeholder into the document. A placeholder appears as the name of the field surrounded by << and >>. For example, the first name field looks like <<First name>>.

4. Repeat steps 1 through 3 for the rest of the fields you want to insert. When all the field placeholders are in place, the holiday letter looks like Figure 10.30.

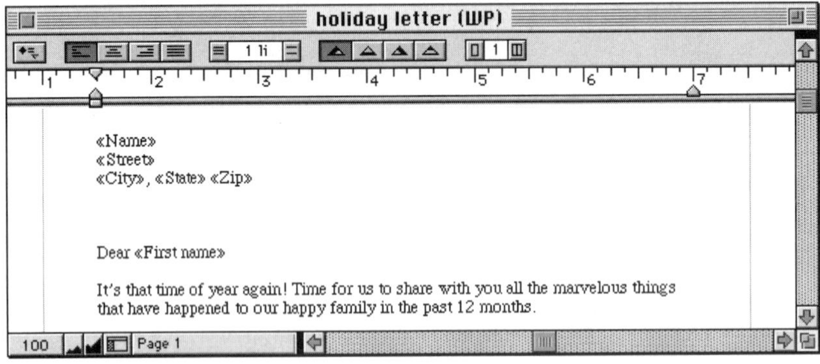

Figure 10.30 A word processing document with field placeholders

You can format field placeholders just like any other text in a word processing document. However, be sure that you include the << and >> in the formatting.

Previewing the Mail Merge

By default, ClarisWorks shows you the field placeholders in a mail merge document. If you want to preview the document as it will appear when printed, do the following:

1. Click in the Show Field Data check box in the Mail Merge window to place a check in it. ClarisWorks replaces the placeholders in the merge document with data from the first visible record in the database file.

2. Click the up and down arrows in the Mail Merge window to scroll through the records in the database file, as in Figure 10.31.

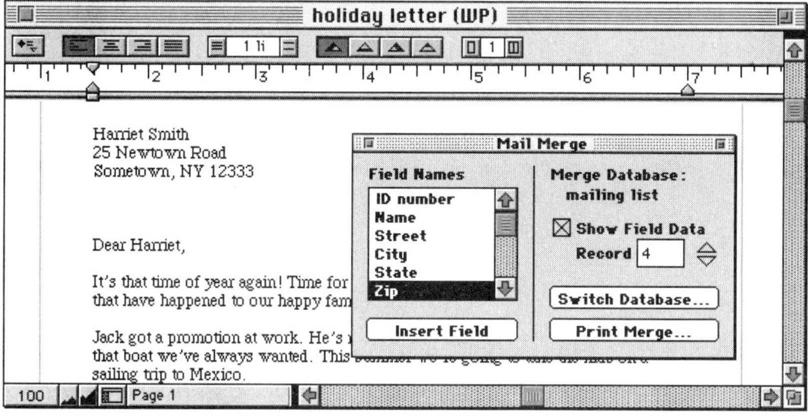

Figure 10.31 Previewing mail merge documents

Printing Merged Documents

To print the merged documents:

1. Click the Print Merge button in the Mail Merge window. ClarisWorks displays a Print dialog box.

2. Configure print options as you would if you were printing any other document.

3. Click the OK button or press Enter to begin printing.

11

Customizing ClarisWorks

The ClarisWorks working environment can be customized to meet your personal needs in a variety of ways. In this chapter we will explore customizing button bars, creating macros to automate common actions, setting environment preferences, and configuring the graphics palettes.

Button Bars

As you know, the Button bar contains shortcut buttons that make it easier to perform common tasks. The particular buttons that appear depend on which Clarisworks module you are using. You can change any of the Button bars that ClarisWorks provides for you. In addition, you can create new buttons bars and connect them to individual documents. You can even create your own buttons.

Positioning and Resizing a Button Bar

At any given time, ClarisWorks displays one Button bar. It can be positioned at any edge of the screen, or it can be a floating palette that you can place anywhere that is convenient.

Placing the Button Bar at a Different Screen Edge

To position the Button bar at an edge of the screen other than the top:

1. Place the mouse pointer over any part of the Button bar not occupied by a button or a popup menu.

2. Drag the Button bar to its new location until an outline of that location appears. In Figure 11.1, for example, the Button bar is being moved from the top to the left edge of the screen.

3. Release the mouse button.

You can also move the Button Bar by dragging its "grab bar," the two lines that appear at the left or top edge, depending on the Button Bar's current position.

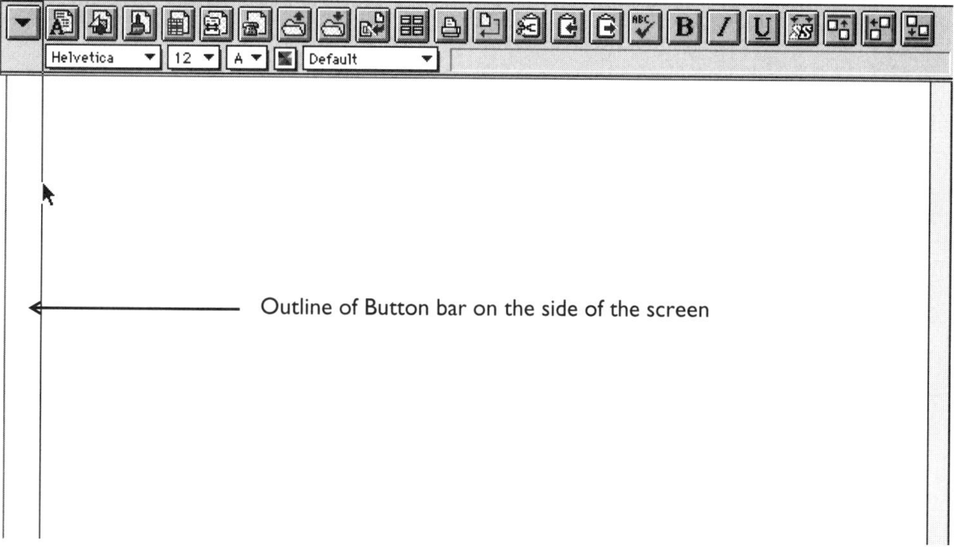

Figure 11.1 Moving the Button bar

Resizing the Button Bar

If there are more buttons than will fit on one line, ClarisWorks expands the Button bar to make room for additional rows of buttons. The drawback to this is that the Button bar takes up space that might otherwise be used to display the contents of a document. You can therefore change the size of the Button bar as needed.

To resize the button bar:

1. Place the mouse pointer over the border of the Button bar that is next to the document workspace. The mouse pointer turns into the resize cursor (⇳).

2. Drag the border of the Button bar toward the document workspace to change its size. As you can see in Figure 11.2, an outline of the bottom border of a

Button bar at the top the screen follows the mouse pointer as you drag.

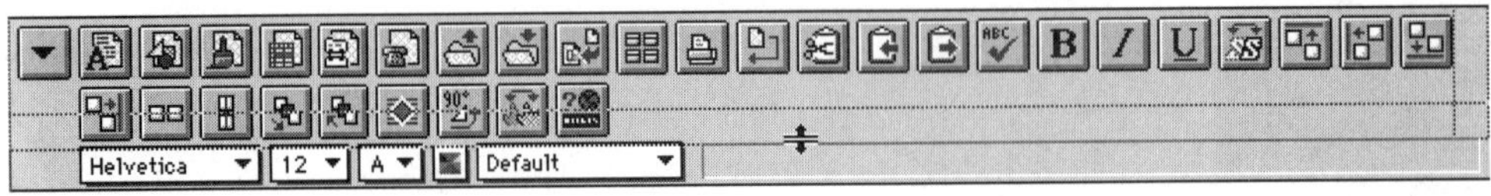

Figure 11.2 Resizing the Button bar

3. Release the mouse button when the Button bar is the size you want.

While the Button bar is positioned at the top or bottom of the screen, you can change only its height, not its width. When the Button bar is at the left or right edge of the screen, you can change its width but not its height.

Turning the Button Bar into a Floating Palette

To turn the Button bar at the top of the screen into a floating palette:

1. Place the mouse pointer anywhere in the Button bar not occupied by a button or a popup menu.
2. Drag down until you see the outline of a window, as in Figure 11.3.
3. Release the mouse button. ClarisWorks removes the Button bar from the top of the screen and displays the floating palette (Figure 11.4).

If the floating Button bar isn't large enough to show all the buttons, you can enlarge it just as you would any other window. Because the Button bar window is a floating palette, it will always be on top of all open document windows.

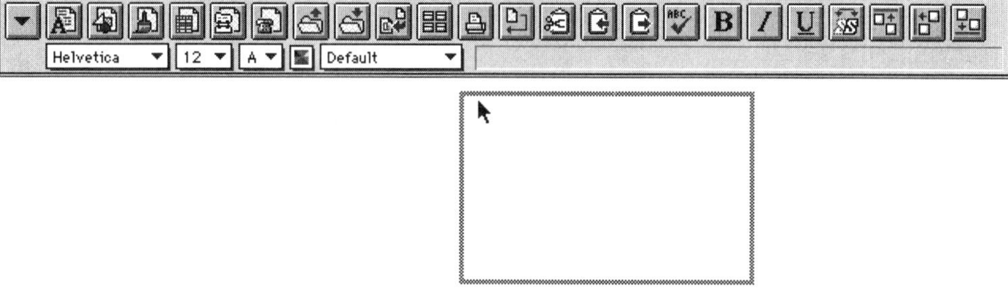

Figure 11.3 Dragging to turn the Button bar into a floating palette

Figure 11.4 The Button bar as a floating palette

Returning the Button Bar to the Top of the Screen

To return a palette Button bar to the top of the screen, drag the palette to the top of the screen. Release the mouse button when the outline of the palette disappears.

Hiding and Showing the Button Bar

If you don't want to use a Button bar, you can remove it from the screen. Doing so will give you the maximum amount of space for viewing your document.

The process for removing the Button bar depends on whether it is displayed on the screen or in a floating palette:

- If the Button bar is at the top of the screen

Macintosh	Choose Window->Hide Button Bar or press SHIFT-⌘-X.
Windows	Choose Window->Hide Button Bar, press SHIFT-CTRL-X, or press ALT-W, B.

- If the Button bar is a floating palette, click the palette window's close box.

  To show the Button bar after it has been hidden

Macintosh	Choose Window->Show Button Bar or press SHIFT-⌘-X.
Windows	Choose Window->Show Button Bar, press SHIFT-CTRL-X, or press ALT-W, B.

Setting Initial Button Bar Placement

By default, the Button bar appears at the top of the screen and includes popup menus for text characteristics. You can change the default by doing the following:

1. Choose Button Bar Setup from the Configure popup menu at the top left of the Button bar (see Figure 11.5). The Button Bar Setup dialog box appears (Figure 11.6).

2. Choose a default position (Top, Bottom, Left, Right, or Floating) from the Position popup menu.

3. Enter the number of rows of buttons in the Rows edit box.

4. Place check marks in the Show Popups and Indicators check boxes to indicate which items should appear. The Info Line check box determines whether text describing a button or popup menu appears in the

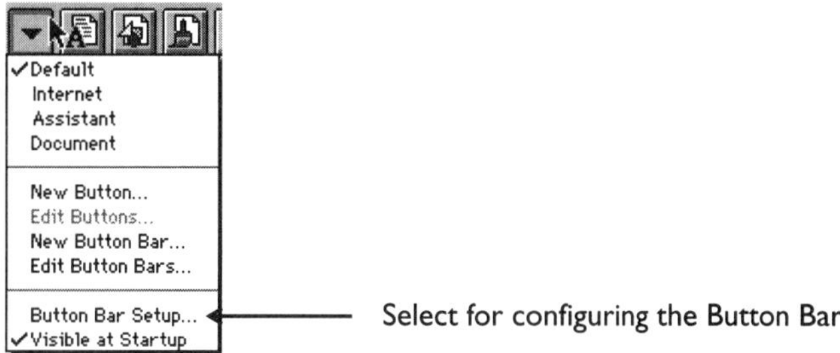

Figure 11.5 The Configure menu

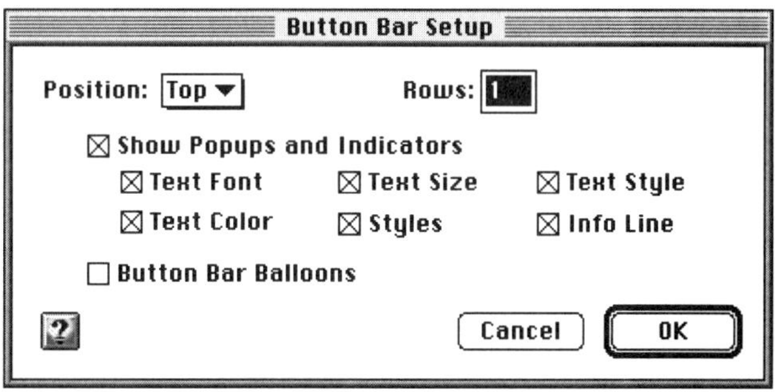

Figure 11.6 The Button Bar Setup dialog box

Button bar when the mouse pointer passes over it. The other check boxes relate to the text formatting popup menus.

5. Click the OK button or press Enter to save your default settings.

Macintosh users can also check the Button Bar Balloons check box. When this box is checked and Balloon Help is turned on, help balloons will appear when the mouse pointer passes over an element in the Button bar.

Choosing a Button Bar

ClarisWorks provides four Button bars for you. To switch between them (and any other Button bars you may add), choose the name of the Button bar from the Configure popup menu at the far left of the Button bar (see Figure 11.7).

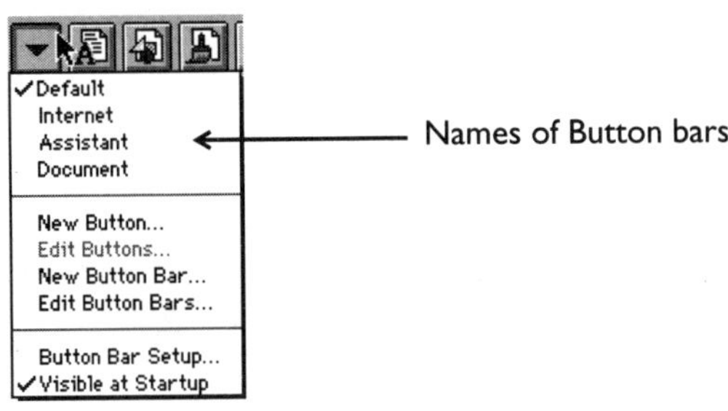

Figure 11.7 Choosing a Button bar

Changing the Buttons in a Button Bar

To change the Buttons that appear in a Button bar:

1. Choose Edit Button Bars from the Configure menu at the top left of the Button bar. The Edit Button Bars dialog box appears (Figure 11.8).

2. Highlight the name of the Button bar you want to change in the Defined Button Bars list.

3. Click the Modify button or press Enter. An Edit Button Bar dialog box appears (for example, see Figure 11.9).

The buttons that ClarisWorks provides for you are divided into 12 categories (see Figure 11.10). These categories are for convenience only; you can place any available button on any Button bar.

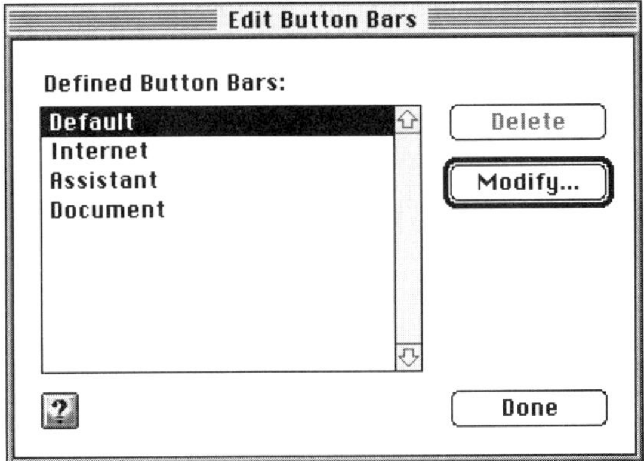

Figure 11.8 The Edit Button Bars dialog box

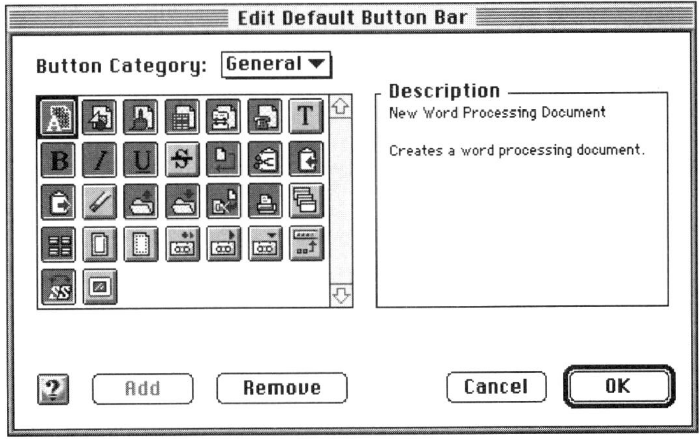

Figure 11.9 An Edit Button Bar dialog box

If you look carefully at Figure 11.9, you'll notice that some of the buttons have a three-dimensional appearance while others appear recessed. The recessed buttons are already part of the Button bar being edited; the 3D buttons are available for inclusion. Notice also that when you highlight a button, ClarisWorks displays a description of what the button does in the Description box at the right of the dialog box.

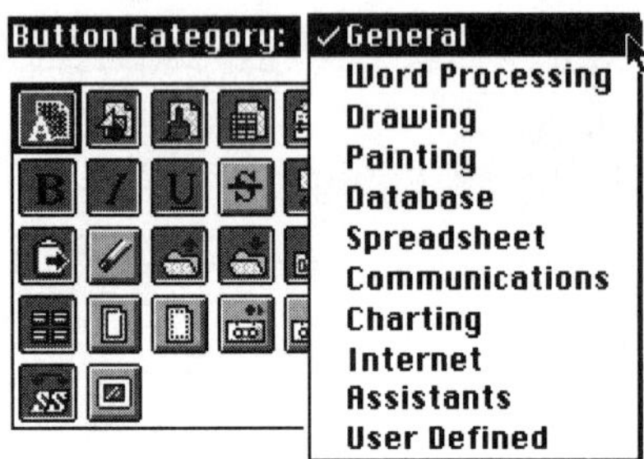

Figure 11.10 Button categories

4. Choose a button category from the Button Category popup menu.

5. To add a new button to the Button bar, click on a 3D button (a button that isn't already part of the button bar). Then click the Add button. To remove a button from the Button bar, click on a recessed button. Then click on the Remove button.

6. Repeat steps 4 and 5 as necessary until the Button bar contains just the buttons you want.

7. Click the OK button or press Enter to close the dialog box and save your changes. You are returned to the Edit Button Bars dialog box.

8. Repeat steps 2 through 7 for any additional Button bars you want to modify.

9. Click the Done button to close the Edit Button Bars dialog box.

Creating a New Button Bar

To create a new Button bar:

1. Choose New Button Bar from the Configure menu at the top left of the Button bar. ClarisWorks displays the New Button Bar dialog box.

2. Enter a name for the Button bar (Figure 11.11).

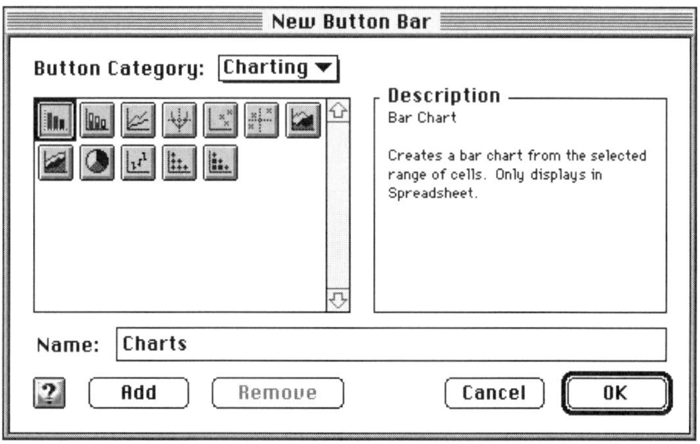

Figure 11.11 Creating a new Button bar

3. Add buttons to the Button bar, using the procedure described in the preceding section of this chapter ("Changing the Buttons in a Button Bar").

4. Click the OK button or press Enter. ClarisWorks closes the New Button Bar dialog box and adds the name of the new Button bar to the bottom of the Configure menu.

Deleting a Button Bar

To delete a Button bar:

1. Choose Edit Button Bars from the Configure menu at the top left of the Button bar. The Edit Button Bars dialog box appears (Figure 11.8).
2. Highlight the name of the Button bar you want to delete.
3. Click the Delete button.
4. Repeat steps 2 and 3 for any other Button bars you want to delete.
5. Click the Done button to close the Edit Button Bars dialog box and save the deletions.

Creating Your Own Buttons

If you look back at Figure 11.10, you'll notice that one of the button categories is "User Defined." This is where buttons that you draw yourself are placed. Creating your own button involves two major steps: drawing the button and indicating what should happen when the button is clicked.

To create a custom button:

1. Choose New Button from the Configure menu at the top left of the Button bar. The New Button dialog box appears (Figure 11.12).
2. Enter a name for the button in the Button Name edit box.

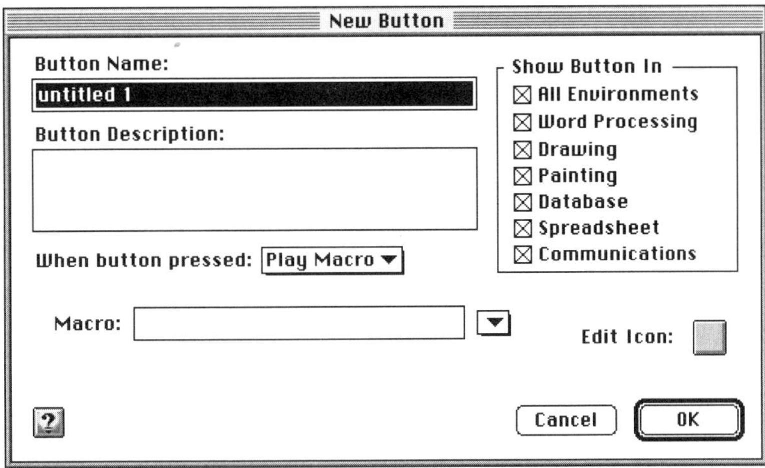

Figure 11.12 The New Button dialog box

3. If you want text to appear in the Button bar when the user moves the mouse pointer over the button, enter that text in the Button Description edit box. (Note that removing the X from the Info Line check box in the Button Bar Setup dialog boxes suppresses the display of the button description.)

4. By default, ClarisWorks makes the button available in all ClarisWorks modules. If you want to restrict where the button is sued, remove the X from the All Environments check box and from the individual modules in which the button shouldn't appear.

5. Choose the action that will occur when the button is clicked from the When button pressed popup menu.

As you can see in Figure 11.13, there are five possible actions:

- Play Macro: A macro is a set of ClarisWorks actions that are recorded for playback in order. You can find detailed information about creating and using macros

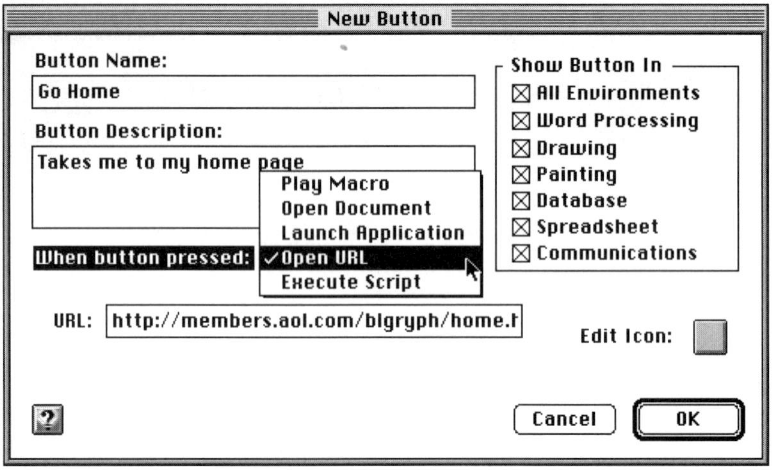

Figure 11.13 Choosing a button action

in the next section of this chapter. When you make this choice, ClarisWorks asks you to fill in the name of the macro in the edit box below the popup menu.

- Open Document: This action allows you to open one specific document. When you choose it, ClarisWorks presents you with a Select Document button. Click that button to display an Open File dialog box from which you can select the document to be opened.

- Launch Application: This action allows you to run another program. When you choose it, ClarisWorks presents you with a Select Application button. Click that button to display an Open File dialog box from which you can select the program to run.

- Open URL: The action connects to a World Wide Web site using the site's URL. When you choose this action, ClarisWorks asks you to fill in the URL in an edit box under the popup menu.

- Execute Script (Macintosh only): The Execute Script action runs an operating system script, such as an AppleScript. When you select this action, ClarisWorks presents you with a Select Script button. Click the button to display an Open File dialog box from which you can select the script.

6. Click the Edit Icon button to display the Edit Button Icon window (Figure 11.14). Notice that you have a palette of 16 colors at the right edge of the window and a gray drawing area at the left.

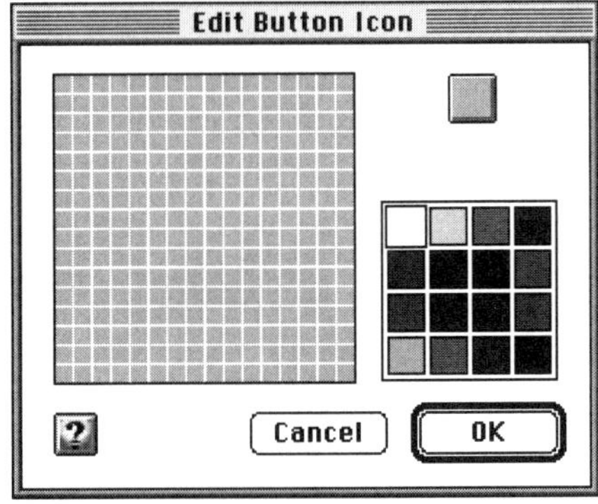

Figure 11.14 The Edit Button Icon window

Whenever you create a button to open a document or run an application, ClarisWorks automatically uses the document or application's icon as the icon for the button.

7. Click on a color in the palette to select it.

8. Click anywhere in the gray drawing area to change a gray square for a colored square.

Clicking a colored square with the same color turns it back into a gray square.

9. Repeat steps 7 and 8 as necessary until the button's icon contains the image you want. As you work, the image in the gray drawing area will be transferred to the sample button at the top right of the window so that you can see exactly how it will look (Figure 11.15).

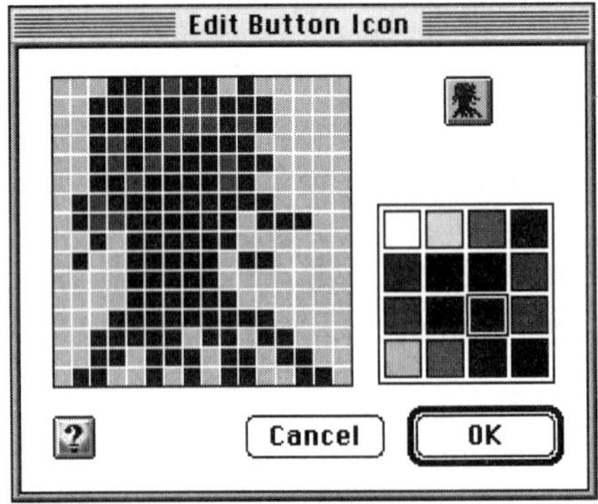

Figure 11.15 A custom button icon

10. Click the OK button or press Enter. You are returned to the New Button dialog box.

11. Click the OK button or press Enter. ClarisWorks closes the New Button dialog box and saves the button you have just created. You can now add the button to a Button bar, using the procedure described earlier in this section.

Macros

A *macro* is a named sequence of actions that are executed automatically when you press an associated key combination. As you read in the preceding section of this chapter, a macro can also be associated with a Button bar button. In addition, you can specify some macros to be executed during specific actions, such as when you first launch ClarisWorks.

What should you do with macros? Anything that you do regularly that you would like to automate. For example, if you have a favorite quotation that you put at the bottom of every letter you send, you can create a macro that types that quotation. If you have a favorite style sheet that you want to use every time you open a specific type of document, you can create a macro that selects the style sheet and then play it whenever you want to use the style sheet for formatting.

Recording a Macro

You create a macro by performing the steps you want the macro to execute. While you are going through those steps, ClarisWorks records your actions. When the recording is finished, you can then ask ClarisWorks to play the macro, repeating exactly what you recorded.

ClarisWorks is very literal when it comes to recording a macro. It records everything you do, even your mistakes. You should therefore test the actions you are planning to record to make sure they work properly before you record.

To record a macro:

1. Figure out exactly what you want the macro to do. As an example, we will be creating a macro that draws a bar graph from data in a spreadsheet document. The macro assumes that the cells containing the data are already selected.

2.

Macintosh	Choose File->Macros->Record Macro or press SHIFT-⌘-J.
Windows	Choose File->Macros->Record Macro, press SHIFT-CTRL-J, or press ALT-F, R, R.

The Record Macro dialog box appears.

3. Enter a name for the macro. For example, in Figure 11.16, the macro is called "Make bar graph."

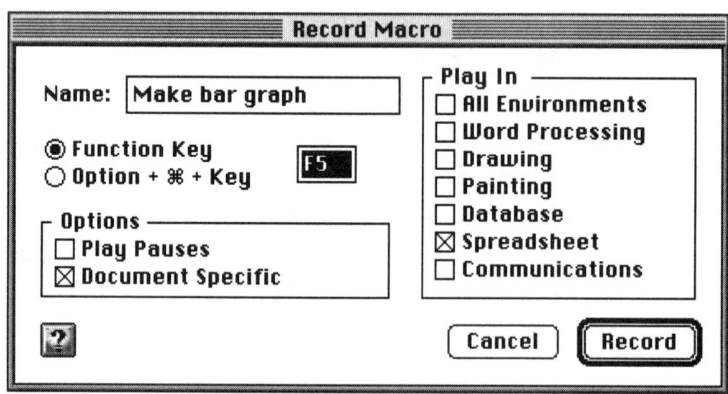

Figure 11.16 The Record Macro dialog box

4. Choose the key combination that will play the macro. If you want to associate it with a function key, click the Function Key radio button and enter F and the number of the function key in the edit box to the right of the radio buttons.

To associate the macro with an alternative key combination, click the Option + ⌘ + Key radio button (Macintosh) or the Control + Alt + Key radio button (Windows). Enter the key in the edit box to the right of the radio buttons.

5. Use the Play In check boxes to indicate where the macro should be available. Check the All Environments check box to make the macro available in all ClarisWorks modules. Otherwise, check just the specific modules you want.

6. If you want the macro associated with only the current document, place a check in the Document Specific check box.

7. Click the Record button or press Enter. From this point on, ClarisWorks records every action you take.

8. Perform the actions you want to record. For the bar graph example you would choose the menu option that creates a graph and then make all necessary settings in the Chart Options dialog box.

9. To stop recording and save the macro:

Macintosh	Choose File->Macros->Stop Recording or press SHIFT-⌘-J.
Windows	Choose File->Macros->Stop Recording, press SHIFT-CTRL-J. (There is no accelerator key for the Stop Recording option.).

Playing a Macro

There are several ways to play a macro:

- Press the macro's key combination.

- Choose File->Macros->Play Macro. (Windows users can also press ALT-F, R, P.) The Play Macro dialog box appears (Figure 11.17). Highlight the name of the macro in the list and click the Play button or press Enter.

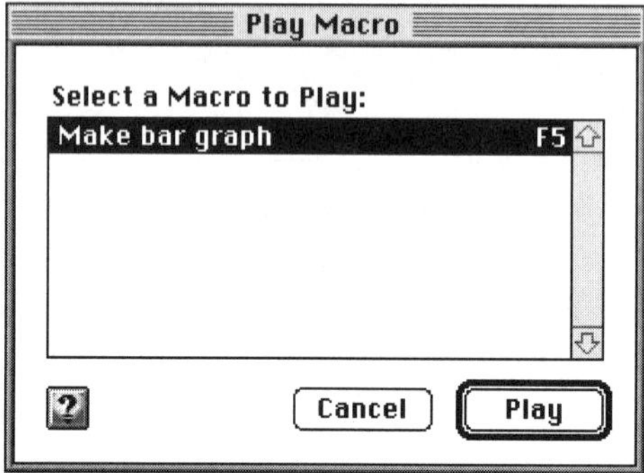

Figure 11.17 Playing a macro from the Play Macro dialog box

- Associate the macro with a custom button and place that button on a Button bar. Then, clicking the button will play the macro.

Modifying and Deleting Macros

Once you've recorded steps for a macro, you can't modify those steps. You will need to delete the macro and create it again from scratch. However, you can change the macro's name, key sequence, and accessibility (the options available in the Record Macro dialog box).

To modify or delete a macro:

1. Choose File->Macros->Edit Macros. (Windows users can also press ALT-F, R, M.) The Edit Macros dialog box appears (Figure 11.18).

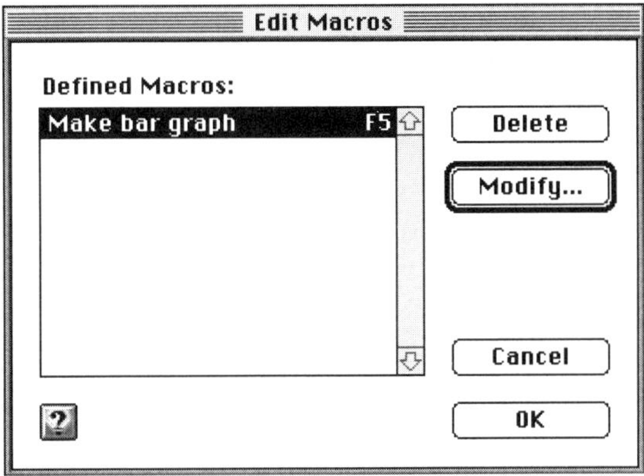

Figure 11.18 The Edit Macros dialog box

2. Highlight the name of the macro you want to modify or delete.

3. To Delete the macro, click the Delete button. To edit the macro, click the Modify button or press Enter.

ClarisWorks will not ask you to confirm the deletion of a macro. Once you click the OK button to close the Edit Macros window, a deleted macro will be unrecoverable.

4. If you are editing the macro, the Edit Macro dialog box appears. (This is the same as the Record Macro dialog box; it simply has a different title.)

5. Make any necessary changes. Click the OK button or press Enter. You are returned to the Edit Macros dialog box.

6. Click the OK button to close the Edit Macros dialog box.

Creating Automatic Macros

You can create macros that run automatically when you launch ClarisWorks, open a document, or create a new document. ClarisWorks recognizes specific macro names and runs them at the appropriate time. The macro names you must use and when they will be run are summarized in Table 11.1.

Table 11.1 Automatic Macro Names and Execution Times

Macro name	When executed
Auto-Startup	When ClarisWorks is launched
Auto-Open WP	When you open a word processing document
Auto-Open DR	When you open a drawing document
Auto-Open PT	When you open a painting document
Auto-Open SS	When you open a spreadsheet document
Auto-Open DB	When you open a database document
Auto-Open CM	When you open a communications document
Auto-New WP	When you create a new word processing document
Auto-New DR	When you create a new drawing document
Auto-New PT	When you create a new painting document
Auto-New SS	When you create a new spreadsheet document
Auto-New DB	When you create a new spreadsheet document
Auto-New CM	When you create a new communications document

There are two additional things you need to keep in mind when creating automatic macros:

- The name of an automatic macro must match one of the names in Table 11.1 exactly, including spacing and capitalization. Otherwise, ClarisWorks won't recognize it as an automatic macro and won't play it at the appropriate time.

- An automatic macro must be enabled for the environments in which the macro will be played. For example, a macro that plays automatically when you open a word processing document must have either All Environments or Word Processing checked in the Play In group of check boxes.

Setting Preferences

ClarisWorks provides a group of "preferences" settings that help you tailor your ClarisWorks working environment to your particular needs. Some preferences affect the entire program; others apply to specific modules.

To set preferences, choose Edit->Preferences. (Windows users can also press ALT-P,N.) The Preferences dialog box appears. However, exactly what you see depends on the type of document open at the time because the preferences dialog box is made up of a group of panels among which you can choose from a popup menu at the top of the dialog box. Regardless of the panel that appears first, you can always switch to another by choosing its name from the popup menu.

Scope of Preferences

Unless you indicate otherwise, the preferences that you set apply to the current document only. However, each panel in the Preferences dialog box has a Make Default button. Clicking this button makes the settings in that panel the default for every new document that you open.

Setting General Preferences

The General preferences panel (Figure 11.19) configures the ClarisWorks environment as a whole.

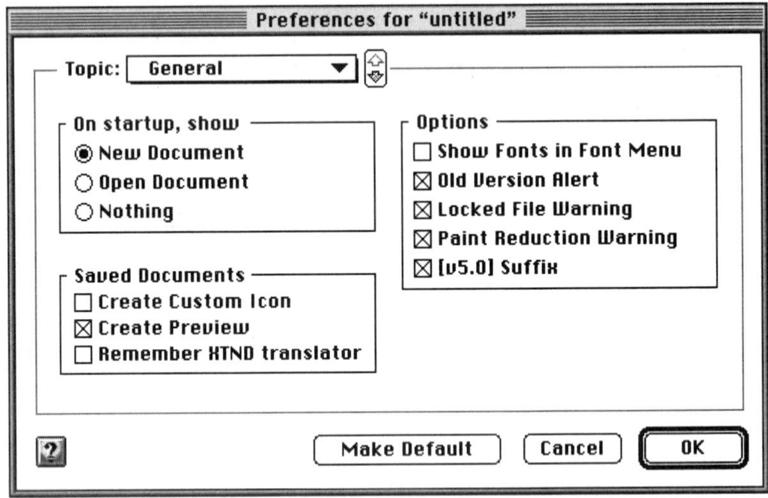

Figure 11.19 General preferences

Its options include:

- Indicating what happens when you launch ClarisWorks, determined by the radio buttons in the On startup, show group. The New Document radio button indicates that you want to see the New Document dialog box. The Open Document radio button displays an Open File dialog box. If you choose the Nothing radio button, then ClarisWorks won't show anything but the default Button bar when you start up the program.

- Choosing features for saved documents, configured by the check boxes in the Saved Documents group:

- A check in the Create Custom Icon box causes ClarisWorks to use a miniature version of the document's contents for its icon. This works only with drawing and painting documents.

- A check in the Create Preview box causes ClarisWorks to create a miniature of the document's contents that will be visible in the Open File dialog box whenever the file's name is highlighted.

- A check in the Remember XTND translator box instructs ClarisWorks to remember the translator used to open a file created by an application other than ClarisWorks. Then, when you issue the Save As command, ClarisWorks will select the translator in the Save File dialog box, making it easier for you to save the file back in its original format. (You can nonetheless always choose any format you want from the Save As popup menu.)

• Choosing a variety of configuration options:

  - (Macintosh only) A check in the Show Fonts in Font Menu box causes font names to appear in their respective typefaces, as in Figure 11.20.

The fancy font menu may look "cute," but it can be a problem if you have specialty fonts installed (fonts that have pictures or symbols rather than letters for their character sets). You may not be able to determine the font name for fonts that don't include letters. However, you can bypass the fancy fonts by holding down the Option key when you drop down the Fonts menu.

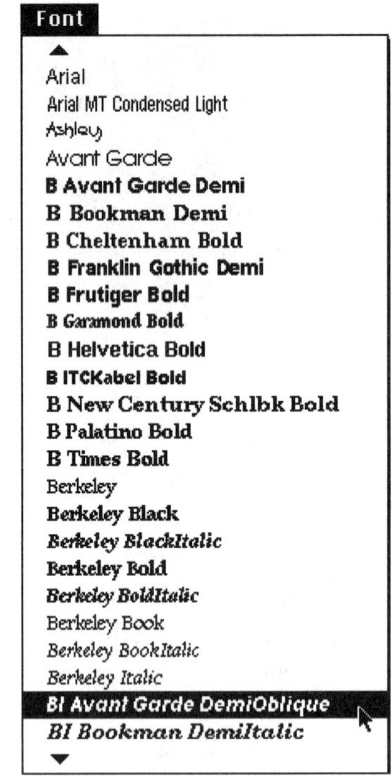

Figure 11.20 Typefaces displayed in the Font menu

- A check in the Old Version Alert box instructs ClarisWorks to warn you whenever you open a document created in an older version of the program. If you go ahead and open the document and then save it using the current version of ClarisWorks, you won't be able to open it again using the older version.

- A check in the Locked File Warning box instructs ClarisWorks to warn you when you open a file that is read-only (its contents can't be changed).

- A check in the Paint Reduction Warning instructs ClarisWorks to warn you when it must crop a paint document because there wasn't enough memory available to display the entire document.

- A check in the [v5.0] Suffix box instructs ClarisWorks to append [v5.0] to the name of any file created with an earlier version of ClarisWorks. In this way you won't accidentally overwrite the original version when you save the document with ClarisWorks 5.0.

Setting Text Preferences

If you are working with a word processing document, you will see the Text preferences first (Figure 11.21).

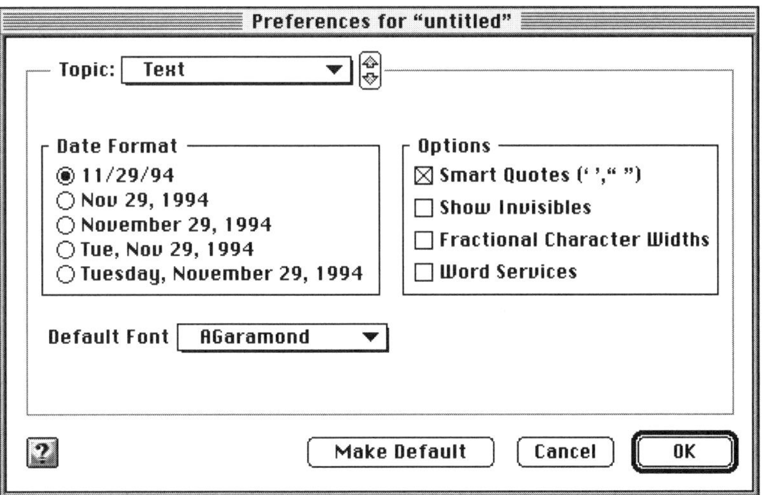

Figure 11.21 Text preferences

The options you can set include:

- Choosing a date format: Click on one of the radio buttons in the Date Format group.
- Choosing whether to use smart quotes: Place a check in the Smart Quotes check box to turn Smart Quotes on. Remove the check to turn Smart Quotes off.
- Choosing whether to show invisible characters: Place a check mark in the Show Invisibles check box to display formatting characters such as carriage returns and tabs. Remove the check to hide invisible characters.
- Choosing better output for laser printers: If you are printing to a laser printer, you can get better looking output if you place a check in the Fractional Character Widths check box.
- Choose a default font for the document from the Default Font popup menu.

Setting Graphics Preferences

The Graphics preferences panel (Figure 11.22) appears first whenever you have a drawing or painting document active. Its options include:

- Deciding whether polygons are closed automatically: If you want ClarisWorks to close polygons automatically, choose the Automatic radio button in the Polygon Closing group. However, if you don't want polygons closed for you, but prefer to leave them open or close them yourself, choose the Manual radio button.

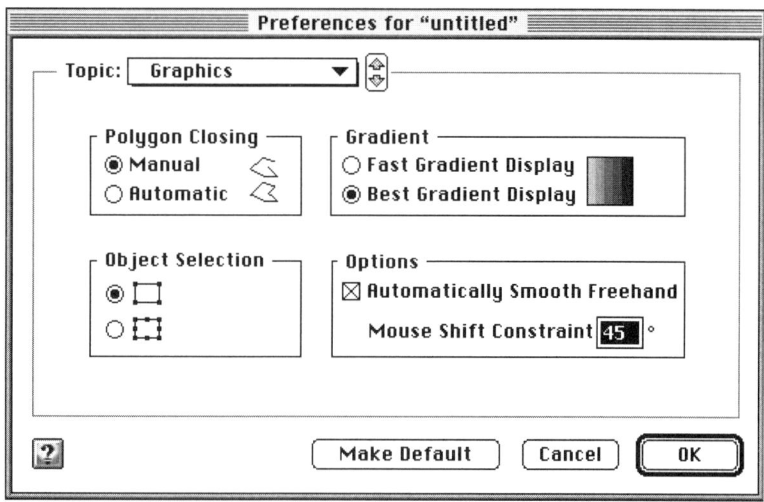

Figure 11.22 Graphics preferences

- Deciding on the number of selected object handles: If you want only four handles (one at each corner of a rectangle surrounding the object), choose the top radio button in the Object Selection group. If you want eight handles (one at each corner and one in the middle of each side of a rectangle surrounding the object), choose the bottom radio button.

- Choosing the speed and quality of gradient displays: There is a trade-off between the quality and speed with which gradients are drawn on the screen. If you want fast display and are willing to sacrifice on-screen quality, choose the Fast Gradient Display radio button in the Gradient group. However, if you want better on-screen quality and are willing to wait a bit longer for the image to be drawn, choose the Best Gradient Display button.

- Deciding whether to smooth freehand shapes: If you want ClarisWorks to smooth freehand shapes automatically, place a check in the Automatically Smooth Freehand check box. To prevent automatic smoothing, remove the check from the box.

- Choosing the angle to which holding the SHIFT key constrains drawing, painting, and free rotation: By default, the SHIFT key constrains the drawing and painting of regular shapes and free rotation to 45°. To change that angle, place a new value in the Mouse Shift Constraint edit box.

Spreadsheet Preferences

The Spreadsheet preferences panel (Figure 11.23) appears first when you are working with a spreadsheet document.

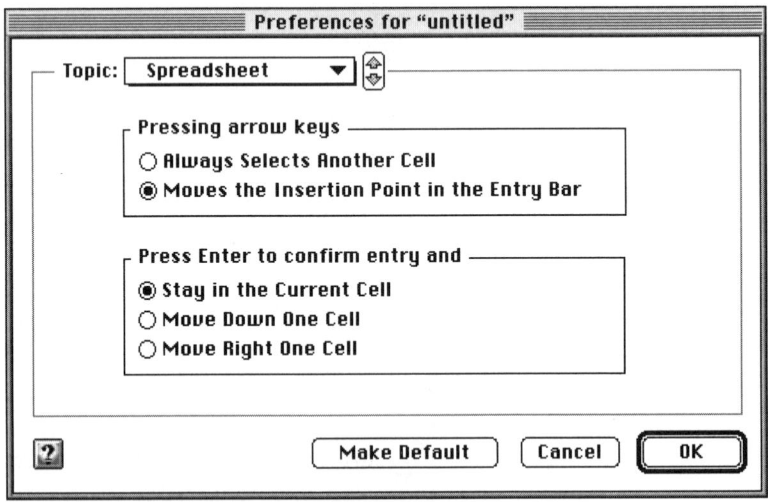

Figure 11.23 Spreadsheet preferences

Its options include:

- Choosing the behavior of the arrow keys: If you want the arrow keys to change the selected cell, choose the

Always Selects Another Cell radio button in the Pressing arrow keys group. If you want the arrow keys to move the insertion point in the entry bar, choose the Moves the Insertion Point in the Entry Bar radio button.

- Determining what happens when you press the Enter key: There are three possible actions when you press the Enter key, determined by the radio buttons in the "Press Enter to confirm entry and" group. Choose the Stay in the Current Cell radio button to prevent the selected cell from changing when you press Enter. To move down one cell in the current column, choose the Move Down One Cell radio button. To move right one cell in the current row, choose the Move Right One Cell radio button.

Palettes Preferences

The Palettes preferences panel (Figure 11.24) lets you choose the type of color palette you want as well as giving you the opportunity to import and export all types of graphics palettes. If you have customized the graphics palettes, you can use this preferences panel to save your work and import it into another document:

- To get fill and pen color palettes that are tailored to the number of colors your monitor can display, click the Colors radio button. Then choose the Drawing and Text Colors radio button. To get a 256-color palette whose colors you can change, click the Editable 256 Color Palette radio button. (Editing these colors is discussed in the last section of this chapter.)

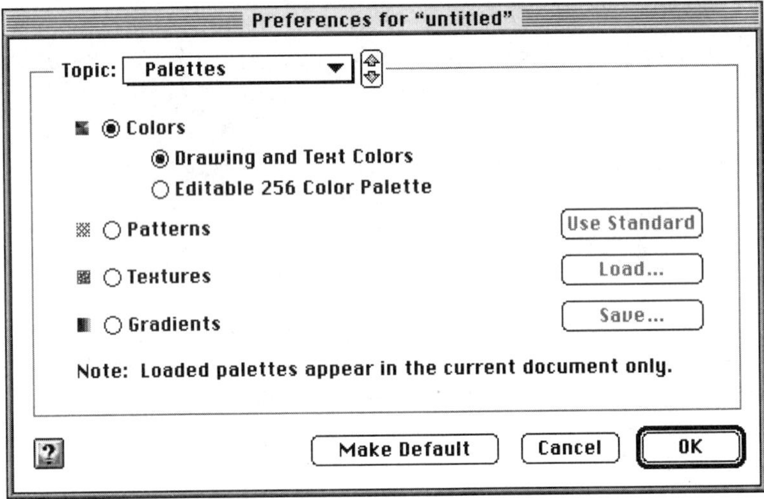

Figure 11.24 Palettes preferences

- To save customized color, pattern, texture, or gradient palettes, click the radio button that corresponds to the palette you want to save in a file. (Note that to save colors, you must be working with an editable color palette.) Click the Save button to display a Save File dialog box in which you can name the file where the palette's contents will be saved.

- To load colors, patterns, textures, or gradients that have been saved in a file, click the radio button that corresponds to the palette you want to modify. (Note that to load colors, you must be working with an editable color palette.) Then click the Load button to display an Open File dialog box from which you can choose the file containing the palette you want to load.

Customizing Textures

ClarisWorks provides a Texture Editor that lets you change any of the patterns in the texture palette. To change a texture:

1. Tear off the texture palette so that it becomes a floating window.

2. Double-click on the pattern you want to change. The Texture Editor appears, as in Figure 11.25.

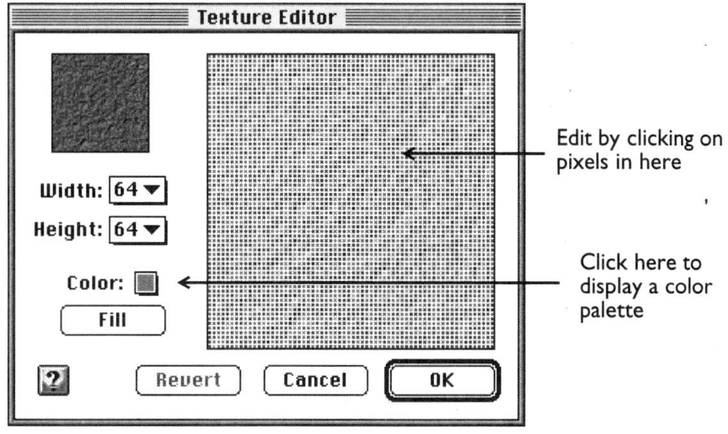

Figure 11.25 The Texture Editor

3. Choose the width and height (in pixels) of the sample with which you want to work from the Width and Height popup menus. Windows 95 users are limited to an 8-pixel square grid. Macintosh and Windows NT users, however, can work with the 64-pixel square that you see in Figure 11.25 to create a larger pattern. The pixels in the larger editing area are quite small. Even if your computer supports a larger pattern, you may find it easier to work with either a 16- or 8-pixel grid.

4. Choose the current pen color from the Color popup palette.

5. Click on a pixel in the editing area to change the color of the pixel to the current pen color. Alternatively, click on the Fill button to fill the entire editing area with the current pen color.

6. Repeat steps 4 and 5 until the pattern appears as you want.

7. Click the OK button or press Enter to save the modified pattern.

Customizing Gradients

ClarisWorks provides a Gradient Editor that lets you change the gradients that appear in the gradients palette. To modify a gradient:

1. Tear off the gradient palette so that it becomes a floating window.

2. Double-click on the gradient you want to modify. The Gradient Editor appears (for example, Figure 11.26).

3. Choose the type of gradient you want from the Sweep popup menu. The exact appearance of the Gradient Editor will vary depending on the sweep setting. In Figure 11.26, you can see the settings for a shape burst gradient. You can also choose a circular gradient (Figure 11.27) or a directional gradient (Figure 11.28).

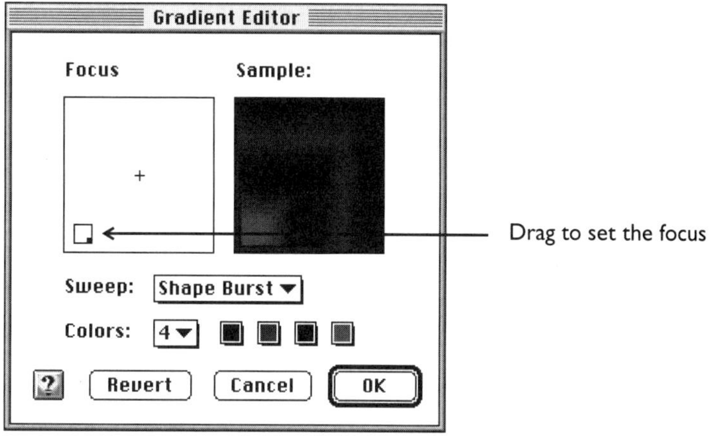

Figure 11.26 The Gradient Editor for a shape burst gradient

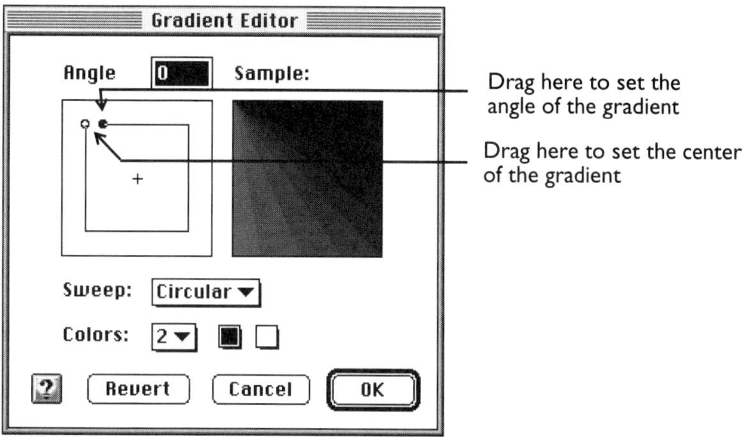

Figure 11.27 The Gradient Editor for a circular gradient

4. Drag to set the focus or angle of the gradient. (You can also enter angles for circular and directional gradients directly in the Angle edit box.)

5. Choose the number of colors for the gradient (2, 3, or 4) from the Colors popup menu. Clarisworks displays

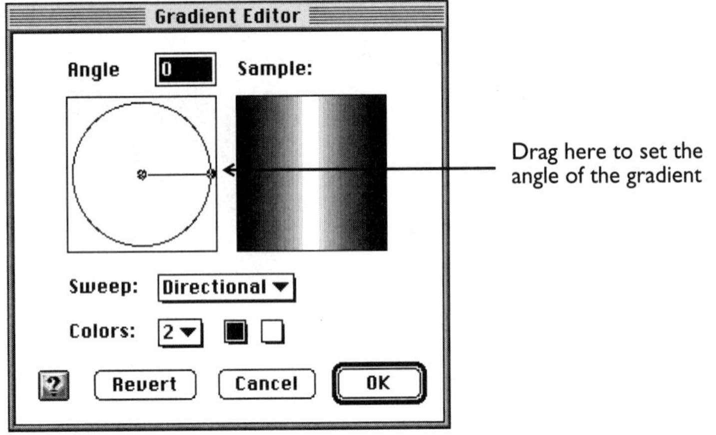

Figure 11.28 The Gradient Editor for a directional gradient

a square for each color to the right of the popup menu.

6. Choose the colors for the gradient by using the popup color palette associated with each color square.

7. Click the OK button or press Enter to save your changes.

Changing Colors in the Fill and Pen Color Palettes

When you are working with an editable color palette, you can change any of the colors. To change a color:

1. Drag the fill or pen color palette so that it becomes a floating window.

2. Double-click on the color you want to change. A color editor appears (Figure 11.29 for the Macintosh and Figure 11.30 for Windows).

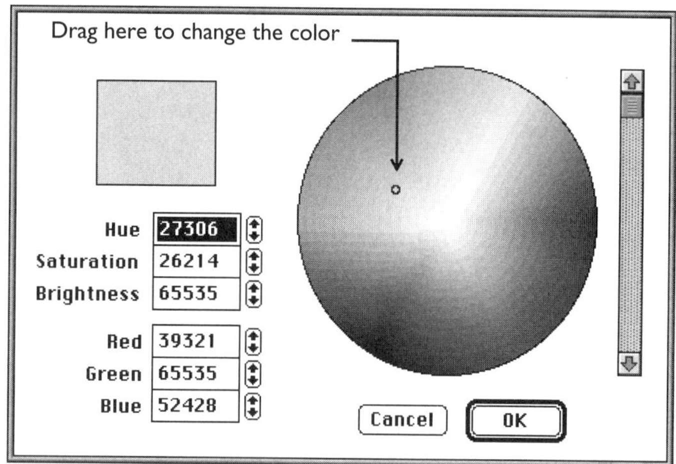

Figure 11.29 The Macintosh color picker

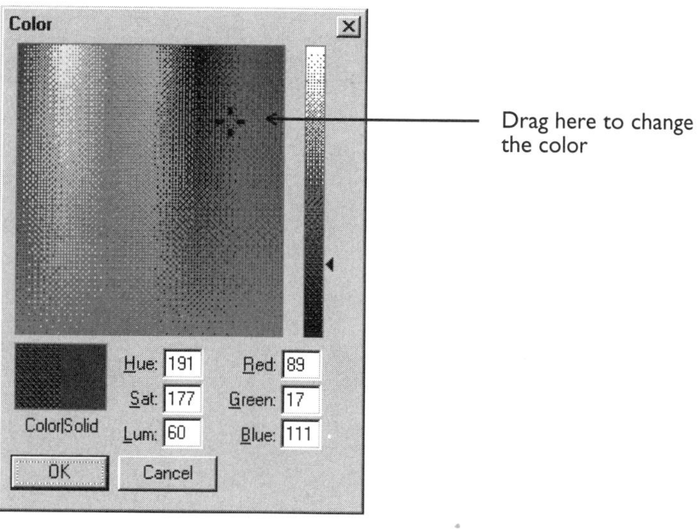

Figure 11.30 The Windows Color window

3. Use one of the following three methods to change the color:

   - Drag the circle in the Macintosh color wheel or the cursor in the Windows color rectangle to set the color.
   - Enter values for hue, saturation, and brightness.
   - Enter values for red, green, and blue.

It you aren't very familiar with color mixing, then the easiest way to change a color is simply to drag until you see the color you want.

4. Click the OK button or press Enter to save your changes.

A

Creating HTML for the Web

Most documents that you see on the World Wide Web are formatted using HTML (Hypertext Markup Language). ClarisWorks lets you save a formatted text document, including one that has embedded graphics, as an HTML document. ClarisWorks will also let you create hypertext links to locations in the same document and to locations specified by a URL (Universal Resource Locator). You can then upload the HTML document to a web server, from which networked users can download and open the document with a web browser (for example, Netscape or Internet Explorer) to view its contents.

This appendix assumes that you are generally familiar with the operation of the World Wide Web and its basic components, such as HTML documents and URLs.

Preparing a Document for the Web

ClarisWorks can generate a valid HTML document from most word processing documents. However, web browsers aren't word processors; they don't recognize the wide range of formatting options commonly found in word processors, such as fixed margin sizes, multiple typefaces, and multiple column and section layouts. If you want to ensure that your HTML document looks as much as possible like your word processing document, keep the following things in mind:

- Go ahead and vary type sizes, but keep in mind that web browsers work with relative type sizes (for example, bigger versus smaller) rather than the absolute type sizes in points used by word processors. If the largest type size in your document is 24 point, for example, you can be relatively certain that it will be displayed using a web browser's largest type size. There is no guarantee, however, that it will be exactly 24 point. Keep in mind also that the same type size appears 30 percent larger on a Windows computer than it does on the Macintosh. So even if a browser is displaying 12-point type, it will look bigger under Windows than on the Macintosh.

- Don't bother with various typefaces. Most web browsers use the same typeface for just about everything. For example, if you are using Netscape Navigator on the Macintosh or Windows, most characters appear in the Times typeface. In contrast, AOL's browser uses Helvetica. Typeface is something you can't control and can't predict. However, if you stick to Times, you're going to be as close as you can get to what most browsers use.

The only way to control typography on a web page completely is to create the text as a graphics object and save it in a graphics file, using either GIF or JPEG format. Then, import the graphics file into your word processing document.

- Center, left align, or right align text.
- Use plain, bold, and italic text. Because web browsers use underlined text to indicate links, don't use underlining as a type style.
- Use tables created from spreadsheet frames. ClarisWorks creates HTML tables from spreadsheet frames, although you have only minimal control over table placement.
- Use embedded graphics. When you create an HTML file, ClarisWorks saves each graphic image in a separate file and translates the graphic to GIF or JPEG format. (More information about the treatment of graphics comes later in this appendix.)
- Create bulleted lists using the Bullet, Diamond, or Checklist style or numbered lists using the Harvard, Legal, or Number style.
- Change the background color. By default, a web page has a gray background. Gray, however, makes many things hard to see. If you want to change the color,

display the Internet Button Bar and click the button to display the HTML Configuration dialog box (Figure A.1). Then choose a color from the Color popup menu. When in doubt, white is always a good choice.

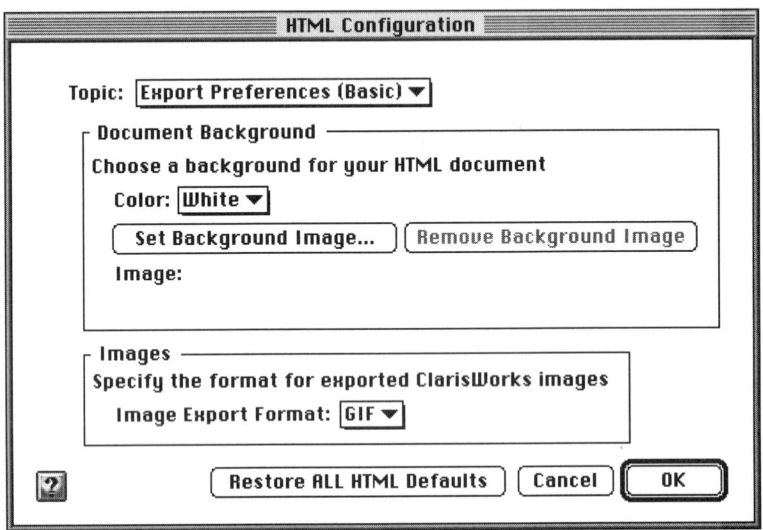

Figure A.1 Setting basic preferences for HTML export

The HTML Configuration dialog box also lets you specify a background image. This image, which must be a GIF or JPEG file, will be tiled to fill the entire web page's background. In addition, you can use this dialog box to specify whether you want ClarisWorks to create GIF or JPEG graphics files when you save a word processing document as HTML.

Turn off ClarisWorks's smart quotes feature before entering the text of a document that is going to be saved as HTML. Web browsers can't interpret smart quotes and will therefore ignore any smart quotes found in your document.

As an example of a simple word processing document that tranlsates relatively well to HTML, take a look at Figure A.2. The larger type is 24-point bold and has been centered. This is a good choice because it corresponds fairly closely to a web browser's level 1 heading format (largest font size and bold). The rest of the text is 12 point, the size most commonly used to display body text in a web page. The document also includes a spreadsheet frame used as a table, a bulleted list, and a link to a *fictional* web site. (You will read about creating links in the next sections of this chapter.)

After being saved as an HTML document and then viewed using a web browser, the word processing document looks like that in Figure A.3. Notice that the text translates rather well, as do the bulleted list and the embedded graphic. However, the table looks considerably different. First of all, it isn't centered. Second, the table's original typeface has been replaced with Times, the display typeface used by the web browser. Finally, the table has a typical web browser border, rather than the spreadsheet-style border it had in the original document.

Creating a Link to a URL

A link to a URL instructs a web browser to download and display another web page. The link can point to a document on the same computer or to a document anywhere on the World Wide Web. The only requirement is that the location of the document must be specified with a valid URL.

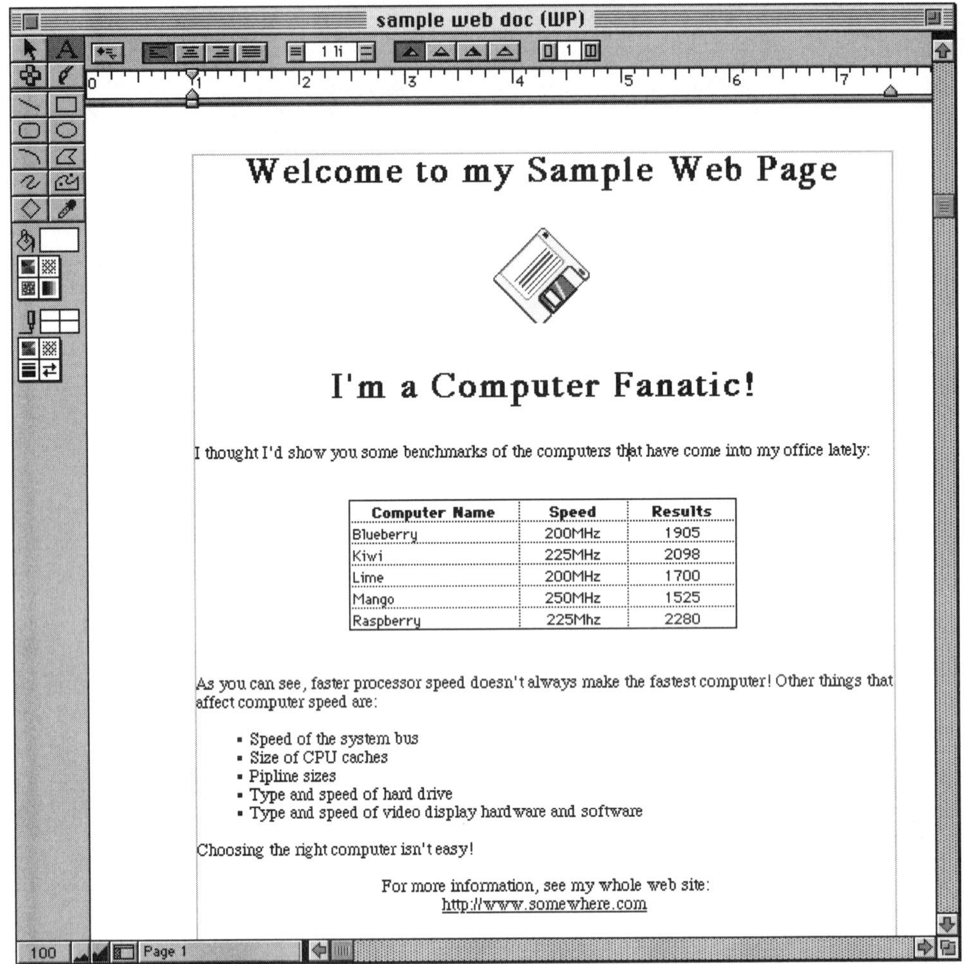

Figure A.2 A word processing document that will translate well to HTML

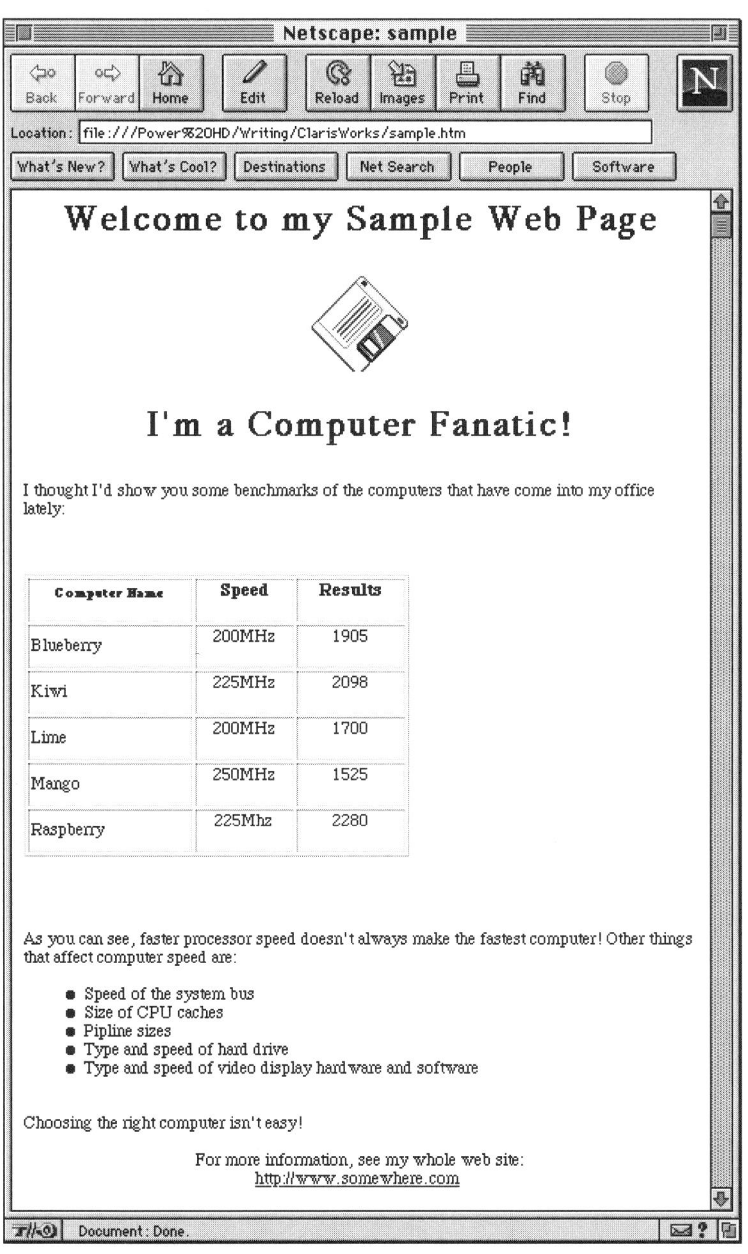

Figure A.3 The HTML document viewed in a web browser

To create a link:

1. Select the text, graphic object, paint frame, or spreadsheet frame that you want to turn into a link.

2. If necessary, display the Internet Button Bar.

3. Click the button in the Button Bar. The New URL Link dialog box appears.

4. If the link is text, the selected text will appear in the Name box (see Figure A.4). If the link is a graphic, then the Name box will be empty.

Figure A.4 Making a new link

5. Type the URL of the link in the URL box.

6. Click the OK button or press Enter. If it is not already visible, the Links palette will appear. This palette (Figure A.5) floats above all currently open documents to give you access to your links. (Instructions on using the Links palette to edit links appear later in this section.)

Figure A.5 The Links palette

To use a URL *link, place the mouse pointer over the links. The cursor changes to* *. Click the link once to activate it. Note that the link will work only if the Live Links check box in the bottom left corner of the Links palette is checked . You can also toggle live links on and off by clicking the button in the Internet Button Bar.*

Creating Internal Links

Not all links need to go to documents on the World Wide Web. Instead, you can use links to make a long document or set of related documents easier to navigate. For example, if you wrote a user's guide to a product and stored the guide in several files (perhaps one file per chapter), then you could use links in an "index" document to open other chapters for the user.

There are two types of internal links:

- A *Document link* opens another document and places the user at the beginning of the document.
- *Book marks* are attached to a specific point in a document. They can take the user to another place in the same document or to a specific location in another document.

Creating Document Links to Open Other Documents

To create a link that opens another document:

1. Open the document that will contain the link.
2. Select the text, graphics object, paint frame, or spreadsheet frame that will represent the link.
3. Click the button in the Internet Button Bar. The New Document Link dialog box appears (Figure A.6).

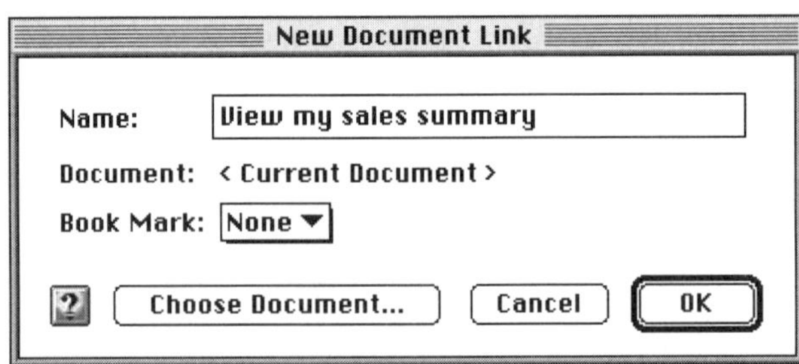

Figure A.6 Creating a document link

4. Click the Choose Document button. An Open File dialog box appears.

5. Choose the document to which you want to link. Click the OK button or press Enter to close the Open File dialog box.

6. Click the OK button or press Enter to close the New Document Link dialog box.

To use a document link, place the mouse pointer over the links. The cursor changes to . Click the link once to activate it. Note that the link will work only if the Live Links check box in the bottom left corner of the Links palette is checked . You can also toggle live links on and off by clicking the  *button in the Internet Button Bar.*

Creating Document Links to Book Marks

A book mark is typically used to make it easy to jump to locations within the same document. It is particularly handy for helping users navigate long web pages. It can also be used within a group of related documents that aren't on the web to open a document and jump to a specific location within that document.

Configuring a document so that you can click on a link to jump to a book marked position is actually a two-step process. First you must place a book mark (an anchor) at the target location. Then you create a document link that goes to that book mark.

To create a book mark and a link to it:

1. Open the document that will contain the book mark.

2. Select the text, graphics object, painting frame, or spreadsheet frame that represents the target location within the document.

3. Click the button in the Internet Button Bar. The New Book Mark dialog box appears (Figure A.7).

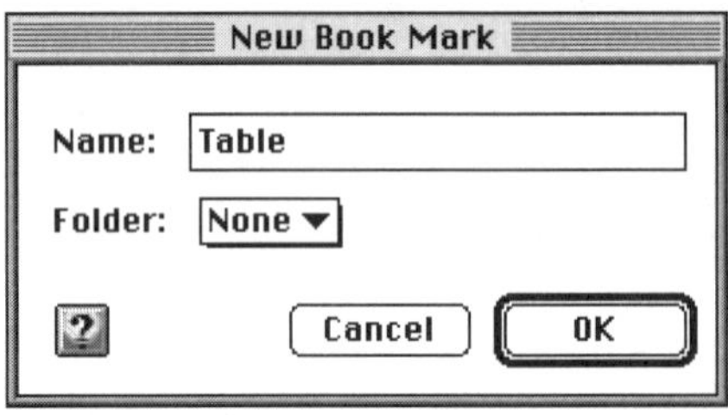

Figure A.7 Creating a new book mark

4. If the target of the book mark is text, its name appears in the Name box. If the target is a graphic or frame, the Name box will be empty. In that case, type a name for the book mark.

5. Click the OK button or press Enter. At this point, nothing will appear in the document, but the book mark will show up in the Link palette's Book Marks list.

6. If necessary, open the document that will contain the link to the book mark.

7. Select the text, graphic object, painting frame, or spreadsheet frame that will represent the link.

8. Click the button in the Internet Button Bar. The New Document Link dialog box appears.

9. If necessary, enter a name for the link.

10. If the book mark to which you are linking is in the same document, leave Document as <Current Document>. If the book mark is in a different document, click the Choose Document button and select the document.

11. Choose the name of the book mark to which you want to link from the Book Mark popup menu (Figure A.8).

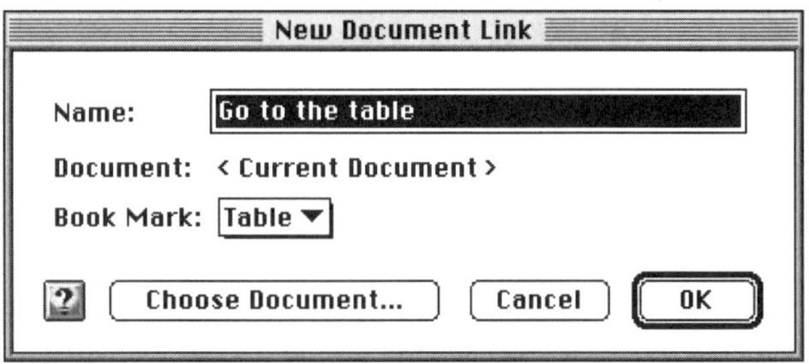

Figure A.8 Creating a link to a book mark

12. Click the OK button or press Enter.

Managing Links

Once you have created a link, you manage that link from the Links palette. By default, the Links palette appears each time you create a new link. If you close the palette, ClarisWorks asks if you want it to continue to pop up (see Figure A.9). Respond by clicking the No button and the Links palette will stay closed until you open it explicity.

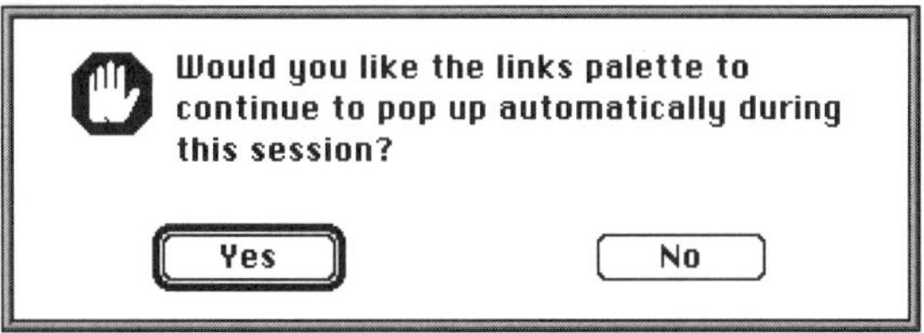

Figure A.9 Choosing or refusing automatic display of the Links palette

To make the links palette appear manually:

Macintosh	Choose Window->Show Links Palette or press SHIFT-⌘-M.
Windows	Choose Window->Show Links Palette, press SHIFT-CTRL-M, or press ALT-W, K.

To modify or delete a link:

1. If necessary, display the Links palette.

2. Choose the type of link you want to modify from the popup menu above the list of links (see Figure A.10).

Figure A.10 Choosing a type of link

3. Highlight the name of the link you want to modify.

4. To edit a link, choose Edit *type* Link from the Link palette's Links menu, where *type* is the type of link you have selected (Figure A.11). The dialog box that you used to create the link appears. (In this case, its title says "Edit" rather than "New.")

5. Make any desired changed to the link.

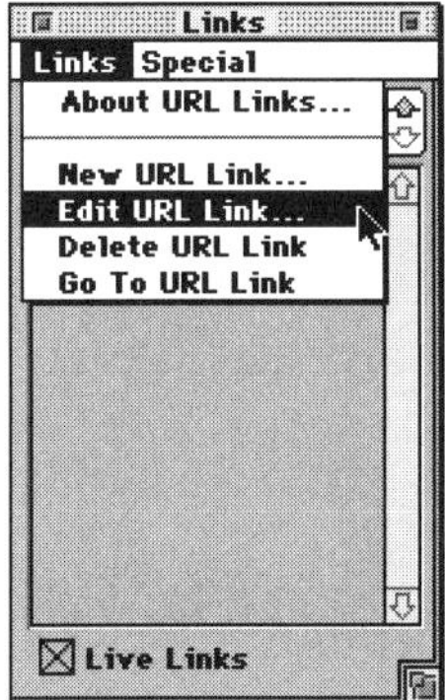

Figure A.11 The Link palette's Links menu

6. Click the OK button or press Enter to close the dialog box.

To delete a link, select the link you want to delete using the procedure described for choosing a link to edit. Then, choose Delete *type* Link from the Link palette's Links menu, where *type* is the type of link you have selected.

Generating the HTML

Because HTML documents can look somewhat different when they are displayed in a web browser, it makes sense to generate HTML often to check how your document is progressing.

There are two ways to generate an HTML document. One is quick and easy but doesn't give you any control over the file name or where it is placed. The other takes a little longer but gives you complete control over file naming and placement.

To generate a quick HTML file, click the button in the Internet Button Bar. ClarisWorks saves an HTML version of your file in the current directory (whichever disk directory you used last). The file's name will be the name of the word processing document with a *.htm* extension. Each graphic in the file will be saved in a separate file. Its name will be created by adding a number to the name of the HTML file's name. For example, if your word processing document is named *web_sample*, then the HTML file will be *web_sample.htm*, and the graphics files will be *web_sample1.gif*, *web_sample2.gif*, and so on. (This assumes that you have selected GIF graphics. The extension will be *.jpg* if you selected JPEG graphics.)

To generate an HTML file manually:

1. Display the Save File dialog box:

Macintosh	Choose File->Save As or press SHIFT-⌘-S.
Windows	Choose File->Save As, press SHIFT-CTRL-S, or press ALT-F, A..

2. Choose a location for the HTML document and its accompanying graphics files.

3. Enter a name for the HTML document. It should have a *.htm* or *.html* extension.

Although the Macintosh and Windows 95 have no trouble with file names containing spaces, the same is not true for some web servers (in particular, many of those running UNIX). You should therefore give HTML files that are going to be used with a web server names without spaces.

4. Choose HTML from the Save As popup menu.

5. Click the Save button or press Enter. ClarisWorks creates the HTML file and its graphics files.

Viewing HTML Documents in a Web Browser

To view your newly created HTML document in a web browser, first make sure that all the graphics files needed by your document are in the same directory (folder) as the HTML document. (If you upload the files to a server, you must also be certain to place the graphics in the same directory as the document.) Then, run the browser. When the browser is running, use File->Open to open and display your document.

For in-depth coverage of ClarisWorks and the Internet, see "ClarisWorks: The Internet, New Media, and Paperless Documents" by Jesse Feiler (Claris Press, 1997).

B

Using the Equation Editor

Part of the ClarisWorks package for the Macintosh is an equation editor that you can use to typeset mathematical and scientific formulas. Once created, a formula can be added as a graphic object to word processing or drawing documents. You can also place an equation on a database layout.

One of the best things about an equation editor is that in most cases, it will correctly space and format equations as you enter numbers, letters, and symbols. The result is that it is much easier to use an equation editor for typesetting equations than it is to attempt to set them using a word processor or graphics program.

This appendix discusses using the equation editor to format equations. It assumes that you are familiar with the mathematical and/or scientific symbols that will be used in the equation you will be typesetting.

Launching the Equation Editor

The equation editor is actually a stand-alone application that is integrated with ClarisWorks. To launch it so that it will copy a formula directly into your document when you have finished formatting:

1. Open a document into which you can insert an equation.

2. In a word processing document, place the insertion point where you want the equation to appear.

3. Choose Edit->Insert Equation. ClarisWorks launches the equation editor and provides you with a window for formatting the equation (Figure B.1).

As you can see in Figure B.1, the equation editor has two rows of popup menus, which the equation editor calls "palettes." These provide access to symbols that you can't type from the keyboard and to formatting options that aren't available with a word processor. The top row contains the symbol palettes that let you insert mathematical and scientific symbols. The bottom row contains template palettes. The remainder of the window is a workspace for formatting a formula. It begins with the outline of a rectangle (a *slot*) into which you can place a number, letter, symbol, or format.

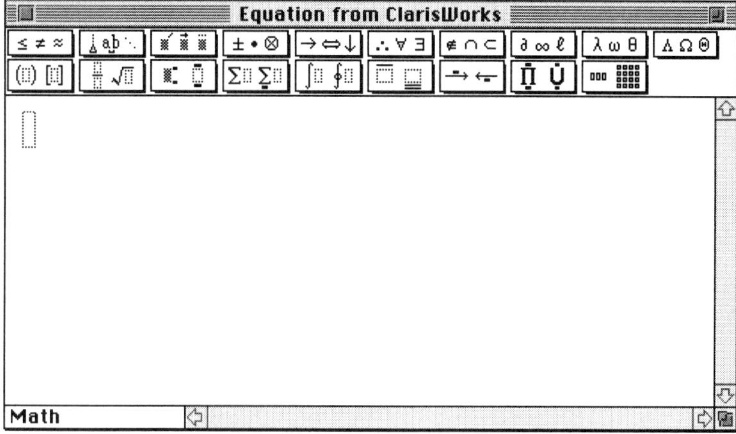

Figure B.1 The equation editor window

Creating a Sample Formula

To give you an overview of how the equation editor works, let's typeset the formula for computing the standard deviation of a group of values. The formula is the square root of the sum of squares of the difference between each value and the mean, divided by the number of values.

The process for creating this formula is as follows:

1. Because the outermost operation is a square root, add the square root symbol by choosing it from the Fractions/Radicals template palette (see Figure B.2). Notice that the symbol in the popup menu indicates that a square root sign will be placed over the slot. As you can see in Figure B.3, the symbol is transferred to the workspace.

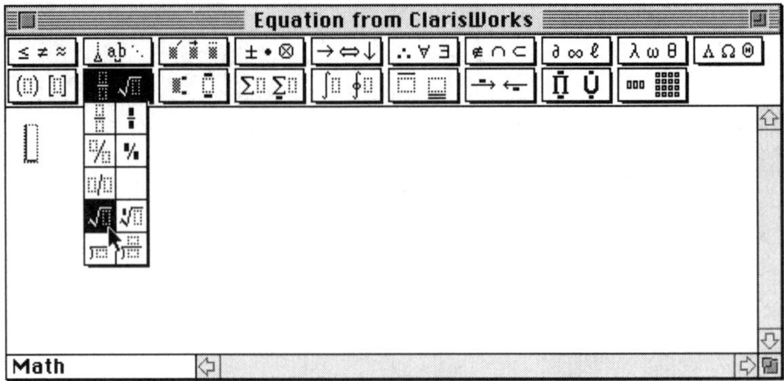

Figure B.2 Inserting the symbol for square root

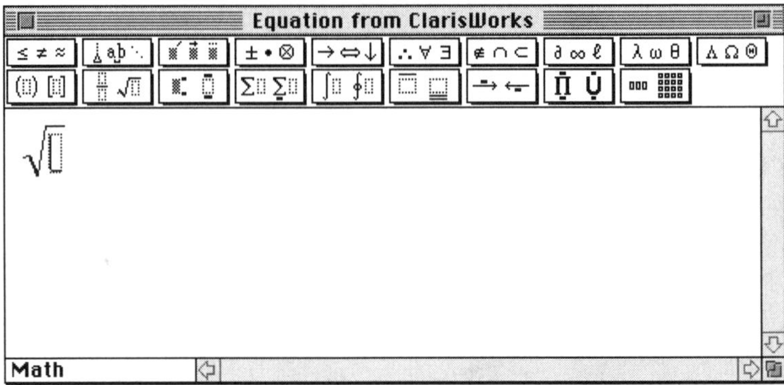

Figure B.3 The square root symbol in the equation editor's workspace

2. Inside the square root symbol, the equation needs to perform a division. The next step is therefore to insert the division symbol, choosing it from the Fractions/Radicals template palette (see Figure B.4).

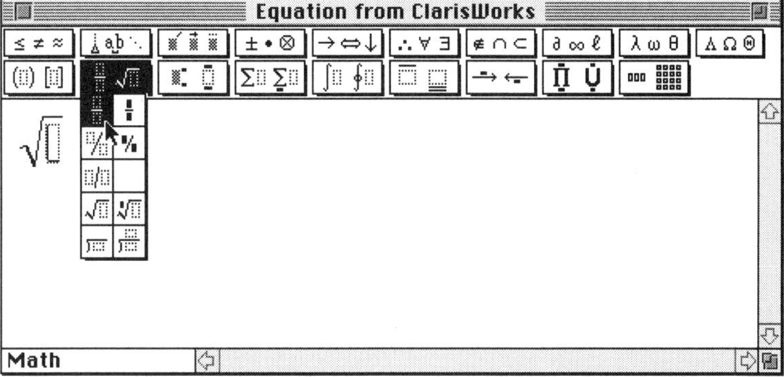

Figure B.4 Inserting a division symbol

The equation now looks like:

3. The denominator of the division needs only an N to indicate the number of values in the group. To enter this value, click in the lower slot and type *N*, producing the following result:

4. The numerator of the division requires a Greek sigma as the sum operator, as well as the difference whose squares will be summed. The first step is to insert the

sigma by choosing it from the Summation palette (Figure B.5).

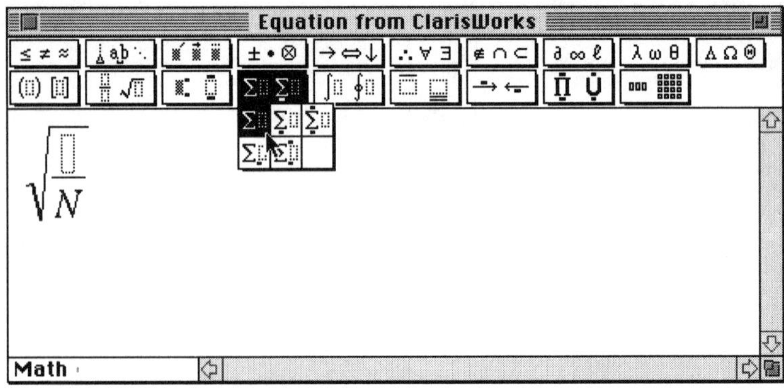

Figure B.5 Inserting a sigma for summation

At this point, the equation looks like:

Notice that the square root symbol has been enlarged so that it covers the entire equation.

5. Now, add a second slot for the exponent by choosing the position of the exponent from the Subscripts/ Superscripts palette (Figure B.6).

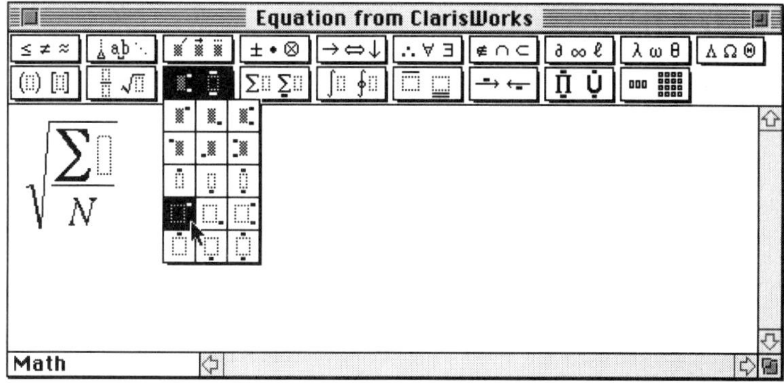

Figure B.6 Inserting an exponent

The resulting equation now has two slots:

6. Click in the larger slot to place the insertion point in it. Add parentheses around it by choosing from the Fences template palette (Figure B.7).

The equation now appears like:

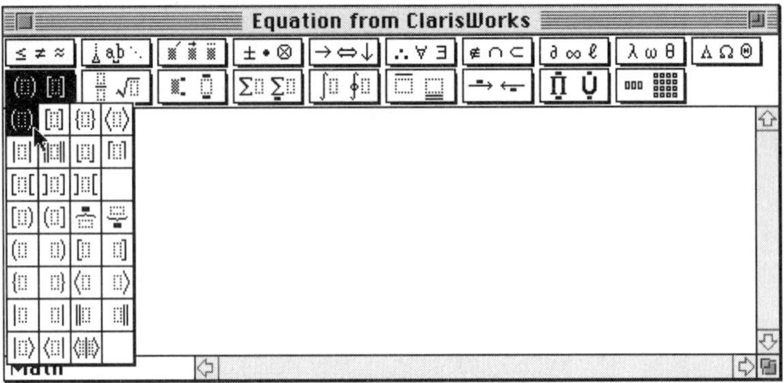

Figure B.7 Inserting parentheses

7. Insert a subscript for the first element in parentheses by choosing a subscript from the Subscripts/Superscripts palette (Figure B.8). A slot appears at the bottom of the large slot within parentheses.

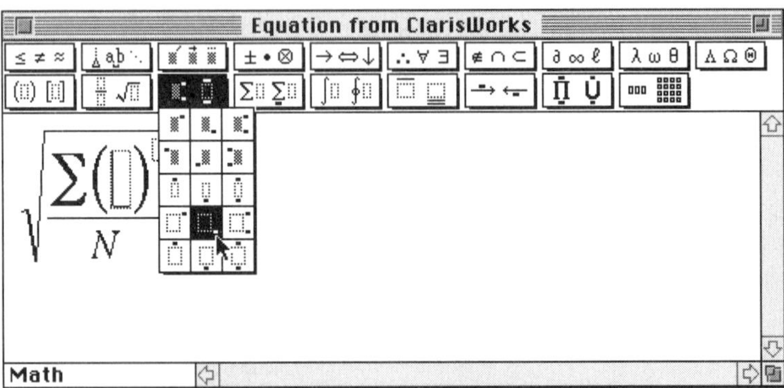

Figure B.8 Inserting a subscript

8. Type an *i* in the small slot within parentheses, producing

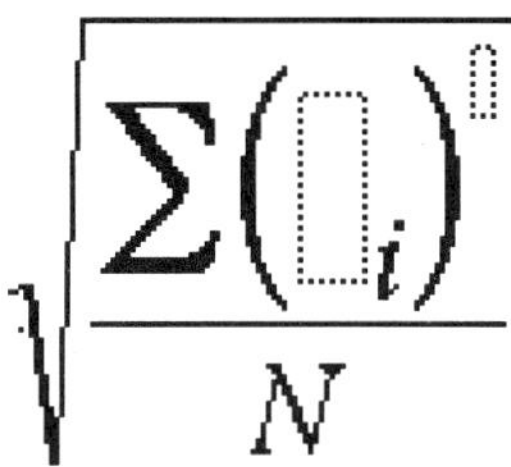

9. Type an X in the large slot within parentheses, giving you

$$\sqrt{\frac{\Sigma\left(X_i\right)^{\square}}{N}}$$

10. Press the right arrow key once to move the insertion point to the right of the *i*. Then type a minus sign and another X. The equation looks like:

$$\sqrt{\frac{\Sigma\left(X_i - X\right)^{\square}}{N}}$$

11. You must add a bar over the second *X* to indicate that it is the mean of the group of values. To add the bar, select the second *X* and choose the bar symbol from the Underbars/Overbars palette (Figure B.9).

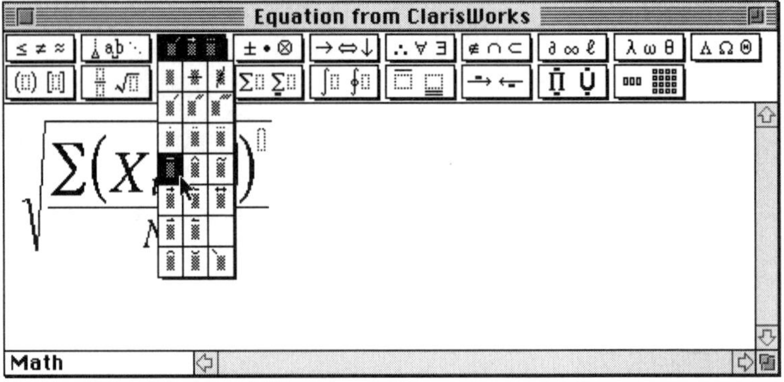

Figure B.9 Adding a bar over an equation element

The almost completed equation now looks like

$$\sqrt{\frac{\sum\left(X_i-\bar{X}\right)^{\square}}{N}}$$

12. The final step is to place the insertion point in the remaining slot and type a 2 for the exponent. The final typeset equation appears in the equation editor as

$$\sqrt{\frac{\sum\left(X_i-\bar{X}\right)^{2}}{N}}$$

Although you can save the equation in a file of its own, you do not necessarily have to do so. When you close the equation editor window, the equation is automatically transferred to the ClarisWorks document that was active when you launched the equation editor. As you can see in Figure B.10, the equation appears as a graphic object. You can move it, resize it by dragging the handle in its lower right corner, and flow text around it, just as you would any other graphic element.

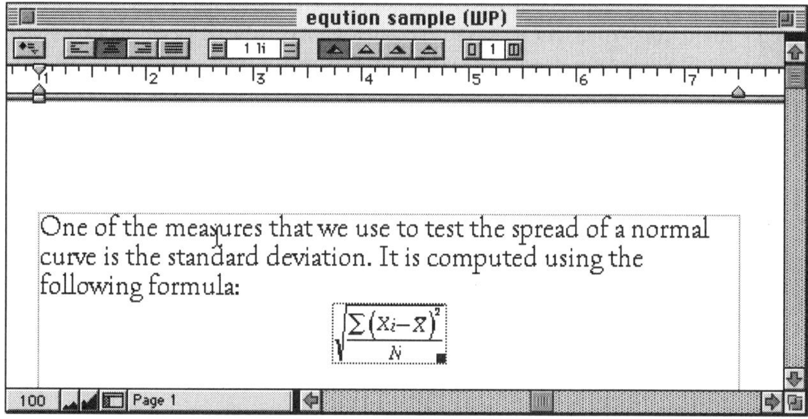

Figure B.10 An equation in a word processing document

To make changes to an equation, you can return to the equation editor by double-clicking on the equation in the ClarisWorks document.

Because the equation editor is a stand-alone application, it will remain running after you transfer an equation back to ClarisWorks. You will therefore need to quit that application just as you would any other program.

The Symbol Palettes

Selections from the symbol palettes insert the symbols directly into an equation at the current insertion point. A symbol may be a stand-alone element such as an arithmetic operator, or it may be added to an existing element in an equation (for example, an overbar).

The 10 symbol palettes, arranged from left to right across the equation editor window, are summarized in Table B.1. The table contains explanations for symbols that aren't typical mathematical or scientific symbols.

Table B.1 The Equation Editor's Symbol Palettes

Palette	Contents
$\leq \neq \approx$ $\leq$ $\geq$ $\prec$ $\succ$ $\lhd$ $\rhd$ $\neq$ $\equiv$ $\approx$ $\cong$ $\propto$	Relational symbols
	Spaces and Ellipses palette. The symbol in the top left corner is an alignment symbol. Place it in the individual equations in a multi-line formula and the equation editor will align the equations on the symbol. (The symbol appears only in the equation editor.) The remaining symbols in the first two rows place explicit spaces between equation elements. The rest of the symbols are ellipses.
	Primes, Hats, and Bars (Embellishments). To insert a symbol from this palette, select the element in the formula to which the symbol should be added. Choose the symbol in the top left corner of the palette to remove all embellishments.

Table B.1 (Continued) The Equation Editor's Symbol Palettes

Palette	Contents
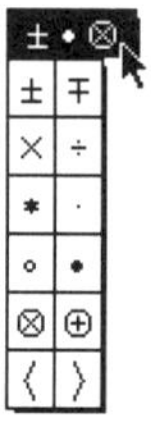 ± • ⊗ ± ∓ × ÷ * · ∘ • ⊗ ⊕ ⟨ ⟩	Operators. This palette contains arithmetic operators that can't be typed from the keyboard. Use the keyboard to insert other operators into an equation.
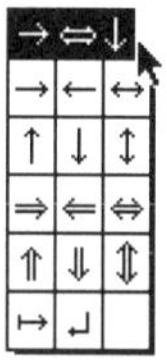 → ⇔ ↓ → ← ↔ ↑ ↓ ↕ ⇒ ⇐ ⇔ ⇑ ⇓ ⇕ ↦ ↲	Arrows
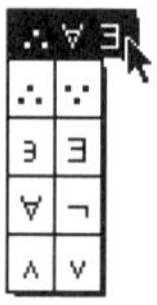 ∴ ∀ ∃ ∴ ∵ ∍ ∃ ∀ ¬ ∧ ∨	Logical symbols
 ∉ ∩ ⊂ ∈ ∉ ∪ ∩ ⋃ ⋂ ⊂ ⊃ ⊆ ⊇ ⊄ ∅	Set theory symbols
 ∂ ∞ ℓ ∂ ∇ ∞ ℑ ℜ ℵ ∠ ⊥ ◊ ℓ ℘ ° ħ ƛ ∫ Σ Π ∐	Miscellaneous symbols

Table B.1 (Continued) The Equation Editor's Symbol Palettes

Palette	Contents
 λ ω θ α β χ δ ε ϕ φ γ η ι κ λ μ ν ο π ϖ θ ϑ ρ σ ς τ υ ω ξ ψ ζ	Greek letters #1
 Λ Ω Θ Α Β Χ Δ Ε Φ Γ Η Ι Κ Λ Μ Ν Ο Π Θ Ρ Σ Τ Υ Ω Ξ Ψ Ζ	Greek letters #2

The Template Palettes

A template inserts one or more slots into an equation in a specific format. What happens when you insert a template depends on where the insertion point is at the time, what parts of the equation are selected, and/or what modifier keys are held down:

- If the insertion point is anywhere except inside another template's slot and nothing is selected, choosing a template inserts the new template into the equation at the insertion point.

- If the insertion point is in a slot, choosing a template replaces the existing template with the new template. Any values in the old template are lost.

- If a template is selected, holding down the Option key while choosing a new template replaces the old template with the new. Values from the old template are copied into the new one.

- If elements in an equation are selected, holding down the 1 key while choosing a template "wraps" the template around the selected elements. This lets you, for example, place parentheses around elements that are already part of an equation. (Not all elements can be wrapped in this way. If you can't select an element by dragging, then it can't be wrapped.)

The nine template palettes are summarized in Table B.2, arranged as they appear from left to right across the second row at the top of the equation editor's window.

Table B.2 The Equation Editor's Template Palettes

Palette	Contents
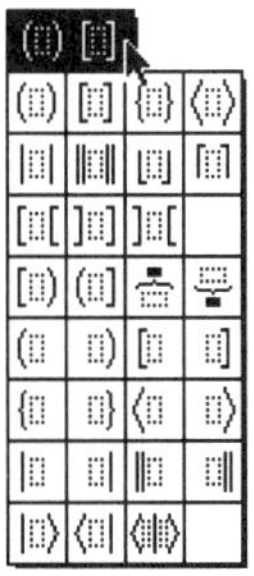	Fences (pairs of matching symbols)
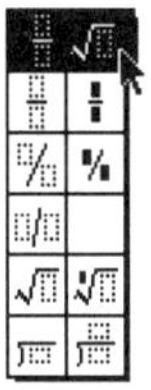	Fractions and radicals

Table B.2 (Continued) The Equation Editor's Template Palettes

Palette	Contents
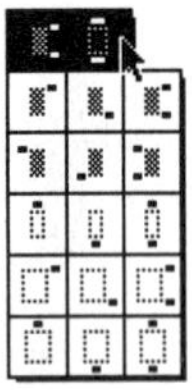	Subscripts and superscripts
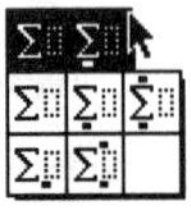	Summation
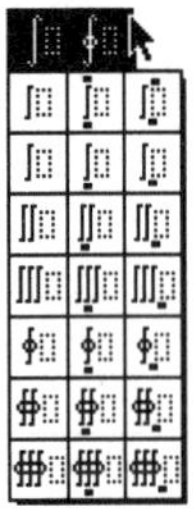	Integrals
	Underbars and overbars
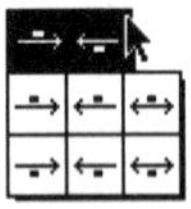	Labeled arrows
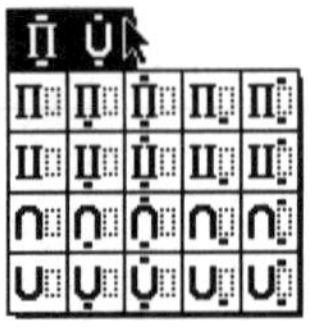	Products and set theory

Table B.2 (Continued) The Equation Editor's Template Palettes

Palette	Contents
	Matrix. Choosing any of the icons in the bottom row of the palette displays a dialog box similar to that in Figure B.11, which lets you determine the size of a matrix. Notice also in Figure B.11 that you can click between matrix elements to add or remove lines between the rows and columns. You can therefore use a matrix to format a table.

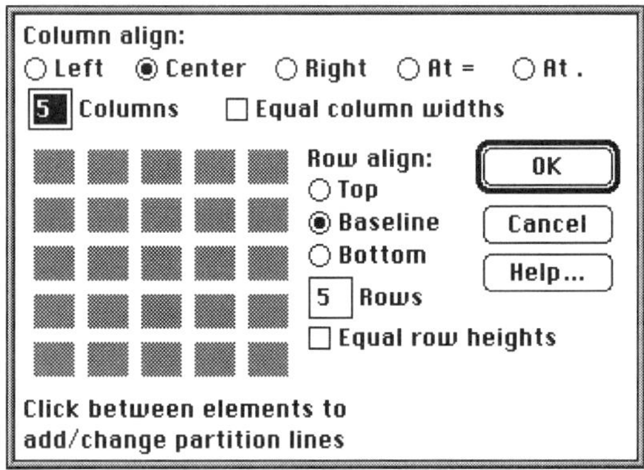

Figure B.11 Setting the size of a matrix

Element Styles

For the most part, the equation editor sets appropriate spacing and element styles for you. However, if you find that the defaults don't produce an equation that meets your needs, you do have control over how elements appear.

Font and Style

The equation editor's Style menu (Figure B.12) is different from a typical Style menu in that it presents style sheets rather than individual styles that you can apply. The settings for these styles are part of the Define Styles dialog box, which you can access by choosing Style->Define. Notice in Figure B.13 that you can choose a font for each style and whether it is bold and/or italic.

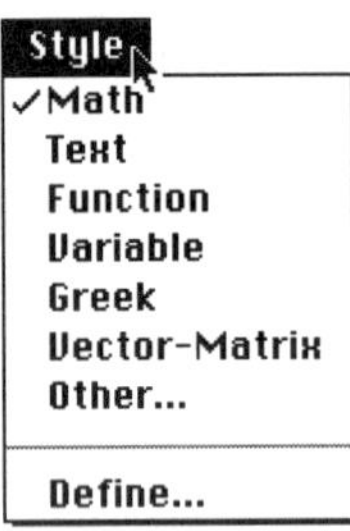

Figure B.12 The equation editor's Style menu

Style	Font	Character Style Bold	Character Style Italic	
Text	Times	☐	☐	OK
Functions	Times	☐	☐	Cancel
Variables	Times	☐	☒	Help...
L. C. Greek	Symbol	☐	☒	
U. C. Greek	Symbol	☐	☐	
Symbols	Symbol	☐	☐	
Vector-Matrix	Times	☒	☐	
Numbers	Times	☐	☐	

Figure B.13 Defining equation editor styles

If one of the predefined styles in the Style menu doesn't meet your needs, you can use another font. Choose Style->Other to display the Other Style dialog box (Figure B.14). Then choose the font you want; check the bold and/or italic check box if you need one or both of those styles.

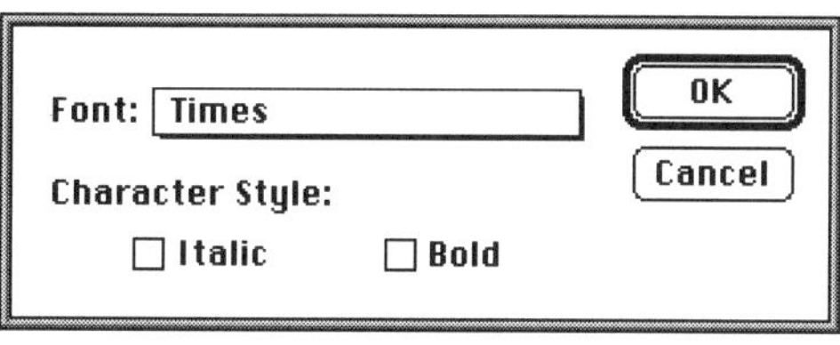

Figure B.14 Setting another style

Type Size

Like its Style menu, the equation editor's Size menu (Figure B.15) contains style sheets rather than individual type sizes. The definitions of the sizes can be found in the Define Sizes dialog box (Figure B.16). To display it, choose Size->Define.

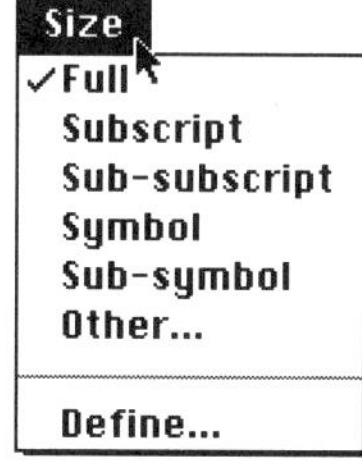

Figure B.15 The equation editor's Size menu

The sizes in the Define Sizes dialog box are associated with specific element positions in an equation. To find the connection, highlight an element in the sample equation at

Define Sizes

Full	12pt
Subscript/Superscript	7pt
Sub-Subscript/Superscript	5pt
Symbol	18pt
Sub-symbol	12pt

$$(1+B)^2 \sum_{p=1} X_{n_k}^{kp}$$

OK
Cancel
Apply
Defaults
Help...

Figure B.16 Defining equation editor type sizes

the right of the dialog box. The equation editor will then highlight the corresponding size name. For example, in Figure B.16, the large X next to the sigma is highlighted; the text "12pt"next to the Full size is highlighted as well, indicating that the Full size is applied to characters that hold the same relative position in an equation as the selected X.

Spacing

The equation editor spaces elements automatically, according to settings in the Define Spacing dialog box (Figure B.17). To see the default settings or to make changes in the spacing, choose Format->Spacing. Any changes that you make will be reflected in the sample at the right of the dialog box.

Define Spacing

Line spacing	150%
Matrix row spacing	150%
Matrix column spacing	100%
Superscript height	45%
Subscript depth	25%
Limit height	25%

$x = a$

$y = c$

OK
Cancel
Apply
Defaults
Help...

Figure B.17 Setting spacing for equation elements

C

ClarisWorks Assistants

ClarisWorks Assistants are miniapplications that guide you through the process of formatting documents for commonly used purposes. The assistants, which are stored in the folder named ClarisWorks Assistants, create documents in eight categories:

- Business Administration: Assistants that can be useful in a small business, such as business cards.
- Certificates: Assistants that help you prepare award certificates.

- General: General-purpose assistants to create documents such as a calendar and to print an envelope.
- Home Budget: An assistant for creating a spreadsheet to manage home finances.
- Names and Addresses: An assistant for managing a mailing list.
- Newsletters: An assistant for creating a newsletter layout.
- Registration: An assistant to help you register your copy of ClarisWorks.
- Slide backgrounds: An assistant that provides a background for documents that will be part of a slide presentation.

This appendix looks at how you can expect assistants to behave. As you will see, assistants are for the most part self-documenting.

Launching an Assistant

To begin using a ClarisWorks Assistant to create and format a document:

1. Launch ClarisWorks.
2. If the New Document dialog box doesn't appear automatically, choose File->New or use any of that menu option's shortcuts.

3. Click the Use Assistant of Stationery radio button in the lower left corner of the dialog box. The file name listing is replaced with a listing of the contents of the ClarisWorks Assistants folder, as in Figure C.1.

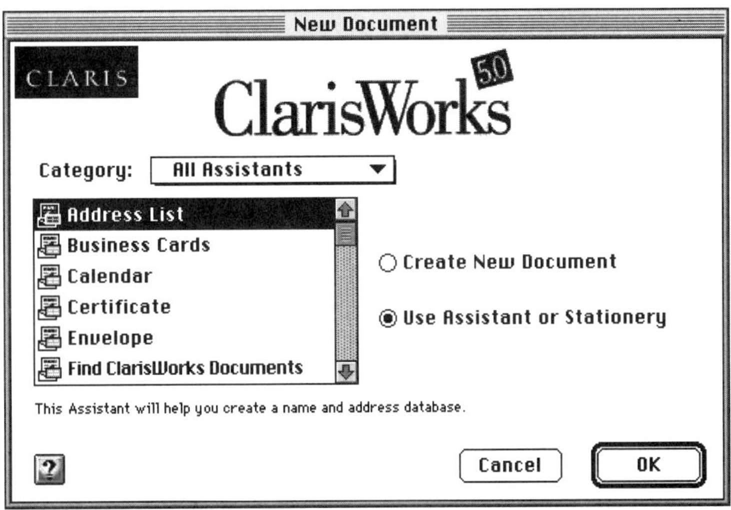

Figure C.1 Getting a listing of available assistants

4. Choose the type of assistant you want to see from the Category popup menu. If you want to see all assistants, leave the menu choice as All Assistants.

5. Double-click on the name of the assistant you want to use. (Alternatively, you can highlight the assistant's name in the scrolling list and click the OK button or press Enter.) ClarisWorks opens the assistant and begins the process of stepping you through the creation of the formatted document.

An Assistant Example: Creating a Calendar

Each assistant collects information from you that it needs to configure the type of document you have requested. Although the specific dialog with the assistant differs from one assistant to another, the general way in which they work is very similar. As an example of one typical assistant that results in a spreadsheet document, let's work through creating a calendar.

1. ClarisWorks displays an opening dialog box, letting you know which assistant you've selected (Figure C.2).

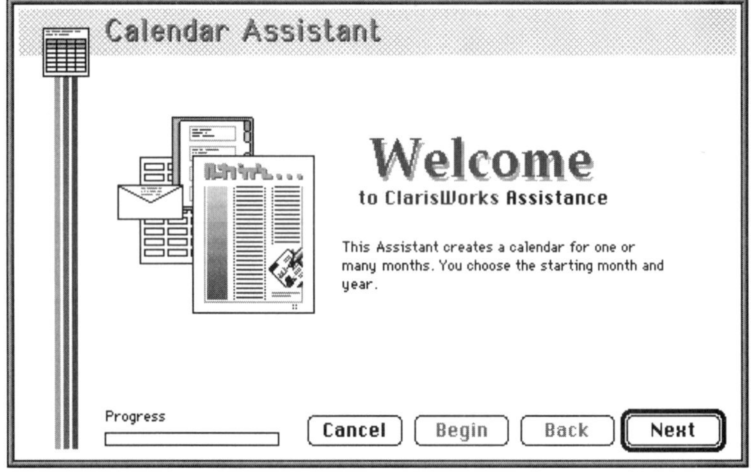

Figure C.2 The opening assistant dialog box

2. Click the Next button or press Enter to proceed. ClarisWorks displays a dialog box to collect information for the calendar (Figure C.3).

3. Choose the month, year, number of months, font, and display style for weekends.

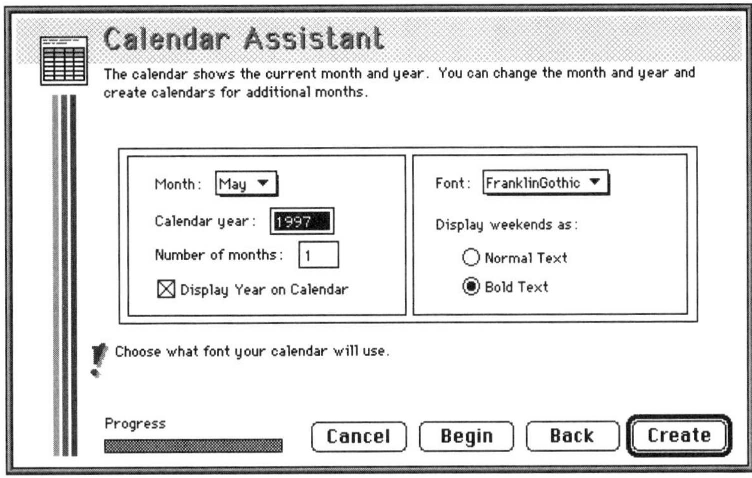

Figure C.3 Entering calendar options

4. Click the Create button or press Enter to create the document. As you can see in Figure C.4, the result is a formatted, untitled spreadsheet document that you can now modify any way you like.

A Second Example: Preparing a Certificate

If you want to give someone a certificate of achievement, ClarisWorks will format a drawing document for you. Because there are so many options for the certificate, the assistant uses more than one dialog box to collect all the necessary information.

1. The certificate assistant begins like the calendar assistant, with an opening dialog box (Figure C.5).

2. Click the Next button or press Enter to move to the next dialog box.

untitled (SS)

B2 Sunday

May 1997

Sunday	Monday	Tuesday	Wednesday	Thursday	Friday	Saturday
				1	2	3
4	5	6	7	8	9	10
11	12	13	14	15	16	17
18	19	20	21	22	23	24
25	26	27	28	29	30	31

100

Figure C.4 The formatted calendar in a spreadsheet document

Figure C.5 Beginning of the certificate assistant

3. Choose the type of certificate you want to produce by clicking one of the radio buttons at the right side of the dialog box (Figure C.6). ClarisWorks displays a miniature of each certificate's layout as you choose radio buttons.

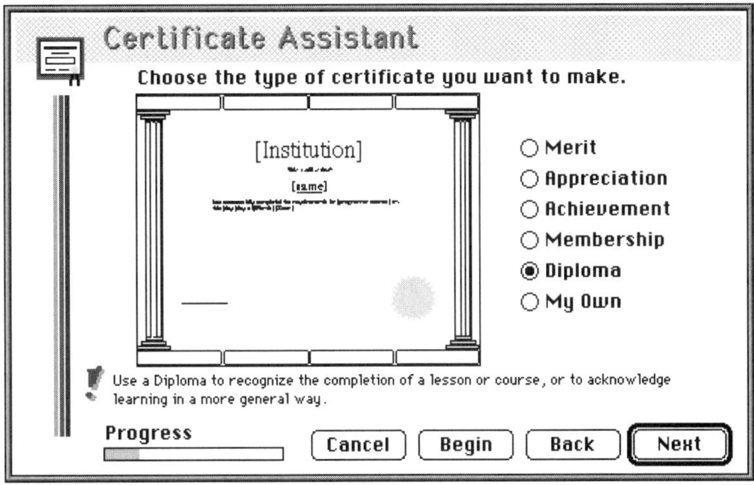

Figure C.6 Choosing a certificate type

4. Click the Next button to move to the next dialog box.

Until the point where you actually create a document, you can move back to dialog boxes you've already seen by clicking the Back button. You therefore are not locked into any choices you make until you click the Create button.

To start over from any point before creating a document, click the Begin button. This erases any changes you have made in any of the assistant's dialog boxes and returns you to the opening dialog box.

5. Enter a title and recipient for the certificate (Figure C.7).

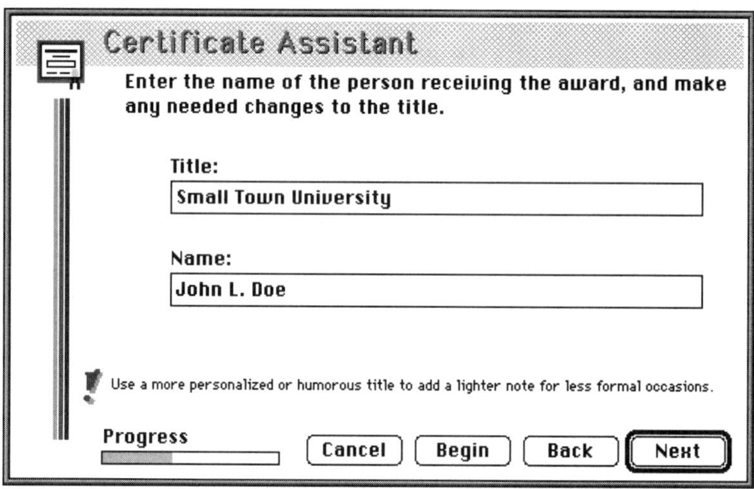

Figure C.7 Entering the title and recipient of a certificate

6. Click the Next button or press Enter to move to the next dialog box.

7. Make changes to the text that will appear in the certificate. In this example, that includes the degree earned and the date on which it is being awarded (Figure C.8).

8. Click the Next button or press Enter to move to the next dialog box.

9. Choose the number of signers from the popup menu at the top left of the dialog box and fill in signer information (Figure C.9).

10. Click the Next button or press Enter to move to the next dialog box

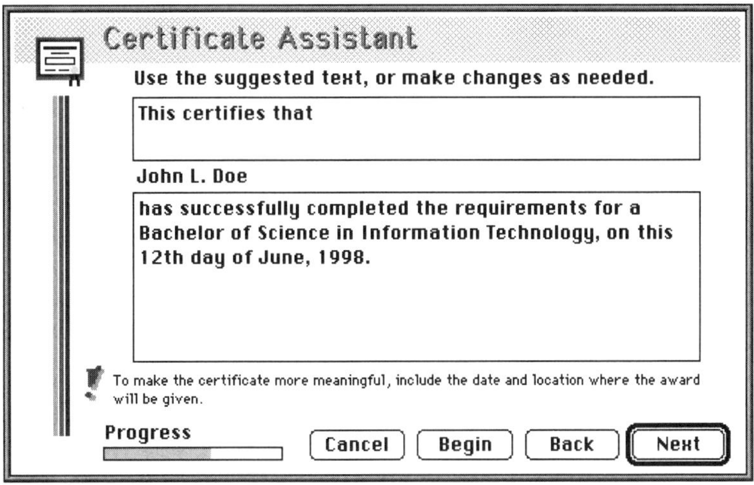

Figure C.8 Modifying certificate text

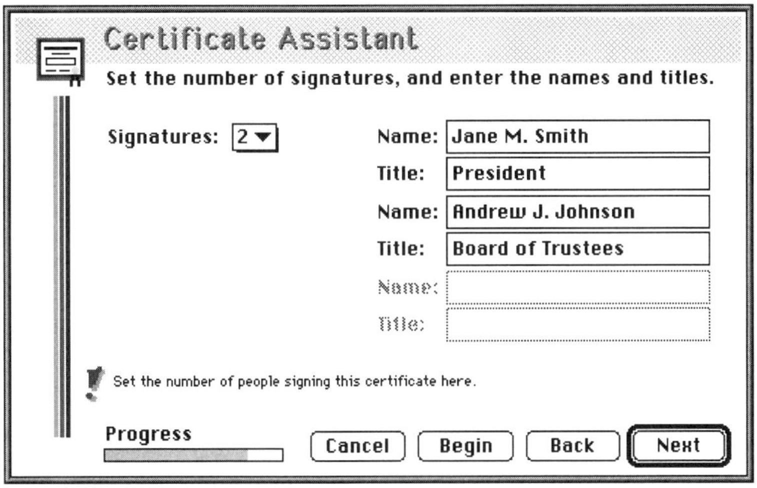

Certificate Assistant

Set the number of signatures, and enter the names and titles.

Signatures: 2

Name: Jane M. Smith

Title: President

Name: Andrew J. Johnson

Title: Board of Trustees

Name:

Title:

Set the number of people signing this certificate here.

Progress

Cancel Begin Back Next

Figure C.9 Entering signer information

11. Choose the type of border the certificate should have, whether it should be printed horizontally or vertically, and how the seal should be handled (Figure C.10).

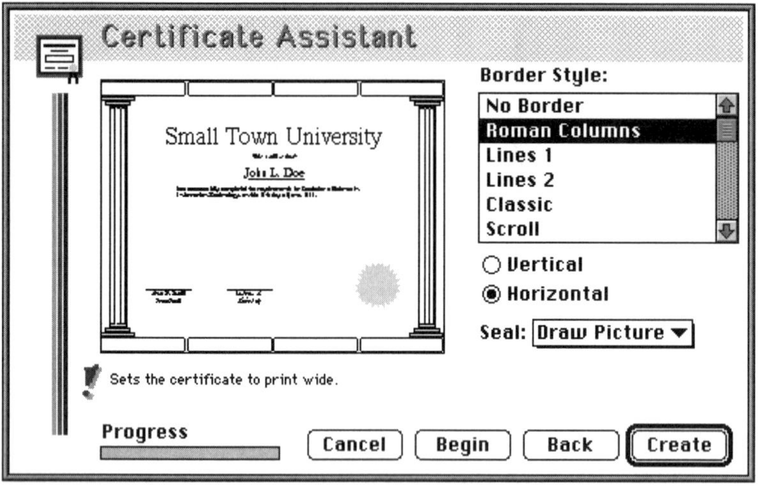

Figure C.10 Adding finishing touches to the certificate

12. Click the Create button or press Enter to create the document. As you can see in Figure C.11, the result is a formatted, untitled drawing document.

There is too great a variety of ClarisWorks Assistants to go through them all here. When you have a bit of time to play, try each assistant to see what it produces. The resulting documents not only are easy to create, but also can be used to generate ideas for documents that you create from scratch.

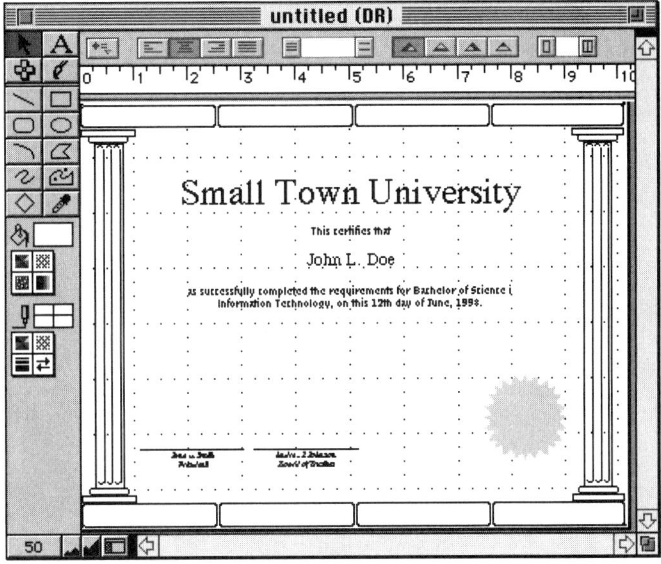

Figure C.11 The completed certificate

D

ClarisWorks Functions

ClarisWorks provides over 100 functions that can be used in formulas throughout spreadsheet and database documents. (A few functions are not available in the database module, however.) This appendix documents each of those functions. They are arranged alphabetically by function name.

The syntax for each function includes the following symbols:

- | between two elements indicates that you can choose one or the other.
- … indicates that an element can be repeated as many times as necessary.

- [ ] surrounding an element indicates that the element is optional.

Through this appendix, the arguments in the examples are expressed as constants so you can see the actual values used. However, when functions are used in a spreadsheet document, the arguments can also be expressed as cell addresses, or expressions involving constants and cell addresses. In a database document, arguments can be constants, field names, or expressions involving constants and field names.

ABS

Action Computes the absolute value of a numeric quantity.

Syntax ABS (*number* | *numeric expression*)

Argument A number or an expression that generates a number.

Examples ABS (-12) = 12; ABS (25/-5) = 5.

Availability Spreadsheet and database modules

ACOS

Action Computes the arc cosine of a cosine. The result is expressed as an angle, in radians from 0 to π.

Syntax ACOS (*number* | *numeric expression*)

Argument A number or expression that generates a number in the range -1.0 to 1.0. To be meaningful, the number or numeric expression should be a cosine.

Examples ACOS (-.9) = 2.69057; ACOS (12/15) = .06435

Availability Spreadsheet and database modules

ALERT

Action Displays a dialog box containing a text message, like that in Figure D.1 .

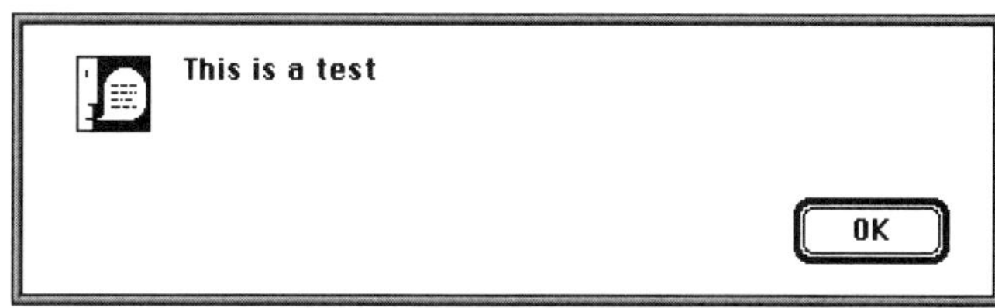

Figure D.1 A dialog box created by the ALERT function

Syntax ALERT (*text value* | *number value*)

Argument Any text or number expression or constant.

Example ALERT ("This is a test") produces the dialog box in Figure D.1.

Availability Spreadsheet module

AND

Action Performs a logical AND on its arguments, returning TRUE if all the arguments are TRUE, FALSE if any one of the arguments is FALSE.

Syntax AND (*expression1, expression2, ...*)

Arguments Each argument must be a logical expression that produces a TRUE or FALSE result or a number or numeric expression. When an argument is a number or numeric expression, a value of 0 is FALSE; any other value is TRUE.

Examples AND (5 > 9, 3 < 5) = FALSE; AND (10/2) = TRUE

Availability Spreadsheet and database modules

ASIN

Action Computes the arc sine of a sine. The result is an angle, expressed in radians in the range -π/2 to π/2.

Syntax ASIN (*number* | *numeric expression*)

Argument A number or expression that generates a number in the range -1.0 to 1.0. To be meaningful, the number or numeric expression should be a sine.

Examples ASIN (-.9) = -1.11977; ASIN (12/15) = 0.92730

Availability Spreadsheet and database modules

ATAN

Action Computes the arc tangent of a tangent. The result is an angle, expressed in radians in the range $-\pi/2$ to $\pi/2$.

Syntax ATAN (*number* | *numeric expression*)

Argument A number or expression that generates a number. To be meaningful, the number or numeric expression should be a tangent.

Examples ATAN (-.9) = -1.46014; ATAN (12/15) = 0.67474

Availability Spreadsheet and database modules

ATAN2

Action Computes an arc tangent directly from its arguments rather than taking the inverse of a tangent. Returns the angle between an X-axis and a line beginning at coordinates 0,0 and ending at coordinates specified as arguments to the function.

Syntax ATAN2 (*x-coordinate, y-coordinate*)

Arguments X-coordinate: the x-coordinate of a point on the line; Y-coordinate: the y-coordinate of a point on the line.

Example ATAN (4,5) = 0.89606

Availability Spreadsheet and database modules

AVERAGE

Action Computes the average of a group of numeric values.

Syntax AVERAGE (*number1, number2, ...*)

Arguments Numeric constants, cell or field references, or (in a spreadsheet document) cell range.

Example AVERAGE (80, 95, 100, 87, 93) = 91

Availability Spreadsheet and database modules

BASETONUM

Action Converts a value in a specified base to its base 10 equivalent.

Syntax BASETONUM (*text of numeric value, base*)

Arguments The first argument is the text representation of the number to be converted. This argument is text so that you can include bases such as hexadecimal that use letters as digits (maximum length = 255 characters). Note that when you are including letters, the letters must be in uppercase; the entire value must be surrounded by double quotes. The second argument is the base in the range 1 to 36.

Examples BASETONUM ("1AB2",16) = 6834
BASETONUM (100011,2) = 35

Availability Spreadsheet and database modules

BEEP

Action Beeps the computer's speaker.

Syntax BEEP( )

Arguments None

Example BEEP( )

Availability Spreadsheet and database modules

CHAR

Action Returns the character that corresponds to an ASCII code.

Syntax CHAR (*number* | *numeric expression*)

Argument A number or numeric expression that represents an ASCII code.

Example CHAR 101 = i

Availability Spreadsheet and database modules

CHOOSE

Action Returns a value from a list of values based on the position of the value in the list.

Syntax CHOOSE (*index, value1, value2, ...*)

Arguments The first argument is the position in the list whose value you want. The remaining arguments are the list of values (maximum length of entire list = 250 characters) from which selection will be made.

Example CHOOSE
(4, "Andrew","Barbara","Chuck","Denise") = Denise

Availability Spreadsheet and database modules

CODE

Action Returns the ASCII code of the first character in a string of text.

Syntax CODE (*text* | *text expression*)

Argument A single character, a string of characters, or an expression that produces a text result.

Example CODE ("This is a test") = 84; CODE ("T") = 84

Availability Spreadsheet and database modules

COLUMN

Action Returns the column of the cell in which the formula is defined or the column of a specified cell.

Syntax COLUMN( )

COLUMN (*cell*)

Argument A cell reference

Examples If the formula is in cell C6, COLUMN( ) = 3, because C is the third column. COLUMN (D1) = 4, because D is the fourth column.

Availability Spreadsheet module

CONCAT

Action Concatenates two or more strings of text.

Syntax CONCAT (*text1, text2, ...*)

Arguments Two or more strings of text, expressed as either literal strings, cell references, or field names.

Example CONCAT ("This is"," a ","test.") = This is a test

Availability Spreadsheet and database modules

COS

Action Computes the cosine of a value.

Syntax COS (*number* | *numeric expression*)

Argument An angle, expressed in radians.

Example COS (2) = -0.41615

Availability Spreadsheet and database modules

COUNT

Action Counts the number of values in a list, ignoring blank values.

Syntax COUNT (*value1, value2, …*)

Arguments A list of any types of values. The values can be constants, cell references, cell ranges, or field names.

Example COUNT ("Test",17,12/16/98,"Jack") = 4

Availability Spreadsheet and database modules

COUNT2

Action Counts the number of times a requested value appears in a list of values.

Syntax COUNT2 (*searchvalue, value1, value2 …*)

Arguments The value whose occurrences you want to count, followed by the list of values to search for the first value.

Example COUNT2 ("tina","tom","dick","tina","mary","tina") = 2

Availability Spreadsheet and database modules

DATE

Action Given individual values for day, month, and year, returns ClarisWorks's internal format for a date (a serial number).

Syntax DATE (*year, month, day*)

Arguments A year in the range 1 to 29941, a month number (1 through 12), a day number (1 through 31). Note that two-digit years are interpreted as being in the first century!

Example DATE (1998, 12, 18) = 34685

Availability Spreadsheet and database module

DATETOTEXT

Action Converts ClarisWorks's internal date format (a serial number) into a formatted date.

Syntax DATETOTEXT (*serial number, [format number]*)

Arguments The first argument is the serial number representation of a date. The second argument is an optional format number, taken from Table D.1.

Table D.1 Date formats

Format Number	Format
0	(Default) MM/DD/YY
1	MON DD, YYYY
2	MONTH DD, YYYY
3	SHORT_DAY, MON DD, YYYY
4	LONG_DAY, MONTH DD, YYYY

Example DATETOTEXT (34685, 4) = Friday, December 18, 1998

Availability Spreadsheet and database modules

DAY

Action Returns the day of the month from ClarisWorks's internal representation of a date (a serial number).

Syntax DAY (*serial number*)

Argument The serial number representation of a date.

Example DAY (34685) = 18

Availability Spreadsheet and database modules

DAYNAME

Action Converts a number representing a day of the week into text.

Syntax DAYNAME (*number* | *numeric expression*)

Argument A number from 1 through 7.

Example DAYNAME (2) = Monday

Availability Spreadsheet and database modules

DAYOFYEAR

Action Converts ClarisWorks's internal representation of a date into the day of the year.

Syntax DAYOFYEAR (*serial number*)

Argument The serial number representation of a date.

Example DAYOFYEAR(34685) = 352

Availability Spreadsheet and database modules

DEGREES

Action Converts radians to degrees.

Syntax DEGREES (*radians value)*

Argument A numeric value or numeric expression in radians.

Example DEGREES (2.094395103) = 120

Availability Spreadsheet and database modules

ERROR

Action Returns ERROR!

Syntax ERROR ( )

Argument None

Example ERROR ( ) = ERROR!

Availability Spreadsheet and database modules

EXACT

Action Returns TRUE if the arguments are exactly alike, FALSE if they are not. The comparison is case sensitive.

Syntax EXACT (*text1, text2*)

Arguments Text constants, cells containing text, or fields containing text.

Example EXACT ("This is a test","THIS IS A TEST") = FALSE

Availability Spreadsheet and database modules

EXP

Action Computes $e^{argument}$.

Syntax EXP (*number* | *numeric expression*)

Argument The power to which e is to be raised.

Example EXP (1.5) = 4.48168907

Availability Spreadsheet and database modules

FACT

Action Computes the factorial of a value.

Syntax FACT (*number* | *numeric expression*)

Argument The number for which you want to find the factorial.

Example FACT (10) = 3628800

Availability Spreadsheet and database modules

FIND

Action Locates the starting position of one string of text within the other.

Syntax FIND (*text to locate, text to search* [*,starting position*])

Arguments The first argument is the text whose position you want to find. The second is the text to be searched. The third argument, which is optional, is the position in the text where the search should start. If the third argument isn't used, searching will begin with the first character in the search string. Note that the search is case sensitive.

Example FIND ("heaven","Oh, heavens!") = 4

Availability Spreadsheet and database modules

FRAC

Action Returns the absolute value of the fractional part of a number.

Syntax FRAC (*number* | *numeric expression*)

Argument Any number.

Example FRAC (123.4567) = 0.4567

Availability Spreadsheet and database modules

FV

Action Computes the future value of an investment.

Syntax FV (*interest rate, number of periods, -payment* [*, present value, type of payment*])

Arguments

- Interest rate: Interest rate per period
- Number of periods: Number of periods during which money is added to the investment
- Payment: Amount added to the investment each period
- Present value: Current value of the investment
- Type of payment: 0 (default) if payments are made at the end of the period, 1 if payments are made at the beginning of the period.

Example FV(5%/12,120,-50,1000) = 6117.104475

An investment of $1000 to which $50 payments are added every month for 10 years. The interest rate is 5% per year and is therefore divided by 12 to get the interest rate per month.

Availability Spreadsheet and database modules

HLOOKUP

Action Searches the first row in a range of spreadsheet cells and returns some value from the column in which the search is successful.

Syntax HLOOKUP (*value to find, table range, offset* [,*method*])

Arguments

- Value to find: A text or numeric expression that will be compared to values in the search range.
- Table range: A range containing a table of values.
- Offset: Indicates the row in the table from which a value is to be taken. The row being searched is row 0; therefore, the row below it has an offset of 1, and so on.
- Method: The way in which the search should be performed.
  - 1 (default; assumes values increase from left to right): Finds the largest value that is less than or equal to the value being found.
  - -1 (assumes values decrease from left to right): Finds the smallest value that is greater than or equal to the value being found.
  - 0: Finds an exact match.

Examples Assume the sample spreadsheet in Figure D.2. Then,

=HLOOKUP(G1,A1..E4,1) = 50
=HLOOKUP(G2,A2..E4,2,-1) = Jane

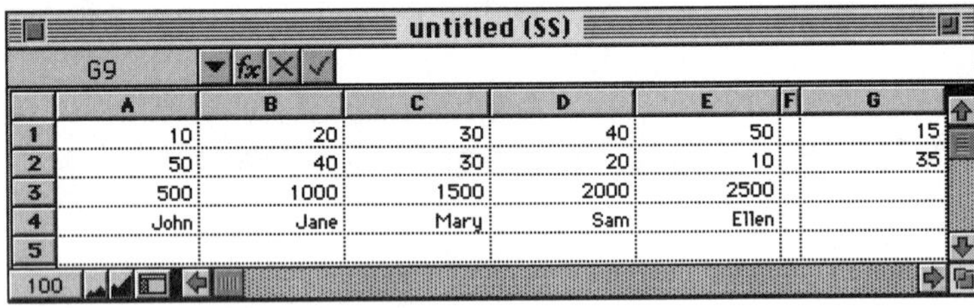

untitled (SS)

G9

	A	B	C	D	E	F	G
1	10	20	30	40	50		15
2	50	40	30	20	10		35
3	500	1000	1500	2000	2500		
4	John	Jane	Mary	Sam	Ellen		
5							

100

Figure D.2 Spreadsheet for HLOOKUP examples

Availability Spreadsheet module

HOUR

Action Extracts the hour portion from ClarisWorks's internal time format (the fractional portion of a serial number).

Syntax HOUR (*serial number*)

Argument The serial number representation of a time.

Example HOUR (.75) = 18 (18:00 or 6 p.m.)

Availability Spreadsheet and database modules

IF

Action Returns one of two values depending on whether a logical expression is TRUE or FALSE.

Syntax IF (*logical expression, true value, false value*)

Arguments

The first argument is a logical expression. The second is the value to return or the action to perform if the logical expression is TRUE; the third is the value to return or the action to perform if the logical expression is FALSE.

Examples

IF (5 > 10, "This is true", BEEP( )) = a beep
IF (5 < 10, "This is true", BEEP( )) = This is true

Availability

Spreadsheet and database modules

INDEX

Action

Returns the value in a spreadsheet cell whose location is specified by row and column offsets from a starting cell.

Syntax

INDEX (*range, row offset, column offset*)

Arguments

The first argument is the range from which you want to take a value. The second argument is the row offset from the top left cell in the range; the top left cell has an offset of 1. The third argument is the column offset from the top left cell in the range; the top left cell has an offset of 1.

Example

Assume the sample spreadsheet in Figure D.3. Then
=INDEX(A1..D3,2,2) = 550

untitled (SS)

D5

	A	B	C	D
1	10	15	20	25
2	500	550	600	650
3	1000	1500	2000	2500
4				

100

Figure D.3 Sample spreadsheet for INDEX examples

Availability Spreadsheet module

INT

Action Converts a real number to a fraction. Positive numbers are truncated; negative numbers are rounded down.

Syntax INT (*number* | *numeric expression*)

Argument Any real number.

Examples INT (9.876) = 9
INT (-9.876) = -9

Availability Spreadsheet and database modules

IRR

Action Calculates an internal rate of return (IRR), based on an initial investment and a group of cash flows. This function allows you to make a guess about the IRR (10% if you make no guess).

Syntax IRR (*range*, [*IRR guess*])

Arguments The first argument is a range of cells containing the initial investment (a negative value) followed by cash flow values in the order in which they are expended or received.

Example Assume the sample spreadsheet in Figure D.4. Then,
IRR (A1..A6) = 22.82%
indicating that for an initial investment of $100,000 and cash

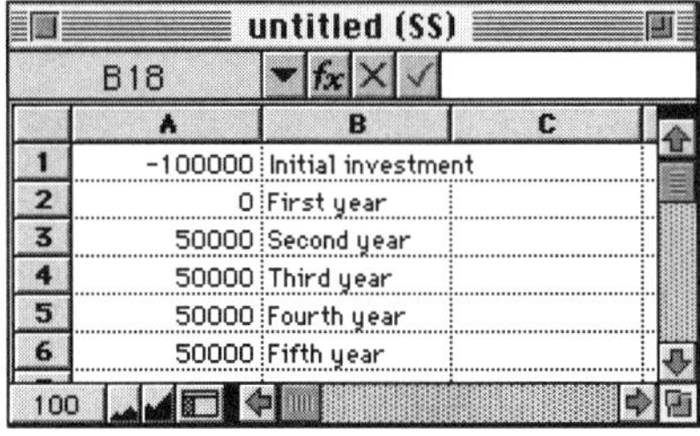

Figure D.4 Spreadsheet for IRR example

flows of $50,000 in the second through fifth years, the rate of return will be 22.82%.

Availability Spreadsheet module

ISBLANK

Action Determines whether a cell or field contains text or a number (TRUE) or is empty (FALSE).

Syntax ISBLANK (*value*)

Argument A text or numeric value or expression, most commonly a cell address or field name.

Example ISBLANK ("This is a test") = FALSE

Availability Spreadsheet and database modules

ISERROR

Action

Determines whether an expression generates an error when it is evaluated. The functions returns TRUE if an error occurred, FALSE if it did not.

Syntax

ISERROR (*value*, [,*type_of_error*])

Arguments

The first argument is the value you want to check, usually specified as a cell reference, field name, or an expression using one of the two. The second argument restricts the function to checking for one specific type of error. Acceptable values can be found in Table D.2.

Table D.2 Error types

Error Type	Meaning
#N/A!	Not available
#DIV/0!	Divide by zero
#VALUE!	Invalid value
#NUM!	Invalid number
#REF!	Reference to incorrect cell
#ARG!	Wrong number of arguments or incorrect argument type
#USER!	User-defined error
#DATE!	Invalid date
#TIME	Invalid time
#ERROR!	Not an error

Example

Assume that cell B5 contains 10/2. Then,

ISERROR (B5) = FALSE

Availability

Spreadsheet and database modules

ISLOGICAL

Action Determines whether an expression is a logical expression (i.e., evaluates to either TRUE or FALSE). The function returns TRUE if the expression is a logical expression, FALSE if it is not.

Syntax ISLOGICAL (*value*)

Argument An expression to be tested, usually specified as a cell reference, field name, or an expression including one of the two.

Examples ISLOGICAL (5 > 10) = TRUE
ISLOGICAL (5/12) = FALSE

Availability Spreadsheet and database modules

ISNA

Action Tests for the not available (#NA!) error. The function returns TRUE if the error is found and FALSE if it is not. You can use this function to test for valid results of lookup functions such as HLOOKUP, LOOKUP, MATCH, or VLOOKUP.

Syntax ISNA (*value*)

Argument A value to be tested, usually specified as a cell reference or an expression including a cell reference.

Example ISNA (55) = FALSE

Availability Spreadsheet module

ISNUMBER

Action Determines whether a value is a number. The function returns TRUE if the argument is a valid number, FALSE if it is not.

Syntax ISNUMBER (*value*)

Argument A value, cell reference, database field, or expression containing any of the three.

Examples ISNUMBER (6) = TRUE
ISNUMBER ("6") = FALSE

Availability Database and spreadsheet modules

ISTEXT

Action Determines whether a value is text. The function returns TRUE if the argument is text, FALSE if it is not.

Syntax ISTEXT (*value*)

Argument A value, cell reference, database field, or expression containing any of the three.

Examples ISTEXT (6) = FALSE
ISTEXT ("6") = TRUE

LEFT

Action Extracts a specified number of characters from a string of text, beginning at the leftmost character in the string.

Syntax LEFT (*text, number_of_characters*)

Arguments The first argument is the text from which characters are to be extracted. It can be specified as a cell reference, database field, or an expression involving either of the two. The second argument is the number of characters to extract.

Example LEFT ("This is a test",6) = This i

Availability Spreadsheet and database modules

LEN

Action Returns the number of characters in a string of text.

Syntax LEN (*text*)

Argument A string of text.

Example LEN ("This is a test") = 14

LN

Action Computes the natural logarithm of a number.

Syntax LN (*number* | *numeric expression*)

Argument A positive number or a numeric expression that produces a positive number.

Example LN(2) = 0.69315

Availability Spreadsheet and database modules

LOG

Action Computes the logarithm of a number. If no base is specified, the function returns the base 10 logarithm.

Syntax LOG (*number* | *numeric expression* [, *base*])

Arguments The first argument a positive number or a numeric expression that produces a positive number. The second argument is the base of the logarithm.

Examples LOG (100) = 2
LOG (100,2) = 6.64385618

Availability Spreadsheet and database modules

LOG10

Action Computes the logarithm of a number to base 10. (Note that this is the inverse of *e*.)

Syntax LOG10 (*number* | *numeric expression*)

Argument A positive number or an expression that produces a positive number.

Example LOG10 (100) = 2

Availability Spreadsheet and database modules

LOOKUP

Action Searches for a value in a range of spreadsheet cells and returns the corresponding value in a second range of cells. If no match is found, the result is an error.

Syntax LOOKUP (*value to find, comparison range, result range* [, *method*])

Arguments

- Value to find: A value for which you are searching.
- Comparison range: A range of cells containing values to be search.
- Result range: A range of cells from which the result should be taken.
- Method: The way in which the search should be performed.
  - 1 (default; assumes values increase from left to right): Finds the largest value that is less than or equal to the value being found.
  - -1 (assumes values decrease from left to right): Finds the smallest value that is greater than or equal to the value being found.
  - 0: Finds an exact match.

Example Assume the spreadsheet in Figure D.5. Then,

LOOKUP(75,A1..A11,B1..B11) = C

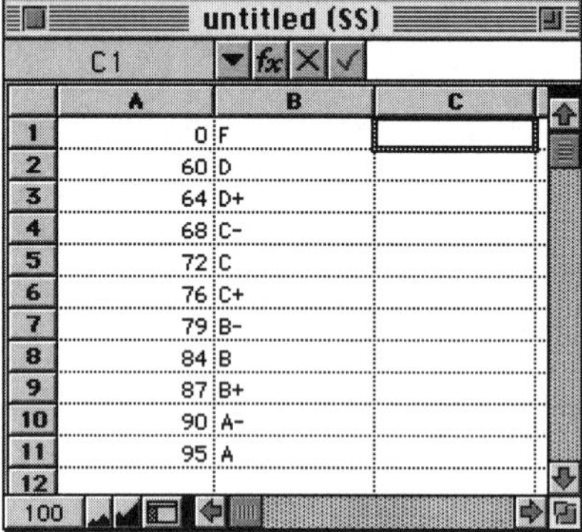

Figure D.5 LOOKUP spreadsheet example

Availability Spreadsheet module

LOWER

Action Converts all characters in a string of text to lowercase.

Syntax LOWER (*text*)

Argument A string of text or an expression that generates a string.

Example LOWER ("This is a test") = this is a test

Availability Spreadsheet and database modules

MACRO

Action Plays a ClarisWorks macro.

Syntax MACRO (*name of macro*)

Argument The name of a ClarisWorks macro. Enclose the name in double quotes. Match capitalization with the name of the macro exactly.

Example MACRO ("Print labels") runs a macro that prints mailing labels.

Availability Spreadsheet and database modules

MATCH

Action Finds a value in a range of spreadsheet cells and returns the position of that value's first appearance in the range.

Syntax MATCH (*value to find, comparison range* [, *type*])

Arguments

- Value to find: The value for which you want to search.
- Comparison range: The range in which the search should take place. If the range contains more than one row, ClarisWorks searches across the top row from left to right and then drops down one row.
- Method: The way in which the search should be performed.
  - 1 (default; assumes values increase from left to right): Finds the largest value that is less than or equal to the value being found.
  - -1 (assumes values decrease from left to right): Finds the smallest value that is greater than or equal to the value being found.
  - 0: Finds an exact match.

Example Assume the spreadsheet in Figure D.6

MATCH(15,A1..A6, 0) = 2

	A	B	C
1	12		
2	15		
3	20		
4	12		
5	15		
6	20		
7			

Figure D.6 Sample spreadsheet for MATCH example

Availability Spreadsheet module

MAX

Action Returns the maximum value in a group of values.

Syntax MAX (*number1, number2, ...*)

Arguments Any numbers, expressed as cell references, a range of cells, or database fields.

Example MAX (75, 90, 55, 100, 4) = 100

Availability Spreadsheet and database modules

MERGEFIELD

Action Formats a field placeholder for mail merge.

Syntax MERGEFIELD (*text*)

Argument The name of a database field or spreadsheet cell containing the name of a database field.

Example MERGEFIELD ("This is a test") = <<This is a test>>

Availability Spreadsheet and database modules

MID

Action Extract characters from the middle of a string of text.

Syntax MID (*text, starting position, number of characters*)

Arguments

- Text: A string of text or an expression that produces a string of text.
- Starting position: The position in the string where character extraction should begin. Characters are counted from the left edge of the string, beginning with 1.
- Number of characters: The number of characters to extract.

Example MID ("This is a test", 6, 2) = is

Availability Spreadsheet and database modules

MIN

Action Returns the smallest value in a group of values.

Syntax MIN (*number1, number2, ...*)

Arguments Any numbers, expressed as cell references, a range of cells, or database fields.

Example MIN(75, 90, 55, 100, 4) = 4

Availability Spreadsheet and database modules

MINUTE

Action Extracts the minutes portion of a time stored in ClarisWorks's internal time format (a serial number).

Syntax MINUTE (*serial number*)

Argument A time stored in ClarisWorks's internal time format

Example MINUTE (.25201) = 2. Given that HOUR (.25201) = 6, this time is 6:02 a.m.

Availability Spreadsheet and database modules

MIRR

Action Computes the modified internal rate of return (MIRR), based on a group of cash flows and safe and risk investment rates.

Syntax MIRR (*safe investment rate, risk investment rate, cash flow1, cash flow2, ...*)

Arguments

- Safe investment rate: Rate produced by investment that covers negative cash flows.
- Risk investment rate: Rate for reinvesting positive cash flows.
- Cash flow: A group of cash flow values, positive or negative. These arguments can be expressed as a range of spreadsheet cells or as a set of individual values separated by commas.

Example

Assume the spreadsheet in Figure D.7. Then,

MIRR(0.05,0.075,A1..A5) = 41.58%

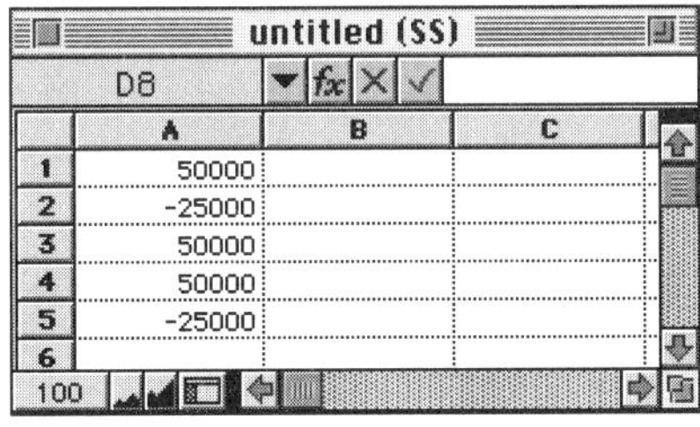

Figure D.7 MIRR spreadsheet example

Availability

Spreadsheet and database modules

MOD

Action

Performs a modulo division, returning the remainder of a division.

Syntax

MOD (*dividend, divisor*)

Arguments

The first argument is the number being divided. The second argument is the divisor. Both values can be constants, cell or field references, or expressions that generate numbers.

Example MOD (11,5) = 1

Availability Spreadsheet and database modules

MONTH

Action Extracts the month portion from a ClarisWorks internal date format (serial number). The result is the month number.

Syntax MONTH (*serial number*)

Argument A date in ClarisWorks's internal date format.

Example MONTH (2532) = 12. Given that DAY (2532) = 7 and YEAR (2532) = 1910, the date is December 7, 1910.

Availability Spreadsheet and database modules

MONTHNAME

Action Translates a month number into the name of the month.

Syntax MONTHNAME (*month number*)

Argument A number or expression that generates a number in the range 1 through 12.

Example MONTHNAME (12) = December

Availability Spreadsheet and database modules

NA

Action Returns the value #N/A!

Syntax NA ( )

Argument None

Examples IF (ISNUMBER (6), 6, NA( )) = 6
IF (ISNUMBER ("a"),"a",NA( )) = #N/A!

Availability Spreadsheet module

NOT

Action Inverts the value of a logical expression. Returns TRUE if the logical expression is FALSE, FALSE if the logical expression is TRUE.

Syntax NOT (*logical expression*)

Argument Any logical expression.

Examples NOT (1 > 2) = TRUE
NOT (2 > 1) = FALSE

Availability Spreadsheet and database modules

NOW

Action Returns the current system date and time as a ClarisWorks serial number

Syntax NOW ( )

Argument None

Example On 12-12-2002, NOW( ) = 34093.470139 (Note: you must format this serial number as a date and/or time to translate it from ClarisWorks's internal format to a readable value.)

Availability Spreadsheet and database modules

NPER

Action Computes the length of an investment, in periods, based on a constant cash flow.

Syntax NPER (*interest rate, payment, present value* [, *type*])

Arguments

- Interest rate: The interest rate per period. Divide an annual interest rate by 12 if payments are made monthly.
- Payment: Payment made each period.
- Present value: The current value of the investment.
- Type: An indication of when payments are made. If type is 0 (the default), payments are assumed to be made at the end of the period. If type is 1, payments are assumed to be made at the beginning of the period.

Example NPER(18%/12,-300,7500) = 31.57, indicating that at an annual interest rate of 18% and payments of $300 per month, a $7500 loan will take 32 months to pay off.

Availability Spreadsheet and database modules

NPV

Action Computes the net present value of an investment, assuming variable payments and a fixed interest rate.

Syntax NPV (*interest rate, payment1, payment2, ...*)

Arguments The first argument is the interest rate. The remaining arguments are payments or income. Usually the first payment value is the initial investment, followed by income from the investment.

Example NPV(6%,-500,0,1000,1000,1500,1500) = 3338.34

Availability Spreadsheet and database modules

NUMTOBASE

Action Converts a base 10 number into its representation in another base. The result is a string to accommodate bases such as 16, which use letters as digits.

Syntax NUMTOBASE (*number* | *numeric expression, base*
[*, minimum digits*])

Arguments

- Number: A number or numeric expression.

- Base: The base to which the number is to be converted (range = 1 to 36)
- Minimum digits: The minimum number of digits to be included in the result. If the result has fewer digits, it will be padded with leading zeros.

Examples NUMTOBASE(12575,16) = 311F
NUMTOBASE(75,2,10) = 0001001011

Availability Spreadsheet and database modules

NUMTOTEXT

Action Converts a number to a string of text so the number can be used in functions that require text as arguments.

Syntax NUMTOTEXT (*number* | *numeric expression*)

Argument A number or numeric expression

Example NUMTOTEXT (575) returns three characters, one for each digit in the number.

Availability Spreadsheet and database modules

OR

Action Performs a logical OR operation on two or more logical expressions. The function will be TRUE if at least one of the logical expressions is true. If all logical expressions are FALSE, the function returns FALSE.

Syntax OR (*logical expression1, logical expression2, ...*)

Arguments Any logical expressions or other expressions that can be evaluated as 0 (FALSE) or nonzero (TRUE).

Examples OR (1 > 2, 2 > 3, 3 > 4) = FALSE
OR (4 + 5, 0 * 6) = TRUE

Availability Spreadsheet and database modules

PI

Action Returns a decimal approximation of π (pi).

Syntax PI ( )

Arguments None

Example PI ( ) = 3.1415926 ... The number of digits you see depends on the current number formatting.

Availability Spreadsheet and database modules

PMT

Action Computes the payments required by an investment given a known number of periods, the current value of the investment, the future value of the investment, and when payments are made.

Syntax PMT (*interest rate, number of periods, present value* [, *future value, type*])

Arguments

- Interest rate: The interest rate per period. Divide an annual interest rate by 12 to get the monthly rate.
- Number of periods: The number of payments to be made.
- Present value: The current value of the investment.
- Future value: The value of the investment at the end of the payments. If you leave this argument off, it defaults to 0.
- Type: If type if 0 (the default) payments are assumed to be made at the end of the period. If you set type to 1, payments are assumed to be made at the beginning of the period.

Example PMT(7.5%/12,360,150000) = 1048.82, indicating that a 30-year mortgage of $150,000 at 7.5% interest will require payments of $1048.82 per month.

Availability Spreadsheet and database modules

PRODUCT

Action Multiplies a set of numbers.

Syntax PRODUCT (*number1, number2, ...*)

Arguments Any numbers or expressions that produce numbers, including spreadsheet ranges.

Example PRODUCT (5, 4, 3, 2) = 120

Availability Spreadsheet and database modules

PROPER

Action Capitalizes the first letter in each word of a string of text.

Syntax PROPER (*text)*

Argument A literal text string or an expression that produces a text string.

Example PROPER ("this is a test") = This Is A Test

Availability Spreadsheet and database modules

PV

Action Computes the present value of an investment, based on a series of payments, a specified interest rate, and a specified number of periods.

Syntax PV (*interest rate, number of periods, payment amount* [, *future value, type*])

Arguments

- Interest rate: The interest rate per period. Divide an annual interest rate by 12 to obtain a monthly rate.
- Number of periods: The number of periods during which payments will be made.
- Payment amount: The amount to be paid each period.
- Future value: The amount of the investment to be left after the final payment. If you don't include this argument, it is assumed to be 0.
- Type: If type if 0 (the default) payments are assumed to be made at the end of the period. If you set type to

1, payments are assumed to be made at the beginning of the period.

Example PV(3.25%/12,120,-50) = 5116.71, indicating that if you invest $50 a month in a 3.25% passbook savings account, after 10 years you will have $5116.71.

Availability Spreadsheet and database modules

RADIANS

Action Converts degrees to radians

Syntax RADIANS (*number of degrees*)

Argument A number or numeric expression

Example RADIANS (270) = 4.7124

Availability Spreadsheet and database modules

RAND

Action Generates a pseudo-random number. By default, the range is between 0 and 1.

Syntax RAND ([*number* | *numeric expression*])

Argument If supplied, asks RAND for a number between 0 and the argument value.

Examples RAND ( ) = 0.72
RAND (100) = 40

Availability Spreadsheet and database modules

RATE

Action Computes the interest rate needed to cause a given investment to grow to a specified future value, given a specified term.

Syntax RATE (*future value, present value, term*)

Arguments

- Future value: The final value of the investment. This value must be something other than 0.
- Present value: The initial value of the investment. This value must be something other than 0.
- Term: The number of periods in the investment.

Example RATE(40000,10000,18) = 8.01%, indicating that if you want to have $40,000 for college when your child is 18 and if you start with an initial investment of $10,000, you will need an interest rate of 8.01% to reach your goal.

Availability Spreadsheet and database modules

REPLACE

Action Substitutes one string of text for specified characters within another string of text.

Syntax REPLACE (*destination text, starting position, number of characters, replacement text*)

Arguments

- Destination text: The text in which the replacement is to take place.
- Starting position: The starting position in the destination text where replacement is to begin.
- Number of characters: The number of characters to replace with the *entire* replacement string.
- Replacement text: The text to insert into the destination string.

Example REPLACE("This is a test",11,4,"good job") = This is a good job

Availability Spreadsheet and database modules

REPT

Action Repeats a string of text.

Syntax REPT (*text, times to repeat*)

Arguments The first argument is the text to be repeated. The second is the number of repetitions.

Example REPT ("!-!-", 4) = !-!-!-!-!-!-!-!-

Availability Spreadsheet and database modules

RIGHT

Action Copies characters from the right side of a string of text.

Syntax RIGHT (*text, number of characters*)

Arguments The first argument is the text string from which characters are to be taken. The second is the number of characters to extract.

Example RIGHT ("This is a test", 6) = a test

Availability Spreadsheet and database modules

ROUND

Action Round a number to a specified number of digits to the right of the decimal point.

Syntax ROUND (*number* | *numeric expression, number of digits*)

Arguments The first argument is the number to be rounded. The second is the number of digits to the right of the decimal point.

Example ROUND(123.45667,3) = 123.457

Availability Spreadsheet and database modules

ROW

Action Provides the row number of the current cell or of a specified cell.

Syntax ROW ([*cell reference*])

Argument If no argument is provided, returns the row number of the current cell. If a cell reference is provided, returns the row number of that cell.

Example ROW (G12) = 12

Availability Spreadsheet modules

SECOND

Action Extracts the seconds portion of a ClarisWorks's time (serial number).

Syntax SECOND (*serial number*)

Argument A time stored in ClarisWorks's internal time format (a serial number).

Example SECOND(0.8225) = 24, indicating that the time includes 24 seconds.

Availability Spreadsheet and database modules

SIGN

Action Determines the sign of a number (1 for positive, 0 for equal to zero, -1 for negative).

Syntax SIGN (*number* | *numeric expression*)

Argument The value to be tested.

Examples SIGN (125) = 1
SIGN (-125) = -1

Availability Spreadsheet and database modules

SIN

Action Computes the sine of an angle, which must be expressed in radians.

Syntax SIN (*angle in radians*)

Argument A number or numeric expression in radians

Example SIN (2.5) = 0.60

Availability Spreadsheet and database modules

SQRT

Action Computes the square root of a number or numeric expression.

Syntax SQRT (*number* | *numeric expression*)

Argument A number or numeric expression

Example SQRT (125) = 11.1803

Availability Spreadsheet and database modules

STDEV

Action Computes the standard deviation from the mean of a group of numeric values.

Syntax STDEV (*number1, number2, ...*)

Arguments Numbers or numeric expressions, including a range of spreadsheet cells or a field (when used in a formula for a Summary field).

Example STDEV (80, 90, 75, 62, 95) = 12.973

Availability Spreadsheet and database modules

SUM

Action Computes the sum of a group of numbers.

Syntax SUM (*number1, number2, ...*)

Arguments Numbers or numeric expressions, including a range of spreadsheet cells or a field (when used in a formula for a Summary field).

Example SUM (80, 90, 75, 62, 95) = 402

Availability Spreadsheet and database modules

TAN

Action Computes the tangent of an angle expressed in radians.

Syntax TAN (*angle in radians*)

Argument A number or numeric expression in radians

Example TAN (4) = 1.16

Availability Spreadsheet and database modules

TEXTTODATE

Action Converts the text representation of a date into ClarisWorks's internal date format (a serial number).

Syntax TEXTTODATE (*text*)

Argument A date expressed as text surrounded by double quotes, as in "5/7/97."

Example TEXTTODATE ("5/7/97") = 34095

Availability Spreadsheet and database modules

TEXTTONUM

Action Converts a string of text to a number so it can be used in functions that require numeric arguments. Non-numeric characters are ignored.

Syntax TEXTTONUM (*test*)

Argument A text string enclosed in double quotes.

Examples TEXTTONUM ("$25.00") = 25
TEXTTONUM ("1EFF") = 1

Availability Spreadsheet and database modules

TEXTTOTIME

Action Converts the string representation of a time to ClarisWorks's internal time format (a serial number).

Syntax TEXTTOTIME (*text*)

Argument A text string surrounded by double quotes.

Examples TEXTTOTIME ("18:00") = 0.75000
TEXTTOTIME ("6:00 PM") = 0.75000

Availability Spreadsheet and database modules

TIME

Action Converts a time specified in hours, minutes, and seconds into ClarisWorks's internal time format (a serial number).

Syntax TIME (*hour, minute, second*)

Arguments Numbers or numeric expressions representing hours (range 0 to 12), minutes (range 0 to 59), and seconds (0 to 59).

Example TIME (18,0,0) = 0.75

Availability Spreadsheet and database modules

TIMETOTEXT

Action Converts ClarisWorks's internal time format (a serial number) to a readable time.

Syntax TIMETOTEXT (*serial number* [*, format*])

Arguments The first argument is the internal representation of a time. The second is an optional format, specified using one of the following options:

Format	Effect
0	(Default) HH:MM AM/PM. Uses a 12-hour clock.
1	HH:MM:SS AM/PM. Uses a 12-hour clock.
2	HH:MM. Uses a 24-hour clock.
3	HH:MM:SS. Uses a 24-hour clock.

Example TIMETOTEXT(0.75,1) = 6:00:00 PM

Availability Spreadsheet and database modules

TRIM

Action Extracts extra spaces from a string of text, preserving one space between each word.

Syntax TRIM (*text*)

Argument The string of text from which spaces are to be removed.

Example TRIM("This   is great.   I think, so.") = This is great. I think so.

Availability Spreadsheet and database modules

TRUNC

Action Truncates a number to an integer by removing any fractional portion of the number.

Syntax TRUNC (*number* | *numeric expression*)

Argument A number or numeric expression.

Example TRUNC (1.2345) = 1

Availability Spreadsheet and database modules

TYPE

Action Identifies the data type of the argument: 1 if blank, 2 if logical, 3 if numeric, 4 if text.

Syntax TYPE (*value*)

Argument A logical, numeric, or text value.

Examples TYPE (16.5) = 3
TYPE ("16.6") = 4
TYPE (1 > 2) = 2

Availability Spreadsheet and database modules

UPPER

Action Converts all characters in a string of text to uppercase.

Syntax UPPER (*text*)

Argument A string of text

Example UPPER ("This is a test") = THIS IS A TEST

Availability Spreadsheet and database modules

VAR

Action Computes the variance of a group of numbers.

Syntax VAR (*number1, number2, ...*)

Arguments Numbers or numeric expressions, which may include cell ranges or fields (when used in the formula for a Summary field).

Example VAR (80, 90, 75, 62, 95) = 168.3

Availability Spreadsheet and database modules

VLOOKUP

Action Searches the first column in a range of spreadsheet cells and returns some value from the row in which the search is successful.

Syntax VLOOKUP (*value to find, table range, offset* [*,method*])

Arguments

- Value to find: A text or numeric expression that will be compared to values in the search range.
- Table range: A range containing a table of values.
- Offset: Indicates the column in the table from which a value is to be taken. The column being searched is column 0; therefore, the column to its right has an offset of 1, and so on.
- Method: The way in which the search should be performed.
  - 1 (default; assumes values increase from left to right): Finds the largest value that is less than or equal to the value being found.
  - -1 (assumes values decrease from left to right): Finds the smallest value that is greater than or equal to the value being found.

- 0: Finds an exact match.

Examples Assume the spreadsheet in Figure D.8. Then,

VLOOKUP(E1,A1..D5,1) = 50
VLOOKUP(E1,B1..D5,1,-1) = 2550

untitled (SS)

	A	B	C	D	E
1	10	50	550	John	15
2	20	40	100	Jane	85
3	30	30	1500	Mary	
4	40	20	2550	Sam	
5	50	10	3000	Ellen	

Figure D.8 Sample spreadsheet for VLOOKUP example

Availability Spreadsheet and database modules

WEEKDAY

Action Extracts the day of a week from a date expressed in ClarisWorks's internal date format (a serial number).

Syntax WEEKDAY (*serial number*)

Argument A date expressed in ClarisWorks's internal date format.

Example WEEKDAY(45229) = 1, indicating that the day is Sunday.

Availability Spreadsheet and database modules

WEEKOFYEAR

Action Extracts the week of the year from a date expressed in ClarisWorks's internal date format (a serial number).

Syntax WEEKOFYEAR (*serial number*)

Argument A date expressed in ClarisWorks's internal date format.

Example WEEKOFYEAR(45229) = 45, indicating the 45th week of the year

Availability Spreadsheet and database modules

YEAR

Action Extracts the year from a date expressed in ClarisWorks's internal date format (a serial number).

Syntax YEAR (*serial number*)

Argument A date expressed in ClarisWorks's internal date format.

Example YEAR(45229) = 2027

Availability Spreadsheet and database modules

Glossary

Absolute address: In a spreadsheet, a cell reference stored as the cell's actual address.

Absolute rotation: The number of degrees an object is to be rotated from its original position in the document.

Active cell: In a spreadsheet, the currently selected cell, which will be affected by actions taken with the spreadsheet.

Address: In a spreadsheet, the location of a cell, made up of the cell's column letter followed by its row number.

Alignment: The justification of text within a paragraph.

Application software: Software that performs useful work for the user, such as a word processor or graphics program.

Argument: An input value to a function.

Ascender: A character that rises above the line of type, such as "h" or "b."

Attribute: A piece of data that describes an entity in a database.

Bit: In a painting document, one dot in the painting. More formally, one digit in a binary number.

Bit-mapped graphics: Illustrations made up of a pattern of colored dots that is only one layer thick.

Case sensitive: Paying attention to the difference between uppercase and lowercase letters.

Cell: In a spreadsheet, the intersection of a column and a row.

Circular reference: In a spreadsheet, a formula that in some way uses itself in its formula.

Clip art: Electronic images that are sold for use in printed form.

Clipboard: A temporary holding area for a single item—text, graphics, data, and so on—that is available to all applications running on a computer.

Control break report: A report that groups data based on the value in a field.

Cut: Remove an item from a document and place it on the Clipboard.

Database: Storage for data along with information about the relationships between the data.

Database management system: Software that manipulates the data and relationships stored in a database.

Depth (of a painting): The total number of colors available for use.

Descender: A character that descends below the line of type, such as "y" or "g."

Document: A container for work that a user has performed, represented by a single file icon on the desktop.

Drag and drop: A technique for moving or copying text in which selected text is dragged with the mouse.

Drag cursor: A mouse pointer indicating that highlighted text can be dragged.

Entity: Something about which we store data in a database.

Field: A storage location for a single piece of data in a database file.

File manager: A piece of software that manipulates the data stored in a single data file.

File manager: A program that stores lists of data that can be viewed, ordered, and searched in many ways.

Find request: A layout in Find mode that contains search criteria.

Font: A single typeface in a single size and style. For example, traditionally 9-point Times boldface is considered a font.

Found set: The records identified by a Find search of a database file.

Function: A small program that performs one specific action, such as finding the average of a range of cells in a spreadsheet.

Hanging indent: A paragraph in which the first line is further to the left than the rest of the paragraph.

Hot links: Ranges of text that, when clicked, take the user to another document or to another place in the same document.

Integrated package: A piece of software that has more than one type of program combined together into a single unit.

Landscape: A page orientation in which the page is wider than it is tall.

Layout: In a database document, formatting specifications for viewing data.

Legend: In a spreadsheet chart, a directory identifying the series.

Macro: A named sequence of actions that are executed automatically when you press an associated key combination.

Mail merge: Creating customized documents by inserting data from a database file into a word processing document or frame.

Module: A component of an integrated package.

Named report: In a database document, a collection of a layout, a named search, and a named sort that are applied together.

Null: In a database, a value that means "unknown."

Object graphics: A graphics program in which the elements of an illustration retain their identity as objects.

Paint graphics: Illustrations made up of a pattern of colored dots that is only one layer thick.

Part (of a layout): A section of a layout, such as Header or Body.

Paste: Copy an item from the Clipboard into a document.

Pixel: One dot on a computer screen.

Portrait: A page orientation in which the page is taller than it is wide.

Precedence: The rules by which a computer determines the order in which it will evaluate parts of an arithmetic expression.

Printer driver: Software that acts as an intermediary between an application program and a printer.

Range: In a spreadsheet, a contiguous rectangular block of selected cells.

Record: All the data values describing one occurrence of an entity in a database file.

Relative address: In a spreadsheet, a cell reference that is expressed as the distance from the current cell rather than by an absolute cell address.

Resolution: The density of pixels in a painting, measured in dots per inch.

Section: A portion of a word processing document with its own layout, page numbering, and headers and footers.

Select: Highlight a portion of a document to indicate that that portion should be affected by the next actions you take.

Series: In a spreadsheet chart, a group of data, taken from either one row or one column of the spreadsheet.

Spelling checker: A word processing tool that identifies incorrectly spelled words in a document and suggests correct spellings.

Spreadsheet: The electronic equivalent of the paper-based ledger sheets used by bookkeepers and accountants.

Style sheet: A group of formatting characteristics that can be applied together to a portion of a document.

System software: Software that performs management functions for the computer, such as the operating system.

Terminal emulation: Using software to make a personal computer appear to a remote host computer like a computer terminal.

Text frame: A region of a document other than a word processing document that behaves exactly like a stand-alone word processing document.

Text wrap: The way in which text flows around, under, or above a graphic object in a document.

Transformation: A special effect used on a selected area of a painting, usually to distort the shape of the area in some way.

Type size: The height of type, measured in points, such as 9 point or 12 point.

Type style: The style of type, such as plain, boldface, italic, or underlined.

Typeface: A style of type, such as Times or Palatino.

User interface: The medium through which a human interacts with a computer.

"What if" analysis: Changing one or more values in a spreadsheet formula to see what effect the changing values have on the end result.

Word processing: A computer program that enters, modifies, deletes, and formats text.

Word wrap: Word processing feature in which the software automatically moves entire words (or hyphenated parts of words) to a new line within a paragraph.

X-height: The height of characters such as "x" or "n."

Index

E

F

M

N

T

U

V

W

GIVE YOUR KIDS EVERYTHING THEY WANT. (AND EVERYTHING THEY NEED.)

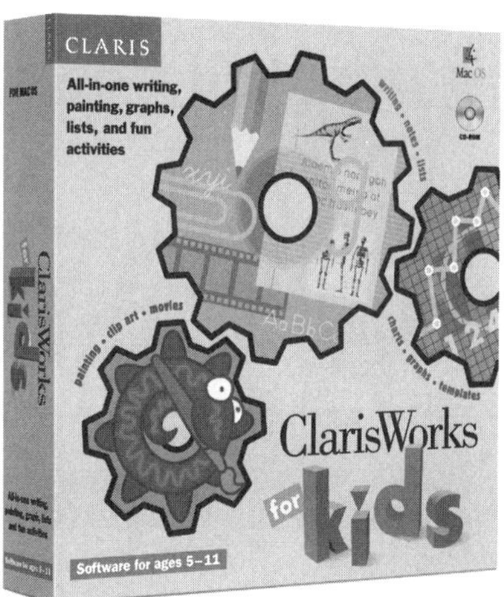

These days, kids and computers go hand in hand. That's why we've developed ClarisWorks® for Kids: the software solution* specifically designed to give kids everything they want (not to mention what they need).

ClarisWorks software for Kids is the all-in-one writing, painting, graphing, list-making educational software package. Kids, ages 5-11, can build creative graphs, lists, slide shows and pictures with our thematically organized collection of clip-art images, sound bites, movies and templates. More than 75 age-appropriate activities are included too, like weather forecasting, school newspaper-making and lunch nutrition measurement. From word-processing for journal keeping to pie charts for learning fractions to easy-to-use spreadsheets for allowance tracking, ClarisWorks for Kids familiarizes children with programs they'll encounter later, giving them a head start. And its kid-friendly filing system, teachers-only password mode, standard school fonts and integrated Web launcher** all make it easy to use for younger children as well. On top of all this, ClarisWorks for Kids offers a unique "family" advantage because it's document compatible with ClarisWorks 4.0.

So give 'em everything they ask for. Give 'em ClarisWorks for Kids.

FOR MORE INFORMATION OR TO PURCHASE CLARISWORKS FOR KIDS, VISIT US AT WWW.CLARIS.COM.

Simply powerful software.™

At Claris our mission is to create and publish award-winning, cross-platform "simply powerful software" that propels business, educational, and home users to greater creativity and productivity. Sound lofty? Well our angle is simple: meet the goal by blending true power with industry-leading ease of use. And our approach has paid off. In fact, in the past two years we've established ourselves as one of the world's largest software vendors. And by continuing to create powerful, usable products that rank high in customer satisfaction, such success is ensured well into the future.

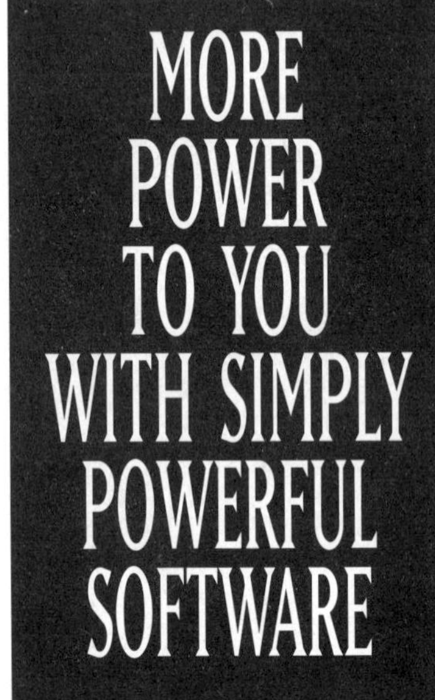

FILEMAKER PRO

FileMaker® Pro software is a relational database application designed to help you manage and share information in the easiest way imaginable. With FileMaker Pro, creating databases for Windows 95, NT, or 3.1, and Mac® OS, is incredibly fast and easy. It comes with a complete set of templates for quick business, education and home solutions, and is one of the leading solutions for database publishing on the Web. It's the ultimate time-saver.

CLARISWORKS

With a full-featured word processor that lets you integrate text, outlines, spreadsheets, charts, presentations, graphics and painting all in a single page, ClarisWorks® software is the all-in-one solution for Windows and Mac OS. And with its incredible Spreadsheet and Charting tools, Assistants and Shortcuts, ClarisWorks guides you and gives expert advice. It's one powerful application to help you accomplish more, faster.

CLARISWORKS FOR KIDS

ClarisWorks for Kids is the complete productivity solution* designed specifically for kids ages 5-11. This unique, all-in-one writing, painting, graphing, list-making educational software program also offers a unique "family" advantage for students and teachers because it's compatible with ClarisWorks 4.0, one of the most popular K-12 software solutions of all time.

CLARIS EM@ILER

No matter how many different Internet or online services you rely on for your email, whether you use it at the office, at home, or on the road, Claris Em@iler™ software is an easy, quick, convenient way for your Mac OS computer to manage it all. With powerful message filing and storing, automated mail management, easy attachments management and the Easy Set-Up, Claris Em@iler turns your email labyrinth into a well-oiled machine.

CLARIS HOME PAGE

Claris Home Page™ software makes it easy for anyone to create and manage their very own dynamic web pages. You don't have to be an HTML guru or a programming genius either, because Claris Home Page handles all that tricky stuff behind the scenes. But if you are experienced in such things, it lets you edit html code, create tables and frames, and play with its advanced features all you want.

VISIT CLARIS AT WWW.CLARIS.COM FOR MORE INFORMATION.

Simply powerful software.™